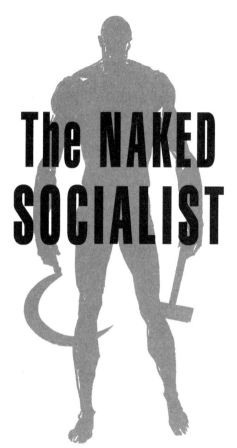

The NAKED SOCIALIST

by Paul B. Skousen

The Ensign Publishing Company, Riverton, Utah

Published by:

Ensign Publishing Company
PO Box 298
Riverton, Utah 84065

www.thenakedsocialist.com

Softback ISBN: 978-1478273486
Hardback ISBN: 978-0910558730
eBook ISBN: 978-0910558723

Cover illustration and design by Arnold Friberg, J. Rich Skousen, and Benjamin C. Skousen

First paperback edition: July 2012
First hardback edition: September 2012

10 9 8 7 6 5 4 3 2 1

Thomas Jefferson
November 29, 1802:

"I predict future happiness for Americans if they can prevent the government from wasting the labors of the people under the pretense of taking care of them."

CONTENTS

PART I—WHAT IS SOCIALISM?

Socialism At Work...1

The Eternal Conflict: Force Versus Choice........................ 3

PART II—SOCIALISM IN ANCIENT HISTORY

First, There Was Force 28

Ancient Sumer, The Earliest Socialists............................ 29

Pharaoh, The Demigod Socialist.....................................33

Nimrod, The Anti-God Socialist 36

China: Dynasties Of Socialism 38

Assyrians: Ruthless, Blood-Drenched Socialists.............. 42

PART III—SOCIALISM IN CLASSICAL HISTORY

Draco And His Draconian Ideas 50

Sparta: Warrior Socialists 52

Of Beards, Words, And Wisdom.....................................56

A Caste Of Millions 60

Aristophanes: Socialist Ideas "In The Round" 62

Rome's Recipe: Bread & Circuses 64

Israel: The Elusive Essenes...65

China: Wang Mang, A Failed Socialist 66

How Socialism Killed Rome 67

PART IV—SOCIALISM IN THE MIDDLE AGES

Socialism And The Rise Of Christianity 74

Feudalism And Rulers' Law 80

Socialism In The Middle Ages... 82

Socialism And The Reformation...................................... 88

Rise Of The Guilds 96

How The French "Revolutionized" Socialism 103

PART V—SOCIALISM IN THE EARLY AMERICAS

Meanwhile, Over In The Americas 122

Incas: Model Socialists 123

Jesuit Priests Socialize Paraguay 129

Jamestown: Socializing The New World 131

Plymouth: No Thanksgiving For Socialism 135

PART VI—SOCIALISM IN RELIGION

Socialism In Religion 144

The Universal Religion 155

Was Jesus A Socialist? 156

Did the Early Christians Practice Communism? 159

The Word That Can't Be Defined 163

Socialism Du Jour 167

PART VII—THE MIRACLE THAT STOPPED SOCIALISM

The Miracle That Stopped Socialism 176

Abolishing Pillar #1: "The Ruler" 181

Abolishing Pillar #2: "The Caste" 192

Abolishing Pillar #3: "All Things In Common" 194

Abolishing Pillar #4: "All Things Regulated" 197

Abolishing Pillar #5: "Force" 199

Abolishing Pillar #6: "Information Control" 201

Abolishing Pillar #7: "No Rights" 204

Does It Work? 212

Founding Fathers Speak On Socialism 214

Is It "Old Fashioned"? 218

Democracy vs. Republic 219

PART VIII—REVOLUTION OF THE SOCIALISTS, I

Conspiracy To Socialize America 224

There's Nothing Progressive About Progressives 225

America's First Progressive 227

The Revolution Of The Socialists 237

Revolutionary: Ned Ludd 239

Revolutionary: Unions & The King 240

Revolutionary: Napoleon Bonaparte 241

Revolutionary: Robert Owen 244

PART IX—REVOLUTION OF THE SOCIALISTS, II

Revolutionary: Union Organizers 250

Revolutionary: Religious Revivalists 260

Revolutionary: The Thinkers...266

Revolutionary: Top Ten Books 274

PART X—REVOLUTION OF THE SOCIALISTS, III

Revolutionary: Bad Amendments 280

Revolutionary: U.S. Supreme Court 291

Revolutionary: The Neo-Progressives 301

Revolutionary: The Socialist Party................................ 309

Revolutionary: Law Schools.. 312

Revolutionary: Federal Power 316

PART XI—THE LAST TEMPTATION, PART 1: COMPULSORY CARE

The Last Temptation: Compulsory Care 326

Franklin Speaks 327

Bastiat Speaks 329

The Twisted Roots Of Modern Welfare 330

Modern Welfare Born In Prussia....................................339

The Roots Of American Welfare.....................................343

PART XII—THE LAST TEMPTATION, PART 2: HEALTH CARE

Death By National Health Care 348

Top 6 Flaws Of Universal Health Coverage 350

PART XIII—SOCIALIZING THE MONEY

John Law's Trillion Dollar Idea 372

The Ruling Power Of Central Banks 376

Progressives Finally Get Their Central Bank.................379

Broken Promises Of The Federal Reserve 385

The Great Concession... 390

The New Deal Constitution 397

PART XIV—SOCIALISM TODAY IN AMERICA

Thinking Like A Socialist 404

U.S. Presidents And Socialism:
  Lincoln, Cleveland, Teddy Roosevelt 405

U.S. Presidents And Socialism:
  Taft, Wilson, Hoover, FDR, Truman 409

U.S. Presidents And Socialism:
  Kennedy, Johnson, Nixon, Carter, Reagan 417

U.S. Presidents And Socialism:
  Bush, Clinton, G.W. Bush 427

U.S. Presidents And Socialism:
  Obama 434

PART XV—SOCIALISM AROUND THE WORLD

The Rise And Fall Of Socialist Europe 446

Grandma Was Right 451

A Snap Shot Of World Socialism:
  Australia, Argentina, Canada, China, Cuba 453

A Snap Shot Of World Socialism:
  France, Germany, Greece, Iran, Ireland, Italy 460

A Snap Shot Of World Socialism:
  North Korea, Peru, Portugal, Russia, Spain 465

A Snap Shot Of World Socialism:
  Sweden, U.K., U.S., Venezuela, Vietnam,
  Zimbabwe 470

Socialism Needs A Host: Three Examples.....................476

PART XVI—THE 46 GOALS OF SOCIALISM

The 46 Goals Of Socialism 482

PART XVII—THE PROPER ROLE OF GOVERNMENT

The Proper Role of Government 494

PART XVIII—THE NEW BEGINNING

The New Beginning... 500

APPENDIX

The Day The Socialists Took My Honey and Nectar 510

"ObamaCare" 514

A President's Private Army? 516

Why Is Socialism So Appealing? 518

Sample Fruits of Ruler's Law 524

It Takes A Family 530

A Khrushchev Quote 533

Acknowledgements 534

About The Author 535

Selected Bibliography 536

Quotes On Major Section Headings 546

Factoid Sources 547

Index 548

The Seven Pillars of Socialism

Socialism stands atop seven pillars of control rooted in the power and authority of Rulers' Law.

1. All-Powerful RULERS
2. Society Divided into a CASTES or CLASSES
3. All Things in COMMON
4. All Things REGULATED
5. Compliance is FORCED
6. Control of INFORMATION
7. No Unalienable RIGHTS

Part I

WHAT IS SOCIALISM?

"Socialism is government force to change society."

—Author—

The Ouroboros—from the Greek meaning
"tail" (ouro) and "eating" (boros)

THE OUROBOROS

". . . Socialism progresses like a snake eating its tail . . . ."
—Author—

How this book was named: In 1958, W. Cleon Skousen took his book manuscript to movie producer and friend Cecil B. DeMille for review. After reading it, DeMille said "Cleon, what you've done here is strip away all the lies and foolishness of Communism. ..." (cont'd)

CHAPTER 1:
SOCIALISM AT WORK

In 2010, President Barack Obama committed the American people to their first-ever national health-care program. He told them it was against the law to say no. If they did, they would be fined. At the same time, Greece, Portugal, Italy, and Spain were in the middle of massive financial meltdowns brought on by their own national health-care programs and enormous entitlement expenses.

That's socialism at work.

In 1787, the Founding Fathers sat uneasy while Alexander Hamilton paced back and forth at the U.S. Continental Congress, speaking for five hours in support of a strong, all-powerful president and state executives appointed for life. At the same time, the crowned monarchs all across Europe watched with worry as the discontented masses in France were agitating for a proper way to remove their own "head" of state.

That's socialism at work.

In 1607, emaciated survivors of Jamestown's first terrible winter looked at their scant food supply and the buried remains of 66 of their company who starved to death, and wondered what went wrong with their "ideal" colony. Meanwhile, far to the south, Jesuit Priests in Paraguay were leading thousands of natives into a life of such regimentation that the men and women wouldn't even sleep together unless they were ordered.

That's socialism at work.

In A.D. 500, a widespread Christian heresy in Persia, called the Mazdakians, won followers by calling for all things in common, including wives and women. So confused were the biological connections, some of the members didn't even know their own children. Meanwhile, far to the east, Shang Yang in China was teaching a doctrine of how to make the working peasants weak so they could be ruled with greater ease.

That's socialism at work.

In the pages that follow we will see that all techniques and methods of force used to rule a group or a mass of people have remained more or less the same throughout history. They've appeared under different names, leaders, and places, but at their root, all ruling control—ancient and modern—has rested on the same ideas. Those ideas have won greater mobility due to changing technologies, but the untold thousands of forms that have evolved over time are still, essentially, all the same.

This is socialism at work. It progresses slowly and methodically, spreading from nation to nation, handing down to each successive generation of socialistic leaders an expanded realm of domination.

The Naked Socialist explains these dark arts of control and power. Without using the confusing jargon of economics and political science, it strips away and lays bare the lies and deceit, the smoke and mirrors, the promises and guarantees, and points to the awful ending place where socialism always leads.

First, we briefly explore the traits and characteristics of force, and contrast that with the principles of freedom. All of us recognize freedom, and innately strive to obtain it. In *The Naked Socialist*, we explain why that human drive for freedom is in direct opposition to socialism, and why the two will never mix for very long.

Second, we look at examples of socialism in history—events that proved the futility of socialism in several of its many forms.

And last, we take a snapshot of socialism in the world today, a survey of a few countries to see how the use of socialism has ruined the fullest capacities of countless generations. Along the way, we'll discover the arrival of a miracle, an astonishing enlightenment that swept around the earth and stopped socialism dead in its tracks.

We conclude with the 46 goals of socialism now being put into effect—goals to replace natural rights and liberty with a type of government that has never worked, and by its very nature, can't work, for reasons that will become clear.

In the end we discuss the way to stop socialism and return to the principles of lasting freedom. The steps forward are not complicated but the labor to get there will take effort and time. Pinning hopes to a changing administration in the White House or in parliaments around the world is not where the true rescue will be made. Reversing socialism is much more personal than that.

What follows is a tale of false hopes and empty promises, of conflict and demands, of personal freedom willingly surrendered for a little bit of peace and security. It is the real story of socialism.

"You cannot make men good by law, and without good men you cannot have a good society."
—C.S. Lewis

CHAPTER 2:

THE ETERNAL CONFLICT: FORCE VERSUS CHOICE

For most people the word "socialism" suggests two very different ideas.

1. BEAUTIFUL PROMISE: The first is an abstract proposition, a utopian promise, a pathway to a different way of living—it is the socialism of the future.

2. THE REGIME: The second idea is very concrete—an actual structure or formation in society, the socialism of the present.

Examples of both are everywhere. John Lennon's enormously popular song, *Imagine*[1], illustrates the first idea—the beautiful promise of life under a future socialistic society.

"Imagine there's no heaven," he proposed, "it's easy if you try. No hell below us—above us only sky—imagine all the people—living for today ..."

Living for today is a tricky proposition. It implies a life with no planning for the future, shirking responsibility, consuming instead of producing—a suggestion to eat, drink, and be merry, for tomorrow we die. To the untold millions of fans, these words conjured up hope for a painless pathway to a different way of living.

Lennon's tune also advanced his beautiful utopian idea of no countries, nothing for people to fight over, "and no religion, too."

No religion, no countries, no possessions, and no worries—what a *great* life. This wasn't the first time such a suggestion was made. Lennon's song was actually a lyrical retelling of the ancient teachings of Plato, Marx, Engels, and Mao. Lennon himself said his song was "virtually the *Communist Manifesto*, even though I am not particularly a communist and I do not belong to any movement."[2]

---

1 *Imagine*, written by John Lennon, produced by John Lennon, Yoki Ono, Phil Spector, 1971, copyright by the John Lennon estate and Yoko Ono.
2 Geoffrey Giuliano, *Lennon in America*, Cooper Square Press, 2000.

Socialism is expensive: In 2012, Canada raised its retirement age from 65 to 67 to defray the rising costs of its government-guaranteed old age pension plans.

THE SECOND IDEA OF SOCIALISM

Examples of the second idea—the actual structure and formation of socialism—can be found in North Korea, where malnutrition has stunted the growth of its children, where large ghost cities stand as empty mirages and facades to fool the world, where three million people starved to death in the mid-1990s because of their government's stupefying policies, and where Dear Leader's image flashes across television screens day and night, gushing the doctrine of Lenin while whistling the tune of Lennon.

Or, Cuba, where fifty years of socialism have produced rampant crime, corruption, prostitution, drugs, and white collar crime. Where the country has to rely on other socialist nations for such basics as food, medicine, and energy. Where the Castro regime uses torture, arbitrary imprisonment, false trials, and executions to keep the population under control.

Or, Red China, where Mao's great leap forward created a famine so intense that it killed at least 30 million people. On top of those dead, Mao heaped at least 40 million more in a purge to purify the formidable ranks of his loyal followers.

Or, the USSR, where the transition to communism killed more than 60 million people over seven miserable decades. Where the Soviet's international thuggery and bullying was used to threaten, steal, and fight its way to world prominence. Where its failure formula brought about the empire's predictable collapse in the 1990s, leaving its 15 republics buried in wreckage and still struggling for survival by 2012.

Or, the European Union, where the massive treasuries of the world's mightiest trading partners, regulated under socialistic ideals, began imploding with uncontrollable spending, borrowing, and debt. By 2010, their circumstances were so desperate, they made a last ditch attempt to rescue their excessive welfare entitlement programs with loans, bailouts, and austerity programs. Europe's highly touted dream of "with socialism, we can do it better," became painful proof that they couldn't.

Such examples show that socialism in the "here and now" never achieves the beautiful promise, the dream, the pathway to a different life as suggested by Lennon's *Imagine*. They also show that socialism is horribly incapable to exert innovation and creativity to solve any of its problems. Today's socialists don't know how to improve

"My people are destroyed for lack of knowledge: because thou hast rejected knowledge, I will also reject thee..." Hosea 4:6 KJV

people's lives. The only outcome that emerges from the abstract dream of "imagine all the people living for today" is the consolidation of power by the leaders. From that has come a stagnated mass of desperate misery, widespread decay, and agonizing death.

THE MECHANICS OF SOCIALISM

Stepping back from all of the arm waving and shouting, it becomes clear that the socialists have just one main goal: the destruction of the current way of living. Their reasoning becomes clear after the dust settles and the bodies are buried—socialism just can't work where freedom of individual action is secured.

The attempt to wipe out an existing culture has been tried from the barrel of communism's gun with no lasting success. The other way is gradual change, using the slower democratic processes—voting away protected rights one by one, gradually wrapping the chains around the ankles, then the arms, then the neck.

Either way, the end goal has remained the same: destroy the successful culture of the past and destroy natural rights.

And then? And then, Marx declared "shall I stride through the wreckage a creator!"[3] Marx truly believed he could recreate the world in his own image. But he died.

THE SEVEN PILLARS OF SOCIALISM

Socializing a people does not build on principles. It operates in violation of principles. The methods to advance socialism's changes are called the Seven Pillars of Socialism:

PILLAR #1—All Powerful Ruler. The first and most important goal is the crowning of the all-powerful ruler—an individual or a group. The ruler operates according to oppressive Ruler's Law (explained later) and does not bow to the people's will, nor obey any written law. When the ruler starts making his own laws, bypasses Congress, or Parliament, or any consortium of representatives, and no one dares stop him, this is a sign that Pillar #1 is well underway.

PILLAR #2—Caste or Classes. Socialists claim they know how to make society fair and equal, but as we will explain, just the opposite takes place. Under socialism, society is divided into classes. The upper class consists of party members who receive special privileges

---

3　Edmund Wilson, *To the Finland Station*, New York Review of Books, 2003, p. 115.

as a reward for their loyalty. The middle caste, or class, is a massive bureaucracy of well-paid enforcers—an overlapping maze of guards and spies dispatched to all levels of society. At the bottom are the most abused and least privileged of all: the workers, the peasants, and the slaves. When the government grants privileges to some classes and not others (bailouts, tax breaks, or refusal to enforce laws equally), this is a sign that Pillar #2 is well underway.

PILLAR #3—Things In Common. Basic socialist doctrine teaches that the ownership of property is the cause of all discord and envy. Therefore, material things must be made equal—and then private ownership must be eliminated altogether. Socialists are not consistent with how this part works, they're all over the map. In some cases, this "commonality" has included sharing wives, and children. When the government imposes graduated taxes, confiscates property for the common good, is uneven in taking from the "haves" and giving to the "have nots," then Pillar #3 is well underway.

PILLAR #4—Regulation. Total control means total regulation. By issuing a regular stream of new laws and requirements, the Rulers control all economic activities and production. Too much broccoli? Reassign the acreage. Too many babies? Stop the pregnancies (see China's one-child policy). Grandpa's cabin standing in the way of a public road, and grandpa won't sell? Condemn the property and exercise eminent domain. Or just nationalize it, take it over. When government passes laws without the legislature involved, when it violates human rights, and sues sovereign states or private companies to have its way, that means Pillar #4 is well underway.

PILLAR #5—Force. In socialism, force and fear go hand in hand. All human activity is restrained or compelled to action with the appropriate use of force—penalties, fines, restrictions, hidden laws, and a multitude of taxes. Under Ruler's Law, force is always controlled by the Ruler. When government begins violating basic rights with force, and the people are powerless to stop it, then Pillar #5 is well underway. When that force becomes deadly and the people are fearful of the government, and for their lives, that is communism.

PILLAR #6—Information Control. To acquire the friendly consent of the people to live under socialism, the regime must convince the masses that the old way was bad, and the new way is good. When a government begins to work hand-in-glove with entertainment and the media, separates the currency from precious metals so only the government can declare its official value, and controls official statistics about job growth, unemployment, national output, national production, etc., then Pillar #6 is well underway.

PILLAR #7—Vested Rights. The ruling body grants all rights. They do not accept the idea of natural or unalienable rights. When government selectively enforces some laws and ignores others, refuses to protect property rights, and favors the whole over protecting rights of the individual, then Pillar #7 is well underway.

NOBODY KNOWS, NOBODY AGREES

Socialists can't agree on what they want. They will defend one or several of these seven pillars as necessary evils to achieve a maximum outcome, while promoting the remainder, and then promise a utopia that is, they say, well worth the wait and suffering.

Other socialists choose differently. They brag that the final outcome of socialism is an exciting unknown. They predict that when it is fully unleashed, socialism will evolve naturally until it reaches a perfect harmony of balance and fairness and prosperity that is too fantastic to even imagine.

Whatever form or scheme the socialists choose, this definition works every time: Socialism is government force to change society.

RULERS MAKE IT HAPPEN

Since the dawn of time, nearly all of humanity has lived under some form of government whereby society was forced to change. The Founders associated this force with the monarch, England's king. They pointed to other forms that operated at the time: A plutocracy, when a monarch invites the support of loyal followers, the wealthy class, to control the people. An aristocracy, when these titles of nobility are passed to the next generation, and people assume authority over others because they are "privileged." And the emperor with his empire, when the military gets involved and one of its generals rises up to use Ruler's Law against the people.

Other leaders of regimes include queens, nobles, lords, barons, czars, princes, regents, chiefs, deans, bosses, priests, caliphs, Chinese wangs, pharaohs, presidents, sovereigns, chairmen, shamans, etc.

THE POLITICAL SPECTRUM

The greatest contribution by America's Founding Fathers was bringing to light the principles of true freedom, and at the same time identifying the common destructive elements of Ruler's Law. They pointed out that governments are not powerful because of their political party, platform, or philosophy. They become powerful to the degree that they hold a monopoly on the use of force.

This is illustrated with a yardstick serving as a scale, a sliding scale, with all power and force to the far left, and no law or anarchy to the far right.

All tyrants must take a seat toward the left: communists, totalitarians, monarchists, fascists, socialists, Fabian-socialists, demagogs, social democrats, Christian socialists, parliamentary republicans, single-party governments, or any other form that denies the people their natural rights and direct control of their government.

On the far right is no law, or anarchy. Examples range from the Articles of Confederation, to mobs. This is basically mob rule, like the mobs during the French revolution, and the 20 years of no central government in Somalia. The Articles of Confederation came close to causing mob rule in some places. These weak or absent regimes must take seats to the far right as examples of how too little power breeds chaos, lawlessness, and lack of sufficient control.

THE GOLDEN MEAN

The correct balance between force and chaos is difficult to achieve. The best balance yet invented is the U.S. Constitution. In this, America's Founders delivered to generations unborn the true, balanced center between the extremes of *all force* and *no force*. They gave the world a carefully crafted system of representation, checks, and balances. It was the miracle that stopped socialism.

THE TEN TRAITS OF RULER'S LAW

The Founders seemed intent on exposing the seven pillars of socialism so that the people could learn to recognize and avoid them. The basic characteristics of Ruler's Law are laced with all seven pillars. Most of humanity has experienced or witnessed one or more of these acts of Ruler's Law in recent decades.[4]

---

4 See W. Cleon Skousen, *The Five Thousand Year Leap*, pp. 12-13.

"Let us tenderly and kindly cherish therefore, the means of knowledge. Let us dare to read, think, speak, and write."—John Adams

1. **BULLY TACTICS**: Authority under Ruler's Law is nearly always put in place by force, violence, and conquest.

2. **MIGHT MAKES RIGHT**: All sovereign power is considered to be in the hands of the conquerors or their descendants.

3. **CLASSES**: The people are not treated equally, but are divided into classes, and are looked upon as subjects of the king.

4. **NO PROPERTY**: The entire country is considered to be the property of the ruler, who speaks of it as his "realm."

5. **HELPLESS MASSES**: The thrust of government power is from the top down, not from the people upward.

6. **NO RIGHTS**: The people have no unalienable rights. The king giveth and the king taketh away.

7. **FLIP-FLOPPERS**: Government is by the whims of the king, not by the fixed rule of law. Rulers know that fixed law governs even the king, a tool that emboldens the people with confidence to act against a ruler's continual gluttonous greed. Therefore, a ruler must prevent and destroy written laws, constitutions, charters, or corpus juris laws that would interfere with his complete power and control.

8. **BENCH RULINGS**: The ruler issues edicts which are called "The Law," and interprets the law whichever way best suits the ruler's ultimate goals, and enforces it, thus maintaining tyrannical control over the people.

9. **GROWING NEW MASTERS**: Problems are always solved by issuing more edicts or laws, setting up more bureaus, setting up more regulatory agencies, harassing the people with more regulations, and charging the people for these "services" by continually adding to their burden of taxes.

10. **REJECTING THE OBVIOUS**: Freedom is never discussed as a solution. The rulers are afraid of the people—they're afraid the people will take away the power. The rulers do what they can to make the people weak and fully dependent on government for everything.

Free market at work: With 4% of the world's population, the U.S. produces more than 50% of the world's soybeans.

THE PRIVILEGED LEADERS

The long history of Ruler's Law is dyed red in blood, terror, and conquest. In all instances, the people are found stratified under the ruler's aristocracy and retinue who lord over the common people with relative ease. The masses are left to suffer under perpetual poverty, excessive taxation, stringent regulations, and a continuous existence of misery.

ETERNAL STAGNATION

As socialism raises its grizzled head in any setting or nation, these elements of Ruler's Law may always be discovered in one form or another. Resistance is impossible because Ruler's Law will accommodate no form of rebellion—and will fight it to the death.

WHY A KING—ANY KING—IS A BAD IDEA

A ruler with kingly power has no place in human society. No matter what name or controls are placed upon this person, that much power always corrupts.

Didn't the Bible promote kings? Deuteronomy tells of the Lord knowing that one day, Israel would demand a king. The Israelites would eventually abandon their open society of a theo-democracy, and choose to become subject to the arbitrary whims of a central, all-powerful authority figure.

Perhaps unknown to these ancient Israelites was the fact that no matter when or how this kind of concentrated kingly power had been allowed to rise, it eventually unraveled into tyranny.

The Lord knew, however, that it *was* possible to have a righteous king, provided he adhered to His law. A "good" king's traits were outlined in Deuteronomy[5]:

1. **CITIZEN**—He must be a citizen of Israel and not a stranger.

2. **CHOSEN**—He should be a person whom "the Lord thy God shall choose."

3. **CIRCUMSPECT**—He should not "multiply horses" (build private armies) which was a common characteristic of heathen kings, especially the extravagant and war-making kings of Egypt.

4. **VIRTUOUS**—The king was not to "multiply wives."

5. **THRIFTY**—The king was not to "multiply to himself silver and gold," which would be at the expense of his people through taxes.

---

5 See Deuteronomy 17:15-19, KJV.

Urban Russia: 3 out of every 4 people grow some of their own food just to survive.

6. WISE—The task of the king was to be a great scholar, judge, general, and righteous policy maker. To do this, he was to have his own personal copy of the law, and he was to "read therein all the days of his life: that he may learn to fear the Lord his God, to keep all the words of this law and these statutes, to do them." In other words, have a constitution, read it often, and rule accordingly.

CAN A PRESIDENT MEET THE REQUIREMENTS?

The Founders labored long and hard to instill the Lord's leadership requirements into the presidency, through the Constitution, so that America's executive officer would, at least, meet this minimum expectation. As it turned out, very few presidents have measured up to the Lord's requirements—and, neither have those in the other branches of government.

THE FOUNDERS' INTENSE INTEREST IN PEOPLE'S LAW

To find what form of government worked best, the Founders studied ancient examples of successful government, starting with Moses.

Exodus tells about Moses leading Israel—an estimated 600,000 families—from Egypt, sometime between 1490 and 1290 B.C. With the help of his father-in-law, Jethro[6], Moses learned how to organize the Israelites under People's Law.

To bring order, Jethro advised Moses to organize the people into small manageable units where everyone had a representative and a vote. When the organization was finished, Moses had divided the families into tens, fifties, hundreds, and thousands, each with a representative. At the very top he added a council of 70.[7]

This provided strong local self-government from the highest to the lowest unit of organization. It allowed problems to be solved at the local level where personalities and local constraints were best known and understood.

If a local problem could not be solved, the leader of ten families carried it to the leader of 50 families of which he was a part—or higher as needed. This process of appealing up the chain spared Moses from dealing with a million problems. Only the most severe issues reached his desk. "The hard cases they brought to Moses," Exodus 18:26 says, "but every small matter they judged themselves."

---

6   See Exodus 18:13-26.
7   Number 11:16.

PEOPLE'S LAW

The Founders identified a number of principles from Moses' experiences that led them to pinpoint the power of People's Law and the requirements for lasting liberty and good government—

1.   SELF-GOVERNMENT The people organized themselves to be self-governing, not servants to a king. They were jealous about their liberty. "Proclaim liberty throughout all the land," Moses declared, "and unto all the inhabitants thereof."[8]

2.   SELF-POLICING: A strong code of virtue and morality was always taught and encouraged. This was a brilliant tactic for self-policing—if the people's hearts were governed by themselves, they had no need for more masters to do it for them.

3.   FREE ELECTIONS: The adults were all organized into small units, with everyone having a voice in all matters—and a vote. All leadership was selected by consent of the people.[9]

4.   LOCAL RULE: Local government was strongly emphasized.

5.   GOLD STANDARD: Their money was reliable, based on gold and silver. They had a uniform system of weights and measures.[10]

6.   PROPERTY: The land was the people's, not the government's.

7.   SACRED PRIVATE RIGHTS: Life and private property rights were protected for each lawful individual.

8.   NO ARBITRARY LAWS: All laws had to be approved by the people or their representatives before they were enacted.[11]

9.   FAIRNESS UNDER THE LAW: People were presumed innocent until proven guilty.[12] Justice was based on giving reparations to the victim, not to the government.[13]

10. PEOPLE IN CONTROL: The power of government originated with the will of the people upwards. Only in times of crises, such as war, could the government exert power from the top downwards.

11. WRITTEN LAW: The government had to comply with the written laws—a constitution—it could not make up laws or ignore certain laws of its choosing.

This carefully balanced system allowed the Israelites to transfer political power from one administration to the next without a massive uprising or bloodbath—as was typical for deposing a tyrannical king.

---

8   Leviticus 25:10, KJV.
9   See 2 Samuel 2:4; 1 Chronicles 29:22; for the rejection of a leader, see 2 Chronicles 10:16.
10   See Deuteronomy 25:13-15.
11   Exodus 19:8.
12   For example, see the law of witnesses, Deuteronomy 19:15, and 24:3.
13   See references to this process in Exodus 21 and 22. There could be no "satisfaction" for first-degree murder. The killer had to be executed. Numbers 35:31.

ANGLO-SAXONS LIVE THE ISRAELITES' SYSTEM

Thomas Jefferson learned that the Anglo-Saxons practiced People's Law. He became so fascinated with that, he decided to learn their language so he could read their original laws himself.

The Anglo-Saxons came from the Black Sea area in the first century B.C., and built settlements all across Northern Europe. They entered Britain around A.D. 450, at the behest of the king of Kent. Hengist and Horsa were the first, settling their families in the south to help guard the frontiers and borderlands. They multiplied, prospered, and eventually took over the island. They renamed the land Anglo-land, or Engle-land, or England.

The Anglo-Saxons embraced the Israelite's form of government and practiced it for centuries with great success. About A.D. 700-750, unfortunately, corruption crept in and things started falling apart.

Jefferson took these ancient ideas as a great breath of fresh air, and encouraged that they be copied. "Are we not better for what we have hitherto abolished of the feudal system," he wrote in 1776. "Has not every restitution of the ancient Saxon laws had happy effects? Is it not better now that we return at once into that happy system of our ancestors, the wisest and most perfect ever yet devised by the wit of man, as it stood before the eighth century?"[14]

SOCIALISM CONTINUES FOR LACK OF KNOWLEDGE

The history of socialism is thick with Ruler's Law and the violation of basic human rights. One of the reasons this mayhem has continued is because succeeding generations have failed to pass along knowledge about People's Law and rights.

SOCIALISM DESTROYS NATURAL RIGHTS

Understanding human rights is to understand socialism.

A "right" is a legal or ethical entitlement. The Founding Fathers identified two basic rights: (1) Those vested by the government, and (2) those natural or unalienable rights that are gifts from the Creator. Many people confuse the two, thinking some parts of life are simply theirs because, well, because it's their *right*.

Vested rights are granted by the government. They can be revoked just as easily as they are granted. That doesn't automati-

---

14   Julian P. Boyd, editor, *The Papers of Thomas Jefferson*, 1:492.

cally make vested rights bad—quite the contrary. They serve many important purposes.

Vested rights include the right to operate a car, build a house, patent an idea, drive on a road, practice medicine, cross borders, participate in health insurance, buy a piece of ground, copyright music, sell paintings, start a business, go fishing, etc.

Vested rights is the set of rules that allows people to participate and interact together without killing each other in the process. If certain rules and regulations are not met, the people empower the government to revoke the vested rights to keep the peace. To a socialist's way of thinking, *all* rights are given by the government.

NATURAL RIGHTS HAVE THREE PARTS

Natural rights, or unalienable rights, are universal and established by the Creator. Every person is born with them, and they may not be revoked or legislated away. They frequently are, but governments have no moral authority to do so. The struggle for freedom is the struggle to exercise unalienable rights.

An unalienable right has three parts.

1. It is universal. It applies equally to every living soul.

2. It imposes no obligation on another person. It doesn't infringe on the rights of other people or make any impositions on them.

3. It carries the responsibility to use the natural right respectfully. Rights must not be misused to harm others except in the defense of moral law.

Therefore, health care is not a natural right. It imposes on doctors, nurses, pharmaceutical manufacturers, etc. For that imposition, people pay a fee to get the services. If a person can't pay, the provider is under no obligation to provide—at least in a free country. When health-care providers receive payment, they are motivated to continue providing the service. The same applies to food, housing, transportation, unemployment, retirement pay, etc. If it imposes on others, people do not have an unalienable or natural right to receive it without giving compensation of some kind.

THE EIGHT RIGHTS

There are eight basic unalienable rights or categories of rights. All eight are necessary for freedom. Remove any one of them, and the remainder quickly fall. Only by destroying these rights may socialism flourish.

RIGHT #1—INDEPENDENT INDIVIDUALS.

The individual human being is the single most important entity upon which all else is created, built, and focused. The individual is a sovereign, self-standing unit of creation with unalienable rights to his own life. Individuals are not born as commodities to be consumed by society—it is society that is built upon the independent individual. To protect society, first protect the individual.

Socialism degrades the independent human to an anonymous, faceless insect dependent on the edicts of the community to survive.

RIGHT #2—CHOICE.

By definition, an independent entity has free will—he or she is capable of making choices. Choosing wisely or foolishly is a measure of a person's level of experience and ability to judge. There are always consequences for choices, and avoiding negative consequences is everyone's constant challenge. Incentives play an important role in making choices, and the responsibility attached to this right is to never violate the same moral rights of others.

Under socialism, all choices are controlled to benefit the rulers.

RIGHT #3—PROPERTY.

Property is the defining attribute of existence. A person's body is his or her first piece of wholly owned and controlled property. A person must work to support his existence, and that labor produces private property. Deny people their property, and you deny them their lives.

Without property, there can be no freedom—an individual cannot express his or her choices. Those denied their property are called slaves—or ghosts.

Socialists believe property is the root of all human problems. They deny an individual the free use of his own property, and claim a superior understanding of how best to use it properly.

RIGHT #4—ASSOCIATION.

Freedom of association means that people may join together with others who share common interests to promote, defend, study,

Socialism kills—Soviet Union death count under Stalin from 1924-1953, from famine, terror, purges and executions: 30,000,000.

and express those interests without interference from the state or anyone else. The Founders believed this freedom was the strongest prevention of centralized power.

Socialists refuse unauthorized associations because discontent and rebellion can grow and overthrow the rulers. Groups must be tightly watched and controlled in a socialist society.

RIGHT #5—EQUALITY.

All humans are endowed with the same set of entitlements or rights. These are natural rights common to all and may not be arbitrarily violated except in consequence of criminal activity.

Equal rights must not be confused with equal opportunity, equal outcome, or equal things. Opportunities are not equal for everyone, and the outcome or fruits of labor are never guaranteed. Equal things for all, the foundation stone of socialism, is impossible.

RIGHT #6. DEFENSE.

The right of self-defense is the unalienable right to defend your own life and property, or that of other people.

This includes the use of deadly force, the use of legal procedures such as a law suit, the use of expression in a private or public forum, the use of legal representation in the presence of a judge and jury, the use of a gun or other weapon, or the use of a militia or military power.

Socialism must deny the right of defense because it allows a person to act in opposition to the rulers, to insist on private choice to protect his or her rights defensively, to raise a rebellion against a dictator—or, to question the declarations of the rulers and to disobey their unlawful writs and rules.

RIGHT #7—COMPASSION.

Compassion is a cornerstone of human emotion and action. It separates humans from animals. It encourages cooperation and prosperity. It serves to correct flaws in society and allow for progress in spite of failings. Compassion is the gentle equalizer of human imperfections.

Socialism destroys compassion by forcing people to pay for government-sponsored welfare with taxes. People naturally dislike taxes and avoid them at all costs. The sad consequence is that people stop being compassionate and turn their backs on those in need, thinking that some agency or shelter will "handle it." Forced compassion is slavery, and it dulls a sense of caring for others.

RIGHT #8—FAILURE.

Failure is the most important of all freedoms. Failure is life's greatest teacher—it exposes weaknesses so that people may be made strong. Failure is unforgiving. It exacts a price that can be costly—sometimes a person pays with his life to learn that some things are dangerous, risky, or foolish.

Failure teaches people tenacity and perseverance. It encourages invention and cooperation, patience and understanding. It can be discouraging, painful, frustrating, and costly—but it teaches, and therefore, advances society. It is an unalienable right to fall flat on our faces.

Socialism seeks to eliminate failure by building safety nets at every level of society—tax-funded supports that thwart the natural consequences of life, and always weigh down a national economy.

"THE INDIVIDUAL HAS REIGNED LONG ENOUGH"

The socialists have been calling for abolishing individual rights for a long time. It's their only way to calm down the world so they can control it from their elitist places of power—

❖ **G. BROCK CHISHOLM (1896-1971)**: "To achieve world government, it is necessary to remove from the minds of men their individualism, loyalty to family traditions, national patriotism and religious dogmas..."[15]

❖ **KARL MARX (1818-1883)**: "The essence of man is not an abstract quality inherent in a separate individual. In reality it is the aggregate of all social relations."[16]

❖ **HERBERT MARCUSE (1898-1979)**: Marcuse said that Freud's most important contribution to understanding humans was to undermine "one of the strongest ideological fortifications of modern culture—namely, the notion of the autonomous individual."[17]

---

15   Quote attributed to G. Brock Chisholm, psychiatrist and co-founder of the World Federation of Mental Health.

16   Quoted in Igor Shafarevich, *The Socialist Phenomenon,* from *Works,* by Marx and Engels, in Russian, vol IV, p. 590, Moscow-Leningrad, 1928-48.

17   Herbert Marcuse, *Eros and Civilization. A philosophical Inquiry into Freud,* Routledge & Kegan Paul Ltd., England, 1956, p. 57.

◆ **JEAN-PAUL SARTRE (1905-1980)**: "I believe that the thinking of the group is where the truth is. ... I always considered group thinking to be better than thinking alone. ...I don't believe a separate individual to be capable of doing anything."[18]

◆ **LOUIS BAUDIN (1887-1964)**, writing about the Inca, "Life itself was torn out of that geometrical and sad empire, where everything occurred with the inevitability of *fatum*. ... The Indian lost his personality."[19] (*fatum*—fate, destiny, doom, lot, etc.)

◆ **DOM DESCHAMPS (1716-1774)** envisioned how his perfect world with "identical morals would make, so to say, one man of all men and one woman of all women. I mean by this that ultimately they would resemble each other more than animals of the same species."[20] He further proposed banishing "all terms presently used to express our good and bad qualities, even all terms unnecessarily distinguishing us from other things."[21]

◆ **LESTER F. WARD (1841-1913)**. In 1893, Ward called for a revolution against the individual:

> "The individual has reigned long enough. The day has come for society to take its affairs into its own hands and shape its own destinies. The individual has acted as best he could. He has acted in the only way he could. With a consciousness, will, and intellect of his own he could do nothing else than pursue his natural ends.
>
> "He should not be denounced nor called any names. He should not even be blamed. Nay, he should be praised, and even imitated.
>
> "Society should learn its great lesson from him, should follow the path he has so clearly laid out that leads to success. It should imagine itself an individual, with all the interests of an individual, and becoming fully conscious of these interests it should pursue them with the same indomitable will with which the individual pursues his interests. Not only this, it must be guided, and as he is guided, by the social intellect, armed with

---

18   Jean-Paul Sartre, *The Right to Rebel*, Ph. Gavi, Satre, P. Victor, Paris, 1974, pp. 170-171.
19   Louis Baudin, *Daily Life of the Incas*, Paris, 2003, pp. 135-136.
20   Dom Deschamps, La Verite ou le Veritable Systeme, Moscow, 1973, p. 176.
21   Ibid., p. 503.

"A collective tyrant spread over the length and breadth of the land, is no more acceptable than a single tyrant ensconced on his throne."—Georges Clemenceau

all the knowledge that all individuals combined, with so great labor, zeal, and talent have placed in its possession, constituting the social intelligence."[22]

The elimination of the individual—the creation of the anonymous society—is making strong headway. Its best progress has come by advancing the clever abuse of one of mankind's most basic generators of conflict: *Envy*.

FORCE AND ENVY

Socialism is a blatant contradiction. It sets out to accuse the world of inequality, injustice, and lack of freedom. Yet history has always shown that once socialism is put in place, it imposes a far greater inequality, injustice, and lack of freedom than that which existed before—all in the name of fairness.

To achieve fairness, socialists must crush the human attributes that create inequality. One way they achieve this is by appealing to the most base and common human weaknesses of envy and force— an appeal to a primitive state that smothers the highest ideals, the most sophisticated and multifaceted human qualities of choice, compassion, and innovation—qualities that philosopher John Locke said are a reflection of the very attributes of God.[23]

STICKS AND STONES WILL BREAK MY BONES ...

Calling on envy to justify force is an easy sell for most populations. Envy appeals to the brutish attributes of the "natural man." Summoning greed, envy, jealousy, and arrogance to any social or political issue is the socialist's main tool of proselytizing.

STIRRING UP ENVY—Hillary Clinton: "The rich are not paying their fair share in any issue."[24]

STIRRING UP ENVY—Barack Obama: "I think when you spread the wealth around, it's good for everybody."[25]

STIRRING UP ENVY—Barack Obama: "It's not that I want to punish your success, I just want to make sure that everybody who is behind you, that they've got a chance at success too."[26]

---

22 Lester F. Ward, "Sociocracy," *American Thought: Civil War to World War I,* pp. 113-114.
23 John Locke, *An Essay Concerning Human Understanding*, Chapter X, "Of our Knowledge of the Existence of a God," see *The Great Books*, pp. 349-354.
24 Hillary Clinton, remarks at the Brookings Institution, FOX News, May 28, 2010.
25 October 14, 2008, said to Joe "the Plumber" Wurzelbacher at a rally in Holland, Ohio.
26 Ibid.

"Equality may exist only among slaves."—Aristotle (384 BC—322 B.C.)
"Equality absolutely carried out leads to communism."—Francis Lieber (1798—1872)

STIRRING UP ENVY—Hillary Clinton: "Too many people have made too much money off of eliminating opportunities for caring for people instead of expanding those."[27]

STIRRING UP ENVY—Franklin D. Roosevelt: "Not only our future economic soundness but the very soundness of our democratic institutions depends on the determination of our government to give employment to idle men."[28]

STIRRING UP ENVY—Howard Dean: "We know that no one person can succeed unless everybody else succeeds."[29]

STIRRING UP ENVY—Michelle Obama: "The truth is, in order to get things like universal health care and a revamped education system, then someone is going to have to give up a piece of their pie so that someone else can have more."[30]

FORGOTTEN AND LEFT OUT

These statements, among others, appeal to the envious side of the "have nots." It suggests their place in life is not their fault, not their doing, and not their responsibility. To fix it, to make things fair, to satiate the demands of envy, the socialists use government force to change society by taking from the real producers, the "haves," and giving unearned riches and benefits to the "have nots."

THREATENING FORCE—Maxine Waters: "And guess what this liberal will be all about? This liberal will be all about socializing—uh, uh-um—will be about ... basically ... taking over and the government, running all of your companies."[31]

THREATENING FORCE—Joe Biden: "You know we're going to control the insurance companies."[32]

THREATENING FORCE—Jim Moran: "Because we have been guided by a Republican administration who believes in the simplistic notion that people who have wealth are entitled to keep it and they

---

27   Quoted in Stephen Chapman, The Chicago Tribune, May 30, 1993.
28   Franklin D. Roosevelt, fire side chat, 1938.
29   Howard Dean, religious conference in Washington D.C., June 27, 2006.
30   Michelle Obama, April 8, 2008, as quoted in the Charlotte Observer, April 9, 2008.
31   Maxine Waters, televised hearing on May 22, 2008.
32   Joe Biden interview on ABC News, May 18, 2010.

In 2012, a Taliban commander in northwest Pakistan threatened America, saying that children in his district would no longer receive polio vaccines until the U.S. stopped its drone (remote-controlled aircraft) attacks. The region is considered a safe haven for fleeing terrorists.

have an antipathy to our means of redistributing wealth."[33]

THREATENING FORCE—Bill Clinton: [Speaking about crime-ridden slum areas] "A lot of people say there's too much personal freedom. When personal freedom's being abused, you have to move to limit it."[34]

THREATENING FORCE—Bill Clinton: "If the personal freedoms guaranteed by the Constitution inhibit the government's ability to govern the people, we should look to limit those guarantees."[35]

THREATENING FORCE—Hillary Clinton: "We're going to take things away from you on behalf of the common good."[36]

THREATENING FORCE—John Dingell: "The harsh fact of the matter is when you're passing legislation that will cover 300 million American people in different ways, it takes a long time to do the necessary administrative steps that have to be taken to put the legislation together to control the people."[37]

THREATENING FORCE—Barack Obama: "I do think at a certain point you've made enough money."[38]

THREATENING FORCE—Jan Schakowsky: "You don't deserve to keep all of it [private money] and it's not a question of *deserving* because what government is, is those things that we decide to do together."[39]

SOCIALISM IS FORCE

According to the socialists, force is a necessary evil for the simple reason that people are more interested in their own pursuits than the needs of the whole. Therefore, people must be forced into socialism. Consider a few of the instances where the freedom of choice has been replaced by the government—

---

33 Congressman Jim Moran (D-VA), comments recorded November 10, 2008, and rebroadcast on The O'Reilly Factor, FOX News, November 14, 2008.
34 Bill Clinton, Interview on MTV's "Enough is Enough," April 19, 1994.
35 Bill Clinton, August 12, 1993.
36 Hillary Clinton, quoted in Associated Press: "San Francisco rolls out the red carpet for the Clintons," by Beth Fouhy, June 29, 2004.
37 Congressman John Dingell (D-MI), comment on Chicago radio WJR, hosted by Paul W. Smith, aired March 23, 2010.
38 Barack Obama, comment on Wall Street reform, Quincy, Ill, April 29, 2010.
39 Congresswoman Jan Schakowsky (D-IL); see transcript at http://www.wlsam.com.

The free market pays: Scavengers in Istanbul make a living digging through people's trash for recyclables. One man found a silver statue, earning him enough to purchase a car. In some U.S. states you would be arrested for digging through people's trash.

- Forcing people to give to the poor (taxes).

- Forcing people to save for retirement (social security).

- Forcing people to hire incompetent employees (EEO regulations).

- Forcing people to stop smoking (taxes and regulations).

- Forcing people to be compassionate (taxes).

- Forcing people to use one kind of light bulb (regulations).

- Forcing the rich to pay more taxes; force the poor to pay none (graduated income taxes).

- Forcing people to pay for unrelated projects a thousand miles from home (redistribution of the wealth).

- Forcing children to attend school, or certain schools (forced busing and government mandates).

- Forcing people to bail out bad businesses (TARP and so-called stimulus bailouts).

- Forcing people to solve other nation's problems (taxes, wars, and foreign aid).

- Forcing people to produce a particular type of car (EPA and OSHA regulations).

- Forcing people to cater to coercive monopolies (post office, utilities, railroads, cable television, water, etc.).

- Forcing people to support media control and regulation, and publicly supported outlets—and the list goes on and on.

WHAT'S WRONG WITH THAT?

In the opinion of many millions, the above list makes good sense. Why not use government resources for these purposes? It's worked so far, hasn't it?

The Founders understood that granting government the power to meddle in private life, to the extent listed above, is a two-edged sword. Government is a fearful master, George Washington warned, and when given too much power, it will turn quickly on its own supporters, and force on them somebody's idea of "good" change, whether the population approves of it or not. The Founders wanted these kinds issues left to the states, where the people could exert

Socialism in America: In 2012, Miami Beach started forcing residents to recycle or face fines up to $2,500. The city said it didn't have money to enforce the ban but hoped citizens would volunteer to support it.

tighter control on the use of force, and adjust the laws according to their individual needs and populations.

For example, suppose the regime in power is opposed to eating meat. They declare that cruelty to animals exists at all stages of the meat production process. They say every aspect of the meat industry contributes to greenhouse gases and global warming.[40] They supply charts and statistics and a multitude of studies proving hundreds of negative impacts on personal health.

The *coup de gras* comes when a host of government experts provide an estimate of meat's impact on people's arteries, and likewise, on the country's insurance and health-care system. The only viable solution, they say, is to reduce consumption of meat by imposing crippling higher taxes at every level—from the farmer's grazing fields, to the butcher, and finally to the restaurant.

This fictitious scenario isn't that far from reality. It has several recent precedents—taxes or fines leveled on alcohol and tobacco to control consumption habits, forcing people to wear helmets and seat belts, and more recently, taxes on tanning salons.

Along the same lines of "government must fix all bad choices," a few states have taken up the responsibility of controlling obesity among their numbers. As poorly crafted as those laws are, at least they are on the state level where the population has more direct control. But on the federal level, the original U.S. Constitution prohibited Congress from such activities, or from extracting taxes for such purposes (see Article 1.2.8). Yet, the federal government does things like this anyway, ignoring the Constitution.

USING THE "EIGHT RIGHTS" AS A TEST

Every action by a government may be tested for principled behavior by asking this simple question: Does the new law or bill or act violate an unalienable right? If it does, that law is probably bad for a nation, and an example of expanding power that will lead to difficulties as time passes. Such laws should be immediately challenged.

For example, the U.S. adopted national health care in 2010. Going down the list of eight rights, and applying each to the new health-care law, will help frame the act as being something wonderfully liberating, or something arduous and despotic—

---

40   The 2006 U.N. Food and Agriculture Organization says meat production contributes 14-22% of the world's annual 36 billion tons of "CO2-equivalent" greenhouse gases.

Being "Created Equal" ends at birth ... after that you're on your own.

RIGHT #1—INDEPENDENT INDIVIDUALS. Does national health care protect my right to be independent, and beholden to no one? No, it forces me into a class of dependency on the government.

RIGHT #2—CHOICE. Does national health care protect my right to choose? No, it forces me to accept the government's decisions about providers, levels of care, facilities, options, etc.

RIGHT #3— PROPERTY. Does national health care protect my property rights? No, it forces me to surrender private property (taxes) to support what the government orders—not what I choose.

RIGHT #4—ASSOCIATION. Does national health care protect my right to associate? No, it violates my right to associate with *my choice* of doctor or health-care facility.

RIGHT #5—EQUALITY. Does national health care protect everyone equally? No, not everyone is covered, some people may opt out for various reasons. Worse, it forces the "haves" to contribute so that the "have nots" can have health-care coverage.

RIGHT #6.—DEFENSE. Does national health care protect my right to defend myself against this imposition? No.

RIGHT #7—COMPASSION. Does national health care protect my right to practice compassion? No. Higher taxes will undermine philanthropic donations, and prevent doctors and nurses from volunteering their services because of regulations, constraints, allocation of resources, and use of personal time, among other impositions.

RIGHT #8—FAILURE. Does national health care protect my freedom to fail? No. Free or reduced-price health care ruins people's motivation to change their lives to afford private health-care services, or to help themselves first before going to the doctor. Medical practitioners lose motivation to be more efficient, cost effective, and innovative. The quality of care and the excitement to invent always suffer without a powerful profit motive.

By asking these eight questions, a person may gain a quick understanding about *any* government act, and learn which unalienable rights are being violated. This equips an individual to better consider, *Is this good or bad?* To the socialists, it's always good, of course. They never entertain freedom as a possible solution. Their goal is power, control, and their professed pursuits of "fairness."

THE APPEAL OF SOCIALISM

The appeal of socialism is not just the many things that socialists are against (unfairness, inequality, etc.) but also because of those things for which they stand.

Socialism claims to have all the answers—

Will there be money in the new society? No, everything is shared from a distribution center *without* money.

How do I buy a house? You don't, everything belongs to everyone else. So do the cars, the stadiums, the theaters—no tickets needed to gain entrance. Health care, laundry services, transportation, communications, food, everything is free to the workers.

But, what if I don't want to stay in socialism? No problem, you are free to go, they say.

Am I freed from religion and the Bible? Of course, they say. There is a new morality, and we will decide what is moral or not. It will be more fair, more logical, and more natural.

May I save a little to get ahead? No, it's no longer about you, it's about *us*.

For the direct quotes from various socialists making all of these promises, see the Appendix, *The Appeal of Socialism*.

THE HISTORICAL RECORD SAYS IT ALL

Socialism is structured so that it will never achieve its stated goals. It is a self-perpetuating consumption of other people's labors. When those labors fall short or run out, the whole system dies. Past events in world history reiterate over and over that whenever those who work the hardest to produce the most are not properly compensated, as the free market does, they will eventually grow weary, and stop producing—despite the appealing allure of the socialists' promises. *That* is human nature at work, and such failings show up everywhere in history, even as far back as Caveman Dad.

(cont'd) "... by a little sophistry on the words 'general welfare,' a right to do, not only the acts to effect that, which are specifically enumerated and permitted, but whatsoever they shall think, or pretend will be for the general welfare. And what is our resource for the preservation of the constitution? Reason and argument?"—Thomas Jefferson

Part II

SOCIALISM IN ANCIENT HISTORY

"Socialism is a time-released poison pill with a 100% success rate."

—Author—

CHAPTER 3:

FIRST, THERE WAS FORCE

The earliest records are scant, but they show that socialism in its most raw form existed more than 6,000 years ago.

S ome researchers believe that socialism is a natural state of ancient cooperation. They surmise that at the dawn of human history the earliest peoples voluntarily resorted to communal living as a necessary part of staying alive. The theory suggests that only by living in large, strong groups could the huddled masses procure food and provide mutual protection.

This theory further surmises that the invention of farming and irrigation made food more accessible—and introduced independent living. Researchers speculate this is the period when the concept of private ownership entered the world—*I planted this field, it's all mine, now get out!*

DIFFICULT QUESTIONS—If this idea is true—that socialism is natural, and therefore, good—then the "early communal" theory leaves unanswered a number of critical questions: Who assigned the workers to their various labors, or did they all just jump in like bees in a hive? Could people be lazy and not be punished and take from others? Who directed the equal distribution of food? What if the director showed favoritism? In times of scarcity, what about the needs of the very young, the sick, or the very old? What was to prevent gangs of bullies rising up at harvest time and taking all that they pleased?[41]

CAVEMAN DAD—One solution might have been family—parents directing children to participate in providing food and protection. But that doesn't resolve the constant risk of other families raiding a village or campground—hunger awakens the beast in all creation.

It's a story that may never be known. However, history shows that communal or collectivist living in any setting required leadership directed by someone, and that dictatorship was fraught with the numerous built-in problems of sustained leadership, rules, regulations, fairness, obedience, punishment—and the ever-present use of force. Here's a sampling of those forces down through history—

---

41 See Ludwig von Mises, *Socialism*, (1922), chapter 5, "Theories of the Evolution of Property," pp. 41-44.

"Innovators and creative geniuses cannot be reared in schools. They are precisely the men who defy what the school has taught them."— Ludwig von Mises

CHAPTER 4:

ANCIENT SUMER, THE EARLIEST SOCIALISTS

It's difficult to peg a start date for Sumer, but many scholars estimate this civilization took form before 4000 B.C.

STORY: Ancient Sumerians built their form of socialism around their temples in a dozen city-states at the south end of today's Iraq. Eventually, there were about 30 large and small cities, some with populations of 10,000 or more. The whole region was known as Sumer. Their prosperity came from intensive year-round cultivation and large-scale irrigation projects. With a reliable source of storable food, the people could settle down in one place instead of migrating to greener pastures, as was their ancestors' custom.

The temples were the center of everyone's life. The priestly governor (*ensi*) or king (*lugal*) was both civic leader and spokes-man for the gods. From him came the commands to keep the temple granaries full and the workers tightly organized and busy.

The societies of Sumer were highly stratified: a ruling class with all power; an aristocracy or nobility class that leeched off everyone; and the lowly workers.

PEASANTS DOING ALL THE WORK, AS USUAL

At the bottom of the caste system were the common people. Some of them were owned by the temple and spent their lives working its lands. Everything necessary to raise food was given to them, including a place to live. However, they had no private property and they couldn't store or save anything as their own.

The earliest Sumerian cuneiform records don't indicate many slaves in Sumerian society. The soldiers won plenty of wars, but rarely brought back prisoners—a strong indicator that the defeated foes were executed on the battle field or marched to death camps.

THE CENTRAL STOREHOUSE

In the Sumerian cities, the storehouse was everything. Workers' equipment, animals, seed grain, and a monthly sustenance all flowed from the storehouse. Quotas were important. The storehouse got stingy if workers failed to reach the quota. If a harvest came in

---

shorter than that which was ordered, the workers were expected to make up the difference the following year—or suffer accordingly.

Igor Shafarevich provides several good examples of life in ancient civilizations in his book, *The Socialist Phenomenon.*[42] Among those is the Sumerians' Temple of Bau, built about 2500 B.C. in Lagash. These temple priests controlled the whole region. The temple was serviced by the "Shub-Iugal," a workforce that received small land grants and government-issued plows, grain, cattle, yokes, collars, tools, etc. Chief farmers supervised them and all their work.

Everything the Bau worshippers produced had to be given to the storehouse, even the skin of a dead animal. Craftsmen who were bonded to the temple used the skins and other materials to manufacture clothing, tools, artwork, and other necessities—all of it surrendered back again to the central storehouse.

Other industries were obligated to do the same. The fishermen had to deliver their entire catch, the foresters their entire load, and the cattlemen every head to the storehouse coffers.

MISERABLE MORTALITY RATES

The cost for these operations was horrific. Copious baked-clay tablets meticulously included the name "deceased" next to names of those who died from the work. Researchers calculate that 35 percent of the field workers died each year. Many of these were women and children involved in unskilled labor and strenuous work such as hauling barges. The average mortality rate for the whole society is calculated to be between 20-25 percent. Over the centuries, the aristocracy grew while the peasants worked, toiled, and poured out their lives until death—all of this to benefit the storehouse.

STATE CONTROL CREATES STATE COLLAPSE

After a thousand years of heavy-handed central regulation, misery, and exploitation, the huge bureaucratic state was ripe for collapse. Their main city was Ur, thought to have been the largest city in the world with some 65,000 inhabitants. Their central god was Nanna, the Sumerian moon god. The temple and shrine for Nanna was built in the 21st century B.C., known today as the Great Ziggurat of Ur. This highly centralized and top-heavy society couldn't sustain itself and started to decay. After repeated assaults,

---

42 See Igor Shafarevich, *The Socialist Phenomenon,"* 1980.

Ur finally fell to the Elamites in 1940 B.C. Other doomed Sumerian cities followed.

The Sumerians wrote a lament for Ur, similar to the book of Lamentations in the Bible. In the aftermath of the destruction of their cities, they described complete wreckage—corpses decaying in the streets, the storehouses stripped down, the towns destroyed, women kidnapped to foreign lands, and other Sumerian cities falling to the sword. Their long and stifling experiment in socialism had ended, with every life sacrificed for the central storehouse—a sad and sorry waste.[43]

THE SEVEN PILLARS

Ruler. Top-down control, the common theme of human domination that would recreate itself hundreds of times for thousands of years, apparently was easily imposed on the early Sumer people. The human tendency to relinquish responsibility to the initiatives of another served well to sustain a man claiming to be a god or god's representative for temple worship.

Caste. Stratified society was enforced with death. The rulers and nobility kept it this way to sustain their own selfish lives and perpetuate power. As a result, untold numbers were denied their contributions to a better society.

Things in Common. It's an easy sell to say all things belong to the ruler when the people believe their ruler is a god. Even though land and resources were not owned in common, they were deployed, dispensed, and used in common, as directed by the rulers to supposedly support the city's survival. With no private ownership, a sense of common use of the land prevailed—and with it, an acceptance of force to ensure production best fit for the whole.

Natural Rights. Central control meant few natural rights could be exercised. The people were obligated to obey every command from the ruler. It was a harsh way of living.

Regimentation. All aspects of society were controlled by a

---

43 For several good references on Sumer, see Will Durant, *The Story of Civilization: Our Oriental History* (1935); Peter Bogucki, *The Origins of Human Society* (1990); Petr Charvat, *Mesopotamia Before History* (2002); Hans J. Nissen, *The Early History of the Ancient Near East, 9000-2000 B.C.*, (1990); Chandler Tertium, *Four Thousand Years of Urban Growth: An Historical Census*; A. I. Tiumenev, *The Economy of Ancient Sumer*, Moscow-Leningrad, 1956, as quoted in Shafarevich, 1980.

"Knowledge will forever govern ignorance; and a people who mean to be their own Governors, \must arm themselves with the power which knowledge gives." James Madison

crude form of modern communism's "scientific method." This is where needs were anticipated whether they materialized or not, and laborers were compelled to fulfill those needs—scientifically.

Information. The people were controlled and probably pacified by the spirit of ignorance that was cultivated around them. By maintaining a sense of pending warfare, and preying upon the superstitions of the people to support temple worship, kept them focused and grateful for the Ruler's benevolence and protection.

Force. Violent retribution for the least infraction made strong control feasible in Sumer. Complainers could have their tongues cut out, or worse. Finally, by around 1800 B.C. or so, Hammurabi brought some order to these laws, but they remained severe. A doctor whose patient did not get better, especially if the person got worse, was liable—even unto death. If a house collapsed because of an architect's bad design, he could be executed. On the other hand, if you were in an upper class, it made a big difference. A noble blinding another noble or breaking his bone could be punished by being blinded with a hot poker or having his own bone broken by a heavy club. However, if a noble blinded or broke the bone of someone in a lower caste or class, he only had to pay a fine.

* * * * *

HUMAN NATURE AT WORK

"It is the common error of socialists to overlook the natural indolence of mankind; their tendency to be passive, to be the slaves of habit, to persist indefinitely in a course once chosen. Let them once attain any state of existence which they consider tolerable, and the danger to be apprehended is that they will thenceforth stagnate; will not exert themselves to improve, and by letting their faculties rust, will lose even the energy required to preserve them from deterioration. Competition may not be the best conceivable stimulus, but it is at present a necessary one, and no one can foresee the time when it will not be indispensable to progress."—John Stuart Mill[44]

---

44   John Stuart Mill, *The Principles of Political Economy*, Book IV, Chapter 7.

CHAPTER 5:

PHARAOH, THE
DEMIGOD SOCIALIST

*Egypt built a civilization on the flood plains of the Nile, extracting
prosperity from the toils of thousands that grew into
millions—starting sometime around 2700 B.C.*

S TORY: The pattern of temple worship and top-down
control was not unique to Sumer. It was representative of
other civilizations during the same period—Egypt, Greece,
Turkey, Crete, Mesopotamia, with shades of the same in the Indus
Valley civilizations. By the middle of the third millennium B.C.,
life in the ancient world underwent a big change. The friendlier
conclaves of temple society and city-states were replaced by the all-
encompassing power of the state—a new power of absolute force
that changed the world forever.

PHARAOH AND THE NILE, GIFTS FROM THE GODS

Ancient Egypt is a good example of the new and expansive
state. The land was ruled by Pharaoh, a god incarnate who united
far-flung villages under his rule. He was advertised as being without
parents, miraculously formed in the womb by the gods. They said
he knew all, saw all, and as the gods' chosen one, he therefore
owned all the land, people and animals. He was revered as the high
priest to Ra and favored of Horus, son of Osiris. He was Pharaoh—
the deified king.

THE NO-ABILITY NOBILITY

Helping Pharaoh, but later competing with him, was a class
of nobility—the royal administrators. This rich upper class ruled in
Pharaoh's stead, checking every part of people's lives—spiritual,
social, and economic. They kept track of all things with a small
army of scribes. These scribes were sent across the land every year
or two to take inventory of people's possessions and taxed them
accordingly. Naturally, the scribes took along a few beefy-looking
soldiers to enforce the peasant's cooperation. It was levelling at the
most intimate place in a person's life.

THE QUILL IS MIGHTIER THAN THE ROD

The scribes were well educated, themselves forming a class of intelligentsia who were better educated than the nobility. Knowing how to read and write led many scribes into positions of administration or pursuits of political agendas later in life.

This massive bureaucracy of administrators was everywhere in Egypt—village judge, village scribe, builder of palaces, overseer of grains and granaries, chief of canals, chief of the fleet, butlers of the palace, leaders of the land, the Sherden, cowherds, priests, warriors, swineherds, shopkeepers, interpreters, boatmen, husbandmen, noblemen, administrators, personal attendants, etc.

OBEDIENCE IS BETTER THAN SACRIFICE

Peasants and farm workers made up the largest part of the population. The snooty upper classes looked down on them. Many worked the Pharaoh's lands in exchange for a home and food. Others were their own masters and owned their own homes and land. They engaged in producing, buying, and selling as they pleased. However, they were still supervised by a scribe from a temple or private estate or some bureaucrat.

Masters were reasonably kind to their workers. They kept them fed, clothed, housed, and protected from mobbing and bullying— they were, after all, the real producers. A maxim from the 19th dynasty proclaimed, "Give one loaf to your laborer, receive two from (the work of) his arms. Give one loaf to the one who labors, give two to the one who gives orders."

The storehouse typically released food only once a month. Some depictions on tombs show workers on the verge of starvation while the beasts of burden are fat and healthy—a telling display of priorities.

WE KEEP YOU ALIVE TO SERVE THIS PHARAOH

Unlike Sumer, the Egyptians prided themselves in keeping their workers alive. Both they and their supervisors were subject to beatings for laziness, tardiness, or desertion. Pharaoh appreciated the fact that with no workers, there was no work—they were too valuable to lose, so there was some protection in this.

While the upper classes enjoyed the richness of life, thanks to the workers, the peasants were on a bare subsistence level. The central planners determined that to stay alive for a year, a working class family required: 380 pounds of wheat (about a pound a day), 44 pounds of lentils, and 11 pounds of meat. Most peasants could earn 50-90 percent of those minimums, thus requiring the women and children to work just to avoid starvation.[45]

And so grew Egypt through thick and thin, for dozens of centuries, to rise and fall and rise again—steeped in Ruler's Law.

THE SEVEN PILLARS

Egyptian culture made an enormous investment in supervising management at every level of society. This multi-layered involvement created a mid-level in the caste system that was strong, well-funded, well-organized, and perpetuated itself down through the generations.

As with Sumer, few natural rights were acknowledged and there was no private ownership of property.

Whatever Pharaoh said was declared as truth—*let it be written, let it be done.* Obedience to him or her (yes, there were female Pharaohs) was extracted by force because disobedience to Pharaoh's law was deemed also as disobedience to the gods.

---

45 For several good references on Egypt's use of Ruler's Law, see Will Durant, *The Story of Civilization: Our Oriental History,* Egypt (1935); Walter Scheidel, *Real wages in early economies: Evidence for living standards from 1800 B.C. to A.D. 1300,* Version 4.0 September 2009, Princeton/Stanford Working Papers in Classics; Andre Bollinger, www.reshafim.org.il/ad/egypt/; The Encyclopedia Britannica, Egypt, 13th Edition, 1926.

What's in a name? The New York phone book listed 11 Hitlers prior to World War II ... and after the war? None.

CHAPTER 6:

NIMROD, THE ANTI-GOD SOCIALIST

*The story here begins approximately 2200 B.C.,
a short time after the Great Flood.*

STORY: According to Josephus, the ancient Roman-Jewish historian from the first century A.D., Nimrod is the fellow who re-introduced centralized power and socialistic tyranny into the world after the deluge—the Great Flood.

Those who know their Bible take interest in Nimrod because he was a great-grandson of Noah. Genesis implies that Nimrod ordered the building of the tower of Babel so his people could survive another flood should God send one. The Bible describes Nimrod as a mighty hunter before the Lord who ruled over several major cities in Mesopotamia. Thanks to Josephus[46] and other scholars, this is what is known about Nimrod: ·

❖   Nimrod comes from the Hebrew verb "marad," meaning "to rebel." Adding "n" changes the meaning to "the rebel" or "we will revolt." The man's name may not be Nimrod at all, but a derisive term. Some scholars believe he might be the king of Uruk, also known throughout history as Gilgamesh.[47]

❖   Genesis 10:9 says "He was a mighty hunter before the Lord: wherefore it is said, Even as Nimrod the mighty hunter before the Lord." Most scholars since A.D. 100 point out that the phrase "before the Lord" should be understood negatively, to mean in opposition or defiance of the Lord.

❖   Genesis 10:10 continues with, "And the beginning of his kingdom was Babel, and Erech, and Accad, and Calneh, in the land of Shinar." Scholars conclude that Nimrod's great kingdom was built of men, explaining that the term "great hunter" really means "great hunter of men." That is, he hunted men to build his empire in opposition to God.[48]

---

46   Josephus, *Jewish Antiquities.*
47   See Kautzsch 1910, as cited by David P. Livingston, www.christiananswers.net/dictionary/nimrod.html.
48   Genesis 10:8-10; 11:1-9, KJV.

"Only the individual thinks. Only the individual reasons. Only the individual acts."
—Ludwig von Mises

Ancient writers said Nimrod turned the people from God, telling them that true joy came not from the Lord, but by their own hand. He instituted pagan worship, idolatry, and the worship of fire. He changed the government and put himself in charge, declaring "I am God." He forced the people to become dependent on him for everything they required—an ancient version of today's food stamps, pensions, and general government welfare. Genesis says Nimrod's reign of tyranny and force was ultimately conquered by the confusion of tongues at the Tower of Babel when all were scattered.[49]

AFTER THE FLOOD, SEVEN SOGGY PILLARS

Nimrod was a devoted adherent to the seven pillars of socialism.

⬥ He set himself up as the all-powerful ruler.

⬥ He created classes of leaders and followers, with him at the top.

⬥ He managed his power base with corruption, drawing support from his followers for the basest of reasons.

⬥ He held all things in common for himself, doling out favors or necessities as he best saw fit.

⬥ He controlled information and dismissed the belief in an intervening or judgmental God, urging his followers to develop their own intellect and self-realization as the best guide for happiness and prosperity.

⬥ He regulated society with ruthless force, passing laws according to his own whims at the time.

⬥ The people had no rights except what he granted them.

The pattern Nimrod followed was the same as other dictators and tyrants. For example, far to the east, similar ideas about Ruler's Law were taking root among the ancient Chinese.

---

49   C. F. Keil, and P. Delitzsch, *Commentary on the Old Testament*, vol. 1, 1975.

During prohibition, New Your City's 16,000 saloons grew to more than 100,000 "speakeasies."

CHAPTER 7:

CHINA: DYNASTIES OF SOCIALISM

From about 1600 to 300 B.C., the elements of Ruler's Law kept order down to the most personal levels of life in China.

STORY: Henri Maspero was a pioneering scholar of ancient China and researched the amazing history of rigid rule and control that existed in the earliest non-mythical period of China.[50]

Most of what is known about the Shang Dynasty (1750-1100 B.C.) comes from inscriptions on tortoise shells, cattle bones, and other oracle bones. Scribes used bronze pins to scratch ancient characters into the bones, telling of a society ruled by an all-powerful king, the leader of Chinese nobility, a ruler called Wang.[51]

RELIGIOUS TYRANT

Wang was leader, military commander, and the high priest. He offered sacrifice to royal ancestors and communed with the divine to bring wind and rain. Should war erupt, Wang kept a personal force of 1,000 men for protection from uprisings, and also to personally lead into battle with other soldiers.

During Wang's rule, the use of bronze was widespread. He ordered an enormous slave labor force to mine the copper, lead, and tin ores, haul them for processing, and deliver the metal to artisans and manufacturers. Bronze was used everywhere—for vessels, weapons, decorations, clothing items, and even chariot wheels.

3,000 CRIMES AND GROWING

The Wang ruled the people with force. He called them his "cattle and people," and on the disobedient he inflicted torture. One of the Wangs had a list of 3,000 crimes for which he imposed fear to extract obedience. For 1,000 of these offenses, the punishment was branding with a hot iron. For another 1,000, the punishment was cutting off the nose. There were 300 offenses punishable with castration, and 500

---

50   Henri Maspero, *Ancient China*, 1927, as quoted in *The Socialist Phenomenon*, Igor Shafarevich, pp. 167-171.
51   Also see Will Durant, *Our Oriental Heritage*, book three, *China* pp. 636-823.

"Give me four years to teach the children and the seed I have sown will never be uprooted."
—Vladimir Lenin

others for which they would cut off the heel. Two hundred were capital crimes for which the person was killed.

WANG OWNS ALL

The Wang owned everything. One script declared, "Under the heavens there is no land that does not belong to the Wang, in the whole world from one end to the other there are no people who are not the Wang's underlings." Children were raised by the elders to age 10. The following year, they were forced to work. At age 20 they received a field whereby they made their subsistence. At age 60 they returned ownership of the field to Wang. When workers reached 70, they became wards of the state—cared for until death,

Wang granted authority to other officials to supervise agriculture, public works, and war. These leaders held tight rein on the fields, deciding when to plant, what to plant, and when to rotate crops. One of their songs declared, "Our ruler summons us all ... orders you to lead the plowmen to sow grain....quickly take your instruments and begin to plow. ...Let ten thousand pairs go out... this will be enough ... the Wang was not angry; he said, 'You peasants have labored gloriously.'" Other songs told of their land and grounds being theirs in common.

MARRIAGE OR UNIONS, NOT BOTH

Marriage was regulated. As a religious bond, only the nobility could marry. The peasants were ordered into "unions"—men had to take a spouse by age 30, the girls by age 20. A day for marrying in the spring was declared and local officials enforced it.

THEN CAME CONFUCIUS

Winding down through the dynasties, from Shang (1600-1046 B.C.) through the Western Zhou (1046-771 B.C.), Confucius finally arrived around 500 B.C. He taught about man's ethical and moral progression and the importance of his nobility and justice, his love of all things. But socialism continued to strengthen its grip on Chinese culture.

SHANG YANG WEAKENS THE PEOPLE

By A.D. 350, a more rigid and centralized state took form. Shang Yang worked hard to strengthen the central government. He viewed the people as raw material that required smelting or molding like clay by a potter. He wrote, "When the people are weak the state is strong; when the state is weak the people are strong. Hence the state that follows a true course strives to weaken the people." Shang Yang put these thoughts in a book that included a chapter, "How to Weaken the People."

THE STATE IS CENTRAL IN ALL THINGS

Shang Yang ruled with punishment and reward. He abandoned all other virtues, saying that love and justice only invited crime and weakness into the people. Igor Shafarevich[52] found several excellent quotes from Shang Yang's book that show that the seven pillars of socialism were well entrenched in ancient Chinese culture.[53]

◆ **MAKE THEM DEPENDENT:** Sever ties that bind people together and build trust in the government: "If the people are ruled as virtuous, they will love those closest to them; if they are ruled as depraved, they will become fond of this system."

◆ **INJECT MISTRUST**: The ruler "should issue a law on mutual surveillance; he should issue a decree that the people ought to correct each other."

◆ **REWARD "WHISTLE BLOWERS"**: "Regardless of whether the informer is of the nobility or of low origin, he inherits fully the nobility, the fields and the salary of the senior official whose misconduct he reports to the ruler."

◆ **THE ENDS JUSTIFY THE MEANS**: "If by war, war can be abolished, then even war is permissible; if by murder, murder can be abolished, then even murder is permissible; if by punishment, punishment can be abolished, then even harsh punishment is permissible."

◆ **STAYING FOCUSED ON THE ONE THING**: Shang Yang considered the "One Thing" to be agriculture and war. Putting everyone's attention to these prevented the peasants from considering other pursuits in life: "He who wants the flowering of the state should inspire in the people the knowledge that official posts and ranks of nobility can be obtained only by engaging in the One Thing."

52　Ibid., Shafarevich.
53　*The Book of Lord Shang*, translated by J. J.-L. Duyvendak, 1928.

Same-Sex Parenting Not the Same: In 2012, a study published in the *Social Science Research* journal reported children raised by same-sex parents have more problems in social, emotional, and relationships issues. They have lower income levels, poorer physical health, ... (cont'd)

❖ **GIMMICK FOR CONTROL:** Part of the "One Thing" strategy was to control the peasants with farming: "When all thoughts are turned to agriculture, people are simple and easily governed."

❖ **POLICING THE RULERS:** The other part of the "One Thing" was to control the nobility: "All privileges and salaries, official posts and ranks of nobility, must be given only for service in the army; there must be no other way. For only by this path is it possible to take a clever man and a fool, nobles and common folk, brave men and cowards, worthy men and those good for nothing, and extract all that is in their heads and their backs and force them to risk their lives for the sake of the ruler."

❖ **INFORMATION CONTROL:** There could be nothing outside of the "One Thing" because the people might start thinking on their own: "It is necessary to drive people into such a state that they should suffer if not engaged in agriculture, that they should live in fear if they are not engaged in war."

❖ **IGNORANCE MUST BE CULTIVATED:** "If knowledge is encouraged and not nipped in the bud, it will increase, and when it will have increased, it will become impossible to rule the land. ...The art of ruling well consists precisely in the ability of removing the clever and the gifted. ...If the people are stupid, they can be easily governed."

These ideas were added upon with other heavy-handed practices: elaborate and staged book burnings to prevent independent thought, guilt by association where relatives and friends of criminals were killed or otherwise punished, and burying the teachings of Confucius—literally. The record says Ch'in Shih Huang buried alive 460 Confucian scholars and exiled others to keep the kingdom purged of the kind of independent thinking promoted by Confucius and his followers.[54]

---

54 Ibid.

(cont'd) ... poorer mental health, and troubles in romantic relationships. Of the 40 measures, differences were found in 25. Researchers said it's not that same-sex couples can't be good parents, it appears the lack of biological parents creates problems and risks as children age into adulthood.

CHAPTER 8:

ASSYRIANS: RUTHLESS, BLOOD-DRENCHED SOCIALISTS

The Assyrians built their mighty power sometime around 750 B.C. Ruthless bloodshed seemed the typical enforcement tool of Assyria and other ancient tyrannies of the Mesopotamia region during that period.

STORY: There's a familiar pattern of reckless disregard for human life among many of the ancient kingdoms. These patterns of mass slaughter are not unique to the ancients— slaughters more reprehensible have been repeated on different levels and to different degrees in modern socialist and communist countries.

It was rare when a tyrant in ancient times could anticipate a nice, quiet retirement after ruling his realm. Leadership often changed hands through assassination, outright murder, uprisings, rebellions, and palace intrigue. If a king's son wanted power, killing good old Dad was the quickest way to get promoted. If the son was not liked by the people or the army, he was made a corpse before he could ascend his father's throne. For example, of the first 47 Roman emperors, 24 were assassinated.

EXTREME VIOLENCE A WAY OF LIFE

Assyria is a shocking example of violence and gore. Enough records were left behind to show that the Assyrians had no regard for their foes or citizens who didn't obey. As historian Will Durant describes it, "The Assyrians seemed to find satisfaction—or a necessary tutelage for their sons—in torturing captives, blinding children before the eyes of their parents, flaying men alive, roasting them in kilns, chaining them in cages for the amusement of the populace, and then sending the survivors off to execution."[55]

Assyrian King Ashurnasirpal (about 860 B.C.) describes putting down an uprising and how "all the chiefs who had revolted I flayed,

---

55   Will Durant, *Our Oriental Heritage, Assyria*, pp. 265-284; *The Encyclopedia Britannica*, 13th Edition, 1926, *Assyria*.

"The mass of mankind has not been born with saddles on their backs, nor a favored few booted and spurred, ready to ride them legitimately, by the grace of God."—Thomas Jefferson

with their skins I covered the pillar, some in the midst I walled up, others on stakes I impaled, still others I arranged around the pillar on stakes .... As for the chieftains and royal officers who had rebelled, I cut off their members."[56]

NO WONDER JONAH SKIPPED OUT ON THE LORD

Assyria and Nineveh have an additional place of importance for students of the Bible. Knowing these added details about Assyria suddenly makes it clear why Jonah disobeyed God. Jonah had been ordered by God to visit the Assyrian capital city of Nineveh, "for their great wickedness is come up before me."[57]

Rather than endure the extreme atrocities for which Assyria was famous, Jonah fled from his assignment and took a ship in exactly the opposite direction toward Tarshish. It required a violent storm and a large fish swallowing Jonah and keeping him for three days and nights to convince Jonah that obedience is more important than the burning, flaying, cutting, dismemberment, blinding, tongue-lopping, beheading, roasting tortures of Nineveh.

And so, in fear and trembling, Jonah went to the great city and began calling them to repentance.

Much to Jonah's surprise, the people of Nineveh hearkened to his message and actually started to repent. Jonah fully expected the Lord to destroy them for their great wickedness, but the Lord later explained there were innocents in that city who needed saving.[58]

ELEMENTS OF SOCIALISM

Long before Jonah was even born, the Assyrian kings told their subjects that they ruled with a heavenly mandate, that they were the incarnation of the god *Shamash*, the sun. The king's lieutenants were anxious that everyone support this doctrine, and assured the masses that the king owned all things because of his divine connec-tions.—*So pay attention and do your job*, they told the quivering masses.

The Assyrian government was an instrument of war, ever striving toward progress in the military arts. The king's troops were organized and trained to be quickly adaptable—as effective against the enemy as against the king's own citizens.

---

56 Quoted by Georges Roux, *Ancient Iraq* (3rd ed.), 1992, pp. 290-291.
57 Jonah 1:2.
58 For full story see See *Bible*, the Book of Jonah.

FIVE-LAYERED CASTE

The people were divided into five classes—the nobility, the craftsmen who were organized into guilds, the free workmen and peasants, and the hordes of slaves captured in war.

There was no private ownership for the workers. They were bound to the land of the great estates and had all things provided for them in exchange for working the land and raising the animals.

The only science that flourished was that of war. The philosophers of the time showed no effort to explain life or the world around them. Instead, they filled their time listing objects—all objects—and attempted to catalogue them. From those lists, the modern world has adopted several words translated through the Greek such as camel, shekel, rose, ammonia, cane, cherry, sesame, and myrrh, among others.

HOW THE MIGHTY FALL

As with all such kingdoms, Assyria relied on the wrong system to retain power and its place in history. Instead of strengthening its populace with freedom, it relied on iron-fisted force and the pillars of Ruler's Law to demand prosperity.

In 626 B.C., the Babylonians and several allies swept through the Assyrian strongholds and set the land to ruin. Palaces fell into mounds of burned-out rubble, Nineveh was smashed and set afire, and its population was slaughtered or hauled away as slaves.

And just that quickly, in an instant of horrible bloodshed, the mighty and seemingly unconquerable Assyrian dynasty of terror and ruthlessness was suddenly and simply ... no more.

SEVEN PILLARS IN ANCIENT TIMES

The predominant pillars of socialism in operation for the first three thousand years of recorded human history were the all-powerful rulers and the suppression and destruction of personal rights. In whatever form the leader maintained control, ownership of all things rested in the priest, Pharaoh, Wang, and whatever classes of nobility were allowed to wallow in the spoils.

Dispensing material necessities came at the whim of the rulers. All things went to a storehouse or treasure city, and were granted to the masses according to levels of production. In times of war, the allegiance and loyalty of their soldiers was secured with additional

"This and no other is the root from which a tyrant springs; when he first appears he is a protector."
—Plato

dispensations of allowances, but always tied to strict obedience to the hand that fed them.

THE PILLARS OF SOCIALISM

Future tyrants would exact similar atrocities as the Assyrians to force the population to bow to the rulers—in particular the Inca, the Maya, Soviet Russia, and Communist China. With such terror exacted on enemies and conquered peoples, the fear of death by dismemberment was a reminder to the populous to support all edicts from the throne.

LEARNING TO RECOGNIZE SOCIALISM

People in the ancient world had to be tricked with superstitions into following the regimented life. The idea of god in the form of their leader solved one of socialism's greatest challenges: how to properly train the human heart to serve as policeman of the brain.

A sign of socialism is compelling people to believe a lie. With no other information available, lies can be masked very well and the people's ignorance used against them.

Today, the lies come in many forms. A nation's currency that is not based on precious metals is a good example. The intrinsic value of money is simply made up. No one really knows how much a dollar is worth—or a yen or a shekel or a ruble or a euro. The worth is hidden by official government policy that manipulates the value as needed.

Another lie is that freedom or free enterprise or capitalism could never solve a host of national problems. Painting the best solution in the darkest light creates a false image and people willingly surrender the freedom to try, buy, sell, and fail, for regulation by the government.

The record of ancient times may not tell us much in the way of early economies and the advancement of human rights. But there is evidence that human nature doesn't change. Most people are content to be followers so long as their needs are met. But as the government requires more, it must extract more from the people, and with that comes more force plus all the associated controls, lies, enticements, and masters. Top-down government *must* function in this fashion.

Freedom to self-defense helps: "Violent-crime rates were rising consistently before the right-to-carry laws and [fell] thereafter ... For each additional year the laws were in effect, murders fell by an additional 1.5%, while rape, robbery and aggravated assaults all fell by about 3% each year."—John R. Lott, Jr.

When the people have lost control of who rules them, a class of elites rises up, and *true to human nature*, they'll resort to anything necessary to stay in power, no matter what rights they violate in others. "Might makes right" is the mantra of the despot.

With that pattern of kingly authority and control well established in the early periods of human history, a break to try out self-government in America truly was a revolutionary act. For most of human history, self-government was rejected by rulers as ludicrous, unfathomable, and unimaginable. The elites presumed that the masses were simply too stupid to manage all of their society's complex affairs.

But when the Founders sat down with a chance to try something different, they rejected such assumptions and concluded that all of mankind *is* able to self-rule, *if* they can first rule their own hearts. As Franklin cautioned, the form of government they created was a republic "*if* you can keep it."

With that opportunity lying in the future, and the lessons necessary for implementation of freedom yet to be learned, more human blood would flow through hundreds of generations while the bad ideas embraced by socialism remained in control.

*   *   *   *   *

SPOKEN LIKE A TRUE SOCIALIST

"I am a Socialist, not through reading a textbook that has caught my intellectual fancy, nor through unthinking tradition, but because I believe that, at its best, Socialism corresponds most closely to an existence that is both rational and moral. It stands for cooperation, not confrontation; for fellowship, not fear. It stands for equality, not because it wants people to be the same but because only through equality in our economic circumstances can our individuality develop properly."—Tony Blair[59], 1983

---

59   Tony Blair, 1983 Hansard, House of Commons, 6th Series, vol. 45, col. 316. Maiden speech by Tony Blair as MP for Sedgefield, July 6, 1983.

Socialism is expensive: Norway adds 8% sales tax to all bus rides.

With only 4.5% of the world's population, the U.S. produces 44% of the world's corn.

Part III

SOCIALISM IN CLASSICAL HISTORY

"From Rome to ruins,
the classical forms
marched bravely toward
the chasm, determined
and assured that
all was well."

—Author—

CHAPTER 9:

DRACO AND HIS DRACONIAN IDEAS

This fellow seems to have coined his own motto: "In death we trust."
It was 621 B.C. when Draco rose to power, feverishly
bent on forcing people to be good.

STORY: Before 621 B.C., the Greeks didn't do a very good job of writing things down, especially their laws. Many of their provincial customs and "whatever worked" rules were passed along orally from ruler to ruler and arbitrarily enforced—but not written. That made problems.

AND THEN CAME DRACO

Historians don't know a lot about Draco, and guess that he came from the nobility class. He apparently rose to take power as Athens' chief magistrate sometime around 621 B.C. According to Aristotle,[60] Draco wrote down an elaborate code of laws—a constitution of sorts—that reached into every aspect of Athenian life. Ridding Athens of deeply rooted problems was Draco's good and worthy goal. It's how he went about doing it that won him a place in infamy.

OFF WITH THEIR HEADS

Draco's strict and unforgiving laws put the death penalty on almost everything. Plutarch wrote that Draco's death penalty "was appointed for almost all offenses, insomuch that those that were convicted of idleness were to die, and those that stole a cabbage or an apple to suffer even as villains that committed sacrilege or murder."[61]

Plutarch also recorded a comment by Draco showing his callous attitude toward death. When asked why Draco had made so many offenses punishable with execution, Draco replied, "Small ones deserve that [death], and I have no higher [punishment] for the greater crimes."[62]

---

60 Aristotle, *The Athenian Constitution.*
61 Plutarch, *The Life of Solon.*
62 Ibid.

Besides his fixation on the death penalty, Draco was a typical ruler. He poured out benefits on the privileged class so they would keep him in power. He granted them private property ownership and the right to vote. The masses were generally denied these rights.

INSTANT RESULTS

As was expected, the harsh punishment for the least little infraction virtually paralyzed the actions of Athenians in every regard. Crime was reduced, but at the horrible cost of perpetual fear among the people, and the loss of their personal freedoms. Nevertheless, Draco's drastic impositions did rid the city of age-old problems. His ruthless actions led to a new word in English vocabulary— "draconian," meaning cruel and harsh.

KILLING WITH LOVE

Draco's overnight elimination of crime was so popular that the people believed he had actually performed a miracle. In gratitude and respect, he was surrounded with cheering, adoring crowds everywhere he went.

And then one day, he entered an Athenian theater and the enamored spectators rose to their feet in a raucous cheer of accolades for their great leader. He was at the height of his popularity and strode to a center place so that all might cherish him. As tokens of the people's high esteem for Draco, or at least to curry his benevolence should they befall one of his laws, several hundred admirers rushed to honor him by casting to him their cloaks, robes, hats, and flowers. The outpouring was so sudden and massive that he was completely covered by their gifts and was literally smothered to death.

They buried him right where he died.

A man named Solon (638-539 B.C.),[63] the so-called father of democracy in Greece, came along later and abolished nearly all of Draco's laws except death for murder.

---

63   Ibid.

Socialism is the squalor of human envy; prosperity the offspring of liberty.

CHAPTER 10:

SPARTA:
WARRIOR SOCIALISTS

*Making war central to their existence from 650 to about 371 B.C.
is a good example of information control to retain power.
Mussolini tried it in Italy some 2,500 years later
under the moniker of fascism.*

S TORY: Hanging off the southern end of Greece is a hand-shaped peninsula that was invaded around 1000 B.C. The invaders were a primitive and rude people called the Dorians. They settled in Sparta and quickly spread and enslaved the local Greeks in Laconia. Although outnumbered by perhaps 20 to 1, the invaders inflicted such horrors that the Laconians acquiesced. And so began Sparta, the most powerful city-state in ancient Greece.

Over the centuries, Sparta became fanatical about producing the finest warriors in the world. It's entire social and economic structure was built around that goal. No greater honor existed than to die in glorious battle for the state.

GRANDSONS OF ZEUS

Sparta was ruled by two kings who traced their genealogy to Hercules, son of Zeus and a divine hero in Greek mythology. The two kings were equal in power and ruled at the same time.

The kings operated their society around agriculture—no industry allowed. The kings owned all the land but gave temporary land grants to support the city. Helping them with civil and judicial affairs was a council of 28 Spartan elders.

RAISING WARRIORS

There were only two types of people who could have tombstones in Sparta—a warrior who died in battle or a mother who died in child birth because both were honored sacrifices of giving your life for the state. Child bearing and child rearing is not for the parents, not for the family, but for the state—that is the sole purpose of any human born into that society. If a newborn was deemed too weak to grow into a good warrior, it was left alone to die. The boys were taken from their mothers at age seven and enrolled in military training called the Agoge to become hardened.

Socialism is expensive: Norway adds 25% sales tax on most non-food purchases.

The training included making them cut reeds to make a bed, being underfed to encourage theft of food, as well as the basics of reading, writing, music, and dancing. They were sometimes flogged as a group to see which of them would be the first to cry out or pass out. Their families would watch at the wayside shouting to them not to pass out or cry or shed tears. The toughest was honored by everyone.

This whole structure and society was designed to strip people of their individual identity—to cement the idea they were nothing more than tools of society.

ALL CONTROL IN THE STATE

By age 12, the boys had to take an older male mentor who functioned as a substitute father and role model. Sexual relations between the two usually followed. At age 18, they were in the military reserve, and by age 20, they joined a group of 15 others to bond with and rely on for times of war.

Marriage was encouraged at age 20, but the men did not live with their families until age 30. For those reluctant to tie the knot, marriage was required by age 30, like it or not.

Young Spartans were granted land to work, and were allowed to own gold and silver. They were forbidden from engaging in commerce or trade. Their houses had to be crude, built with an axe to discourage time-wasting labors to beautify or sculpt the interiors. The women enjoyed more freedoms than others of that time—owning properties and being treated equally in divorce. Some scholars estimate that women owned at least 35% of all land and property in Sparta.

The rest of society consisted of a slightly larger class called the free men—people who escaped the original Dorian invaders but still lived in Sparta.

THE DISPOSABLE SLAVES

At the bottom of society were the Greek slaves from Laconia. They were called Helots, wholly owned by the state. The Helots farmed the soil but were required to surrender the produce to the state, sometimes all of it.

Young Spartan warriors just graduating from military school practiced their arts on Helots. Each autumn the Spartans declared war on the Helots and sent their young soldiers in training to slay rebellious or otherwise threatening slaves. This kept the Helots submissive and emaciated of strength.

SOCIALIST AND REGIMENTED

In Sparta, all land was granted by the state, a citizen's place in society was determined at birth, children were raised by the state, any commerce or trade was outlawed. There was no private property, and most of those restrictions were conveniently set aside for the elite who received such privileges for reasons of birth, status, or loyalty. It was a period of warrior socialism—the first fascists.

Spartans were very religious and would turn to the Oracle at Delphi for guidance. This had been a Greek tradition since about 1400 B.C.[64]

MAGIC ALWAYS WORKS

The all-powerful ruler was exalted and revered as a deity. Worship was a convenient self-avowed devotion that required no force and simplified securing complete obedience. By making himself an object of worship he could control the beliefs and knowledge of the people. This technique kept him securely ensconced on his throne of power and embraced in the sanctity of his international powers with the mysterious and eternal unknown.

Deifying the ruler was common everywhere. The practice continued through dozens of centuries, and took on the forms of regal appointment and majesty during the post-Christian era. In Europe this was known as the *Divine Right of Kings*—another way of saying the king was all powerful in the eyes of God so long as he was in accord with the Bible. In Asia, the Chinese called it the *Mandate from Heaven* with similar responsibilities and authority laid on the shoulders of the ruler.

DESTRUCTION OF FAMILY BONDS

Preventing the formation of rebellion and uprising was managed by breaking down the family. Sometimes Spartan families were left intact and sold, or rented with the land—other times divided according to the needs of the state.

GUNS VS BUTTER ... OR SLAVERY VS STARVATION

Perhaps in that hand-to-mouth bare subsistence level of living the politics of human organization mattered little compared to an

---

64   See John P. McKay, Bennett D. Hill, John Buckler, *A History of World Societies*, 1996; *The Encyclopedia Britannica, Sparta*, 13th Edition, 1926.

"The meaning of peace is the absence of opposition to socialism."—Karl Marx

empty stomach. Starving people generally don't care who feeds them. But the undying traits of human nature simmered from warm to hot. As indicated by the records left behind, every effort was exhaustively required to coerce or restrain normal human behaviors to protect the elites.

A more pleasing cooperative among the masses was encouraged in the classical period. Central to this era is Plato, father of the *bad idea*.

NEVER TRUST THE PEOPLE

Breaking down society by destroying the family and putting all trust in the leaders is demonstrated among the Spartans. Lost to history are the details of much day-to-day living, but enough remains to paint a picture of a society built on warfare. This would not be possible were leaders not in complete control over a culture of allegiance to conquering power rather than cooperation with other peoples.

* * * * *

WORTH READING THRICE

"I've always doubted that the socialists had a leg to stand on intellectually. They have improved their argument somehow, but once you begin to understand that prices are an instrument of communication and guidance which embody more information than we directly have, the whole idea that you can bring about the same order based on the division of labor by simple direction falls to the ground. Similarly, the idea [that] you can arrange for distributions of incomes which correspond to some conception of merit or need. If you need prices, including the prices of labor, to direct people to go where they are needed, you cannot have another distribution except the one from the market principle. I think that intellectually there is just nothing left of socialism."—F. A. Hayek, interviewed by Thomas W. Hazlett.

CHAPTER 11:
OF BEARDS, WORDS, AND WISDOM

Plato is among the impassioned few who received a lot of press for ideas that appealed more to meeting immediate lapses in society rather than promoting long-term solutions.

At the dawn of western culture there sprang forth another form of socialism, a kinder, gentler enslavement. As the ancient city-states took shape, the seven pillars of socialism become prominent. It was during these formative years that the idea of Ruler's Law in a less violent form became the intellectual brainchild of philosophers and kings. There were many "if only" ideas put forth by thinkers as a means of calming down the wild aggressions of mankind.

The ideas themselves sounded great on the surface, but under scrutiny, they offered nothing new—they were the usual servings of socialism in other packages.

SOCIALIST: Plato (427-347 B.C.)
PLACE IN HISTORY: Wrote "The Republic" and "The Laws"
LIFE: Born in Athens, Plato was a Classical Greek philosopher, mathematician, writer of philosophical dialogues, and founder of one of the first schools of higher learning in the Western world called the Academy in Athens. He had good company in those days—his mentor Socrates and his student Aristotle. Plato's writings laid the foundations of Western philosophy and science.

He wrote his ten-volume work, "The Republic," during his middle years to depict an ideal state structure. "The Laws" was written in his older years depicting his best estimation of how his ideals would be put into practice.[65]

IMPACT: In "The Republic," Plato laid the foundation for all other socialist schemes that followed for 1,500 years. In his perfect society Plato said that nature would decide who was strong or not. Leaving these evolutionary processes alone was, according to Plato, the least confrontational means of choosing out leaders and followers. It was the caste system all over again—

---

65   Will Durant, The Story of Civilization, 3:510-511, *Plato*.

"Socialism means slavery."—Lord Acton (1834-1902)

Ruler: There were the philosopher kings, smarter than everybody else, therefore, naturally deserving of unlimited powers to control everyone else. Their focus was to be on ever servicing the state, and staying focused on the broad state of affairs and their place in the universe.

Soldiers: The guardians were supposed to be gentle to friends but vicious to enemies. They were never to criticize the leaders and were true warriors, fearing no death. Their education could not include divinity stories of the gods or the injustice of fate. From childhood onwards, guardians were to be taught new myths to secure their devotions to the state. Plato said any desires for property would be bred out of them so they would live exclusively for the state.

The artisans and peasants: As usual, the lowest case had to do most of the work. They were to be ruled by the other two groups and were expected to surrender their lives for the defense of the city. Human personality and egoism were supposed to be reduced to the level of an ant hill—not through armed struggle, but by changing human nature from within.

PLATO ON SUBMISSION: "In a word, [man] should teach his soul, by long habit, never to dream of acting independently, and to become utterly incapable of it."[66]

PLATO ON SOCIALISM: "Our object in the construction of the state is the greatest happiness of the whole, and not that of any one class." [67]

"The community which has neither poverty nor riches will always have the noblest principles." [68]

"Tyranny naturally arises out of democracy."[69]

"There will be no end to the troubles of states, or of humanity itself, till philosophers become kings in this world, or till those we now call kings and rulers really and truly become philosophers, and political power and philosophy thus come into the same hands."[70]

---

66 Plato, *The Republic*, see Karl Raimund Popper, *The Open Society and Its Enemies, Plato*; 1962, pp. 7, 90 (Chapter 6/notes 34).
67 Plato, *The Republic*, Book IV, Great Books of the Western World, p. 342.
68 Plato, *The Dialogues of Plato*, translated by Benjamin Jowett, Vol. IV, *The Laws*, 1908, p. 208.
69 Ibid., Vol. III, *The Republic*, p. 455.
70 *Plato*, translated by Sir Henry Desmond Lee, Part VII [Book V], p. 191-192 (473 d-e).

"Real socialism is inside man. It wasn't born with Marx. It was in the communes of Italy in the Middle Ages. You can't say it is finished."—Dario Fo, Italian playwright

PLATO ON LYING: "Then if anyone at all is to have the privilege of lying, the rulers of the State should be the persons; and they, in their dealings either with enemies or with their own citizens, may be allowed to lie for the public good."[71]

PLATO ON PREDESTINATION: "You are brothers, yet God has framed you differently. Some of you have the power to command, and in these he has mingled gold ... others he has made of silver [to be soldiers] ... and others again he has composed of brass and iron [the common people] ... a golden parent will sometimes have a silver son."[72]

PLATO ON LAWS: "Good people do not need laws to tell them to act responsibly, while bad people will find a way around the laws."[73]

PLATO ON SUPPRESSING INITIATIVE: "All things will be produced in superior quantity and quality, and with greater ease, when each man works at a single occupation, in accordance with his natural gifts, and at the right moment, without meddling with anything else."[74]

"For the introduction of a new kind of music must be shunned as imperiling the whole state; since styles of music are never disturbed without affecting the most important political institutions."[75]

PLATO ON DEATH: "No one knows whether death, which people fear to be the greatest evil, may not be the greatest good."[76]

PLATO ON CULTIVATING IGNORANCE: "Entire ignorance is not so terrible or extreme an evil, and is far from being the greatest of all; too much cleverness and too much learning, accompanied with ill bringing-up, are far more fatal."[77]

---

71 Plato, *The Republic*, Book III, Great Books of the Western World, p. 326.
72 Ibid., pp. 340-341.
73 Quotation frequently attributed to Plato, but not yet sourced.
74 Plato, *The Republic*, Book II, Wordsworth Classics, p. 51 (369d-370d).
75 Plato, *The Republic*, Book IV, Wordsworth Classics, p. 118 (423a-424d).
76 Plato, *Apology*, Classics of Western Philosophy, 6th ed., 2002, p. 35 (29a).
77 Plato, *The Dialogues of Plato*, Vol. IV, translated by Benjamin Jowett, p. 332 (p. 819).

"They talk about the failure of socialism but where is the success of capitalism in Africa, Asia and Latin America?"—Fidel Castro

THE FOUNDERS DISMISSED PLATO'S IDEAS

Thomas Jefferson: "While wading through the whimsies, the puerilities, and unintelligible jargon of [Plato's] work, I laid it down often to ask myself how it could have been that the world should have so long consented to give reputation to such nonsense as this."[78]

John Adams: "My disappointment was very great, my astonishment was greater, my disgust shocking .... His Laws and his Republic, from which I expected most, disappointed me most."[79]

Thomas Jefferson: "The doctrines which flowed from the lips of Jesus himself are within the comprehension of a child, but thousands of volumes have not yet explained the Platonisms engrafted on them; and for this obvious reason, that nonsense can never be explained."[80]

PLATO'S SEVEN PILLARS

The writings of Plato reveal his vision of how the seven pillars would best function in society. The ruling class answered to no one. With no lies allowed, except by the ruler to achieve some ultimate goal, the free-flow of information would remain suspect at all times. The caste was a permanent part of Plato's society as a means to keep the feeble-minded in their places, and the overly aggressive people in theirs. All things in common was the ultimate goal, and having sufficient force to fully smother all other rights was to be upheld by the warriors. As with all schemers for the perfect society, Plato fell far short from having it all worked out.

---

78   Thomas Jefferson, Bergh, *The Writings of Thomas Jefferson*, 14:147-149.
79   John Adams, Howe, *The Changing Political Thought of John Adams*, p. 382.
80   H. Colburn and R. Bentley, *Memoir, Correspondence, and Miscellanies From the Papers of Thomas Jefferson*, 1829, p. 242.

Good ideas spread without force, like the Bible, and unlike socialism. Of the 6,909 world languages, the Bible or portions of it have been translated into at least 2,287.

CHAPTER 12

A CASTE OF MILLIONS

Roll the dice, show up among a family of untouchables and suffer the consequences—or, live right and be reborn a king or queen, it's the very way of things among the Indian Hindus.

S TORY: Beginning some time before 2500 B.C., the ancient empire of the Indus River Valley apparently was the largest on earth, looming larger than Egypt and Mesopotamia. Sometime around 1500 B.C., this empire came to an end, possibly at the hands of Aryan troops. The destruction was so severe, the records tell of thousands of the dead strewn in the streets of several abandoned cities.

Meanwhile, in the southern regions, those populations were spared from the attacks. They organized themselves and incorporated socialist ideas that were well developed by the 5th century B.C.

Imagine a system where simply being born in the wrong place and time locks a person into his or her permanent and limited choices of friends, food, job, marriage, housing, associations, and many other aspects of life—and no one had any say over any of it.

FOUR CASTES—There have existed thousands of castes over the centuries, but four major groups that survive till today. At the top are the spiritual leaders, the Brahman priests. The warrior and aristocracy follows second. The merchants follow third, with the Sundras or the laborers last. Excluded from these are the outcasts, a group set apart all by themselves consisting of the poor, the diseased or the otherwise rejected from society.

REGIMENTING LIFE

Hinduism and India's ancient caste system were intimately involved in almost every aspect of a person's life. The system strictly regulated the labor force at all levels—it set boundaries for marriage, ordered obeisance to those of the higher classes, itemized the foods that could be grown and consumed, jobs, housing, travel, communications, and more. Attempting to break loose from this regime could cost a man and his family their lives. The lower classes usually had no hope of ever changing jobs, improving their lives, or altering their future.[81]

---

81   See Kiran Kumar Thaplyal, *Guilds in Ancient India*, 1966.

In socialist Sweden, the average wait to see doctor is 12 weeks.

GUILDS AND UNIONS

Most of India's early population was concentrated in villages. These were usually isolated and self-sufficient. They took care of their own food and nutrition needs, and food production kept the majority of people busy and employed.

This environment was perfect for the rise of specialists—ivory sculptors, craftsmen, barbers, weavers, carpenters, goldsmiths, doctors, etc. To harness this financial power, various associations were formed called shrenis (singular "shreni").[82] These were guilds—early forms of unions.

NO WOMEN ALLOWED

The shrenis excluded women to protect all the family secrets—economic, trade, or craft secrets. The cultural norm was that married daughters moved in with their husband's family. Fathers worried their daughters' loyalties would give way to the in-laws' pressure to reveal carefully guarded methods or processes. One way to ensure secrecy was to exclude daughters from any such knowledge, and instead, carefully pass along the knowledge to the sons who were more likely to stay put after marriage.

MIXING PRIVATE WITH PUBLIC

Some shrenis grew so large that entire villages developed around them with every villager focused on just one task or service. The caste system, the religion, and the shrenis subordinated individual rights at every level. With local governments enforcing the protectionist rules, any artisan seeking independence could be punished or banished for attempting to compete outside of the established shreni.

The caste system was so entrenched in early Indian society that those of a lower class felt intensely uncomfortable being around those of a higher class. It was an automatic suppression that was achieved without soldier or weapon. It perpetuated itself by way of cultural control of knowledge about freedom and rights. Even today the influence of the caste system dominates society.

---

82 See Romila Thapar, *Ancient Indian Social History: Some Interpretations*, pp. 129-133.

Tax-funded socialism kills jobs. From 1981-2003, low-tax Ireland had 56% job growth—high-tax Sweden and Finland had 0% job growth.

CHAPTER 13:
ARISTOPHANES: SOCIALIST IDEAS "IN THE ROUND"

*People from all ages love entertainment, as demonstrated with
ancient coliseums and records. As early as 400 B.C.,
plays promoting socialism became popular.*

W**HEN**: 400 B.C.
WHERE: Greece
STORY: Not much is known about Aristophanes (446
B.C.-386 B.C.) except for glimpses he gives of himself in his plays.
He was a prolific writer, winning local competitions, and producing
fantastic productions that won him a place in history.

Aristophanes is most well-known for his great sense of comedy,
and a knack for ridiculing the famous and powerful—something that
people in high positions actually worried about. Some scholars give
Aristophanes credit for providing the most accurate information and
description of ancient Athenian culture than any other writer.

SOCIALISM "LIVE ON STAGE"

Aristophanes also used his plays to proselytize his view of
Plato's socialism. In his play, *The Ecclesiazusae*, he has a woman
named Praxagora joining several other women who dress in men's
clothing with beards to attend the "men only" political Assembly. In
a discussion afterwards with her husband Blepyrus, she explains her
views on the ideal society. Says Praxagora:

"I want all to have a share of everything, and all property to be
in common; there will no longer be either rich or poor; no longer
shall we see one man harvesting vast tracts of land, while another
has not ground enough to be buried in ... I intend that there shall
only be one and the same condition of life for all ... I shall begin by
making land, money, everything that is private property, common to
all."

ALL THINGS IN COMMON—INCLUDING WOMEN

But alas and forsooth, that is not all the characters in the play
hoped to achieve. Aristophanes foreshadows future socialistic

---

"My object in life is to dethrone God and destroy capitalism."—Karl Marx

experiments regarding marriage when he has his fictional Praxagora discuss men and women in common:

"I intend that women shall belong to all men in common, and each shall beget children by any man that wishes to have her."

Then Blepyrus observes the obvious, "But all will go to the prettiest woman and try to lay her."

To which Praxagora explains the socialist's solution, "The ugliest and the most flat-nosed will be side by side with the most charming, and to win the latter's favours, a man will first have to get to the former."

Aristophanes' theme of "all things in common" is sprinkled through several of his surviving plays.[83]

WHEN: 100 BC

WHERE: Mediterranean Lands—more socialist literature

STORY: The Greek Historian Diodorus was re-creating Plato's ideas in his writings about two centuries after Plato's death. In one dreamy place that Diodorus called the "sunny islands" in the Indian Ocean—he manufactures a fictitious re-creation of Plato's Republic. On these islands the 400 inhabitants labored for each other and freely shared in all things.

"Marriage is unknown to them; instead they enjoy communal wives; children are brought up in common as they belong to the whole of the community and are equally loved by all. Frequently, it so happens that nurses exchange babies that are suckling so that even mothers do not recognize their children."

These fictional people lived to age 150, were unusually tall, and anyone with a physical defect was expected to commit suicide.[84]

---

83 See Aristophanes, *The Ecclesiazusae*, translated by Thomas Bushnell.

84 Robert von Pohlmann, *The Sunny Islands*, as quoted in *The Socialist Phenomenon*, Igor Shafarevich, p. 15.

CHAPTER 14:

ROME'S RECIPE: BREAD & CIRCUSES

In the Roman Senate, support for Ruler's Law came as cheaply as a free loaf of bread or a small sack of grain

STORY: Around 140 B.C., Roman politicians discovered a great way to stay in power—buy votes with bread. Their easiest target were the poor people who happily exchanged their supporting votes for food and entertainment.

At the time things were not well in Rome. Much of the populace had neglected their participation in the political affairs of the Republic. The average Roman was content to leave the drama and intrigue of national leadership in the able hands of professional politicians. National neglect left a dangerous void. But with free bread—oftentimes small bags of wheat—handed out through the benevolence of those in power, why worry?

The free lunch strategy wasn't enough to settle the concerns of the politicians. The fact the country was falling apart proved another concern. The politicians tried to hide the problems with the best anesthesia they had—Monday Night Football—or, in their day, The Circus. These huge parades of blood and action grew into grand spectacles and extravaganzas of the exotic. They drew thousands of spectators.

This distraction worked well for more than a century. While people were glued to the drama at the stadiums to watch chariot races or helpless slaves shredded by lions, or battle re-enactments with real killings, an emperor slipped into the Senate and rose to take power. His name was Julius Caesar.

Caesar changed Rome's weakening republic into the iron-booted force of an empire. The Roman citizens could do little to stop the takeover—but the prevailing attitude was, why worry so long as we have bread and circuses?

The Roman promise of bread and circuses (panem et cirenses) has since been translated around the world as Spain's "bread and bullfights" (pan y toros), Russia's "bread and spectacle," and America's "tax, spend and bailout," among others.

Socialism is expensive—Average tax burdens for socialist Europe from 1970-2003: Sweden–61%, Denmark–58%, Finland–55%, compared to U.S. federal, state and local combined: 25%.

CHAPTER 15:

ISRAEL:
THE ELUSIVE ESSENES

Religious extremists were some of the first to discover "all things in common" is a really bad idea. The Essenes tried it between 100 B.C. and A.D. 100. Did it work?

S TORY: Josephus, Philo and other early writers report the Essenes were the smaller of three Jewish sects that included the Pharisees and the Sadducees. They kept most of the traditional Jewish observances but would not sacrifice animals or eat meat. They were scattered among several cities according to Philo, but Pliny the Elder (died A.D. 79) puts them off the shores of the Dead Sea at Ein Gedi and probably at Qumran.[85]

ALL IN COMMON: The Essenes lived a strict life of celibacy and had no private property—all money and property was held in common. It was a self-imposed socialism—practicing religious rites of communalism—for the purposes of worshiping God.

THE RULER: The leader was supreme in all things and whatever orders he issued, everyone obeyed. There is evidence the leader might also have had traditional Jewish authority in his blood from his ancestry in Levi or Cohen.

REGULATIONS: The Essenes practiced daily baptisms, voluntary poverty, swearing oaths to no one, committed to controlling their tempers, and vowed abstinence from all worldly pleasures including marriage and sexual intimacy.

2,000 YEAR OLD BEST SELLER

Knowledge of their existence came alive with the discovery of the Dead Sea Scrolls in nearby Qumran. Some scholars believe these scrolls belonged to the Essenes' community library. Many of the scrolls have since been translated and found to include several copies and versions of the Hebrew Bible dating back to 300 B.C.

---

85 See references to Essenes in Josephus, *The Wars of the Jews, Antiquities of the Jews*; Philo; Epiphanius, among others.

"Socialism in general has a record of failure so blatant that only an intellectual could ignore or evade it." Thomas Sowell

CHAPTER 16:
CHINA: WANG MANG, A FAILED SOCIALIST

S TORY: After a thousand years of all-powerful emperors controlling everyone and everything, a man came along who was the epitome of utopian scheming—Wang Mang. Was he a great visionary or a royal incompetent? It is still undecided.

Wang Mang[86] ruled from A.D. 9-23. He hoped to be remembered as a selfless social reformer who ended the Han Dynasty and its wealthy class of land owners. He named his dynasty Xin, meaning "new."

Once in power, he nationalized gold, imposed government monopolies, and went after the large-land owners to break up their power. He imposed communal farming and forced families to farm a plot shared by others. The food they raised went to the rulers who then gave part to Wang Mang as tribute.

In addition to his tyrannical ways, it turned out Wang Mang was not a good diplomat. His arrogance and frequent faux pas when dealing with foreign heads of state ruined international relations. Diplomatic relations collapsed. This led to wars that absorbed a great deal of national treasure and cost lives.

If that wasn't enough, the Yellow River suddenly changed course and started flowing south—not his fault, but his socialism offered no solutions. The lack of water ruined the agriculture and caused panic, famine, and epidemics. Great masses of people started moving around for greener pastures.

The people finally became fed up with Wang Mang. The wealthy and nobility banded together with the military and took their country back, reinstating the Han dynasty. But it was too little too late. The final straw came when enemies watching from afar saw a vulnerable and fractured country, and launched an attack. They sacked the capital city of Chang'an. Wang Mang and his personal guard of 1,000 took their last stand and were all killed. Thus ended his short and confusing reign.

History remembers Wang Mang as a failure, and China learned once again in its chaos and ruins of A.D. 23 that socialism had failed.

---

86   See Rudi Thomsen, *Ambition and Confucianism: A biography of Wang Mang,* 1988.

In socialist Sweden, the average wait for medical treatment *after* seeing a doctor is 12 more weeks.

CHAPTER 17:

HOW SOCIALISM KILLED ROME

Meanwhile, at about the same time over in Rome, the slow death of Rome's love affair with "the dole" finally took its toll.

STORY: We take one final visit to Rome to see how socialism destroyed that world power from within, in just a few centuries.[87]

Civil war had sapped the strength of Rome in the first century B.C.[88] Mark Antony led rebellious troops to conquer Octavian for control, but Mark Antony was defeated. This was supposed to mean a return to economic freedom. However, the Roman empire was drained of its endurance. The army was sucking huge taxes from the people. Heavy inflation was underway and the means to rejuvenate the economy were blocked by closed trade routes. Over time the people concluded that only by putting all power into one individual could they get Rome's financial house in order. They gave that power to Octavian who took the name Augustus, the first emperor of Rome in 27 B.C.

THE DOLE DRAINS

Since about 140 B.C., Rome had informally adopted its expensive policy of bread and circuses. This steady drain on resources was tolerable at first. When the policy hit full stride under Gracchus in 123 B.C., its popularity was drawing crowds by the thousands. Some 80 years later (40 B.C.) the empire was supporting more than 320,000 Romans. This number dropped to a steady 200,000 by A.D. 30. Bread was not the only handout in those days—sometimes free pork, oil, and wine were added.[89]

WELFARE PUSHES TAXES HIGHER

The free food forced taxes up. For two centuries the tax rate had hovered between the miniscule margins of .01 and .03

---

87 See Bruce Bartlett, *How Excessive Government Killed Ancient Rome*, The Cato Journal, Vol. 14 Number 2, Fall 1994.

88 See The Encyclopedia Britannica, 13th Edition, 1926, *Rome*.

89 See M. Rostovtzeff, *The Social and Economic History of the Roman Empire*.

"There can be no freedom in art and literature where the government determines who shall create them."—Ludwig von Mises,

percent.[90] By the early A.D. 100s, taxes rose to 1 percent. Roman coinage began to suffer. The denarius started to lose precious metal content—down to 90 percent during Nero's time. By A.D. 300, there was hardly 5 percent silver in the coins. With high taxes, money becoming worthless, and military costs skyrocketing, the government was forced to take extreme measures. It began confiscating what it needed directly from the individual citizens. Soldiers went about taking people's cows, pigs, harvests, and crafted goods, whenever the need arose.[91]

This mess locked everyone into their jobs—nobody could easily change. The state compelled them to work their jobs to support the army. This caused many to hide their wealth so the state couldn't take it.

PEOPLE SEEK ESCAPE

As the economy broke down, people fled to work their own plots, or took safety with a wealthy land owner. By A.D. 270, the denarius was down to .02 percent silver, causing food prices to explode. One estimate put inflation at 15,000 percent during the third century.

The crisis was so severe, extreme actions were taken to stabilize the economy. For example, the death penalty was imposed on those caught fixing prices. Hundreds were executed for the least little infractions.

A local historian, Lactantius, reported that so much blood was shed that products were no longer brought to market for fear some oversight or suspicion would result in instant death. Fortunately the death law was finally repealed. But that didn't stop the oppression—there were still wars to be fought.

THE COST OF DEFENSE

To distribute the burden of the Rome's expensive wars, the state calculated what one soldier required for food and supplies. This multiplied by all the soldiers told them how much each individual Roman had to provide.

Then they conducted a monstrous inventory, counting every fruit tree and vine, every square foot of cultivatable land, every

---

90   A. H. M. Jones, *Taxation in Antiquity*, published in *The Roman Economy: Studies in Ancient Economic and Administrative History*, 1974, p. 161.

91   Aurelio Bernardi, *The Economic Problems of the Roman Empire at the Time of Its Decline*, in *The Economic Decline of Empires*, pp. 16-83.

animal, and every living soul. Using the information to determine each citizen's responsibility, the government could give citizens an idea of what they had to pay in advance, instead of the surprise confiscations.

FORCED UNIONIZATION

Another approach to calming the raging inflation was forcing workers to organize into guilds, and businesses into collegia, both controlled from above. This structure forced workers to remain chained to their jobs. People hated that and rebelled by abandoning their farms, hoarding, refusing to trade, and suddenly the number of people dependent on bread grew to exceed the capacity of those producing all the bread.

COLLAPSING CURRENCY

Efforts to restore the currency failed to stem the tide of collapse. The wealthy had managed to bribe their way out of paying taxes, and the impoverished workers had been shouldering almost all the financial burdens. Taxes climbed to 4.5 percent in A.D. 444, but revenues continued to fall. The reason revenues collapsed was because the people started to withdraw from society. They could see their country coming apart—the government, the economy, and the security of the borderlands.

ROME'S COLLAPSE A RELIEF

The final few years saw no income to finance Rome's mighty army, its ships and forts, or to fight the invading forces. When Rome finally collapsed, the scattered citizens grouped around the churches and villas, and willingly offered themselves as servants, slaves or tenants—anything to just stay alive. By then, the collapse was seen more as a relief than anything else—a relief to be out from under the decay and tyranny and burdens of that society.

With the former empire's defenses dissolved away into the countrysides, the invaders had free reign of the great production that once dominated the land. But unlike other conquering hoards, the barbarians were not bent on wiping out every last person— only the Roman government. With that disposed of, the invaders allowed the business people, the landowners, and their workers to remain because such concentrations of wealth gave the invaders more resources to tax, tax, and tax. It was the late A.D. 400s, and so began western Europe's dark ages.

"To cure the British disease with socialism was like trying to cure leukemia with leeches."
—Margaret Thatcher

LEARNING TO RECOGNIZE SOCIALISM

A sign of socialism is the control of information. For ages, the European continent was under various dictators who suppressed the growth of cultures and civilizations to maintain their power. Once those shackles began to fall off by the A.D. 1200s, an enormous enlightenment unfolded.

The Greek influence had already been popular and widespread before Rome's rise and had a large influence after Rome's fall. Monuments, statues, ceremony with pomp and circumstance to institutionalize the coronation of the new ruler was very appealing to both friend and foe. Spiritual stability in the worship of Greek and Roman gods developed along side economic prosperity. In short, the individual in the Mediterranean region enjoyed more freedom of action after Rome's fall than did his predecessors living under Rome's imperialism.

As populations across Europe began to grow and expand during the middle ages, there was a shift from agricultural life to the rise of city-states and large concentrated populations. Power became consolidated in centralized groups, local rulers and businessmen, and the farmers became the paid or indentured laborers for the wealthy. Trade became important and the profitable benefits of peace and cooperation between regions, realms and budding countries were secured as best as times would allow.

Another advancement that grew out of the middle ages was an improved value on life—people were not as easily expendable as centuries past. Individuals took a more active part in social life. They saw the world much differently than before. Instead of rule by the gods and the whims of the deities, people began to reason and formulate advantages for personal gain.

Curiosity about the world and the mechanisms for its operation triggered the growth of philosophers and their schools of thought. Balance and harmony with the universe became the new pursuit. The study of astrology, languages, the arts, politics, literature, music, painting, sculpture, architecture, and philosophy flourished. It was the dawning of a new age, the age of enlightenment.

POLYBIUS DESCRIBES SOCIALISM'S DEADLY PATTERN

Polybius was an ancient Greek historian who lived 200-118 B.C. He is known for his 40-volume work, *The Histories*, covering the

Socialism's promise of heaven on earth sounds delectable to a fast-food mentality addicted to instant gratification.

period 220-146 B.C. He describes the growing power of the Roman Republic and how it eventually overshadowed Greece. His insights were extremely valuable in the writing of the U.S. Constitution.

In this particular passage below,[92] Polybius summarizes man's eternal cycle of savagery to freedom, then corruption, and back again to savagery—and he explains why this cycle continually unfolds, suggesting the best way to stop it is proper education about freedom. As he points out, there is nothing new to socialism.

Polybius said—

SURVIVORS OF OPPRESSION: "Then as long as some of those survive who experienced the evils of oligarchical dominion [all power in the rulers], they are well pleased with the present form of government, and set a high value on equality and freedom of speech. But when a new generation arises and the democracy falls into the hands of the grandchildren of its founders, they have become so accustomed to freedom and equality that they no longer value them, and begin to aim at pre-eminence; and it is chiefly those of ample fortune who fall into this error.

SECOND GENERATION DOESN'T VALUE FREEDOM: "So when they begin to lust for power and cannot attain it through themselves or their own good qualities, they ruin their estates, tempting and corrupting the people in every possible way. And hence when by their foolish thirst for reputation they have created among the masses an appetite for gifts and the habit of receiving them, democracy in its turn is abolished and changes into a rule of force and violence.

SOCIALISM CONSUMES, THEN DESTROYS: "For the people, having grown accustomed to feed at the expense of others and to depend for their livelihood on the property of others, as soon as they find a leader who is enterprising but is excluded from the honors of office by his penury, institute the rule of violence; and now uniting their forces massacre, banish, and plunder, until they degenerate again into perfect savages and find once more a master and monarch."

—Polybius

---

92. See William Ebenstein, *Great Political Thinkers, Plato to the Present*, Rhinehart & Co., Inc., New York, p. 115.

"The theory of Communism may be summed up in the single sentence: Abolition of private property."—Marx and Engels

Part IV

SOCIALISM IN THE MIDDLE AGES

"They advocated having all things in common—including wives. Early Church fathers stated, 'They lead lives of unrestrained indulgence'..."

—Author—

CHAPTER 18:

SOCIALISM AND THE RISE OF CHRISTIANITY

*True Christianity blessed the world. The frauds
used it to wreak havoc.*

With the rise of Christianity the roots of socialism found rich soil. Socialist doctrine aligned well with the basic Christian ideals of charitable giving, sharing, and a belief in a future "last days" when all wickedness would be wiped off the earth. Socialists found harmony with the Christian teachings that a millennium of peace and joy was coming, when all things would be had in common.

The Catholic monasteries and convents provided good models of the socialist life style—no private property, all things in common, self-interests and initiative subordinated to abject obedience, and all forms of family abandoned. As the Christian heresies gained power and influence through the middle ages, they adopted several perversions of the Christian model and used force and death to impose their beliefs on others.

SOCIALISM IN THE CHRISTIAN ERA

The first 500 years after Christ were important to the growth of Christianity. During this same period, unfortunately, the heresies strove to rework Jesus' Gospel of peace and good news. They liked the idea of all things in common, but what Jesus taught (voluntary) and what the heretics practiced (force) were poles apart.

The heretics' misunderstanding was rooted in events described in Acts 2:44-45 and 4:32, where the idea of lumping all property together and living a life of pious poverty received Biblical authority. For the heretics, common property was a sign of humility and an overt signal to everyone that they were rejecting the imperfect material world. Rejecting material goods remained a common theme for the heretics.

WHAT IS A HERESY?

A *heretic* is someone who makes a change to the official dogma, the tenets, or declared beliefs of a religion. It is not the same as *apostasy* which is the complete rejection of a belief system. It is

**Socialism is expensive: In 2012, India barred its airlines from complying with European Union
carbon taxes, and refused to hand over their emissions data, saying compliance to ecosocialists'
demands would cost the airline industry thousands of jobs and trigger price wars.**

also not the same as *blasphemy*—being rude or irreverent toward a religion.

The 1,500 years of Christian heresies are good examples of how the pillars of socialism found power under the guise of sincere association with Christianity. The drifting away from the simple concepts taught by Jesus led many tens of thousands into behavior completely contrary to his Gospel. Likewise, the heretical descent into debauched paganism violated the most basic truths of happy human existence that had been embraced ever since Moses had delivered God's commandments to ancient Israel.

It is particularly curious how many of these groups frequently descended into a "jungle morality" of uninhibited sexual union. Scholar Igor Shafarevich must be credited for locating much of the Middle Ages information for his book, *The Socialist Phenomenon*, wherein these religious movements are described in greater detail.[93]

WHEN: 1st Century AD
HERESY: Nicolaites—first Christian socialists[94]
STORY: As the original Apostles died away, various break-away Christian factions began to interpret scripture in strange ways, and injected their own ideas. They began forming various sects to create their form of a perfect society. The Nicolaites took their name from Nicholas, one of the seven deacons in Jerusalem. They are mentioned negatively in the Book of Revelations.[95] They preached no private property, and having all things in common—including wives. Early Church fathers stated "they lead lives of unrestrained indulgence," and "ate things offered to idols."[96] Nicholas supposedly allowed other men to marry his wife. Eusebius said this socialistic sect was short-lived.[97]

WHEN: 2nd Century AD
HERESY: Carpocratians—also had wives in common
STORY: Carpocrates[98] taught a few principles of Christianity and then brayed off into the wilderness by falsely attributing to God a

---

93   Igor Shafarevich, *The Socialist Phenomenon*, foreword by Aleksandr I. Solzhenitsyn, in Russian in 1975 by YMCA Press; in English by Harper & Row, 1980.
94   Acts 6:5; Apocalypse 2:6-15.
95   Revelations 2:14.
96   Translated by Alexander Roberts and William Rambaut, *Ante-Nicene Fathers*, Vol. 1 edited by Alexander Roberts, James Donaldson, and A. Cleveland Coxe, 1885.
97   See Irenaeus, *Against Heresies*, http://www.ccel.org/ccel/schaff/anf01.ix.html; Catholic Encyclopedia, *Nicolaites*.
98   New Advent, *Refutation of All Heresies*, Book VII, chapter 20.

desire that they practice the socialist ideals of all things in common and no private property: "God's justice consists in community and equality," wrote Epiphanes, the son of Carpocrates. "He who takes a wife, let him posses her. But they can possess all in common as the animals do."

Epiphanes continued: "It is therefore laughable to hear the giver of laws saying: 'Do not covet' and more laughable still the addition: 'that which is your neighbor's.' For he himself invested us with desires, which moreover must be safeguarded as they are necessary for procreation. But even more laughable is the phrase 'your neighbor's wife,' for in this way that which is common is forcibly turned into private property."

This sect was reported to have spread as far as Rome. Having women in common appears to be a distinguishing enticement that helped the sect grow so rapidly.

WHEN: 3rd Century AD
HERESY: Manicheism—also shared wives
STORY: Followers of Manicheism believed in the socialist ideals of all things in common and no private property. The group's founder, Mani (A.D. 216-276), lived in Babylonia and became the founding prophet of his sect after some personal spiritual experience. He wrote six sacred books that he claimed corrected the corruption of Adam, Zoroaster, Buddha, and Jesus.

Plato's class socialism can be detected among Manicheism followers. They organized themselves into the upper "Elect" and the mainstream "Hearers."[99] The Elect fasted once a week, sometimes twice. The Catholic Encyclopedia reports Mani's followers were rigidly regulated with elements of socialism. "They were forbidden to have property, to eat meat or drink wine, to gratify any sexual desire, to engage in any servile occupation, commerce or trade, to possess house or home, to practice magic, or to practice any other religion." They were opposed to marriage and viewed maternity as a calamity and sin because having children interfered in "the blissful consummation of all things." [100]

Mani's religion endured about 400 years, from around A.D. 200 until the A.D. 600s. It was one of the most widespread religions in the world and spawned other sects that adopted his social-

99   This group is discussed in more detail in *The Socialist Phenomenon*, I. Shafarevich 1980.
100   Catholic Encyclopedia, *Manichaeism*.

The quickest way to create a problem is to take a process that has no problems and try to fix it.

ist doctrines. At its peak, Manicheism stretched from the Roman Empire to China. Mani's six holy books were translated into Persian, Chinese, Greek, Coptic, and Latin, among others, and this helped prosper the sect. Among its membership was St. Augustine for 9 or 10 years before converting to Christianity—then he became its fierce opponent. The sect finally faded from sight in the A.D. 600s.

WHEN: 4th Century AD
HERESY: Mazdakism—early communists[101]
STORY: The Mazdakians tried to practice the socialistic ideals of no private property and having all in common. They used strange ideas and perverted conclusions to control and coerce followers into strange behaviors.

The namesake for Mazdakism is a fellow named Mazdak. Not a lot is known about him, and some wonder if it was an earlier Mazdak who named the religion. Most information comes from his opponents in such diverse places as Syria, Persia, Greece and Arabian territories.

Like other religions of this period, Mazdak taught there were two main forces in the universe—light and dark—that were meant to remain separated but accidently mixed together here on earth. The living were supposed to rid themselves of the dark so more light could be released into the world.

To this end Mazdak discarded the Church's religious formalities and emphasized good personal conduct. This included no killing or shedding of blood, no eating flesh, never oppressing others or inflicting harm, always standing on best manners to be friendly, giving and kind—and, oh yes, sharing wealth and women.

Mazdak believed God gifted the earth's resources to everyone so they could be divided up and shared equally among all men. However, the greedy and strong hoarded the resources and began dominating the weak, thereby creating an evil inequality.[102]

Mazdak taught that inequality unleashed the evil demons of Envy, Wrath, Vengeance, Need, and Greed into the earth. He said the only way to get rid of these evils was by eliminating family

---

101   Remy, Arthur F.J. "The Avesta." *The Catholic Encyclopedia*. Vol. 2. New York: Robert Appleton Company, 1907.
102   *The Cambridge History of Iran*, volume 2. p. 995-997.

In 2009, Obama struck a deal with pharmaceutical manufacturers to buy their support for his national health care legislation. The back door deal-making by Obama who promised transparency and "an end to the game playing," was kept from the public and the House of Representatives.

and property, and making women and wealth common among all people. And that's just what they tried to do: destroy family and live off of each other. The historian Abu Tabari (A.D. 838-923) wrote, "Frequently, a man did not know his son nor the son his own father, and no one possessed enough to be guaranteed life and livelihood."[103]

Modern historians brand Mazdak as an early socialist, and his philosophy as early communism.

MAZDAKISM WAS APPEALING

Over the years, Mazdakism spread across Persia, even converting Persia's King Kavadh. Local Zoroastrians feared the sect's growing popularity, and in A.D. 524, they received permission from the king to rise up, attack the Mazdakians, and cleanse the land of the evil heresy. The band of attackers successfully slaughtered most of the Mazdakians, including Mazdak whom they hanged. A few small remnants fled for survival, and kept the movement going for centuries. By the 1700s, only a small handful of Mazdakians remained, continuing to practice their observances among their Muslim neighbors in secretive modesty.

A CHRISTIAN IS AS A CHRISTIAN DOES

These assorted heresies relied on distortions, perversions and complete destruction of the ideas Jesus originally taught to create their religious empires. The closest Jesus ever came to using force was to drive the money changers out of the Temple. However, he was well justified by both Jewish law and tradition, so no one dared complain. The lax Jews had allowed their Temple to become a place of mercantilism rather than a common gateway for people of all walks to bring their sacrifices and petitions to God.

When Jesus began his ministry, his message was consistent and powerful: *freedom*—freedom to choose, to act, to impart or withhold, freedom to show love and caring compassion for others. The personal salvation of the human soul and a path to a fullness of joy was what Jesus offered. It was voluntary, never forced, and required nothing but a willingness to embrace the basic principles of freedom and personal accountability.

---

103 Wherry, Rev. E. M., *A Comprehensive Commentary on the Quran and Preliminary Discourse*, 1896. pp 66; http://www.worldlingo.com/ma/enwiki/en/Iranian_philosophy.

"A government can't control the economy without controlling people. And [America's Founding Fathers] knew when a government sets out to do that, it must use force and coercion to achieve its purpose."—Ronald Reagan

Jesus' teaching about having problems in common, not things, was misunderstood and lost in the centuries after Jesus' crucifixion. Much of the Mediterranean and European region fell into a dark age of masters and slaves. In the name of religion and Christianity, the worst elements of socialism were propagated through time and throughout the continent.

Socialists of today hold Christianity guilty for the atrocities of the medieval period. In truth, it wasn't the philosophy and teachings of true Christianity that were at fault. The fighting popes, the crusades and inquisitions—all uses of force—were opposite to Jesus' message of freedom, charity, compassion, hard work, friendly persuasion, and love. True Christianity is completely compatible with all the principles of freedom—it sustains every unalienable right. It might be said that Christianity is the embodiment of every principle required to acquire and perpetuate freedom. All other systems use variations of uncontrolled force—the elements of Ruler's Law.

LEARNING TO RECOGNIZE SOCIALISM

The heresies provide a good example of how control of information can lead normal people into abnormal behavior. The followers just had to *believe* what they were doing was right, and the ancient pied pipers could lead their flocks to waste away their lives.

For several centuries, a whole movement of heresies looked forward to a great "last days" when destruction would cleanse the earth of the polluted man-made societies, and replace them with a thousand years of utopian life style.

To achieve this end, most heretics believed they were supposed to help. They were supposed to take part in the destruction and cleansing so the new societies could be created. Many were happy to hurry the process forward—with arson, killing, torture, raping, robbing, and destruction.

"The family is now one of the major obstacles to improved mental health, and hence should be weakened, if possible, so as to free individuals and especially children from the coercion of family life."—International Congress on Mental Health, London, 1948

CHAPTER 19:
FEUDALISM AND RULERS LAW

Feudalism was no futile philosophy—it was socialism

From the A.D. 700s to the 1400s, socialism was practiced by landholders in Europe who provided security and a place to stay in exchange for labor and loyalty from the tenants. It was no established system of government, but became an orderly way to preserve a degree of peace in the land.

Long before Rome fell in A.D. 476, local seats of power or landholdings were established with the construction of Roman villas. Originally these were country dwellings for the nobility, and were scattered all over Europe. When Rome fell and Europe became decentralized, the local churches and villas became the new power centers. The families with land and the means of protecting it cordoned off their claims and dared anyone to take it away.

The peasants were left with nowhere to turn except to align with the churches or one of the landholders. And so evolved a crude replacement of Roman rule. The tenants willingly gave labor and loyalty for a place to till the land and raise a family.

❖ **THE NON-WORD EVERYONE USES**: "Feudalism" is used to describe this desperate "land for loyalty" arrangement. The origins and correct use of feudalism is regularly debated because the word didn't exist back in the day. Italian Renaissance thinkers apparently invented it in the late A.D. 800s. The French Revolutionaries used it to describe the system they were overthrowing in the late 1700s, and the rest of us equate it with Europe during a difficult and dark time.[104]

❖ **THE RULER**: At the top was the feudal lord. This was a landowner who presumed superiority for the simple lucky happenstance that he inherited some land from his forefathers. That made him the boss. His rentable land was called a fief.

❖ **THE PEASANTS:** At the bottom of the feudal caste system were the vassals. In exchange for providing service to the lord or

---

104 See Will Durant, *The Story of Civilization, The Age of Faith,* 1950.

"Comparison" Means "Confiscated": In 2012, China announced it would compare the production of vegetables, grain, pigs, poultry, sheep and cattle in several major cities to ensure they met environmental standards set for the end of the 12th Five Year Plan.

king, the peasants were allowed to use the land and benefit from the king's protection inside the castle.

Making a peasant a vassal was quite the formal and ceremonial event. It included a great feast and everyone showed up in their Sunday best. At the conclusion of the dinner, the vassal gave an oath to the lord—to obey and observe their contract of cooperation. This ceremony rendered the contract formally consummated.

THE FEUDAL ARRANGEMENT: These contracts gave the lords of the land a body of farmer-warriors who he could call upon to defend his lands or to pursue other goals. It also gave the farmer a fairly reliable place to settle down and raise his family. He paid for this safety by giving away part or all of his agriculture work, or by taking up the sword, if so commanded.

The vassals were not all farmers. They performed an assortment of other duties, but usually they could not own anything. Those who were particularly valiant were granted favors or were elevated to a class of nobility—a knight, counselors, guards, etc. These promotion ceremonies were mixed with Christian sacraments to give the whole structure a degree of God-sanctioned authority. The religious anointing of kings and sacred oaths of knights were viewed as binding before God and king.

FIEF: The word *fief* has a long history but was used to mean possessions or duties in a feudal relationship. A person's fief could be any number of things: land, money, animals, an office, a task such as hunting or fishing. These could be passed down to the next generation but the original property right or authority always remained with the king—and what the king giveth he could also taketh away.

CASTLES: Those beautiful buildings romanticized in legend and lore were the private fortified residences of the lords. They originated in the A.D. 800s, and many were actually the glorified expansions of the Roman villas. They were symbols of a king's power and influence, and became centers for administration of the lands and fiefs under his control. The more powerful the king, the larger the castle. Finally, by the 1700s, cities and borders were well-entrenched and most of that constructive bragging and building of the elaborate castles finally wound down. [105]

105　Kenyon, J., *Medieval Fortifications*, 1991.

"If one rejects laissez faire on account of man's fallibility and moral weakness, one must for the same reason also reject every kind of government action."—Ludwig von Mises

CHAPTER 20:
SOCIALISM IN THE MIDDLE AGES

*For parts of Europe, these were the dark and
suffering years, with crazies running amok.*

T he first few centuries after the turn of the new millennium
(A.D. 1000) saw an astonishing period of fanaticism
and backwardness in Europe. People lost their heads—
figuratively and literally. Where the existence of the Church was
intended to bring order to life and a deeper soul-searching pursuit
of happiness, a few over-zealous fanatics managed to rise to the top
of various religious movements. They drew away thousands into
acts of brazen paganism that were so extreme they might even have
ashamed hardened warriors like Attila the Hun and Genghis Khan.

W HEN: A.D. 1100s-1200s
HERESY: Catharism—violent "Christian" socialists[106]
STORY: The Cathars used the socialistic ideas of
information control to live with all things in common and complete
regulation of every aspect of the followers' lives. They degraded to
the point of forcing people to kill themselves, or be murdered if they
disagreed.

In Greek, cathar meant "the pure." Over the centuries this
heresy expanded into at least 40 different sects including numerous
non-Cathars sharing the same doctrinal tenets. Its beginning was
around A.D. 1000 and swept across Europe in a matter of decades.
A former Cathar bishop in Italy wrote in A.D. 1190, "Are not all
townships, cities and castles overrun with these pseudo-prophets?"

EVIL GODS, GOOD GODS—TAKE YOUR PICK

The Cathars believed the physical world was the source of all
evil, and was created by an evil God or perhaps by God's fallen
son, Satan—they weren't sure. The spiritual world was the essence
of good, and was created by a good God. There was to be no

---

106   See Will Durant, *The Story of Civilization, The Reformation* (1957); Tony Perrottet, New
York Times, *The Besieged and the Beautiful in Languedoc*, May 9, 2010; Catholic Encyclopedia, *Cathari*; The Encyclopedia Britannica, 13th Edition, 1926, *Cathars.*

**Do the communists gain power through the socialists? Yes: "The vital interests of the working-
class movement demand that the Communist and Social-Democratic Parties take joint action ...
Both in the struggle for the improvement of the living condition of working people, ..." (cont'd)**

mingling between physical and spiritual. They supposed that Jesus, being good, had to be a spiritual being while on earth—although the circumstances of mortality obligated Him to make Himself appear as a physical man.

Cathars called themselves "New Adams," and viewed the Church as a hostile enemy. This philosophy is viewed by many as the precursor to humanism that would later take root.

ALL MATERIAL THINGS ARE EVIL

Cathars considered their own bodies to be the creation of the evil God. Their bodies, and all other physical creation, were doomed to destruction. Their essence or matter wasn't destroyed but was recycled into new creations by the evil God. They believed the ultimate goal of mankind was, therefore, to throw off the physical—that is, commit universal species suicide—to free their spirits so they could join the good spiritual God.

Plato's teachings about family and society gained practical support in the Cathar's religious beliefs. They rejected property as a product of the evil God, and they forbade marriage. Sexual relations were okay so long as they didn't propagate the species. Pregnancy was seen as the means whereby spirits became trapped in material bodies. Pregnant women were considered possessed by demons, and so were their children.

SAY THAT AGAIN—SEX BAD, DEATH GOOD?

Cathars didn't eat anything that came from mating (meaning meat of any kind), or participate in anything considered physical or material that was a creation of the evil God. They opposed legal proceedings, giving oaths, owning a weapon, fighting in war, or even contacting non-Cathars unless it was to proselytize.

They firmly believed that becoming freed from the body was a good thing—and the sooner the better. If one among their numbers was terminally ill, he or she was given a deathbed "consolation." However, if that "consoled" person suddenly recovered and didn't die, it was expected that he would still honor the consolation, by committing suicide. Suicide was viewed by Cathars as a lawful act—it was also encouraged and commendable. They called it "endura."

(cont'd) " ...the extension and preservation of their democratic rights, the achievement and defence of national independence, for peace among nations, and also in the struggle to win power and build socialism, the Communist Parties advocate cooperation with the Socialist Parties." **Communist and Workers' Parties' Manifesto, 1960**

Very few people wanted endura, especially after recovering their health. In those instances the happy restored person would receive involuntary endura—basically they were murdered.

According to some researchers, more Cathars in France died from endura than from the pope's crusade in A.D. 1208, sent from Rome to eradicate the Cathars.[107]

CATHARS HATED THE CATHOLIC CHURCH

Cathars viewed the Church as the whore of Babylon and the source of all error. Cathars denied Catholic sacraments, such as baptism of children (declaring that children were too young to believe), marriage, and communion. They hated the cross as a symbol of the evil material God. Some sects felt justified in attacking churches—burning, looting, plundering, defiling, and killing.

WAR AND CRUSADES

The pope launched several crusades against the Cathars, once trapping them in castles in the southwest corner of France, where many hundreds of their leadership were finally killed, burned, or captured. In Béziers, more than 15,000 men, women, and children were butchered. When the Crusaders asked who among their prisoners were Cathars or Catholics, the crusader monk Armond Amaury told his troops, "Kill them all, God will know his own."

By A.D. 1220, the Cathars were no longer a threat in Germany and England. Within another century, they were exterminated in France, Belgium, and Spain. By A.D. 1400, remaining believers in Italy were executed, and the Balkan States chased out the remainder a few years later. In A.D. 1416, some 40,000 Cathars left Bosnia for Herzegovina, where they finally disappeared after the Turks conquered those provinces and imposed Islam.

WHEN: A.D. 1200-1400s
HERESY: Brethren of the Free Spirit
STORY: The Brethren of the Free Spirit used the socialistic principles of information control, force, and all things in common to spread destruction in the lives of others in preparation for the coming cleansing of the world.

Joachim of Fiore (A.D. 1135-1202) and Amalric of Bena (died A.D. 1204) were the pioneering brains behind many of the Middle

---

107   Ibid., Shafarevich.

Ages heresies. They shared the belief that the corrupted world was about to end. It had already passed through two of its three epochs—Moses' law, then Christ's Law—and in A.D. 1260, according to their calculations, the world would finally enter the third epoch, a new age of freedom.

This era of perfection was supposed to be wonderful—a time when the words "mine" and "thine" would be unknown, and the renewed church would serve all mankind equally and fairly.

However, arriving at this blissful state required passage through a terrible period of war and bloodshed when the Antichrist would appear. Joachim taught that the Catholic Church was proof of the prophesied decay, and said the Antichrist would appear and rise up to become its pope. He told followers that if they would revert to apostolic poverty (no property or money), they would become strong enough to defeat the Antichrist. The result would be all of mankind uniting in Christianity.

MUST DESTROY AT ALL COSTS

The destruction of the Church, Joachim promised, would open the door to a leaderless communal world run by the people. This teaching is said to have influenced—or at least, been a precursor to—Marx's call to abolish the state and install rule and order through the dictatorship of the proletariat.

Meanwhile, Amalric told everyone he was the embodiment of this budding third epoch—the man into whom all revelation was imbued, just as revelation was imbued into Christ.

GO HAVE FUN—THERE IS NO LONGER ANY SIN

Amalric taught that he and his faithful inner circle members were above sin because they were received and accepted of God. And, God being the author of all things, both good and evil, whatever they did was, therefore, God's will. This relationship made them surprisingly incapable of sin. To achieve that holy state, they had to surrender all property, their families, even their own will, and go about begging for survival. They called themselves the "The Brethren of the Free Spirit."

With no moral restrictions, the Free Spirits believed they owned everything and they could do with it as they pleased. Anyone standing in their way could be killed. Nothing worldly could further

Religious socialism in Saudi Arabia: Non-Muslims may not enter Mecca. A sign over the freeway directing three left lanes into the holy city reads "Arafat Makkah, Muslims only." The sign directing two right lanes off the freeway, "Jeddah, Obligatory for non muslims."

exalt or diminish a Free Spirit. Once they achieved their state of "godliness" and understood that God works through everything, Free Spirits believed they could engage in sexual relations with any woman—stranger, sister, mother—and it could not stain him and would only improve her holiness.

By the early A.D. 1300s, the Free Spirits movement had spread far and wide. Those opposed to the Catholic Church were particularly drawn to it because the Free Spirits taught that this life is their actual resurrection—there is no other life, and man's greatest joys are in this life alone, so get out there and live it up.

FORCE AND MORE FORCE

The longed-for Third Epoch that Joachim and Amalric had promised wouldn't come until first there was a cleansing of the Church from the earth. Once that was out of the way, the wonderful and new way would have room to finally establish itself. So, mobs of Free Spirits began attacking any establishment of the Church they could lay their torches to. They rained down upon villages and towns, slaughtering men, women, and children. Count Montefeltro (A.D. 1290-1364), boasted about plundering villages and churches, and raping nuns. According to records from the Inquisitions, members of the sect openly embraced Satan as their supreme deity because they concluded that even the existence of evil had to be a creation of God, made for God's purposes.

Similar to the Cathars, the Free Spirits had a caste. At the top level—an "inner circle" of the most elevated—the group leadership declared that any act, regardless of its depravity, was not a sin. At the lower level—the "outer circle"—were the great masses of followers who evidently didn't realize what atrocities the inner circle was perpetrating. Still, they all lived by the doctrine of no private property, no family, no church, and no state.

W HEN: 1200-1400s
HERESY: Dolcino and the Apostolic Brethren
STORY: Followers of Dolcino submitted to the socialistic ideals of a supreme ruler whose every utterance was truth. He deployed all the usual suspect ideas: things in common, stringent regimentation, control of all information, force, and no rights.

The Free Spirit movement of the early millennium spawned this

Saudi Arabian women are forbidden from driving or cycling on public roads. Saudi clerics considered bicycles "the Horse of Satan" in the 1960s. Things have changed since then, though women moving about like that is still frowned on.

group in the 1350s. These people ran around telling everyone that the fulfillment of Joachim's prophecy (see above) of the coming Antichrist was near, and the Catholic Church's corruption had finally reached the point of total collapse. Like many others, the Apostolic Brethren pointed to Emperor Constantine in A.D. 300 as the beginning time of the Catholic decay. They taught that the pope was possessed by the devil, and set themselves up as the new righteous leadership. At their head was a man named Dolcino.

Dolcino demanded strict obedience to his every command, and declared that violence against anyone was permitted because it helped to further cleanse the earth. He also ordered that wives, property, and all things be held in common. As before, nobody recorded what the women thought about this religious tenet of wife-swapping, but the husbands seemed agreeable.

In 1404, Dolcino summoned 5,000 Apostolic Brethren to the mountains of northern Italy and began a guerilla warfare campaign, attacking villages and destroying churches. This war lasted for three years until his followers were finally beaten back. Dolcino and his "spiritual sister," Margareta, were given the chance to recant their heretical beliefs, but they refused. They were burned at the stake on June 1, 1307.

War on women in America: In 2012, democrat Representatives made it clear they supported sex-selective abortions, allowing mothers to abort their babies depending on gender. If she wanted a boy, the democrats insisted, she should be free to kill the girl baby and try for a boy later.

CHAPTER 21:

SOCIALISM AND THE REFORMATION

Frustration leads to rebellion against the Church.

As populations in Europe grew in size, so did their frustration with the tyranny of renegade priests. Wanting to gain freedom from oppression, large groups left the Catholic Church and joined reformers who sought to force change on the Church. Even though many of the Church's official teachings were aligned with the Christianity Jesus introduced, the abuse that renegade clergy exercised was a constant reality. The people's complaints were very justified and their suffering quite real.

WHEN: A.D. 1300-1400s
HERESY: Taborites and the reformation
STORY: The Taborites adopted the socialist principles of severe top-down control. They built armies to force their belief systems on others, or at least break the grip the Catholics had on alternative religious viewpoints and beliefs. However, the Taborites went about violating the very same rights in others when they destroyed and fought and killed their way to dominance.

Our story begins with two forerunners of the Protestant Reformation—the English theologian John Wycliffe (1328-1384) and a Catholic priest named Jan Hus (1369-1415) from the Czech Republic.

They were among a growing number across western Europe who were angry with the evolving role of the Church in civic affairs. Political power, material possessions, and privileged position became the chief focus of local Church leaders. Many bishops and abbots acted as if they were secular rulers instead of representatives of the Church. They labored more to increase power and income than to help the poor. Celibacy wasn't uniformly practiced (with all the local problems that ignited), and misgivings about Church doctrine and goals were festering in many locations.

WYCLIFFE CALLS FOR CLEANSING

John Wycliffe began publicly criticizing the Church for these lapses, saying it should renounce its massive land holdings and

"We learn from history that we don't learn from history"—Georg Eilhelm Hegel

wealth and become poor as in the days of Jesus. He held aloft the Bible as the sole source of Christian doctrine, not the pope, and believed the bread and wine of the Eucharist (the sacrament or Holy Communion) *remained* bread and wine once consumed—they didn't turn into the actual flesh and blood of Christ when administered to the membership.

WAR

Meanwhile, over in the Czech Republic, Jan Hus read Wycliffe's writings and embraced his ideas. He went so far as to translate them into Czech, and taught the same ideas in his own writings. He gained many supporters and followers, but at a cost—Hus fell in serious disfavor with Church leaders.

In 1415, Hus was lured to Constance, a city on the German-Swiss border, to an ecumenical council that had been called to settle the thorny issue of who exactly was the legal pope. The justification of Hus's presence was to give him opportunity to air his grievances face-to-face with leading church authorities.

It was a trap. After a couple of weeks, the church guards suddenly confined Hus to quarters, and then one day brought him out for a contrived trial. The council members found him guilty of heresy, led him in chains to a meadow beyond town, and burned him at the stake.

Hus's death triggered a revolt by his followers. Within five years, Hus's original followers and others who aligned themselves started a series of wars against the Church. These lasted from 1420 to 1434, and became known as the Hussite Wars.

An army leader of the Hussites set up a fortified headquarters just outside of Prague, a town they named Tabor. This became a gathering place for preachers who were opposed to the Church. Though united in their opposition to the Church, the groups eventually splintered into various sects.

FIRST PRIORITY: DESTROY THE CHURCH

The Taborites sent their armies to fight the pope's crusaders along various fronts. They were victorious, defeating the pope's armies on numerous occasions.

"Pull down trees and destroy houses, churches and monasteries," they ordered. "... All church property must be demolished, and

---

"Your goose is cooked," meaning you're caught or doomed, was sardonically coined to mock the burning of Jan Hus at the stake. Why? Because "Hus" in Czech means "goose."

the churches, altars and monasteries destroyed."[108]

In the process, thousands of priests were chased, burned and killed. The Taborite invaders destroyed libraries, works of art, sacramental candelabras, and gold and silver ornaments. The order was issued, "All human institutions and human laws must be abolished, for none of them were created by the Heavenly Father."[109]

ALL THINGS IN COMMON

Meanwhile, back in Tabor, the Taborites put all their money and wealth in barrels to be distributed evenly. There was to be nothing "which is mine or thine, but all possess everything in common and no one is to have anything apart, and whoever does is a sinner."[110] All things were to be communal, including wives: "There will be free sons and daughters of God and there will be no marriage as union of two—husband and wife."[111]

ADAMITES GO CRAZY

The Adamites carried the destruction of the Catholics even further. They attacked villages and towns at night, setting them ablaze, killing both young and old.

At their meetings, they wore no clothing as a sign of purity and separation from the ways of the world. They taught that marriage was wrong, and any man could take any woman by merely declaring "she inflames my spirit."[112] They practiced unlimited sexual liberty, mimicking the earlier established Free Spirit movement. This debased behavior couldn't endure—it never does—and the Adamites eventually weakened, fell prey to attack, and were exterminated under the leadership of Hussite commander Ian Zizka in 1421.

LEGACY

The Hussite wars did more than just ravage nearby countries and Church holdings. They also served to spread the utopian ideas of a necessary cleansing of the land as preparation for a coming millennium of peace with all things in common—no more oppressive overlords in the form of the Church, the monarchs, or any other tyrant. But first, they had to get rid of the corruption—

---

108   J. Macek, *Tabor in the Hussite Revolutionary Movement*, vol. 2, 1959, p. 85.
109   Ibid., Macek, p. 94.
110   Ibid., pp. 99-100.
111   Ibid., p. 113.
112   Ibid., p 478.

Socialist Health Care in Europe (2008): Survival for prostate cancer in Europe—57.1%; in U.S.—91.1%.

W HEN: 1525-1540
HERESY: The Anabaptists
STORY: The Anabaptists tried all the usual socialistic
ideals—things in common, no private property, and the destruction
of the existing society—to further their cause. Their plan was struggling to get off the ground, and then suddenly appeared some help.

Gutenberg's printing press did a lot to spread the influence
of the heretical off-shoots during 16th century Europe. With the
Peasant's War in Germany, the Anabaptist movement was enabled
to more quickly expand their rate of conversions through Germany
to Switzerland, The Netherlands, Austria, Denmark, Czechia, and
decades later, over into England.

The name "Anabaptist" implied re-baptism, from the belief that
infants were too young to make such religious decisions. Infant
baptism was a tenet of the Catholics, and Anabaptists taught that it
was meaningless—therefore, all must be rebaptized.

OPPOSING THE CHURCH ON ALL FRONTS

The Anabaptists rejected the Catholic Church, saying it had
been in apostasy since Constantine (A.D. 300). The Anabaptists
claimed their own authority came directly through the bloodlines
of the original Apostles. They rejected any sacrament or Church
structure that wasn't in the Bible, and claimed for scripture only
those words spoken by Jesus Himself.

Their doctrine was inconsistent. Some Anabaptists believed
that baptism made them impervious to sin and they could do as
they pleased. A 16th century German free thinker, Sebastian Franck,
described these inconsistencies: "Some believe themselves to be
holy and pure; they have everything in common. ... Others practice
commonality only to the extent that they do not permit need to arise
among themselves. ...Among them a sect appeared which wished to
make wives, as well as belongings, communal."[113]

WEALTH, WIVES, AND WORSHIP IN COMMON

It went further: their clothing was dictated—the fabric, shape,
style, length, and size. Then came the broad gray hat, mandatory
for all to wear. They also had rules for eating, drinking, sleeping,
free time, and when and how to stand or walk about. A group of

---

113   L. Keller, *Johann von Staupitz un die Anfange der Reformation*, 1888, p. 306, cited in
Shafarevich, p. 35.

**"The socialist system will eventually replace the capitalist system; this is an objective law
independent of man's will. However much the reactionaries try to hold back the wheel of history,
sooner or later revolution will take place and will inevitably triumph."—Mao Zedong**

enforcers checked on people's upbringing of children, their marriages, assigned them their work, wouldn't allow private cooking or eating, separated children at age 2 to be raised in common nurseries, and were not allowed contact with the state. Wives could be taken as desired by whomever—all in common.

FORCE LOVE AND HUMANITY WITH THE SWORD

After the Peasant Wars in which the Anabaptists played a role against Germany, the authorities unleashed a wave of persecution against the movement. It weakened them for a while, but they rose again in 1530. Their new doctrine of self defense was proscribed: "The saints must be joyful and must take up double-edge swords," said Apostle Hans Hut, "in order to wreak vengeance in the nations. ...slaughter of all overlords and powers that be."[114]

ANOTHER TYRANT MEETS HIS MAKER

By 1535, the Anabaptists had angered enough Germans that a large coordinated attack was organized to neutralize the heretics once and for all. The "saints" gathered to Munster, Germany, where Jan Bokelson was made their ruler as well as king of the world. He had a huge court of luxury, and many wives. He wielded all justice, and personally beheaded evil-doers in the town square.

Surrounded by all his utopian dreams, all the riches and benefits a poor mortal soul could want, Bokelson was captured and the city of Munster fell, He and his Anabaptist leadership were executed, and the rest of his followers were hunted and killed up until about 1660. To escape the persecution, thousands migrated to North America, taking upon themselves various names such as the Amish, the Hutterites, and the Mennonites.

W
HEN: 1640s
HERESY: The Diggers—spreading atheism
STORY: The Diggers took hold of the socialistic idea of all things in common, and went about pushing it as far and wide as they could.

The mid-1600s was a time of upheaval in England. Corruption in the government gave rise to conflicting opinions about the best form of rule. Some wanted to return a king to the throne; others led

114   F. Bezold, *Geschichte der deutschen Reformation*, 1886, p. 703, cited in Shafarevich, p. 39.

Socialism in North Korea: In 2012, two reporters for *The Sun* bluffed their way into North Korea. They discovered all the six-story buildings dotting the river border with China were windowless and empty. Why? To make it appear they were prosperous and "living well."

by Oliver Cromwell wanted property owners to have more say. Still others wanted to build a parliamentary government that represented all male leaders of a household. Some wanted a theocracy, and then there were The Diggers.

The nickname of Gerrard Winstanley's group, the Diggers, came about because they believed in digging the land as a common ownership and equally sharing in the harvest and fruits of labor. These Protestant socialists preached the gospel of knocking down enclosures, disposing of borders, and making everything free to everyone. They called themselves the True Levellers, a term associated with socialism to distinguish themselves from other levellers groups.

NO WALLS, NO FENCES

Winstanley's pamphlets served as the Diggers' guiding articles of faith. These condemned private property as the root of all evil. Of land, he said, "Not enclosing any part into any particular hand, but all as one man, working together, and feeding together as Sons of one Father, members of one Family; not one Lording over another, but all looking upon each other, as equals in the Creation."[115]

In April 1649, food prices were at record highs. When The Diggers came into Weybridge, and offered communal land and harvest to freely share, local farmers blew their stacks. Landowners were irate that free food was undermining their efforts to get maximum pricing. This triggered a revolt against The Diggers.

CHASED FROM TOWN TO TOWN

After the local farmers exhausted their efforts to reclaim control over pricing, they grabbed their pitchforks and turned to violence. They began harassing, arresting, and burning until the Diggers pulled up stakes and moved to Cobham. The Diggers were not appreciated there, either.

Another settlement was started in Wellingborough, Northamptonshire. After similar clashes and troubles, some sect members were arrested without charges and held in prison indefinitely.

By 1651, the farmers finally crushed the upstart, forcing its members to disband. Even though their numbers probably didn't exceed 200 people, their impact was felt far and wide.

---

115   Gerrard Winstanley, *The True Levellers Standard Advanced*, 1649.

The Socialist Prophets get it wrong again: "The Soviet economy is proof that, contrary to what many skeptics had earlier believed, a socialist command economy can function and even thrive."—Paul Samuelson, 1989, just before the Soviet Union imploded.

LEGACY

The Diggers' tactics for proselytizing their cause introduced to the rest of Europe the effective use of pamphlets, the media, and petitions to magnify their pursuit of political goals. They had friends in a newspaper called *The Moderate* in which defense of their actions was supported. Using these techniques to rouse public sympathy and support for their cause helped expand the Digger movement, but also proved the power of the written word.

W HEN: 1649-1660
HERESY: The Ranters—Leaderless fanatics
STORY: The Ranters' socialistic ideas included having all things in common, including wives, and no private property.

There remain questions about this strange group, but what is known is that they embraced many of the teachings of the Brethren of the Free Spirit of the 14th century. They rejected a personal God, and some denounced immortality or a life hereafter. They didn't believe they had to obey anyone, including local governments and leaders.

Their most well-known member was Laurence Claxton, who declared in a 1650 pamphlet he called *A Single Eye*, "[Ranters believe] that a believer is free from all traditional restraints, that sin is a product only of the imagination, and that private ownership of property is wrong."

POPULAR THEME: WOMEN IN COMMON

From another of their pamphlets, *The Ranters' Last Sermon,* came the teaching, "...for one man to be tied to one woman, or one woman to be tied to one man, is a fruit of the curse; but they say we are freed from the curse; therefore it is our liberty to make use of whom we please."

Ranters went around nude as a means of social protest and as a demonstration of abandoning earthly and material things. They also engaged in unlimited sexual contact.

The Ranters as a distinct group were lost when most of the members joined the Quakers in the 1650s.

LEARNING TO RECOGNIZE SOCIALISM

Destruction of the existing moral codes and institutions contin-ued the basic theme of socialism under the guise of Christianity, or whichever religious leaning the assorted and varied heresies liked to claim.

Predominant among their teachings was abolishing private property, including no possible claim to spouse and children. This direct assault on the family reduced their perch atop higher moral ground, seeking to institutionalize permissible orgies.

Friedrich Engels commented on the tendency of rebellions to frequently turn to sexual liberties: "It is a curious fact that in every large revolutionary movement the question of 'free love' comes to the foreground."[116]

The heresies exerted strict regulations of their followers' social and economic lives, but had difficulties in generating incomes to support themselves. They took what they wanted from others, and when sufficiently large in numbers they attempted common farms and gardens.

Fortunately, as their stridency finally calmed, there arose a unity in the faith that put a rational work ethic back into the groups. True Christianity started to make its comeback—sort of. As countries established national religions, persecution took on a new form in the guise of local law—*If you're not one of us, you're not welcome.* For many, they had no only viable option to exercise their free choice and religion except to leave and start fresh in the New World. Besides religious freedom, they also brought to the America's the ancient idea of *guilds.*

---

116 Engels, *The Book of Revelation*, in ME: On Religion (Moscow, FLPH, 1957), p. 205.

Regulating knowledge: In 2012, Florida's Board of Education lowered the passing grade for a state-wide writing test because not enough students could pass.

CHAPTER 22:

RISE OF THE GUILDS

Meanwhile, back in Europe: Before socialism infiltrated free trade under the guise of unions, there were first the ancient associations and guilds.

The butcher, the baker and candlestick maker conjure up pleasant images of a simpler time in faraway medieval European towns where everyone looked like roly-poly cartoon characters and there was no violent crime, disease or outhouses.

WELL—MAYBE NOT

In earlier centuries the cobblers, tinkerers and craft makers were members of a guild—an association of specialists organized in Middle Ages Europe to guard and protect trade secrets. The guild movement was a great engine of self interest at work, established to protect their businesses and exclude competition.

"Guild" is from the Anglo-Saxon *gildan*, meaning "to pay" or "to contribute." Guild members paid regular dues to the central fund to pool the risks of life and business. This helped secure against an emergency such as sickness, accidents, funerals, financial collapse, bad economic times, etc.

EARLY MILESTONE DATES

Organizing skilled people into groups was not a medieval invention. Associations of talented people appear to have existed in many eras and numerous places. They were not always so organized or retained bargaining power as those of recent centuries, but pooling talent appeared to be popular.

800 B.C.—Homer mentions associations of builders, potters, carpenters, and specialists in metal and leather in ancient Greece.

700 B.C.—Numa, thought to be the second king of Rome, divided craftsmen into nine guilds or collegia.

400 B.C.—India's caste system evolved guilds called shrenis.

200 B.C.—A Chinese guild system began to form at least during the Han Dynasty (206 B.C.-A.D. 200), called the hanghui. Chinese guilds were well established by the Sui Dynasty (A.D. 589-618).

Corrupting American Culture: In 2012, the Obama administration's Department of Justice ordered the University of Arkansas at Fort Smith to allow a male student who was undergoing sex-change surgeries to use women's bathrooms on campus.

A.D. 600—Earliest guilds reported in England.

A.D. 900—Craftsmen started organizing in Iran.

MERCHANT GUILDS—IN LIKE A LAMB ...

The most powerful associations during the medieval period were the merchant guilds—associations of people selling and trading, including many artisans and craftsmen.

Membership was voluntary. The Christian church played a large role in the overall philanthropy adopted by most guilds, even though the Church as an institution was not connected. The Church opposed the binding oaths that guild members swore to keep the secrets among themselves.

The medieval merchant guilds were organized to resist the arbitrary tax hikes imposed by the land-owning lords and kings. An individual could have no say in such matters—he was too insignificant to do anything about it.

By uniting with others in a guild, by forming a group, they could wield enough influence to refuse services or products unless certain demands were met. For example, the guilds challenged high taxes, insisting these be set and locked in for a year or more. Those agreements were drawn up as charters or letter patents, which are the predecessors of today's patent and trademark system.

Guilds built their own meeting places called the guildhall. The buildings gave the members a safe and distinguished place of privilege to conduct business and receive payment of guild taxes. They wore special apparel to advertise their guild association at formal occasions and parades, and hung signs out in front of their businesses to let people know that only the best was available there.

... AND OUT LIKE A LION

The merchant guilds grew so powerful, they melded in with the town structure and began to monopolize everything—including the craftsmen.

The craftsmen didn't like being smothered. They wanted to break the iron grip of the merchants and form their own associations to control their business destinies. It wasn't always a scene of pitchforks and torches, with peasants shaking fists and shouting insults at the gates of the guildhall, but the craftsmen succeeded in starting their own silent revolution. Over time, these craft guilds eventually overpowered and replaced many of the merchant guilds.

CRAFTSMEN UNITE

The first to form a craft guild were the weavers and fullers in England in A.D. 1130. They successfully fought the power of the merchant guilds, established their own authority over various trades, and other craftsmen soon followed suit.

The craft guilds were organized along similar lines as the merchants. They built guild halls, they corralled skills into a pool, and they controlled the sale and availability of their services in a way to strengthen their business profits and foot traffic. After a few years no one could practice a particular craft without being a member of the local guild.

The new guilds prevented outside competition and the various guilds worked together to fix prices as well as to ensure high levels of quality. They conspired to keep their products in great demand by limiting the numbers of craftsmen working in any particular art or trade.

TUTORING THE APPRENTICE

The craftsmen monitored their art with patience. The son of a guild member typically joined the guild as an "apprentice" who worked under the professional tutorship of a "master." This training lasted 5-9 years. The youth received no income during this period except free room and board. He couldn't even marry until he graduated to the level of "journeyman."

A journeyman could receive wages for his work. His goal was to make the next level of master. To qualify for the top job a journeyman had to successfully create an acceptable "masterpiece." This was a work of such precision and professionalism (he hoped) that it would convince the guild leadership and other masters he was ready to be craft guild master.

When he achieved the level of master, he could set up his own shop and begin training (and exploiting) apprentices.

101 MODELS OF CRAFTS ON THE WALL ...

The craftsmen formed hundreds of guilds from apothecaries to armor makers, bakers, barbers, surgeons, dentists, embroiderers, butchers, carpenters, candle makers, leather workers (cordwainers), cutlers, dyers, farriers, fishmongers, arrow makers (fletchers), girdle makers, goldsmiths, stirrup and harness makers, masons, needle makers, plasterers, plumbers, writers of legal documents, skinners, winders and packers of wool—and more.

CHURCH AND EMPERORS NOT HAPPY

During the reign of the Carlovingians (also known as the Carolinians, the family dynasty that ruled Germany, France and Italy during A.D. 700-900) the guilds' control threatened those emperors' ruling power. One of the emperors declared in A.D. 779,

"Let no one dare to take the oath by which people are wont to form guilds. Whatever may be the conditions which have been agreed upon, let no one bind himself by oaths concerning the payment of contributions in case of fire or shipwreck."[117]

Other emperors issued similar decrees.

There was little the emperors could do to stop these organizations. Their feudal co-dependencies complicated matters even more—exerting too much force could chase away the hired help.

Lost in all of these machinations was the individual. The best way up the ladder of success was guild membership, but what if a person wanted to go solo, do it alone, venture into entrepreneurship, innovate and invent in competition with the guild? Those who tried it were punished by the guilds or by the town fathers, who were one and the same in some places.

LEGAL AUTHORITY TO OPPRESS

By the turn of the new millennium, merchant guilds in England were asking for government sanctions, or charters—and were getting them. They started popping up everywhere. By A.D. 1093, they had large organizations in Bristol, Carlisle, Durham, Lincoln, Oxford, Salisbury, and Southhampton. Chartering gave the guilds power to make legal rules of conduct that often carried the authority of local law.

Participation records from the parliaments of Edward I (1272-1307) showed there were some 160 towns represented in his government. Of these, at least 92 were known to have merchant guilds—it's easy to surmise from the business and trading activities of the time that all villages and towns had guilds of one kind or another.

---

117 Burton, E., & Marique, P. (1910). *Guilds*, paragraph 7, In The Catholic Encyclopedia.
For China's Mao Zedong, it was all about force: "The army must become one with the people so that they see it as their own army. Such an army will be invincible...."

Similar organizations were forming elsewhere—Gilde and Confrerie (France and the low countries); Zunft, Bruderschaft, and Hansa (Germany); Komtoor (Bruges), and others in Novgorod (Russia), Prussia, Westphalia, Livonia, Sweden, and just about everywhere a man could buy a good plow and horse collar, and a woman a good stove pot and sewing needles.

EQUAL OPPORTUNITY GUILDS?

Widows were allowed to participate in guilds if their husbands had been members in good standing when they died. Women and children could resume the trade to bring in some income so long as the quality and production standards were met.

GOVERNMENT FORCE MADE THEM SOCIALISTS

The story of guilds is important in the history of socialism because they corrupted the free market with elements of Ruler's Law.

For the most part, guilds were capitalistic. They tried to control wealth for private benefit. Freedom to associate and form a guild did not violate the rights of others. Setting rules for participation, and out-producing with superior products didn't hurt either.

But when the guilds' rules carried the force of public law, when they created monopolies and prevented workers from switching jobs—such as something so rigid as preventing a shoemaker from becoming the obvious related job of shoe repairer, or more broad, such as a carpenter from becoming a plumber—that's when they became little combines of socialism.

Violating the basic freedom to *try*, by using coercion and violence to keep competition away from guilds was the precursor to today's modern trade unions. Thugs and mobs of guild members found a fresh way to kill the competition—literally.

◆   **EARLY THUGGERY**: In 1397, a case was brought before the Lord Chancellor in England complaining of local merchants who had attacked a competitor:

"... Because he sold his merchandise at a less price than other merchants of the said town of Yaxley did theirs ... [angry merchants] and many other evil-doers of their coven, lay in wait with force and arms to kill the said William Lonesdale, and they

Socialism is amoral: Socialists believe all things evolve, therefore "right conduct" is defined according to the traditions and standards of the times. These will change over time, they say, therefore there really is no such thing as "right" and "wrong."

assaulted him, beat him and ill-treated him, and left him there for dead, so that he despaired of his life."[118]

❖ **DYING DYERS**: Another case in that same period dealt with snuffing out a competitor who offered to dye cloth at below the going rates. Official court records of the late 1300s report:

"Dyers guild undertook to work only at certain rates; and when a number of dyers refused to be bound by these rates, the guild hired Welshmen and Irishmen to waylay and kill them."[119]

❖ **FIRST PICKET LINE**: What might be the first union-type picket line recorded in history was formed in 1538. A bishop reported to Oliver Cromwell that:

"...twenty-one journeymen shoemakers of Wisbech have assembled on a hill without the town, and sent three of their number to summon all the master shoemakers to meet them, in order to insist upon an advance in their wages, threatening that 'there shall none come into the town to serve for that wages within a twelve month and a day, but we will have an arm or a leg of him, except they will take an oath as we have done."[120]

With lethal force taking care of business on the outside, secret handshakes and ceremonial initiations among the associations were taking care of business on the inside.

SUPER SECRET SOCIETIES

The *compagnonnages*[121] were secretive societies of journeymen in medieval Europe. Unlike the local guilds, the compagnonnages were international, with groups all over the western continent. There is little mention of these before the 1400s, but the Masons participated, and developed their own secretive initiations and recognitions. The Masons claimed their origins stretched clear back to the stonework performed on the temple of Solomon around 900 B.C. However, a more probable origin for the Masons was during the heydays of cathedral building that started in the A.D. 700s in Germany or A.D. 1040 in England. To join the Mason's building

118   Great Britain, Court of Chancery; Baildon, W. Paley (William Paley), 1859-1924, *Select Cases in Chancery, A.D. 1364 to 1471*, London, B. Quaritch, 1896.
119   Quoted in Howard Dickman, *Industrial Democracy In America*, 1987, p. 28.
120   *Calendars of State Papers: Letters and Papers, Foreign and Domestic, Henry VIII.*, vol. xiii. Part i. 1538, No. 1454, p. 537.
121   George Francois Renard (1847-1930), *Guilds of the Middle Ages*, pp. 87-89.

Socialist health care in Canada (2004): One in 13 patients treated in Canadian hospitals will fall victim to surgical error or incorrectly prescribed drugs.

construction fraternities, a person was initiated into the mysticism with secret handshakes, oaths, passwords, and ceremonies. Violating these oaths could mean death.

That's how the guilds held their ground, and set the stage for the collective bargaining power in trade unions that followed a few centuries later.

The strength of the guilds began to decline in the 1600-1700s. When France was teetering on the brink of complete conflagration in the 1790s, the king banished the guilds to restore peace. He allowed any craftsman to freely compete by paying a fee for a business license. Suddenly that made things fair again—but it was short-lived, and then abandoned. At the time, the French people had much larger issues exploding in their faces.

* * * * *

SOCIALISTS BY NATURE?

Julius Nyerere, the first President of Tanzania, believed Africans were socialists by nature, and promoted the collectivist ideal of "ujamaa" or "familyhood" in the villages. His socialist program abolished capitalism, but required a massive bureaucracy and high taxes. Then came bribery and corruption. The utopian idea of ujamaa collapsed and Tanzania changed from being Africa's largest exporter of food to the largest importer of food. From 1974-1977, cereal grain production plummeted—a million tons shy each year. With 90% of the people living in the ujamaa villages, they were producing barely 5% of their needed food. Socialism was a disaster in Tanzania. Collapsing prices, the oil crisis, lack of investors, and war with Uganda were too much for the fragile economy—only loans and grants prevented Tanzania from going bankrupt and the people starving. Nyerere retired in 1985.[122]

---

122 Cranford Pratt, *Ujamaa—Essays on Socialism*, 1977; *Julius Nyerere: Reflections on the Legacy of his Socialism*, Canadian Journal of African Studies 33 (1), pp. 137–52.

John Lennon said his famous Beatles song, *Imagine*, was meant to be, in Lennon's words, an "anti-religious, anti-nationalistic, anti-conventional, anti-capitalistic [song]." He said the message that ran so contrary to western culture and tradition wasn't rejected. ... (cont'd)

CHAPTER 23:

HOW THE FRENCH "REVOLUTIONIZED" SOCIALISM

*Centuries of socialistic management under a monarch changed when
France's citizens woke up to the possibilities of freedom. The
potential to be free was theirs—but they missed it. They
ended up replacing one socialism with another.*

Before the great revolution in 1789, France had all the earmarks
of a typical socialist society.

It was feudalism, it was a monarchy, it was regimented,
regulated, and maddening.

Its name was *Ancien Régime*, the "old system." Everyone—old,
young, rich, poor, high, low—knew it was failing to meet the needs
of the growing populous and had to be replaced.

SETTING THE STAGE

Here's where the country stood in 1774 when Louis XVI took
the throne.[123]

◆ **SCATTERED VILLAGES:** France was not an all-together
nation. For centuries, the various kings had patched it together by
conquest and deal-making—even marrying heiresses for political
purposes. The kings broke down the old feudal dynasties and drew
new lines. Some provinces came on board with their own laws,
customs, and system of government. So long as they paid taxes,
the kings didn't see a need to impose a universal law on everyone.
Some of these districts were very self-sufficient with their own as-
semblies and historical independence.

◆ **SCATTERED LAWS:** In France's west and north, there were
at least 285 separate codes of law. If you moved from one village
to another, you might get arrested for some crime you never knew
existed.

---

123 James Harvey Robinson and James T. Shotwell, *An Introduction to the History of
Western Europe*, 1902, pp 537-605.

(cont'd) "... because it's sugar-coated, it's accepted." Lennon explained his song's message was
"virtually the Communist Manifesto, even though I am not particularly
a communist and I do not belong to any movement."

◆　**GRIDLOCK:** Attempting to trade goods between towns and regions was like trading to a foreign country. Merchants had to pay duties to cross "state" lines.

◆　**THE SALT TAX:** The government had a monopoly on salt. This earned the king a ton of money. Once a year every household was compelled to purchase from the state warehouse seven pounds per person over age seven—the price was arbitrarily set at any given place or time.

Some of the districts paid horrific prices, perhaps 30 times more than their neighbors. For example, if people in Dijon wanted to salt their potato fries, they paid seven francs. But go east a few miles in Franche-Comté and it was 25 francs. Up in Burgundy, it was 58 francs, but over in Gex, it was zero. (Gex must have made great fries). A man caught smuggling this precious commodity could be fined, flogged, sent to the gallows, and executed.

◆　**CLASS DIFFERENCES**: Not all Frenchmen enjoyed the same rights. The French caste system had three classes called the Estates.

The First Estate was the clergy—probably because God was supposed to be first in everything.

The Second Estate was the nobility—no doubt because they wanted to be first.

And the Third Estate was the peasants—as usual, the workers who did everything important but were always being listed last. In 1789, this Third Estate of peasants numbered 25 million, while the other two Estates totaled 275,000.

But change was coming. It was a time when the French believed they could climb out from the ancient ways, become more modern, and overhaul the government, the economy, and even human nature. The pieces were all falling into place.

ABOUT THE CHURCH ...

The Catholic Church was a ruling power in France for centuries. It played a key role in public life by handling education, providing relief for the sick and poor, and was a rallying point for the discouraged and spiritually downtrodden.

Records indicate that the Church owned as much as a fifth of all the land. The clergy said church property was sanctified for God's work, and therefore it shouldn't, and wasn't, taxed (but the clergy were smart enough to give the king a "free gift" every so often).

FORCED TITHES: The Church collected tithes from all the people. This was enforced by the government like a tax, and amounted to 183 million francs in 1789 ($780 million in 2012 dollars[124]). But things were not friendly if you were not Catholic. A Protestant, for example, could not be legally married, make a legal will, or register the births of his children.

CLERGY PROFITS: Huge sums of Church funds went into the pockets of the bishops, archbishops, and abbots. These fellows were not selected by the pope—they were the king's buddies and were simply appointed to the jobs. They didn't do much for the Church or the people, and just enjoyed the handout. When the French Revolution began, the lower clergy, those who carried the heavy load of actually serving the people as originally intended, didn't side with their higher-up leaders—they joined the people.

THE CASTE

As kings before him had done, King Louis XVI claimed authority from God and wouldn't let anybody forget it. "The sovereign authority resides exclusively in my person. To me solely belongs the power of making the laws, and without dependence or cooperation. ...I am its supreme protector ... by the grace of God." He also insisted on continuing that terrible taille, a direct tax on land that raised a sixth of the country's entire income. Nobody knew how much money was gathered every year, but the sums were estimated to be enormous.

ALL POWER

The king had power to arrest anyone at any time and throw him into prison, lock the door, and forget him. Such arrest orders were called *lettres de cachet* (sealed letters). These arbitrary orders were hated by medieval Europeans and were specifically outlawed in the

---

124 The 1839 *Penny Cyclopaedia of the Society for the Diffusion of Useful Knowledge* (London) reported the U.S. dollar contained 416 grains of silver to the franc's 69.453 grains of silver, or approximately $1 = 6 francs, or $30,500,000 in 1789, or $780 million adjusted for inflation in 2012 dollars.

(cont'd) ... only nine studies had been studied. The study of the study of studies concluded the Pentagon's study of studies was incomplete. The GAO has not released the cost of its study.

Magna Carta (1215 A.D.). Some people were being locked away for a pamphlet they published or a speech they gave that offended the king or one of his groupies—and they were never heard of again.

CHECKS AND BALANCES

Next to the king were the higher courts of law called the parlements. Not to be confused with English Parliaments, the French version helped check the king's edicts. The people insisted that any law the king issued had to be looked at by parlement—read, reviewed, understood, and registered. If not, the people argued, how could the king expect them to enforce a new law that conflicted with others, or simply made no sense?

PROTEST LETTERS: When the parlements didn't like a new law, they sent the king a "protest" explaining their objections. But that wasn't all—they had the protest printed and distributed so the masses would support them in opposition to the king's tyranny. This kept the debate public and conveyed the idea that the king wasn't as all powerful as he tried to act—that there were fundamental laws even he couldn't break.

NASTY FEUDALISM REMAINED: By 1774, the nobility class no longer enjoyed the power it retained during the prior 500 years. Nevertheless, some remnants of serfdom let these lords extract some time-honored dues from those who lived nearby or inside the boundaries of what used to be their villas and manors.

The dues included part of a peasant's crops or a toll on animals driven past a lord's home. The lord usually obligated the peasants to use his mill, oven, or wine press, and charged heavily for the privilege. And any of the lord's animals and birds that wandered onto peasants' lands could not be hunted because those were his property.

SURPRISE! NOT VERY POOR? The commoners of the 1780s were not as down-trodden and miserable as some said. Thomas Jefferson reported in 1787 that the peasants in France had plenty to eat and were comfortable.[125] An English traveler named Arthur Young reported that the country people had prosperity and were contented.

---

125   James Harvey Robinson, *An Introduction to the History of Western Europe*, p. 417.

At the peak of its power, Sparta had 25,000 citizens and 500,000 slaves. Though vastly outnumbered, the Spartans maintained control with horrific terror tactics and brutal treatment of their slaves.

IF NOT POVERTY, WHY THEN A REVOLUTION? The reason the peasantry finally rose up in a revolution in 1789 wasn't necessarily because of their impoverishment. They finally rose to a level of education, understanding, and freedom where they realized that they simply didn't have to take it anymore.

They rejected the old ways, those remnants of serfdom that still haunted their culture. They resisted the nobility's continued attempts to act the part of common robbers, skulking around to extract a portion of the harvest, or hiding in the trees to take a toll at a river crossing, or refusing to compensate for damage from His Lordship's animals that might have ruined a commoner's crops during a hunt.

WEARY OF THE SLAVE SOCIETY: In short, the whole country was tired—tired of the absurd and abusive laws, rules, and customs of top-down regimentation, of thievery and control, of oppression and domination. Those relics of the old system that perpetuated the seven pillars of socialism at work would no longer be tolerated—the French wanted them gone. Helping to push things along, some great thinkers came forward.

GREAT THINKERS SET THE STAGE

❖ **VOLTAIRE (1694-1778)** was a popular reformer whose writings unified the cause of freedom and rebellion in France.

❖ **CATCHING THE VISION:** Understanding Voltaire is understanding France before their revolution. He had no patience or sympathy for the old traditions and wore out his quill exposing absurdity after absurdity in the existing norms. His prolific ways spanned the written word in published editorials, histories, plays, dramas, romances, letters, and more—reaching out to all levels of society where he put forth his persistent question, why not freedom?

❖ **GREED IS AS GREED DOES:** Voltaire was no atheist, but the Catholics and Protestants he attacked accused him of it, and of corruption and hypocrisy. He credited God for all things wholesome and good—as a good deist would—but his creative pen lobed fireballs at the worldly religions that showed themselves bent on greed, power, and gain.

He somehow missed or at least he avoided acknowledging the

centuries of good works by the Church, and instead focused on ridiculing them for their tragic lapses. The French commoners loved his writings.

❖ **JEAN JACQUES ROUSSEAU (1712-1778)** did a great job stirring discontent. His famous little pamphlet, *The Social Contract*, boldly declared it is the people who should make the laws because it is the people who must obey them. France's first constitution in 1789, the Declaration of the Rights of Man and of the Citizens, included Rousseau's doctrine:

"Law is the expression of the general will. Every citizen has a right to participate personally, or through his representative, in its foundation. It must be the same for all, whether it protects or punishes."[126]

❖ **MONTESQUIEU (1689-1755)** pointed out how Englishmen kept control over their limited monarchy with a clever idea called separation of powers. The English, Montesquieu observed, had three powers in government—Parliament making the laws, the king executing them, and the independent courts enforcing them. France would be stronger, Montesquieu reasoned, if these three functions were removed from the same individual's hands as the English had done, and spread them out to check one another's powers and choices.

TAXES AND THE SCIENCE OF POLITICAL ECONOMY.

When Louis XVI (1754-1793) took the throne in 1774 as a young 20-year-old with his beautiful wife Marie Antoinette, he was anxious to turn around the financial mess in which the country was buried. The chicanery of prior monarchs had plunged the country deeply into a fiscal nightmare.

But poor Louis XVI had to keep up appearances, too.[127]

❖ **STAFF**: The on-site military retinue of the king included 9,050 people. His civil household numbered around 4,000. The palace at Versailles also kept on the payroll 150 pages, 128 musicians, 48 physicians and assistants, 383 officers of the table, and 198 persons to wait personally upon the king.

---

126   *The Works of Jeremy Bentham, Part III,* Simpkin, 1839, p. 507.
127   Frederic Austin Ogg, *Social progress in Contemporary Europe,* 1912, pp. 17-18.
"In Mexico the oil industry is completely socialized. If you discover oil on your property the following applies: Failure to report the discovery it is a crime; failure to accept the government's offer for your house and land results in automatic loss of the house and land, without compensation."

❖ **NEW BABY**: When the queen delivered little Princess Marie-Thérèse-Charlotte, the royal couple negotiated a compromise with the royal court that the one-month-old child could be adequately cared for by only 80 persons.[128]

❖ **"HOMES"**: The king had a dozen residencies always kept in readiness. These had 1,857 horses, 217 vehicles, and 1,458 men in livery. Marie Antoinette's stables in 1780 had 75 vehicles and 330 horses.

❖ **WEEKLY ALLOWANCE**: The cost of these extravagances was at least $120 million a year in adjusted 2010 dollars. Pensions to the king's courtiers cost another $120 million a year.

❖ **FAVORITISM**: The upper class enjoyed benefits that others did not, such as the unjust taxes that exempted the rich from paying, and the horrific and unequal methods of tax collection.

❖ **SELF-DEFEATING**: Interior tariffs paralyzed free trade among districts and cities.

❖ **GREED**: Kings of the past had bought support from the upper clergy, and meddling in the market was slowing the economy. The opulence was very one sided—while the king lived the lavish life-style, his people were arrested for hoarding food, even during times of plenty. The fiscal mess brought various economists to Versailles, begging on bended knee for the king to please stay out of the people's private market, *laissez faire*—(French: "leave it alone").

LOUIS XVI LISTENED. The king knew wasn't totally detached from his country's economic crises, and looked for smart people to help him get things righted again. He summoned the ablest econo-mist in the land, Turgot, and made him controller general to clean up the mess. Turgot made a good stab at things and even induced the king to abolish the guilds (this lasted only a short time). But the privileged class won the day and undermined Turgot until he was fired in May, 1776. And then came—

❖ **NEXT MINISTER**: Jacques Necker, took over in as minister of finance in 1776. He sought to calm the troubled financial waters by

---

128   Shailer Mathews, *The French Revolution*, New York: Longmans, Green, and Co., 1914, p. 33.

Socialism kills: The body count from Cambodia's reign of terror, executions, and starvations from 1975 to 1987 (12 years) is estimated at 2,627,000.

making the taille more fair to all citizens, and arranged to borrow vast sums to help France support Americans in the War for Independence against the British.

Necker's undoing was publishing the great secret of income and expenses in France, a report on France's financial condition that he delivered to the king in 1781. It wasn't so much what the report said that caused the problems, but that he also had the information publicly printed and widely distributed. It told how much was raised from the hated taille and the salt tax, and how much the king lavished on himself, his court, and his friends. Necker was promptly fired. And then came—

♦ **NEXT MINISTER**: Charles Calonne was next in 1783. He is the man credited/accused of precipitating the great reforms that led to the French Revolution in 1789.

Calonne was a lavish spender, also known as Monsieur Déficit for that obvious reason. After settling into his new job and looking at the books he realized France was in deeply in debt, mostly from helping in the American Revolution. How was that to be handled? The country had no means to borrow more—everyone was taxed to the hilt—so just what was this powdered-wig dignitary to do?

IT'S NOT NICE TO FOOL PARLIAMENT. Calonne by-passed the parliaments and went straight to the king with a proposal to fix things. He would reduce the taille, equalize the salt and tobacco taxes, create free trade, correct the abuses of the guilds, start a universal land tax, allow the sale of church property, and last, but not least—force the nobility and privileged classes to give up their exemptions and start paying taxes like everyone else. That's where the fight started.

Calonne knew the powder puffs wouldn't go along so he schemed with the king to bring important people in church and state together as a representative body to give their stamp of approval. This group was called the Notables.

The Notables were all of the upper classes and seemed willing to help bail out the nation from looming bankruptcy. However, when they heard Calonne's plan, they didn't trust him and refused to go along. So, naturally, the king fired Calonne.

Socialism promotes free love: August Bebel (1840-1913), a German socialist politician wrote: "Woman may love whom she pleases and as long as she pleases. If she is not satisfied with one alliance, she may loose the knot and bless some other with her love. Married or unmarried, she is to enjoy perfect equality with the sterner sex." ... (cont'd)

The king tried to make the reforms himself and sent them to the parliaments to be registered as law. Those fellows refused unless the king would call an assembly of all the three Estates, the *Estates General*, to take charge and really fix things.

THE KING'S MINISTERS LIGHT THE FUSE

The king agreed, but then the evil ministers of the king threw a monkey wrench into the whole mess: they started maneuvering for a way to remove the ability of the parliaments to review all the king's decisions. This would let the king make law by simple royal edict with no check or challenge to worry about.

The parliament of Paris was the first to hear of this scheme, and they blew their lids. Word quickly spread to the provinces. Fear and doubt spread—would the king and his ministers actually make laws for the entire realm, and ignore the special privileges granted some provinces, privileges that went back centuries as conditions for their joining with France? It was unthinkable!

ESTATES GENERAL: With rumblings of alarm rolling through the kingdom, the king decided the only way out was to go ahead and call the Estates General and let them duke it out.

The last time the Estates General had been assembled was way back in 1614—that was about 175 years before. No one knew exactly how the meeting should go. The group was made up of hundreds of delegates, but each was supposed to vote together as a bloc, and each bloc got one vote—a vote by the clergy, a vote by the nobility, and a vote by the commoners. No matter what happened, the commoners could be outvoted 2 to 1 every time. To make it more unfair, there were clergy and nobility who sided with the commoners, but their votes didn't matter so long as the majority of their blocs wanted it this way or that.

ONE MAN, ONE VOTE: Realizing the "old way" was creeping up again, the commoners demanded "one man, one vote" of all the delegates.

After six weeks of haggling and being outvoted, the commoners grew impatient and just took over. They met at an indoor tennis court building, took an oath to remain until a constitution was created, and declared themselves the "National Assembly." It was

(cont'd) ...Bebel continued, saying that the human animal is no different than farm animals: "In a book published in Leipsic we find the following thought expressed: 'Sexual impulse is neither moral nor immoral; it is simply natural like hunger and thirst. Nature knows nothing of morality.' But organized society is very far from recognizing the truth of this sentence."

an amazing and long overdue power grab that made them the first modern representative assembly in continental Europe.

The king was eventually forced to concede authority to the new national body and told the others to go join the whole. But Louis XVI wasn't happy with the loss of control and power, and considered dissolving the Assembly and sending everyone home.

THE MINISTERS THROW ANOTHER WRENCH: As if things weren't tense enough, the king's ministers advised the king to beef up his personal guard. If he was going to dismiss the Assembly, chances of an uprising were pretty high, and he should be prepared with more troops.

The king agreed and summoned more troops—just in case.

When the people of Paris saw the king's private troops receiving reinforcements, they panicked. What was he up to? Without arms, how could they protect themselves once the shooting began? They knew where the arms were—the Hôtel des Invalides—and decided to take action and grab the guns. They forced their way in and gathered up 30,000 muskets—but they had no powder or shot.

STORMING THE BASTILLE: The Paris mob was now more than 8,000, and believed there was a cache of 30,000 pounds of powder holed up in the Bastille. They stormed the gates for admittance and a gun fight broke out. About a hundred were killed before the governor capitulated and opened the gates. The mob rushed the defenders, freed 7 poor souls still imprisoned there, and killed the governor and the guard. With weapons and ammunition, the demolition of the hated Bastille was next on the list.

And so began this first blow for freedom on July 14, 1789.

Word of the revolution in Paris spread through France. In other cities, similar acts took place as the peasants took control of their futures by rising up against the tyranny of the nobility and the corrupted clergy.

In hundreds of villages, people gathered at the commons or the parish churches and voted to stop paying feudal taxes. They turned on the old regime and burned their castles, thus destroying records showing any obligation of money or servitude to their feudal lords.

As news of a general revolution reached Paris, the National

Socialism in America: In 1981, the U.S. government ordered oranges destroyed to keep prices high: "From afar, it looks like a red haze on the horizon. But . . . it [later] becomes clear that what lies in the distance is actually mounds of oranges. ... (cont'd)

Assembly they moved forward with confidence and passed their first important reforms:

⬧ They abolished serfdom and feudalism.

⬧ The lords, nobility, and independent provinces had to surrender their ancient privileges. Even the exclusive right of the nobility to hunt was abolished—now anyone could hunt.

⬧ Mandatory church tithes were abolished.

⬧ Taxes were made uniform and equal to all.

⬧ It was decreed that anyone could run for any public office.

⬧ All laws in all provinces were wiped out—all of France now had one law applicable to everyone, regardless of earlier promises or privileges.

The passage of these historic reforms was another great day for France—August 5, 1789.

CHANGES CAME RAPIDLY

The Assembly moved to secure more changes. They unified the whole country, erased the old province boundary lines, and divided the country into departments of appropriate size. They named them after nearby landmarks, such as mountains and rivers to further erase remnants of the old feudal distinctions.

On August 26, 1789, the Assembly then approved an important document that assured freedom and prepared the foundation for a constitution. It was called the Declaration of the Rights of Man and of the Citizen. It established that—

⬧ **CREATED EQUAL:** "Men are born and remain equal in rights."

⬧ **LAW IS SUPREME:** "Law is the expression of the general will. Every citizen has a right to participate, personally or through his representative, in its formation. It must be the same for all."

⬧ **WRIT OF HABEAS CORPUS:** "No person shall be accused, arrested, or imprisoned except in the cases and according to the forms prescribed by law."

(cont'd) " ... Stretching in all directions are millions and millions of navel oranges . . . all abandoned to rot under the California sun. The oranges have been dumped under what is known as a Federal marketing order."—Ann Crittenden, New York Times

◆ **FREEDOM OF RELIGION:** "No one shall be disquieted on account of his opinions, including his religious views, provided that their manifestation does not disturb the public order established by law."

◆ **FREEDOM OF SPEECH:** "The free communications of ideas and opinions is one of the most precious of the rights of man. Every citizen may, accordingly, speak, write, and print with freedom as shall be defined by law."

◆ **TAXES:** "All citizens have a right to decide either personally or by their representative, as to the necessity of the public contribution, to grant this freely to know to what uses it is put, and to fix the proportion, the mode of assessment and of collection, and the duration of the taxes."

◆ **PUBLIC ACCOUNTABILITY:** "Society has the right to require of every public agent an account of his administration."

THE KING DIDN'T WANT TO SURRENDER POWER

It took two years for the Assembly to clean feudalism off the map, and create a new constitution. The king didn't like the rapid erosions of power and thought fleeing was the best way to regroup with supporters and find a way back into power. On the night of June 20, 1791, he fled Paris with his family. He didn't get very far before he was recognized and hauled back.

Three months later, the new constitution was finished and presented to the king for his approval. This pointed the way to abolish the monarchy, making France a republic with a congress called the Legislative Assembly.

CHAOS AND MISERY. Swirling around the revolutionary changes were confusion, poverty and hunger. The Legislative Assembly had their hands full trying to purge the country of lingering threats, and trying to feed the starving at the same time. By the spring of 1792, matters worsened significantly when war broke out with Prussia and Austria—talk about a lousy time for a war.

"EVERY MAN FOR HIMSELF!" The war panicked members of the Legislative Assembly. They had enemy troops at the border,

---

Socialist Vs. Socialist: In 2011, U.S. trade unions balked at Obama's pollution rules aimed at coal-fired power plants because they could lead to "higher electric bills, billions of dollars in new costs, and the closing of plants that employ thousands of workers."—Wall Street Journal, March 14, 2011

mobs in the streets, all of Paris calling for the abdication of the king, and there the politicians sat paralyzed, wondering what to do. For half of that august body, the answer was simple—flee Paris and run for the hills.

RISE OF THE NATIONAL CONVENTION. So, power changed hands again, this time to a group called the National Convention.

Lenin liked this part of France's revolutionary period. In 1917, Lenin stood atop the ruins of his own revolution and declared that the French events of August 10, 1792, had successfully revolutionized the revolution. It showed the world, he said, how the lower classes should rise up and claim what was theirs.

Meanwhile, back in 1792, the National Convention held an iron grip on the affairs of the country and used terror to achieve its ends. They deported some priests, sold off property claimed by recent immigrants, took away all dues owed to landlords, and made everyone start calling each other "Citizen."

FROM FRENZY TO FEAR. By September 2, 1792, patriotic enthusiasm had switched to fearful paranoia. In just five days, ruthless mobs raged through Paris, freeing fellow citizens from the prisons, and hunting down the aristocracy. Members of the upper class who were accused of abusing the people received brief trials and were executed. By week's end some 1,400 were killed.

FOURTH HORSEMAN OF THE APOCALYPSE. And thus came to be installed a fourth governmental power, *Terror*, that replaced *Democracy* which had already won out over the *Monarch* and the *Aristocrat*.

BACK TO BUSINESS. On September 21, 1792, the National Convention finally and formally replaced the monarchy with a republic. It was a great day because good news came in from the war front— the troops had stopped the Prussians and liberated other lands in Savoy, Frankfurt, and Belgium.

MEANWHILE, WHAT ABOUT THE KING? Louis XVI remained a formal figure head, but he had to be eliminated. That came about by way of accusations that he had cavorted with the enemy. He was arrested, put on trial for treason, found guilty, and guillotined on January 21, 1793.

The king's death didn't calm or solve France's problems.

With food shortages, crime, mobs, and fighting among those in power, the National Convention stepped in to control the economy. They set up a wide system of price controls on 50 necessities. This included foodstuffs, fuel, clothing, and wages.

The National Convention also formed the Committee of Public Safety to watch over France's internal security. One of its leaders, a man named Robespierre, rose to total control by having others in the Committee of Safety condemned and executed. "To punish the oppressors of humanity is clemency," he said in 1794. "To forgive them is barbarity." It was his philosophy that the revolutionary government adopted—his strange combination of both virtue and terror.

REIGN OF TERROR SPREADS

The Committee of Safety sent commissioners all over France to root out those suspected of contributing to the tensions of the time or challenging the committee's authority. The purge began with the aristocrats, including Marie Antoinette. The sound of carts lumbering through the streets of Paris toward Madam Guillotine became far too familiar as the famous and the unknown were taken to their deaths.

SYSTEMATIC KILLINGS

After the aristocrats were eliminated, the moderates went next, including those formerly on the National Assembly who opposed the power of the Committee of Safety. The feast for blood and power then turned on itself and executions were conducted everywhere—drownings, shootings, the guillotine—anyone suspected was put on trial with no legal representation.

GREASING THE SKIDS

In the fever of the times, Robespierre lent his support to a new law that simplified the judicial process of convicting the accused. "Every citizen is empowered to seize conspirators and counterrevolutionaries, and to bring them before the magistrates. He is required to denounce them as soon as he knows of them." It gave the Revolutionary Tribunal more power to kill.

Joseph-Ignace Guillotin (1738-1814) was an elected member of the French National Assembly in 1789. He suggested a more humane way of executing people. The decapitating device was actually built by Tobias Schmidt with advice from Dr. Antoine Louis.

TIRED OF THE BLOOD

And then great news came in July 1794, that French troops had swept through Belgium, successfully extending the revolution and securing another border. This brought a national sigh of relief from one village to another. The crisis atmosphere that had hung heavy for so long finally seemed to lift. The fatigue of all that hate and suspicion turned on Robespierre and Saint-Just, the two leaders who fomented the Reign of Terror. They were accused of conspiring to wrest complete control for themselves.

GETTING A HEAD'S UP

On July 28, 1794, Robespierre and 21 of his closest associates were gathered at the Hotel de Ville to consider their next move. It was 2 a.m. when suddenly, army troops surrounded the compound and ordered them to surrender. Fighting broke out. Several tried to escape, others tried to commit suicide.

There are mixed reports about injuries Robespierre received that night. Either he shot himself in the face in a failed suicide attempt or he was shot by one of the troops. However it happened, the bullet shattered his jaw and he was bleeding profusely when they captured him. He used a handkerchief to secure his jaw, and remained bandaged all the way to his appointment with the guillotine. When the executioners laid him at the blade facing up, a man removed the bandage. Robespierre screamed in pain—until the blade silenced him forever.

BEFORE THE EMPEROR

The revolutionary fervor abated after this, but France's financial and national security concerns did not go away. The people wanted more security in their lives and thought a stronger central government was needed. What they got was Napoleon, first emperor of France.

THE FRENCH REVOLUTION AND SOCIALISM

The ten-year revolution in France is an excellent study in socialism. A major theme for socialists is the destruction of the existing society. The French Revolution did just that—it got rid of Christianity, it got rid of the Church, it got rid of the aristocracy and the nobility, it got rid of the king, it was a major change. It brought bread to the poor and democracy to France, and established a

Without the guillotine, it took longer: Dominique Larrey, Napoleon's chief surgeon who saw a lot of military action, could amputate a leg in 13 seconds.

grand new society. But it failed to finish the work. To establish freedom and the protection of natural rights for all.

AMERICANS SUPPORT THEN REJECT

During this time, Americans applauded the overthrow of the Bourbon monarchy. However, when the ghastly Reign of Terror began, the Americans turned against them.[129]

The rampages through the countryside, the short and unfair trials, the hundreds of deaths with no legal support, gave ample proof to most Americans that the French were not ready for freedom. It was evidence the uneducated and property-less masses were motivated mostly by greed and envy to despoil the propertied class. They were not ready for self-government.

LEARNING TO RECOGNIZE SOCIALISM

The French governments that rose and fell during that decade of 1789-1799 exhibited all seven pillars of socialism in action.

❖   An all-powerful ruler was present as first the king, whom they failed to retire, and then the various all-powerful groups and committees that fought each other for power instead of serving the people.

❖   The government retained economic control. It set prices for at least 50 essential commodities and managed production and trade.

❖   It eventually allowed more freedom of information, but turned this against the people by allowing suspicion, opinion, and simple finger pointing to send a man or woman to the guillotine.

❖   It imposed behavior patterns such as the title of "Citizen" as a means for testing loyalty, or the new colors and styles that were forced on the people.

❖   The use of force to compel citizens to comply with the rulers could be no better illustrated than during the reign of terror, the beheadings, and other forms of destruction and execution. France missed its chance for real freedom and prosperity, and suffered accordingly for decades.

---

129   Alfred H. Kelly & Winfred A. Harrison, *The American Constitution—Its Origins and Development*, Fourth Edition 1970, pp. 205-206.

Socialism kills—Death count under Hitler from singling out Jews for execution: at least 6,000,000.

Eye witness: "Living in North Korea is a life filled with difficulties, every day. The authorities are always trying to crack down on people and find ways to put them into prison because that's how they get bribes."—Jiro Ishimaru, editor of Aisiapress Internationa.

Part V

SOCIALISM IN THE AMERICAS

"The sober and godly men ... evince the vanity of that conceit of Plato's ... as if they were wiser than God."

—Governor William Bradford—

CHAPTER 24:

MEANWHILE, OVER IN THE AMERICAS . . .

Socialism was not strictly a European invention.

Most of the pre-Columbian Indians of north America did not leave behind much in the way of record-keeping. This makes understanding their culture more difficult. Tradition, art, and legend is all that remain in some instances.

NORTH AMERICAN NATIVES

What little is known about the earliest inhabitants of north America, generally speaking, is that most American Indians were on the move. Some of them did put down roots, such as the Pacific Northwest people, but the majority were frequently relocating to follow the food or find a more suitable climate.

There were thousands of groups, small and independent, led by a chief who was chosen for his superior material wealth, or in some instances on account of his ancestry. For some tribes power was passed down along matriarchal lines. Many were bonded by tradition and blood to large decentralized nations.

PUBLIC AND PRIVATE PROPERTY

On the level of the individual tribe, it was common to have basic village needs held in common—housing, the cook fire, sometimes canoes and teepees, or hunting and fishing grounds. There was, however, plenty of self-aggrandizement going on. Private ownership and building up personal wealth was a sign of superior wisdom and capacity. Commercial trading of shells or copper or unique craft goods have been found far removed from their places of manufacture.

MAKING DO ...

Most of the groups practiced slavery; a few were cannibals. It also appears their hand-to-mouth "on the go" bare subsistence level of living imposed a dependence that was more cooperative than in the larger civilizations. It is in the larger groups that the rise of the seven despotic pillars of socialism are found well established, entrenched, and floating in human blood.

Socialism in America: In 2011, the Environmental Protection Agency began issuing new regulations to control greenhouse gasses from stationary sources such as power plants, refineries and factories, unconstitutionally bypassing Congressional authority.

CHAPTER 25:

INCAS:
MODEL SOCIALISTS

*Nobody did socialism better than the Incas from about 1200
to 1573—for them there were no problems a few
thousands of human sacrifices couldn't solve.*

S TORY: When Pizarro arrived in Peru in 1532, he had Spain's
royal decree to conquer the land. It was a daunting challenge.
They had to force some 12 million people scattered over
Ecuador, Bolivia, Peru and northern parts of Chile and Argentina
to capitulate to Spain's military authority. With hardly 200 men at
his command, the prospects were ridiculously remote.[130]

Fortunately for Pizarro, he had two things going for him: a
civil war between two brothers and their followers was underway,
and 200 years of socialism that had sapped the entire culture of its
ability to organize an adaptable means of defending itself.

BEAUTIFUL CITIES FROM STRICT REGULATION

The prize was worth the effort. Pizarro and his men were struck
by the fantastic achievements of the Incas. Their capital city Cuzco
was as advanced as any major city in Europe, and this without the
advantages of iron or centuries of evolving European technologies.

The Incas had marshaled their people and resources to build
magnificent fortresses, temples, palaces, paved roads, bridges and
aqueducts. Giant blocks of stone weighing 10-12 tons each were
fitted together for walls with such carved precision that even a
knife blade could not fit between them. Cuzco was the center of
everything, and was connected to the empire with excellent roads
cut as needed through solid rock or that spanned gorges with
suspension bridges. Foot messengers ran the routes to keep Inca
informed of the doings in his kingdom.

CENTRAL STOREHOUSES

The Inca storehouses were all full of food and supplies. llamas

---

130 For more information, see Louis Baudin, *A Socialist Empire: The Incas of Peru*, 1961;
and, William H. Prescott, *History of the conquest of Peru, with a preliminary view of the
civilization of the Incas*, 1883, in two volumes.

**Socialism in America: In 2011, Obama had 4,257 new regulations in the works, 219
of these would cost $100 million apiece, annually.**

did the heavy labor and also provided meat and wool. Weapons, clothing, houses, utensils, tools, everything was finely developed and orderly—an amazing achievement considering the people had only wood and stone to work with.

CASTE SYSTEM

The Inca society was organized into a three-level caste system. At the top were the Inca rulers, the direct descendants of the original tribe. This class provided leadership at all levels, but the levels were highly regimented. Each official could communicate only with his direct supervisor and those directly beneath him, thereby designating immediate accountability for all things good and bad.

The next level down were the peasants and workers. This vast majority did all the work to support the empire. They were the soldiers and defenders of the empire. When a village was conquered, these people were sent to set up the Inca way of life. They also sustained the kingdom with everything from farming, raising llamas, and producing clothing and other handcrafted items. And, they also provided their young daughters for human sacrifice. The Inca gods were hungry for such rituals, especially at the great festivals when a new Inca was installed as leader.

The lowest level were the state slaves. The largest of this slave class apparently descended from an earlier group that once tried to rebel against Inca. They were condemned to die but legend says Inca's wife pled for their preservation and the tribes were instead made slaves in perpetuity. They were servants to the Incas.

NO INDIVIDUAL RIGHTS

There was no private land ownership—Inca owned all. He distributed land as needed for farming, but the produce went to the ruling class. When a peasant married, he received a parcel large enough to sustain he and his wife. When children were born, the family received more. When the man died the land went back to Inca.

Low-level administrators supervised the peasants working the land. Work began each day with the sound of a conch, and everyone filed out to his or her assigned duties. Their labors included building the temples, repairing the palaces and roads, working the gold and silver mines, or any other state project assigned to them.

TIGHTLY ORGANIZED

The people were grouped as families into 10s, 50s, 100s, up to 10,000—each group had an assigned official watching them closely. Houses were all the same size and design—doors had to be open to anyone. They all ate at the same time, and they were forbidden to change anything from the standardized size, look, and feel, or they would be executed. If anyone wanted to leave a village for any purpose at all, permission was always required.

SHAVE AND A HAIRCUT, TWO BITS

The Incas devised an excellent policing system for runaways. They forced everyone to have certain haircuts and uniform styles of clothing. The only variation in these appearances was from province to province. This smothered the temptation to use style, clothing, and looks to appear better. Also, if someone tried to run away, those in other districts could spot them immediately because of their different hair style and cut and color of their cloak.

"BRISTLE WHILE YOU WORK ..."

The law imposed constant production from everyone. Men's lives were divided into ten periods with appropriate duties and requirements for each period. Women had similar duties, and when en route from here to there they were expected to take along some wool to spin along the way. The elderly or infirm had work assignments suited to their abilities. If slaves had no work to do, their masters would give them useless chores such as moving rocks from here to there or digging pits and filling them again. Work, work, work—no slackers allowed.

MATCH MADE IN HEAVEN—OR SOMEWHERE ...

Marriage was strictly regulated. Once each year in every village a ruler would conduct marriages for all those who had reached a certain age. If they had not paired off, they would be forced to. A man might express a preference but a woman had no say—objecting to the ruler's choices was punishable by death.

There was no sharing of wives but a man could have concubines in addition to his first wife. Depending on the man's place in the caste system dictated how many concubines he could have—10, 20, 40, or more.

When children were old enough for school, only those of the upper class were allowed to learn—education among the lower classes was punishable by death. The privileged children learned their nation's history, laws and culture, as well as hymns that conveyed similar messages that were recited around the campfires. A village scholar was assigned the duty to teach.

FOOD FOR THE GODS

Females were treated like disposable property. Every year representatives of Inca visited all the villages to choose out girls eight years old. They were taken from their families and raised in a commune. Also every year, those who turned 13 were taken to Cuzco and presented to Inca himself. He picked a third who would attend to matters of the Inca worship of the sun, moon, and stars. Another third was given away as wives or concubines to the nobility class.

The last third was reserved for human sacrifice. If parents grieved over their daughter's selection for the sacrifice they could be punished with death.

OBEY OR ELSE

Punishment for disobedience was extremely severe. Violation of the state laws was viewed as a direct affront to the state's authority. Even the most minor infractions such as picking berries or catching a fish on state-owned property resulted in death. Other capital crimes included causing an abortion or seducing someone of a higher class. The law allowed for forced labor instead of death, but terms could extend beyond life and include the lives of the criminal's descendents. But the laws did not apply equally to all. Incas often got off with just a scolding and a sour look.

FATE WORSE THAN DEATH

Executions by stoning, hanging by the hair, being thrown off a cliff, or dropped into a pit of snakes wasn't necessarily the worst of it. The Incas had underground prisons that housed meat-eating animals or deadly scorpions. An accused conspirator's guilt was tested by throwing them into just such a prison. If a person was guilty, the creatures would kill him—if innocent ... well, it was a miracle.

"It is ordained in the eternal constitution of things , that men of intemperate minds cannot be free. Their passions forge their fetters.:—Edmond Burke

IGNORANCE AND FEAR

With all things identical, all things regulated, and all things standardized, the Incas were naturally suspicious of anything out of the ordinary—an eclipse, an earthquake, twins or triplets, strange anomalies in nature—these were feared and shunned as manifestations sent as warnings from the evil gods.

CRUSHING THE HUMAN SPIRIT

The Inca system of socialism weakened the people terribly. It took away their drive to achieve and initiate anything from their own creativity. They became indifferent, apathetic, and stopped thinking for themselves. They lost the connective tissue and the emotional bond in their family circles. They apparently didn't care about elderly parents who were no longer able to care for themselves. They didn't care about the suffering by those closest to them. They didn't care about the Inca state. They had become accustomed to being told by someone what to do, when to do it, and when to do it over if things didn't measure up.

It is little wonder then why a small group of 200 Spaniards could come among them and dispatch the Inca leadership and take over with relative ease. The Spaniards used faction against faction to gain complete control, and waged battles and wars. But in the end, the final tally showed that the Inca's thousands always lost against Pizarro's hundreds.

SOCIALISM ERUPTS ON ITS OWN

The interesting message from the rise and fall of the Inca empire is that nearly every element of socialism that was promoted in Plato's "perfect" Republic or More's "ideal" Utopia were independently invented and implemented among the Incas—with devastating and miserable results. Also important is the fact the Incas didn't have access to the writings of western philosophers—they came up with the horrible ideas of socialism all by themselves.

NO PRECEDENT

This leads to the conclusion that socialism as a set of tyrannical aspirations needs no precedent to come into existence. Lacking any better code of moral existence, tyranny will rise of its own accord. The seven despotic pillars of socialism in Europe or the Americas

"Good men are unwilling to rule, either for money's sake or for honour.... So they must be forced to consent under threat of penalty.... The heaviest penalty for declining to rule is to be ruled by someone inferior to yourself. That is the fear, I believe, that makes decent people accept power...." —Plato

cannot be dismissed as mere coincidence or accidental commonality. They are the magnification of mankind's natural desires to survive at any cost, including the extermination of their fellow beings.

LEARNING TO RECOGNIZE SOCIALISM

If socialism can spontaneously spring up in a place as removed from Europe and Africa as is Peru, then it comes as no surprise that it appears in modern society where communication, access, and resources can spread its failure formula that much quicker. Popular entertainment has painted numerous and horrible prophetic fantasies of a world under socialism, with all the rot and discouragement that the Inca had, but mixed with modern advances. For example—

1984: Richard Burton's last film. Cameras are everywhere in futuristic 1984. Big Brother is always listening and watching, only crimes of the heart escape scrutiny—for a while, anyway.

Fahrenheit 451: The totalitarian government does not want books, they spark notions of freedom. So-called "Firemen" are given authority to check anyone, anywhere, any time, for hidden books, and may burn them on the spot. It works until one of the Firemen meets a pretty school teacher named Clarisse. She *likes* books....

THX 1138: It's a great socialist idea—drug everyone's emotions and sex drive so they stop bothering others and obey the robot cops without question. It works until someone dodges the drug—and then human nature awakens, demanding a mate *and freedom.* In true socialist fashion, the tense chase scene lasts as long as the budget.

V for Vendetta: Remember, remember the 5th of November. A freedom loving terrorist awakens London from its stupor of obedience to the Chancellor and his socialism using Truth against their Lies.

The Village: Conspiracy of ignorance to control the populous. All the socialistic tricks are there: deceit, control, no innovation allowed, terror to keep the populous subservient to the fathers, until desperation requires a messenger to procure medicine from *the evil capitalists.*

The Matrix: The perfect socialist society, all humans in a coma, their brains running a program that grants them a fulfilling life while their bodies float in life sustaining fluids with wires taking away electrical energy to support the vast communal intricacies of the Matrix.

Superstition: In 2012, archaeologists in Bulgaria dug up skeletons dated to A.D. 1300-1700, with iron rods driven through their chests to keep them from becoming the un-dead. The vampire myth is a good example of information control and how sensible people can be led to believe lies—such as the utopian promises made by socialists.

CHAPTER 26:
JESUIT PRIESTS SOCIALIZE PARAGUAY

In the name of Christianity, Jesuit missionaries socialized native converts with baptism, the whip, and Ruler's Law.

In 1609, Jesuit priests rode into the jungles and valleys of central South America to search for converts.

The regional Spanish governor was in favor of these evangelical labors because there was a frontier border he needed to protect. He granted the Jesuits permission to proselytize provided they would organize the people into hamlets at strategic points along the Paraná River. The Jesuits complied and went about their labors.

In a fascinating description provided by Yves Guyot in his book, *Socialistic Fallacies* (1910),[131] this is how socialism worked among the natives of Paraguay—

❖   **NO FREEDOM TO ASSOCIATE**: It took only a few hundred Jesuits to conquer villages. They would invade the selected tribe, set the huts on fire, and take men, women and children as their prisoners. They divided the people among their missions to prevent them from combining again to rebel. Some of the settlements (called a Jesuit Reduction) controlled as many as 3,500 or more at a time with just a pair or so of Jesuits as overseers.

❖   **FIRST THINGS FIRST**: A native was considered baptized when the Jesuit touched him or her with a damp cloth. A record of this baptism was sent to Rome.

❖   **RULER'S LAW BY EDICT**: After the baptisms, things relaxed a little—each tribe was ruled by a spiritual leader and a temporal leader. There was no uniform or formal law put in place—the only laws were those set by the whim and wit of the Jesuits in charge.

❖   **ALL THINGS IN COMMON**: All possessions were held in common—there was no private property. There was no inheritance to pass along or, for a while at least, no property boundaries to define or debate. The children were also communally raised by the village.

---

131   Yves Guyot, *Socialistic Fallacies,* 1910, Chapter V: Paraguay.

In China before 1997, extra-marital behavior, called "group licentiousness," was severely punished. The instigator was executed and all others imprisoned for 15 years to life. Since the 1997 Cultural Revolution, things have lightened up—offenders go to prison for only 3 years, or so.

❖ **SMALL PERMISSIONS GRANTED**: Even though the natives had to labor exactly as ordered, the Jesuits found things went smoother if they allotted a small piece of land the people could farm two days a week. They also allowed fishing and hunting, provided they returned a gift of fish or game to the missionaries.

❖ **REGIMENTED LIFE**: Before sun-up, the entire village met at the church for hymns, prayers, and roll call. After filing by to kiss the hands of the missionaries, they were fed a broth of barley meal—no fat or salt. Salt was scarce, so was meat, and very little of either was served except maybe on an occasional Sunday. Then, off to work. The men went to the fields or shops, the women worked over the fires, roasting a day's worth of corn—later they went to work spinning at least an ounce of cotton. At lunch, the same broth was served but this time thickened up with peas and beans, some flour and maize. After lunch, they again kissed the missionaries' hands and headed back to work.

❖ **BREAKDOWN**: When a native became a convert and "confessed," he or she was forced to become an informer on others. Lashes with leather whips punished men in public and women in private for neglecting their duties or from committing other crimes. The problem of "all things in common" allegedly infected some missionaries who took advantage of the native women and girls. The Jesuits were confessor, legislator and judge, and supervised everything—the natives complained of many abuses.

❖ **RIGID RESTRICTIONS**: The natives could never ride the horses, and had no money or commerce outside the set boundaries.

❖ **LIFELESS AUTOMATONS**: Before the Jesuits were expelled in 1768, observers reported the populations had become spiritually dead. Some 70 workers could hardly perform what eight or ten mediocre Europeans could perform in the allotted same time. The natives loathed their wretched lives. Even a nightly bell rung by the Jesuits to signal the start of sexual relations to repopulate their numbers failed to produce an increase. Disinterest in their spouses was the last and most horrible testimony of the smothering impact of socialistic life. After 160 years of ruinous regimentation, the Jesuits left behind an entire people in misery, stagnation, and broken spirits.

American Bureaucracy: In 2010, the Federal government employed on average 2,580,000 people and paid them $16,000,000,000 every month—that adds up to about $194 billion a year.

CHAPTER 27:

JAMESTOWN: SOCIALIZING THE NEW WORLD

It was 1607 when the ancient ideas of 'all things in common' began to wreak havoc in North America.

S TORY: The first English settlement in America is significant for several reasons.

The climate of Virginia was harsh compared to the relative ease of warmer climes farther south. A study by Ellsworth Huntington of Yale University indicated that cooler climates make people more active, alert and efficient. His study suggested that the New England region, the birth place of the U.S. Constitution, might have been best suited for innovative thinking because of its cooler temperatures.

The best temperatures for physical activity, Huntington concluded, was 60-65-degrees F for a 24-hour period. The best for mental efficiency was an average 38-degrees F. The hotter equatorial regions may have been easier to settle, but they didn't spawn the level of industry that took place in the cooler north.

FIRST SETTLEMENTS FAILED

After Sir Walter Raleigh's attempts to establish a colony in Roanoke had failed, a group of investors obtained a charter to try again somewhere along the Virginia coastline. In 1607 a group of 104 entrepreneurs and explorers tied off at an island about 40 miles inland from Virginia's Atlantic coast. They had discovered a natural deepwater port that was easily defendable.

IMPOSING RULER'S LAW

Once ashore, their first chore was to divide the colonists roughly into thirds—a group to build a fort, another to start a farm, and the remainder to look for gold. A central storehouse was established to receive all supplies from which each could take as needed. Each man was required to put back all that he could. Marx would later codify the regimen as "From each according to his

American Bureaucracy: In 2010, the State and local governments employed a country-wide total of more 19,000,000 people who were paid and average $70,000,000,000 every month---that adds up to about $840 billion in a year.

ability, to each according to his needs."[132]

Did it work? Not at all. The lack of incentive to work for each other, even to avoid starvation, left them severely hurting for food. By Christmas the death toll was high—66 had already died from starvation and disease. The remaining 38 suffered through the winter while they waited on England to deliver food, supplies, and a fresh crop of settlers.

SOCIALISM FLOPS AGAIN

Why did this initial group of settlers fail to provide for themselves? A host of modern voices point to everything for the colony's miserable failings except to the antagonistic assault on human nature that was used to coerce labor. Threats, deprivations, punishments, and even execution couldn't stir the men to work. They hated working for others, as if they were slaves or servants.

The following year a few hundred more settlers arrived. They faced the same problems. The expected free handouts from the central storehouse couldn't supply the needs. Only 40 of the men did any appreciable work while the others shirked their duties. That winter, death by starvation nearly wiped out all of them.

THE STARVING TIME

In 1609, another 500 settlers arrived. Unfortunately, this didn't solve anything because the principles of socialism continued to be in operation: no private ownership, top-down control, total and complete regulation.

That winter, their journals record a horrid time of suffering they named the "starving time." The unfortunate entrepreneurs initially exhausted their stores of food and had to turn to eating their work animals. When those were gone, they ate any small rodents they could find. When that failed to satisfy, they finally resorted to boiling shoe leather. With the leather gone they ate the bodies of the dead. By the spring of 1610, only 61 were alive.

PROPERTY RIGHTS TO THE RESCUE

This communal misery of "all in common" was finally abandoned after the arrival of Sir Thomas Dale. He brought whips and cruelty to the village, and a code he called "Articles, Lawes,

---

132   Karl Marx, *Critique of the Gotha Program, Part 1*, 1875, published after Marx's death.

Socialism in Venezuela: "When food shortages became critical in Venezuela last year [2007], Helen Mercado and Luis Boada visited store after store searching for milk ... (cont'd)

and Orders—Divine, Politique, and Martial."[133] It was tyranny of the worst kind. He imposed capital punishment for trivial crimes. For example, one of his punishments for a man caught stealing food was to tie him to a tree to starve to death as a message to others about Dale's new strict and strait ways.

However, Thomas Dale brought salvation to the colony in a most unexpected way: It was the miracle of private ownership. After two years of imposing force to make the settlers rebuild and become industrious about their plight, Dale saw that the men had no investment in the colony. So, he abandoned the communal farming plan in 1613, and handed out parcels of land—private ownership. For those longest settled, he granted three acres of land. Smaller plots were given to the newer arrivals. In return, he asked for 2-1/2 barrels of corn for the central storehouse.[134]

The settlers were delighted. They dropped their half-hearted communal labors and raced to improve their own property. With their own little farm to work, plow, and plant, the settlers came alive, putting in a new level of anxious enthusiasm they had lacked under the old system. That fall, private land ownership unleashed an industry that resulted in enough food production for the colony to survive all through the winter, and the storehouse was stocked with plenty.

FIRST-HAND ACCOUNT

In 1614, Jamestown's colony secretary, Ralph Harmor, affirmed that socialism resulted in laziness and a plague of disinterest:

"When our people were fed out of the common store, and labored jointly together, glad was he [who] could slip from his labor, or slumber over his tasks he cared not how, nay, the most honest among them would hardly take so much true pains in a week, as now for themselves they will do in a day, neither cared they for the increase, presuming that however the harvest prospered, the general store must maintain them, so that we reaped not so much corn from the labors of thirty as now three or four do provide for themselves."[135]

---

133   See Peter Force, *Historical Tracts*, vol. iii, no. 11; Walter F. Prince, *Annual Report of the American Historical Association*, vol. i, 1899, Washington, D.C., 1900; Lawrence M. Friedman, *A History of American Law*, third edition, Touchstone, 2005.

134   See Alexander Brown, *The First Republic in America*, Houghton, Mifflin and Co., 1898.

135   See John Smith, *Generall Historie of Virginia*, for the summary of Ralph Harmor's *True*

(cont'd) ... for their three-year-old son. But many times the young couple had to settle for liquid yogurt, which is more widely available because it is unregulated."
—National Geographic, July 2008

PROPERTY OWNERSHIP

According to this same eyewitness, giving the people an investment in the land saved the colony. Ralph Harmor continued:

"To prevent which, Sir Thomas Dale hath allotted every man three acres of clear ground, in the nature of farms ... for which doing, no other duty they pay yearly to the store, but two barrels and a half of corn. ...for the industrious, there is reward sufficient."[136]

FREEDOM TO TRY, BUY, SELL, AND FAIL

A short time later, John Rolf discovered that tobacco grew well in Virginia, and an interest in smoking it back home in Europe encouraged the colony's first cash crop. That's when Jamestown began to take form and strength. The lessons learned from the 1607 disaster were not forgotten in the U.S. Constitution—180 years later the Founders made socialism illegal and unconstitutional. No one wanted another starving time.

Discourse of the Present Estate of Virginia ... till the 18 of June 1614, Library of Congress.
136   Ibid.

"In a democracy it's your vote that counts. In feudalism it's your count that votes."

CHAPTER 28:

PLYMOUTH: NO THANKSGIVING FOR SOCIALISM

*Like Jamestown, the Plymouth settlers were obligated to follow a
certain business model that was, in fact, the same
old tired fraud of socialism. The experiment
ran from 1620 to 1624.*

STORY: William Bradford served as governor of the Plymouth colony and provided rich details about their failed experiment with socialism.

After two months at sea, the 102 Pilgrim settlers stepped ashore to their new but cold and desolate wilderness home. They carried with them their freshly penned Mayflower Compact—a charter of laws that declared authority over believers and non-believers alike.

The voyage had been stressful and exacted a terrible price from the Pilgrims. Upon arrival some of them were too ill to do anything more than just linger onboard, attempting to recover. Those able to do the work went ashore for extended periods to construct housing. Their large "common house" of wattle and daub was finished first. Before winter ended, they had completed three more common houses plus seven residences.

DEATH THE FIRST YEAR

The colony suffered terribly that first winter—45 people died of disease and exposure. By fall of the following year more had died leaving just 53 alive in the colony.

ALL THINGS IN COMMON

Prosperity eluded them for reasons similar to those in Jamestown. The colony's merchant-sponsors in London had ordered a very regimented system for living. Everything the colonists produced went into the central storehouse. All the land they cleared and houses they built were held in common—there would be no private ownership.

Guiding this arrangement was a seven-year contract. Point 3 said (all quotes from Gov. Bradford's writings), "...All profits and benefits that are got by trade, traffic, trucking, working, fishing, or any other means of any person or persons, remain still in the common stock until the division."[137] And stated again in point 10, "That all such persons as are of this colony, are to have their meat, drink, apparel, and all provisions out of the common stock and goods of the said colony."[138]

Land, homes and gardens were in common as well: "...That the houses, and lands improved, especially gardens and home lots should remain undivided wholly to the planters at the seven years end."

SOCIALISM FLOPS AGAIN

As with Jamestown, the rules and needs were abundantly clear, but getting the people to cooperate for their mutual survival just didn't work. Those able to work complained about working for others. They complained about receiving the same compensation as those who didn't work. As Bradford told it,

"For the young men that were most able and fit for labor and service did repine that they should spend their time and strength to work for other men's wives and children, without any recompense."

INDUSTRIOUS BECOME ANGRY WITH THE LAZY

Those who were more industrious and fit for the rigors of hard physical labor were angry they had to do all the work while others did less or none at all. Bradford reported:

"The strong, or man of parts, had no more in division of victuals and clothes, than he that was weak and not able to do a quarter the other could; this was thought injustice. The aged and graver men to be ranked and equalized in labors, and victuals, clothes, etc., with the meaner and younger sort, thought it some indignity and disrespect unto them."[139]

The industrious women objected to being treated like maids or slaves for others, and their husbands objected as well. Bradford writes:

"And for men's wives to be commanded to do service for other

---

137   William Bradford, *Of Plymouth Plantation*, Bradford's History of Plymouth Plantation, 1606-1646, Ed. William T. Davis, 1908, p. 75.
138   Ibid., p. 82.
139   Ibid., p. 83.

Smuggled journalists' videos out of North Korea: "In one dramatic clip, a woman who is trying to board a truck to take her to work flies into a rage after a uniformed policeman demands a bribe. She shouts at him and waves her finger in his face until he backs away. ... (cont'd)

men, as dressing their meat, washing their clothes, etc., they deemed it a kind of slavery, neither could many husbands well brooke it."[140]

The 1855 History of Massachusetts by John S. Barry, helps emphasize how socialism self-destructs because it runs so contrary to human nature. He observed the damage of false security in the free handout, and how this let the lazy avoid work or stop it altogether at Plymouth:

"The indolent, sure of a living, would labor only when compelled to; the willing were discouraged by the severity of their toils."[141]

STARVATION FORCES DESPERATION

In Bradford's narration, he continued explaining how the whole system was corrupt and the crops yielded little because people kept sneaking around taking what they wished. Bradford wrote:

"Also much was stolen both by night and day, before it became scarce eatable, and much more afterward. And though many were well whipped (when they were taken) for a few ears of corn, yet hunger made others (whom conscience did not restrain) to venture."[142]

Bradford pointed out specifically the decay and corruption that spread among otherwise good and religious God fearing people:

"For this community (so far as it was) was found to breed much confusion and discontent, and retard much employment that would have been to their benefit and comfort. ..."[143]

A THANKSGIVING AT DEATH'S DOOR

As for the famous first Thanksgivings of 1621 and 1622, the grand feasts that are bragged about in legend and lore were hardly representative of a surplus of overflowing bounty.

The people feasted alright, but that didn't mean they had much to live on afterwards. They didn't know how to raise Indian corn, and they didn't pay much attention to it anyway. Bradford wrote,

"Now the welcome time of harvest approached, in which all had their hungry bellies filled. But it arose but to a little, in compari-

---

140   Ibid., p. 217.
141   John Stetson Barry, *The History of Massachusetts, The Colonial Period*, 1855, p. 121.
142   Ibid., Davis, p. 204.
143   Ibid., Davis, p. 147.

(cont'd) ... Emboldened, other people come to her aid, shouting at the officer. The clip ends with the unidentified woman yelling: 'This cop is an idiot!'"—Excerpt from article in *The Telegraph*, November 28, 2010

son of a full year's supply; partly by reason they were not yet well acquainted with the manner of Indian corn, (and they had no other), also their many other employments, but chiefly their weakness for want of food, to tend it as they should have done."[144]

A comment in Mourt's Relation, a first-person account of the Thanksgiving event, repeats the same: "...Although it be not always so plentiful, as it was at this time with us, yet by the goodness of God, we are so far from want ..."[145]

SOCIALISM ABANDONED

After two deadly years of starvation and suffering, the nightmare of collectivism was ejected in 1623. The more industrious among the settlers approached Gov. Bradford and asked that some land be given to them. Bradford wrote, "That they might therefore increase their tillage to better advantage, they made suit to the Govr to have some portion of land given them for continuance, and not by yearly lot. ..."[146]

Bradford recognized that private ownership was the answer to their problems. He said,

"And to every person was given only one acre of land, to them and theirs, as near the town as might be, and they had no more until the seven years were expired. The reason was, that they might be kept close together both for more safety and defense, and the better improvement of the general employments."[147]

Those with an excuse not to work suddenly wanted to work. For example, Bradford said, "The women now went willingly into the field, and took their little ones with them to set corn, which before would allege weakness, and inability; whom to have compelled would have been thought great tyranny and oppression."[148]

PLATO IS LAUGHED OUT OF PLYMOUTH

Bradford analyzed the change that came after private property ownership was implemented. He blamed Plato's socialistic ideas for the earlier failures:

---

144   Ibid., Davis, p. 204.
145   Henry Martyn Dexter, *Mourt's Relation Or Journal of the Plantation at Plymouth*, John Kimball Wiggin, 1865, p. 133.
146   Samuel Eliot Morison, *Of Plymouth Plantation, 1620-1647*, p. 145.
147   Ibid.
148   Ibid., p. 20.

Socialism in Nazi Germany: Human brains from the "killing centers" were delivered to Nazi doctors in batches of 150 or 250. Dr. Hallervorden was delighted. Said he, "There was ... " (cont'd)

"The experience that was had in this common course and condition, tried sundry years, and that amongst godly and sober men, may well evince the vanity of that conceit of Plato's and other ancients, applauded by some of later times; that the taking away of property, and bringing in community into a common-wealth, would make them happy and flourishing; as if they were wiser then God."[149]

PRIVATE OWNERSHIP WINS AGAIN

With private property finally rescuing the colonists from the multiple failures of all things in common, Gov. Bradford happily concludes, "This had very good success for it made all hands industrious, so as much more corn was planted than otherwise would have been."[150]

CONDEMNATION OF COMMUNISM

Of this amazing failure and salvation at Plymouth, modern economist E. A. J. Johnson observed (1961), "One would have to search long for such a damning criticism of communism, or such a penetrating analysis of the causes for its failure as a practical expedient. It restricts production by increasing the real costs involved; it breeds confusion and discontent; it creates a feeling of injustice in the minds of the young and old, the strong and weak, the married or unmarried."[151]

SUCCESS BREEDS SUCCESS

Because of the success of Bradford's changes and the industry of the early Pilgrims, the Plymouth colony became prosperous. It attracted additional settlers who made the risky overseas journey, and it ignited the Great Puritan Migration. This great movement was not just of individual men, but of whole families—educated and capable—who ventured to New England to be free. During the following two decades some 20,000 migrated to the colony and nearby towns.

SEVEN PILLARS OF SOCIALISM IN THE AMERICAS

There is no better example of all seven pillars than among these early inhabitants of the American continents, beginning with the

---

149 Ibid., Morison, p. 120.
150 Ibid.
151 E. A. J. Johnson, *American Economic Thought in the Seventeenth Century*, 1961, p. 234.

(cont'd) "...wonderful material among those brains, beautiful mental defectives ... I accepted those brains, of course. Where they came from ... was really none of my business."

Inca—the despotic ruler, his obedient nobility, the fraud of human sacrifice to appease the gods, the complete destruction of all human rights, keeping all things in common so long as it belonged to Inca, and the miserable use of force.

THE INCA AFFECT

It is interesting to note that more than a century after the Inca empire fell, Jesuit Priests in Paraguay attempted to salvage the local culture from extinction under the spread of European settlements.

The priests tried to force large groups of people into socialistic society at remotely scattered missions. From the start, the missionaries were frustrated with the native's doleful lack of initiative—a problem they tried to resolve with the whip. Unknown to the priests, the native workers had a long-nurtured proclivity to simply take orders, to do as they were told, or to do nothing if they were not told. This was not a change in biological human nature, it was the outcome of the all-powerful Inca ruler meeting all their needs without demanding personal responsibility.

The Jesuits attributed the Paraguayan's despondency to the lingering impact of the Inca's socialistic control. They called it the "Inca affect."

DIFFERENT FORMS OF HUMAN SACRIFICE

Meanwhile, the first colonists in New England didn't fare much better than the Inca or the Indians of Paraguay. The English were spared the formal rites of human sacrifices, but they were sacrificed just as well. Their deaths from starvation and harsh conditions came in exchange for a business venture. Instead of having their beating hearts cut out and their heads lopped off while strapped atop some pagan temple, the colonists had to endure death by starvation and related diseases brought about by the violation of the natural rights to own property. In all cases, the ultimate answer came in the form of private, unhampered control over *property*.

Killing their own: In North Korea, 30 officials involved in re-unification talks with South Korea were executed by firing squads or in staged traffic accidents, according to the 2012 report by Amnesty International. Another 37 were executed for "financial crimes."

* * * * *   -

KNOWLEDGE NECESSARY FOR FREEDOM

"Liberty cannot be preserved without a general knowledge among the people, who have a right, from the frame of their nature, to knowledge, as their great Creator, who does nothing in vain, has given them understandings, and a desire to know; but besides this, they have a right, an indisputable, unalienable, indefeasible, divine right to that most dreaded and envied kind of knowledge, I mean, of the characters and conduct of their rulers. Rulers are no more than attorneys, agents, and trustees, of the people; and if the cause, the interest, and trust, is insidiously betrayed, or wantonly trifled away, the people have a right to revoke the authority that they themselves have deputed, and to constitute other and better agents, attorneys and trustees."[152]—John Adams

---

152   John Adams, *A Dissertation on the Canon and Feudal Law*, 1765.

"God is dead. Marx is dead. And I don't feel too well myself."—Eugene Ionesco

Part VI

SOCIALISM IN RELIGION

"All major world religions have experienced periods when members, or its leaders, practiced Ruler's Law in one form or another."

—Author—

CHAPTER 29:

SOCIALISM IN RELIGION

For all the good that people try to do for God and individuals, some religions take it a step too far—they resort to tyranny on their own members—or nonmembers alike—to force obedience.

The eternal clash between religion and socialism is choice versus force: Is a person free to join and leave a religious order rather than obey its strict and strait rules? May a person voluntarily refuse a dominant religion's teachings?

PERSONAL AND VOLUNTARY

Religion is an intimately personal form of private conduct. An individual voluntarily follows the tenets and commandments of a belief system because of his or her conscience and free choice.

A religion that compels or restrains people against their will, whether they be adherents or not, is the embodiment of Ruler's Law. The Bible provides an example in the form of Shadrach, Meshach, and Abed-nego who refused to bow down to a golden image that Nebuchadnezzar ordered them to worship. As punishment, they were cast into a fiery furnace, but were delivered by the power of God.[153]

A common flaw in cultures that are strictly dominated by a religion is that they honor institutional rights above individual rights. They sustain the overall culture at the expense of the individual. This is unacceptable to western cultures and creates automatic conflict whenever the two cross paths over the role of religion.

IMPERFECT PEOPLE DOING AN IMPERFECT JOB

All major world religions have experienced periods when members or its leaders practiced Ruler's Law in one form or another. The actions of those imperfect and short-sighted humans should not automatically become an excuse for outsiders to re-define that religion's core belief as evil or degrading.

But when a religion's leaders or membership stand by doing nothing to rectify the excesses and anomalies of force and terror committed in their name, or even engage in propagating the abuse

---

153   Daniel, chapter 3 KJV.

The head of Iran's Chastity Headquarters in Isfahan announced in 2006 that taxis were not allowed to pick up women inappropriately dressed—that includes unauthorized makeup, clothes that show any part of the hair or legs, or bright colors.

themselves, that leaves the rest of the world wondering if that religion is really everything that it says it is.

It's a murky and difficult subject to tackle. Here is one approach—

RELIGION: Catholic Church and Christianity
ADHERENTS: 2.1 billion worldwide[154]
STORY: The life of Jesus Christ is recorded as one of service, compassion, love, healing, and the ultimate sacrifice of his own life to benefit others. The message of obedience to God, loving others as yourself, and the promise of forgiveness and resurrection are key foundation stones that helped his apostles spread "the good news." Today, that message has been embraced by at least a third of the world.

CHRISTIAN SOCIALISM

As a political distinction, Christian socialism can be traced to a meeting of Christian Socialists in London in the mid-1800s. They rejected individual rights and the selfish aggression brought on by market-place competition. They thought Christian-type cooperation was the best replacement for competitiveness, and gave it a test drive by financing co-partnerships and profit sharing in industry. Henri de Saint-Simon was an early advocate, Frederick Denison Maurice, Charles Kingsley and others followed suit.

Today, Christian Socialists have melted into the background of so much ranting, arm waving, noise and messages. These are not much different than any other beleaguered attempt at securing governmental power for their own best interests.

After the death of the apostles, Ruler's Law in Christianity was found erupting in a variety of ways. Some examples:

❖ **BELIEVE OR ELSE:** Killing people for their negative opinions about Christianity (the heretics) began as early as A.D. 385 when the Church had Priscillian, the bishop of Ávila in Spain, executed by Roman officials. The actual civil charge was practicing magic.[155]

❖ **HERETICS:** The Cathars, starting about A.D. 1150, is an example of heretics targeted for slaughter by a formal Church-sanctioned Crusade. After killing and driving the Cathars away, the

---

154   See Adherents, *Religions*, www.adherents.com.
155   The Catholic Encyclopedia, *Priscillianism*.

pope permitted the army to confiscate the Cathars' lands.[156]

◆ **CHURCH ARMIES:** The Crusades (1095-1798 A.D.) were nine major military campaigns (and dozens of lesser campaigns), launched by the pope to regain control over the Holy Land, and to fight Muslims, heretics, and pagans. The pope gave his blessing to the troops and an indulgence to those killed in battle. The invaders were hardly Christian. Crusaders were guilty of massacring civilian men, women and children—and instances of cannibalism.

◆ **EXECUTED FOR THINKING:** Jan Hus (1374-1415) was a Czech priest who berated the Church for its lofty arrogance. He was excommunicated. During this same time, a fight over who was the real pope had been raging since 1378. The *Council of Constance* was convened to resolve the matter in 1414. Hus was invited to attend the Council and express his concerns and apparent reasons for apostasy. It was actually a dirty trick—after Hus's arrival the soldiers grabbed him, threw him in prison for heresy, held a fast trial, and burned him at the stake.[157]

◆ **TORTURE:** The inquisitions were extreme efforts to suppress heresy in the Church using torture and death. They didn't start out ugly like that, but abusers twisted it so. They began around A.D. 1184, and continued in various forms, including death, in different countries until about 1860.

◆ **FORCED TITHES:** Many of the clergy in medieval countries, especially France, benefitted from royal decrees that let them force extraction of tithes from the peasantry. They also avoided paying taxes on Church-owned land.

THE GREAT REFORMATION: This was a rebellion by Christians who didn't believe the leadership of the Catholic Church had the right to rule and reign in civic affairs, or had the right to oppress others. The Reformers called for a return to the original teachings of Jesus and to put the Bible at the head of the Church. The Reformers were not guiltless in their rebellions—they drove out, killed, and burned devout Catholics.

---

156 See Tony Perrottet, *The Besieged and the Beautiful in Languedoc*, May 9, 2010.
157 The last name of Jan Hus mans "goose" in Czech. Those who mocked his entrapment and death told other heretics they had "cooked his goose," a phrase that has come to mean you've been caught or ruined.

No natural law: "Where do correct ideas come from? Do they drop from the skies? No. Are they innate in the mind? No. They come from social practice, and from it alone; they come from three kinds of social practice, the struggle for production, the class struggle and scientific experiment."—Mao Zedong

Over the centuries, Catholic clergy functioning closer to the people on the local level remained diligent and, for the most part, practiced true Christianity. They served their flocks with devotion and compassion, often in conditions of extreme poverty and stress.

The primary problem of socialism in the Catholic Church during its first 1,500 years was the upper clergy's penchant for entangling alliances with the powers of the monarchies to force religious obedience. In places where this grew into an all-powerful culture from which no one could escape, Catholic or not, that was Ruler's Law replacing the Gospel of peace. The fruit of that shift away from free religious practice was misery, heavy burdens, taxation, punishment, war, and death.

In recent centuries, many dozens of Christian churches have been formed with the declared intent to return Christianity to be more in line with the New Testament. These assorted churches encompass approximately one billion followers outside of the Catholic church.[158]

CATHOLIC CHURCH TODAY: Despite some bad apples and abject foolishness among some that do great harm against the true teachings of Jesus Christ, for the vast numbers aligned with Christianity, a refining and refreshing spirit of love, service, and selfless labor dominates the Catholic Church and Christians everywhere.

RELIGION: Buddhism
ADHERENTS: 376 million[159]
STORY: Buddhism is both a religion and a philosophy that dates back to about 450 B.C. Its founder, the young prince Buddha, desired to learn more about life and left the sheltered care of his father's palace to learn the normal earthly pain and suffering of others. Along the way he learned important lessons about his own mortal desires, stresses, and failings, and a pathway to control them, a pathway toward enlightenment.

HUNTING FOR PERFECTION: Seeking to conquer his mortality, Buddha experimented with forms of meditation. The end result was an earthly perfection of his body and soul through complete

---

158 See Adherents, *Religions*, www.adherents.com/Religions_By_Adherents.html.
159 Ibid.

"Men are built, not born.... Give me the baby, and I'll make it climb and use its hands in constructing buildings of stone or wood.... I'll make it a thief, a gunman or a dope'fiend. The possibilities of shaping in any direction are almost endless..."—John B. Watson, psychologist

personal control. Buddha formed a monastic society and taught his discoveries to others.

MODERN LEADER: Buddhadasa (1906-1993) was a modern-day philosopher of Buddhism in his native Thailand. He taught that socialism is a natural state of being. "Look at the birds; we will see that they eat only as much food as their stomachs can hold. ... Therefore a system in which people cannot encroach on each other's rights or plunder their possessions is in accordance with nature and occurs naturally ... The freedom to hoard was tightly controlled by nature in the form of natural socialism."[160]

NOT FORCED: Buddhism is voluntary, although some fringe groups have used force to regain members who convert to other religions, but these are rare. Buddhism's modern view is to seek world harmony through natural socialism—to live within one's own sphere, share what nature provides, and don't be an exploitative capitalist.

SURPLUS IS WASTEFUL: While Buddhadasa called for mankind to become like the birds and eat only until they're full, he implied at the same time that any surplus must therefore be evil. His problem that remains unanswered is that the *surplus* he objects to as wasteful is not an extravagance. It is the only means whereby people may serve one another. After they eat, are there no crumbs for the hungry? Surplus is how people are able to care for themselves and also help others less fortunate at the same time.[161]

RELIGION: Islam
ADHERENTS: 1.5 billion[162]
STORY: Islam is the only major world religion that mixes civic and religious law as one. Islam's doctrine, tenets, and commandments mandate death and violence against apostates and non-believers. However, that orthodoxy is generally practiced by only a minority of its followers.

The religious movement had its beginnings with Muhammad (570-632 A.D.). He was a merchant who started receiving revela-

---

160   Buddhadasa Bhikkhu, *No Religion*, www.abuddhistlibrary.com.
161   Buddhadasa Bhikkhu, *Dhammic Socialism—Political Thought of Buddhadasa Bhikkhu*, see www.stc.arts.chula.ac.th/.
162   See Adherents, *Religions*, www.adherents.com/Religions_By_Adherents.html.

"Many people consider the things government does for *them* to be social progress but they regard the things government does for *others* as socialism."—Earl Warren

tions from the Angel Gabriel at age 40. These messages were written down as the Qur'an, and embodied the restoration of all God's teachings from Adam through Moses, Jesus, and others.

Muhammad's religion was intended to put followers on a path away from worldly ways and toward obedience to God's commandments. Today it does this by force in countries where it has been allowed to rule society—imposing a way of life that must be obeyed or the rebellious must face punishments that have included dismemberment or death.

QUR'AN

The Qur'an is the cornerstone of all Islamic belief. The book is viewed as sacred scripture. It is organized in sections that are not chronological, but roughly according to size, approximately from longest chapter to shortest chapter.

The verses written by Muhammad while in Mecca are mostly peaceful and encourage cooperation with people of other beliefs.

After Muhammad became a rich and powerful warlord in Medina, and established his theocratic government, the new verses added to the Qur'an take on a much more forceful and violent spirit. These verses express a very intolerant view toward other religions. For example, Surah 2:256, written in A.D. 614 (the more peaceful years in Mecca), says, "There is no compulsion in religion ...." meaning no one should be forced into a religious belief system—they should be free to choose participation or not.

Surah 9:5, written in A.D. 627 (written in Medina), says just the opposite—threaten them with death if they don't join, and actually kill them if they refuse: "Kill the unbelievers wherever you find them. ... But if they repent and accept Islam ... then leave their way free."

LAW OF THE LAND: Religion and state are not separated in Islam. It is a complete way of living. In Muslim nations, Islam governs all moral, spiritual, social, political, economical, and intellectual aspects of life. This made breaking away, or expressing opinions critical of Islam, not only blasphemous but against civic law—and very punishable.[163]

There is an extensive record of Islamic warfare all through the middle ages.[164] The aim was not necessarily to win more converts

---

163 Oussani, G. (1911). *Mohammed and Mohammedanism*. In The Catholic Encyclopedia.
164 Rudolph Peters, *Jihad in Medieval and Modern Islam*, 1977, p. 3.

Socialists must destroy religion: "Religion is an illusion and it derives its strength from the fact that it falls in with our instinctual desires."—Sigmund Freud, 1932

to Islam but to protect the Islamic empire. There is debate over interpretation of the Qur'an's role regarding jihads during this period—whether or not the wars and battles were for an offensive or defensive purpose. In either case, bloody conflict has continued up until the present time.

THE INDIVIDUAL MUSLIM: The nuclear family and vast populations of the Islamic community looking to make God the center of their lives stand apart from today's Islamic political activism.

When the extremists (or more correctly, the orthodox Muslims) dominate the world's top news stories day after day, Muslim families truly ignoring the Ruler's Law aspects of Islam can only hope others will understand that the monster parading in front of the media is brutal fanaticism—evil expressions of compulsion and slavish indulgence—and nothing like their peaceful version of Islam.

ON DISPLAY: The public appearance of Islamic tenets extracted to an extreme have been forming and molding western opinions about Islam for several decades. It's a public relations nightmare for many Muslims, especially those enjoying freedom of religion in the West.

UNALIENABLE RIGHTS DENIED: In terms of natural and unalienable rights, the western view is that Islamic traditions of managing all human rights has cost untold millions of people the joy and prosperity that true religious freedom brings. It is Ruler's Law of tyranny and force rather than choice and conscience.

DYING IN THE NAME OF ALLAH

Suicide bombers are not really suicidal because that is contrary to the Qur'an. But dying while killing nonbelievers is a good thing.

According to Surah 9:111, "Verily, Allah has purchased of the believers their lives and their properties for (the price) that theirs shall be the Paradise. They fight in Allah's Cause, so they kill (others) and are killed. It is a promise in truth which is binding on Him in the Taurat (Torah) and the Injeel (Gospel) and the Qur'an. And who is truer to his covenant than Allah? Then rejoice in the bargain which you have concluded. That is the supreme success."

It is possible to have periods of truce and coexistence with Islam, but some authorities view these are more likely waiting games by orthodox Muslims as they build their numbers to become strong. "Allah's Apostle said, 'I have been ordered to fight with people till they say, *None has the right to be worshipped but Allah.*'"[165]

NO CENTRAL AUTHORITY: There is no top-level governing body in Islam to guide, restrain, instruct, and advise all the people. Competing factions for leadership, such as Sunni and Shi'a Muslims, have long clashed over opinion—most often with violence—to argue points of doctrine or settle prejudices.

For lack of the cultural virtue necessary to enjoy true freedom, various pockets of extremists froth their way to the world's attention with stonings and beheadings.

RULER'S LAW AND THE SEVEN PILLARS OF SOCIALISM

The pillars of socialism most prevalent in Muslim-majority nations include the iron-clad use of force to impose religious obedience; an all-powerful ruling class that will punish the violation of laws; the destruction of personal freedoms of choice; strict control over all associations (especially between men and women); and the violation of property ownership rights for women. This slavery mentality is forced on millions who are trapped into obedience. In some Muslim countries these extremes are being challenged, and support for more individual rights is growing.

RELIGION: Judaism
ADHERENTS: 14 million[166]
STORY: The Jews descend from Abraham through Jacob. Their great forefather, Judah (1700 B.C.), was one of Jacob's 12 sons. With the political breakup of the twelve tribes around 930 B.C., only the tribes of Judah and Benjamin, with some remnants of Levi and Simeon, remained in the regions around today's Jerusalem—they formed the southern kingdom of Judah. Later, they were joined by members of Ephraim and Manasseh.

SCATTERED: For 3,000 years, the Jews have been driven and scattered to all corners of the earth. At the same time, they developed a remarkable reputation for outstanding scholarship, science, business, and artistic talents that are exceptional from such a rela-

---

165   Sahib Al-Bukhazi, vol. 1, Bk 8, number 387.
166   See Adherents, *Religions*, http://www.adherents.com/Religions_By_Adherents.html.

"If anything is certain, it is that I myself am not a Marxist."—Karl Marx

tively small group.

The modern development of the state of Israel initially embraced socialism. In the early 1900s many Jews were driven from Russia, most going to America but some settling in Palestine. Being too poor to buy land or start farms individually, they pooled their labors and funds to create a collective.

The kibbutz (meaning "community") began as "... a voluntary collective community, mainly agricultural, in which there is no private wealth and was responsible for all the needs of its members and their families." [167]

❖ **DECLINING:** The number of kibbutz in operation has been declining but has stayed around 270 nationwide, with about 117,000 people participating.

❖ The earliest kibbutz pioneers cleared thousands of acres, first around Galilee. They planted orchards, crops, raised poultry, dairy and fish farming. They made the barren lands bloom.

❖ Membership ranges from 40-50 to more than 1,000, with most of them averaging around 400-500 residents. The median age is 30.

❖ The kibbutz is a pure democracy, "one man, one vote, the majority rules." Both men and women vote.

❖ Members are assigned their work positions. Routine duties such as kitchen and laundry are rotated.

❖ For many years, children were raised in communal children's houses. Modern times have changed that, and the family unit has become more important to new couples moving in.[168]

❖ With only 2.5 percent of the nation's population, the kibuttzim produce about 33 percent of the agriculture farm produce and 6.3 percent of manufactured goods.

The kibbutz have struggled to keep up with changing times. Where large investments would upgrade and modernize their equipment and facilities, the collectives are generally too poor to handle large capital improvements. An association of kibbutzim

---

167   Encyclopedia Judaica, *Kibbutz*, 1989.
168   See Abraham Pavin, *The Kibbutz Movement, facts and figures*, Central Bureau of Statistics, State of Israel, 2006.

Socialism is Atheistic: To have pure equality, socialists must reject God, who, through commandments and counsel, directs people toward refinement and self-improvement, the very antithesis of equality.

has helped solve that problem, but the greatest improvements have come when the lands and facilities were privatized as profit-making operations.

An important difference in the socialistic nature of the kibbutz and similar farming communities called a moshav (plural = moshavim) is that these establishments are all voluntary—people may join or leave at their pleasure without being arrested, punished, or forced to remain.

FREE RELIGION: The tourist to Israel will find that Jewish beliefs and traditions are not imposed by law. Even so, many Jews observe tenets at their businesses. For example, most Jewish establishments in Israel will close for the Sabbath, elevators will go into automatic mode and stop on every floor of hotels (so a person doesn't "work" by pressing a button for the desired floor), and only Arab-operated taxis and shops are open for business.

But come Sunday morning, it's business as usual—and time for the Christians living in Israel to put on their Sunday best and attend church—freely, encouraged, and welcomed.

RELIGION: Hinduism
ADHERENTS: 1.1 billion
STORY: Hinduism is the most predominant group of religious beliefs in South Asia. There is no record of a single founder, no single religious or traditional style, and no singular code of beliefs— it is the combination of several ancient religions with strains of beliefs reaching far back into antiquity. They call it the oldest living religion.

In fact, Hinduism is not a religion in the traditional sense but more like a way of life. A person doesn't really convert to Hinduism, he just melds in with the rest.

BELIEF IN AFTERLIFE: The Hindus put a great deal of importance into breaking the cycle of birth and death, which is the main goal of their search for a loftier state of awareness and connection with the eternities.

Some believe in gods who occasionally visit the earth to rectify imbalances and to guide humans the right way. One method Hindus employ to find the right way is yoga. Yoga is one of any number of

In 2012, Barack Obama vandalized the official presidential biographies on the White House website by inserting his own name and performance in contrast to or in support of prior presidents.

practices performed in temples as a ritual, or anywhere the person desires to seek peace. These rituals include chanting mantras, offering sacrifices, reciting scripture, and meditating.

In several countries Hindu society is a caste with four divisions. There is debate about this being sanctioned by scripture or simply a leftover social custom, but it dates back thousands of years.

The four classes of Varna (meaning order, type or color) are 1) the Brahmins who are scholars and teachers, 2) the warriors and kings, 3) the agriculturists and merchants, and 4) the artisans and service providers. At the bottom are the untouchables. The untouchables' job is the dirty work—haul away corpses, execute criminals, dispose of night soil, basically your on-call disaster or stinky mess cleanup crew. In the past they were forbidden to learn from holy books and lived together in their own ghettos outside of the villages.

This regimentation gave each individual a place in society, and if they were moral about it they would be reborn after death into a higher caste as a reward—or lower caste if they were immoral.

YOU ARE WHAT YOU WERE: Hindus consider their places in life simply the consequence of their own earlier actions in a previous existence. Therefore, they just put up with life and life's challenges. A person born rich is rich because of his karma. But if he was born poor and suffering, he has only himself to blame. Getting out of the mess is a chore viewed as his only. Enduring his plight is proof of his worthiness for a higher state of existence in the next life.

The same view is taken toward electing leaders or being invaded by foreigners. Hindus put up with the resulting hardships of corrupt leaders, wars, or conquerors. They believe a bad leader or a conquering army is the result of their own lapses or fault. They believe they are personally responsible, and must endure the suffering for its cleansing effects.

SOCIALISM SIMPLY WON'T WORK IN HINDUISM

Hindu's beliefs encourage such an independent and personal responsibility that any form of collective or socialist action among them is simply impossible. The individual pursuit for karma makes a group or socialistic society completely incompatible.

These self-interested people wouldn't want wealth sharing,

Socialism in America: The food czars are patrolling public schools to control what people eat. In 2012, Davis High School in Utah was fined more than $16,000 for allowing students to buy soda and candy during the lunch hour.

or their freedom to suffer or improve, impeded by socialism—it is illogical and contradictory to personal perfection. Likewise, free enterprise is very much in harmony with Hinduism. It blends wonderfully with independent action and personal responsibility.

THE UNIVERSAL RELIGION

Benjamin Franklin and other Founders defined religion as a belief system based on faith that these five elements are true:

1. There is a Creator.

2. We are his creations.

3. He has revealed laws that govern our actions toward one another, and we are responsible to treat one another well.

4. There is life after death.

5. We will be judged for our treatment of others.[169]

Samuel Adams said these basic beliefs constituted "the religion of America," which he said was also "the religion of all mankind."[170] In other words, these beliefs belonged to all world faiths—Christianity, Islam, Judaism, and the others—and could be taught without being offensive.

John Adams called them the "general principles" on which the American civilization had been founded.[171]

Thomas Jefferson called them the principles "in which God has united us all." [172]

CAREFUL NOT TO MENTION THE "FORCE" WORD ...

Socialists avoid mentioning the necessity of Ruler's Law as the enforcing power in their utopian schemes, and skip over the negative consequences of force directed against those who will not obey the rulers.

---

169   Benjamin Franklin, "Here is my creed: I believe in one God, the Creator of the universe. That he governs it by his providence. That he ought to be worshiped. That the most acceptable service we render to him is in doing good to his other children. That the soul of man is immortal, and will be treated with justice in another life respecting its conduct in this. These I take to be the fundamental points in all sound religion." Smith, *Writings of Benjamin Franklin*, 10:84.
170   Wells, *Life of Samuel Adams*, 3:23.
171   John Adams, letter to Thomas Jefferson, *Writings of Thomas Jefferson*, 13:293.
172   Thomas Jefferson, *Writings of Thomas Jefferson*, 14:198.

King John never actually affixed his signature to the original Magna Carta in A.D. 1215, he sealed it by pressing his seal into hot wax.

As with medieval Christianity and Islam, the use of force at any level quickly backfires. History shows the downward spiral of coercion always goes to the same ending place—torture, death, burnings, beheadings, and war.

RELIGIOUS LEADERS NOT RELIGIOUS GOVERNMENT

Religion changes the man on the inside so that he can change his world on the outside. Extremists try to change the outside to force change on the man's inside. It never works. Religion is best separated from government as a tool of free personal refinement.

Jesus clarified the importance of keeping religion and government carefully separated when he said "Render therefore unto Caesar the things which are Caesar's, and unto God the things that are God's."[173]

Moses clarified the power of rational organization and God-centered government among the children of Israel without force.

The Founding Fathers clarified the beneficial powers of religious influence in good government when they founded the United States.

When individuals and their culture freely embrace the positives of religious belief, the fruits of those choices are quickly manifested by an increase in cooperation, harmony, neighborliness, and prosperity. When any form of religious force is imposed on the people, the whole society eventually explodes with misery.

W AS JESUS A SOCIALIST?

Some socialists try to justify compelling others to "be good" and "do good" by misinterpreting Jesus' teachings. In their attempt to formulate the true heart and spirit of their benevolent socialism, they twist things to mean ...

❖ ... Jesus said to have all things in common by admonishing followers to share, to give to the poor, to sell worldly possessions, to help others, and to dispose of material wealth—no private property.

❖ ... Jesus said it was okay to tax the rich more than others because "For unto whomsoever much is given, of him shall be much required."[174]

---

173   Matthew 22:21 KJV.
174   Luke 12:48 KJV.

Socialism in Mexico: It's no wonder why Mexico has so many problems—the people have only three bad choices at election time: PRI-Institutional Revolution Party (liberal and environmental), PAN-National Action Party (socialist), and PRD-Democratic Revolution Party (communist).

❖   ... Jesus taught taking from the "haves" and giving to the "have nots" was okay when he said, "Thou shalt love thy neighbor as thyself."

❖   ... and in the early Christian Church, communalism was encouraged because new converts "had all things common, And sold their possessions and goods, and parted them to all men, as every man had need."[175]—Once again, no private property.

FORCE VERSUS CHOICE

Usually forgotten in these blissful considerations is that Jesus' acts of compassion and his call to do likewise were not acts of compulsion, but free-will and *voluntary*. Socialism is *force*.

Is force bad when it's used to help the poor and needy? Should people be forced to sell their goods and give to the poor? Should they be forced to have all things in common?

USING GODLY FORCE?

Early in his ministry, Jesus showed that force is not the way to get things done, even if it's to help the hungry. After he had fasted 40 days, Jesus was tempted by the devil:

"And the devil said unto him, If thou be the Son of God, command this stone that it be made bread."[176]

If Jesus had used his Godly powers to *force* a solution, to force the changing of stone to bread for the positive purpose of feeding the hungry (in this case, Himself), his mission would have been an immediate failure.

A hungry man using a shortcut to turn stone to bread would show himself a slave to human appetites, a slave to the craving for instant self gratification, a slave to the vice of wanting something for nothing. Such miracles apparently were in His power, but Jesus would save those for another day—to teach his followers and bolster their faith, not to gratify selfish hunger pains.

But on this day, the devil tempted Jesus in the solitude of privacy, with no one else there to witness a little cheating to eat bread, to indulge just a little, and thereby succumb to the powerful mortal temptation and human flaw that Jesus had come to conquer.

---

175   Acts 2:44-45 KJV.
176   Luke 4:3 KJV.

Socialism in America: In 2008, the average compensation for federal workers, including health, pension and other benefits, was $108,476. For the same mix of jobs and benefits in the private sector, the average compensation was $69,928.

Jesus could not be swayed. Later in his ministry he would teach that only by resisting such urges would true peace and happiness ever be found. He would teach his followers to hold fast to the iron rod of true principles that runs along the pathway of provident living as established by his Father in Heaven—and never let go.

As for the bread, Jesus knew God's commandment was to work for what you eat.

"In the sweat of thy face," God commanded in Genesis 3:19, "shalt thou eat bread." Jesus was obedient to all of His father's commandments. He refused to set himself above any law his Father gave to everyone else, and forthwith rejected Satan out of hand:

"And Jesus answered him, saying, It is written, That man shall not live by bread alone, but by every word of God." (Luke 4:4) Jesus waited until he could procure food himself, a very real and tangible example to everyone else who suffers for want and is tempted to indulge against honesty or principle, and shrink.

FORCED GOODNESS?

When charity for others is imposed by force, people are denied the benefits of carrying the entire responsibility of compassion on their own shoulders. Forced compassion always short-circuits the human heart and destroys the integrity of true and loving charity.

Sincere and voluntary charity is kind, it doesn't envy, it doesn't boast, it endures, and never fails. People enjoy helping when they can, it is part of human nature. But when people are forced to pay heavy taxes for entitlement programs, food stamps, and welfare, they hate it. Some will go so far as to skip, cheat, or dodge paying for them by any means available. Paying taxes so somebody can eat—or buy cigarettes and lottery tickets using food stamps—doesn't ignite feelings of compassion. It ignites feelings of anger and frustration, the antithesis of a helpful attitude. So—which process has the better outcome, government's policy of force, or voluntary charity?

Force will always and inevitably frustrate the simplicity of pure compassion. The positive messages Jesus taught are in no way connected to the seven despotic pillars of socialism. Jesus' message was precisely the opposite: be free to choose—and choose wisely.

Spoken like a true socialist: After Mao Zedong killed and starved 75 million people, David Rockefeller said, "Whatever the price of the Chinese Revolution, it has obviously succeeded not only in producing more efficient and dedicated administration, but also ..." (cont'd)

CHAPTER 30:

DID THE EARLY CHRISTIANS PRACTICE COMMUNISM?

By W. Cleon Skousen[177]

A few students have secretly or even openly defended Communism because they considered it to be an important set of principles practiced by the early Christians. Such persons often say that they definitely do not condone the ruthlessness of Communism as presently practiced in Russia, but that they do consider it to be of Christian origin and morally sound when practiced on a "brotherhood basis."

This was exactly the attitude of the Pilgrim Fathers when they undertook to practice Communism immediately after their arrival in the New World. Not only did the project fail miserably, but it was typical of hundreds of other attempts to make Communism work on a "brotherhood basis." Without exception, all of them failed. One cannot help wondering why.

"BROTHERHOOD COMMUNISM" IS UNCHRISTIAN

Certain scholars feel they have verified what Governor Bradford has said concerning "brotherhood Communism," namely, that it is un-Christian and immoral because it strikes at the very roots of human liberty. Communism—even on a brotherhood basis—can only be set up under a dictatorship administered within the framework of force or fear. Governor Bradford found this to be true. Leaders in literally hundreds of similar experiments concur. Students are therefore returning to ancient texts with this question: "Did the early Christians really practice Communism?"

TWO BIBLE PASSAGES CREATE CONFUSION

The belief that the early Christians may have practiced Communism is based on two passages. Here is the first one:

"And all that believed were together, and had all things in

---

177 Reprinted with permission from *The Naked Communist* by W. Cleon Skousen, 1958, 2006.

(cont'd) "... in fostering high morale and community of purpose. The social experiment in China under Chairman Mao's leadership is one of the most important and successful in human history."—David Rockefeller, 1973

common; and sold their possessions and goods, and parted them to all men as every man had need." (Acts 2:44-45)

Two things might be noted here. First, the people formed a community effort by coming together; second, they sold their possessions and goods as they appeared to need cash proceeds for the assistance of their fellow members. It does not say that they sold all their possessions and goods although it is granted that at first reading this may be inferred. Neither does it say that they pooled their resources in a common fund although this has been assumed from the statement that they "had all things common."

COMMON PROBLEMS, NOT COMMON THINGS

What they actually did is more clearly stated in the second passage which is often quoted

"And the multitude of them that believed were of one heart and of one soul; neither said any of them that ought of the things which he possessed was his own; but they had all things common." (Acts 4:32)

Here we have a declaration indicating that the common effort was not a legal pooling of resources in a communal fund but rather a feeling of unity in dealing with common problems so that no man "said" his possessions were his own but developed and used them in such a way that they would fill the needs of the group as well as himself.

That this is a correct reading of this passage may be verified by events which are described in the next chapter of Acts.

ANANIAS AND SAPPHIRA TRY TO CHEAT PETER

There we read of Ananias and Sapphira. They had a piece of property which they decided to sell. They intended to give the proceeds to the Apostle Peter. But the author of Acts says that when they had sold the property they decided to hold back some of the proceeds even though they represented to Peter that their contribution was the entire value of the property received at the sale. For this deceit, Peter severely criticized them, and then, in the process, he explained the legal relationship existing between these two people and their property. Said he, "While it (the property) remained, was it not thine own? and after it was sold, was it (the money) not in thine power?" (Acts 5:4)

In other words, this property had never been required for any communal fund. It belonged to Ananias and Sapphira. It was completely in their power. After the property was sold the money they received from the sale was also in their power. They could spend it or contribute it. If contributed, the money was a freewill, voluntary offering. It will be seen immediately that this is altogether different from a Communist's relationship to property where there is a confiscation or expropriation of each member's possessions, and the proceeds are distributed by a single person or a small committee. The member thereby loses his independence and becomes subservient to the whims and capriciousness of those who rule over him.

CHRISTIANS KEPT LEGAL TITLE TO PROPERTY

It would appear, therefore, that the early Christians did keep legal title to their property but "said" it was for the benefit of the whole community.

This is precisely the conclusion reached in Dummelow's *Bible Commentary*. It discusses the two passages we have just quoted and then says: "The Church of Jerusalem recognized the principle of private property. A disciple's property really was his own, but he did not say it was his own; he treated it as if it were common property."

Dr. Adam Clarke's commentary also makes this significant observation concerning the Apostolic collections for the poor: "If there has been a *community of goods* in the Church, there could have been no ground for such (collections) ... as there could have been no such distinction as *rich* and *poor*, if everyone, on entering the Church, gave up his goods to a common stock."

JESUS TAUGHT PROPERTY IS INDIVIDUALLY OWNED

This, then, brings us to our final comment on this subject, namely, that the Master Teacher made it very clear in one of His parables (Matthew 25:14-30) that property was not to be owned in common nor in equal quantities.

In this parable He said the members of the kingdom of God were servants who had been given various stewardships "every man according to his several ability." One man was given a stewardship of five talents of silver and when he "traded with the same

Socialism kills: In North Korea, an estimated 3,000,000 starved to death in 1998 because the country failed to develop a self-sustaining system of food production. When the Soviet Union fell, North Korea was left without the handouts its communist regime required to keep going.

and made them other five talents," his Lord said, "Well done!" However, another servant who had been given only one talent of silver feared he might somehow lose it, so he buried it in the earth. To this man his Lord said, "Thou wicked and slothful servant!" He then took this man's one talent and gave it to the servant where it could be developed profitably.

ENJOY PROPERTY AS A STEWARDSHIP

Two things appear very clear in this Parable of the Talents: first, that every man was to enjoy his own private property as a stewardship from God. Second, that he was responsible to the earth's Creator for the profitable use of his property.

All of the evidence before us seems to clearly show that the early Christians did not practice Communism. They did not have their *property* in common. Instead, they had their *problems* in common. To solve their problems, each man was asked to voluntarily contribute according to his ability "as God had prospered him." (1 Corinthians 16:2)

When carefully analyzed, this was simply free enterprise capitalism *with a heart!*

The student will also probably recognize that whenever modern capitalism is practiced "with a heart" it showers blessings of wealth, generosity, good will and happy living on every community it touches.

The ancient Christian order was a great idea.

Free Speech in China: In 2012, a blind lawyer, Chen Guangcheng, who was outspoken about China's fierce one-child police (he protested the government forcing women with one child to undergo an abortion), escaped to the U.S. Embassy in China. China's internal security was... (cont'd)

THE WORD THAT CAN'T BE DEFINED

Socialism is often defined to promote a particular brand of the perfect dream. In truth, they're all nightmares.

With this preceding historical summary to give context, what then can be the best definition for socialism? The traditional definitions include something about the government controlling parts of the economy, portions that typically are controlled by private businesses. Outside of that, definitions of socialism are all over the map. This sampling includes both pro- and anti-socialism observations—

SOURCE: Encyclopaedia Britannica, 13th Edition
DEFINITION: "Socialism is that policy or theory which aims at securing by the action of the central democratic authority a better distribution, and in due subordination thereunto a better production, of wealth than now prevails."[178]
    COMMENT: This sentence is loaded with pitfalls: A *central authority*, "democratic" or not, must use unchecked force to make anything "better." To "make" is the same as "to force."

SOURCE: Alexis de Tocqueville, defender of freedom
DEFINITION: "Democracy extends the sphere of individual freedom, socialism restricts it. Democracy attaches all possible value to each man; socialism makes each man a mere agent, a mere number. Democracy and socialism have nothing in common but one word, equality. But notice the difference: while democracy seeks equality in liberty, socialism seeks equality in restraint and servitude."[179]
    COMMENT: As precisely stated, socialism means force.

SOURCE: Paul Hubert Casselman, Labor Dictionary, 1949
DEFINITION: "An economic theory which holds that ownership of property should be in the group and not in the individuals who make up the group. Collectivism may be partial or complete. Partial

---

178   Encyclopaedia Britannica, 13th Edition.
179   Cited in Hayek, *The Road to Serfdom*.

(cont'd) ... embarrassed and delicate political negotiations followed, and Mr. Chen was allowed to visit the U.S. But then China scrubbed their social media of all references to Chen including his name, initials, "blind lawyer," "embassy," "U.S. embassy," "blind person," and more.

collectivism is exemplified by public ownership of schools, hospitals, recreational centers, etc., in the capitalistic system. Complete collectivism exists under communism where all wealth is owned in common."[180]

> **COMMENT**: Casselman assumes socialism retains some private ownership to keep things orderly and functioning as planned. If the free market works so well to sustain a regulated market, then why not just let it loose and forget the regulated part?

SOURCE: Robert V. Daniels, U.S. author and educator
DEFINITION: "I take as my general working definition of socialism, 'any theory or practice of social control over economic activity.' This definition is purposely vague. It embraces any degree of social control in the economy, from the U.S. Post Office to the completely nationalized economy of the USSR. It covers both state socialism and non-state (cooperatives, syndicalism, etc.). It permits democratic as well as dictatorial forms of political control."[181]

> **COMMENT**: "Social control" means top-down government control without power by the people—the loss of freedom.

SOURCE: Ludwig von Mises, pro-liberty scholar and teacher
DEFINITION: "My own definition of socialism, as a policy which aims at constructing a society in which the means of production are socialized, is in agreement with all that scientists have written on the subject. I submit that one must be historically blind not to see that this and nothing else is what has stood for Socialism for the past hundred years, and that it is in this sense that the great socialist movement was and is socialistic."[182]

> **COMMENT**: Von Mises accurately points out that any name or label describing the regulation of society is still and will always remain socialism.

SOURCE: Benjamin Tucker, publisher, proponent of socialism
DEFINITION: "First, then, State Socialism, which may be described as the doctrine that all the affairs of men should be managed by the government, regardless of individual choice."[183]

---

180 Paul Hubert Casselman, Labor Dictionary, *Socialism*, 1949.
181 Quoted in J.D. Bales, *What is Socialism?*
182 Ludwig von Mises, *Socialism*, 1951, p. 20.
183 Benjamin Tucker, *State Socialism and Anarchism: How Far They Agree, and Wherein They Differ*, paragraphs 11 and 12, 1888.

Socialism kills: Cuba's death count from purges, executions and terror from 1949 to 1987 is approximately 70,000.

COMMENT: Tucker cuts to the chase: Under socialism, there are no unalienable rights, no choice, and no property.

SOURCE: Roger Nash Baldwin, a founder of ACLU
DEFINITION: "I am for socialism, disarmament, and, ultimately, for abolishing the state itself ... I seek the social ownership of property, the abolition of the properties class, and the sole control of those who produce wealth. Communism is, of course, the goal."[184]
   COMMENT: Baldwin echoes the major goals of all socialists. Communism does it by abrupt force—socialism does it by gradual infiltration and change. Both aim for the same goal.

SOURCE: H. G. Wells, author and outspoken socialist
DEFINITION: "The New Deal is plainly an attempt to achieve a working socialism and avert a social collapse in America; it is extraordinarily parallel to the successive 'policies' and 'Plans' of the Russian experiment. Americans shirk at the word 'socialism,' but what else can one call it?"[185]
   COMMENT: H. G. Wells points out the New Deal was the socializing of the United States—and an otherwise inattentive America embraced it with hopeful smiles.

SOURCE: Episcopal Bishop Franklin Spencer Spalding, 1914 **DEFINITION**: "The Christian Church exists for the sole purpose of saving the human race. So far she has failed, but I think that Socialism shows her how she may succeed. It insists that men cannot be made right until the material conditions be made right. Although man cannot live by bread alone, he must have bread. Therefore the Church must destroy a system of society which inevitably creates and perpetuates unequal and unfair conditions of life. These unequal and unfair conditions have been created by competition. Therefore competition must cease and cooperation take its place."[186]
   COMMENT: Bishop Spalding sees force in everything—the church must destroy capitalism, it must destroy competition, it must save the human race. The bishop neglected to consider free choice as originally taught by Christianity, and the words of the strongest proponent of free choice among all religions, namely, Jesus Christ.

---

184   Robert C. Cottrell, *Roger Nash Baldwin and the American Civil Liberties Union,* pp. 228-229.
185   H. G. Wells, *The New World Order,* p. 46.
186   Franklin Spencer Spalding, *The Christian Socialist,* November 1914.

Socialism in Brazil: The Brazilian government is the country's largest single employer, taking in 21% of the workforce, and it pays salaries 56% higher than its private sector counterparts.

SOURCE: Frederic Bastiat, French economist and politician

DEFINITION: "Socialism, like the ancient ideas from which it springs, confuses the distinction between government and society. As a result of this, every time we object to a thing being done by the government, the socialists conclude that we object to its being done at all. We disapprove of state education. Then the socialists say that we are opposed to any education. We object to a state religion. Then the socialists say that we want no religion at all. We object to a state-enforced equality. Then they say that we are against equality. And so on, and so on. It is as if the socialists were to accuse us of not wanting persons to eat because we do not want the state to raise grain."[187]

COMMENT: Bastiat illustrates the fifth pillar of Socialism (force)—while free people choose what they want in their society, socialism deems it necessary to impose on everyone "what is good for us" by government *force*. The problem is and will forever be, who decides? As Bastiat observes, the best answer is "We the People" must remain free to decide our future. We do this by way of a free representative government, not through tyrants who will dictate what best benefits them and their power base.

LEARNING TO RECOGNIZE SOCIALISM

These examples illustrate the difficulty in parading tyranny in a positive light. It takes a lot of careful work to gloss over the details of Ruler's Law and cast it as worthy of attention, or as a viable solution to human problems. Socialists try to get around this by inventing a good name or category or leader around which others who want change may rally. There are hundreds of these groups, but only a few have achieved widespread recognition.

---

187 Frederic Bastiat, *The Law*, par. L. 102 (1850 edition).

"We should be modest and prudent, guard against arrogance and rashness, and serve the Chinese people heart and soul...."—Mao Zedong. And then 73,000,000 Chinese died (1949-1987), half of those starved to death.

CHAPTER 32:

SOCIALISM DU JOUR

*With more variations, brands, flavors and combinations of
socialistic ideas than you can shake a stick at, nobody
can figure out what the socialists really want.*

W**HAT ARE THE MAJOR GROUPS?** This list is not all-inclusive, but presents a few of the more common forms of modern socialism. After plowing through a million words of sickening boredom, the various major socialisms have been painfully distilled into a single paragraph—a task assuredly more daunting than actually attempting to implement the freakish ideas themselves. It goes without saying that a socialist could do a much better job of confusing the subject even more.

BRAND: Utopian socialism
UNIQUE FEATURE: Impossible, but delightfully hypothetical
STORY: First envisioned by Plato and then given a name by Sir Thomas More (1516 A.D.), this brand of socialism found roots in the early 1800s. It promised a perfect society brought about through the harmonious cooperation of like-minded people. Everyone shares everything happily—a garden of earthly delights with no fights, no poverty, and no crime.[188]

BRAND: Democratic socialism
UNIQUE FEATURE: People vote for socialistic policies
STORY: This brand is hard to define. In general, it has deeper involvement of the masses who vote democratically for policy instead of relying on an elite class of leaders to impose it. Some see capitalism and basic property ownership (house, car) as engines of prosperity benevolently tolerated to prop up a democratic socialistic society. Others see it as a transitory mechanism, an in-between that leads from evil capitalism to righteous Marxist socialism without those nasty revolutionary wars and upheavals. Democratic socialism means voting to be impoverished and miserable rather than having it forced upon you.[189]

---

188 Ludwig Von Mises, *Socialism An Economic and Sociological Analysis*, p. 249; Clarence B. Carson, *The Utopian Vision*, The Freeman, February 1965, pp. 20-34; The Encyclopaedia Britannica, 13th edition, 1926, Vol. 27, p. 823.
189 See Alex de Tocqueville, *Democracy in America*, 2:336; W. Cleon Skousen, *The Majesty of God's Law*, pp. 556-558.

North Korea requires a license from the government to operate cars, motorcycles and bicycles. In 2007, motorcycle licenses for anything but a North Korean motorcycle was made impossibly expensive to force people to purchase locally produced models.

BRAND: Marxist socialism (communism)
UNIQUE FEATURE: Quickly imposed with violent uprising
STORY: It's the culmination of an evolution. Marx envisioned capitalism reaching a breaking point at which time the working class would rise up and take over everything. These masses of laborers are managed by the State until order is restored, and then the State supposedly dissolves away so science can direct everything. Find yourself short on decaf? Plug your problem into the master planning computer. Workers are moved from one job to the other, more decaf is produced, and suddenly you have less to be fidgety about. The end goal is no property, no state, and no religion—just communism.[190]

BRAND: Scientific socialism
UNIQUE FEATURE: Adjusts according to supply and demand
STORY: Similar to Marxism, this brand relies on evolution. By looking back in history at how the needs of a society expand and change, the scientific socialist strives to predict future needs. He adjusts his production and distribution to meet those needs—and then hopes he is right. If he's wrong, millions starve to death, or barges of unused tofu go rotting on some distant loading dock, but that's okay—the ends always justify the means, better luck next time.[191]

BRAND: Market socialism
UNIQUE FEATURE: Price fixing by trial and error
STORY: This version has the state owning all resources and setting prices by trial and error. The idea is to lower prices on surpluses to get rid of the excess, and raise prices on scarce items to encourage more production to make more money and employ more workers (sounds very capitalistic). In this back and forth trial and error, a nation is eventually supposed to reach a point where everyone is producing what the country uses, everyone is employed, and their united labors happily grow the economy.[192]

---

190   See W. Cleon Skousen, *The Naked Communist*, pp. 47-59; The Encyclopaedia Britannica, 13th edition, 1926, Vol. 17, pp. 809-810; Encyclopedia of Marxism, *Marxism and Marxist*.
191   Friedrich Engels, *Socialism: Utopian and Scientific*, 1880.
192   See Mark Skousen, *The Making of Modern Economics*, pp. 414-415; Encyclopedia of Marxism, *Market Socialism*.

Socialism in America: In 2010, the only company making the drug used for lethal injections to carry out capital punishments ceased making the drug. States began importing it from overseas. But then in 2012, a Washington State judge ... (cont'd)

BRAND: Fabian Socialism

UNIQUE FEATURE: Secretive, subtle, sneak up and infiltrate

STORY: Founded in London in 1884. Its supporters advanced communism through gradual, easily swallowed means, not sudden revolutionary action. Socialism imposed slowly will last longer than a revolution, they said, provided it isn't obviously anti-democracy or too bossy. The Fabians proposed minimum wage, national health care, "social justice," and nationalization of the land, among other things. They promoted forced schooling and eugenics (selective breeding). Famous people embraced it wholeheartedly: George Bernard Shaw, H.G. Wells (for a while), Virginia Woolf, Bertrand Russell (for a while), Jawaharlal Nehru, Tony Blair, etc. It's the same ol' same ol' socialism—when fully matured there would be no private property, no free choice, and no liberty or personal rights.[193]

BRAND: Christian Socialism

UNIQUE FEATURE: Bless them with benevolent socialism

STORY: There is nothing new here in Christian socialism. The same doctrines of taking from the "haves" and giving to the "have nots" by government force is couched in the pleasant church cushions of common Christian beliefs. They call for national health care, welfare, taxing the job-providers, minimum wage—the usual list of typical socialist causes, all in the name of Jesus. They claim moral justification from Acts 2:44-47, the oft misapplied justification to give away one's goods to the poor and have things in common—a misunderstanding that is ages old. For a discussion on these scripture verses and what the early Christians actually did by having "things in common," see page 159, for *Did the Early Christians Practice Communism?*[194]

BRAND: Fascism

UNIQUE FEATURE: Turns family against family

STORY: "Fascism" has become a colloquialism for anything that is rash and brutal. For Italy's Mussolini during WWII, fascism meant centering all power in him. His secret police spied on everyone to crush all opposition and dissent. Support for fascism was promoted

---

193 See Paul Hubert Casselman, *Labor Dictionary*, p. 132; A. M. McBriar, *Fabian Socialism and English Politics, 1884-1918*, pp. 8-11; Anne Fremantle, *This Little Band of Prophets: The British Fabians*, p. 263; Margaret Cole, *The Story of Fabian Socialism*, 1961.

194 Also see http://www.christiansocialists.com/Faith_in_Politics.html.

(cont'd) ... blocked the importation because the Food and Drug Administration had not approved the drug for "safety and effectiveness," a requirement for all imported drugs. At least 15 states asked for the ruling to be overturned.

as a patriotic duty and anyone opposed was viewed a traitor. To maintain popular support, Mussolini cultivated a state of ignorance about his activities by controlling all media, and restricting travel and association. It fomented a war-like state of crisis, convincing people of a threat they must be prepared for, and then employing many in the government to prepare and make armaments. The wealthy supported it because it protected their private properties. But once established, Italy's fascist forces turned on the propertied classes to take from the "haves" and spread around the wealth.[195]

BRAND: Environmental Socialism
UNIQUE FEATURE: Destroy rights to save the environment
STORY: The so-named "green movement" has taken root in recent years to expand government power at the expense of individual liberties. Carbon taxes, global warming, capitalism's supposed penchant for using too much energy, limited natural resources, cap and trade, the hole in the ozone layer, evil filament light bulbs, flatulence-prone cows—just about anything that puts humans below all things to regiment or eliminate them altogether, is today euphemistically called *going green.*

Ecosocialists say that Marxism already contains many pro-earth ideals, but today's movement is designed to give teeth to the abstract—such as empowering Americans to sue companies that are not "green" enough, or shutting down coal-powered power plants (and driving up energy costs), or stopping oil drilling (and driving up energy costs), or stopping land development (make everything a no-touch national park), or imposing mandatory regulations to create ultra-expensive alternatives that are theoretically kinder to the earth.

In 2009 and 2011, suspicions about the political motivations of the global warming movement were validated when batches of 5,000 emails were posted on the Internet.[196] Among the messages are cleanly stated the intentions of prominent scientists to conceal underlying data that went contrary to their political agenda, to promote political causes instead of making unbiased scientific

195   See Ludwig Von Mises, *Socialism—An Economic and Sociological Analysis,* pp. 524-528; Friedrich A. Hayek, *The Road to Serfdom,* pp. 168-169; *Dictatorship, Its History and Theory,* 1939, pp. 131-135. 275-279; Whittaker Chambers, *Witness Whittaker Chambers,* p. 462; Walter Lippmann, *A Preface to Morals,* p. 251; Norman Thomas, *A Socialist's Faith,* 1951 pp. 52-53.
196   Forbes, *Climategate 2.0: New E-Mails Rock the Global Warming Debate,* Nov. 23, 2011.
"We all accept the need for some form of socialism to enable our people to catch up with the advanced countries of this world and to overcome their legacy of extreme poverty. But this does not mean we are Marxists."—Nelson Mandela, 1964.

inquiry, and admissions that science is dependent on manipulation of the facts.

Ecosocialism has developed into a filthy assault on liberty that many Americans are supporting at the expense of their own innovation and freedom.[197]

PRICKLES OFF THE SAME WEED

The growing number of socialisms are prickles off the same weed. Each destroys property rights with force. Each brand has its own elitist class of egotists leeching off the masses for sustenance and justification. The misery they create brings out the worst in humans. Fighting, lawlessness, protests, and occupy movements that such oppression produce also conveniently provide the excuses needed for an increase in police power. The rulers use police power to punish and crush with multi-layered regulations, and to project more control and top-down Ruler's Law.

LEARNING TO RECOGNIZE SOCIALISM

Socialism is the organized pursuit of something for nothing. It feeds on human nature with false assurances. It claims the power to satisfy all needs with minimal or no effort. In the end, only an elite class enjoys the advantages while everyone else must suffer.

The philosopher Ayn Rand spoke about the dark tide of socialism that swept across her homeland of Russia, and warned that no good will come of it for the rest of the world.

"Socialism is the doctrine that man has no right to exist for his own sake," Rand wrote, "that his life and his work do not belong to him, but belong to society, that the only justification of his existence is his service to society, and that society may dispose of him in any way it pleases for the sake of whatever it deems to be its own tribal, collective good."[198]

Rand was an eyewitness to the modern-day spread of socialism and the power it wields over individuals—

"Socialism may be established by force, as in the Union of

---

197   Jon Basil Utley, *Obama and the Alternative Energy Fiasco*, Reason.com, May 13, 2009; Joel Kovel, *The Enemy of Nature*, 2002; Robyn Eckersley, *Environmentalism and Political Theory*, 1992; John Clark, *The Anarchist Moment*, 1984); John Belemy Foster, *Marx's Ecology in Historical Perspective*, International Socialism Journal, Winter 2002.
198   Ayn Rand, *The Ayn Rand Lexicon*, edited by Harry Binswanger, p. 463.

"The historical experience of socialist countries has sadly demonstrated that collectivism does not do away with alienation but rather increases it, adding to it a lack of basic necessities and economic inefficiency."—Pope John Paul II

Soviet Socialist Republics—or by vote, as in Nazi (National Social-ist) Germany. The degree of socialization may be total, as in Russia—or partial, as in England. Theoretically, the differences are superficial; practically, they are only a matter of time. The basic principle, in all cases, is the same.

"The alleged goals of socialism were: the abolition of poverty, the achievement of general prosperity, progress, peace and human brotherhood. The results have been a terrifying failure—terrifying, that is, if one's motive is men's welfare.

"Instead of prosperity, socialism has brought economic paralysis and/or collapse of every country that tried it. The degree of social-ization has been the degree of disaster. The consequences have varied accordingly."[199]

Rand said the right to property was the single most important and consistent field of battle between freedom and socialism—

"When you consider socialism, do not fool yourself about its nature," she wrote in the early 1960s. "Remember that there is no dichotomy as 'human rights' versus 'property rights.' No human rights can exist without property rights. Since material goods are produced by the mind and effort of individual men, and are needed to sustain their lives, if the producer does not own the result of his effort, he does not own his life. To deny property rights means to turn men into property owned by the state. Whoever claims the 'right' to 'redistribute' the wealth produced by others is claiming the 'right' to treat human beings as chattel."[200]

All forms of dictatorship eventually crumble from within. They are built on corruption, revolution, and anger, and they come crashing down for the same violations. The great nations of the world were never conquered from without until they first had decayed and collapsed from within. Socialism has bred that cycle of peaks and valleys into nearly all of human history.

The seven pillars of socialism are not applied equally through time, but are applied according to world circumstances and changing tolerances. In every instance, all seven methods to violate human rights become part of a painful test of endurance for the populous. When the ruling class, having finally exhausted their

199   Ayn Rand, "The Monument Builders," in *For the New Intellectual*, 1963, pp. 100-101.
200   Ibid., p. 120.

Socialism in North Korea: In 2012, two reporters for *The Sun* bluffed their way into North Korea. Besides empty apartment buildings along the river border with China, there were watchtowers manned 24x7. Soldiers had orders to shoot anyone trying to flee to a better life.

consumptions on the people, becomes weak, as they always do, a revolution erupts and new forms are installed to guide the people.

Are these ever any better than the originals?

It is the sad experience of generations past that replacement governments, once installed, eventually decay into abuse, like their predecessors—except for one grand exception: the government formed by the U.S. Constitution.

The assorted experiments in government practiced through the ages prove the brilliance of the Founding Fathers' wisdom when they drafted the ideal framework for correct management of political power.

The Constitution was not a set of laws per se, but rather a structure to accommodate laws that would be as fair, as managed, and as carefully controlled as humanly possible. It was the great happy news on Planet Earth when history's miserable tide of blood and misery came to a halt—at least in one part of the world. And from there, freedom and liberty were positioned to spread to the rest of the nations. It was a historical and time-altering moment that forever changed history.

Here, then, is the genesis, the unfolding, the brilliant beginning of that sparkling pause for freedom—

As of 2012, the "pink tide" of socialism overtly sweeping through Latin American nations has been openly embraced by: Venezuelan President Hugo Chávez, Nicaraguan President Daniel Ortega, Bolivian President Evo Morales, and Ecuadorian President Rafael Correa.

Part VII

THE MIRACLE THAT STOPPED SOCIALISM

"The utopian schemes of leveling ... are arbitrary, despotic, and in our government, unconstitutional."

—Samuel Adams—

CHAPTER 33:
THE MIRACLE THAT STOPPED SOCIALISM

*It was 1787, and for the first time in history, a nation rose to its
feet firmly planted on the correct principles of freedom.
They built a structure that banned forever the
seven despotic pillars of socialism.*

As pointed out earlier, America's Founding Fathers had an interesting perspective about political systems. They didn't look at the *issues* or *causes* that governments sought to uphold. Instead, they examined how much political power a government had.

Their sliding scale had on the far left Ruler's Law and nations that placed all power in the tyrant—or 100% Ruler's Law.

To the far right was no power and no law at all—anarchy and mob rule.

THE BALANCED CENTER

The Founders' quandary was how to find the balanced center. How could they find just enough power in government to run the country effectively without infringing on individual rights?[201]

Their first experiment was a miserable failure. The Articles of Confederation, adopted in 1777, were so weak that the central government could hardly supply George Washington's troops with their most basic needs. Congress had to go to the states begging with hat in hand for rifles, uniforms, and powder. The Articles of Confederation failed because:

◈ There was no strong executive

◈ There was no judiciary

◈ There was no taxing power

◈ There was no enforcement power.

---

201   See W. Cleon Skousen, *The Five Thousand Year Leap*, Ensign Publishing, 1981, 2009.

Socialist Cuba: "In Castro's Cuba, it is a crime to meet to discuss the economy, to write letters to the government, to report on political developments, to speak to international reporters, ... (cont'd)

NOT ENOUGH GOVERNMENT POWER

At Valley Forge, Washington watched his troops suffer on a steady diet of fire cakes—flour, water, and salt—that were baked morning, noon and night, day after day. Of his 8,000 troops, about 3,000 abandoned him and went home. Some 200 of his officers resigned their commissions. More than 2,000 of his men died of starvation and disease.

Washington pointed directly to the Articles of Confederation for the near disaster, blaming them for the inability of Congress to rally financial support for the War for Independence.

TOO LOOSE, TOO LAME, TOO INEPT

The Articles were too far to the right, too close to no law at all, with too little power to exercise the needs and demands of the young fledgling nation.

Even though the Founding Fathers recognized the flaw in their new government, none of them had a workable solution.

After the war was won and independence from England was firmly in hand, the new nation almost fell apart in a civil war.

13 FOREIGN ENEMIES

The states started fighting one against another, guarding their borders as if King George himself was trying to enter.

The Continental Dollar was inflated beyond value. The economy was in a severe depression. Riots were breaking out. The New England states were threatening to secede. And Spain and England were standing by waiting for the in-fighting to explode into anarchy so they could march in and snatch up the treasures.

CHAOS RULED SUPREME

Things were falling apart so badly after four years of freedom that the Founding Fathers knew something had to be done—and quickly. A convention was called to repair the Articles, and delegates assembled in Philadelphia on May 25, 1787. Their first order of business? Abandon the Articles and start over.

THE 116-DAY ARGUMENT

After four months of ragged debate and drawn-out discussion, the Founders reached general agreement on just about everything—except three great compromises: allowing slavery to continue for

(cont'd) ... to advocate human rights, to visit friends or relatives outside your local area of residence without government permission."—Larry Solomon

a short time before being phased out, allowing proportionate representation (a congressmen for every 30,000 people), and federal control over interstate trade and commerce between the states.

When the new Constitution was signed on September 17, 1789, and the famous Bill of Rights attached a short time later, it was a purely unique invention unlike anything the world had ever seen. For the very first time, power and authority was held and controlled by *We the People*.

SOCIALISM MADE UNCONSTITUTIONAL

The abolishment of socialism and Ruler's Law was written right into the words and sentences of the Constitution itself. The debates surrounding the crafting of those words were recorded in the journals of James Madison.

The Founders discussed these issues at great length before hand, leaving written record of their difficult struggle on how best to tie down a national government with chains that would endure the foolish unpredictability of human nature.

The foundation stone upon which the Founders discovered good government are the principles of People's Law. These principles were practiced by Moses and Israel (about 1500-1200 B.C.), and later by the Anglo-Saxons (A.D. 550 to 1066).

PEOPLE'S LAW AS PRACTICED BY THE ANGLO-SAXONS

1. The Anglo-Saxons considered themselves a commonwealth of freemen.

2. All decisions and the selection of leaders had to be with the consent of the people, preferably by full consensus, not just a majority.

3. The laws by which they were governed were considered natural laws given by divine dispensation, and were so well known by the people they did not have to be written down.

4. Power was dispersed among the people and never allowed to concentrate in any one person or group. Even in time of war, the authority granted to the leaders was temporary and the power of the people to remove them was direct and simple.

5. Responsibility for resolving problems rested first with the individual, then the family, then the tribe or community, then the region, and finally, the nation.

Socialism must deploy rulers at every level of society: "Policy and tactics are the life of the Party; leading comrades at all levels must give them full attention and must never on any account be negligent."—Mao Zedong

6.   They were organized into small, manageable groups where every adult had a voice and a vote. They divided the people into units of ten families, then fifty families, a hundred families, and then a thousand families—each level choosing a representative.

7.   They believed the rights of the individual were unalienable and could not be violated without risking the wrath of divine justice as well as civil retribution by the people's judges.

8.   Justice was structured on the basis of severe punishment unless there was complete reparation to the person wronged.

9.   They solved problems on the level where the problem originated. If this was impossible, they went no higher than absolutely necessary to get a remedy. Rarely did problems become escalated to the top leaders for solution.[202]

A SENSE OF MANIFEST DESTINY

It is, without a doubt, a rare and exhilarating sense of opportunity to actually start a new nation. John Adams thought so.

"I always consider the settlement of America with reverence and wonder," he wrote in 1765, "as the opening of a grand scene and design in Providence for the illumination of the ignorant and the emancipation of the slavish part of mankind all over the earth."[203]

Thomas Jefferson expressed his view that the Constitution was "the world's best hope," and in 1801, he predicted that the United States "will be a standing monument and example for the aim and imitation of the people of other countries."[204]

CAN RULER'S LAW BE ABOLISHED?

Alexander Hamilton put the American people on notice that their Constitution had the capacity to change the world:

"It has been frequently remarked that it seems to have been reserved to the people of this country, by their conduct and example, to decide the important question, whether societies of men are really capable or not of establishing good government from reflection and choice, or whether they are forever destined to depend for their political constitutions on accident and force."[205]

---

202   See Skousen, *The Making Of America*, 1985 pp. 41-62.
203   Quoted in Conrad Cherry, *God's New Israel*, 1971, p. 65.
204   Thomas Jefferson, *Writings of Thomas Jefferson*, 10:217, Bergh.
205   The Federalist Papers, No. 1, p. 33.

Socialism in America: In 2012, New Jersey ordered car drivers to put their pets in seat belts or face a fine of up to $1,000. The official reason? Unbuckled Rover or Kitty is "dangerous for the driver ... other drivers ... and that pet."

Hamilton added that if the American people failed in their mission to abolish Ruler's Law, it would serve to "the general misfortune of mankind."[206]

John Adams agreed, saying if the first free people in modern times abandoned the freedom given them in their Constitution, it would be "treason against the hopes of the world."[207]

The Founding Fathers laid an excellent foundation for true freedom and liberty. The very words of the Constitution reveal their labors to institutionalize People's Law as the best alternative to Ruler's Law. They succeeded far better than any of them might have imagined.

---

206   Ibid., p. 33.
207   Koch, *The American Enlightenment*, p. 367.

Benjamin Franklin warned "Only a virtuous people are capable of freedom." Facilitating a shocking trend in the decline of virtue are the abuses of new technologies. In 2012, the hugely popular Facebook was noted as a main facilitator for some form of crime every 40 minutes, ... (cont'd)

CHAPTER 34:

ABOLISHING PILLAR #1: "THE RULER"

B ecause this first pillar of socialism was the strongest, it required the most work to abolish. That's why the Founders carefully wove layers of protections to strike an excellent balance between power and freedom.

In order to remove the despotism of "all power in the ruler," the Founders put two brilliant devices into the Constitution.

❖ **Dilute**: The first device controls the ruling body by spreading political power out among all the people.

❖ **Define**: The second specifies exactly what that ruling body can do—and then it is chained down with laws, checks, and balances.

HOW IS POWER SPREAD OUT?

The idea of spreading out power to keep it under the people's control had ancient roots. Polybius (Greece, 204-122 B.C.) proposed a mixed constitution with political power shared among "the many." He envisioned the ruler being assigned the executive duties of the government. The interests of the nobility or the "established order" would be represented in the Senate. The general population would be represented in the popular Assembly.

Polybius' insight led to the idea of three separate powers, each accountable and dependent on the other two. It was a great idea that unfortunately died when Polybius died.

About 1,800 years later, it was given new life by Baron Charles de Montesquieu (1689-1755) as America's now-famous *Separation of Powers*. Thomas Jefferson explained why this idea was so effective for retaining freedom:

"The way to have good and safe government is not to trust it all to one," Jefferson wrote, "but to divide it among the many, distributing to everyone exactly the functions he is competent to [perform best]. Let the national government be entrusted with the defense of the nation, and its foreign and federal relations; the State governments with the civil rights, laws, police, and adminis-

(cont'd) ... **according to international police reports. Crimes ranged from harassment or intimidation, to stalking, grooming children by pedophiles, bilking people out of money, and murder. For the record, Facebook has also been used very effectively by investigators to catch many such criminals.**

tration of what concerns the State generally; the counties with the local concerns of the counties, and each ward [township] direct the interests within itself.

"It is by dividing and subdividing these republics," Jefferson continued, "from the great national one down through all its subordinations, until it ends in the administration of every man's farm by himself; by placing under everyone what his own eye may superintend, that all will be done for the best."

Jefferson then asks, "What has destroyed liberty and the rights of man in every government which has ever existed under the sun? The generalizing and concentrating all cares and powers into one body, no matter whether of the autocrats of Russia or France, or of the aristocrats of a Venetian senate."[208]

The results of *Separation of Powers* was ingenious. It was a three-headed eagle—executive, legislative, judicial—each watching the others for bad behavior.

❖   **EXECUTIVE**: This is the president, with strong but well-defined powers.

❖   **LEGISLATIVE**: The law-making body was divided into two houses, each watched closely by the other.

The House: 435 congressmen are divided according to population among the many states—the larger the state, the more representatives. Today, each congressman represents about 760,000 people.

The Senate: This "upper house" has two representatives for each state. The Founders gave the state legislatures the responsibility for choosing their two senators. This made the senator beholden to the legislature on a daily basis instead of hiding behind the voters for five years and suddenly appearing for re-election in the sixth year. As Kenneth Ballard explained:

"Before the Seventeenth Amendment, Senators were appointed by the State Legislatures. This kept representation of the people and the States distinct, but it also kept distinct the States themselves by recognizing individual State sovereignty at the federal level."[209] America is a federation of sovereign states.

---

208   Bergh, et al, 14:421.
209   Kenneth Ballard, *Observations*, www.kennethballard.com, June 5, 2010.

Socialism in America: In 2012, Dawn Paulus, 75, displayed three small flags for Memorial Day on the 6th floor balcony of her New Jersey housing project apartment. The official Philipsburg Housing Authority immediately shot over a cease order threatening eviction if the flags were not removed.

❖ **JUDICIARY**: The Supreme Court is appointed to test the validity of the law against the principles of freedom in the Constitution—*not* to interpret or twist the Constitution to meet "changing times." That's what amendments are for.

The lower courts are empowered to resolve all issues unless specifically identified to be handled on a higher level.

❖ **CHECKS AND BALANCES**: The three branches of government stand together and support each other, but guard their responsibilities carefully. If one branch tries to step across the line, the other two branches have power to push it back.

❖ **THE STATE LEGISLATURES**: The idea was that neighbors would vote for neighbors. A state legislator was the first and most easily reached representative of the people. That person carried the will of his or her district or precinct to the state level where issues were presented and voted on. From there, the people's desires were carried to the halls of Congress in Washington, DC, for further action by two senators (until the 17th amendment ruined that chain of representation).

❖ **THE PEOPLE**: The right to elect representatives begins with the individual voter who must be left alone and free to ponder, consider, and make a choice.

TYING DOWN THE POWER

Thomas Jefferson said Americans should view government power with jealousy and suspicion, not confidence. Americans may love their leaders, he observed, but that is no excuse to release them from careful control. The power is the people's, not government's.

"Free government is founded in jealousy, and not in confidence," Jefferson wrote in 1798. "In questions of power, then, let no more be said of confidence in man, but bind him down from mischief by the chains of the Constitution."

WHAT ARE THE CHAINS ON THE PRESIDENT?

The president's job description is written up in Article 2. This section makes it clear the Founders did not want this leader to have power to make law like a king—on a whim.

They gave him six responsibilities: 1—Chief of State, 2—Commander in Chief, 3—Executive over the whole executive branch of government, 4—Chief diplomat in foreign affairs, 5—Chief

"After the collapse of central planning in Eastern Europe and the former U.S.S.R., the only place in the world where Marxists were still thriving was the Harvard political science department."—Peter G. Klein, 2006

architect for needed legislation, and 6—Conscience of the nation in granting pardons and reprieves. (Article 2.2)

The Founders wanted a leader with enough power to act with vigor but not escape accountability. If he or she acted foolishly, they wanted very real and legal punishments available.

The Founders opposed political parties. They saw their corrupting influence in Europe and tried very hard to do without. The system they proposed did a much better job at vetting a presidential candidate. It shut the door on hype and hyperbole, and allowed personal, face-to-face contact by those who did the actual voting. From that came understanding, promises, commitments, and explanations. It was called the Electoral College. See Article 2.1.

❖ **BUILT-IN TERM LIMIT**: The length of term was hotly debated. The Founders wanted the terms long enough so the president wouldn't be wasting all his time fighting for re-election when there was only so much time to get the work done. Seven years was deemed too long, three was too short, so they settled on four.

The Founders decided a president should be rewarded for good service with the chance to be reelected. The elections act as referendums on the president's capacity to govern well. (Article 2.1)

WHAT ARE THE CHAINS ON CONGRESS?

The Founders opposed how Europe wasted the labors of the people with massive welfare projects. In Article 1, they gave the House and Senate power to take care of the nation's general welfare, but drastically shortened the list of things they could do.

WHAT IS "WELFARE"?

Noah Webster's dictionary of 1828 defined *welfare* in the days of the Founders as "exemption from any unusual evil or calamity; the enjoyment of peace and prosperity, or the ordinary blessings of society and civil government."[210] This had nothing to do with public relief, as claimed by tax-hungry bureaucrats in later years.

WHAT IS "GENERAL WELFARE"?

The intent of "general welfare" was clearly a restriction, not a free-for-all blank check. Madison defended that specific list of do's and don'ts as necessary to prevent runaway taxation and spending. In *Federalist* No. 41 he said:

---

210   Noah Webster, *An American Dictionary of the English Language*, 1828.

Self Interest is inborn: "Men always strive for an improvement in their conditions and always will. This is man's inescapable destiny."—Ludwig von Mises

"For what purpose could the enumeration [a numbered list] of particular powers be inserted, if these and all others were meant to be included in the preceding general power?"

Immediately, Congress tried to twist and turn the restrictions and definitions of welfare. They used the opening paragraph of Article 1.8 as the excuse, words they said authorized them to care for the "general welfare." In defense, Madison said that paragraph was an introduction only, and what followed was the actual authority:

"Nothing is more natural nor common than first to use a general phrase, and then to explain and qualify it by a recital of particulars. But the idea of an enumeration of particulars which neither explain nor qualify the general meaning, can have no other effect than to confound and mislead, is an absurdity, ..." (*Federalist* No. 41)

Madison called it an absurd misconstruction to believe that "general welfare" amounted to an "unlimited commission to exercise every power which may be alleged to be necessary for the common defense or general welfare...." (*Federalist* No. 41)

Hamilton said the same thing (using some $5 words to do so):

"This specification of particulars evidently excludes all pretension to a general legislative authority, because an affirmative grant of special powers would be absurd, as well as useless, if a general authority was intended...." (*Federalist* No. 83)

Jefferson observed that if "general welfare" truly meant any taxation for *any* purpose, "it would reduce the whole instrument to a single phrase, that of instituting a Congress with power to do whatever would be for the good of the United States; and, as they would be the sole judges of the good or evil, it would be also a power to do whatever evil they please."[211] Unfortunately, those early controls were eventually eroded away by aggressive presidents and Congresses, and a willing Supreme Court. But in the beginning, the chains were brilliant, well-crafted, and would have kept America out of the trouble it's in today:

---

211 Jefferson's Works, *Official Papers*, Vol. III-I, p. 148. See *Federalist Papers* No. 14 (eighth paragraph), No. 27 (last paragraph), No. 39 (last three paragraphs), No. 45 (ninth paragraph), and the 10th Amendment where all powers not listed in the Constitution revert to the States or the people.

Socialism kills: Leopold II of Belgium swept into the Congo in 1885 to extract sap from rubber plants, ruling the people as his private labor force, compelling obedience with his private army. His atrocities against the people took the lives of 8,000,000 or more—about half the population.

RULE BY LAW, NOT "WHIM"

The House puts forth reasons to raise money for various needs of the country. The Senate may agree or suggest changes. Extracting a tax must be equal for everyone and not graduated as it is today (Article 1.2.3). The use of those taxes is highly restricted—a laundry list of acceptable expenses is written right into Article 1.8.

1. **BORROWING**: Authority to borrow money, and ...

2. **COMMERCE**: to regulate State and Foreign commerce

3. **RULES**: to establish uniform rules of citizenship

4. **FAILURES**: to establish laws regarding bankruptcies

5. **COINAGE**: to coin money and establish its value

6. **STANDARDS**: to fix standards of weights and measures

7. **PUNISHMENTS**: to set the punishment for counterfeiters

8. **MAIL**: To establish post offices

9. **POSTAL ROADS**: to establish roads connecting the post offices, but *not*, Madison said, "a power to construct roads and canals." That job is the responsibility of the states.[212]

10. **INTELLECTUAL PROPERTY**: to promote science and art by protecting copyrights

11. **COURTS**: to organize a court system beneath the Supreme Court

12. **FELONIES**: to set the punishment of certain felony crimes

13. **WAR**: to declare war and set certain rules

14. **DEFENSE—ARMY**: to raise an army

15. **DEFENSE—NAVY**: to raise a navy

16. **RULES OF WAR**: to set rules of military engagement

17. **MILITIA**: to call forth a militia for national security concerns

18. **INTERNAL STRIFE**: to organize, arm and set rules for militia in cooperation with the states

19. **SEAT OF GOVERNMENT**: to exercise legislative authority over Washington DC

---

212 James Madison, *Veto Message, To the House of Representatives of the United States,* March 3, 1817.

Thinking Like A Socialist: In 2012, American actress Amanda Bynes, 26, was arrested twice for driving under the influence. After the second arrest, she appealed ("Tweeted") to Barack Obama to hit back: "Please fire the cop who arrested me."

20. **LAW-MAKING POWER**: to make all laws necessary to carry out these responsibilities.

EXTRA CHAINS JUST TO MAKE SURE

After the list of 20 permissions, the Constitution further controlled the powers of Congress with 14 restrictions and obligations outlined in Article I.9.

1. **ANTI-SLAVERY**: Congress may not interfere with importation of slaves for 20 years, but after that time (1808) it could terminate the slave trade.

2. **ANTI-SLAVERY**: Congress may impose a $10 tax for each immigrant or slave. This was meant to make the importation of slaves more costly.

3. **HABEAS CORPUS**: Congress may not keep a person in jail without cause (writ of habeas corpus).

4. **INNOCENT UNTIL ...:** Congress may not declare a person a criminal without a trial and conviction.

5. **EX POST FACTO**: Congress may not pass laws after an act has occurred that makes that act illegal.

6. **EQUAL TAXES**: Congress may not extract taxes unequally

7. **EQUAL TAXES, Part II**: Congress may not extract direct taxes unequally. These are taxes the business can't cover by raising prices on the goods it sells.

8. **COMMERCE**: Congress may not tax articles that the states export to foreign countries.

9. **TAXES & FEES**: Congress may not tax shipping ports unequally, thereby giving one an advantage over others.

10. **SHIPPING**: Congress may not force ships and boats traveling from one port to another to pay fees or get permission—this was designed to ensure freedom of the coastal seas.

11. **STEALING**: Congress may not take any funds from the Treasury unless the expenditure has been approved by the people's elected representative.

12. **ACCOUNTABILITY**: Congress must publish all receipts and expenditures.

"A major source of objection to a free economy is precisely that it gives people what they want instead of what a particular group thinks they ought to want. Underlying most arguments against the free market is a lack of belief in freedom itself."—Milton Friedman

13. **CASTE SYSTEM**: Congress may not create an upper class, an aristocracy, nobility or privileged class.

14. **BRIBERY**: Members of Congress, and any other office holder in the U.S. government, may not accept gifts or titles of nobility, from foreign governments or agency.

Keeping control of these enumerated powers and preventing them from expanding to become all-inclusive, was the Founders' goal. "If Congress can apply money indefinitely to the general welfare," Madison told Congress, "and are the sole and supreme judges of the general welfare, they may take the care of religion ... education ... schools ... roads ... In short, everything from the highest object of State legislation, down to the most minute object of policy." Madison was prophetic—that's exactly what happened.[213]

WHAT ARE THE CHAINS ON THE STATES?

The Founders learned by sad experience that the Articles of Confederation gave the states far too much power over the federal government, and this prevented the country from making progress. The challenge was to balance the power just right so both governments would function well within their own spheres of influence.

Article 1.10 puts the states under authority of the Constitution and explains what they may do. In addition, Amendments 9 and 10 gave yet one more restriction on the federal level, clarifying that powers not given the federal government defaulted to the states or people themselves.

RULE BY LAW, NOT "WHIM"

❖ **TREATIES**: States may not enter into treaties and alliances.

❖ **BULLYING**: States may not instigate actions or authorize anyone to commit acts that could bring the nation into war (such as issuing letters of marque and reprisal).

❖ **CURRENCY**: States may not coin money or issue credit.

❖ **DEBTS**: States may not pay debts with anything but gold and silver.

❖ **HABEAS CORPUS**: States may not jail someone without a trial and conviction.

---

213 James Madison, remarks, debates on the Cod Fishery Bill, February 7, 1792, p. 429.

Clouded thinking justifies force: "I maintain that the civil authorities are under obligation to compel the people to send their children to school .... If the government can compel such citizens as are fit for military service to bear spear and rifle, to mount ramparts, ..." (cont'd)

◆ **EX POST-FACTO**: States may not pass laws after an act has occurred that makes the act illegal.

◆ **CONTRACTS**: States may not pass laws that undo contracts or make their provisions illegal after such contracts have been agreed upon. For example, neither Congress nor state legislatures can suspend the payment of house mortgages during a depression—that is none of government's authorized business.

◆ **SNOBBERY**: States may not grant titles of nobility.

◆ **COMMERCE**: States may not charge taxes (duties) on imports or exports of other states.

◆ **FAIR FEES**: States must allow Congress to control any import fees charged to offset the costs of inspecting things at the border.

◆ **SHIPPING**: States may not charge fees on ships according to their tonnage (which, of course, varies with each ship), but are required to all charge the same fees.

◆ **MILITIAS**: States may have state militias, but may not keep troops or build up a military—that is the job of Congress.

◆ **WARS**: States may not start a war except for self-defense. For any other purpose, Congress must give its consent.

◆ **ALL OTHER RIGHTS …** States are responsible and obligated to handle everything else not specified in the Constitution—a privilege and right that has been foolishly abrogated and delegated to the whims of Congress.

WHAT ARE THE CHAINS ON THE JUDICIARY?

During the Revolutionary War, the people had no top court to settle squabbles between the states. The Founders realized that some form of new judiciary had to be invented to handle national-level problems.

The Supreme Court was intended to be a third branch of the federal government, an independent branch at that. As will be discussed later, the Court quickly evolved into the last and final word on *anything*, including the actions of the other two "equal" branches. It became the new Ruler.

Jefferson was extremely disturbed with the Court's role as an un-checkable ultimate authority. This, Jefferson warned, would

(cont'd) "... and perform other martial duties in time of war, how much more has it a right to the people to send their children to school, because in this case we are warring with the devil, whose object it is secretly to exhaust our cities and principalities."—Martin Luther, 1524

result in the Court one day twisting and interpreting the Constitution as a means of amending it without due process, simply by reading it this way or that way. "Our peculiar security is in the possession of a written Constitution," Jefferson warned. "Let us not make it a blank paper by construction."[214]

Jefferson suggested an amendment giving power to Congress or the state legislatures to veto Supreme Court decisions, giving the people a remedy when the Court strayed from the Constitution.

JOB DESCRIPTION: Article 3 describes the duties of the Supreme Court and related courts in America.

RULE BY LAW, NOT "WHIM"

⬥ **SUPREMACY**: The judicial power of the U.S. is vested in one Supreme Court and such inferior courts as Congress shall establish.

⬥ **LIFE-LONG**: Judges in the federal courts are appointed for life, provided they serve with "good behavior."

⬥ **SALARIED**: Judges will receive a salary that can't be diminished during their terms.

⬥ **EQUALITY**: The judiciary handles all cases of law and equality. Even thought equality is not guaranteed under the Constitution, it becomes an issue when people are legally taken advantage of, just because they were forced into situations of hardship or misfortune. The federal court system is supposed to look at those cases, too.

⬥ **CONSTITUTIONAL**: The federal courts shall deal with all questions concerning the Constitution.

⬥ **APPEALS**: The federal courts must accept appeals from lower courts when the case involves enforcement or interpretation of U.S. law.

⬥ **TREATIES**: Federal courts are responsible for problems arising from treaties or agreements made with foreign powers.

⬥ **AMBASSADORS**: The delicate legal entanglements of foreign ambassadors and consuls shall be handled only by the federal courts.

⬥ **NON-STATES**: Federal courts handle all cases involving maritime issues outside of a state's jurisdiction (off its coastal waters, for example).

---

214   For an explanation of Jefferson's position, see Skousen, *The Making of America,* p. 576.

❖ **SUING**: The federal courts deal with any lawsuit or legal action involving the U.S. government.

❖ **INTERSTATE**: Problems between the states shall be handled by the federal courts.

❖ **CITIZENS**: Controversies between citizens of different states shall be handled by the federal courts.

❖ **PROPERTIES**: Controversies between citizens in the same state over lands or issues in other states may find a neutral hearing on the federal level.

❖ **FOREIGNERS**: Any individual or states having difficulties with a foreign state or group may have the case heard on the federal level.

❖ **DIPLOMATS**: Top diplomats may have access to the highest court in the land if they run into trouble in America.

❖ **STATES**: If a state is involved in a legal issue, it has the right to be heard by the highest court in the land.

❖ **CASE LOAD**: Congress may limit the number of cases appealed to the Supreme Court so the justices don't get buried in a mountain of trivial issues that should be resolved at the lower levels.

ABOLISHING THE RULER

Forging all the links necessary to chain down federal power includes more than what is listed above. Additional controls can be found interlaced with all other restrictions, responsibilities, and declarations throughout the Constitution. The all-powerful Ruler is prevented from tyranny and kingly dictatorship in the United States, thanks to the chains put down with wisdom and foresight by America's Founding Fathers.

The U.S. spends an average $32 billion a month for interest payments on its national debt.

CHAPTER 35:

ABOLISHING PILLAR #2:
"THE CASTE"

The Founders disrupted the natural tendency toward divisions in society with the creation of a republic.

A republic is a state where power is held by the people, who express their desires and control through elected representatives. This means even the smallest class in society (the individual) has a voice and someone close by to hear it and convey those concerns into the limelight of public consideration.

IT TAKES A FAMILY ... THEN THE VILLAGE

The beginning place for power by the people is first the family, then the village. Jefferson called these little populations *wards*, meaning "watched over."

"These wards, called townships in New England," Jefferson wrote, "are the vital principle of their governments, and have proved themselves the wisest invention ever devised by the wit of man for the perfect exercise of self-government."[215]

Jefferson pointed to this strong local self-control as the means to protect freedom. "The way to have good and safe government is not to trust it all to one, but to divide it among the many ..."[216]

James Madison said that division of power is best made by putting the bulk of the power at the lowest possible levels. "The powers delegated by the proposed Constitution to the federal government are few and defined," Madison wrote. "Those which are to remain in the State governments are numerous and indefinite." (*The Federalist Papers* #45)

THE REPUBLICAN FORM WORKS BEST

Madison explained, "In a democracy the people meet and exercise the government in person; in a republic they assemble and administer it by their representatives and agents. A democracy, consequently, must be confined to a small spot. A republic may be extended over a large region." (*The Federalist Papers* #15)

---

215 Bergh, Writings of Thomas Jefferson, 15:38.
216 Bergh, et al, 14:421.

Adolf Hitler, 1927: "We are socialists, we are enemies of today's capitalistic economic system for the exploitation of the economically weak, with its unfair salaries, with its unseemly evaluation ..." (cont'd)

With the power so disbursed, the various classes cannot usurp political control to create advantages for themselves at the expense of others.

IT'S THE LAW

These concerns were dealt with in Article 3.4: "The United States shall guarantee to every State in this Union a Republican Form of Government ...."

So long as representation exists in every state and community in America, the caste system of a ruling class, an aristocracy, and a working class cannot take root.

NO LOCAL CONTROL: Historian Richard Frothingham pointed out how local control was constantly under attack by monarchs. Regarding England's history of local control, he wrote:

"In the course of events the Crown deprived the body of the people of this power of local rule, and vested it in a small number of persons in each locality, who were called municipal councils, were clothed with the power of filling vacancies in their number, and were thus self-perpetuating bodies. In this way, the ancient freedom of the municipalities was undermined, and the power of the ruling classes was installed in its place. Such was the nature of the local self-government in England, not merely during the period of the planting of her American colonies (1607 to 1732), but for a century later.... It was a noble form robbed of its life-giving spirit."

FAMILIES OF TENS: As mentioned earlier, republicanism or the process of elected representation, was used by Moses. After leading Israel out of Egypt, his father-in-law, Jethro, suggested a way to manage the 2-3 million who followed them into the desert: Divide them into families of 10s, 50s, 100s, 1,000s, and so on, each with a representative.

Some 2,000 years later, the Anglo-Saxons implemented the same pattern among themselves. Thomas Jefferson, Benjamin Franklin, John Adams, and others were students of Anglo-Saxon culture and carried those concepts to the Constitutional Convention. To this day, Americans continue to benefit from the wisdom of that inspired system of management. It helps keep power and responsibility where it belongs: with the people.

(cont'd) "... of a human being according to wealth and property instead of responsibility and performance, and we are all determined to destroy this system under all conditions."

CHAPTER 36:

ABOLISHING PILLAR #3: "ALL IN COMMON"

*Of all the socialistic promises made to lure people into surrendering
their rights, the promise to deliver something they didn't
earn has been the most difficult to eradicate.*

The proper role of government is to ensure equal rights, not
equal things.

At the foundation of all socialist thought is the stated
goal of taking from the "haves" and giving to the "have nots."
The Founders called this "leveling." The fallacious fiction that
equality in things is in some way the same as prosperity is dismissed
out of hand by the lessons learned at Jamestown, Plymouth, and
elsewhere. The Founders were not going to let America fall for that
one again. Said Samuel Adams,

"The utopian schemes of leveling [redistribution of the wealth],
and a community of goods, are as visionary and impracticable
as those which vest all property in the Crown. [These ideas] are
arbitrary, despotic, and, in our government, unconstitutional."[217]

OWNERSHIP NECESSARY FOR LIFE: John Locke (1632-1704)
was a keystone revelator for the Founding Fathers. He brought the
correct perspective to property into the discussion surrounding good
government. Locke pointed out that mankind received the earth as
their common gift, but were expected to improve it.

"God, who hath given the world to men in common," Locke
wrote, "hath also given them reason to make use of it to the best
advantage of life and convenience."

THE FOUR HORSEMEN OF APOCALYPSE: If property rights
did not exist, history demonstrates that four things would take place
that would return mankind to chaos and tyranny.

1.   The incentive to develop property would be destroyed;

2.   The industrious would be deprived of the fruits of their
labors and freedom of choice;

3.   Mobs of the desperate or power-mongering would eventually form and go about confiscating by force whatever they pleased;

---

217   Sam Adams, 1768 letter to Massachusetts's agent in London.

Socialists hate this: "Every step of progress is a change involving heavy risks."—Ludwig von Mises

4. Peoples everywhere would become forced to live on bare subsistence levels because accumulating *anything* would invite attack. It would be a return to the feudal times of old.

"ALL IN COMMON" AND FREEDOM IS NOT POSSIBLE: Locke clarified the importance of property and freedom. He drew from the Bible, saying the Creator's command to have "dominion" and to "subdue" the earth required control and exclusiveness:

❖ All property lawfully acquired and developed is an extension of that person's life, energy, and ingenuity.

❖ To destroy or confiscate another person's property is an attack on the life of that very person.

❖ "Every man has a property in his own person," Locke said.

❖ Whatever a person removes out of nature and mixes with his own labor thereby makes it his property: "It is allowed to be his goods who hath bestowed his labor upon it, though, before, it was the common right of everyone," Locke said. For example, a man comes upon a tree in the wild. He turns it into lumber, makes a table and chair, and sells them. It is his labor that made the tree of value in the marketplace, and by natural law he can't be deprived of his labors and property except with fair compensation.[218]

❖ "The supreme power cannot take from any man any part of his property without his own consent," Locke said. "For the preservation of property being the end of government, and that for which men enter into society, it necessarily supposes and requires that the people should have property, without which they must be supposed to lose that [property] by entering into society, which was the end for which they entered into it."[219]

THE RIGHT TO PROPERTY: Justice George Sutherland of the U.S. Supreme Court once made an important distinction about property rights that reflected the Founding Fathers' position:

"It is not the right *of* property which is protected, but the right *to* property," he said in a speech given in 1921. "Property, per se, has no rights; but the individual, the man, has three great rights, equally sacred from arbitrary interference: the right to his *life*, the right to his *liberty*, the right to his *property*... The three rights are so bound

218 John Locke, Second Treatise of Civil Government, Chapter 5, section 30.
219 John Locke, ibid., Chapter 11, section 138.

When survival is threatened, a socialist government always gives up a fundamental principle of socialism: China, Soviet Russia, North Korea, Vietnam, et al, adopted levels of limited free market trade; Stalin halted religious persecution during World War II; the EU imposed austerity (cuts), etc.

together as to be essentially one right. To give a man his *life* but deny him his *liberty*, is to take from him all that makes his life worth living. To give him his liberty but take from him the property which is the fruit and badge of his liberty, is to still leave him a slave."

PROPERTY RIGHTS NECESSARY TO FREEDOM

John Adams made it clear that the right to property was the most important foundation stone for liberty.

"The moment the idea is admitted into society that property is not as sacred as the laws of God, and that there is not a force of law and public justice to protect it, anarchy and tyranny commence. *Property must be secured or liberty cannot exist.*"[220]

James Madison said the same thing in his Essay on Property (1792) where he rejected all excessive spending and future raids on the U.S. people and treasury in the form of taxation:

"Government is instituted to protect property of every sort.... This being the end of government, that alone is not a just government, ... nor is property secure under it, where the property which a man has in his personal safety and personal liberty is violated by arbitrary seizures of one class of citizens for the service of the rest."

And from these building blocks of freedom came these declarations inside the Constitution and Bill of Rights:

◆ **INTELLECTUAL PROPERTY**: "To promote the Progress of Science and useful Arts, by securing for limited Times to Authors and Inventors the exclusive Right to their respective Writings and Discoveries." (Article 1.8)

◆ **EQUAL TAXATION (PROPERTY)**: "... Direct Taxes shall be apportioned among the several States ... according to their respective Numbers ...." (Article 1.2.3)

◆ **TAKING TAXES (PROPERTY)**: "No Capitation, or other direct Taxes shall be laid, unless in Proportion to the Census or Enumeration herein before directed to be taken." (Article 1.9)

◆ **PROPERTY RIGHTS**: "...Nor shall private property be taken for public use without just compensation." (5th Amendment)

◆ **SEIZURE OF PROPERTY**: "The right of the people to be secure ... against unreasonable searches and seizures, shall not be violated ..." (6th Amendment)

---

220   John Adams, Works, 6:8-9.

"Destroy the family, you destroy the country."—Vladimir Lenin

ABOLISHING PILLAR #4: "ALL THINGS REGULATED"

T he attempt to regulate the market to achieve prosperity has proved a consistent failure. Regulating freedoms simply doesn't work, and each attempt to do so always backfires. The Founders clearly understood that when they gathered in 1787 to talk about how to balance power and freedom.

To abolish the abuse of regulatory powers, the Founders gave the new American government a very simple chore: protect the freedom to fail.

Allowing for equal failure meant certain rules of fairness had to be enforced—no monopolies, no fraud, no collusion, no restrictions of trade or access, no artificial limits or subsidies, no violation of free trade and competition, no violation of personal rights.

If the government ever found itself getting in the way of any enterprise falling flat on its face, that was proof positive the government had overstepped its bounds.

GEORGE WASHINGTON SAID: "Let vigorous measures be adopted; not to limit the prices of articles, for this I believe is inconsistent with the very nature of things, and impracticable in itself, but to punish speculators, forestallers, and extortioners, and above all to sink the money by heavy taxes. To promote public and private economy; encourage manufacturers, etc."[221]

To chain down the government from encroaching on regulating commercial activities, the Founders wrote this into the Constitution:

❖ **FOREIGN COMMERCE**: "The Congress shall have Power ... To regulate Commerce with foreign Nations..." (Article 1.8.2). This gave the Congress the right to represent the American people in regulating commerce with other nations.

❖ **INTERSTATE COMMERCE**: "...and [to regulate commerce]

---

221   Letter from George Washington to James Warren, in Massachusetts, March 31, 1779.

among the several States..." (Article 1.8.2). This gave Congress the right to create a common market of free trade between all the states and regulate interstate commerce of all kinds.

When these responsibilities were drafted, the emphasis was on the commerce—to prevent the states from trying to gain advantages over each other by interfering in the fair exchange of goods across state lines.

The government is further restricted from regulating American's lives with:

✦ **THE BILL OF RIGHTS** (Amendments 1-10): These ten amendments spell out several aspects of personal and commercial life that may not be interfered with or regulated by the government.

✦ **THE ENUMERATED POWERS (Article 1.8)**: The laundry list of activities for which Congress may tax the people and otherwise regulate their lives is limited to just those things enumerated and no others.

✦ **ADDITIONAL CHAINS**: Article I, Sections 9 and 10, put additional restrictions on the government's proclivity to regulate. Fairness is made a matter of constitutional mandate, and there are strong distinguishing separations between federal responsibilities and State powers.

So long as the American people could keep their national government chained down, there would be no fear of the government agency heads regulating aspects of American lives for which they should have no power.

LASTLY: If there was ever any doubt about the powers of regulation, the Founders included the tenth Amendment to the Constitution:

"The powers not delegated to the United States by the Constitution, nor prohibited by it to the States, are reserved to the States respectively, or to the people." (Amendment 10)

It is very clear—unless the federal government was granted specific powers of regulation, it's the States' job to do the regulation (for example, capital punishment, gay marriage, unions, guns, abortion, immigration reform, speed limits, etc.).

"The true foundation of republican government is the equal right of every citizen, in his person and property, and in their management ..."—Thomas Jefferson

CHAPTER 38:

ABOLISHING PILLAR #5: "FORCE"

The failure of the Articles of Confederation taught the Founders an important lesson: authority without sufficient power of force is no authority at all.

For the Founders, the critical question of the day was, *how much force should be granted so the ruling power doesn't grow into another ruling monarchy?*

THE KEY WAS "WE THE PEOPLE"

Putting reins on the power, having it emanate from the people themselves, was how the Founders intended to keep control of "force." This wholly unique invention was designed to tolerate only definite and limited powers. As James Madison wrote[222]:

"The powers delegated by the proposed Constitution to the federal government are few and defined. Those which are to remain in the State governments are numerous and indefinite."

It was a common-sense choice. Generally speaking, Madison said the federal government was responsible for the *whole* and the *outside*, and the States were responsible for the *individual* issues on the *inside*.

"The former," Madison continued, "will be exercised principally on external objects, as war, peace, negotiation, and foreign commerce ... The powers reserved to the several States will extend to all the objects which, in the ordinary course of affairs, concern the lives, liberties, and properties of the people, and the internal order, improvement, and prosperity of the State."

A NATION OF LAWS, NOT MEN

It wasn't enough to declare restraints and responsibilities. The Founders wanted a written law controlled by the people, under which all government power was required to perform and otherwise required to be restrained, according to the Constitution.

---

222   All Madison quotes on these two pages are from The Federalist Papers, #45.

Socialism (force) in religion costs lives: In 2011, the ongoing trend of honor killings, primarily women, reached a new his in Pakistan with 943 reported murders of women and girls killed for defaming their family's honor. In 2010, the murdered numbered 791.

DOUBTS REMAINED

Even with their very best efforts to forge all the necessary chains around government finally talked out and described as cleanly as thought possible, there remained doubts about unseen loopholes.

As a double-safety net, they added these interesting and well-crafted words: "The enumeration in the Constitution of certain rights shall not be construed to deny or disparage others retained by the people." (Amendment 9)

This passage is an expression of ultimate distrust of government—that it will corrupt, usurp, and creep into realms where it doesn't belong. To this was added: "The powers not delegated to the United States by the Constitution, nor prohibited by it to the States, are reserved to the States respectively, or to the people." (Amendment 10)

If ever there was conflict over power and rights, the Founders wanted the default resolution to point *away* from the centers of power and into the control of the individuals. Their systems of checks and balances were meant to encourage the flow of force to the lowest logical level.

"This balance between the national and state governments," Alexander Hamilton wrote, "ought to be dwelt on with peculiar attention, as it is of the utmost importance. It forms a double security to the people. If one encroaches on their rights, they will find a powerful protection in the other. Indeed, they will both be prevented from over-passing their constitutional limits, by certain rivalship which will ever subsist between them."[223]

And lastly, James Madison laid his axe at the root of the problem and foreshadowed America's greatest threat: "I believe there are more instances of the abridgement of the freedom of the people by gradual and silent encroachments of those in power, than by violent and sudden usurpations.... This danger ought to be wisely guarded against."[224]

As shall be seen a little later, the "gradual and silent encroach-ments of those in power" is precisely what eventually started to unfold. Today, that crafty invasion is burying Americans in a pit of destroyed culture, lost freedoms, and a mountain of obligations approaching 100 *trillion* dollars.

---

223   Alexander Hamilton, speech at the New York Ratifying Convention, June 17, 1788.
224   James Madison, speech at the Virginia Ratifying Convention,, June 6, 1788.

"Can the liberties of a nation be thought secure when we have removed their only firm basis, a conviction in the minds of the people that these liberties are of the gift of God? That they are not to be violated but with his wrath?"—Thomas Jefferson

CHAPTER 39:

ABOLISHING PILLAR #6: "INFORMATION CONTROL"

Among the seven pillars of socialism, controlling information is the next most powerful tool after raw force. Information control is necessary to keep a dictator in power. Even if conditions are bad, the illusion of stability will keep the people under control because a natural human trait is to put up with bad things so long as hope and change are on the horizon.

Jefferson made that very point in the Declaration of Independence: "... all Experience hath shewn, that Mankind are more disposed to suffer, while Evils are sufferable, than to right themselves by abolishing the Forms to which they are accustomed."

He continued, saying that when the abuses become intolerable, "it is their right, it is their duty, to throw off such Government, and to provide new Guards for their future security."

Throwing off the old tyranny and installing new guards with the Constitution included unhampered information flow.

ABOLISHING INFORMATION CONTROL

America's founding documents include several statements enforcing freedom of information and government transparency.

❖ **FREEDOM TO BELIEVE AS YOU WISH**: "Congress shall make no law respecting an establishment of religion, or prohibiting the free exercise thereof; ..." (Amendment 1)

❖ **FREEDOM TO EXPRESS OPINIONS**: "...or abridging the freedom of speech, ..." (Amendment I)

❖ **FREEDOM TO PRINT WHAT YOU WANT**: "... or of the press, ..." (Amendment I)

❖ **FREEDOM TO ASSOCIATE**: "... or the right of the people peaceably to assemble, ..." (Amendment I)

❖ **FREEDOM TO COMPLAIN**: "...and to petition the Government for a redress of grievances." (Amendment I)

The Founders also insisted the activities of the nation be open for scrutiny. Among their requirements for openness are:

❖ **RESPONSIBILITY TO REPORT**: "Each House shall keep a Journal of its Proceedings, and from time to time publish the same..." (Article 1.5.3)

❖ **STATE OF THE UNION**: The President "shall from time to time give to the Congress Information of the State of the Union ..." (Article 2.3.1)

REVERSING THE TREND TOWARD IGNORANCE

Cultivating a culture of ignorance helps the grip of socialism tighten. As long as the people don't know what's going on around them, so long as they are fed and housed and entertained, those in charge feel more free to do as they please. Preventing parents from teaching their children, abolishing Bible study, regulating what can be spoken and taught, controlling the media's bias to one side or the other, these and all other inhibitors of the free flow of information keep people ignorant.

NORTHWEST ORDINANCE

The very year the Constitution was written (1787) the Founders' intention of spreading information was codified as a pre-requisite for statehood: "Religion, morality, and knowledge, being necessary to good government and the happiness of mankind, schools and the means of education shall forever be encouraged." (Northwest Ordinance, 1787, Article 3)

TOP SECRET CODE WORD

There are some exceptions to the free flow of information, such as activities necessary for national security. Elected representatives have oversight responsibility on intelligence committees to keep an eye on U.S. government activities. Unfortunately, moles, spies and reckless comments by self-enamored politicians for personal gain have cost this nation untold billions of dollars and thousands of lives in lost advantages and increased risks by spilling the beans on classified information.

MANIPULATING MONEY

Another tool of information control comes from changing a nation's medium of currency from actual gold and silver to paper notes that cannot be cashed in for gold or silver. Once a baseless paper is admitted into circulation, it may be inflated and traded without the natural controls of the marketplace, and without the knowledge of the people—it is an insidious and powerful form of information control.

George Washington advised, "We should avoid ... the depreciation of our currency; but I conceive this end would be answered, as far as might be necessary, by stipulating that all money payments should be made in gold and silver, being the common medium of commerce among nations."[225]

Thomas Jefferson saw oppressive power in the control of money that was not based on gold. The following quote is attributed to Jefferson, but some believe it is a combination of his statements. Either way, it is a prophetic: "If the American people ever allow the banks to control the issuance of their currency, first by inflation and then by deflation, the banks and corporations that will grow up around them will deprive the people of all property until their children will wake up homeless on the continent their fathers occupied. The issuing power of money should be taken from the banks and restored to Congress and the people to whom it belongs."[226]

Restoration of control that Jefferson promoted meant keeping money tied to gold and silver reserves on hand.

"We are overdone with banking institutions," Jefferson wrote toward the end of his life, "which have banished the precious metals, and substituted a more fluctuating and unsafe medium... These have withdrawn capital from useful improvements and employments to nourish idleness... [These] are evils more easily to be deplored than remedied." (*The Writings of Thomas Jefferson*, Vol. 12, p. 379.)

A free market is best at conveying accurate economic information. Each dollar spent is a vote for or against products they purchase. Such exchanges convey volumes of information about the worth of products, if supply is meeting demand, and where opportunities for profit-making investments can be found. Once the government intervenes to remove the precious metal backing from the dollar, the people have nothing but faith in which to assume their dollar's true value. All that glitters is not gold—sometimes it's the vapidness of the government's brave smile.

---

225   *The Writings of George Washington*, Volume 6, page 461, G.P. Putnam' Sons, 1890.
226   For a discussion on the origins of the quote, see www.wikiquote.org, "Talk: Thomas Jefferson."

A 160-page book, "A Gift for Muslim Couple," by Hazrat Maulana Ashraf Ali Thanvi (2010), says a husband my beat his wife "by hand or stick" or "pull by the ears" if she doesn't obey him. Muslim wives are not to "leave his house without his permission." The book sold out in Toronto in 2012.

CHAPTER 40:
ABOLISHING PILLAR #7: "NO NATURAL RIGHTS"

At the very heart of tyranny is the demand that only the ruler can declare rights and permissions. In the real world, nothing could be further from the truth.

By the time the Founding Fathers completed the Constitution and its Bill of Rights, they had sufficiently defined *natural rights* so they could be protected within the strong fortress of the Constitution. That sifting process was difficult. One of the teachers who guided them along the way was a man named Cicero.

CICERO (106-43 B.C.) was a Roman statesman, lawyer and constitutionalist. His excellent understanding of natural law laid the foundation for protecting natural rights, a breakthrough to which Thomas Jefferson was particular attracted.

Cicero lived in pagan Rome. It was unusual in that society to find a man speaking of a one true God, but so declared Cicero. He made his reliance upon and advocacy of God the center of his political philosophy. He taught:

❖ **GOD EXISTS**: God is the Creator, and man shares with Him the divine gift of reason.

❖ **REASON**: Not just any reason, but *right reason*. Right reason is law, therefore man must have law in common with God.

❖ **LAW**: True law is right reason in agreement with nature.

❖ **JUSTICE**: Those who share reason and law must also share justice.

❖ **ETERNAL**: It is a sin to alter this law or repeal any part of it— in fact, "it is impossible to abolish it entirely," Cicero said.

❖ **SELF-EVIDENT**: Everyone knows instinctively this natural law: "We need not look outside ourselves for an expounder or interpreter of it."

❖ **NATURAL LAW IS CONSISTENT**: "There will not be dif-

"Every successful revolution puts on in time the robes of the tyrant it has deposed."
—Barbara Tuchman

ferent laws at Rome and Athens, or different laws now and in the future," he said. "But one eternal and unchangeable law that will be valid for all nations and all times, and there will be one master and ruler, that is God...."

With the foundation of Natural Law from which to work, the Founders built a structure to delineate and protect natural rights from abuses. Here is a sampling from the Founding Documents:

DECLARATION OF INDEPENDENCE

❖ **EQUALITY:** All people are born with "the separate and equal station to which the Laws of Nature and of Nature's God entitle them..."

❖ **CREATED EQUAL:** "We hold these truths to be self-evident, that all men are created equal, that they are endowed by their Creator with certain unalienable Rights, that among these are Life, Liberty and the pursuit of Happiness."

❖ **GOVERNMENT DIDN'T INVENT RIGHTS**: "That to *secure* these rights, Governments are instituted among Men, deriving their just powers from the consent of the governed."

❖ **NATURAL RIGHT TO BE FREE**: "...it is the Right of the People to alter or to abolish [destructive government], and to institute new Government..."

❖ **NATURAL RIGHT TO FORM GOVERNMENTS**: "...it is their right, it is their duty, to throw off such Government, and to provide new Guards for their future security."

❖ **NATURAL RIGHT TO CONTROL DESTINY**: "...and that as Free and Independent States, they have full Power to levy War, conclude Peace, contract Alliances, establish Commerce, and to do all other Acts and Things which Independent States may of right do."

CONSTITUTION OF THE
UNITED STATES OF AMERICA

The Constitution is a very thorough declaration of natural rights from its opening preamble to its conclusion. At least 286 rights are specified (for the complete list see *The Making of America*, by W. Cleon Skousen).

"Poverty has no causes. Only prosperity has causes ... Poverty can be overcome only if the relevant economic processes are in motion."—Economist Jane Jacobs

The people feared, however, that since England's King George was so lax in his interpretation of natural rights, they should make a specific list of natural rights so there would be no question.

THE PROBLEM OF LISTED RIGHTS

Alexander Hamilton didn't like a list of specific ideas. In Federalist Papers No. 84, he points out that the federal government had only 20 specific enumerated powers—nothing more. "I go further and affirm that bills of rights, in the sense and to the extent in which they are contended for, are not only unnecessary in the proposed Constitution but would even be dangerous. They would contain various exceptions to powers which are not granted; and, on this very account, would afford a colorable pretext to claim more than were granted. For why declare that things shall not be done which there is no power to do? Why, for instance, should it be said that the liberty of the press shall not be restrained, when no power is given by which restrictions be imposed?"[227]

George Washington and others had to give personal assurances that if the states would accept the Constitution as is, Congress would accept suggestions to improve it—including a Bill of Rights. The states submitted 189 amendments that James Madison boiled down to 17. Congress approved only 12, and the states ratified only 10—today's Bill of Rights.

THE BILL OF RIGHTS

The Bill of Rights comprises the first ten amendments to the Constitution. Their stated purpose is laid out in the preamble, "... the States ... expressed a desire, in order to prevent misconstruction or abuse of its powers, that further declaratory and restrictive clauses should be added ...," and thereby provided these 27 protections of individual rights:

1. **RELIGION**: Congress may not interfere in the free exercise of religion.

2. **SPEECH & PRESS**: Congress may not interfere in the free exercise of speech and the press.

3. **ASSEMBLY**: Congress may not interfere in the right of the people to peaceably assemble.

---

227   The Federalist Papers, No. 84: Hamilton.

In 2011, at least 943 women and girls were murdered in Pakistan in "honor killings" For defaming their family's honor. The toll was 791 in 2010. Police dismiss the murders as "private family affairs."

4. **PETITION**: Congress may not interfere in the right of the people to petition the Government for a redress of grievances.

5. **ARMS**: The people may possess arms without interference from the government.

6. **SOLDIERS**: The people will not be forced to house the military except as the people's representatives describe it according to law.

7. **PRIVACY**: The people have the right to the privacy of their homes, their businesses, and all their private papers and effects.

8. **SEARCH AND SEIZURE**: The people have the right to be free from unreasonable searches and seizures.

9. **WARRANTS**: The people may not be arrested without a properly issued warrant.

10. **ACCUSED**: People accused of a felony do not need to answer for it unless a formal charge is brought against them that has been heard by a grand jury and formal charges issued.

11. **MILITARY CRIME**: Military personnel charged with crimes may be tried by a civilian court except during times of war.

12. **DOUBLE JEOPARDY**: An individual passing through the criminal trial process is free of any additional prosecution for that same crime.

13. **SELF-INCRIMINATION**: People may not be forced to testify against themselves in court unless they freely choose to do so.

14. **DUE PROCESS**: People may not be deprived of life, liberty or property without due process of law.

15. **PROPERTY**: Private property may not be taken without just compensation.

16. **TRIALS**: The accused shall enjoy the right to a speedy, fair and public trial in the state and district where the crime was committed.

17. **ARBITRARY EXCUSES**: The accused has the right to have explained the nature of the crime of which he is accused.

Unconstitutional: In 2012, Barack Obama bypassed Congress and unilaterally declared that children of illegal immigrants would no longer be deported. While Article 2.2 does give the president power to grant pardons and reprieves, that is for individual cases. He may not make a blanket law, which is the Legislative's duty. Article 1.8.4 is clear: The job of Congress is "To establish an uniform Rule of Naturalization."

18. **WITNESSES**: The accused has the right to confront witnesses brought against him.

19. **POVERTY**: The accused will be provided the means to obtain witnesses in his favor using the compulsory powers of the court.

20. **DEFENSE**: The accused has the right to a defense attorney whether he can afford it or not.

21. **CIVIL CASES**: The accused in a civil case has the same right to trial by jury as does an accused in a criminal case, provided the suit involves $20 or more.

22. **APPEALS**: The facts of a case may not be altered, added to, or adjusted during the appeal process.

23. **BAIL**: The accused of a bailable crime will be released without providing a bail that would be considered excessive and unreasonable.

24. **FINES**: The convicted has the right to penalties that are reasonable and not excessive.

25. **PUNISHMENT**: The convicted will not suffer cruel or unusual punishment.

26. **ALL RIGHTS NOT MENTIONED** ... Americans may claim any and all rights that belong to them whether or not they are listed in the Constitution.

27. **ALL POWERS NOT DELEGATED** ... Americans and their sovereign states retain all powers not delegated to the federal government.

IT'S ALL ABOUT RIGHTS

The important distinction between the U.S. Constitution and other forms of government is that natural rights are not presumed to be invented by government, but instead are declared pre-existing and therefore receive *protection* by government. The great modern clash between socialistic governments and freedom always points back to this fundamental part of human creation. Cicero said it best:

"The animal which we call man, endowed with foresight and quick intelligence, complex, keen, possessing memory, full of reason and prudence, has been given a certain distinguished status by the Supreme God who created him; for his is the only one among so many different kinds and varieties of living beings who has a share in reason and thought, while all the rest are deprived of it. But what is more divine, I will not say in man only, but in all heaven and earth, than reason? And reason, when it is full grown and perfected, is rightly called wisdom. Therefore, since there is nothing better than reason, and since it exists both in man and God, the first common possession of man and God is reason.

"But those who have reason in common must also have *right reason* in common. And since right reason is law we must believe that men have Law also in common with the gods. Further, those who share law must also share Justice; and those who share these are to be regarded as members of the same commonwealth. If indeed they obey the same authorities and powers, this is true in a far greater degree; but as a matter of fact they do obey this celestial system, the divine mind, and the God of transcendent power. Hence we must now conceive of this whole universe as one commonwealth of which both gods and men are members."[228]

CICERO ALSO WROTE:

"True law is *right reason* in agreement with nature. It is of universal application, unchanging and everlasting."[229]

"God ... is the author of this law, its promulgator, and its enforcing judge. ...Whoever is disobedient is fleeing from himself and denying his human nature, and by reason of this very fact he will suffer the worst punishment."[230]

LEARNING TO RECOGNIZE SOCIALISM

The "Miracle" that stopped socialism was brilliant—and it worked. All seven pillars of socialism were handily dealt with, but the Founders knew this would survive only if the people wanted it.

NO RULER: The executive was locked down so he couldn't become a king and declare edicts on a whim. So long as Congress and the Court could reign him in, the president had little authority except to manage the government and make the hard decisions.

---

228   Alan O. Ebenstein, *Great Political Thinkers*, p. 134.
229   Ibid., p. 133.
230   Ibid.

(cont'd) ... cable TV (63.7%), cell phones (54.5%), a computer (38.2%), 2 or more cars (33%), 2 or more TVs (32.2%), a dishwasher (25%). Money spent to eradicate poverty since 1965: $16 trillion.

NO CASTE: Classes and casts among the populous could not develop because the Constitution gave each individual a raw chance at freedom, and the responsibility to bear the full weight of their own choices, their own industry, and their own ability to make opportunities where none existed.

When a people knows their salvation rests in their own hands, history proves they are more apt to labor their way out of difficulties. The American system promoted that to everyone's advantage.

NO THINGS IN COMMON: Things in common, or the effort to level the producers and the consumers was outlawed by both culture and the Constitution. Taking a handout was once humbling proof of failure or laziness, and made anathema. But failure also allowed true human compassion to rise to the challenge.

The Constitution wisely prevented such help from eating up the labors of the people by becoming an issue of taxation or national responsibility.

MINIMAL REGULATION: The constipating drag on prosperity that over-regulation creates was carefully guarded against. Government was denied the power to shadow every human action and manipulate it toward some national goal.

It was every man and woman for themselves—the pioneering spirit that broke the land in Jamestown, Plymouth, Oregon, Utah, the prairie, the mountains, the rivers and streams. The best government is small government, and American prosperity proved the adage true.

BALANCED FORCE: Force was held down to just the minimum necessary to meet national goals. The proper role of government was enshrined with chains and guards so it remained the servant of the people instead of vice-a-versa. Unrestrained prosperity grew beyond anyone's imaginations.

FREE FLOWING INFORMATION: The free flow of information promotes prosperity, it is the key to wealth. With a free press, free association, and a money based on sound value of precious metals, the flow of information lifted the American body and soul to heights of achievement and satisfaction unlike ever in the history of mankind.

The Fisher Space Pen will write in zero gravity, underwater, on wet or greasy paper, at any angle, and at extreme temperatures. It was privately invented in 1965 and sold to NASA.

NATURAL RIGHTS: The Constitution did not create any rights, it only defined those already existing and put arms of protection around them. The Founders built their model government on the simple premise that a national government should have no more rights than those of any individual. The individuals may delegate rights, but the government may not take them.

Upon that simple formula was the greatest nation in the history of the world scratched out of the prairie sod and coastal swamps to become a land littered with light, growth, and peace. It was indeed the miracle that stopped socialism.

* * * * *

THE CONSTITUTION IS A LIST OF RESTRAINTS, NOT A BLANK CHECK

"The plan of the convention," Alexander Hamilton wrote, "declares that the power of Congress, or, in other words, of the national legislature, shall extend to certain enumerated [listed by number] cases. This specification of particulars evidently excludes all pretension to a general legislative authority, because an affirmative grant of special powers would be absurd, as well as useless, if a general authority was intended."[231]

---

231   Alexander Hamilton, *The Federalist Papers*, #83.

"When plunder becomes a way of life for a group of men in a society, over the course of time they create for themselves a legal system that authorizes it and a moral code that glorifies it."
—Frederic Bastiat

CHAPTER 41:

DOES IT WORK?

Did the U.S. Constitution work? Here is one of countless millions of ideas that proves the workings of the phenomenon of free choice.

In 1945, one of the hottest-selling gadgets at Gimbels in New York City was the first-ever ball-point pen. It was bragged about as a "fantastic ... miraculous fountain pen guaranteed to write for two years without refilling." More than 5,000 people jammed the store that day and snatched up the entire supply of 10,000 pens, paying $12.50 apiece—that's $145 in today's dollars.

The ingenious invention of a loose ball set in a socket that smeared ink on paper was not new. The idea had been around since 1888, but it was Laszlo Jozsef Biro, a Hungarian refugee, who first brought it to market.

The Milton Reynolds Company grabbed Biro's idea, developed it, and struck gold. For the first time in history there was a viable solution to the maddening frustration of charcoal pencils or quill pens with all their spilled ink, blotting, and smearing that these ancient tools brought to the art of written communications.

And everybody wanted one. That's when America's amazing free market took over.

Competing companies saw the popularity of the ball-point pen and started working on their own designs.

By the 1950s, inventors discovered a better ink so people could hold the pen at an angle, upside down, or even in water, and it still worked.

Another company made it retractable. With just a click, the ball point disappeared inside so ink wouldn't leak all over someone's shirt. Others invented clips to hold it in a pocket.

One company boasted that their ink would not stain clothing, and sent salesmen into offices to write all over the shirt of the boss. If the ink didn't wash out, they would provide a more expensive shirt. But the ink *did* wash out—each and every time. The company made a fortune.

What did all these new features do to the price of pens? Instead of making them more expensive, the competition forced the prices

In 2012, there were only four socialist republic nations (one- or multi-party nations that vote for socialism), down from 22 before 1958: Republic of India, Democratic People's Republic of Korea, Democratic Socialist Republic of Sri Lanka, United Republic of Tanzania.

down—and the quality up. Companies all over the world began manufacturing their brand of a better pen in hopes of cornering the lucrative market. By 1952, a ball-point pen could be purchased in almost any store in America for only 19 cents.

By 1964, annual sales topped $80 million with nearly a billion pens sold worldwide.

In 2005, the Bic pen company sold its one-hundred-billionth pen (that's 100,000,000,000). That's enough pens to draw a line from Earth to Pluto and back, 33 times.

The story of the ballpoint pen is a wonderful example of how freedom in America works. No one forced Mr. Biro to invent his pen, and no one forced Milton Reynolds to market it. Nobody forced anybody to make it better. Every individual involved did it for one reason: to make millions.

They tried different ideas, they lowered the price, they advertised—anything to lure dollars away from competitors and into their own pockets.

For the consumer, all the competition and fighting was delightful. Pens were invented and re-invented, improved, and made cheaper, and as prices fell their availability went up.

Along the way many inventors and marketers succeeded, and others failed. But everyone benefitted. At first, only the well-to-do could afford the ball-point pen, but over time, everyone could get one, rich and poor alike. Predictably, the tide of freedom lifted all boats. That's how the free market works. It makes life better for the greatest number of people at the lowest possible cost.

Are there still $12.50 ballpoint pens out there? Indeed there are. In fact, there are some designer pens that sell for thousands of dollars—many of those are just flamboyant gimmicks flaunted for attention—but inside, the ink, the roller ball, and the technology are essentially the same ideas at work.

The final fruit of that remarkable combine of energy is this: If you happen to know a good insurance salesman, you can get a pocket-clipping, ink-safe, button-clicking, non-leaking, long-lasting gravity-defying amazing ball-point pen for absolutely free.

And that's how *freedom to choose* works in America.

Does Socialism lead to Communism? "The two Russian revolutions of 1917 are the classic example of the impossibility of maintaining a social democratic position against determined communist pressure ... the communists could not have come to power if the social democrats had not first paved the way."—Ivor Thomas, 1951

CHAPTER 42:

FOUNDING FATHERS SPEAK ON SOCIALISM

Socialism is unconstitutional.

T he Founders did everything they could to preserve choice and make socialism, communism and any other scheme of leveling, clearly and unquestionably unconstitutional.

SOCIALISM IS UNCONSTITUTIONAL

Sam Adams: "The Utopian schemes of leveling and a community of goods, are as visionary and impractical as those ideas which vest all property in the Crown ... [these ideas] are arbitrary, despotic, and in our government, unconstitutional."[232]

SOCIALISM IS THEFT

Thomas Jefferson: "To take from one, because it is thought his own industry and that of his fathers has acquired too much, in order to spare to others, who, or whose fathers, have not exercised equal industry and skill, is to violate arbitrarily the first principle of association, the guarantee to everyone the free exercise of his industry and the fruits acquired by it."[233]

SOCIALISM ERASES PROPERTY RIGHTS

John Adams: "The moment the idea is admitted into society that property is not as sacred as the laws of God, and that there is not a force of law and public justice to protect it, anarchy and tyranny commence. If 'Thou shalt not covet' and 'Thou shalt not steal' were not commandments of Heaven, they must be made inviolable precepts in every society before it can be civilized or made free."[234]

SOCIALISM DESTROYS PROFIT

Thomas Jefferson: "A wise and frugal government... shall restrain men from injuring one another, shall leave them otherwise free to regulate their own pursuits of industry and improvement, and shall not take from the mouth of labor the bread it has earned. This is the sum of good government."[235]

---

232 Sam Adams, 1768 letter to Massachusetts's agent in London.
233 Thomas Jefferson, letter to Joseph Milligan, April 6, 1816.
234 John Adams, *A Defense of the Constitutions of Government of the United States of America*, 1787.
235 Thomas Jefferson, First Inaugural Address, March 4, 1801.

"A liberal is a person whose interests aren't at stake at the moment."—Willis Player

SOCIALISM STOPS PROGRESS

Thomas Jefferson: "I predict future happiness for Americans if they can prevent the government from wasting the labors of the people under the pretense of taking care of them."[236]

ARTICLE 1.8 PREVENTS SOCIALISM

Thomas Jefferson: "Congress has not unlimited powers to provide for the general welfare, but only those specifically enumerated."[237]

ARTICLE 1.8 PREVENTS SOCIALISM

James Madison: "With respect to the two words 'general welfare,' I have always regarded them as qualified by the detail of powers connected with them. To take them in a literal and unlimited sense would be a metamorphosis of the Constitution into a character which there is a host of proofs was not contemplated by its creators." [238]

SOCIALISM BENEFITS ONLY A FEW

James Madison: In 1794, Congress appropriated $15,000 for relief of French refugees coming to America. James Madison objected, saying, "I cannot undertake to lay my finger on that Article of the Constitution which granted a right to Congress of expending, on objects of benevolence, the money of their constituents."[239]

SOCIALISM IS FORCED WELFARE

James Madison: "The government of the United States is a definite government, confined to specified objects. It is not like the state governments, whose powers are more general. Charity is no part of the legislative duty of the government."[240]

SOCIALISM CENTRALIZES POWER

James Madison: "An elective despotism was not the government we fought for; but one in which the powers of government should be so divided and balanced among the several bodies of magistracy as that no one could transcend their legal limits without being effectually checked and restrained by the others."[241]

---

236 Thomas Jefferson letter to Thomas Cooper, November 29, 1802.
237 Thomas Jefferson letter to Albert Gallatin, June 16, 1817.
238 James Madison letter to James Robertson.
239 James Madison, 4 Annals of Congress 179, 1794.
240 James Madison speech at the House of Representatives, January 10, 1794.
241 James Madison, Federalist No. 58, February 20, 1788.

"Inequality will exist as long as liberty exists. It unavoidably results from that very liberty itself."
—Alexander Hamilton

SOCIALISM DESTROYS "POWER BY THE PEOPLE"

James Madison: "Wherever the real power in a Government lies, there is the danger of oppression."[242]

SOCIALISM ALWAYS BECOMES TYRANNY

James Madison: "If Congress can do whatever in their discretion can be done by money, and will promote the general welfare, the government is no longer a limited one possessing enumerated powers, but an indefinite one subject to particular exceptions." [243]

SOCIALISM UNCHECKED CREATES TYRANNY

James Madison: "There are more instances of the abridgment of the freedom of the people by gradual and silent encroachments of those in power than by violent and sudden usurpations." [244]

SOCIALISM BEGINS WITH EASY MONEY

Benjamin Franklin: "When the people find that they can vote themselves money, that will herald the end of the republic."[245]

SOCIALISM TRAPS PEOPLE INTO WELFARE

Benjamin Franklin: "I am for doing good to the poor, but I differ in opinion of the means. I think the best way of doing good to the poor, is not making them easy in poverty, but leading or driving them out of it."[246]

FREEDOM ENDS WITH SOCIALISM

Thomas Jefferson: "To compel a man to furnish contributions of money for the propagation of opinions which he disbelieves and abhors, is sinful and tyrannical."[247]

SOCIALISM OFFERS FALSE SECURITY

Benjamin Franklin: "They who can give up essential liberty to obtain a little temporary safety, deserve neither liberty nor safety."[248]

---

242   James Madison letter to Thomas Jefferson, October 17, 1788.
243   James Madison, "Letter to Edmund Pendleton," January 21, 1792, in The Papers of James Madison, vol. 14.
244   James Madison, speech to the Virginia Ratifying Convention, June 16, 1788.
245   Attributed to Benjamin Franklin; similar quote also attributed to Alexander Fraser Tytler.
246   Benjamin Franklin in On the Price of Corn and Management of the Poor, Nov. 29, 1766.
247   Thomas Jefferson in An Act for establishing Religious Freedom, passed in the Assembly of Virginia in the beginning of the year 1786.
248   Benjamin Franklin and William Temple Franklin, Memoirs of the life and writings of Benjamin Franklin, London: British and Foreign Public Library, 1818, p. 270.

Honoring Great Leaders: In Washington D.C., there can never be a building that is greater in height than the Washington Monument. On the east face of the monument's aluminum cap are the words, LAUS DEO, "Praise be to God."

SOCIALISM CAN ONLY BE REPLACED BY WAR

John Adams: "A Constitution of Government once changed from Freedom, can never be restored. Liberty, once lost, is lost forever."[249]

CENTRALIZATION OF POWER LEADS TO SOCIALISM

Thomas Jefferson: "Our country is too large to have all its affairs directed by a single government. Public servants at such a distance from under the eye of their constituents, must, from the circumstance of distance, be unable to administer and over-look all the details necessary for the good government of the citizens, and the same circumstance, by rendering detection impossible to their constituents, will invite the public agents to corruption, plunder and waste. And I do verily believe, that if the principle were to prevail, of a common law being in force in the United States ..., it would become the most corrupt government on earth....

"What an augmentation of the field of jobbing, speculating, plundering, office-building and office-hunting would be produced by an assumption of all the State powers into the hands of the General Government. The true theory of our Constitution is surely the wisest and best, that the States are independent as to everything within themselves, and united as to everything respecting foreign nations. Let the General Government be reduced to foreign concerns only, and let our affairs be disentangled from those of all other nations, except as to commerce, which the merchants will manage the better, the more they are left free to manage for themselves, and our General Government may be reduced to a very simple organization and a very unexpensive one; a few plain duties to be performed by a few servants."[250]

---

249   John Adams, Letter to Abigail Adams, July 17, 1775.
250   Thomas Jefferson letter to Gideon Granger, 1800.

Drowning in rules: In 2011, President Obama's administration swamped the *Federal Register* with 23,193 new Rules and 31,258 Notices for regulating American businesses. Unfortunately, these additions generally followed a growing trend that was already decades old.

CHAPTER 43:
"OLD FASHIONED"?

Critics dismiss the Constitution as a creation ideal for a bunch of farmers, but no longer applicable to today's modern problems.

A merica has made unprecedented progress since the Declaration of Independence in 1776. Some people clamor for reform, claiming that America has outgrown her founding Declaration and Constitution. They suggest these antiquated ideas be abandoned for something more modern. But can anything more modern be offered?

EQUALITY: The Declaration of Independence declares "all men are created equal"—Is equality old fashioned?

RIGHTS: The Declaration of Independence declares we "are endowed with unalienable rights"—Are rights old fashioned?

LIBERTY: The Declaration of Independence defines those rights as "life, liberty, and the pursuit of happiness"—which of those three is old fashioned or can be improved or replaced?

The Constitution of the United States lays out the mechanisms and restraints for those absolute truths to abide.

There is no improvement of liberty possible—no new plan or new approach that can advance human beings forward as have the Declaration of Independence and the U.S. Constitution. To *refuse* those truths is to turn back to Ruler's Law.

On the 150th anniversary of the Declaration of Independence, Calvin Coolidge said about these absolute truths,

"No advance, no progress can be made beyond these propositions. If anyone wishes to deny their truth or their soundness, the only direction in which he can proceed historically is not forward, but backward toward the time when there was no equality, no rights of the individual, no rule of the people. Those who wish to proceed in that direction cannot lay claim to progress. They are reactionary. Their ideas are not more modern, but more ancient, than those of the Revolutionary fathers."[251]

Those clamoring for reform are *really* clamoring for control.

---

251 Calvin Coolidge, July 5, 1926, Philadelphia Pennsylvania.

"Education should aim at destroying free will so that after pupils are thus schooled they will be incapable throughout the rest of their lives of thinking or acting otherwise than as their school masters would have wished ..."—Bertrand Russell quoting Johann Gottlieb Fichte (1810)

CHAPTER 44:
DEMOCRACY VS. REPUBLIC

*There has been a great deal of confusion about the terms
'democracy' and 'republic'—does it really matter?*

JOHN ADAMS SAID, "Remember, democracy never lasts long. It soon wastes, exhausts and murders itself. There was never a democracy yet that did not commit suicide."[252]

Is democracy really that bad? In the literal sense, yes. The word democracy combines two Greek words—*demos*, the people, and *kratia*, the government.

A democracy involves the mass of the people participating in the government and making all the decisions as a whole. This is very inefficient because who wants to assemble the millions of masses to argue the mundane of day-to-day governing?

In a republic, the people's representatives meet to pass the laws and run the government—that is more efficient.

The Founders organized liberty with pure democracy at the very bottom of society for the masses to elect representatives, and then turned to the principle of a republic to have those representatives carry the will of the people up the line to the proper levels of government. That is why America is correctly called a democratic republic; also, a constitutional republic.

DEMOCRACY ALSO MEANS: Democracy means one-man, one-vote. It is the basic political model of socialism. Having all things in common as socialism mandates means the common masses must be heard in pursuit of their common goals and their commonality.

The Founders frowned on this form of government because it always means the majority wins and the minority loses. Minority rights are not protected or even discussed under majority rule.

HISTORY EXPOSES PURE DEMOCRACY AS FLAWED

Mass participation in the government only works with small groups like a family or a voting precinct. On a state or national level, one-man-one-vote democracy has always been a big flop.

Around 450 B.C. when Pericles was in power in Greece, Athens gave democracy a try. The outcome? Totally self-defeating.

---

252 Writings of John Adams, vol. xviii, p. 484, April 15, 1814.

"My God! how little do my countrymen know what precious blessings they are in possession of and which no other people on earth enjoy."—Thomas Jefferson

❖ The only voters were the rich who were free of daily woes so they could focus on issues of State—this excluded all others.

❖ These masses eventually become bored with the tedium of minutia. For example, the government required 6,000 voting members to pass *any* law, and juries had to have anywhere from 201 to 2,001 jury members to hear a case.

❖ The most exciting thing these "democrats" discovered was the power to "soak the rich" and rob the treasury. With the unstoppable power of the majority, they raised taxes on the rich and give themselves special financial favors and compensations.

❖ After the passage of time a few bureaucrats eventually took over and manipulated laws and policies to their private advantages. These men became known as the "Thirty Tyrants."

HISTORY PROVES REPUBLIC FORM IS BEST

Examples of the republican form of government prove it the most efficient and fair of all. Ancient Israel, the Anglo-Saxons, Rome, and the United States, all survived hundreds of years by operating under the principles of a "republic."

When the pillars of socialism crept in, usually by consolidating power in rulers and destroying representation, those listed civilizations collapsed—from King Saul to Augustus to Hitler to American progressives—the list of precursors to destruction of freedom is long and disappointing, and thriving to this very day.

THREE KINDS OF REPUBLICS

Historically there have been three kinds of "republics."

❖ **UNITARY**: All power vested in the central government. Great Britain is an example with all power in Parliament.

❖ **CONFEDERATION OF STATES**: Very little power in the central government but all power in the local states. This was the weakness of the Articles of Confederation and the Southern States' confederacy during the Civil War era—both flopped.

❖ **CONSTITUTIONAL REPUBLIC** or federal republic is ruled by written law that divides all power horizontally and vertically with powers spelled out in writing and all of it under control of the people through their representatives. That's the United States of America, the soundest government of all. So—technically speaking, "our great democracy" isn't and shouldn't.

"Where there is no vision, the people perish."—Proverbs 29:18

LEARNING TO RECOGNIZE SOCIALISM

The timeless magnificence of the U.S. Constitution is lost on people who have accepted Ruler's Law as a way of life.

Where the government today is eating up the labors of the people, the original Constitution prevented such abuse by restricting how it may tax the people and for what purposes.

Where the government today is dictating the minutia of day-to-day living, the Constitution prevented such abuse by restricting with a written list the powers delegated to the federal government.

Where the government today is abusing its authority by delving into the private marketplace to bail out one industry but not another, to grant massive sums of money to one pursuit but not another, to build power bases to perpetuate one political faction against all others and then saddling the citizens with the tax burden to pay for it all, the Constitution prevented such favoritism and do or die abuse by limiting all things the federal government could do to just a few bare essentials.

The mess America is in today is not the fault of the original Constitution. It is the lapse of careful protection and tending by the very guardians placed over it—we the people.

SUGGESTED AMENDMENTS

If the Constitution is to regain its original intended purposes, it may require some amendments to further tighten down loose interpretations that many generations of Congresses have recklessly applied to gain political power. A good starting place would be an amendment to specifically limit the General Welfare Clause to those powers listed. Another would be an amendment to prevent the government from borrowing, except, perhaps, in times of war. It would force the government to cut expenses, to "pay as you go"—a policy of frugality practiced with tremendous results by many millions of families.

Next, we look at how decay and abuse were allowed to flourish unchecked in the U.S., revealing a pattern of failure and enslavement that is being adopted by the entire world. It was a revolution of sorts, a revolution by the socialists that continues today.

Capitalism works: In 2011, Walmart made $46,206 in *profit* every single *minute*. That same year its philanthropy group voluntarily gave away $2 billion.

Part VIII

REVOLUTION OF THE SOCIALISTS, SECTION I

"When the people
find that they can vote
themselves money,
that will herald
the end of the republic."

—Often attributed to Benjamin Franklin—

CHAPTER 45:

CONSPIRACY TO SOCIALIZE AMERICA

While the United States pushed forward with a new standard in human freedom and potential, its powerful engine of productivity was looked upon with greed and envy.

The Founding Fathers did such a good job of protecting the nation from the spread of socialism that the socialists had to invest an enormously difficult and costly amount of time and infiltration to upend the Founders' best efforts.

In 1895, the Fabian Socialists complained, "England's [unwritten] Constitution readily admits of constant though gradual modification. Our American Constitution does not readily admit of such change. England can thus move into Socialism almost imperceptibly. Our Constitution being largely individualistic must be changed to admit of Socialism, and each change necessitates a political crisis. This means the raising of great new issues ..."[253]

Ramsay MacDonald, a British Fabian socialist greatly vexed by the Constitution's "roadblock to reform," complained that "The great bar to progress is the written constitutions, Federal and State, which give ultimate power to a law court."[254]

U.S. CONSTITUTION BLOCKS SOCIALISM

Because of a *written* Constitution, the shift toward top-down socialistic control of the American economy and culture was thwarted. But that didn't ensure the American way was impervious to collapse. The carefully prepared structure of the Constitution was built to work only if the people managing it (*that would be us*) kept all of its necessary protections in place.

Those protections relied upon a voluntary and *freely embraced* national virtue, morality, religion, education, participation, and knowledge. As those guardrails on the road to freedom were refused, ignored, and taken down, so was freedom, a little at a time. For many ignorant people this drift toward Ruler's Law was a *good* change—they called it *progressive*.

---

253 Introduction to The American Fabian, 1895.
254 Fabian News, February 1898.

In 1776, the 2nd Continental Congress borrowed the Philadelphia Carpenter's Guild meeting hall to adopt the Declaration of Independence.

CHAPTER 46:

THERE'S NOTHING *PROGRESSIVE* ABOUT PROGRESSIVES

The so-called Progressive Movement in the U.S. did not begin around 1900 as many might believe—its beginnings can be traced to more than a century earlier, back when the ink on the Constitution had not even dried.

An otherwise unknown woman remembered only as "Mrs. Powel of Philadelphia," caught Benjamin Franklin after the Constitutional Convention and asked, "Well, Doctor, what have we got, a republic or a monarchy?"

Franklin responded, "A republic, if you can keep it."[255]

Franklin's answer was both prophetic and factual. "*If* you can keep it" was a piercing expression of both hope and doubt: the hope of unrealized capacity because of freedom—and some degree of doubt that weak and gullible humans could sustain it as long as might be hoped.

Already by 1787 the seeds of erosion were planted at the top levels of the new government, and Franklin probably knew of it as he stood in front of Independence Hall to briefly converse with Mrs. Powel. He was more than likely well aware that forces lay in wait to undo the hard work of birthing freedom the Founders had so recently completed.

HERE WE GO AGAIN ...

Since America's break with England, various efforts to replace the republic and impose unrestrained top-down control had been urgently promoted by self-proclaimed reformers seeking an overthrow of nearly every aspect of American life.

For more than a century historians have called that drift toward reforming the Constitution the *Progressive Movement*—a generalization of the plethora of efforts to socialize America.

---

255 See James McHenry's diary, reproduced in the 1906 American Historical Review, see New American, November 6, 2000.

Judicial activism is unconstitutional: "The Constitution which at any time exists, till changed by an explicit and authentic act of the whole people, is sacredly obligatory upon all."
—George Washington

TERMS OF ENSLAVEMENT

A progressive is someone who seeks to cut the chains of the Constitution that hold back the consuming powers of the federal government. With such chains cut, there is only one way the federal government can grow—bigger, fatter, more meddlesome, and more expensive.

A progressive seeks to install top-down government power and destroy control from the bottom up. He does this in the name of fairness or equality or social justice or economic justice or civic responsibility or equal opportunity, or some other appeal to the free lunch mentality. A progressive strives to take advantage of the ever-changing whims and frustrations wrought by the natural inclinations of human nature to trod the path of least resistance.

The very term "progressive movement" is an oxymoron. There is nothing progressive or positive or beneficial about the work to destroy freedom. Progressives would not see it that way, of course, but why call going backwards going forwards except to deceive and mask their true intentions? A more suitable name for progressivism is just what it is—"socialism."

Each and every progressive effort, regulation, plan, law, court decision, and legislation has worked to remove freedom from individuals or the nation as a whole. Many of these changes came to America with a great amount of pomp and circumstance, of pontificating and proclamations promising some utopian dream.

The passage of time eventually wears away those empty promises and facades, and exposes progressivism for what it really is—the systematic and carefully crafted violations of true principles. There is nothing new here. Progressivism is simply another flavor, another version, another strategy, another deception to take a great forward-moving people backwards.

Progressivism has unleashed multiple chain reactions that give us today's national meltdown in which Americans are now trapped. When did it actually start?

Socialized Medicine in Mexico: A woman in Zapopan, Mexico, suffered a bone break so severe her foot was literally detached from her leg. She had to wait one week for surgery, a luxury made possible because she knew someone "higher up." Other bone break patients have waited months.

CHAPTER 47:

AMERICA'S FIRST PROGRESSIVE

America's first big-league progressive was also a respected and brilliant Founding Father. What went wrong?

W̲e pause in our world-wide view of socialism to focus on America for this important reason: the dominant power in the earth tends to draw all other nations to it through trade, alliances and example. With America standing as the sole practitioner of actual liberty, its resulting prosperity has blessed the entire world. All other peoples have sought to emulate its patterns of success, and have succeeded to varying degrees.

But then, as America's integrity was weakened, so began the shrinking of freedoms everywhere. Liberty and prosperity in the Earth today do not rise any higher than the level established by the United States. It will remain that way unless America's demise becomes so severe that one day it is unseated as the major influential power over all nations.

Discovering the starting place for that weakening helps us find a cure and a solution. One day, that solution will be required, but until then it is critical to discover why and who and when. It starts with a dismal doubt in the heart of an original Founding Father.

ALEXANDER HAMILTON (1755-1804)

For all of Alexander Hamilton's brilliant and inspiring insights into principles of freedom, he had a dangerous blind side: he liked some aspects of Ruler's Law, of the "British system."

Hamilton was one of America's Founding Fathers and the first Secretary of the Treasury. He was born and raised in the Caribbean and attended Columbia University in New York. He was elected to Congress from New York and later founded the Bank of New York. He represented New York at the Constitution Convention in 1787, and wrote 52 of the 87 essays in *The Federalist Papers* to explain and define the new Constitution, and get it ratified.

Hamilton's admiration for the British system was his downfall. While his role in setting up the new government is highly admired,

"The strongest reason for the people to retain the right to keep and bear arms is, as a last resort, to protect themselves against tyranny in government."—Thomas Jefferson

quoted, and celebrated, his corruption of its authorities in favor of a stronger central government spoiled an otherwise honored place among the defenders of freedom. His policies as Treasury Secretary reverberate to this day in the form of bottomless national debt and incurable federal intrusion.

PROMOTED BRITISH SYSTEM

Hamilton wanted a strong ruler in the nation's capital, an all-powerful leader similar to the monarchy of England. He wrote:

"I have no scruple in declaring ... that the British government is the best in the world; and that I doubt much whether anything short of it will do in America. ...It is the only government in the world which unites public strength with individual security."[256]

Hamilton gave a 5-hour speech at the very beginning of the Constitutional Convention celebrating the British system as the model of government that America should follow. The speech didn't sparkle with his usual flourish, but listeners knew he was trying to stir up the comforting memories of old loyalties to crown and country.

The speech probably wore everyone out. It received polite applause but that was about it. William Samuel Johnson from Connecticut panned it saying Hamilton was "praised by everybody" but "supported by none."[257]

Hamilton was so disappointed in the lack of appreciation (no discussion or votes were called), that he left the convention discouraged and angry. Except for a couple of times when he dropped in to see what was happening, he didn't return until it was about time to sign the finished document. As a result, Hamilton missed all the debates on the important issues.

The ideas Hamilton proposed in his speech read like the "to-do list" of a modern-day progressive.

HAMILTON'S PLAN

Hamilton said it was too dangerous to tread the untried waters of representative government. The British system, he said, was the best way to go.[258] His plan called for:

---

256   Madison's Report, Works, i. pp. 388, 389; see Frederick Scott Oliver, *Alexander Hamilton: An Essay on American Union*, 1918, p. 155.
257   Forest McDonald, *Alexander Hamilton*, 1979, p. 105.
258   "Hamilton's Plan" from *The Majesty of God's Law* by Skousen, pp. 366-367.

Socialism creates a class of elitists: During the 1980s, Romanian President Nicolae Ceausescu built the lavish *Palace of the Parliament*, the world's largest and most expensive civilian building—12 stories high, 1,100 rooms with 3,700,000 square feet of floor space. ... (cont'd)

◆ **LIFETIME RULER**: A single executive chosen for life by electors from the states. Hamilton wanted the President to have an absolute veto over any legislation, similar to the veto power of the king of England. In the notes for his speech, Hamilton referred to the executive as the "Monarch," and said the office "ought to be hereditary." [259]

> **THAT'S BAD BECAUSE ...** The people can't get rid of a bad president who is appointed to office for life. He'll give favors, bribes and freebies to others to keep himself in power. Bribes are corrupting and create a class of privilege and power—it's Ruler's Law all over again.

◆ **ALL-POWERFUL, EXCEPT ...** Hamilton insisted the office of president have all power to do anything except what it was forbidden to do in the Constitution. "The general doctrine of our Constitution, then, is that the executive power of the nation is vested in the President; subject only to the exceptions and qualifications which are expressed in the instrument."[260]

> **THAT'S BAD BECAUSE ...** A president with all-power, except for a few listed restrictions, is essentially a king. Jefferson and Madison were totally opposed to Hamilton's theory because it removed the chains on the executive office that would keep it from growing beyond the people's control, which today it has.

◆ **LIFETIME SENATORS**: Senators were also to be appointed for life similar to the English House of Lords.[261]

> **THAT'S BAD BECAUSE ...** Life-time senators will always vote to keep the president in power and his policies in force. They would tend to never bite the hand that feeds them for fear of falling out of favor.

◆ **THREE YEARS**: The House of Representatives, like the British House of Commons, would be chosen for a limited term. Hamilton recommended three years.

---

259. Noemie Emery, *Alexander Hamilton, An Intimate Portrait*, New York: G. P. Putnam's Sons, 1982, p. 98.

260 The Federalist, *On the New Constitution, 1788*, Letters of Pacificus (Hamilton), p. 408, Hallowell et al, 1852.

261 Alexander Hamilton comments to the Convention, Monday, June 19, 1787.

(cont'd) ... The workers created gold-leaf walls, crystal chandeliers, marble columns, intricate parquets, handwoven carpets. While the $4.5 billion dollar building was under construction, most of Romania was standing in breadlines and suffering through winters without heat.

THAT'S BAD BECAUSE ... Two years is more than enough time for those with control over the money to prove their worth of office. If they do poorly it shows quickly—they can be kicked out with the next election before too much damage can be done. Their incentive, therefore, is to be wise.

❖ **FEDERAL AGENTS IN STATES**: Governors of the states would be appointed by the federal government, just as the king of England appointed governors for each of the colonies before the War for Independence.[262]

THAT'S BAD BECAUSE ... Appointed executives over the states totally destroys states' rights and puts the states under the thumb of the federal government. It's the model of the old USSR where a Communist Party member was required to be present at all local government events to ensure that Party policies were being obeyed.

❖ **TOTAL VETO POWER**: Hamilton proposed a president who could veto any and all laws passed by the states.

THAT'S BAD BECAUSE ... Consolidating all power in one leader who could tell states what they could or couldn't do violated the separation of powers, destroyed state sovereignty, and was simply going back to government by monarchy, the very power and enslavement the colonists had so recently rebelled against at the cost of so much American blood.

HAMILTON TRIES TO INSTALL A KING

In 1786, Hamilton and some friends tried to convince 50-year-old Prince Henry of Prussia to be king of the new United States.[263] The plot came dangerously close to success. Prince Henry hesitated just long enough to allow an investigation to expose him as one of Europe's most debauched and notorious philanderers—with *both* sexes.[264]

---

262 Alexander Hamilton at the Convention, Monday, June 18, 1787.
263 Extracted from *The Majesty of God's Law*, 2nd ed., 1st printing, by W. Cleon Skousen, p. 380.
264 Eugen Wilhem, "Die Homosexualitat des Prinzen Heinrich von Preussen, des Bruders Friedrichs des Grossen", Zeitschrift fur Sexualwissenschaft 15, 1929; and David Wallechinsky and Irving Wallace, Peoples Almanac, 1978, 2:400.

"When one makes a Revolution, one cannot mark time; one must always go forward—or go back. He who now talks about the 'freedom of the press' goes backward, and halts our headlong course toward Socialism."—Vladimir Lenin

NEW GOVERNMENT INCLUDES HAMILTON

On April 30, 1789, George Washington was inaugurated as the first President of the new United States of America.

On September 11, President Washington chose Alexander Hamilton as his Secretary of the Treasury. Two weeks later the federal court system was set up with a Supreme Court presiding over federal district courts in each state. John Jay was appointed the Chief Justice. A week later President Washington created the United States Army.

HAMILTON WANTED TO BE PRIME MINISTER

Hamilton was a star-struck student of England's history and was intrigued by the ruling power of its Prime Minister.

In 1727, King George II inherited his father's throne. He reigned for about 33 years, and was the last British monarch to be born outside of Great Britain. Like his father, he was a German elector and spent nearly all his time away in Germany with his mistress. For England's Prime Minister, the king's absence opened the door for him to keep things running practically any way he saw fit. That Prime Minister was named Sir Robert Walpole.

Hamilton like the way Walpole was able to run things as an almost all-powerful monarch.

There was one more angle that Hamilton liked about Walpole—the man also served as the secretary of the treasure, or more formally, "chancellor of the exchequer."

As Hamilton began his new duties as the U.S. Secretary of the Treasury, that chance to wear many hats was playing in his mind. As one biographer writes:

"Hamilton contemplated an American adaptation of the British scheme of things—with Washington as George II and himself as Sir Robert Walpole."[265] It fit nicely his idea of a strong executive authority as practiced in Great Britain. Jefferson and Madison were disgusted by this attitude, as noted in their journals.

AN INTERESTING DIALOGUE

Hamilton took many opportunities to emphasize the superiority of the British political system over that of the Constitution.

---

265. McDonald, *Alexander Hamilton*, op. cit., p. 126.

Potemkin Village ("fake village"), is a name given villages built to fool others. During World War II, the Nazi Germans established "the Paradise Ghetto" to fool the Red Cross into believing it was a model Jewish settlement. Instead, more than 33,000 were brutally killed by starvation, sickness and torture.

One day while John Adams was serving as Vice President under Washington, he apparently tried to humor Hamilton and poke fun at Hamilton's pet project, the British system. Said Adams,

"Purge that [British] constitution of its corruption, and give to its popular branch [House of Commons] equality of representation, and it would be the most perfect constitution ever devised by the wit of man."

Hamilton shot right back:

"Purge it of its corruption and give to its popular branch equality of representation, and it would become an *impracticable* government; as it stands at present, with all its supposed defects, it is the most perfect government which ever existed." [266]

Thomas Jefferson, who recorded this conversation, wrote, "Hamilton ... [was] so bewitched and perverted by the British example, as to be under thorough conviction that corruption was essential to the government of a nation."[267]

WHAT IS "CORRUPTION"?

The "corruption" Jefferson loathed was Hamilton's introduction of the same kinds of "buddy networking" that England's King enjoyed: appointing all leaders of influence, rewarding loyalty, paying for obedience, ensuring perpetuity of private wealth and income, wrapping his arms around the aristocracy with money and privilege, viewing all the rest of society as peasant masses requiring the seasoned guidance of aristocratic leadership.

Said Jefferson, "Hamilton was not only a monarchist, but for a monarchy bottomed on corruption."[268]

HAMILTON'S IDEAS TO IGNITE THE ECONOMY

As Secretary of Treasury, Hamilton wanted to fire up the economy of the new nation and attract leaders of industry, shipping, and commercial enterprises, He proposed doing this by using several techniques:

❖ **SPECIAL FAVORS**—Hamilton liked the king's ability to grant generous favors to key people in Parliament, to the landed gentry, to certain investors, and others who held political power so the king could get things done.

266. Ibid.
267. Ibid.
268 Thomas Jefferson, The Anas, p. 278.
Socialism kills—In Khomeini's Iran of 1988, a religious purge to "purify the culture" resulted in the execution of 30,000, some of them children, hanged six at a time from cranes.

THAT'S BAD BECAUSE ... Instead of outright bribes, these special royal favors usually came in another form—inside investment tips, lucrative contracts, prestigious appointments or nominations to high offices in the government. In other words, politics as usual, rewarding supporters with advantages the others don't get—dishonesty the other Founders thought they had outlawed in the Constitution.

❖ **TAX FAVORITISM**—Use tax revenue to subsidize risky investments by private people, or give them tax breaks or even cash bonuses for just trying. That was the kind of political corruption he felt was necessary to turn America into a great industrial nation "after the manner of England."

THAT'S BAD BECAUSE ... In the Founders' wisdom, the Constitution forbade the government from taking money from some and giving it to others, as either a handout or a tax break. It is wiser to let the free market dictate what works and what fails, and leave the people's hard-earned taxes out of it.

❖ **MONETIZE THE NATIONAL DEBT**—Hamilton wanted to invite the affluent to pay off the country's debts in exchange for repayment with interest. Hamilton knew this would entrap investors into supporting his schemes for bigger taxes and bigger government, all in violation of the Constitution. Did it create bigger taxes and government? Yes.

THAT'S BAD BECAUSE ... Every working man or woman knows you're never free to do what you please with your money until you are debt free. Jefferson argued to Washington that paying off the national debt is the responsible, smart, and morally mandated direction to take, but Hamilton's position prevailed. As a result, the affluent were always first in line for bailouts and handouts—then and now.

❖ **A PRIVATE CENTRAL BANK**—Hamilton's idea for a central bank was to have it handle all financial affairs of the government and the country, lend money, borrow, control the money supply, and tell other banks what they could and couldn't do, similar to the Bank of England.

In 2012, Tehran police enforced a new dress code, fining or arresting women wearing "bad headscarves, bad dress, and model-type women in vulgar dress." Those taken to jail were held until relatives could rescue them with a modest change of clothing.

THAT'S BAD BECAUSE ... The Constitution gave those fiscal responsibilities to Congress where the people could keep an eye on how coins and the value thereof were managed.

Hamilton won congressional support for a central bank by corrupting their personal principles—he offered Congressmen generous stock in the new private bank. Many of them happily accepted, hoping to secure a nice fat portfolio.

The awful fallout from the bank's attempt to regulate the money supply was a horrific 72 percent inflation in its first five years of operation.

A central bank prevents private banks from flourishing—it sets all rules and forces compliance without any power by the people to manage the efficiency, elect new directors, etc.

A central bank can inflate or devalue the currency to control the market. It has power to instantly reduce the buying power of the dollar. Such power created America's first boom and bust cycle, and the banking panic of 1819.

Today's incarnation of Hamilton's central bank is the Federal Reserve—to be discussed later.

❖ **CONTINENTAL BUYBACK**—Washington was very concerned about the money owed after the war. Many people who financed the war were suffering financially for lack of payback. Hamilton proposed that the worthless Continental Dollars used in those days be exchanged for good currency at face value.

THAT'S BAD BECAUSE ... Hamilton's suggestion was that Continentals be exchanged for their face value, not what they were actually worth. Hamilton bragged about the plan to a friend and when word got out, schemers scattered far and wide offering to buy up worthless Continentals for pennies on the dollar. This dishonest scheme was underway long before the holders of the old Continentals even knew they could get more. The crooks then presented the Continentals to Congress for full exchange value.[269]

Jefferson never forgave Hamilton for his loose talk that resulted in the organized cheating and betrayal of the veterans,

---

269. Ibid., p. 1208.

farmers, and business houses who had sacrificed so much to support the war effort.

❖ **BUYING VOTES**—Hamilton promised special favors to the states and politicians in exchange for their support of his programs by voting for them whenever possible.

THAT'S BAD BECAUSE ... This was the very corruption that Jefferson and the other Founders worried over as Hamilton sought a more *progressive* way to run things.

Hamilton told the states the federal government would assume all their war debts, even if they couldn't provide documentation proving what debts they owed. An "estimate" was okay.

JEFFERSON TRIES TO CONVINCE WASHINGTON

Jefferson hated Hamilton's plans. At his first opportunity Jefferson sat down with Washington and carefully explained to him what the monetizing of the debt meant to future generations. Instead of paying off this debt, Jefferson explained that Hamilton and his moneyed friends were buying the right to receive interest checks taken from the taxpayers for generations to come.

But Washington told Jefferson that high finance was something he didn't entirely understand. He was impressed, however, that Hamilton's plan had made the country's credit first rate.

Jefferson sadly returned to his office and later recorded:

"Unversed in financial projects ... his [Washington's] approbation of them was bottomed in his confidence in the man [Alexander Hamilton]." [270]

How shocked Washington would have been if Jefferson could have shown him our own day—two hundred years hence—when the national debt Hamilton so gleefully promoted would exceed 16 trillion dollars and the interest payments would amount to more than 400 billion dollars per year, with many of those payments (taken from working Americans in the form of taxes) going to foreign investors.

HAMILTON PAYS BRIBES TO COVER ADULTERY

It was during the same period that Hamilton was extremely worried over threats of exposure by the husband of Maria Reynolds

---

270.   Ibid., p. 1211.

A two-year study by Cornell, Chicago and Hebrew Universities released in 2011 showed that voters glimpsing the American flag were swayed toward Republican candidates, attitudes and beliefs.

with whom he had established extra-marital relations. The liaisons began soon after the government offices were moved from New York to Philadelphia in 1790.

Mrs. Reynolds had gained Hamilton's sympathies by claiming her husband had deserted her, but after their affair had continued for some time, the husband suddenly returned and threatened Hamilton with exposure if he did not provide immediate satisfaction. At first Hamilton paid $600, then $400, and apparently other payments from time to time. By 1797 the scandal broke in the press and Hamilton eventually issued a public confession setting forth a complete recitation of the whole sordid affair.[271]

By this time, however, Hamilton had long since resigned as Secretary of the Treasury and was practicing law. Hamilton had also gone through a bitter and long-standing dispute with Thomas Jefferson who considered Hamilton one of the foremost enemies of the Constitution as it was originally designed by the Founders.

DEATH AND LEGACY

In 1804, Hamilton settled an issue of honor in a pistol duel with Vice President Aaron Burr. Hamilton was mortally wounded and died the next day, July 12, 1804.

Many biographers attribute to Hamilton a keen insight into changes necessary to stabilize the early American economy. There is no doubt he did a great deal to help in other areas, but this brief review is meant to highlight Hamilton's damaging socialistic policies, not present other achievements in his life that promoted principles of constitutional freedoms.

Hamilton fell victim of the socialist lie—that the people cannot be trusted to govern themselves, that intellectual superiors should be put in charge. It was this attitude and his actions as Secretary of the Treasury to centralize control in the Executive that opened the doors to dismantling chains and protections put forth in the Constitution. These were the early blows of progressivism that would evolve into stronger influences as the decades wore on.

Alexander Hamilton *was* the first progressive.

---

271.   Emery, *Alexander Hamilton, An Intimate Portrait*, op. cit., pp. 163-164.

"The press should be not only a collective propagandist and a collective agitator, but also a collective organizer of the masses."—Vladimir Lenin

CHAPTER 48:

THE REVOLUTION OF THE SOCIALISTS

Industry wasn't the only thing being revolutionized in the 1800s.

After America's break from England, a spirit of individual freedom spread throughout Europe. People saw an opening to finally unshackle themselves from the lingering remains of the dying feudal system. They demanded a say in political affairs. They looked to throw off the tyranny of kings and lords. They sought ways to apply their own ideas to politics and economics, to create, invent, invest, and expand the freedom to exercise and protect their individual rights. It was a renaissance of liberty, of self-rule, of creativity, of inventiveness. It was the dawning of the Age of the Machine.

INDUSTRIAL REVOLUTION CHANGES THE WORLD

The so-called Industrial Revolution was really an industrial evolution that spanned more than 100 years. It was a time of opportunity, invention, investment and creativity.

This *revolution* has roots back to the age of the guilds when governments were sponsoring and protecting certain industries. By the 1700s, major advancements appeared in England, most of them in the textile industry. Assorted innovations in weaving and thread-making gave birth to new jobs, new machines and new industries.

STEAM POWER: Steam engines contributed to every aspect of society where traditional manufacturing processes suffered for want of some kind of power to run large machines.

IRON AND CEMENT: Construction materials were invented for better performance and cheaper production. This led to improvements in construction, mining, machinery, mills, housing, and all of the related employment.

LIKE A GIANT VORTEX: All this creativity was unleashed and began overlapping to advance engineering, metallurgy, chemistry, and medicine. Thousands more came together to build inventions, discoveries and ideas, one atop another, until the tide toward a

"Those who make peaceful revolution impossible will make violent revolution inevitable."
—John F. Kennedy

whole new age had swelled beyond imagination: automated loom, spinning wheel, flyer-and-bobbin, steam engine, steam power, spinning mills, rotary machinery, power tools, glass making, paper manufacturing, food productions, pharmaceuticals, ploughs, harvesting equipment, steamboats, steam locomotives, steel manufacturing, weaponry, and so much more.

GENIUS ON PARADE: The new ideas were displayed and paraded around at symposiums and fairs and international expositions. Details and descriptions of the achievements were printed in books, encyclopedias, and periodicals. The means to spread this amazing knowledge were improved by the very act of spreading such knowledge.

It was a wonderful time of enlightenment and progress for the world, and Europe in particular.

MAKING DO ON THE CONTINENT: For Europe, the joys of actual *freedom* remained largely just headlines boasting the fantastic prosperity taking off in America. Could Europe follow suit, or would socialism get in the way? On both sides of the ocean during the 1800s, the principles of socialism started taking root. Who were the socialist revolutionaries of recent history?

Here are some of them, the more prominent revolutionaries of the past two centuries—some forgotten, others remembered with fondness or disdain.

"What is the freedom of expression? Without the freedom to offend, it ceases to exist."
—Salman Rushdie

CHAPTER 49:
REVOLUTIONARY: NED LUDD

He attacked a machine with a hammer and became a legend.

Not a lot is known about Ned Ludd but his legacy lives on as the lad who fought the machine and launched a revolution.

The Industrial Revolution had a worrisome impact on craftsmen and others who believed their handmade skills were put to flight with machines. It was a love-hate relationship. Craftsmen boasted of their high quality handmade goods, and their ability to manufacture them with careful attention to detail and patient processes. But the machines! They magnified everything. Those amazing technologies could do it faster and better than humans, thus increasing profits for manufacturers.

Ned Ludd was born in England, and hailed from the little village of Anstey on the outskirts of Leicester. He was a weaver who, in 1799, exploded "in a fit of insane rage," and took a hammer and broke two stocking frames (knitting machines). Such machines had been putting knitters out of work for 200 years before the Industrial Revolution, so Ned's outburst doesn't seem motivated by resentment of the newness of the machines per se'. He remains a puzzle, some records calling him a half-wit, dull, etc.

Nevertheless, Ned's vigorous and single-handed attack on the machine was admired and gave birth to the 1812 movement in England of machine busters called the Luddites.

The Luddites were anonymous, masked, and well organized men. They went about destroying machinery, mostly in the textile industry, to keep the demand for handmade goods high. The conspirators' loyalty was to no one but the now mythical "King Ludd," and their goal was to preserve jobs. As with the guildsmen of old and the trade unions of the future, the Luddites learned they could destroy the property of other people as a means of propping up their own sources of income and thereby prevent the competition from getting a leg up on them in the hosiery business.[272]

---

272 *English Historical Documents*, XI, Oxford University Press, 1959, pp. 532-33.

"Truth will ultimately prevail where there is pains to bring it to light."
—George Washington

CHAPTER 50:

REVOLUTIONARY: UNIONS & THE KING

Circa 1795-1825
*The king giveth and the king taketh away—anything
more or less than that meant death.*

The problem of the Luddites was not new. Other groups were forming, in particular the trade unions that were striking for more pay, fewer hours, and other demands.

As a step to stop this breakout of free assembly and action, England's king declared in 1795 that 50 was the maximum number of people allowed to gather for any purpose outside of his official decrees—especially if they met for political reform. If the number exceeded 50, the local sheriff could force the crowd to disburse. After an hour, if 12 or more remained, they could be arrested. If any were found guilty of seditious talk, they could be hanged.

These draconian measures against the freedom to associate were called the Seditious Assembling Act of 1795.

By 1799, a similar proclamation against seditious assembling, The Combination Act of 1799 and 1800, prevented workers from forming trade unions and collective bargaining. They were not allowed to strike "for obtaining an advance on wages ... or altering their usual hours of working ... or decreasing the quantity of work."

The anti-union laws remained in force until 1824. Sympathy for the problems that workers faced, and the necessity of resolving them outside the view of the king's guards, brought about a repeal of the Combination Act in 1824. Almost immediately a series of strikes broke out by workers wanting to settle old and festering grievances. A short time later, the Combination Act of 1825 was passed making labor unions legal.[273]

And so began the complex era of unions that would slowly erode the property rights of business owners. It was a power given teeth by the iron fist of law and government. This brand of socialism had already spread to America.

---

273   Ibid., vol. XI, pp. 749-52; and *Statutes at Large* XL.

The Constitution is not an amalgamation of compromises. The Founders talked out every issue until everyone understood and voted "yes." There were only 3 compromises.

CHAPTER 51:
REVOLUTIONARY: NAPOLEON BONAPARTE

Circa 1779-1815

In a strange contradiction of goals, Napoleon used force and Ruler's Law to export into his conquered European subordinates many of the freedoms gained from the French Revolution.

The failure of France to figure out permanent freedom with its first revolution in 1789 continued to haunt the country for sixty more years. The first decade was a topsy-turvy confusion of competing forces that sought to de-throne the king or at least sharply curtail his powers. Several versions of constitutions and declarations rose and fell until France found herself embroiled in despotism, war, runaway inflation, tyranny, and confusion.

By 1799 the country was tired of the revolutions and turmoil, and submitted almost with relief to the rise of Napoleon Bonaparte, the brilliant strategist who headed France's armed forces through several decisive victories.

FOR THE FOLLOWING 15 YEARS, Napoleon ruled France and expanded French dominion into Italy and most of Europe. He created a vast empire of states, threatening to dominate them militarily if they refused to accept the monarchs he gave them.

Most of Europe was already under the rule of kings with their confusing patchwork of feudal laws. As Napoleon's troops swept across the landscape, he gave the sitting monarchs the option to capitulate or die. Many stepped down, others fled. In this way Napoleon was able to put loyal friends on the various thrones and extend France's new-found freedoms across the continent—his new law became known as the *Napoleonic Code.*

NAPOLEON'S CODE abolished the old feudal ways of ancient monarchs, serfs, and lords. In their places he installed a code of relatively broad-based freedoms, such as—

◇ No special privileges based on birth.

The Declaration of Independence references God four times: Nature's God, Creator, Supreme Judge, Diving Providence

❖ Freedom of religion—but not the press. Emperor Napoleon insisted he be spoken about kindly and positively.

❖ Freedom to vote and run for office.

❖ Freedom to private property and unrestricted access to the marketplace.

❖ No more secret laws—all laws had to be properly examined, well defined, clearly described, and published for the public to review before they could be put in force. No *ex post facto* laws (laws created *after* a crime was committed to convict a person).

❖ Judges could not be activists and make up laws to suit their own personal desires or pursuits for power.

❖ The criminally accused were innocent until proven guilty, and were promised a defense attorney.

❖ Trial by jury.

❖ Husbands were made legal heads of family, although divorce was allowed.

❖ In Spain, Napoleon abolished the Inquisition, feudal dues, internal customs fees, and 2/3rds of the Catholic cloisters (cloisters were walled-off living places that separated monks from serfs and workmen who performed their labors outside and beyond the high walls. These church-owned compounds encompassed thousands of acres throughout Europe).

❖ Freedoms to try, buy, sell, and fail were guaranteed.

❖ Peasants who were once locked to the land as serfs were freed to buy such lands, to sell or work them—even move away if they pleased.

OTHER NATIONS COPY NAPOLEON

As that spirit of newly-found freedom spread, the Napoleonic Code was adopted by many other European countries including Poland, Holland, Portugal, Spain, England, Russia, Prussia, the lands of Germany, and Italy. Leaders saw how well such freedoms were working and decided that the best way to retain strength and

"Only the individual thinks. Only the individual reasons. Only the individual acts."
— Ludwig von Mises

national harmony was to adopt those same principles. Even to this day the Napoleonic Code remains the foundation for many European nations' jurisprudence.

Napoleon was finally deposed in 1814. He escaped his prison island, built an army, was re-conquered, and deposed a second time in 1815—this time permanently.

CLEANING UP THE MESS

Napoleon's demise left Europe in a mess. It took the Congress of Vienna, with delegates from the largest countries, to try to sort things out. They labored for more than a year (1814-15) to carefully re-draw European borders so no single nation could rise up and dominate the others as had Napoleon's France.

BACKWARDS IS THEIR IDEA OF GOING FORWARDS

When the dust settled, Europe's borders were returned to their pre-Napoleon boundaries *and* rulers.

France returned to its 1789 borders, and its old line of Bourbon kings was put back in power. Most nations took back their own kings and re-instituted the old ways, dissolving natural rights as if those were some form of contagious plague. And in just a matter of a few years, Europe was back in the grip of the seven pillars of socialism. But the taste of freedom was hard to erase—it lingered in the memories of millions for a long time.

"Let us tenderly and kindly cherish, therefore, the means of knowledge. Let us dare to read, think, speak, and write."—John Adams

CHAPTER 52:
REVOLUTIONARY:
ROBERT OWEN

*They call him the father of modern socialism—his capitalistic
experiments helped him build a fortune, and then his
socialistic experiments lost it all just a few years later.*

SOCIALIST: Robert Owen (1771-1858)
LIFE: Born in Wales, sixth of seven children, became famous
for buying textile mills in Scotland and giving his paid workers
and their families good educational and living opportunities. He
encouraged self sufficiency within the whole.

When Owen tried his utopian schemes in New Harmony,
Indiana in 1824, he abandoned what he called "private property,
irrational religion, and marriage" for the hollow ideals of socialism.
His experiment was an expensive failure, costing him 4/5ths of the
fortune he had built with capitalism back in Scotland.

IMPACT: Considered the "father" of modern-day socialism, Owen
pioneered the "cooperative movement" in Great Britain where villagers jointly owned and operated the town's businesses.

FAMOUS WORDS: "Man is the creature of circumstances."[274]

FALLACY: It's the old nature vs. nurture argument. Owen taught
that no one was "responsible for his will and his own actions"
because "his whole character is formed independently of himself" by
his nurturing.[275] Throughout all ages in all places, men and women
resist slavery and stagnation. They bristle against tyranny. Whether
they ultimately escape or not, nurture doesn't matter—all people
demand just the same: the freedom to choose.

FAMOUS WORDS: "[Religions] have made man the most inconsistent, and the most miserable being in existence. By the errors of
these systems he has been made a weak, imbecile animal; a furious
bigot and fanatic or a miserable hypocrite..."[276]

---

274 Quoted in *The History of Co-operation in England*, by George Jacob Holyoake, 1875.
275 Quoted in Joshua Muravchik, *Heaven on Earth: The Rise and Fall of Socialism*, p. 37.
276 Robert Owen, from a speech delivered August 21, 1817, an extract of which is included in
"The Parliamentary Debates," Vol. 41 (Nov. 23, 1819 to Feb. 28, 1820), p. 1201.

**Arab socialism differs from Soviet and Chinese socialism because it is not atheist. It acknowledges
the role of Allah, even though Arab societies tolerate abuse, brutality and violation of
human rights for both civic and religious infractions.**

Believing that to be true, Owen tried to make the ideal workplace at his textile mills. He invested heavily to provide nice homes for workers and a school for the children. He insisted there be no child labor, created shorter work days, and instead of punishing poor performers he rewarded excellence. Like all good capitalists, Owen believed proper incentive would encourage better performance. He was right, of course, and he made millions.

NATURE VERSUS NURTURE: One of Owen's ruling philosophies declared that a person's personality and ethics are molded by the environment—the better the environment, the better the person becomes in all aspects. He said no one was "responsible for his will and his own actions" because "his whole character—physical, mental and moral—is formed independently of himself."[277]

INSPIRED MARX AND ENGELS: Owen's ideas helped lay the philosophical groundwork for Marx and Engels that human nature has no pre-disposed or built-in tendencies. He believed that human nature was the product of interaction with others, and that such nature is under constant revision and change.

If you change the environment, he said, you can change human nature. He was convinced that people are not born with certain attributes and proclivities, but they develop these according to the world in which they are born. And that's just what Marx and Engels concluded some two decades later.[278]

CHANGING INTO A SOCIALIST: Then a strange thing happened. Owen turned from a capitalist into a socialist. He believed that planning and regulation could create the same prosperity *without* the capitalistic principles of incentive and ownership that had worked so well for him before.

Owen thought the incentive of working together for the *common good* would be sufficient motivation for people to work hard. He and his followers even coined a word for Owen's approach: *socialism*.

INFECTING AMERICA: In 1824, Owen sailed to America to launch his idea. He was welcomed everywhere—he spoke to

---

277 Ibid., Muravchik, p. 37.
278 Steven Pinker, *The Blank Slate: The Modern Denial of Human Nature*, pp. 287-88.

"Socialism: nothing more than the theory that the slave is always more virtuous than his master."
—Henry Louis Mencken

Congress, the president, and justices of the Supreme Court. His socialist ideas spread about into many rural areas where people seeking a better way in "the land of the free" decided to give it a try.

SEEKING HARMONY IN INDIANA: Owen's own choice for his blissful experiment in socialism was New Harmony, Indiana in 1825. Here he invested his treasure to create the perfect utopian society with everyone happily working for the benefit of everyone else. All things were tightly regulated and there was no private ownership—all was in common.

About 900 families joined Owen in his enterprise. They sold their properties, invested with the commune, and took their place in Owen's new socialist village.

New Harmony lasted only two years before falling flat on its face, taking with it 4/5ths of Owen's fortune.

SAME PROBLEM AS ALWAYS ...

The culprit was the same as always: no private property, no personal rights, and top-down control. According to Josiah Warren, an original participant at New Harmony, the incontrovertible truth remained: human nature and socialism simply don't mix. Warren wrote of his woes in a series of magazine articles, and concluded:

"[Owen] showed us that in Communism, instead of working against each other as in competition, we should all work for each other while working for ourselves.[279] ...It appeared that it was nature's own inherent law of diversity that had conquered us ...our 'united interests' were directly at war with the individualities of persons and circumstances and the instinct of self-preservation..."[280]

From the very pen of that regretful adherent to socialism, it could not have been said better: *"nature's laws conquered us."*

---

279 Josiah Warren, *The Motives for Communism—How It Worked and What It Led To*, Woodhull and Claflin's *Weekly*, IV, 15 (Feb. 24, 1872).
280 Josiah Warren, *Periodical Letter*, II (July, 1856), pp. 55-56.

"All the great things are simple, and many can be expressed in a single word: freedom, justice, honor, duty, mercy, hope."—Winston Churchill

The Constitution doesn't create law, it gives fair form to all laws created.

Part IX

REVOLUTION OF THE SOCIALISTS, SECTION 2

"When virtue suffers neglect and death, the historian knows an end to the whole is not far behind."

—Author—

CHAPTER 53:
REVOLUTIONARY: UNION ORGANIZERS

Circa 1740-2010

*After a thousand years of looking for an easier way to
make a buck, the guilds finally found traction
as trade unions in the 1800s.*

One of the intriguing legacies left by the guilds (see Chapter 22) is their ingenious strategy of organizing themselves with government control in such a way that other people were not given the fair opportunity to participate or compete. In the free market, competition pushes prices lower and ignites the creation of better quality or new inventions—that's how a civilization grows. But the guilds had complete control over pricing, availability, value, and quality. They held a firm grip on the market of *try, buy, sell,* and *fail.*

EARLY UNIONS: The guild system worked pretty well for a while. They became powerful small-business associations, or cartels. Small towns benefitted enormously from their local guilds and zealously protected all the sources of revenue the guilds helped generate. Town leaders passed laws favoring the guilds, and helped them preserve the secrets of their trade—an early form of patent and copyright protection.

DECLINE OF THE GUILDS

With the passage of time and the growth of populations, the tables turned against the guilds. People started blaming guilds for having too much control, for stifling innovation and business development, for preventing technology from advancing, or benefitting their friends and relatives in other communities. The guilds also ignited fights over sales territory. The fighting and control turned towns against villages and cousins against relatives. It was bad PR for the guilds, and helped lead to the guild system's eventual collapse.

How to Remember the seven Articles of the Constitution (in correct order): Remember those *Star Wars* **characters—Jar Jar Binks, R2D2, Chewbacca? How about Lej Sasr? LEJ SASR—** **Legislature, Executive, Judiciary, States, Amendments, Supremacy clause,** **Ratification. (There's really no Lej Sasr in** *Star Wars***, I made that up.)**

WERE GUILDS FORERUNNERS TO LABOR UNIONS?

Modern scholars debate whether or not there exists a direct connection between guilds and modern trade unions. Whatever the technical definitions are that create such debates, to an outsider it seems fairly clear that guilds led to unions.

Like unions of today, the guilds united craftsmen into what amounted to an exclusive members-only club. For example, with all the skilled shoemakers in a particular region strongly united to create only *so many* shoes in a week, and demanding a sales price of *so much* money per shoe, and setting standards of skill so that only *so many* shoemakers were servicing a population, they could control the shoe market and get rich.

PRO-LABOR POLITICIANS NOT NEW

That exclusive control across hundreds of crafts and services was further entrenched when pro-guild candidates ran for election. Those who won office carried forward the guilds' agenda into town hall to pass pro-guild laws: *lace sold in this town must be made with locally produced thread; shoes sold in this town must be made of local leather; candles sold in this town must be made with locally produced wax and wicks*, etc.

To the guild members this was fantastic progress. To everyone else, it made life more restricted. And to competitors, it was the loss of liberty.

MINORITY BECOMES THE RULER

The labor movement in the 1800-1900s had similar goals and tactics as did the ancient guilds. Most histories of trade unions list a time-line of strikes and violence, and show how the courts and society gradually accepted the unions as if they really were necessary for progress.

In the beginning, only a minority typically joined a union. The unions were led by a small group of leaders. The select groups, with the strong backing of the government, demanded that the rest of the industry, the country, and the world to obey their commands.

UNIONS ARE 'SOCIALISM IN ACTION'

From the perspective of the spread of socialism, union "milestones" in history do not represent progress—they represent battles won in the war to take away property rights of business owners. As unions gained more power, so did the laws that protected their actions on all fronts. Unions constituted the socialization of a nation—as unions grew, so did socialism.

LIKE THE GUILDS: Trade unions organized themselves to restrict or prevent competition. They gained the legal power of the strike or the walk-out to force their demands. They created exclusive markets and centers of production. They illegally confiscated advantages with the backing of legal entities. It was, in short, the imposition of Ruler's Law in the marketplace.

COLONIAL UNIONS

By the mid-1700s, there was already a good working relationship among employers and employees throughout the colonies. Walk-outs and strikes in this early setting were viewed more as greedy conspiracies that fostered antagonisms than as the means to bargain over wages or working hours.

✦ **IN 1740,** bakers in New York City went on strike. They refused to bake until they received a pay raise. The constables arrested the strikers and charged them with conspiracy to ruin the otherwise honestly-run bakeries.

✦ **IN 1776,** New York City was occupied by British troops and the young country was in the very throes of declaring independence. With newspapers owning the Goliath portion of communications in those days, printers had a lot of clout and influence in all the major cities. The New York printers decided they deserved a wage increase, and demanded it. The employers refused, so the printers went on strike to get their raise.

✦ **IN 1794,** an association of printers in New York went on strike for shorter work hours and higher pay. The same demands were made by cabinet makers in 1796, carpenters in 1797, and cordwainers (shoemakers specializing in soft leather) in 1799.

✦ **BY THE 1800s,** the idea that workers could gang up on their employers was widespread and popular. It became the most effective means whereby workers could garner some degree of leverage against employers whom they believed were abusive, or to otherwise extract treatment they considered more fair or more safe.

❖ **IN 1803,** the Sailors' Strike enticed sailors from all over New York to march through the city encouraging sailors from other ships to join them as they demanded higher wages. Although the crowds swelled, the leader was arrested and the strike failed.

❖ **IN 1805**, the Shoemakers' Strike in New York and Philadelphia was the first time the factory owners turned to the courts for relief. The Journeyman Shoemakers' Association launched a strike to raise prices from 25 cents to 75 cents per shoe. The strike dragged on for six weeks. The leaders were finally arrested and prosecuted for criminal conspiracy. The jury declared the union members to be guilty of "a combination to raise their wages."[281]

❖ **IN 1809**, New York cordwainers went on strike for better pay. During the strike, the bosses slipped away with the shoe-making materials to other shops where non-strikers would finish the work, thereby defeating the strikers' strategy. But when the strikers discovered what the bosses had done, almost 200 men joined in a new strike in an attempt to shut down *all* the shoe-making shops.

❖ **IN 1827,** workers in several diverse occupations were invited to join together in the Mechanic's Union Trade Association. The goal was to give a unified setting and airing of all mutual concerns, regardless of trade or specialty. Supporting and backing strikes together carried more support and additional pressure tactics. Other associations and unions were encouraged by the unified effort.

STRIKES INCREASE: The number of strikes in the first 35 years of the 19th century grew so rampant and widespread in America, the strikers starting behaving as if this was standard procedure to get pay raises. Union leaders advertised their newly-found *easy pickings* by advertising the possibilities in the newspapers. In 1835, *The New York Daily Advertiser* boasted that strikes "are all the fashion," and encouraged others to get in on the action, saying it was "an excellent time for the journeymen to come from the country to the city."[282]

CROSSING THE LINE AND CHANGING THE WORLD

In 1842, the Massachusetts Supreme Judicial Court broke the last chain preventing socialism from entering American labor when it declared that labor unions were not criminal conspiracies.

---

281 *Monthly Labor Review*, May 1938, by Florence Peterson, Bureau of Labor Statistics.
282 *The New York Daily Advertiser*, June 6, 1835.

With only 4.5% of the world's population, the U.S. produces 18% of the world's wheat.

At issue was the Boston Journeymen Bootmakers' Society that tried to force boot factories to hire union members only. In modern terms, they tried to create a "closed shop."

The bootmakers went on strike in 1839 for a "closed shop," and the strike leaders were arrested on charges of conspiracy to restrain trade. The lower court found them guilty, but the union appealed to the state supreme court. Chief Justice Lemuel Shaw identified their constitutional right to assemble, but only if they never used force to get their way.[283]

The shaky ground on which Shaw made his ruling was this: unions have but one purpose—to use the force of the strike to get their way. Shaw's ruling was contradictory. Can an institution founded on the use of force and created to violate the rights of others be made legal so long as it doesn't use force, or violate the rights of others?

Shaw declared that the union could exist regardless of its purpose (seeking a closed shop) or the means whereby it would seek those ends (the power to strike).

The ruling gave unions a legal foundation to exist. That's all they needed to launch strikes and make other demands for control across multiple issues and multiple decades.

UNIONS MORE IMPORTANT THAN PROPERTY OWNERS

Since the 1842 Bootmakers case, the courts have given legal teeth to widespread union organizing, even when business owners don't want that on their property.

◆ **STRIKES MADE LEGAL:** In 1914, the Clayton Antitrust Act[284] gave unions the legal permission to conduct peaceful strikes, to picket, and to boycott.

◆ **CAN'T PREVENT UNIONS:** In 1932, the Norris-La Guardia Act prevented business owners from going to the courts to stop union organizing in their companies. If workers wanted to join a union, owners could do nothing to stop it. Union organizers were given legal permission to trespass on private property, and to peace-

---

283   Commonwealth vs. Hunt, 45 Mass. 111 (1842), Farwell v. Boston & Worcester RR, The Law of the Commonwealth and Chief Justice Shaw cited in Orth, John V. (2010). "Commonwealth v. Hunt, 45 Mass. 111 (1842).

284   Title 15 of the United States Code, Section 6.

"We are on the verge of a global transformation. All we need is the right major crisis and the nations will accept the New World Order."—David Rockefeller, Statement to the United Nations Business Council, September 23, 1994. Or sept 14, `994, p. 109

fully pass out pro-union literature.[285]

❖ **LOSS OF FREEDOM TO NEGOTIATE:** In 1935, the National Labor Relations Act forced workers to let unions set their wages and benefits. Workers and employers could not make their own contracts at union-controlled businesses without the blessing of the union.[286]

❖ **INTERSTATE COMMERCE CLAUSE VIOLATED:** In 1937, the Supreme Court broke a major chain binding down Congress. There was a steel plant that manufactured goods in Pennsylvania. When the unions tried to organize its workers, the company fired them. The workers sued, saying the National Labor Relations Board had jurisdictions, but they lost in the lower courts. When the case reached the Supreme Court, that's when the damage was done.

The problem was that Congress and its NLRB only had constitutional authority over trade between states. The steel plant issue was *inside* Pennsylvania, and it did not extend to other states.

Justice Hughes said even though the company didn't engage in trade outside the state, its close relationship to those that *did* meant Congress and the NLRB could indeed control them. The court ordered the company to rehire the ten employees and give back their lost wages.

The justices who disagreed said Congress shouldn't be allowed to interfere with a company that was just in-state. The dissenters were outvoted 5-4.[287]

This decision warped the restrictions on Article 1.8, the so-called Commerce Clause that restricted congressional powers. Without amending the Constitution, the Court gave Congress the power to control intrastate businesses if unions wanted to organize there.

❖ **VIOLENCE, DAMAGE IS LEGAL:** In 1972, power company union workers who were striking for higher pay shot bullets into three electric transformers, drained the oil out of another, and dynamited an electric company substation.

The Supreme Court said this was okay because the union had a legitimate claim to higher wages—destroying property was accept-

---

285   Norris-La Guardia Act (1932).
286   See *National Labor Relations Act of 1935*, and the *Federal Labor Relations Act of 1978*.
287   National Labor Relations Board vs. Jones & Laughlin Steel Corporation, 301 U.S. (1937).

Socialism in Brazil: The media in Brazil is subsidized by the government. It must, therefore, report whatever the government wishes.

able in pursuit of that claim.[288] Violent acts against a business, including assaults, destruction of property and even murder, are not punishable under federal law, but they can be punishable under state law. In the 25 years after that 1973 ruling, there were 8,799 incidents of violence recorded, but there were only 258 convictions.[289]

❖ **UNION FORCE RUINS PROSPERITY:** In 2007, just as the collapse of the U.S. economy was beginning, the American auto industry was screaming for help. Instead of cutting back and going through a self-imposed austerity program, the unions held firm, threatening the bankruptcy of the major U.S. auto makers. And that's just what happened.

❖ **UNIONS BANKRUPT THEIR COMPANIES:** In 2008-2010, a perfect storm of rising oil prices, rising material prices, rising union demands, and foreign competition all combined to hit U.S. auto makers hard. The Big Three—Ford, General Motors and Chrysler— were dying. They petitioned the government for bailout help—that is, they wanted the U.S. taxpayer to pay for their extravagances and poor planning. In all, they wanted $50 billion from Congress to pay for union-mandated health care and to avoid bankruptcy. Despite the help, GM and Chrysler declared bankruptcy in 2009.

Union demands cost the Big Three a great deal. For example, between 2006 and 2008, GM lost $2,500 per vehicle while Toyota made $1,500 per vehicle. GM fired more than 35,000 while Toyota fired zero. GM's union insisted that workers be paid an average of $73.26 per hour, while Toyota's average wage was $48.

Like socialists, the unions successfully advance their causes until they run out of other people's money. The "other people's money" ran out with the big auto makers, and in the end, a great industrial giant was reduced to a skeleton. But in a free market, innovation can overcome downturns in the market—just ask Toyota.

❖ **UNIONS MAY MISUSE FUNDS:** In 2010, the Supreme Court decided that unions, among others, may spend unlimited amounts of union dues on information supporting or opposing federal candidates of the union's choosing. They said such action was a First Amendment right. There are stipulations, but the fact remains, union

288   United States vs. Enmons, 410 U.S. 396 (1973).
289   Carl F. Horowitz, *Union Corruption: Why it Happens, How to Combat It.*, 1999.

bosses can inundate union members with literature supporting their favorite candidates, and dues-paying members have no say in it.[290]

Union members pay into pension plans so they have money to retire. The pension funds have been in trouble for years. The Pension Benefit Guaranty Corporation, a U.S. government agency, seeks billions to secure union pensions from failure. This ongoing pursuit will not let up until the socialism train wreck either explodes in bankruptcy, or a firm resolve is made to return to the principles of freedom.[291]

DECLINE OF THE UNIONS?

With the passage of time and the growth of populations, the tables are turning against the unions. People have been blaming unions for having too much control, for stifling innovation and business development, for preventing technology from advancing or benefitting their friends and relatives in other communities.

Unions have a history of igniting fights over sales territory. The fighting and control has turned cities against towns, and friends against competitors. There is a lot of bad PR for the unions, and the right-to-work states are prospering from an influx of businesses fleeing the union-heavy states. This shift away from unions is nearly identical with the shift away from the guild system centuries earlier.

In 1944, union membership accounted for almost 36 percent of the U.S. work force. The U.S. Bureau of Labor Statistics[292] reported that in 1983, union membership stood at 20.1 percent of the labor force, or about 17.7 million union workers. By 2011, membership had dropped to 11.9 percent, or 14.7 million of the current number of employed Americans. That decline was spread across 33 states that saw a drop in membership during 2010.

About half of the American workers in unions live in only six states: California (2.4 million), New York (2 million), Illinois (800,000), Pennsylvania (800,000), Ohio (700,000), and New Jersey (600,000).

As government grew, so did the benefits extracted from taxpayers. In 2010, union membership for people working for the government stood at 36.2%, while the rate for private-sector union

---

290   Citizens United vs. Federal Election Commission, 558 U.S. 08-205 (2010).

291   PBGC website www.pbgc.gov.

292   Bureau of Labor Statistics U.S. Department of Labor, News Release, USDL-11-0063, January 21, 2011.

(cont'd) "... in his relations to others as to develop an illusion of being really able to stand and act alone—an unnamed form of insanity which is responsible for a large part of the remedial suffering of the world."—John Dewey

membership dropped to 6.9%. The pay difference? Average pay per week for union members in 2010 was $917, and for non-union members it was $717.

SLOW EROSION OF LIBERTY

The golden era of unions rose and fell at the expense of human rights. The right to compete on a fair playing ground, and to exercise their unalienable rights, had fallen prey to the ever-increasing bully tactics of unions.

There is no question that labor disputes are a complex issue. On the one hand are the needs of the desperately unemployed, those who are willing to do anything for a paycheck. On the other hand are those employers needing workers, who often give in to the temptation to take unfair advantage of people, such as hiring illegal immigrants to work at below-market wages.

The strike, with all its connected coercion, intimidation, and violence, was the lever to steal from a property owner his right to develop his idea in the fashion that freedom allows.

To their credit, the unions did launch strikes to correct lapses in the workplace. They correctly identified abuses, safety issues, and other risks.

But such discovery didn't *require* a union. Men and women are capable of noticing, all by themselves, that rats in the kitchen, lopped-off fingers in the ground beef, and more pay for men than women doing the same work, are all *bad*. Was union-instigated force the only alternative to correcting such problems?

WAS UNION FORCE THE ONLY ANSWER?

Pro-union people stand aghast with shocked annoyance that anyone would dare question the contributions of violent and non-violent strikes to force change in the working environment.

What they ignore, squash, squander, and kick under the rug are all of the positives that the free market might have brought.

The free market has a way of improving everything it touches with a unique durability that expands into other corners of civilization. The question of how life might be different were unions not the driving force for such corrections in the workplace must remain unanswered for the 1700-1800s.

However, letting freedom back into the workplace portends a more satisfying solution to employment issues in the future. A 2011 study[293] showed that during the period 1977 to 2008,

◇   ... right-to-work states enjoyed a 100% growth in employment while union-friendly states grew only 56.5%. The national average was 71%;

◇   ... the unemployment rate in right-to-work states was 7.9% while the national average was 9.1%;

◇   ... real per capita income grew 62.3% in right-to-work states, while union-friendly states averaged 52.8%. The national average was 54.7%.

◇   Between 2005-09, some 5 million people relocated to right-to-work states.

◇   The bottom 14 states for slowest income growth from 1999 to 2009 were all union-friendly states.

◇   In 2011, a survey by CNBC found that measuring for quality of work force, all 22 of America's right-to-work states ranked in the top 25.[294]

FREEDOM IN THE WORKPLACE

How different might today's world be if companies had to actually compete for good employees. *Come work here, we don't have rats. Come work here, our machines are finger safe. Come work here, we offer a shorter work week, fewer hours, better pay, equal pay, and fantastic benefits such as insurance.*

Obviously, everyone would rush to the employment office of companies offering so many positives, and ignore those that didn't. *Competing to compete* is a novel idea that freedom allows.

---

293   First five points attributed to Sean Higgins, *Investor's Business Daily*, June 29, 2011, citing Richard Vedder, Ohio University, January 2011.
294   *Washington Examiner*, July 2, 2011.

CHAPTER 54:

REVOLUTIONARY: RELIGIOUS REVIVALISTS

There are hundreds of examples of socialism entering the rank and file of religions and religious movements. The following is just a random sample from the 1800s.

W**HO**: Frederick Denison Maurice
WHAT: His book, *The Kingdom of Christ,* 1836
WHERE: Normanstone, England
STORY: Maurice was a professor of theology at Kings College and the University of Cambridge. He was attracted to the socialist ideas of Robert Owen, and pressed those ideas forward to start a movement that later became known as Christian socialism. The foundation of his viewpoint was a dislike for competition in the marketplace. He called it unchristian.

In 1838, Maurice spelled out his version of the ideal relationship between religion and society in *The Kingdom of Christ*. He expressed his philosophy that politics and religion were one and the same, and that the church should be involved in both.

Maurice believed that individual rights and the pursuit of self-interest, with all of its inherent selfishness, were wrong. He rejected the economic principles of laissez faire, and looked to compulsory change through socialism as the best solution.

He encouraged profit-sharing as a means of creating the perfect Christian society, and added numerous tracts and writings to support Christian socialism until his death in 1872.

W**HO:** Adin Ballou
WHAT: Created a utopia in America, 1842
WHERE: Hopedale, Massachusetts
STORY: In the early 1840s, Ballou set out to create the ideal society that would be blissfully set apart from the wicked ways of the world. With the help of his 31 followers, he purchased 600 acres in Worcester County, Massachusetts. It was supposed to be the seed of the ideal community. They built churches, homes for members of the commune, and factories to make an income.

In 2012, a woman seven months pregnant was forced to undergo an abortion because she failed to pay a hefty fine ($6,300) to local officials for violating China's draconian one-child policy. A lethal injection was given to the unborn baby. A photo of the woman and her dead baby raced... (cont'd)

Unlike other socialist societies, members were free to leave if they wanted, and could take their original investment, or 90 percent of what they earned. Although they attempted to treat men and women as equals, women were usually relegated to domestic chores and men became the political leaders.

Members could own their homes but all other facilities and tools were owned in common by the cooperative.

EQUALITY COMES FIRST

The societal foundation Hopedale was on built on equality more than Christianity, although basic Christian tenets were emphasized.

Their constitution listed important commitments made by the members: Avoid all evils mentioned in the Bible, never hold political office or have any dealings with the rest of the country, never file lawsuits, or join a posse, or serve in the military, or vote, or gamble, or drink, or be unchaste.

After 14 years, the commune used up all its member's money and went bankrupt.[295] For Hopedale, the lesson was clear: For economic survival, competition is inevitable and is a law irrevocable. The Hopedale community survived from 1842-1856.

W**HO**: Sidney Rigdon
WHAT: A socialist in the Mormon Church, 1844
WHERE: Kirtland, Ohio
STORY: When the Church of Jesus Christ of Latter-day Saints (the Mormons) was founded in 1830, one of its early converts was a man named Sidney Rigdon. He was a successful Baptist minister who formed his own communal religion based on the ideas of Robert Owen. When the Mormon missionaries found Rigdon he was already living with "all things in common," and had about 50 followers in a commune he called his "family."[296] Rigdon and the congregation converted to Mormonism.

Rigdon's "communal family" lifestyle didn't sit well with Mormon teachings of self-sufficiency and independence. The founder of the Mormon Church, Joseph Smith, saw "no private property" as an

---

295 Hopedale, Massachusetts, www.hopel842.com.
296 Joseph A. Geddes, *The Mormons, Missouri Phase: An Unfinished Experiment*, pp. 16-21; see also, Larson, Andrew Karl, *I Was Called to Dixie: The Virgin River Basin: Unique Experiences on Mormon Pioneering*. 1961.

(cont'd) ... around the Internet, prompting Chinese officials to formally investigate. Late-term abortions have been discouraged since the early 2000s. China's one-child policy from the 1970s resulted in millions of forced abortions—the number peaking in 1983 at 14.37 million. Officials claim the policy has prevented the population of 1.37 billion from growing an additional 400 million.

unworkable flaw in Rigdon's organization.

REPENT, ALL YE SOCIALISTS!

Smith asked Rigdon and his followers to abandon the practice, calling the ideas of socialism "dreadful." Writing from Liberty Jail in Missouri, Smith condemned the communalist society: "We further suggest ... that there be no organization of large bodies upon common stock principles, in property, or of large companies of firms, until the Lord shall signify it in a proper manner, as it opens such a dreadful field for the avaricious, the indolent, and the corrupt-hearted to prey upon the innocent and virtuous, and honest."[297]

OBEDIENCE FOLLOWS CONVERSION

Rigdon and his followers were obedient and abandoned their socialist lifestyle.

The following year, Smith set up his own organization for funding the Church's activities. He called it the United Order where members retained private ownership of their property but were asked to voluntarily put it to work in behalf of the Church.

Retaining property ownership in their common religious labors was a clever process that actually worked and provided the needed support that saved the Church from financial collapse. Many Christian societies have attempted common ownership without success. They've based their authority on Acts 2:44-45 and Acts 4:32 where a cursory reading creates the impression that Jesus Christ's original church practiced all things in common. As explained on page 159,[298] this interpretation is wrong—private ownership remained a part of that earliest practice.

UNITED ORDER BECOMES UNITED DISORDER

After the Mormons settled in the Rocky Mountains in 1847, Smith's successor, Brigham Young, deployed the United Order to about 200 start-up communities. The members gave it a good try beginning in 1855—but this time they made the serious error of trying to have "all things in common," with no private property ownership The usual problems crept in with the industrious

---

297   Joseph Smith, March 25, 1839, *The Personal Writings of Joseph Smith: To the Church of Latter-day Saints at Quincy, Illinois, and Scattered Abroad,* Letter from Liberty Jail, March 25, 1839, p. 389.

298   See page 159, *Did the Early Christians Practice Communism?*

Socialism kills—One aspect of Nazi Germany's death count under Hitler was in 1939, from carbon monoxide and cyanide gas poisoning of chronically ill and mentally deficient: 275,000 killed.

doing more work than the feeble or lazy, so most of the collectives failed by 1858. Community leaders responded by turning to more traditional and successful means (i.e., free market) to sustain themselves, and after that, the whole region started growing.

W**HO**: Pope Leo XIII
WHAT: Pro-union *encyclical* issued May 15, 1891
WHERE: Europe and the world
STORY: In response to what the Catholic Church called "The misery and wretchedness pressing so unjustly on the majority of the working class" from the industrial revolution, the pope issued an open letter on labor, unions, wages, and working conditions. It was called *On the Conditions of Labor*, or *Rerum Novarum*.[299]

PROMOTED MINIMUM WAGE

"Let the working man and the employer make free agreements," the letter stated, "and in particular let them agree freely as to the wages; nevertheless, there underlies a dictate of natural justice more imperious and ancient than any bargain between man and man, namely, that wages ought not to be insufficient to support a frugal and well-behaved wage-earner."

PROMOTED STATE FORCE AS NECESSARY

"...It is advisable that recourse be had to societies or boards such as we shall mention presently, or to some other mode of safeguarding the interests of the wage-earners; the State being appealed to, should circumstances require, for its sanction and protection."

PROMOTED LABOR UNIONS

"History attests what excellent results were brought about by the artificers' guilds of olden times. They were the means of affording not only many advantages to the workmen, but in no small degree of promoting the advancement of art ... Such unions should be suited to the requirements of this our age. ..."

CONTRADICTING PRINCIPLES

The letter further called for life to be made rosy for the worker but neglected to consider the property rights of the factory owner. The Church viewed the owners as profit-hungry and willing to

---

299   All quotes from Encyclical, May 15, 1891.

"Freedom granted only when it is known beforehand that its effects will be beneficial is not freedom."—F.A. Hayek

abuse workers where possible:

"... If through necessity or fear of a worse evil the workman accepts harder conditions because an employer or contractor will afford him no better, he is made the victim of force and injustice."

As a solution to the plight of the working class, the letter called for the creation of trade unions, the power of collective bargaining, and the right to a "living wage."

INTERFERING WITH FREE MARKET

The pope's letter appears to view competition with disdain, and called for imposing an orderly process in the market:

"The great mistake made in regard to the matter now under consideration is to take up with the notion that class is naturally hostile to class, and that the wealthy and the working men are intended by nature to live in mutual conflict. So irrational and so false is this view that the direct contrary is the truth."

Class conflict was a favorite theme of Marx. The letter called for labor and capital to work together instead of against each other.

RECOGNIZED EVILS OF SOCIALISM

On the positive side, the letter pointed out that redistribution of wealth doesn't help:

"To remedy these wrongs the socialists, working on the poor man's envy of the rich, are striving to do away with private property, and contend that individual possessions should become the common property of all, to be administered by the State or by municipal bodies. They hold that by thus transferring property from private individuals to the community, the present mischievous state of things will be set to rights, inasmuch as each citizen will then get his fair share of whatever there is to enjoy. But their contentions are so clearly powerless to end the controversy that were they carried into effect the working man himself would be among the first to suffer. They are, moreover, emphatically unjust, for they would rob the lawful possessor, distort the functions of the State, and create utter confusion in the community."

LEARNING TO RECOGNIZE SOCIALISM

It becomes clear that the seven main ideas embodied in socialism reappear from time to time in assorted flavors and styles. Those who happen to become influential in the historical development and

"The best way to destroy the capitalist system is to debauch the currency."
—Vladimir Lenin

perpetuation of socialism do little more than repackage the dark art in the nice wrapping of regurgitated dreams promising an escape from the ever-present nightmares of the day, regardless of epoch or era in history.

As with all those who preceded them, the socialists' "new" concepts continue to be flawed failures from the start. The oft-heralded discoverers of socialism's tired ideas were the revolutionary philosophers and economists—otherwise brilliant thinkers who exhausted their life pursuits to prove that the unworkable works. Of these labors it may be said: Socialism will continue to spread misery until morale improves.

CHAPTER 55:

REVOLUTIONARY: THE THINKERS

Philosophers and Economists

SOCIALIST: Robert Owen (1771-1858)
LEGACY: Promoted a theory that nurture beats nature
STORY: As discussed earlier, Owen proselytized a theory that top-down regulation of the market, culture, and personal rights would create some kind of utopian scheme of happiness. Nurturing people in the right way, he claimed, would make them a *different* people, a better people—less inclined toward selfish interests, and more inclined toward cooperation. He built his workers nice living conditions in hopes that this would make them better employees. While that much of the experiment worked, it was driven by profits and incentives, important elements he removed for his disastrous socialist colony called New Harmony. He would have done better to stay with free-market, incentive-driven capitalism.

SOCIALIST: Robert Malthus (1766-1834)
LEGACY: Worried about unchecked population growth
STORY: Malthus was fascinated by the relationship between human population and the supply of food. According to his extensive collection of data on births, deaths, and changing ages of marriage and childbearing, he concluded that the human race was in for trouble—food production was rising steadily but populations were rising geometrically.

Malthus decided that the most logical solution to an insufficient food supply was to keep population growth on par with food production. In other words, control population growth.

He saw that humanity's ills and flaws could serve to slow down population growth, and "check" the excessive numbers of people. Malthus listed among these natural inhibitors the positives of marrying late or not at all (fewer babies), the withholding of health care (shorter lifespan), higher food prices (malnutrition), diseases or filthy living conditions (early death), warfare (genocide), and even infanticide. Government welfare, he said, was faulty because—while

<hr/>

Punishing success: "We want to take money [from the wealthy] and put it back in the pocket of middle-class people."—US Vice President Joe Biden, 2009.

it helped sustain life—it did nothing to increase the overall food supply for everybody else.[300]

Malthus was fascinated that against all these odds, humans still survived. He said it must be the will of God that such evils are present to keep the Creator's creations active at solving problems.

"Evil exists in the world," he wrote, "not to create despair, but activity. We are not patiently to submit to it, but to exert ourselves to avoid it."[301]

Malthus's ideas spawned a whole generation of socialistic perspective. For example, Darwin and his survival of the fittest; social engineers and their demands for population control; assumptions about global warming; China's one-child policies, etc.[302]

SOCIALIST: Charles Darwin (1809-1882)
LEGACY: Popularized evolution and natural selection
STORY: Darwin is an insightful scholar remembered for his keen attention to detail and his voluminous experimentation with the flora and fauna of raw nature. He wrote several books on botany, including four zoological works that were exhaustive in their depth and observation. He even wrote a short book describing how vegetable mold is formed from action by worms—no doubt that would prove to be, for worm and vegetable experts, hard-to-ignore riveting reading.

Darwin is perhaps best remembered for his works on evolution—in particular, *Origin of Species* and the *Descent of Man*.

EVOLUTION NOT NEW

The idea of evolution was not invented by Darwin, but his research gave the idea some scholarly support. While science today is obliged to reject several of Darwin's theories, he nevertheless made a great impact on the world, pitting people of faith against people of science. True to the theme of his books on evolution, Darwin wrote that his reason for giving up on Christianity was "Because I found no evidence for it."[303]

---

300   Robert Malthus, An Essay on the Principle of Population, 1st ed., 1798.
301   Malthus, Ibid., XIX. 15.
302   For an excellent summary of Malthus's theories, see Mark Skousen, *The Making of Modern Economics,* pp. 67-89.
303   Edward Aveling, *Charles Darwin and Karl Marx: A Comparison,* 1897, p. 13.

'Politicians are the same all over. They promise to build a bridge even where there is no river."
—Nikita Khrushchev

DARWIN AND MARX WERE ACQUAINTED

The parallels between Darwin and Marx are personal. Their lives overlapped by 65 years, and two of their books, *Origin of Species* and Marx's *Criticism of Political Economy* (the foundation work for *Capital*) were published the same year, 1859.

MARX DEVOURED DARWIN'S BOOKS: Darwin wasn't very interested in Marx's writings. He was the true scientist, ever buried in his research. Darwin did once acknowledge receiving one of Marx's books and wrote in reply, "I believe that we both earnestly desire the extension of knowledge; and this, in the long-run is sure to add to the happiness of mankind."[304] Darwin's optimism in Marx's writings saw no fulfillment, but that personal note reflected the close sentiment the two shared via correspondence.

MARX'S SON-IN-LAW: Edward Aveling married one of Marx's daughters, and grew to know both Marx and Darwin very well. He believed their teachings was a confluence of innovative thinking that was both harmonious and mutually supporting. "Socialism is indeed the logical outcome of evolution," Aveling wrote, "and its strongest scientific support is derived from the teaching of Darwin."[305]

The connection between Marx and Darwin can be seen in Marx's later writings that envisioned an evolutionary path growing out of class struggle. Marx's philosophy declared:

❖ **DESTRUCTION:** The existing society must be destroyed with the death of the "parent" (capitalism) as necessary to make way for the "offspring" (socialism).

❖ **EVOLVING SOCIETY:** Mankind is forever evolving and so must his society.

❖ **TRADITION PREVENTS EVOLUTION:** Abandon traditions such as religion, capitalism, the state, and the family to make room for a new society based on equality and economic justice.

❖ **EVOLVING SPECIES:** Evolution laid a framework for advancing socialism. All new ideas are products of steady evolution of human thought. This is why the past must be detached from

304   Ibid., p. 11.
305   Ibid.

Socialism in France: In 2012, France's socialists won 314 of the 577 seats in parliament. Emboldened by the large win, they promptly announced higher taxes on the rich, elimination of loop holes and numerous tax exemptions, and more spending on welfare—all the same things that got France into the hole they vowed to free it from.

expanding into the future, so that free evolution of thought can mature and develop with each generation.

John Dewey, the so-called father of education in America, was a strong proponent of Darwin's evolutionary process and encouraged that the teachings of parents and the Bible be left out of school so young minds could evolve toward undiscovered horizons of knowledge.

SOCIALIST: Karl Heinrich Marx (1818-1883)
LEGACY: Early advocate of revolutionary Communism
STORY: Marx believed that all of the world's ills could be reduced to one common fault: private ownership of property. He surmised that because there are always those who have, and those who don't, all of society is, as a result, constantly in turmoil to beg, earn, or steal its way into the pockets of the more successful.

GUARD PROPERTY: Marx believed that the rich created a culture to protect their property: the *state, religion,* and the *family.* He also lumped in to this mix, as disposable appendages, all the moral restraints, restrictions, and ideas associated with religion and society. Morality, he declared, is what the socialists say it is—nothing more. This idea mimics Plato, who said that only the elite could tell lies to keep the masses pacified. Plato said that all others in his perfect society would be forced or obligated to tell the truth.

WORKERS' WAR: Marx predicted that one day the working class would rise up against their chains of economic restraint and forcibly take what was theirs. He promoted ideas such as labor unions, graduated income taxes, and government intervention in the marketplace to foster and prepare for this destruction of the existing condition and usher in a new utopian age of reason.

IT'S IN MY BOOKS: Marx's vision for the world was put forward in two books prepared with the help of his cohort, Friedrich Engels: *Communist Manifesto* and *Capital.*

WAS NO PROPHET: History has proven Marx wrong in his predictions of a collapsing capitalistic society and a revolution by the working class. Capitalism's erosion has not come from its strengths *or* weaknesses, but rather from the corrupting influence of Marx's

Socialism kills—China's death count from purges, executions and terror from 1949 to 2010 is estimated to be at least 72,260,000, probably more.

socialistic ideas imposed on natural rights and freedom. Relentless pounding over the decades has corrupted the free market's best operations. As the Psalmist asked, "If the foundations be destroyed, what can the righteous do?"[306]

Though idealized as a great thinker and theorist, Marx's philosophy remains confusing and flawed. Like all other shifts toward the seven pillars of socialism, the true outcome of Marx's intentions had to be buried in a lot of empty promises, predictions, and warnings.

Even his supporters didn't "get it." In 1886, an admirer of Marx, Herr Werner Sombart, admitted that Marxism was a "disordered confusion of the most conflicting conceptions. It represents an extremely heavy potpourri of contradictory doctrines."[307] And so it remains today.

S OCIALIST: John Stuart Mill (1806-1873)
LEGACY: Promoted the force of government in society
STORY: Mill was a contradiction. He defended individual rights, he hated paper money that could *not* be traded for gold, he opposed others telling people what their personal religion or morals should be, and he favored women's right to vote.

On the other hand, Mill called himself a socialist. He was in favor of heavy taxes on inheritances and nationalizing private land, he worried about the problems of overpopulation, and he wondered why private property was something people should completely control.

He encouraged the confiscation of the property and land of dead people who had no relatives to inherit it, and supported the redistribution of people's money. He also didn't like people hanging on to land that wasn't being used. "When land is not intended to be cultivated, no good reason can in general be given for its being private property at all."[308]

Like all socialists, Mill saw a wonderful potential dream for humanity—if only the people would get out of the way.

Mill was very influential in economic circles, and his ideas spread far and wide.

---

306   Psalm 11:3 (KJV).
307   Yves Guyot, *Socialistic Fallacies,* Book VI, Chapter 3, 1910, p. 234.
308   John Stuart Mill, *Principles of Political Economy with some of their Applications to Social Philosophy,* Book II, Chapter II, p. 29.

S OCIALIST: John Dewey (1859-1952)
LEGACY: Sometimes called the father of education in America
STORY: John Dewey had an early fascination with Darwin's theories on evolution. He liked Darwin's explanation that creatures could survive their changing world by adapting and evolving. He believed this principle should apply to education.

❖ **I AM THAT I AM:** Dewey taught that the only real truth in the universe was what mankind said it was.

❖ **DON'T LEARN FROM HISTORY:** It is bad, he said, to perpetuate our own beliefs from generation to generation. Our understanding should be evolving in the same fashion as the creature evolves (that creature would be homo sapiens).

❖ **DON'T LEARN FROM HOME:** Passing along values from one generation to the next doesn't let intellectual evolution take place. He advocated that we break free from the foolish traditions of our forefathers that weigh us down with fiction and fantasy.

❖ **NURTURE, NOT NATURE:** Dewey believed that children become what their environment teaches, and said, "Any education given by a group tends to socialize its members, but the quality and value of the socialization depends upon the habits and aims of the group."[309]

❖ **REPLACE GOD:** What were Dewey's "habits and aims" for the future education system in America? In short, to remove God and let "scientific truths" lead the way.

A MISSIONARY FOR MIS-INFORMATION

In the early decades of the 1900s, Dewey spread his ideas on education and teaching in such nationally-published outlets such as *The New Republic* and *Nation* magazines. He was active in political causes such as women's suffrage (right to vote) and unionizing teachers. He was invited to speak at public and academic settings, where he shared his secular and evolutionary views with America's rising generation of educators and decision makers.

---

309   John Dewey, *Democracy and Education*, Chapter 7, 1916.

Hitler tells God His business (1933): "I believe that Providence would never have allowed us to see the victory of the Movement if it had the intention after all to destroy us at the end." Eleven years later, amid the ashes of destruction, Hitler put a bullet in his head.

FRONTAL ASSAULT ON RELIGION

A pivotal document called *A Humanist Manifesto* was published in 1933. Many believe Dewey was one of its primary authors or editors (there were an unknown number who participated). Author or not, the *Manifesto* received Dewey's blessing, along with the signatures of 33 other leading philosophers, educators, and leaders. Among its 15 conclusions are:[310]

❖ **NO GOD**: "Religious humanists regard the universe as self-existing and not created."

❖ **PRO-DARWINISM**: "Humanism believes that man is a part of nature and that he has emerged as a result of a continuous process."

❖ **SCIENTIFIC VALUES TRUMP RELIGION**: "Humanism asserts that the nature of the universe depicted by modern science makes unacceptable any supernatural or cosmic guarantees of human values."

❖ **NO RELIGIOUS VALUES IN EDUCATION**: "Man will learn to face the crises of life in terms of his knowledge of their naturalness and probability. Reasonable and manly attitudes will be fostered by education and supported by custom. We assume that humanism will take the path of social and mental hygiene and discourage sentimental and unreal hopes and wishful thinking."

❖ **LEAVE TRADITIONAL VALUES BEHIND**: "Though we consider the religious forms and ideas of our fathers no longer adequate, the quest of the good life is still the central task for mankind. Man is at last becoming aware that he alone is responsible for the realization of the world of his dreams, that he has within himself the power for its achievement. He must set intelligence and will to the task."

ONE GENERATION

These doctrinal declarations contained in the *Humanist Manifesto* were injected into America's public school system. It took only one generation to make prayer, God, and the Bible illegal in public schools. This fulfilled an important goal for socializing America. It removed 6,000 years of recorded human history that

---

310   For all quotes, see *A Humanist Manifesto*, The New Humanist, Vol 3, pp. 1-5, 1933.

Thomas Jefferson coined a word to describe his suspicions about Alexander Hamilton's true allegiance. Jefferson combined "monarchy" and "aristocrat" and called Hamilton a "Monocrat."

perpetuated values that had proven themselves as the most beneficial to peaceful and prosperous human relations—and replaced them with a new religion called scientific analysis.

While science as a whole is an invaluable extension of people's curiosity and life-enhancing inventiveness, any attempt to make of it a religious belief for its own sake is corrosive and destructive. And so the world suffers as it loses its heart and soul to a god of human invention.

SOCIALIST: Albert Einstein (1879-1955)
LEGACY: Regarded as the father of modern physics
STORY: Revered as one of the world's greatest mathematical thinkers, Einstein was once asked for his theory on how best to run the economics of a society. He chose socialism, showing that great minds do not always ask the right questions, even minds like his.

"The economic anarchy of capitalist society as it exists today is, in my opinion, the real source of the evil," Einstein wrote in 1949. "We see before us a huge community of producers the members of which are unceasingly striving to deprive each other of the fruits of their collective labour... I am convinced there is only one way to eliminate these grave evils, namely through the establishment of a socialist economy, accompanied by an educational system which would be oriented toward social goals."[311]

* * * * *

GENERIC CHRISTIAN NATION

"The general principles on which the fathers achieved independence, were ... the general principles of Christianity, in which all those sects were united, and the general principles of English and American liberty, in which all those young men united, and which had united all parties in America, in majorities sufficient to assert and maintain her independence. Now I will avow, that I then believed and now believe that those general principles of Christianity are as eternal and immutable as the existence and attributes of God; and that those principles of liberty are as unalterable as human nature and our terrestrial, mundane system."—John Adams

311 "Why Socialism?" Essay originally published in the first issue of *Monthly Review*, May 1949.

"There is something to be said... for gently putting aside the mistaken old ways of our elders if that is possible. If it cannot be done gently, it may have to be done roughly or even violently."
—Alger Hiss

CHAPTER 56:

REVOLUTIONARY: TOP TEN BOOKS

Regardless of age, era, or continent, the idea of socialism has been perpetuated for millennia in books.

It didn't seem to matter in what century a person lived—finding the latest writings on how to build a socialist world was not too difficult, provided that person could read, and the writings were translated into the right language. But writers and readers weren't necessarily looking for socialism—they were looking for *fair*.

BOOK: *The Republic*, written around 380 BC
AUTHOR: Plato (428-348 B.C.)
SYNOPSIS: The author engages various speakers to consider the definition of justice and how to create a city where all human frailties and ills are disposed of by proper management—pure socialism that influenced almost 2,500 years of dreamers and inventors seeking to control humans like bees in a beehive.

As modern historian Will Durant says, Plato's Dialogues "are cleverly and yet poorly constructed. ...they seldom achieve unity or continuity, they often wander from subject to subject, and they are frequently cast into a clumsily indirect mode of being presented as narrative reports, by one man, or other men's conversations."

BOOK: *Peach Blossom Spring*, a poem (A.D. 376-397)
AUTHOR: Tao Yuan Ming (A.D. 365-427)
SYNOPSIS: This essay and poem tell of a fisherman rowing upstream from his home. Suddenly he discovers a hidden valley. The people there know nothing of the real world and live in a utopian state of blissful happiness—a type of ancient Shangri-la, the route to which is lost to the fisherman after he leaves, even though he left markers to help him return at a later time.

BOOK: *Al-Madina al-Fadila* (The Virtuous City)
AUTHOR: Abu Nasr al-Farabi (A.D. 872-950)
SYNOPSIS: Some see this book as an Islamic version of Plato's *Republic*, although Islamic philosophers will clarify that the similari-

Socialism in religion leads to the unthinkable: In December 2011, a 7-year-old girl in India was murdered and her liver offered to gods in hopes for a good agricultural harvest. The jungle district of Chhattisgarh is a rebel Maoist stronghold where human sacrifice ... (cont'd)

ties are really superficial. Al-Farabi's perfect city is God-centered. The role of philosopher king in Plato's book is replaced here with a prophet-Imam.

The ruler in the Virtuous City uses his superior human reasoning ability to direct the people, with or without personal divine revelation. It's his job to force the citizens to be obedient to the laws of happiness. The author chose democracy for the ideal system of government, but gave society a rigid stratification with rulers at all levels to make sure—with force—that everyone behaved correctly.

BOOK: *Utopia*, published in 1516—full title: *A Truly Golden Handbook, No Less Beneficial Than Entertaining, About the Best State of the Commonwealth and the New Island of Utopia.*
AUTHOR: Thomas More (A.D. 1478-1535)
SYNOPSIS: Written as a dialogue between two people (More and a friend, Peter Giles), the tale spins around the island of Utopia, where there is no private property or money.

Everyone is forced to work the farms and must learn a craft that will benefit the city. Their clothing, hair styles, and homes are all the same. No locks on doors—in fact, houses are swapped by lottery every 10 years.

Meals are eaten in common and all venues of vice (taverns, brothels, etc.) are forbidden. There are no secret private places, and permission is needed to take a stroll or leave the town.

The Utopians are pagans who found "god" in all things. The narration criticizes European society of the day, and weaves the possibilities of brilliant regimentation among the island's people into humanity's failings—from which solutions to everything are found.

BOOK: *City of the Sun*, published 1602
AUTHOR: Tommaso Campanella (A.D. 1568-1639)
SYNOPSIS: This is another seafarer story where a Grandmaster asks a sea captain to tell about his latest voyage. The spokesman describes an island in the Indian Ocean where a priest rules all. He knows everything and is therefore brilliant, wise, and understanding, and able to meet the needs of all the inhabitants (called Solarians).

All things are held in common, including material goods, women, and children. Everyone receives their needs from the community, and the officials make sure no one gets more than he

(cont'd) ... is still practiced. Two men were arrested and confessed to the crime. Similar tortures and murders have taken place, some at the urging of local holy men who prescribe human sacrifice to cure nightmares and possession by demons.—The Guardian, AFP, others.

deserves, and no one goes wanting. Everyone must work four hours a day—the rest of the time is spent "in pleasant occupation with the sciences, in discourse and in reading."

BOOK: *New Atlantis*, published 1624
AUTHOR: Francis Bacon (1561-1626)
SYNOPSIS: This story takes place on a mysterious island called Bensalem, somewhere in the Pacific Ocean, west of Peru. These people manage to create the perfect socialistic society, including the ideal college, "Salomon's House." Living in such isolation, it is curious how they became Christian and how they acquired so much knowledge from the outside world. These puzzles are resolved in the book—in particular, how they send fellows in disguise around the world to collect the best inventions and ideas (all created, of course, in free societies!) and bring them back to benefit the island.

BOOK: *The Law of Freedom*, published 1652
AUTHOR: Gerrard Winstanley (1609-1676)
SYNOPSIS: As a leader of the Diggers movement, Winstanley complained to Oliver Cromwell that the English revolution did not help improve the poor. His "Law of Freedom" presents his socialistic view of a future day when money and private property are not needed. The government regulates everything, and all production is put into a central storehouse. Regimentation exists on all levels of society, and neighbors can have each other arrested for violating the rules of society.

BOOK: *How the Other Half Lives*, published 1890
AUTHOR: Jacob Riis (1849-1914)
SYNOPSIS: Riis was a so-called muckraker who photographed the poor and their housing in New York City. The shocking exposé served to unite public demand for government intervention—they wanted strict laws to improve housing, standardize the building codes, and improve sanitation.

To everyone's satisfaction, more or less, the government did step in and force change, all at the expense of free-market solutions. Why couldn't the market fix these things? The socialists say it was because of greed. The free market was too slow, too irregular, and too inefficient—or so the socialists said.

Public's view of Political Terms: 60% of Americans dislike "socialism," but only 50% think "capitalism" is good. About 62% of the same group thought "conservative" was good and 67% thought "progressive" was good.

BOOK: *The Jungle*, published 1906
AUTHOR: Upton Sinclair (1878-1968)
SYNOPSIS: It's not too difficult to make a slaughter house look disgusting and unsanitary, but Sinclair's creativity helped launch a nationwide examination of how America's meat supply was processed. The descriptions of filthy handling and packaging processes prompted lawmakers to pass the Meat Inspection Act in 1906.

The free market has a way of fixing things if left to its own devices. To this point, the financial incentives to clean up the meat packing processes were curtailed by government intervention. It was an easy move to regulate, and government control carried popular support. Since then, government regulations have spread into nearly every aspect of American society because of the same concerns and presumptions of control. Proponents of the free market insist, once again, that the free market would do a better job were it left to its own creative ways.

BONUS BOOK: *Communist Manifesto* (1848)
AUTHOR: Karl Marx (1818-1883) & Friedrich Engels (1820-1895)
SYNOPSIS: This short book is mostly Marx's passionate call for a grand revolution. He and Engels tell the workers of the world to unite and overthrow capitalism, abolish private property, install a heavy graduated income tax, eliminate the family as a social unit, abolish all classes, establish industrial armies (unions), overthrow all governments, and enact communism with communal ownership of property in a classless, stateless society. Alas, as with all the other books on socialism, the *Communist Manifesto* has a bad ending.

Socialism in America: A well-to-do couple in Seattle were convicted in 2012 of collecting thousands of dollars in welfare while living in a $1.2 million waterfront home and purchasing expensive luxuries. They had to pay back 2-1/2 times what they took plus jail time.

Part X

REVOLUTION OF THE SOCIALISTS, SECTION III

"God is dead. God remains dead. And we have killed him. How shall we comfort ourselves, the murderers of all murderers?"

—Friedrich Nietzsche—

CHAPTER 57:

REVOLUTIONARY: BAD AMENDMENTS

*For lack of understanding the correct principles of freedom,
Americans busied themselves amending away their
liberties—a little here, a little there—until
suddenly, the country was back on a
path toward Ruler's Law.*

14 TH AMENDMENT (RATIFIED 1868)

Of all the Amendments, the Fourteenth is one of the longest, perhaps the most poorly written, and certainly one of the most difficult to understand.[312] The way it was written shows more of a sense of revenge and anger than the more careful and calculated calmness typically present in other bills and amendments. Several of its provisions were repetitive and impractical. Here's an overview:

GOOD POINTS IN THE FOURTEENTH

❖ **CITIZENSHIP**: Every person born in America is automatically a citizen. This was passed to stop the abuse of former slaves that continued despite the 13th Amendment that abolished slavery.

❖ **RIGHTS**: States may not pass laws that violate the rights belonging to all Americans. This principle actually repeats what was already granted in Article 4.2: "The citizens of each state shall be entitled to all privileges and immunities of citizens in the several states."

❖ **FULL HEARING IN COURT**: No state may deprive anyone of life, liberty, or property without a full hearing provided by law. This principle repeats what was already guaranteed by the Fifth Amendment: "No person shall be ... deprived of life, liberty, or property, without due process of law."

❖ **3/5THS DESIGNATION ABOLISHED**: The anti-slavery provision in Article 1.2 regarding "3/5ths" was to prevent the South

---

312 For a brief and clarifying discussion on the 14th Amendment, see Skousen, *The Making of America*, op cite., pp. 721-727.

The Communist Party USA was established in 1919 with 12,000 members.

from counting slaves for tax and representation advantages. The 14th did away with that 3/5ths designation.

BAD POINTS IN THE FOURTEENTH

After its passage, the Fourteenth Amendment was used as the basis for shifting power away from the states and into the laps of the federal government. Those bad changes include:

❖ **CITIZENSHIP**: Every person born in America is automatically a citizen. Those entering the U.S. illegally who then give birth ("anchor babies") may see their offspring today receive the gifts of citizenship, free hospital care, welfare, Medicaid, education, reduced college tuition, Social Security, and other benefits that legal immigrants often wait years to receive. This expensive American gift has been abused to strengthen a political base.

❖ **UNEQUAL PROTECTION**: The fourteenth amendment was supposed to enforce equal protection of the laws. The unintended consequence of that provision is that it allowed the federal government's rules and regulations to override the states'.

For example, when Congress imposed the graduated income tax, it prevented the states from protecting all of its citizens equally. Congress decided to extract a higher percentage of money from the wealthy (see 16th Amendment), and the states had no say. This is not "equal protection."

❖ **PUNISHMENT OF STATES**: If a state prevented a qualified male from voting, it could have its number of congressmen reduced. This was intended to punish states that prevented former slaves from voting, but was impractical and never utilized. This flew terribly in the face of healing the nation after the war.

❖ **DEPRIVED LEADERSHIP**: The 14th Amendment prevented the South from putting its most experienced, capable, and responsible leadership into federal office. Six months after the 14th was ratified, President Andrew Johnson erased this bad provision by giving a full pardon and full amnesty "unconditionally and without reservation" to all who had been engaged in the Southern cause.[313]

---

313 Andrew Johnson, *Presidential Proclamation*, Dec. 25, 1868.

✦ **ILL-DEFINED**: Because the 14th Amendment was so poorly crafted, enforcement of its provisions has required *more* legislation and judicial proceedings than any other amendment or provision in the Constitution.

IMPACT: The 14th Amendment shifted power away from the states and into the hands of the federal government—it strengthened the role of the ruler to tell the states what to do. It added more regulations, it eliminated the right to equality under that law, and it certainly gave the central authority more force to impose its will. The federal government gained power to override decisions made in the states, breaking another chain controlling the power of Congress and coming a step closer to Ruler's Law. In short, it legislated into law some basic goals of socialism.

16TH AMENDMENT (RATIFIED 1913)

The Sixteenth Amendment was advertised as a "soak the rich" scheme that backfired terribly and is now soaking *everyone*. This Amendment gave Congress the power to extract taxes directly from everyone's personal income.

GOOD POINTS IN THE SIXTEENTH

For the socialists, this Amendment provided the mechanics to generate virtually unlimited funding for their progressive programs. It footed the bill so they could promise anything in exchange for the voters' support: "Keep me in office, and when we retake the White House, think of all the money I can bring to *our* state!"[314]

BAD POINTS IN THE SIXTEENTH

✦ **DIRECT TAXATION**: The Amendment violates the more thoughtful and less intrusive process of taxation given by the Founders in Article 1, Section 2 and 9.

✦ **VIOLATES PRIVACY**: The 16th inadvertently repealed the 4th Amendment by opening up American homes and private lives to the prying examination of snooping tax collectors. The 4th Amendment declares: "The right of the people to be secure in their persons,

---

314   A direct quote from a sitting senator to the author and his two brothers on May 7, 2010.

houses, papers, and effects, against unreasonable searches and seizures, shall not be violated ...''

◆ **DESTROYS CAPITALISM:** The 16th implements Karl Marx's strategy to destroy a capitalist society with steep and unequal taxes. In the *Communist Manifesto*, Marx called for ''... A heavy progressive or graduated income tax.''[315] This supports his oft-repeated maxim, ''From each according to his ability, to each according to his need.''[316] That is, he who makes more (the rich) must pay more.

◆ **DISCRIMINATES:** Graduated taxation takes more from those who have proven themselves better capable of generating great profits than those who don't know how, or are just lazy.

IMPACT: When T. Coleman Andrews, the Commissioner of the IRS, resigned from his post in 1950, he blasted the Sixteenth Amendment as one of the worst course changes America had made: ''I am convinced that the present system,'' Andrews said, ''is leading us right back to the very tyranny from which those who established this land of freedom, risked their lives, their fortunes and their sacred honor to forever free themselves.''

Most of this tax money, taken from Americans unfamiliar with its unconstitutionality, went to federal programs the Founders declared should remain state responsibilities. A whole generation of ''progressive'' thinking is to be blamed for breaking down these chains of protection. The resulting rampant and immoral accumulation of tax power has grown into a futile attempt to fulfill the utopian pursuits of cradle to grave care by the government. Such spending has bankrupted America to the tune of trillions of dollars.

17TH AMENDMENT (RATIFIED 1913)

The original job of a senator was to represent the state as a sovereign entity. The state legislature selected their representative (the senators) to go back to Washington and make sure a state's best interests were protected and represented such as keeping taxes as low as possible, balancing the budget, helping calm the abrupt extremes of the House that might erupt from time

---

315   Karl Marx, Friedrich Engels, *Communist Manifesto,* 1848 (German original) Chapter 2.
316   Karl Marx, *The Criticism of the Gotha Program,* 1875, published after Marx's death.

In 2012, two reporters for *The Sun* bluffed their way into North Korea. At their hotel, where every room was carefully monitored and bugged, the TV had only one station—"pro-regime propaganda," they reported, "including hours of footage of new leader Kim Jong-un watching military displays."

to time, and providing stability in the government as the senior statesmen with seasoned experience in life and government.

The 17th Amendment ruined this important link in representative government. It made both the senators and the house members representatives of the popular ebbs and flows of emotional rambunctiousness, actions that typically lead to bad choices for leaders. That's why congressmen were allotted only two years in office, so they couldn't do too much damage before they could be kicked out. That's why senators were beholden to the legislature— the legislature could fire them immediately. But now, a long six years must expire before the next voting cycle.

The momentum to vote senators into office (instead of appoint) began with prolonged debates over the subject during the Constitutional Convention in 1787. Rumblings opposing appointment continued over the decades and into the early 1900s. The final blow came when Senator William Lorimer (R-Ill) literally purchased his way into office by bribing the whole legislature to appoint him as senator. The nation was in an uproar over the corruption and demanded protection in the form of popular election.

Ever since, nearly all seated senators have pointed to that corruption as justification for keeping the 17th Amendment in place. They do not want to answer to the direct scolding of legislators for being stupid because appealing to the mass of inattentive voters is so much easier with good ad campaigns at election time, than begging forgiveness—and their job back. Many senators like to run on a platform to repeal the 17th, but once in office, they claim their presence in the Senate is so valuable, "let's repeal it later."

GOOD POINTS IN THE SEVENTEENTH

People who do not understand the importance of an appointed Senator are very supportive of this amendment. They point out how the 17th allowed a popular election campaign to vet the candidates for office in a public forum. That much helps—popular elections do give people a chance to vote directly for who will represent them.

BAD POINTS IN THE SEVENTEENTH

For the socialists, this amendment removed an important link of representation between the states and the federal government. With no direct representative of a state's legislature present in Washington, DC, the legislature's immediate concerns cannot resonate outside the halls of their capitol building. Their concerns and decisions are emasculated, and become subject to the whims of political emotions every time a senator comes up for reelection.

The lowest level of representation—state senators and congressmen—are approachable by anyone in that voting precinct. Such representatives are their neighbors and have regular jobs outside their legislative duties. People could visit their state senator during lunch, air their grievance, and expect action on that state's Capitol Hill. If the complaint had enough support, it was relayed through the appointed federal-level senator to Washington, DC.

Now those direct links are broken. The state legislature may communicate concerns to the senators, but there is no controlling or compelling authority to make him or her properly represent the legislature's views in the nation's capital. The 17th Amendment severed that linkage, and America has suffered for it ever since.

❖ Generally speaking, the "popular vote" essentially makes senators no different than congressmen except for a longer term of office. Their duties are different, but even those lines of demarcation have become blurred in recent years.

❖ Without power to appoint their own representative, the legislatures no longer have direct involvement in the decisions taking place in Washington, DC.

❖ The people have much closer contact with their legislators than their federal representatives. As mentioned, a voter may drive to a legislator's office for a chat in person. Today's senators have mazes of well compensated handlers to manage the day-to-day issues because, "Sorry, the senator is so very busy representing you, he/she can't come to the phone." And they like it that way.

Many senators don't even try to cast a shadow across their states except before re-election time, and then suddenly they're everywhere, defending *you* and *your rights* and *your pocketbook* as if they were the next best thing since sliced bread.

For an unfortunate majority—in all parties—that six-year cycle between re-elections has become a predictable sham.

Socialism in America: A school in Massachusetts banned children from playing tag, touch football and other chase games so accidents wouldn't happen and the school gets sued.

❖   The 17th also permits a devious vacancy procedure that has functioned in this fashion in years past:

1. When a senator dies in office or is otherwise removed, the governor happily resigns his office and is replaced by the lieutenant governor.

2. According to a pre-arranged agreement, the new governor then appoints the ex-governor to become the new senator for the remainder of the term.

3. When the new elections roll around, both leaders run as incumbents—and often win reelection.

IMPACT: No senator wants to surrender the power of public aloofness that has worked so well to insulate him or her from the scrutiny of legislators. Putting their fate into the hands of the closely watched bosses is anathema to the sitting senior statesmen.

The state legislature is much closer to the people than those in Washington, DC. If a senator acted foolishly or in opposition to the people's will, the legislator could take the concern to Capitol Hill to discuss it among other legislators and recall the senator to talk it over—or fire him if the lapse was sufficiently egregious.

Concerned citizens do indeed bring issues to their legislators, and the state legislature does indeed bring those concerns to their congressmen and senators. But the iron teeth of accountability and consequences have all been ripped out by the destructive elimination of representation as imposed by the 17th Amendment.

18TH AMENDMENT (RATIFIED 1919)

The problem with the 18th amendment, often referenced as "Prohibition," is that it went beyond the proper role of government and violated the basic right to choose (in this case, the right to chose to consume alcoholic liquor).

TEETOTALERS: Interest in Prohibition had been growing since before the Civil War. Even so, only five states had actually adopted statewide prohibition by 1900. Many other states adopted laws allowing counties to decide on Prohibition if they pleased. These were called the local-option laws.

Does Socialism lead to Communism? It did in Poland: "But the tragedy of the polish Socialist party will not be understood unless it is realized that in its fight with Soviet communism it was ideologically compromised. Its partial acceptance of communist ideology constantly imposed ..." (cont'd)

By 1919, a huge effort by women nationwide was organized into the Anti-Saloon League. This helped push 14 more states to go dry, with many others embracing the local-option laws.

WORLD WAR I: With the war getting under way, Congress passed a prohibition law as a means of food-control in 1917. That same year Congress went further and passed the 18th Amendment and sent it to the states for ratification. It became law in 1919.

ABSENT VOTERS: A problem with troops returning from the war was that they felt left out of the debates and ratification process because of their absence. Resistance to the Amendment over the prohibition of even lighter drinks such as beer and wine compounded the Amendment's unpopularity. Resistance grew until it was repealed with the 21st Amendment in 1933. That Amendment didn't make drinking legal—it just turned the problem back over to the states to solve, where it should have been in the first place.

DRUG PROBLEM: Alcoholism is the number one drug problem in the U.S. Had Prohibition imposed higher taxes and penalties for intoxication from the hard liquors and left the lighter liquors alone, it might have achieved some good while respecting individual rights. But as an amendment to the U.S. Constitution, that was an improper role for government to play.

LOCAL LEVEL BEST: Alcoholic drinks and other social issues that concern society are best managed by the states. Some of these issues include capital punishment, abortion, gun laws, beer and wine distribution, sex education, minimum age of marriage, gambling, the lottery, dog and horse racing, etc. The Founders' good counsel was to push the problem to the lowest possible level. That wisdom was timeless, and America would benefit by returning to it.

23RD AMENDMENT (RATIFIED 1961)

This Amendment gave the seat of government, Washington, DC, its own electors—that is, representatives to the Electoral College—to help choose the president and vice president.

(cont'd) "...upon it dilemmas which hindered the effectiveness of its action, and led first to common action with, and eventually to absorption by, the Communist party; and the Communist party in its conquest of the Polish state found it advantageous to have the facade of an alliance with the socialists."—Ivor Thomas, The Socialist Tragedy, 1951.

GOOD POINTS IN THE 23RD AMENDMENT

❖ The people living in Washington, DC had no ability to participate in the elections for president and vice president. The 23rd Amendment gave them a place on the electoral college.

BAD POINTS IN THE 23RD AMENDMENT

❖ Leaders of the Democratic Party saw an opportunity to stack the political deck against the Republican Party. Washington, DC was very left-leaning and would easily become a deciding factor for *any* legislation if it were allowed two senators and one representative. To achieve this, Congress had to make DC a city-state—that is, grant a city the same powers of representation as a full-fledged, sovereign state.

❖ The first step was achieved with the 23rd Amendment.

❖ The second step was the "Washington, DC Voting Rights Amendment" proposed in 1978. It gave the District of Columbia two senators and one representative. This amendment failed to become ratified, and expired in 1985.

❖ If the failed amendment passed, it would have opened the door for additional city-states to be created, probably beginning with New York, Los Angeles, and Chicago—traditional strongholds for the Democratic Party. If the Republican Party had pushed for the same in strongly-conservative cities, the howling on the other side of the aisle would have been just as loud.

❖ The Founders and other students of history observed that the seat of government in any nation throughout history becomes the recipient of showers of national treasure for its beautification and aggrandizement. The citizens of such cities become happy converts to the money and attention, and anxiously support whichever ruling party can keep the money flow going.

❖ A simpler solution to voting rights was to send the residents of Washington, DC back to Maryland to cast votes because Maryland was the original landowner of the District of Columbia.

25 TH AMENDMENT (RATIFIED 1967)

When the president or vice president dies, resigns, or is removed from office, the one or the other is given authority to fill the vacancy by the 25th Amendment. Before this Amendment, a vacancy in the office of vice president had to remain vacant until the next presidential election, while a vacancy for president already followed a written plan.

GOOD POINTS IN THE 25TH AMENDMENT

❖ The procedure for keeping the top two executive positions filled was streamlined by the 25th Amendment. However, the potential to misuse this process is, and has been, dangerously abused.

BAD POINTS IN THE 25TH AMENDMENT

❖ This amendment allows un-elected people to occupy the highest office in the land. For example:

FORD

In 1973, Spiro T. Agnew resigned as vice president, and President Richard Nixon appointed Congressman Gerald R. Ford of Michigan to fill the spot. This appointment was approved by a majority of the Senate and House.

ROCKEFELLER

In 1974, Nixon resigned as president, and Vice President Ford became the new president. Ford had power to appoint his replacement and called on Nelson A. Rockefeller to become vice president, with approval of a majority of the House and Senate.

UN-ELECTED EXECUTIVES

And with that, the United States suddenly had two men in these important positions who were not elected by the American people.

A wiser process would require a 2/3rds majority vote by the Senate instead of a simple majority vote in these various office-hopping activities. Simple majority allows confirmation to follow party lines instead of forcing cooperation between both parties (assuming neither party has a 2/3rds majority).

❖ The president can turn over his powers to the vice president any time he pleases, and take them up again at a later time without being stopped in either instance by the House or Senate.

❖ An ambitious vice president who can get a majority of the Cabinet to agree with him can summarily take over the president's

---

Hitler's view of freedom of speech (1942): "We have to put a stop to the idea that it is a part of everybody's civil rights to say whatever he pleases."

duties, with or without the president's consent—a type of *coup* to take over the White House.

❖ If the president has relinquished power to the vice president, he may not resume his presidential powers without the consent of the vice president and a majority of the Cabinet—the *coup* may thereby be continued.

❖ A President recovering from some disability that rendered him unfit for office, temporarily, who then seeks to resume his office is still subordinate to the vice president who sits in the Oval Office as acting president. An ambitious vice president controlling a dominant bloc of Congress could stall a return to power by the president long enough to have certain legislations passed and sign into law any number of bills that the original president might otherwise veto.

❖ The potential consequences of the dangerous flaws incorporated into the 25th Amendment are not farfetched, as illustrated by the Nixon administration. America has yet to fully try on the 25th Amendment, should the president become disabled, but as described above, it is fraught with dangerous loopholes and potentials for abuse. It should be repealed and replaced with something putting Congress and the Senate more firmly in control, with 2/3rds majorities required to replace an elected officer of the Executive Branch.

Union contracts forced the maker of Twinkies to pay $100 million a year into pension plans for other companies. In 2012, these demands pushed Hostess into bankruptcy.

REVOLUTIONARY: U.S. SUPREME COURT

Jefferson saw this one coming like a bull charging out of the fog ... and it changed everything.

One of the gaping holes left in the Constitution was how to prevent the U.S. Supreme Court from exercising its prejudiced *will* when it was supposed to exercise an unprejudiced *judgment*. The problem then, and now, is that judgments by the Court pivot on the political biases and social philosophy of the individual justices—instead of the Constitution and the intent of its Founders. Every president hopes to pack the court with *his* kind of justices.

For the other branches, the Founders put restraints on Congress with several good safeguards and constitutional remedies. It was the same for the President. But where were the safeguards for the Court?

This is one of the issues the Founders left undone. They talked about it, they worried over it, they debated it,[317] but the closest they came to crafting controls and a remedy was in these three inadequate restrictions:

❖ **PRESIDENTIAL APPOINTMENT**: All the judges had to be appointed by the president—with the advice and consent of the Senate. This let the president pick a justice who would support his own political aspirations. This is not strong control *by the people*.

❖ **CONGRESSIONAL RESTRICTIONS**: The Congress was authorized to restrict what cases the Court could handle (its jurisdiction), but that has rarely been attempted. (See Article 3.2)

❖ **IMPEACHMENT**: Congress was allowed to impeach the justices and kick them off the bench for treason, bribery, or other crimes, but not for unpopular decisions—even if the Court altered the Constitution with an unconstitutional decision.

---

317 A summary of the Founders' concerns may be found in Skousen, *The Making of America*, pp. 569-581.

Union's control over U.S. government—Percentage of unionized public sector employees in the 1960s: 10%. The percentage in 2007: 36%

JUDICIAL REVIEW

The authority to examine Acts passed by Congress or State legislatures is called the right to "judicial review"—meaning, the Court can review an Act to measure if it violates any provision in the Constitution as designed by the Founding Fathers.

This authority wasn't spelled out very well. There was much discussion on the matter, but it was never really resolved. This resulted in a gradual evolution of the Court's power.

Today, the Court is so independent and all-powerful that it has indeed become despotic—an outcome that Thomas Jefferson warned about very early on, as will be discussed later.

EVOLUTION OF THE COURT'S POWER

The Court passed through four stages of development[318]:

1. **JOHN MARSHALL PERIOD (1801-1835).** Marshall was the fourth chief justice and established the Court as the "last say" on all things constitutional. For reference material the Court used the Constitution, the Federalist Papers, and the words of the Founders to make their decisions.

2. **ROGER B. TANEY PERIOD (1835-1895).** Starting around 1835, the Court began distancing itself from the Founders. It leaned heavily on constitutional doctrines and theories, and the Founders' philosophy, but the justices stopped quoting the Founders and the Federalist Papers in most cases. Justice Taney is remembered for delivering the majority opinion in Dred Scott v. Sanford (1857) that said blacks could not be considered citizens of the United States.

3. **JUDICIAL SUPREMACY (1895-1930s).** Around 1895, the Court took a giant "progressive" step backwards and became more vocal about its opinions being *supreme* instead of the Constitution. The Constitution was no longer what the *Founders* said. It was now what the Supreme Court said.

4. **'SUPER LEGISLATURE' (1930s to today).** The Court today is seriously out of control. It bypasses the amendment process to make law and declares it through interpretation, voiding Congress and the states if an Act happens to hit the justices wrong for any reason. Presidents will pack it with political supporters, and today's Court

---

318 See Edwin S. Corwin, editor, *The Constitution of the United States, Annotated*, Library of Congress, 1953.

has changed the supreme law from a Constitution of *Rights* to a Constitution of *Powers*.

SOME COURT CASES TO ILLUSTRATE

Just as Jefferson had warned, an unchecked Supreme Court began abolishing, little by little, the subtle protections of rights provided by the Constitution. Each weakening of the Constitution gave ground for the establishment of various components of Ruler's Law and the seven pillars of socialism. There are *hundreds* of cases that prove the Court's progressive tendencies.

CASE: Marbury vs. Madison (1803)

PRECEDENT: Declared a congressional bill unconstitutional. **STORY**: This was the first time the Supreme Court declared an Act passed by Congress to be unconstitutional. This decision emphasized that the Constitution was the supreme law of the land, and that's good. But it also emphasized that the Supreme Court justices wanted everyone to understand that *they* were the final authority on what the Constitution actually meant. So long as decisions were handed down based on the actual Constitution, this declaration of supremacy was appropriate. When decisions were based on precedent (what prior courts decided), that's when trouble started.

Judicial activism—the un-checkable power to create new laws by twisting or ignoring the Constitution to mean something the Founders never intended it to mean—found its opening with this case.

CASE: Martin vs. Hunter's Lessee (1816)

PRECEDENT: The Court declared itself the supreme authority. **STORY**: At issue was a state's interpretation of a federal law. The Court denied states any authority to interpret federal law as they saw fit. This case was *good* because it helped unify the new nation under a single, unified, common understanding. It was *bad* because it eroded state sovereignty, making it tough for the states to challenge federal laws that were bad or unfair or conflicted with state law. It contributed to the loss of state's rights and state sovereignty.

CASE: Gibbons vs. Ogden (1824)

PRECEDENT: Unleashed power to regulate almost everything. **STORY**: The case involved New York giving Robert Fulton 100% control of steamboat operations along the Hudson so nobody else could compete. The Supreme Court declared it unconstitutional, saying that competing steamboat operators could engage in trade along a coast—it was an interstate commerce activity. This was later interpreted to mean Congress could also regulate the actual steamboat itself, the means of its construction, all safety issues, loading docks, fares, and just about everything else. This wiped out a state's right to set any of those parameters, clearly a violation of states rights to control their own commerce.

CASE: United States vs. Butler (1936)

PRECEDENT: Removed restrictions on taxing and spending, defined "general welfare" as a blank check.

STORY: Ever since the Constitution had been ratified, Hamilton and Madison had argued over the actual meaning of the Constitution's list of enumerated powers granted to Congress. Hamilton said the list was mere suggestion, and Madison disagreed, stating unequivocally that there is a strong limit for what Congress may tax and spend.

In the Butler case, the Supreme Court settled the debate by siding with Hamilton, saying Congress could raise taxes for anything it deemed important for "the general welfare." Did that change things? Yes. In 1936, the federal budget was under $6 billion. By 1980, it had grown to about $600 billion, and now pushes past $4 *trillion*, and 20 times that amount in national obligations. The Butler case turned America's economic power on its head. Today, the burden of that foolishness is being felt across the country and worldwide.

CASE: Everson vs. Board of Education (1947)

PRECEDENT: Forced Bill of Rights onto the individual states.

STORY: This case involved state support for children attending private religious schools in New Jersey. The Court ruled the practice was unconstitutional, citing "Congress shall make no law respecting an establishment of religion." This case gave the federal government jurisdiction over states if their laws conflicted with federal law. It was the beginning of the removal of religion from America's public institutions. Later on, the courts would stand atop this ruling to stomp all over states' rights by forcing all public schools to eliminate prayer, the Bible, and God from their curriculum and in-school activities.

CASE: Roe vs. Wade (1973)
PRECEDENT: The Court turns state issue into a federal issue.
STORY: Abortion is an enormously complex issue that has consumed billions of words across millions of pages. In Rove vs. Wade, the court mandated that abortion was a legal medical procedure in America, and available for the asking.

The very most the Court should have done was to turn the issue over to the states where it belonged. The "Jane Roe" in the lawsuit, Norma McCorvey, has since regretted her role and petitioned the court to re-hear the case based on evidence that abortion also harms the mother.[319] The court refused.

CASE: Garcia vs. San Antonio Metro. Transit Authority (1985)
PRECEDENT: Destroyed Tenth Amendment.
STORY: The Tenth Amendment reserves to the states all the powers not specifically granted to the federal government. In National League of Cities vs. Usery (1976), the Court declared that Congress had no authority under the Tenth Amendment to dictate wages and overtime rules for local governments. In Garcia, the Court overruled itself and said that Congress could indeed dictate on the local level.

At issue were volunteer government employees, such as policemen volunteering as ambulance drivers, and teachers volunteering for extra duties for their students. The Court ruled that Congress could indeed force the municipalities to pay wages. The point of volunteering was purely to help local governments short on cash to improve their communities. In violation of the Tenth Amendment, the Court said Congress could control those activities. The Court mandated that either the 80,000 employees from state and local governments go without this extra volunteer help, or they must pay wages to get it.

CASE: Kelo vs. New London (2005)
PRECEDENT: Destroyed Fifth Amendment and private property.
STORY: This highly controversial case allowed the transfer of private property from its rightful owner to another private owner whose purposes promised an increase in jobs and tax revenue. The decision destroyed the distinction between private and public use of property. The dissenting justices declared that this action amended

---

319   "Court rejects challenge to abortion ruling," Associated Press, February 22, 2005.

"Almost all the prophecies of Marx and his followers have already proved to be false, but this does not disturb the spiritual certainty of the faithful, any more than it did in the case of chiliastic sects."—Leszek Kolakowski

the Constitution by erasing from the Fifth Amendment the words "for public use" and replacing them with "for whatever use the government decides."

CASE: "ObamaCare," national health care (2012)
PRECEDENT: The Court expanded congressional powers beyond constitutional boundaries, again.
STORY: In its most damaging swipe against freedom in 100 years, the Supreme Court upheld the individual mandate in Obama's national health care program, giving Congress authority to force Americans to buy health insurance under Congress's power to "lay and collect taxes." In a carefully crafted slight of hand, the Court said the government could not order people to buy health insurance, but it could tax those who didn't. The Court also held the federal government could not force states to expand Medicaid to cover millions that were uninsured. It rejected Congress's claim it could force health care as an enumerated right in the Commerce Clause.

ROBERT A. LEVY cites numerous other cases[320] where the Supreme Court ...

- **Radically expanded government**—Helvering vs. Davis (1937) *and* United States vs. Butler (1936)

- **Allowed expanding powers of regulation**—Wickard vs. Filburn 1942; Gonzales vs. Raich 2005

- **Destroyed the sanctity of private contracts**—Home Building & Loan Association vs. Blaisdell 1934; Gold Clase Cases 1935

- **Gave law-making power to government agencies, bypassing the constitutional law-making authority of Congress**—Whitman vs. American Trucking Associations, Inc. 2001

- **Eroded freedom of speech**—McConnell vs. Federal Election Commission 2003; Buckley vs. Valeo 1976

- **Curtailed gun-owners' rights and other civil liberties all in the name of national security**—United States vs. Miller 1939; Koremat-

---

320   Robert A. Levy, *The Dirty Dozen: How Twelve Supreme Court Cases Radically Expanded Government and Eroded Freedom*, 2008.

Socialism in China: In an attempt to silence celebration on the annual anniversary day of the government's bloody crackdown in Tiananmen Square in 1989, China regularly blocks Internet sites, deletes blogs, and prevents search terms such as "six four" (June 4), "candle," and "never forget." Estimates of the number of protesters killed and wounded ... (cont'd)

su vs. United States 1944; Korematsu vs. United States 1944

❖ **Forced people to surrender private property without the opportunity to appeal the judgment in a court of law**—Bennis vs. Michigan 1996

❖ **Infringed on the right to earn an honest living**—United States vs. Carolene Products 1938, and Nebbia vs. New York 1934

❖ **Violated equal protection under the law for reasons of race**—Grutter vs. Bollinger 2003, and Regents of the University of California vs. Bakke 1978

❖ **Protected the rights of unions to destroy private property, intimidate, and commit violence during a strike**—See "Revolutionary: Union Organizers" in Chapter 53).

WHAT CAN BE DONE?

Thomas Jefferson had plenty to say on this topic and offered some solutions. One of those is an amendment allowing the states or their representatives to nullify a decision by the Supreme Court with a 2/3rds majority vote. These ideas were put forward by Thomas Jefferson more than 200 years ago because by the time Jefferson was president, the Court was already taking power it wasn't granted.

JEFFERSON ON JUDICIAL REVIEW

As president, Jefferson expressed his concerns in a letter to Abigail Adams:

"You seem to think it devolved on the judges to decide on the validity of the sedition law, but nothing in the Constitution has given them a right to decide for the executive, more than to the executive to decide for them.

"Both magistrates are equally independent in the sphere of action assigned to them.

"The judges, believing the law constitutional, had a right to pass a sentence of fine and imprisonment, because the power was placed in their hands by the Constitution.

"But the executives, believing the law to be unconstitutional, were bound to remit the execution of it, because that power has

(cont'd) ... range from the hundreds to the thousands who were massacred and imprisoned that day. When interfering with Internet traffic, the Chinese government uses the word "harmonized" to explain why a blog or search term was censored. Former prisoners and dissidents are always warned not to talk to journalists.

been confided to them by the Constitution. That instrument meant that its coordinate branches should be checks on each other.

"But the opinion which gives to the judges the right to decide what laws are constitutional and what not, not only for themselves in their own sphere of action, but for the legislature an executive also in their spheres, would make a judiciary a despotic branch."[321]

JEFFERSON ON MARBURY VS. MADISON

Jefferson objected to the Court taking upon itself unbounded powers of decision, and wished to abolish the precedent the Court established in Marbury vs. Madison—

"The Constitution intended that the three great branches of the government should be coordinate, and independent of each other," Jefferson wrote. "As to acts, therefore, which are to be done by either, it has given no control to another branch.... It did not intend to give the judiciary ... control over the executive.... I have long wished for a proper occasion to have the gratuitous opinion in Marbury vs. Madison brought before the public, and denounced as not law."[322]

JEFFERSON ON CORRUPTION OF JUSTICES

In a letter to William Charles Jarvis in 1820, Jefferson pointed out that Court justices are no more immune from corruption than anyone else, and with life-long appointments, there is little incentive to stay responsible to the people and the Constitution:

"You seem ... to consider the judges as the ultimate arbiters of all constitutional questions; a very dangerous doctrine indeed, and one which would place us under the despotism of an oligarchy.

"Our judges are as honest as other men, and not more so. They have, with others, the same passions for party, for power, and the privilege of their corps.... Their power [is] the more dangerous as they are in office for life, and not responsible, as the other functionaries are, to the elective control.

"The Constitution has erected no such single tribunal, knowing that to whatever hands confided, with the corruptions of time and party, its members would become despots. It has more wisely made all the departments co-equal and co-sovereign within themselves."[323]

---

321 Bergh, 11:50.
322 Bergh, 11:50, p. 213.
323 Ibid., p. 277.

"Young men talk of the future because they have no past. Old men talk of the past because they have no future."—Boyd K. Packer

JEFFERSON ON UNCONSTITUTIONAL DECISIONS

Continuing in his letter to William Charles Jarvis, Jefferson points out that all others in the federal government are responsible to those who elected them. But not the Court, and this is dangerous to freedom:

"When the legislative or executive functionaries act unconstitutionally, they are responsible to the people in their elective capacity. The exemption of the judges from that is quite dangerous enough.

"I know of no safe depository of the ultimate powers of the society but the people themselves; and if we think them not enlightened enough to exercise their control with a wholesome discretion, the remedy is not to take it from them but to inform their discretion by education.

"This is the true corrective of abuses of constitutional power."[324]

JEFFERSON ON ORIGINAL INTENT

Putting the Court in a position to pronounce what the Constitution meant was not what the Founders intended. They wanted the Court to *apply* the Constitution, not interpret or twist its meaning. The Founders wanted the justices to be pro-Constitution, not anti. As president, Jefferson wrote:

"On every question of construction, [let us] carry ourselves back to the time when the Constitution was adopted, recollect the spirit manifested in the debates, and instead of trying what meaning may be squeezed out of the text, or invented against it, conform to the probable one in which it was passed." [325]

CONSTITUTION NOT A BLANK PAPER

Jefferson declared that the Constitution is not an arbitrary set of flexible rules. Had America adhered to that counsel, how many looming problems might never have developed? Said Jefferson:

"When an instrument admits two constructions, the one safe, the other dangerous, the one precise, the other indefinite, I prefer that which is safe and precise. I had rather ask an enlargement of power from the nation, where it is found necessary, than to assume it by a construction which would make our powers boundless. Our peculiar security is in the possession of a written Constitution. Let us not make it a blank paper by construction."[326]

---

324   Ibid.
325   Bergh 15:449; See also Bergh 10:248.
326   Bergh, 10:418.

"All of Marx's major predictions have turned out to be wrong."—Roger Kimball, 2005

AN UNCHECKED FEDERAL JUDICIARY WILL DESTROY DEMOCRACY

Jefferson believed the Supreme Court and its lesser offices posed the greatest danger to liberty. He said,

"...The germ of dissolution of our federal government is in the constitution of the federal judiciary; an irresponsible body working like gravity by night and by day, gaining a little today and little tomorrow, and advancing its noiseless step like a thief, over the field of jurisdiction, until all shall be usurped from the States, and the government of all be consolidated into one. To this I am opposed; because, when all government, domestic and foreign, in little as in great things, shall be drawn to Washington as the center of all power, it will render powerless the checks provided of one government or another, and will become as venal and oppressive as the government from which we separated."[327]

MEANWHILE, OVER IN EUROPE (AND THE U.S.) ...

While the Courts, the people, and economic experimenters tried on new opportunities in the revolutionary 1800s, a more subtle and dangerous manifestation of socialism was quietly eating into the core of national stability. It was a failure system that one day would embrace all seven pillars and all the world's nations. It carried the moniker *state welfare*. But first, before that final temptation towards power could be tried, the ground had to be plowed—

---

327   Thomas Jefferson letter to C. Hammond, 1821.

Socialized medicine is inefficient: A man in Zapopan, Mexico, required surgery on his knee joint, but rather than being provided everything he needed, he was required to purchase the screws and other small parts himself to complete the surgical procedure.

CHAPTER 59:

REVOLUTIONARY: THE NEO-PROGRESSIVES

For a hundred years, American liberty survived the buffeting of usurpers and tyrants. Could it survive another century against the new progressives of the 1900s?

T he progressive era familiar to most people reached prominence from 1880 to 1920. Even though the formal Progressive Party dissolved in 1916, the movement continued to pursue its goals through other means.

STORY: At first, the progressive movement was a sporadic, spontaneous uprising that called for more freedom for some things, but more federal control over others. Big business and stagnation put the Constitution in a tug-of-war, some pulling for a return to constitutional restraints, others pulling for dumping it for socialism. They wanted *change*.

In the progressives' gallery of infamy hang a thousand portraits of change. Here are some samples from its first 50 years—

1 **UNALIENABLE RIGHTS—REJECTED:** Neo-progressives insisted that humans are not born free, nor is freedom a gift ◆ of God. John Dewey (1859-1952) said freedom is not "a ready-made possession ... it is something to be achieved."[328] He said any idea of natural rights and liberties exist only in "the kingdom of mythological social zoology."[329]

NATURAL RIGHTS DISCREDITED. Progressive writer Charles Merriam also rejected the concept of unalienable rights: "The individualistic ideas of the 'natural right' school of political theory, indorsed in the Revolution, are discredited and repudiated.... The origin of the state is regarded, not as the result of a deliberate agreement among men, but as the result of historical

---

328 John Dewey, *The History of Liberalism*, excerpted from Liberalism and Social Action, 1935.
329 Ibid.

In 2012, Massachusetts banned junk food at bake sales or related school activities, declaring that obesity had become the government's responsibility because parents failed to reign in their kids' eating habits. Regulating what people eat, now *that's* thinking like a socialist.

development, instinctive rather than conscious; and rights are considered to have their source not in nature, but in law."[330]

2. LIMITED GOVERNMENT—REJECTED: John Dewey said government's role was to create laws and structure ♦ "not [as] means for obtaining something for individuals, not even happiness. They are means of creating individuals ...." In other words, it was government's role to properly train people, *create them*, and fabricate their lives with education, structure, economy into ideal servants of society.

CHARLES MERRIAM (1874-1953) said the public *wants* unlimited government: "The public, or at least a large portion of it, is ready for the extension of the functions of government in almost any direction where the general welfare may be advanced, regardless of whether individuals as such are benefited thereby or not."[331]

THEODORE WOOLSEY (1801-1889) was president of Yale College. He insisted that government should meet all human needs: "The sphere of the state may reach as far as the nature and needs of man and of men reach, including intellectual and aesthetic wants of the individual, and the religious and moral nature of its citizens."[332]

3. GOD IS DEAD: The *Humanist Manifesto*, published in 1933, was an accumulation of progressive philosophy that re- ♦ jected God, religion, and creation. The Manifesto declared, "Religious humanists regard the universe as self-existing and not created." And, "Humanism believes that man is a part of nature and that he has emerged as a result of a continuous process."[333]

GEORG WILHELM FRIEDRICH HEGEL (1770-1831), the originator of class conflict (dialectics), elevated the state as the "divine idea as it exists on earth." "All the worth which a human being possesses," he said, "all spiritual reality, he possesses only through the State. ..."[334] "We must ... worship the State as the

---

330   Charles Merriam, *A History of American Political Theories*, 1903, Chapter VIII.
331   Ibid., Merriam, p. 333.
332   Theodore Woolsey, Political Science, Vol. I, pp. 23-25.
333   See www.americanhumanist.org.
334   G. W. F. Hegel, Philosophy of History.

Socialism kills—In North Korea from 1948-2010, brutal crackdowns and a needless famine resulting from strident socialist policies caused the deaths of at least 3,163,000.

manifestation of the Divine on Earth."[335] Progressives embraced Hegel and his ideas.

JOHN BURGESS (1844-1931), influential political scientist, echoed Hegel, and said the ultimate end of the state is not heaven above, but the "perfection of humanity, the civilization of the world, the perfect development of the human reason and its attainment to universal command over individualism; the apotheosis of man."[336] *Apotheosis* means "man becoming God."

FRIEDRICH NIETZSCHE (1844-1900), a noted German philosopher, viewed God as either a mythical creation or the rejected founder of western culture who was usurped by materialism. A preoccupation on things secular led Nietzsche to declare, "God is dead. God remains dead. And we have killed him. How shall we comfort ourselves, the murderers of all murderers?"[337]

4 **FREEDOM AND INDEPENDENCE—REJECTED**: Instead of protecting rights, the state declares rights, *every* ◆ right, according to the progressives. John Burgess wrote in 1891, "The state cannot be conceived without sovereignty, i.e. without unlimited power over its subjects." He said the state must have "original, absolute, unlimited, universal power over the individual subject, and all associations of subjects."[338]

5 **REPLACE "REPUBLIC" WITH "DEMOCRACY"**: Progressives pushed for removing representatives and replacing ◆ them with a direct popular vote. They wanted the power to approve new laws by direct vote, remove public officials by direct vote, nominate candidates for election by direct vote, elect senators by direct vote, and legalize the vote by women. The last two goals were achieved with the 17th and 19th amendments to the Constitution—the former (the 17th) turned out to be a foolish mistake, the latter (suffrage) was good, but it was already being adopted in several of the states by the time it was formalized as an amendment.

---

335   G. W. F. Hegel, Philosophy of Law.
336   Merriam, ibid., vol. VIII.
337   Friedrich Nietzsche, *The Gay Science,* Section 125.
338   *Political Science and Comparative Constitutional Law*, I, p. 52, 1891, cited in *A History of American Political Theories* by Charles Edward Merriam, 1915.

Socialism in China: In 2012, China announced ID cards were being abolished and replaced with fingerprint registration. The announcement claimed that providing fingerprints was strictly voluntary and public security groups were not allowed to force mass registration of fingerprints.

6. **TAX INDIVIDUAL INCOME** became a reality during the Civil War with a flat tax of 3% that was expanded to ♦ 5%. Various tax plans were put forward until 1909 when an amendment was passed by Congress. It was ratified in 1913 as the 16th amendment, allowing a direct tax on wages, salaries, commissions, etc. The progressives wanted—and got—the rich to be forced to pay more, a levelling scheme proposed by Marx in 1848.[339]

7. **ELIMINATION OF PRIVATE PROPERTY**: The American dream of building up a business into a large generator of jobs ♦ and prosperity was viewed with envy by the progressives. They called for large monopolies of corporations to be nationalized—taken over by the federal government, or otherwise fiercely regulated. With the outbreak of hostilities in World War I, a preview of the progressive's world was unveiled:

THE FOOD AND FUEL CONTROL ACT, 1917: This set limits on how much food an American could have on pantry shelves. It also regulated the production and consumption of "distilled spirits"—all of this "to support the war effort."

HERBERT HOOVER HAD KINGLY POWERS: During WWI, Hoover could fix food prices, act against hoarding to ensure sufficient food for the troops, control food production and distribution, control profits, and tell farmers what to grow. He set guidelines to reduce consumption with "meatless Tuesdays," "sweetless Saturdays," and "wheatless Mondays." These were voluntary for the private sector.[340]

HARRY GARFIELD HAD KINGLY POWERS: During WWI, Garfield could save coal by closing non-essential factories (which he did), setting prices, and controlling production, shipments, and distribution. Garfield distributed fuel oil in similar fashion, and called for voluntary "gasless Sundays," "lightless nights," and "heatless Mondays."[341]

CAN'T OWN GOLD: In 1933, President Franklin D. Roosevelt signed an executive order "forbidding the hoarding of gold coin,

---

339   Marx, Engels, *The Communist Manifesto*, chapter 2, 1948.
340   New York Times, *Hoover Declares 'Victory Bread' and Cut Rations*, January 27, 1917.
341   David M. Kennedy, *Over Here: The First World War and American Society*, 2004,   pp. 124-125.

"Darwin, by the way, whom I'm reading just now, is absolutely splendid. There was one aspect of teleology that had yet to be demolished, and that has now been done."—Karl Marx

gold bullion, and gold certificates" by American citizens. The theory was this prevented the circulation of money that would help ignite the economy. There were rumors that safety deposit boxes were being searched for gold—in rare instances this did take place, but not as an official government policy.[342]

PRIVATE RAILS: Owners of small railroads lost their freedom to set fees for hauling goods because of the Shreveport Rate Case (1914). Congress said the Commerce Clause (Article 1.8) gave it power to tell a private rail owner to charge the same rates inside a state as those carriers running cross-country through his state. Congress didn't want the little guy competing by charging too little, or "soaking" the carriers with higher rates if his was the only rail line available. The Supreme Court agreed—Congress could force the little guy to set rates the same as the interstate carriers. Ever since the Shreveport Rate Case, this ruling has been used to expand federal power beyond "interstate commerce," and into just about any aspect of life.[343]

PRICE CONTROLS: Theodore Roosevelt believed in top-down control: "We wish to control big business so as to secure among other things good wages for the wage-workers and reasonable prices for the consumers."[344] "I believe in a larger use of the Governmental power to help remedy industrial wrongs."[345]

8 **ELIMINATE FREE CHOICE**: The consequences of alcohol and drunkenness were such a blight on human progress ✦ that the progressives successfully pushed through the 18th amendment prohibiting the consumption of alcoholic beverages. As noted earlier, this action was nothing short of socialism at work. An amendment that does not protect rights is not in harmony with the intent and design of the Constitution.

---

342 Time Magazine, *Josefowitz Gold*, April, 1936.
343 Walter Hines Page, Arthur Wilson Page, *The World's Work*, Vol. 28, 1914, pp. 377-378; United States Reports, vol. 234, p. 342.
344 Effingham Wilson, *Progressive Principles by Theodore Roosevelt, Selections from Addresses*, 1913 p. 139.
345 Ibid., p. 171.

Socialism kills—In the Soviet Union from 1922-1991, the crushing power of totalitarianism killed at least 58,627,000—some estimates go as high as 75,000,000.

9 FORCED MINIMUM WAGES: In 1912, the Progressive Party wrote into their platform a call for set wages. "We ◆ pledge ourselves to work unceasingly in State and Nation for ... Minimum wage standards for working women, to provide a living scale in all industrial occupations...."[346]

10 TARIFFS: Protective Tariffs had already proved counter-productive, but not according to the Progressive plat-◆ form. "We believe in a protective tariff which shall equalize conditions of competition between the United States and foreign countries, both for the farmer and the manufacturer, and which shall maintain for labor an adequate standard of living."[347]

11 ABANDON CONSTITUTION IN LAW SCHOOLS: By the 1920s, American law schools had abandoned teaching ◆ law based on principles in the Constitution. Students were immersed in a study of "casebook law"—that is, the decisions made by judges regardless of application or reference to the Constitution. There was no test for constitutional correctness because people were led to believe what the Court said was law, so why argue? (See brief history of that abandonment beginning in Chapter 61, *Revolutionary: Law Schools*).

12 RULE OTHER COUNTRIES: Charles Merriam called on Western culture to advance its expertise into the core ◆ of other cultures and nations: "The Teutonic [Germanic] races must civilize the politically uncivilized. They must have a colonial policy. Barbaric races, if incapable, may be swept away. ... On the same principle, interference with the affairs of states not wholly barbaric, but nevertheless incapable of effecting political organization for themselves, is fully justified."[348]

13 CREATE CHANGE THROUGH CRISIS: Many revolutionaries before and after the progressives believed the ◆ ideal time to enact change or to violate rights was in the middle of a crisis. World War I came along just in time. Measures to secure the nation included the Espionage Act of 1917—people were threatened with 10-20 years in jail if they "interfered with the

---

346 Ibid., p. 317.
347 Ibid., p. 320.
348 Merriam, Ibid., p. 314.

Socialism in Venezuela: In 2010, Hugo Chavez ordered all national newspapers to cease printing violent photographs to protect the country's children. The definition of "violent" was not stipulated.

draft or encouraged disloyalty [to America]." The Sedition Act of 1918 made it a crime to obstruct the sale of U.S. war bonds, discourage recruitment, use "disloyal or abusive language" about the government or the American flag or the Constitution, or even military uniforms. Some 1,500 were arrested for those very crimes.

14. **NATIONALIZE INDUSTRIES**: Taking over free-market enterprises spooked Americans after World War I. By that time the U.S. government already owned most of the radio facilities and controlled the railroads and a vast merchant fleet. Congress didn't dare take over directly, but it did pass Acts and regulations that over time forced the marketplace to comply with government regulations—a slow grinding down of private investment.

MORE THAN 50: The federal government issues laws, rules, and regulations to control commerce through more than 50 agencies, each with its own set of purposes, rules, requirements, and impact.

ENFORCEMENT: Federal agencies are tasked with enforcing more than 150,000 pages of rules. Not all are bad—some fall within the proper role of government, but the rest are highly debatable or outright unconstitutional by any reasoned review of the powers usurped by such agencies.

STAGGERING COST: A 2005 study put a conservative cost of obedience to government regulations at a crushing $1.1 trillion every year.[349]

KILLS INNOVATION: Regulation stifles innovation in ways not even imagined. For example, decades of communications restrictions by the Federal Communications Commission stalled the invention and development of cell phones, the Internet, and wireless services. When the rules were relaxed, the wireless technology exploded in a worldwide revolution that created jobs and trillions of dollars in new business.

THE PILLARS OF SOCIALISM

In 1912, the progressive movement completed its split from the Republican Party by forming its own Progressive Party. The new

---

349 W. Mark Crain, *The Impact of Regulatory Costs on Small Firms*, Small Business Administration Office of Advocacy, September 2005.

Socialism in Brazil: On average, a Brazilian must pay almost 55% of his or her earnings to the government as taxes in one or more of various forms.

party gave the foundation for candidates seeking office to further progressive ideals. In 1916 the schism was healed and the Progressive Party was dissolved.

Meanwhile, for two decades, the conservative side of the Republican Party refused to let any progressives advance as nominees. When Franklin D. Roosevelt came along in the 1930s with his "new deal" Democrat Party, the progressives flocked to his side. Since that time, the Democrat Party has best represented the progressive goals up to modern times. This does not excuse the Republican Party, which has, for the sake of expediency, adopted support of the same.

CHAPTER 60:

REVOLUTIONARY: THE SOCIALIST PARTY

Another political schism in 1901 brought together the 3-year-old Social Democratic Party and some discouraged dropouts from the Socialist Labor Party. Together they created The Socialist Party of America.

The Socialist Party was popular. Membership grew rapidly in its first couple of decades. Most of its support came from progressive and trade union members, and they succeeded in putting candidates in office everywhere. By 1912, they had nine seats in Congress, a senator, and more than 200 offices all across the country as mayors, city councilmen, and state legislators.

Two influential progressives from this period worth noting created enormous headway that millions later followed—

SOCIALIST: Eugene V. Debs (1855-1926)
REPUTATION: Influential American labor union leader, candidate for president on the Socialist Party ticket.
STORY: Debs began as a Democrat in Indiana and was very active in several unions. He helped form the country's first industrial union, the *American Railway Union*. He led a strike of 3,000 workers against pay cuts by the Pullman Car Company in 1894—and got arrested.

WHILE IN PRISON: Debs spent his incarceration learning all about socialism. When he was released in 1895, he launched his life as a career socialist. He ran for president in 1900, 1904, 1908, 1912, and 1920, the last effort while serving time in jail. His 1912 run was the most successful of all, securing 900,000 votes.

GIFT OF THE GAB: Debs' articulate oratory against America's participation in World War I got him in trouble—he encouraged resistance to the draft. He was arrested and found guilty of sedition. At a hearing on September 14, 1918, he told the judge:

Saparmurat Niyazov, ruler of Turkmenistan (1990-2006), declared himself "President for Life," and erected a golden statue of himself that rotated to always face the sun. He also renamed the months and days of the week to honour himself, his mother, and his favorite national heroes.

"Your honor, I have stated in this court that I am opposed to the form of our present government; that I am opposed to the social system in which we live; that I believe in the change of both but by perfectly peaceable and orderly means...."[350]

ACTING THE MARTYR: Debs made another defiant declaration during his sentencing two months later, November 18, 1918—

"Your Honor, years ago I recognized my kinship with all living beings, and I made up my mind that I was not one bit better than the meanest on earth. I said then, and I say now, that while there is a lower class, I am in it, and while there is a criminal element I am of it, and while there is a soul in prison, I am not free."[351]

INFLUENCE: Debs congealed the progressive movement's scattered and disjointed protagonists into a more cohesive force united against unalienable rights. Socialists, communists, union members, and anarchists rallied around him to achieve Ruler's Law in America.

Debs died of heart failure in 1926. He was 70.

SOCIALIST: Clarence Darrow (1857-1938)
REPUTATION: American lawyer, leading member of ACLU.
STORY: Another prominent progressive socialist was Clarence Darrow. He was described as a sophisticated country lawyer who became famous in America for his wit, oratory, and successful defense of famous cases. He defended Eugene Debs in 1894 after the Pullman Strike, sparing him conviction in one case but losing the other. Over the course of his career, Darrow defended accused killers in 50 murder cases. He lost his very first case, but won the other 49.

Darrow was a strong supporter of labor and defended unions in multiple cases. He also ran for office a few times.

COLORFUL BACKGROUND: Darrow was accused of bribing jurors, and was known for his opposition of the death penalty.

---

350   David Pietrusza, *1920: The Year of Six Presidents*, 2007, pp, 269-70.
351   See E. V. Debs, *Statement to the Court Upon Being Convicted of Violating the Sedition Act.*

"Marxists have never forgotten that violence will be an inevitable accompaniment of the collapse of capitalism ... and at the birth of a socialist society."—Vladimir Lenin

He was also famous for his defense of John Scopes, an evolution-teaching biology teacher in the Scopes Monkey trial. Darrow had a gift of eloquence that was credited for winning him many cases.

Darrow's political and religious views perpetuated the progressive ideals.

❖ **DARROW SUPPORTED JUDICIAL ACTIVISM:** Darrow supported the idea that judges should break from constitutional law and tailor-make laws to fit the circumstances. "Laws should be like clothes," he said. "They should be made to fit the people they serve."[352]

❖ **DARROW REJECTED RELIGION:** "The origin of the absurd idea of immortal life is easy to discover; it is kept alive by hope and fear, by childish faith, and by cowardice."[353]

❖ **DARROW BELIEVED IN UNIONS:** "With all their faults, trade unions have done more for humanity than any other organization of men that ever existed. They have done more for decency, for honesty, for education, for the betterment of the race, for the developing of character in man, than any other association of men."[354]

❖ **DARROW WAS CONFUSED:** Darrow didn't understand the basic principles of freedom, and blamed abuses of rights on the Constitution. "The Constitution is a delusion and a snare if the weakest and humblest man in the land cannot be defended in his right to speak and his right to think as much as the strongest in the land."[355]

Darrow's complaints had merit, but not for the reasons he gave. It is not the Constitution's fault that a judicial or other system denies a person unalienable rights. It is the fault of corruption or failure to sustain the original Constitution. More laws couldn't fix that problem—it is a collapse of virtue among those applying the law where the corruption occurs. The real culprit in Darrow's complaints rightly lies at the feet of the judges and attorneys, those graduated without constitutional training in law school. What was being taught in our law schools back then?

352　Attributed to Clarence Darrow.
353　Attributed to Clarence Darrow.
354　The Railroad Trainman (November 1909).
355　Address to the court in People vs. Lloyd (1920).

Former socialist George Orwell wrote Animal Farm to expose the fallacy of socialism.

CHAPTER 61:

REVOLUTIONARY: LAW SCHOOLS

The progressives' effort to control information made a giant leap when they successfully penetrated education.

One of the pillars of socialism is to control information. The importance of this pillar was not lost on those pushing for change in the early 1900s.

The leading progressives viewed traditional ideas about freedom as archaic remnants holding back revolutionary ideas. Reformers blamed the clergymen for controlling higher education and stifling the natural intellectual evolution of college students. Such stagnation, they warned, was suicide in a rapidly changing industrialized world.

The law schools became an early venue for reform. The first attempt at law school reform started on the tradition-laden campus of America's oldest university.

WHO: Charles W. Eliot, Harvard president 1869-1909

IMPACT: He saved Harvard from bankruptcy, and ignited growth in higher education in America.

STORY: Eliot graduated from Harvard in 1853, and stayed on for a decade to teach math and chemistry. Using family money and savings, Eliot decided to go exploring. He took a two-year hiatus to Europe so he could study other forms of education. He was fascinated by their styles of curriculum and how teachers conveyed information. When he returned to America, Eliot was ready to help American education catch up with the times.

In 1869, Eliot was appointed president of Harvard. He was passionate about education as a tool to expand opportunities of study. That's when he introduced the "electives system," a buffet of top-notch classes from which students could choose how to develop their intellectual lives according to their interests.

Eliot served 40 years as Harvard president, and built the school from near closure to the world's wealthiest private university. He was described as a fearless crusader for education reform and pushed for many goals of the progressive movement. One of his

New World Order: In 2005, the U.S. Supreme Court cited international law to help justify its decision opposing juvenile executions for murder. (Roper v. Simmons)

most eloquent spokesmen for progressive views was Herbert Croly, class of 1889.

WHO: Herbert Croly (1869-1930)

IMPACT: Intellectual leader of the progressive movement; author of the progressive classic, *The Promise of American Life* (1909).

STORY: Croly made three attempts to graduate from Harvard, withdrawing each time for one reason or another. In 1910, after his book, *The Promise of American Life,* was published, Harvard finally awarded Croly an honorary degree.

Croly was enamored by Alexander Hamilton's views of a strong central government. His 1909 book reflected that view as a way to transform America from an agrarian society to a powerhouse in the industrialized world. He also supported Thomas Jefferson's views on individual freedom, but set them secondary as "tantamount to extreme individualism."[356]

Croly's solution to a new America included nationalizing large corporations, building a strong national government, and strengthening the labor unions—calling them "the most effective machinery which has yet been forged for the economic and social amelioration of the laboring class."[357]

The balance of his ideas promoted heavy taxes, creating an aristocratic class of elites, unlimited government, and destruction of individual rights in support of national ideals.

After Croly's death, his unnoticed book took off, imparting socialism to presidents, jurists, and teachers—for decades.

WHO: Christopher Columbus Langdell (1826-1906)

IMPACT: Turned law schools from studying constitutional law to the "casebook method."

STORY: During Eliot's reign at Harvard there came along a teacher and scholar named Christopher Langdell who would advance progressive goals deep into American culture and jurisprudence by changing the way law was studied in college.

Langdell attended Harvard's law school from 1851-1854, long before Eliot came along. But the two joined up in 1870 when Langdell was made dane professor of Law at Harvard Law School.

---

356   Herbert. Croly, *The Promise of American Life*, 1901, p. 194.
357   Ibid., p. 387.

Socialism in Massachusetts: Just before Mother's Day in 2012, armed Environmental Police officers closed down a park's popular ice cream stand because its owner made improvements without permission. Said the owner, "I make improvements *every* day and have for 26 years."

Shortly after, he was made dean of the law faculty, a position he held until 1895.

Langdell introduced two major changes into how law was taught in America. The first is still in use today. It's a system for teaching first-year students the intricacies of contracts, property, torts, criminal law, and civil procedure.

Langdell's second innovation was the case or casebook method. He dropped the Constitution as the deciding factor in law, and had students study how they, and presiding judges in the cases, thought the outcome *should be*. Unfortunately, judges' personal biases and agendas proved contradictory and fluctuated with every major case. Deserting the Constitution as a foundational starting place for law education was foolish.

WHO: Roscoe Pound (1870-1964)
IMPACT: Started the "legal realism" movement that institutionalized judicial activism.
STORY: Roscoe Pound started teaching law at Harvard in 1910, and became dean of the law school in 1916.

Pound was one of the early promoters of the casebook method, and took it a step further. He helped start the so-called "Realism" movement.

"Legal Realism" was the view that law should be used to achieve whatever social purposes seem to fit at the time. Said another way, "the law" is whatever the judges say it is.

Prior to that time, most law schools were teaching "legal formalism." The idea was that the formal written law is unmovable—it is what it is, not what the judge says. And if the law failed for some reason, it wasn't the judge's job to rewrite it, but to apply it as best as he or she could and leave it to the legislature to make necessary clarifications.

Those supporting "formalism" said that judges should be constrained in their interpretations. Allowing judges to say what the law *should* be instead of making them pass judgment according to what the law *does say* violates the Constitution's separation of powers.

Why? Because the legislative branch is supposed to make the law, and the judicial branch is supposed to apply it, not change it according to their own whims.

Pound's approach to teaching law has sent hundreds of thousands of law students into America with the mistaken belief they are empowered to create law if the situation warrants it. It is a progressive's dream come true.

INTERPRETATION VERSUS APPLICATION

Supreme Court Justice Antonin Scalia is one of those former law school students who *didn't* fall for "legal realism." He deeply respected the Constitution and wanted it left alone, and made this clear many times as a justice on the Supreme Court—

❖ **"WE AMERICANS HAVE A METHOD** for making the laws that are over us. We elect representatives to two Houses of Congress, each of which must enact the new law and present it for the approval of a President, whom we also elect. For over two decades now, un-elected federal judges have been usurping this lawmaking power by converting what they regard as norms of international law into American law. Today's opinion approves that process in principle, though urging the lower courts to be more restrained. This Court seems incapable of admitting that some matters—any matters—are none of its business."[358]

❖ **"I THINK IT IS UP TO THE JUDGE** to say what the Constitution provided, even if what it provided is not the best answer, even if you think it should be amended. If that's what it says, that's what it says."[359]

❖ **"THE COURT MUST BE LIVING** in another world. Day by day, case by case, it is busy designing a Constitution for a country I do not recognize."[360]

❖ **"I DON'T THINK IT'S A LIVING** document, I think it's dead. More precisely, I think it's enduring. It doesn't change."[361]

❖ **"I AM LEFT** to defend the 'dead' Constitution."[362]

358 Antonin Scalia, *Sosa vs. Alvarez-Machain et al., 542 U.S. 692* (2004).
359 Antonin Scalia, forum at American University, 2005.
360 Antonin Scalia, *Wabaunsee County vs. Umbehr, 518 U.S. 668* (1966).
361 Antonin Scalia, from a speech in Alexandria, Virginia, April 9, 2008.
362 Antonin Scalia, speech at Marquette University, March 13, 2001.

CHAPTER 62:

REVOLUTIONARY: FEDERAL POWER

Achieving progressive goals required the rousing of public demand for more police power at the highest levels. Starting in 1901, that's what they got.

W hen Theodore Roosevelt became president in 1901, he started decades of destruction of constitutional restraints. This grab for power was supported by the Supreme Court, and unleashed all manner of avoidable problems. This episode shows how the establishment of Ruler's Law was streamlined with the installation of an all-powerful ruler.

THE PROBLEM OF TOO MUCH SUCCESS?

America's amazing growth during the industrial revolution was racing white-hot at the turn of the century—with more to come during the "roaring twenties." For the general public in the early 1900s, all they read and heard about were tycoons taking over businesses, finances, and labor practices. Popular resentment began to spread. People wanted some kind of national police power to step in and get things under control.

Feeding the public frenzy were the muckrakers. Journalists sold millions of books and articles exposing the dirty under-belly of bad conditions—grotesque conditions in the meat-packing industry, packaging of spoiled food, illegal drugs, child labor, and prostitution (white slavery).

For the progressives, this was an important transition opportunity. They saw the chance to break from the Constitution and grant the federal government fantastic control—a new authority to become a national regulatory dispensary outside the Founder's restraints—a top-down, Ruler's Law police power.

TWO WAYS TO DISMANTLE THE CONSTITUTION

Federal power was chained down with purpose, and the progressives somehow needed to break that chain. They had two options:

❖ **AMENDMENTS**—This was not a very practical solution. The amending process opens up an issue to too much analysis and discussion. It takes time and runs the risk of being rejected. For almost a century, the Constitution had remained untouched, except for the fallout from the Civil War and reconstruction. The progressives set this option aside for a while.

❖ **REINTERPRETATION**—The easier route to expand federal power was to assert national authority and then hope the Supreme Court would uphold the claims. Part of the public relations campaign had to promote the notion that the Constitution was a living, growing instrument intended to adjust as the nation and its economic complexity expanded.

The fact that natural law and principles of freedoms never change was beside the point. President Roosevelt and the progressives took the "reinterpretation" route, and fortunately for them, they had a Supreme Court that went along.

MAKING THE CONSTITUTION UNCONSTITUTIONAL

The progressives' first and most important hurdle was to establish the idea that the federal government had police power over everyone. Somehow the boundary between federal and state powers had to be broken. The weapons used to invade the heart of states' rights, it turns out, were the powers of regulating commerce and taxation. The strategy was first to bring to light some widespread problem or social horror, and then arouse public opinion to demand federal legislation to fix it. Here is the evolution:

ACT: Federal Lottery Act (1895)
PRECEDENT: Gave Congress power to outlaw the trade of specific items.
STORY: In 1895, Congress tried to control gambling by outlawing the buying or selling of lottery tickets across state lines. A man was caught trying to ship lottery tickets privately from Texas to California. Could Congress actually *stop* lottery ticket sales inside the state boundaries of California because the tickets arrived from Texas? The Supreme Court said *yes*—Congress could outlaw, forbid, reject, and ban whatever items it chose from being shipped across state lines.

Writing for the majority, Justice Harlan said, "Congress may arbitrarily exclude from commerce among the states any article ...

As of 2010, the total financial promises made by the U.S. government that are not paid for is $61.6 trillion. That's $534,000 per household, at least five times what the average American had borrowed for everything else—car loans, mortgages, credit card debt.

which it may choose, no matter what the motive." That is, Congress could not only regulate commerce but prohibit it altogether if the item being traded met its disapproval.

A CT: The Oleomargarine Act (1886), amended 1902
PRECEDENT: Gave Congress power to use taxes to control society unfairly and manipulate the marketplace.
STORY: An amazing butter substitute called "oleomargarine" appeared on the market and was cutting into the sales of natural butter. In 1902, angry dairymen repeated the actions of their guildsmen ancestors and tried to get government power to eliminate the competition.

The butter-makers sent a national dairymen's lobby to pressure Congress to help. *It worked.* In 1902, Congress raised the tax on artificially colored margarine to $.10 (ten cents) a pound, and taxed un-colored margarine at $.0025 (a fourth of a cent) per pound. The restrictions cut U.S. consumption from 120 million pounds to 48 million pounds a year. The obvious purpose was to restrict and impede the sale of *yellow* margarine that looked and tasted a whole lot more like butter with each innovation.

The tax was attacked in court as an invasion of states' rights (taxing an activity inside state boundaries) in violation of the 10th Amendment, and the tax was so heavy it was confiscatory—it seized private property for the public treasury—in violation of the Fifth Amendment (depriving the margarine-makers of their property without due process of law).

The Court carefully stepped out of this one by refusing to consider why the tax was levied or how it impacted the butter-margarine dilemma. Instead, the Court simply said that Congress had the power to tax—so, violating states' rights really has nothing to do with taxation. If the tax destroyed a business, that didn't matter because the power of Congress to tax was its valid power—therefore, no need for "due process of law."

This case made it clear: there are no limits on what Congress can do with the power to tax. Its motives and the outcome are not reasons enough to warrant a judicial review.

Rewriting History: China and Korea have long disputed their early histories. Korean soap operas are popular in China, winning a large viewership. But when Korea portrayed the regions ancient mythology to their favor, China blacklisted the costly production ($45 million) for distorting history.

ACT: Pure Food and Drug Act (1906)
PRECEDENT: Allowed the federal government to regulate food production inside state boundaries.
STORY: Dr. Harvey Wiley, an employee in the Department of Agriculture, did research that showed a trend of dangerous preservatives, dangerous coloring chemicals, and dangerous preparations of foods becoming "almost universal" in America. Added to this was the impact of Upton Sinclair's *The Jungle*, and actions by other social activists that further inflamed the public. Popular outrage pushed for Congress to pass some kind of regulation to protect the public. And just like that, a federal law requiring inspection of meat and outlawing adulterated products was signed into law on June 30, 1906.

The law demanded that certain drugs and patent medicines had to be accurately labeled showing their content and recommended dosage. Some patent medicines contained cocaine, alcohol, morphine, heroin, or cannabis. Coca-Cola had replaced cocaine with caffeine in 1903, but they were challenged later for having too much caffeine, and they were forced to reduce the amount.

ACT: The Meat Inspection Act (1906)
PRECEDENT: Forced meat packers to obey federal inspectors and federal rules, usurping states' rights.
STORY: On June 30, 1906, the Meat Inspection Act was signed into law. Inspectors were sent to every inter-state meat-packing plant to look for diseased animals or putrefying carcasses. Rejected meat or meat that was not inspected could not be shipped.

If meat packers refused to comply with the inspections, their products could not be shipped out of state. They had no choice but to submit.

ACT: The White Slave Traffic Act (1910)
PRECEDENT: Known as the Mann Act, it invaded state police power by regulating local prostitution.
STORY: The Bureau of Immigration had been watching the ports of entry for international trafficking of prostitutes. In 1907, Congress passed a law making it illegal to keep an alien woman for prostitution. The Supreme Court struck this down as unconstitution-

The free market works: In 2011, Walmart's sales exceeded $429 billion—shareholders earned $19.2 billion.

al. The justices said it was an attempt to regulate local prostitution from the federal level.

Prostitution is another issue the Founders left to the states to control. Congress exceeded its authority with the Mann Act to control prostitution, claiming it was an interstate activity. The bill became law on June 25, 1910, giving the federal government police powers inside a state.

ACT: The Weeks Act (1911)

PRECEDENT: Using "grants-in-aid," the federal government took control of additional state responsibilities.

STORY: The Act gave the federal government power to purchase, preserve, and control watershed areas inside the states and turn them into national forests. Part of the cost was to be carried by the states with the so-called "grant-in-aid."

The idea was to offer money to a state for some specific and mutually beneficial project. To receive the federal money, states had to match the grant with equal money, and allow the federal government to supervise and approve the projects. The Weeks Act originally focused on eastern lands, but it soon became the model for all future joint federal-state projects nationwide.

Similar projects already had been tried—sharing the costs of maternity welfare and helping infants, providing vocational training, and helping disabled veterans.

But something was amiss. People feared this was a means to break down the sovereignty in local self-government. After a dozen years of grants-in-aid, President Calvin Coolidge expressed concern in 1925: "The functions which the Congress are to discharge are not those of local government but of National Government. The greatest solicitude should be exercised to prevent any encroachment upon the rights of the States or their various political subdivisions. Local self-government is one of our most precious possessions .... It ought not to be infringed by assault or undermined by purchase."[363]

People watching this friendly usurpation of state responsibilities made them fear that grants-in-aid were simply a crafty way to expand federal power and destroy state sovereignty. It allowed the national government to take over functions that belonged to the

---

363   Calvin Coolidge, State of the Union Address, December 8, 1925.

It needs a host: From 1996-2000, North Korea was dependent on China to stay alive. The Chinese sold 500,000 tons of grain, 1.3 million tons of crude, 2.5 million tons of coal, plus another 850,000 tons of grain donated by China.

states. States were pressured to participate because, either way, their tax dollars were taken for these programs and the money would go to other states. This was a clear violation of constitutional spending authority in Article 1.8.

A CT: The Child Labor Act (1916)
PRECEDENT: Forced states to comply with federal rules about age and hours for working children.
STORY: The 1900 census showed that 2 million children were working in factories, mines, mills, fields, stores and on the streets all across the U.S. The census result triggered a national clamor for more control over child labor. To further stir alarm, a photographer was hired to document some of the abuses, and the call to spare children from accidents and damage to their health went far and wide.

Most children at this time were in the work force because of dire necessity. Most of them were teenagers. Working in the deplorable factory conditions that existed in those days was in reality a better alternative than unemployment, starvation, and death. They also worked as long as they could to earn what they could.

In 1916, the Child Labor Act relied once again on the interstate commerce side. It made it illegal for anyone to ship products produced by children under age 14, and prohibited labor by children 14-16 for more than 8 hours a day, 6 days a week—and no night work allowed. Preventing the abuse of children at the work place is important. However, allowing the government to dictate labor rules prevented the children, their parents, and the employers to agree on a contract, a right that was protected by the Constitution (Article 1.10.1).

The Act was signed into law, but was declared unconstitutional in 1918. Another attempt was made in 1918—also declared unconstitutional. The Court said the government wasn't regulating, it was prohibiting—a sudden recognition of the true principle involved that apparently was ignored for the lottery, pure food, and white slave laws. Not until 1938 did the government win police power over state's rights with the passage of the Fair Labor Standards Act that fulfilled most of the original intents of the earliest child labor laws.

A CT: The Harrison Narcotics Tax Act (1914)
PRECEDENT: Used the excuse of taxation to get the names of producers and track drug transactions.

Socialism in America: As of 2011, more than 100 million people in the U.S., including illegal immigrants, were receiving some form of federal welfare.

STORY: After the Spanish-American War of 1898, the U.S. acquired the Philippines. The population there had a severe and widespread problem of opium addiction. Opium abuse was becoming a problem in the U.S. as well, particularly among immigrants from that part of the world.

The problem was hoisted up the flag pole and drew a lot of international attention. This resulted in the first international drug control treaty signed in 1912. Meanwhile in America, the importation and abuse of opium was spreading. By 1914, an estimated 1 in 400 U.S. citizens was addicted.[364] This same year, 46 states had laws against cocaine and 29 states had laws against opium, morphine, and heroin.

The Harrison Act of 1914 required everyone who manufactured, sold, or distributed narcotic drugs to register with the government. They had to pay $1 a year in taxes, keep detailed sales records, and use special authorized forms whenever making drug transactions. It also outlawed the use of the drugs for any purpose other than professional or commercial purposes.

The $1 tax really had no value other than to force narcotic dealers to let the government know who they were, where they lived, and how much product went through their hands—another powerful grant of police power to the federal government.

GOOD IDEAS IN BAD PACKAGES

The problems facing America in the early 1900s certainly needed to be rectified. However, the long-range complications that emerged from fast fixes brought a new tyranny to the U.S. that was never meant to be. The states were slow in resolving their problems, and in the face of ignorance and apathy, the powers of Ruler's Law rose up and took their places. No sane person wanted the problems the early Acts resolved, but granting powers of socialism to solve them has proven in the long run to be ruinous. Ruler's Law is now permanently entrenched. If America survives today's onslaught against constitutional liberties, it will only do so by the hand of benevolent intervention from the Creator all freedoms—and by none other.

LEARNING TO RECOGNIZE SOCIALISM

The emphasis on the corruption of the American system helps explain the pattern of destruction that all nations around the world

---

364   New York Times, *Uncle Sam is the Worst Drug Fiend in the World*, March 12, 1911.

"The Chinese Communist Party is the core of leadership of the whole Chinese people. Without this core, the cause of socialism cannot be victorious."—Mao Zedong

have adopted. We learn that just as soon as the ruling powers discover how to rob from the national treasury, they'll also regulate society to support that thievery. Then, it is just a matter of time before a country caves from within. Europe, the former Soviet Union, Asia, Africa, Australia, the U.S., and all others slouching toward socialism did or will in the near term face the same demise if the people fail to wrest back full control of their governments.

In the U.S., that demise was accelerated during the New Deal era. All those massive government bailouts made the people dependent on handouts. They were promised something for nothing. And to hand out *something*, the government had to chip away at property ownership and the freedoms to try, buy, sell, and fail. Dangerous precedents were set. The chains that once bound down the federal government started binding down the people.

It won't be easy turning around that enormous mess because an entire culture is now gratefully dependent upon the freebies.

BEING SKEWERED ON A THREE-PRONGED PITCHFORK

Now we shift gears to look at the way socialism perpetuates itself in today's world. It pins a nation beneath the powers of Ruler's Law with the inescapable efficiency of a three-pronged attack—

The first prong is national health care. This is the quickest route to draw the necessary funding from every person's wallet and get them to the polling place to keep the flewage[365] flowing. "Vote for me," they say, "and I will get you *everything* you need." And what could be more important than health care? Even the homeless and hungry will go without wants and necessities just to find relief from the immediacy of pain and injury.

Next to health care is its twin, state welfare. This is unemployment, pensions, Social Security, school lunches (and breakfasts), publicly-subsidized transportation and utilities, forced hiring practices, meddling in the market, etc.

The third prong is control of the banking system. Controlling the money is how the socialists control the government and its power.

Combining the three into one—welfare, health care, and central banking—creates the most destructive power in the world. Most of the world has embraced all three, and puts its trust in elected dictators who dispense the dole and say, "Want more? Vote for me." And that's exactly what happens—

---

365 Flewage: A mass of disgusting waste that flies past consumers with such velocity, they can't recognize it for what it is, and blithely assume it's important, and let it go by unchallenged.

Cicero on the importance of learning history: "To be ignorant of what occurred before you were born is to remain always a child."

Part XI

THE LAST TEMPTATION, PART 1: COMPULSORY CARE

"The surest path to dictatorship is braced with the promises of universal care."

—Author—

CHAPTER 63:

THE LAST TEMPTATION: COMPULSORY CARE

The number-one contrivance in the socialists' bag of tricks is popular, enticing, addictive, and fools most of the people most of the time.

The most important survival lesson from history is this: Having *problems* in common always works—having *things* in common doesn't. From Rome's free bread to Jamestown's common storehouse, each attempt at "all things in common" has failed.

Whenever the seven pillars of socialism are applied to basic welfare needs, an amazing breakdown of judgment overwhelms common sense.

❖ **GIVERS AND TAKERS:** Welfare easily cultivates a sense of entitlement. Recipients become addicted to welfare and adopt assorted and blurred conclusions that, somehow, society owes them everything—food, clothing, medicine, shelter, employment, disability help, retirement, etc.—they eventually demand it as a *right*.

❖ **TAXPAYERS PAY:** Welfare is circular. As the payouts grow, the tax burden on everyone else also grows. Businesses suffer, some resort to cutting back, laying off workers. The unemployed apply for welfare. This increases the welfare rolls, forcing taxes up even more, and that makes *more* unemployed—it's a snake eating its tail.

❖ **FACELESS, NAMELESS:** State welfare removes the weight of personal responsibility from individuals and puts it on the doorstep of that innocuous, faceless, soulless entity called *government*.

❖ **NUMBS THE SOUL:** State welfare leaves the poor with little incentive to rise any higher because their basic needs are being met. A free ride through life doesn't help people in the long run—it destroys their greatest capacity to learn and grow. That's what Benjamin Franklin discovered during his difficult years in Europe—

CHAPTER 64:

FRANKLIN SPEAKS ...

Benjamin Franklin did more than talk about welfare—he lived it.

Benjamin Franklin was a "have not" in England for several years. He was an eye witness to compulsory welfare in action—and had a lot to say about its failings.

Writing to his friend, Franklin said, "I have long been of your opinion, that your legal provision for the poor [in England] is a very great evil, operating as it does to the encouragement of idleness. We have followed your example, and begin now to see our error, and, I hope, shall reform it."[366]

ADDICTIVE WELFARE NOT NATURAL

The Christian ideals of helping your neighbor were already a part of the American culture in the 1700s. Franklin and the Founders believed helping others was not someone else's job, it was everyone's. But it must be dealt with the right way. This comment by Franklin is worth reading slowly—twice:

"To relieve the misfortune of our fellow creatures is concurring with the Deity; it is godlike; but, if we provide encouragement for laziness, and supports for folly, may we not be found fighting against the order of God and Nature, which perhaps has appointed want and misery as the proper punishments for, and cautions against, as well as necessary consequences of, idleness and extravagance? Whenever we attempt to amend the scheme of Providence, and to interfere with the government of the world, we had need be very circumspect, lest we do more harm than good."[367]

HELPING, NOT HURTING

Franklin said the poor are not helped out of their problems with easy handouts. The goal must always be to help them do more for themselves until they are on their own feet. Too much help achieves precisely the opposite.

"I am for doing good to the poor," Franklin said, "but I differ in opinion of the means. I think the best way of doing good to the

366 Smyth, *The Writings of Benjamin Franklin*, vol. 10 p. 64.
367 Ibid., p. 135.

Does Socialism lead to Communism? It did in Hungary: "There was the same fatal alliance of the socialists with the communists, the same expulsion or suppression of all democratic elements, and the same acquiescence, with notable exceptions, of the former Social Democrats in a totalitarian state."—Ivor Thomas, 1951.

poor, is not making them easy in poverty, but leading or driving them out of it. In my youth I travelled much, and I observed in different countries, that the more public provisions were made for the poor, the less they provided for themselves, and of course became poorer. And, on the contrary, the less was done for them, the more they did for themselves, and became richer."

FOUR FLAWS IN STATE WELFARE

Franklin taught that state welfare is always counterproductive. His personal experience led him to identify four major flaws:

◆ **AVOIDS REAL PROBLEM**: State welfare that helps a drunk indulge in more drunkenness hasn't solved any problem at all. It hasn't fixed a thing. It only perpetuates those failings that already existed in the first place.[368]

◆ **CREATES DEPENDENCY**: State welfare that makes people dependent on others has also failed to get them back on their own feet. The goal, Franklin said, is always to help them become dependent on no one but themselves and their own private work ethic.[369]

◆ **PERMANENTLY DEBILITATING**: State welfare engenders a spirit of entitlement. The entitlement society has become a new class that didn't exist before. It's a new segment of society made up of desperately dependent citizens whose daily work is to "work the system," and make a comfortable living at that.[370]

◆ **RUINS INITIATIVE**: Welfare that numbs any yearning to strive toward excellence and personal progression consigns to the ash heap of history untold millions of otherwise productive people. The wrong kind of help turns people's temporary setbacks into permanent failings of wasted dreams and unfulfilled potentials. When initiative dies, so die a million creative ideas that have the potential of helping countless others in ways unimaginable.[371]

---

368   Ibid., vol. 5, p. 538.
369   Ibid., p. 123.
370   Ibid., vol. 3, pp. 135-36.
371   Ibid., p. 135.

Socialism creates a class of elitists, the very aristocracy it claims to loathe: Leonid Brezhnev, general secretary of the Soviet Communist Party and president of the USSR (1964-1982), had a Rolls Royce, Mercedes, Cadillac, ... (cont'd)

CHAPTER 65:

BASTIAT SPEAKS ...

Reckless welfare corrupts everyone and everything.

Frederic Bastiat was a gifted writer who could clarify in simple terms an amazing array of complex ideas. He issued this excellent caution about welfare in 1848. That was the same year Marx and Engels presented their idea about welfare, their proposed savior of society entitled the *Communist Manifesto*. Bastiat warned that all ideas of levelling are old, tired, worthless traps.

"[THE SOCIALISTS DECLARE] THAT THE STATE owes subsistence, well-being, and education to all its citizens, that it should be generous, charitable, involved in everything, devoted to everybody; ...that it should intervene directly to relieve all suffering, satisfy and anticipate all wants, furnish capital to all enterprises, enlightenment to all minds, balm for all wounds, asylums for all the unfortunate, and even aid to the point of shedding French blood, for all oppressed people on the face of the earth.

"WHO WOULD NOT LIKE TO SEE all these benefits flow forth upon the world from the law, as from an inexhaustible source? ... But is it possible? ... Whence does [the State] draw those resources that it is urged to dispense by way of benefits to individuals? Is it not from the individuals themselves? How, then, can these resources be increased by passing through the hands of a parasitic and voracious intermediary?

"FINALLY ...WE SHALL SEE the entire people transformed into petitioners. Landed property, agriculture, industry, commerce, shipping, industrial companies, all will bestir themselves to claim favors from the State. The public treasury will be literally pillaged. Everyone will have good reasons to prove that legal fraternity should be interpreted in this sense: 'Let me have the benefits, and let others pay the costs.' Everyone's effort will be directed toward snatching a scrap of fraternal privilege from the legislature. The suffering classes, although having the greatest claim, will not always have the greatest success."[372]

---

372   Frederic Bastiat, *Justice and Fraternity*, in Journal des Économistes, June 15, 1848, p. 319.

(cont'd) ... Lincoln Continental, Monte Carlo, Matra, and Lancia Beta automobiles while the rest of his empire was struggling to eat. The value of these high-quality vehicles never showed up in his reported income.

CHAPTER 66:

THE TWISTED ROOTS OF MODERN WELFARE

Several centuries before Franklin and Bastiat, the foundations for State Welfare were laid in the wake of a deadly plague. It was a desperate time in the 1300s—what was a king to do?

T he Black Death did more than kill millions of people around the world. It also inadvertently killed Europe's fabric of private compassion, a safety net for the needy that had been developing for many centuries. This fascinating tale of twisting intrigue, collapse, and interwoven collisions of freedom and force had its beginning after Rome collapsed.

A MILLENNIA OF GOOD WORKS

Soon after the fall of Rome in A.D. 476, various religious aid societies took on the role as civic humanitarians for Europe. They lent a helping hand at the most intimate levels of people's lives— helping the needy, keeping order, attending to marriages, baptisms, child births, burials, local elections, and giving food, shelter, clothing, financial aid, sometimes employment, sometimes education, and sometimes protection and public safety. Not all at first, but over time society's fabric grew strong enough to bear the burdens of caring for one another voluntarily.

As the centuries passed, these activities were institutionalized in the Roman Catholic Church and its thousands of representative parishes scattered all over Europe.

Journeying toward these well-propertied stone edifices, the faithful came to petition God's clerics to have their eternities massaged and secured, and their mortal probations cleansed of impurities—for which they were willing to pay a tithe. These accumulated funds provided help for the poor and expanded Church-owned lands, influence, and certainly helped grow its ever-increasing wealth.

E VENT: French Popes challenge Rome, A.D. 1309-1418
IMPACT: Church infighting leaves a lasting weakness
STORY: Relations between the Roman Catholic Church and its flocks started to change in the 1300s. It began with the new pope,

"We have no government, armed with power, capable of contending with human passions, unbridled by morality and religion. Avarice, ambition, revenge and licentiousness would break the strongest cords of our Constitution, as a whale goes through a net."—John Adams

Clement V, a Frenchman who took office in 1305.

With Rome engaged in local uprisings, Clement V decided the city was too unsafe and chose to stay at Avignon, south of ancient France. The Roman cardinals wanted him to move to Rome for fear he was vulnerable to corruption and collusion with the French king. Clement V refused, and so began the "Babylonian Captivity of the Papacy." The schism lasted through 67 years and seven successive popes until 1376.

E**VENT**: Black Death devastates England, A.D. 1348-1350
IMPACT: King imposes on free market, starts welfare.
STORY: Poor King Edward III ... he had a complete disaster on his hands and didn't know what to do. The Black Death had recently indulged its horrific rampage from A.D. 1348-1350, taking millions of lives from all across the continent and beyond.

England suffered tens of thousands dead, on average perhaps 30-40%[373]—in some villages it was more than 80 percent. London lost in excessive of 35,000 of its 60,000 inhabitants.[374]

◆ **DEATHS MOUNT:** Sporadic outbreaks that followed are said to have precipitated a death toll of 50 million out of an estimated 80 million in Europe. Worldwide, some 75-100 million died.[375]

◆ **HELP WANTED:** Across the grassy knolls of England's farmlands, landowners found themselves in a terrible strait. A significant portion of the farmhands who had reliably worked the land year after year were now dead. They were the backbone of England's agricultural prosperity. Without their help, much of the farmland went fallow. Herds of cattle wandered untended. Farm production fell off, food prices rose, and landowners were left desperate to make an income.

◆ **SHORTAGES:** To entice those few workers who were available, landowners competed against each other by offering higher wages, more benefits, and promises of future prosperity. They were good capitalists and passed along these higher wage costs to the buyers in the form of higher food prices. And so began a period of medieval inflation.

---

373   Suzanne Austin Alchon, *A pest in the land: new world epidemics in a global perspective.* University of New Mexico Press. 2003, p. 21.

374   Barney Sloane, *Black Death in London*, The History Press Ltd., 2011.

375   See Ole J. Benedictow, *The Black Death, 1346-1353, The Complete History,* 2004.

"I have come to the conclusion that politics is too serious a matter to be left to the politicians."
—Charles de Gaulle

* **LOAVES AND LOAFERS:** Increasing food costs wasn't helping King Edward rebuild the country. As he went groping about for some workable solutions, he detested the sight of relatively healthy people loafing around the street corners, begging for handouts. At a time when farm help was so desperately needed, letting capable laborers do nothing was outrageous.

* **BACK TO WORK:** As the plague abated in 1349 and 1350, King Edward passed laws that forced the loafers to go to work—or else. He also tried to force wages and food prices back to the same levels before the plague. These changes seemed to help. More laws were added to keep workers from moving around to other jobs, a practice that was creating havoc.

EVENT: Second round of French popes, A.D. 1378-1418
IMPACT: Schism in Church mortally wounds compassion
STORY: Just when things were looking good for the French popes, another fight broke out in Rome. In protest, the newest pope, Gregory XI, packed his bags and returned to France. For 30 more years the French popes challenged Roman authority, but this time almost everyone considered the French popes illegitimate.

* **BATTLING POPES:** The battle for authority was finally settled at the Council of Constance in 1414-1418. Rome won the tug-of-war, and the papacy was returned to its rightful place in Italy.

* **THE SCHISM LEFT LONG-TERM EFFECTS:** For centuries the Church fortified its presence with massive landholdings, large stone cathedrals, and an involvement in everyone's day-to-day affairs. Many of the nuns and clergy had a living standard far superior to that of the impoverished masses. The poor watched this with envy and discontent. Opulence in the name of Jesus became a dangerous sore spot. Reformers started rallying support for change. They challenged the Church to return to its more humble roots, the simplicity taught by Jesus.

* **FLEECING SEASON:** England's poor found voice for their frustrations in King Henry VIII (1491-1547) and his young son, Edward VI (1537-1553). These Highnesses and other aristocrats decided it was time to fleece the Church of its power and wealth.[376]

---

376   See Geoffrey Baskerville, *English Monks and the Suppression of the Monasteries*, 1937; and Alexander Savine, *English Monasteries on the Eve of the Dissolution*, 1909.

"My reading of history convinces me that most bad government results from too much government."—Thomas Jefferson

❖ **EASY MONEY:** Europe's monarchs liked the idea of raiding the churches. They had tremendous economic burdens to carry—armies to raise, ships to construct, fortifications to build, lavish lifestyles to maintain, plus bribes and rewards to pay for loyalty from the faithful.

❖ **HOLY IMMUNITY NO MORE:** So began the continent-wide church plunder of the late 1400s. No longer were the Church's vast landholdings safe. The sanctified opulence that reclined unmolested and sheltered behind the cross for so many centuries, whetted an appetite for confiscation.

❖ **ANTI-FRENCH:** In the beginning, the Roman Church cheered the monarchs onward to absorb the properties of the "apostate" French popes and their followers. The land and buildings were ultimately turned over to colleges and universities, among others. And then—the kings turned on the Roman Church itself.

EVENT: Invention of the printing press, c. 1440
IMPACT: Further weakened the power of the Church
STORY: Another piece of this amazing story of transition centers on a new German invention. Did Guttenberg's printing press play a part in dismantling the power of the Roman Catholic Church?

In the mid-1440s, Guttenberg's invention took Europe by storm. By the 1500s, the press was warmly welcomed by England's reformers who used it as a missionary tool to spread their discontent and publish religious tracts.

❖ **POWER OF THE PEN:** The press also undermined the monasteries' most valuable service: penmanship. The monarchs often turned to the monks and priests to reproduce important proclamations and manuscripts. Such work came faster and cheaper with the new press. The old fashioned hand work was, by comparison, too slow and expensive. People began to wonder, for what else are these monasteries useful?

EVENT: Anti-begging law passed in 1495
IMPACT: Desperate people are driven to starve or steal
STORY: As turmoil and trouble magnified, England's Parliament continued having trouble kick-starting the economy. They

---

Rats and fleas no longer blamed as carriers of the Black Death plague. Researchers now point to person-to-person contact as the best explanation for the plague's fast spread.

gave it one more try with an Act that made begging even *more* illegal. Anyone found loafing around, refusing to work, or otherwise suspected of loafing, could be put in stocks for three days and fed nothing but bread and water. After the humiliation, the convicted were escorted out of town.

EVENT: Pope wages PR campaign with reforms in 1518
IMPACT: The kings of Europe tell the Church *"No."*
STORY: The pope saw the writing on the wall. A big rebellion was swelling. Something needed to improve.

He issued a few reformations in 1518, hoping to calm things down but these didn't pacify the masses of peasants for long.

In 1529, King Henry forced the pope to backtrack a few steps more. Among other things, Henry had Parliament impose caps on fees the Church was charging for services such as burials, and put a limit on the "right of sanctuary" by criminals seeking refuge behind Church walls.

EVENT: Martin Luther heads reform movement, 1517-1521
IMPACT: Triggered the dismantling of the monasteries
STORY: And then came Luther. In 1517, the legendary reformer wrote up his complaints against the Church, a document now known as the 95 Theses, and he nailed it to a church door in Wittenberg. But that wasn't all.

In 1521 he produced another document, "On the Monastic Vows." He outlined from the Bible how institutions such as the monasteries had no basis in scripture, and the tyranny they exercised over the people certainly didn't support the true teachings of Christianity.

LUTHER'S IDEAS SPREAD LIKE FIRE: Intentional or not, he provided Europe's monarchs with the biblical permission needed to justify dismantling the various monastery institutions—the larger abbeys, the medium-sized priories and nunneries, and the smallest, called the friary. England, France, Sweden, Denmark, Germany, and Switzerland joined in the nationalization of church properties.

Confiscating property forced the clergy and nuns to move out, sell their lands, congregate in larger cities, get married, and otherwise blend into society.

Supreme Court said in 1973—a 14 year old is mature enough to abort a baby without parental consent. In 2005, the Court said—a 17 year old is too immature to be executed for pre-meditated murder.

EVENT: England outlaws monasteries, 1536-1540
IMPACT: Ruined the network of voluntary compassion.
STORY: When King Henry took England's throne in 1509, there were more than 850 religious houses spread throughout England and Wales. Thomas Cromwell was King Henry's chief minister in charge of the daily affairs of the Church. In 1535, Cromwell decided to tighten the Crown's grip on the Church, and ordered an inspection of all Church buildings and properties.

❖ **ENCROACHMENTS:** In the past, such inspections had been conducted by a higher member of the clergy. But this time, Cromwell had other plans in mind—he thought it an ideal opportunity to also take a census so he could start taxing Church property.

❖ **PROOF AT LAST:** With the surveys in hand, Cromwell was ready to make his move. In March 1536, Parliament passed a law declaring that any monastery making less than £200 a year had to be dissolved and all the property turned over to the king. Some 300 religious houses qualified and had to shut down. Those with the right government connections earned a reprieve—for the cost of a year's income, they could stay open. About 60 or 70 managed to survive.

❖ **LET THE LEGAL LOOTING BEGIN:** When the decree was passed, government agents went into the religious houses and confiscated all precious treasures—gold, silver, bronze, lead, paintings, books, anything of value to the Crown. The metals were melted down. The locals were given free rein on the rest—furnishings, fences, windows, bricks. In short order, the churches were reduced to the classic ruins that today dot the English countryside.

❖ **HUNDREDS:** By 1540-41, more than 800 monasteries had been closed. Ten years later, most of the associated religious guilds, hospitals, and almshouses were also closed. The dissolution was complete

❖ **NOBODY LEFT?** Left in the vacuum of this levelling and consumption were the ever-present needs of the poor, the needy, and the unemployed. Who was going to take care of them *now*? The dissolution did more than turn vast resources of wealth over to the king—it also destroyed the institutional fabric of Europe's "good Samaritan" society. Along with the opulence of the Church's wealth, the move also destroyed the network of human compas-

"The strongest reason for the people to retain the right to keep and bear arms is, as a last resort, to protect themselves against tyranny in government."—Thomas Jefferson

sion, the helping hands, the epitome of Christian charity originally intended for those in need.

EVENT: England passes Poor Laws, 1500s-1800s
LIMPACT: Human welfare becomes government's job
STORY: The vacuum left by the rejected Church was poorly filled in England. Numerous attempts were eventually launched and these became known as the Poor Laws.[377]

The Poor Laws proved a permanent turning point in how human welfare was handled. They were put in place just a few years before the monasteries were attacked.

◆ **NO IDLENESS**: In 1530, Henry VIII declared that idleness was the "mother and root of all vices."[378] The vagabonds of that day, if caught, were put in stocks for their leeching on society. Henry had them whipped, then driven out. The elderly and sick were allowed to continue begging, but only if they procured the proper license to beg. For the others, their only options were to starve or break the law by stealing food.

◆ **DONATIONS**: In 1536, the English instructed each parish across the land to collect voluntary weekly donations to help the poor. The parish was the Church organization that served as the basic unit of local government to 50-500 or more people.

◆ **DEATH TO THE BEGGARS**: In 1547, Edward VI tried to impose harsh punishment on beggars. He threatened them with two years in prison and a "V" for vagrant branded on their flesh for the first offense—and death for the second offense. Local magistrates didn't approve of executing beggars simply for their want of food, so the most severe punishments were rarely carried out.[379]

◆ **TRACKING VAGABONDS**: In 1572, a legal distinction was made between professional beggars and those who fell victim to circumstance. The parishes were ordered to track local beggars. Those caught faking it could have their ear bored through, and if caught a second time, hanged. Four years later, counties were ordered to build "houses of correction" for vagrants—a place to keep them cared for and available for work.

---

377 See Paul Slack, *The English Poor Law, 1531-1782*, Macmillan, 1990.
378 The Pictorial History of England, vol. 2, 1839.
379 R. O. Bucholz, Newton Key, *Early Modern England*, 1485-1714, p. 176.

Socialist oxymoron—In 2012, the "Governance Commons" website posted these friendly words: **Peace Through Governance. [NOTE: Hitler, Stalin and Osama bin Laden had the same idea]**

❖ **CHARITY TAXES**: In 1597, the Act for the Relief of the Poor was passed by England's Parliament. Voluntary alms were replaced by mandatory taxes. The local elected position of overseer was created. His job was to collect taxes and administer food, clothing, and money welfare to the poor. Charitable gifts for building hospitals were also authorized.[380]

WHERE HAVE ALL THE CARING PEOPLE GONE?

England's population was swelling during the 1500s, and so were its problems—jobs were scarce, the king's coins were losing their value, and grain prices were skyrocketing. In fact, grain prices tripled from 1490 to 1569, and jumped another 73 percent by the time English settlers arrived in Jamestown in 1607.

On top of the rising prices, England suffered through four crop failures in a row (1595, 1596, 1597, and 1598), almost driving the country into widespread famine. These problems pushed the number of welfare recipients higher every year.

CENTURIES OF POOR LAWS

For more than 350 years, England's evolving Poor Laws were the guiding rules for every assorted welfare problem. The shift from compassionate human welfare to state-run welfare did not significantly re-invent itself after that time except in *degree*. Coverage was expanded and taxes were increased to pay for it, but the underlying philosophy remained the same—we the rulers will take care of you. Some of those changes included—

❖ Orphans and widows were made eligible. Specific classes of workers and people were added—including able-bodied men who needed only temporary help with some stopgap income.

❖ Work houses were built to shelter unemployed work parties.

❖ The parishes were allowed to unionize, to combine their resources, and spread the burden of caring for the needy among more people and assets.

❖ Communities were granted authority to kick people out of their parish if they were not planning to settle permanently—or if they had come just for the "free" handouts.

By the early 1800s, the Poor Laws were extensive and refined.

---

380 Paul Slack, *The English Poor Law, 1531-1782*, 1990.

Socialized America: Regulatory agencies that make all the business rules cost Americans $57.3 billion in 2012, and employed 291,700 bureaucrats.

So many of life's failings were covered that the public viewed Poor Relief as a right, an inalienable right, an entitlement. And they were happy to partake and indulge.

WHAT DOES THIS HAVE TO DO WITH SOCIALISM?

The first pillar of socialism is an all-powerful ruler. Welfare, health care—*any* government sponsored care—cannot be dispensed without the power to extract taxes. That is what rulers use to exert complete control over the people. It is their chain of control—the power to tax in the name of welfare. It works because those who receive the government handout will never vote it away, they are too dependent on it. A government promising a never-ending flow of welfare help will always be sustained by the recipients. It's the tried and true pattern of tax-tax, spend-spend, elect-elect.

Government welfare is popular at every level. The rich like it because it relieves them of the guilt of helping. The poor love it because they need it—the lazy want it. And the middle class likes it because they feel their taxes for welfare are virtuously surrendered for a good cause—a sense of combined resources to help the lowliest. And everyone is pacified in letting others be responsible. This is how everyone is made to feel good about all forms of state welfare.

LIKE A SNAKE EATING ITS TAIL: The luxury of cradle-to-grave care does not feast upon some endless quantity of resources. Once the allowance is given, state welfare grows and expands to consume national treasure—eventually and predictably, the needs of the consumers one day outweigh the provisions of the producers. The desperately hungry begin consuming the creators of prosperity. And so it consumes itself to death. It is a law of nature.

The evolution of dispensing favors to stay in power has grown with the technologies and populations of the world. In these modern times, the bad idea took permanent hold in the heart of Prussia.

Most Important Battle: The Battle of Jumonville Glen in 1754 was a small skirmish meant to protect a fort under construction in Pennsylvania. Unknown at the time, this battle that encroached on French-claimed territory led directly to a cascade of amazing world events: 1) The French & Indian War (Seven Years' War), 2) the Stamp Act debacle, 3) the American Revolution, ... (cont'd)

CHAPTER 67:
MODERN WELFARE BORN IN PRUSSIA

Bismarck knew all about tax-spend-elect—he made it work in Germany and everyone wanted to copy him.

It was 1794, and the Prussian states were finally ready to unite their small fiefdoms and states into a single nation. They wanted to stamp out the last remnants of feudalism and protect the average citizen from arbitrary law-making by local princes.

Their new constitution in 1794 was supposed to do just that—create a single new nation. But what a document! The king expanded it in hopes of preempting every possible legal contrivance whereby his many judges might attempt to gain personal advantages. In the end, the king tried to check that with an unwieldy tome of 17,000 paragraphs.

The people were excited about the new country and changes. Impoverished immigrants started pouring across the borders to begin their new lives. As the people jammed into the cities, a new problem erupted: masses of unclean and diseased people all pushed together in slums. And just that fast, new outbreaks of disease appeared—smallpox, malaria, tuberculosis, typhoid fever, dysentery, influenza, the "sweating sickness," and others.[381]

What does a country do to stem the explosion of rampant disease? In 1811, Bavaria decided the best answer was to force the poor into preventative health care.

They picked two dozen towns and made it mandatory for the poor to pay a regular insurance premium. In exchange, they received "free" medical care in local hospitals. This way the spread of disease could be arrested, a degree of hygiene and cleanliness was introduced into the slums, and the rest of the population would be spared the spread of newly acquired sicknesses.

The idea seemed to work. Other Europeans soon copied it.

---

381   See for example, Stephen J. Kunitz, *Making a Long Story Short: A note on men's height and mortality in England from the first through the nineteenth centuries,"* 1987; and Felinah Memo Hazara Khan-ad-Din, *Common Misconceptions about Medieval England,* 2003.

(cont'd) ... 4) the French Revolution, 5) rise of Napoleon, 6) nationalism, 7) modern revolutionism, 8) Communism, 9) Fascism, and 10) the American Empire. Who started the small skirmish that began this massive unfolding of modern world history? It was a 22-year-old Virginia militia major, Lieutenant Colonel George Washington.

The Prussians liked this idea, too. Some 25 years later, they did the same thing and started preventative medical care for the same reasons. Their system wasn't strictly government-supported. Volunteers pitched in to contribute to basic health and sanitary needs, such as taking away the garbage, making sure the dead were buried, inspecting the food, ensuring the water supply was clean and waste-water was carried safely away.[382]

By 1845, the diseases and problems of the poor were brought under control, and the Prussians decided to expand mandatory health insurance to the entire nation as national health insurance.

Meanwhile, over across the border inside Germany, a curious monarchy watched, wondering if compulsory insurance could work for them too.

BISMARCK VS. SOCIAL DEMOCRATS

In his rise to power, Germany's Chancellor Otto Van Bismarck (1815-1898) was watching these rapid changes with concern. With Prussia turning national treasure loose to support national health care, over the other way in France, the socialist party was demanding the same thing and threatening to overthrow the government to get it. In 1870-71, the French socialists staged a nine-week revolt, their so-called *Second Commune.* In their attempt to storm the government and force change, French troops retaliated and killed some 50,000 socialists and sympathizers. The slaughter sent a shock wave across Europe as monarchs wondered, could that happen here?

The German Social Democrats were winning huge followings to their cause. It was an easy sell: They called for the transformation of capitalism and private ownership of factories to common public ownership. They demanded improved working and living conditions, safety inspections of mines and factories, and other changes. But more than that, they called for a revolution against the status quo—an overthrow of leadership, of Emperor Wilhelm I.

The conflicts between workers and the government led to two assassination attempts on Emperor Wilhelm I. He survived both, and blame was quickly directed toward members of the Social Democrat party. The government vowed retaliation.

---

382   See citation in Fritz Dross, *The Price of Unification—The Emergence of Health & Welfare Policy in Pre-Bismarckian Prussia*, footnote 21 and 22, pp. 31-32.

ANTI-SOCIALIST LAWS

Bismarck struck back in 1878 by passing the Anti-Socialist Laws. Any group, he said, who promoted socialist principles was henceforth banned. Trade unions were outlawed. Some 45 newspapers were closed. Many socialists were arrested or expelled, and their agitations were silenced—for a while.

With the socialists finally put underfoot, Bismarck could then turn his attention to a couple of other problems. The people were clamoring for the ideas the socialists had advanced, and out of frustration, many were leaving for a land where they could have more freedom and prosperity. They were going to America.

THE BRAIN DRAIN

One of Europe's frustrations in the latter part of the 1800s was the lure of American prosperity. Many of Europe's best and brightest emigrated away for the chance at freedom and wealth, and Germany was losing tens of thousands. In one year alone, 1882, more than a quarter million emigrants—250,630—pulled up roots, said goodbye, and left their homeland forever to settle in the U.S.

Bismarck needed to kill several birds with one stone. That's when he came up with a plan to out-promise the socialists, pacify the country's agitated work force, and stop workers from emigrating. The idea he launched was Prussia's own specialized form of insurance. And not just any insurance, but national insurance—state welfare of the highest order. "Stay home in Germany," he said, "and look at how we'll take care of you."

THE FIRST STATE WELFARE PROGRAM

At the core of Bismarck's welfare plan were three new programs:[383]

◆ **HEALTH INSURANCE (1883)**: The costs for basic health-care premiums were divided between the workers who paid 1/3, and their employers who paid 2/3rds. Minimum payments for sick leave were set by law. If health problems forced a person out of work, benefits would begin after two weeks and continue for up to 13 weeks.

◆ **ACCIDENT INSURANCE (1884)**: This picked up where health insurance left off—beginning in the 14th week of absence from work.

---

383   Hajo Holborn, *A History of Modern Germany—1840–1945.* 1969. pp. 291–93.

It guaranteed a pension of 2/3rds of earned wages. Employers had to pay the whole bill for this coverage.

◆ **OLD AGE AND DISABILITY INSURANCE (1889)**: The premiums for retirement were split between workers and employers, and were designed to support workers with a pension when they reached age 70. It's a myth that Bismarck invented the retirement age of 65. Many years after Bismarck's death, Germany lowered the mandatory retirement age to 65, and America copied it.

Did Bismarck's insurance scheme work? Absolutely. By 1898, emigration had plummeted to 17,111, and fell from there.[384]

POWER, NOT PHILANTHROPY

Were the socialists happy that Bismarck's ideas precisely mirrored what they wanted? Not at all. They hated his socialistic programs.

They believed that his handouts took all the foam and steam out of their great proletariat uprising. The socialists wanted discord to spread. They were anticipating Marx's prophecy that one day the angry and frustrated workers would rise up in spontaneous revolution against capitalism and set up the new socialist society. How could that great change in society ever materialize if "evil" leaders like Bismarck made life too soft and too easy? How could they convince German workers to rise up and fight against cushy security and handouts and safety nets like *that*?

Even though compulsory insurance was *socialism in action* and should have been celebrated by the socialists, it wasn't. Their actions betrayed a true desire—a desire to acquire power under the guise of helping the common man with fantastic government handouts.

As a result, whenever the socialists could win seats on the Reichstag, they would go to work to defeat Bismarck's programs. It was their goal to smother Bismarck's bribe of the working class.

Bismarck's government worked for six years to implement his state welfare ideas. For the rest of Europe, Germany became the model. The compulsory insurance laws created there were emulated all over the continent, and later, the world. They became the foundation for today's modern welfare state.

---

384 U.S. Dept. of Commerce, *Historical Statistics of the United States, Colonial Times to 1970*, ser. 95, at 105 and 106 (1975).

Potemkin Villages ("fake villages") are alive and well in today's Tibet. The Chinese built "modernized resettlement villages" for Tibetans to show off to foreign journalists how the Chinese occupation of the land has been so"helpful" to Tibetans. Most observers say all of Tibet is a Potemkin village.

CHAPTER 68:

THE ROOTS OF AMERICAN WELFARE

The creeping temptation to impose the cost of welfare on the taxpayer found an early home in the land of the free.

There was a day in early American history when the government kept its distance. Those in charge left the people alone to go about their business and take care of themselves. If business made someone successful, he or she was free to buy and hire, sell, and invest. The money flowed down from the "haves" to the "have nots" in the form of jobs, buying, selling, investing—in short, America's government stood back so the free market and capitalism were left to themselves to grow and shrink, to adjust and re-tool as needed in freedom, endurance and efficiency.

The spirit of the times was pioneering: Stand on your own feet, make your own way, create your own value, work hard, work harder, and rise as high into the economic and social stratosphere as your creativity could lead you.

Self-sufficiency was a mandate from God—to earn your bread by the sweat of your face; to support those dependent on you; to give liberally to strangers in need. Strong Christian principles governed the spirit and tenacity of many early American settlers.

LETTING GO OF FREEDOM PRINCIPLES

A major shift in that American culture took place when the Civil War erupted in 1861-1865. For a long time, there were unresolved questions about the proper role of government—did the federal government have authority to draw its own lines in the sand separating its powers from the states?

After the war, any lingering questions about the supremacy of the federal government were answered. States couldn't secede, and the federal government could wield heavy control.

From that event onward, the balance of power had shifted. No longer was it hands-off management, but it grew toward direct involvement in local responsibilities. Suddenly, the federal government had to have its hand everywhere—stretching the Constitution's original intent to less than paper thin.

Socialism in China: In the U.S. there are 940 vehicles per 1,000 drivers. In China it is 8. However, thanks to current market freedoms in China, it is expected to surpass the U.S. in 2030.

At first, there were only a few innocent intrusions over that line, intrusions that seemed safe and were not challenged.

In 1861, for example, the U.S. Sanitary Commission was established by the government to help Union soldiers who were wounded or sick. The Commission had all the trappings of a private organization—it was self-funded, run by thousands of volunteers, and effectively supported the war by filling in where the military fell short. It raised $5 million and delivered $15 million in supplies. That help saved untold thousands of lives. For all this valuable good, had the federal government stepped outside its boundaries and into private states' rights? During the Civil War, it didn't seem so.

UNEVEN, UNFAIR, UNCONSTITUTIONAL LAND GRANTS

In 1862, another precedent was set by way of the Morrill Land Grant Act. The Act set aside 30,000 acres of federal land for every senator and representative in each state. The larger states loved this idea—it gave them a great deal to work with. The federal goal was to get this land into the hands of the states so they could sell it to build colleges.

It was a huge shot in the arm for better access to higher education, but the grants were unequal. For example, states with too little federal land were authorized to take their 30,000 or more acres from another larger state—usually in the west—and sell it off for cash. Westerners howled over this unfair federal control.

The Land Grant Act was first put forward during President James Buchanan's administration. He vetoed it as unconstitutional and as an unfair redistribution of national resources. And then came new elections. The Land Grant Act was re-submitted. President Lincoln signed it into law on July 2, 1862.

By the time all the dust settled, the Land Grant Act had re-distributed 17,400,000 acres and raised $7.55 million.[385]

Another federal encroachment into states' rights was the Freedman's Bureau (1865-1872). This was a federal welfare program to care for freed slaves. Lincoln wanted it to last only a year, but it proved so valuable by supplying food, housing, education, health care, employment, and helping reunite families that the expiration date was extended.

---

385   Michael L. Whalen, *A Land-Grant University*, 2001.

The importance of controlling education and information: "Ideological education is the key link to be grasped in uniting the whole Party for great political struggles. Unless this is done, the Party cannot accomplish any of its political tasks."—Mao Zedong

How could so much positive be considered negative? The problem wasn't the fact the programs were supposed to support the war, build college campuses, or feed and house freed slaves and their families. The problem was the federal government stepping into areas it was forbidden to touch—economic and cultural issues reserved to the states.

The transition from "business as usual" and a little-noticed federal government into a totally new creature, was snowballing by the turn of the century. Suddenly, people expected and demanded the federal government to provide all the answers to all the problems.

THE OLD IDEAS RETURN AS NEW

Swirling beneath the upheavals and evolutions and disruptions across nations and war-torn America in the later 1800s was a budding new philosophy that promoted top-down government control to force, manage, and regulate all resources toward common goals.

People thought this was a new idea, a great idea, an evolved idea well suited to the industrial revolution underway around the globe. The political science seemed new and the books and pamphlets all said it was new. Strong central governments controlling the resources of prosperity—yes, socialism as usual—was sold as the *new* way of the future.

CAN'T TRUST THE PEOPLE

Running parallel to this thrust toward Ruler's Law was an undercurrent of finger pointing. There was a growing sense that "it can't be my fault." Agitators pushed the perspective that the world's woes were no one's fault—individuals couldn't possibly be at fault for the miserable nightmares unfolding to their left and right. At fault, the new philosophy declared, was the "system." The system must be broken. The system must be changed. The system must be overthrown and replaced.

Socialists of all stripes and colors were calling for change, many of them pointing to the "enlightened" teachings of socialists Bentham, Mill, Marx, the Fabian Societies, and finally the Progressives in 1900, for economic and moral guidance. These new prophets of prosperity had risen to take their places in the world, all of them chanting in unison, *change the system.* They pushed for prong #2, national health care.

"A large proportion of the estimated 180,000 to 200,000 common criminals in Cuba's 500 prisons are people who broke the law by killing their own pigs, cattle and horses and selling the excess meat on the black market."—Larry Solomon, National Post, May 2003

Part XII

THE LAST TEMPTATION, PART 2: HEALTH CARE

"All modern dictators believe in coercing people into governmentalized medicine."

—Melchoir Palyi—

CHAPTER 69:
DEATH BY NATIONAL HEALTH CARE

"All modern dictators have at least one thing in common. They all believe in Social Security, especially in coercing people into governmentalized medicine."—Melchior Palyi

Health care is not an enumerated power of the U.S. government. It is not on the list of 20 permissible activities in Article 1.8. Regardless, the U.S. government began around the New Deal period to go down the path of welfare, health care, and perpetual economic upheaval and suffering.

Dr. Melchior Palyi, an American of Hungarian descent, astutely observed, "In democracies, the Welfare State is the beginning, and the Police State the end. The two merge sooner or later, in all experience, and for obvious reasons."[386]

The "obvious reasons" Dr. Palyi cites include:

❖ **POLITICAL POWER**: The most personal intrusion into privacy that any society can inflict, besides a bullet to the head, is regulating the people's health care. This gives government the power to decide who gets what treatment—in essence, who lives and who dies.

❖ **FEAR TACTICS:** Becoming dependent on the government scares people into supporting government programs, even if they're expensive. Unemployment, for example, is less stressful because welfare stands ready to rescue the unfortunate victims. A trip to the hospital is less stressful because national health care will rescue everyone, theoretically.

❖ **NATIONAL SICKNESS:** Universal health care is the perfect national virus. It is universally desired, easily justified, and sold to the public as completely necessary to prolong life.

❖ **TAXES ARE THE ANSWER:** The enormous tax burdens for health care are sold to the public as simple redistribution of wealth.

---

386   Melchior Palyi, *Compulsory Medical Care and the Welfare State*, 1949, pp. 13-14.

Socialism in North Korea: At least 37 percent of the country suffers chronic malnutrition.

Those with the most pay the most, and this goes to help those with the least. Is that fair? Under socialism, that's how it works.

* **MOTIVATED BY CRISIS:** Planned chaos is how nations are thrust into socialistic ideas. In an emergency, everything, *anything* seems easily justified. "We have *millions* suffering without health insurance, we *must* rescue them. We'll need more of your money." Really? How many "emergencies" does it take to show that compulsory care just doesn't work? Evidently, there are never enough.

* **TAX INCREASES NORMAL:** Raising the taxes to meet the ever-increasing costs of health care is reported across the media as the only compassionate solution—and people put up with it.

* **HIDING OUT-OF-CONTROL SPENDING:** Shifting around budgets to cover the inevitable shortfalls of health care has become routine in America and most of the industrialized world. Tax funded health care has built-in incentives to become more costly—it's free, so people flock to it, expecting a standard of living prior generations had to work for. Until the pressure of the free market is brought to bear, the governmentalized health industry has no incentive to streamline, reduce waste, or improve services.

* **ROUTINE CRISES:** Creating a crisis around health-care funding becomes a rallying cry every election cycle. "Vote for me, and I will keep you secure" is the election-year slogan. Such crises prevent positive change from saving a country.

Health care is not a right—it is a luxury. The private market does a far superior job providing the highest level of health care because it has built-in incentives. The better the services, the more likely are patients to come and spend their insurance dollars. Mistake, inefficiencies, outdated equipment, aging facilities and antiquated processes keep people away—and their dollars. Those facilities are forced to lower their prices to draw less discerning patients who can't afford otherwise.

The inequalities are what socialized medicine seeks to rectify. The very process of seeking equality with national health care gives government enormous power over national economies. It is indeed the last and greatest gateway whereby Ruler's Law can impose the will of the rulers to the most extreme degree.

Capitalism in America: Every day, about two trillion dollars move to and from banks, in roughly 400,000 wire transfers.

CHAPTER 70:

TOP 6 FLAWS OF UNIVERSAL HEALTH COVERAGE

The flaws are inborn, inescapable and fatal.

The frantic cultural dash that begins at government medicine and ends at the welfare state is too long and too slow to recognize—and that's the trap.

For years—maybe a couple of generations or more—the positives of universal health coverage appear to outweigh the negatives. Enthusiasm charges the decision makers with resolve to edge ever-closer to the brink of health-care utopia.

An amazing phenomenon unfolds along the way: everything becomes unimaginably expensive. The people want more, the doctors want more, the managers want more. The resources shrink, the quality suffers, the complaints increase, the dissatisfaction grows, and then the system's bloated, seething, unwieldy enormity— unable to collapse, explode, exhaust or congeal—simply imbloats.[387]

When this happens, politicians sound the alarm and threaten to raise the taxes, cut the expenses, reduce the services, screen out the extremes, and finally settle on the typical, usual, normal default solution: Get out your wallets, everyone, you must pay *more*.

Missed in these frequent fire drills is the best solution of all: let the free market prevail. But suggestions such as free choice are anathema and sacrilege to the socialist brain.

Instead, a cacophony of assurances is foisted on the national dialogue, seeking cultural triteness through blissful slogans and chants: "New Deal!" "Great Society!" "Hope and Change!"

But nothing rescues—and the six flaws remain.

---

387 "Imbloat," best describing a state of rigid and distended dilation of engorged excess—too large to move, too weak to correct, too seamy to contain, it labors unceasingly to perpetuate its own stagnation.—Author

Socialism in Sweden: Some health clinics require security guards to control angry mobs that form when supplies or services run out or are denied under Sweden's socialized health care program.

1 **UNSUSTAINABLE**
A bottom-less treasure of government insurance creates its
♦ greatest flaw in over-use or "use abuse," to the point of self-destruction. It creates an attitude of, "Because it's free, take all you can get." This is best illustrated by Garrett Hardin's *The Tragedy of the Commons*.[388] In this classic 1968 economic parable, Hardin meant to promote population control. However, he also showed how socialism failed to serve a group of cattle herders.

THINGS IN COMMON: The story starts with Hardin's herders sharing a pasture in common. Naturally, each man works to keep as many of his cows grazing there as possible. Over the decades, wars, theft, and disease keep the numbers of man and beast well in check, so the pasture manages to carry the same load of animals for centuries.

FINALLY, PEACE ARRIVES: Each herdsman decides that to advance himself, to grow his prosperity, he will bring one more cow to graze. This works well, so he adds another, and then another. He is not unique in that pursuit—all of his fellow herdsmen do exactly the same, for the very same reason.

Suddenly, there are a whole lot more cows grazing the commons than initially anticipated.

RUINING THE COMMONS: In a few short weeks, the grassy green meadow is reduced to a barren, overgrazed patch of brown muddy waste. Had the commons been divided among the herdsmen, each would have tended his place with an economy of care, protecting it from overgrazing so it would serve him in the future. Without specific ownership, assumption of equal access is justly employed to advance self-interest. With each herder so engaged, the property in common is ruined for all. Socialized medicine is no different—it's all about use abuse.

EXAMPLES: "Overgrazing" the benefits of free or subsidized health care can fill volumes. Some samples:

♦ **E.R. RE-RUNS:** Dr. Edwin Leap (South Carolina) reported that his emergency room received 37,000 patients each year, but in 2010, some 200 of those patients averaged 27 visits each—that's 5,400

---

388   Garrett Hardin, *The Tragedy of the Commons*, SCIENCE, vol. 162, December 13, 1968, pp. 1243-1248.

Freedom engages a man's strength. Socialism engages his weakness.

visits in one year. Their most requested medical help? Pain medication—most often narcotic.[389] The emergency rooms of America have taken a lot of grief ever since the government forced them to take all visitors, regardless of problem or ability to pay.

CALIFORNIA: In 2004, a report revealed that 250,000 California adults and 60,000 children use high-cost emergency rooms for their regular, routine medical care. The ER costs are about six times those of a regular doctor's office visit.[390]

GEORGIA: In 2006, Northeast Georgia Medical Center's emergency department had 97,000 visits. About 26,000 were non-emergencies, and 40,000 had to be written off because the patients didn't pay the bills.[391]

TEXAS: In 2009, an investigation revealed that nine people made 2,678 visits to an Austin, Texas emergency room over a six-year period, costing taxpayers $3 million. Some of the diagnostic bills totaled $20,000 in one visit. Of the 750,000 under-insured in the surrounding region, 900 were frequent users who racked up 2,123 preventable visits in 2009 costing taxpayers another $2 million.

There are ample examples of the numbing effect that overwhelms the better judgment of honest people who find themselves on the receiving end of free health care:

AUSTRIA: A woman from Vienna was quoted in 1962: "My man and I are seldom ill. We were used to sending our Krankenscheine (sick tickets) to one particular doctor. We considered him our family physician. We wanted to help him. Every three months as we got the tickets I would send them to the doctor whether we were sick or not. Everybody does it. Then one day I really needed a doctor. I had an infection in my eye and he swabbed it out. Then he told me, 'Don't think that your two tickets are enough for this treatment. Send me your father's ticket, too.'"[392] Greed knows no loyalty.

UNITED STATES: Howard E. Kershner, the editor of *Christian Economics*, reported on a personal experience with the free-for-nothing attitude: "Many people still believe that money from Uncle

---

389   Edwin Leap, M.D., *The Problem With 'Free' Health Care*, WND, Dec. 11, 2009.
390   Sacramento State News, *Report Highlights Emergency Room Abuse*, September 1, 2004.
391   Debbie Gilbert, *Hospitals Try To Limit Emergency Room 'Abuse,'* Gainesville Times, October 15, 2007.
392   Chicago Tribune, July 28, 1962.

The Constitution gives no authority to the federal government to meddle in education.

Sam is free and costs nobody anything. That's why otherwise honest people seem to have no conscience about the charges they run up against Medicaid and Medicare. It is widely believed that some druggists and doctors join in the scramble to get as much as they can of Uncle Sam's 'limitless' money.

"The writer went recently to buy a wheel chair for his wife, who had an injured knee and ankle. He picked out a good serviceable chair, but the dealer urged him to buy a far more costly one, saying, 'Medicare will pay 80 percent of it, so why not have the best?' We replied that we did not want to take advantage of the public even by reporting that we had purchased the chair. To this the dealer replied, 'You're very foolish. You've been paying in all your life, so why not take the benefits?'

"That spirit is rampant in America today and it is growing at an astonishing rate of speed. The more socialistic measures we adopt, the more we centralize the government, the more opportunity there will be for individuals and especially strong pressure groups to wangle more and more money out of the taxpayers ..."[393]

UNITED KINGDOM: Dr. E. Lloyd Dawe, formerly with the NHS, wrote in 1961 regarding his decision to move his practice to America. "A curious demand came one day in London from a patient of mine, a middle-aged factory worker. He wanted me to prescribe for him ten pounds of absorbent cotton, which is used in packing open wounds and which could be ordered almost free under Britain's program of nationalized medicine. 'What on earth do you want with that absorbent cotton?' I asked. 'I want to restuff a sofa,' he replied.

"When I refused to approve this improper request, he angrily threatened to withdraw his whole family of six who were my regular patients. This attitude of disdain for the British health-care program and the doctors who serve under it became widespread soon after the National Health Service was established in Great Britain. It is only one—perhaps the least important—of the potential dangers America faces if a system of nationalized medicine is adopted in this country."[394]

SWEDEN: On the ten year anniversary of Sweden's compulsory health insurance, U.S. News & World Report said, "...The present

---

393   Howard E. Kershner, Christian Economics, April 14, 1970.
394   Dr. E. Lloyd Dawe, Nation's Business, July 1961.

Socialism in China: Almost 70% of all illegal copycat products are created in China where socialism makes stealing and copying easier than inventing and innovating.

system is proving anything but a clear-cut success. The average patient here finds his situation is worse rather than improved. It is more difficult for him to get a doctor. He must wait longer to get into a hospital. And he may be forced to leave the hospital before he is medically ready for discharge. The shortage of nurses is acute.

"Over-burdened doctors must turn away thousands of patients annually—many of them old people who badly need medical care ... these crippling shortages are the result of vast increased demands for medical services since the start of Medicare, Swedish authorities say. They point out that since 1950 the total number of practicing doctors has doubled, the number of nurses has nearly doubled. The number of hospital beds has increased by more than 25 per cent. During the same span, population has gone up less than 10 per cent. Yet shortages grow worse ... Everyone, young and old, is demanding more medical services, now that it is free ...."[395]

SOVIET UNION: Famed Soviet nuclear physicist Andrei Sakharov was outspoken about the broken Soviet health system. He told American reporters, "The deplorable condition of popular ... health care is carefully hidden from foreign eyes...."

Russian writer Alexander Solzhenitsyn expressed more of the same in his novel, *Cancer Ward*: "What does 'free' mean? The doctors don't work for nothing, you know. It only means that they're paid out of the national budget and the budget is supported by patients. It isn't free treatment, it is depersonalized treatment ... You would be ready to pay goodness knows how much for a decent reception at the doctor's, but there's no one to go to get it. They all have their schedules and their quotas, and so it's 'Next patient, please.'"[396]

The resulting inferior care in Russia drove American embassy personnel out of country. News reporter Allan H. Rvskind was in Russia for two weeks in 1974. He wrote, "American doctors in Moscow, in fact, are not high on Soviet health care and U.S. Embassy personnel advised us that they go to Finland or to other countries when they are hit by serious illness and have to be hospitalized. They go to Finland for the dentist, too ...."[397]

---

395   U.S. News & World Report, January 24, 1966.
396   Human Events, Nov. 23, 1974.
397   Human Events, December 28, 1974.

Socialism in Russia: In 2011, the policy of any-time abortion was limited to the first 12 weeks of pregnancy to reverse a dangerous decline in population since 1992.

2. FLAWED INCENTIVES

The dangerous possibility of failure constantly haunts the
◆ owners of privately-run clinics and hospitals. They must therefore work harder to achieve maximums, stay efficient, reduce waste, and encourage more customers with the lure of excellent quality care. Government operations have no incentive to achieve superlatives. They don't have to worry about losing business, being closed, or a sudden collapse of funding. They have no real incentive to climb any higher than society's legal minimums. Incentives or the lack thereof make all the difference.

◆ **U.K.**—A 2011 study examining incentives showed that doctors who were promised a bonus for performing certain treatments demonstrated a consistent 4 percent increase for those treatments after three years. They also showed a 5 percent decrease for treatments with no bonus attached. Quality of care that was rewarded went up while non-rewarded care went down.[398]

◆ **GERMANY**—Two health-care options are available, both public and private. It turns out that those opting for private care are healthier, and on average make more money. Although private care is more expensive for them, they also don't use as much. This leaves more money in the private health sector to develop superior services, technology, and pharmaceuticals. The power of incentive is seen every day as doctors are observed giving preferential treatment to patients with high-paying private insurance, over those on the lower-paying public option.

Meanwhile, over in the socialized sector of Germany—the other 90 percent of the population—premiums are based on income. When the rich opt out, the remainder with lower incomes suffer through fewer resources, longer waits, and poorer service.[399]

◆ **CHINA**—Despite China's amazing and recent economic growth, medicine has not kept up. Only one percent of China's medical doctors are PhDs, and are very underpaid. The other 99 percent go straight from high school to medical school (no 4-year college program) and emerge as practicing doctors with the equivalent of a U.S. pre-med experience. Very few pursue the PhD program because there is no financial incentive.

398 Jenny Hope, *GP bonuses 'lead to poor patient care,'* MailOnline, June 29, 2011.
399 Stefan Gress, *Private Health Insurance in Germany: Consequences of a Dual System,* 2006.

Keeping watch: In 2006, Walmart China allowed branches of the *Communist Party of China* to set up offices inside the stores.

Chinese law allows physicians to earn extra cash by selling pharmaceuticals. This gives them an incentive to overprescribe medicines—which they do. The lucrative drug market also attracts most medical school graduates to abandon medical practice and go straight to the higher-paying drug companies.[400]

3. NET LOSS

♦ Funds paid into a politicized, government-run national insurance program will forever fail to reach an equilibrium with need. Growing population, new innovations and treatments, and longer life spans are all good things, but they also put more demand on insurances. Each and every time a government tries to intervene, the whole system slows down, bogs down, and finally breaks down.

Around the world, various incarnations of the bad idea have been mulching national treasure for decades. Some samples:

♦ **UNITED KINGDOM**: At its outset (1946), promoters of the British National Health Service (NHS) promised costs would be £260 million per year ($409 million). That very first year (1948-1949), costs grew to £359 million ($565 million).[401] By 1960, costs rose to £820 million ($1.29 billion).[402] By 2010, costs exceeded £105 billion ($166 billion).[403]

On the 30th anniversary of NHS, the British Medical Association reported there were too many defects in the system to list. Facing bankruptcy in 1978, the surveys declared that the hospitals were outmoded, repairs were minimal, and modern equipment was lacking. They said strikes were common and long waits typical.[404]

♦ **CANADA**: As of 2010, health care is consuming 40% of provincial budgets, and is growing by 6 percent a year, much faster than the rate of inflation and the population. Spending has passed $5,400 per person.[405]

---

400   Chee Hew, *Healthcare in China*, IBM Institute for Business Value, 2006; Bradley Blackburn, *World News Gets Answers on China: Health Care*, November 18, 2010.

401   Senate Joint Economic Committee, Minority Staff, *Are Health Care Reform Costs Estimates Reliable?* July 31, 2009.

402   George Winder, *The British Nationalized Health Service*, The Freeman, August 1962, pp. 3-14; *NHS Summarised Accounts*, www.nao.org.uk.2007-12-11.

403   U.K. Department of Health, *Spending Review 2010*, October 20, 2010.

404   *National Health Insurance—It doesn't work & it's not free*, American Cause, Inc., vol. IV, no. 9, October 1978.

405   CBCNews, *Canadian Health-care spending to top $180B,"* November 19, 1990.

Long road to freedom: Between 1993-1995, about 20,000 of Russia's state enterprises were privatized. For the buyers it was a steal—the new government sold them for 10% of their true value.

⬥ **UNITED STATES**: In 1965, Congress promised that a major component of Medicare—the hospital insurance program—would cost $9 billion by the year 1990. It was $67 billion. But only two years later (1967), Congress estimated the entire Medicare program would cost $12 billion by 1990. It was $98 billion. The facts that follow are taken from the U.S. Senate's Joint Economic Committee report, "Are Health Care Reform Cost Estimates Reliable?"[406]

In **1987**, Congress promised that Medicaid's special relief payments to hospitals would never exceed $1 billion by 1992. It exploded to $17 billion.

In **1988**, Congress promised that Medicare's home-care benefits would slowly and predictably creep up to $4 billion by 1993. It blew past $10 billion.

In **1997**, Congress promised the children's health insurance program (SCHIP) would cost only $5 billion each year. *Every year* Congress must supplement it with hundreds of millions ($283 million in 2006, $650 million in 2007). In 2009, President Obama signed a $33 billion bill that would open SCHIP to four million more children and legal immigrants.[407]

In **2000**, the Health Care Financing Administration estimated an increase of only 1 percent a year for children enrolled in Medicaid, growing from 22.6 million that year to 23.8 million five years later. It ended up at 29.9 million.

In **2010**, the new so-called ObamaCare national health-care plan promised $569 billion in higher taxes, $529 billion in cuts to Medicare, 16 million new recipients of Medicaid, and creation of two bureaucracies, the "Patient-Centered Outcomes Research Institute" and the "Independent Payments Advisory Board" with power to ration the resources.[408] As of this writing, government's record of reliability on *any* project puts ObamaCare into the trillions of dollars projected to be squandered on a national, unconstitutional extravagance that liberty would handle with greater efficiency. In 2012, the U.S. Supreme Court invalidated ObamaCare as an action permissible under the Welfare Clause

---

406   Ibid., Senate Joint Economic Committee.
407   Robert Pear, *Obama Signs Children's Health Insurance Bill*, The New York Times, February 5, 2009.
408   Ibid.

"All the marvelous achievements of Western civilization are fruits grown on the tree of liberty."
—Ludwig von Mises

in Article 1.8, but allowed it to stand as a tax, with penalties for non-payment—a legitimate power of Congress, it said. The Founders would not recognize the America created by actions of progressive congresses and Supreme Court decisions as this.

4 ♦ WASTE, FRAUD AND ABUSE

Regardless of how rigid or lax the controls are on socialized health care—be it dictated from Moscow, London, or Washington—people will always find a way to steal, abuse, or manipulate the system. Some samples:

♦ **WORLD:** A multinational health-care fraud organization concluded in 2010 that outside of the United States, at least $260 billion in fraud and error is stolen from health-care systems worldwide every year. That's more than the GDPs of at least 160 countries around the world. This works out to be about 5.6 percent of the $4.7 trillion spent globally on health care.[409]

♦ **U.S.:** In 2008, the FBI estimated $234 billion was stolen from the American health-care systems, representing as much as ten percent of the $2.34 trillion spent on health care that year.[410] Abuse of the socialized U.S. system is rampant.

MASSACHUSETTS: In 2009, Massachusetts' taxpayers funded millions in false, bogus, or unnecessary procedures: $7 million in claims by *non*-Massachusetts residents (including foreigners); $18 million for fraudulent claims such as foot X-rays for headaches and gynecological exams for men; and $6 million wasted on duplicate claims.[411]

KANSAS: A Kansas doctor and his wife were convicted in 2010 for illegally dispensing controlled prescription drugs, collecting more than $4 million from 93 different insurance companies. The doctor was found responsible for 68 deaths from overdoses over a six-year period.[412]

---

409   Kate Kelland, "Global health care fraud costs put at $260 billion," Reuters, January 18, 2010.
410   National Health Care Anti-fraud Association white paper, *Combating Health Care Fraud in a Post-Reform World*, October 6, 2010—www.nhcaa.org.
411   AP, "Mass. Discovers Abuse of Free Health Care Pool," May 29, 2011.
412   Ibid.

DETROIT: Nine health-care professionals, with the aid of 12 others, filed false Medicare claims to the tune of $23 million for bogus home health care, psychotherapy, physical therapy, and podiatry.[413]

LOS ANGELES: Five people stole $28 million from Medicaid with false claims for medical equipment and home health care.[414]

BROOKLYN: Four health-care professionals with six accomplices submitted $90 million in false Medicare claims for fraudulent physical therapy, proctology, and nerve-conduction testing.[415]

❖ **JAPAN:** In 2004, Japanese dentists lobbied, invested, and worked hard to buy political influence in local elections. They wanted to make sure government-set fees stayed high. Influence peddling has been a way of life for so long, people assume it is part of the cost of doing dental work—and politics.[416]

❖ **CUBA**: Medicare thieves find safety in Cuba's cash-hungry economy after stealing millions from Americans. In 2009, the FBI closed in on a group that had stolen at least $420 million from Medicare with false companies and claims. All but one fled from Florida to Cuba, and he was arrested at the airport. Their scheme involved 85 medical equipment companies that never provided a single piece of equipment to anyone.[417]

❖ **FORMER SOVIET STATES:** An underground system for circumventing socialist health care is institutionalized in the former Soviet empire. It grew out of frustration from such things as poor facilities and long waits to be paid. For example, during the 1990s, caregivers in Lithuania and Ukraine waited up to three months for a paycheck—even longer in Russia.

Dissatisfied with their government-set fees, doctors and nurses began supplementing their income by demanding under-the-table compensation. These "informal payments" are the expected norm across eastern Europe. The degree of these informal exchanges is difficult to measure, but estimates include:[418]

---

413 See LaBovick Law Group at www.whistleblower.labovick.com, July 11, 2011.
414 Ibid.
415 Ibid.
416 Transparency International, *Global Corruption Report 2006*, country reports, p. 183.
417 Myriam Marquex, *Medicare crooks like Cuba—why?* Miami Herald, February 5, 2009.
418 Transparency International, *Global Corruption Report 2006*, Chapter 1, part 4, pp. 62-75.

"A system dependent on one man to make it work right is a bad system."—Milton Friedman

BULGARIA: Doctors reportedly ask—and get—up to $1,100 to augment their average monthly salary of $100. As much as 80 percent of that extra cash reportedly comes from surgeries, thereby creating an incentive for excessive surgeries. These informal payments are now a way of life, averaging 4.4 percent of household income spent on medical care.

CZECH REPUBLIC: Informal payments are not high because doctor's salaries are rising faster than the rate of inflation. In 2000, five percent admitted they gave medical care in exchange for "something more" than a small gift.

AZERBAIJAN: An estimated 84 percent of all health-care expenses are "informal" and "under the table."

GEORGIA: People pay out of pocket 70-80 percent of their health-care costs, and about half of that is "informal."

ROMANIA: Patients pay 41 percent of all out-of-pocket expenses "under the table." And not just the poor. A recent survey showed that 39 percent of those with high incomes paid under the table for health care, while 33 percent of the poor did too. The country adopted a national health insurance program hoping that would help stem the "deal making," and forced everyone to pay monthly. This has not significantly reduced informal payments.

KAZAKHSTAN: In 1991, the government promised that citizens did not have to pay anything out-of-pocket for health care. However, within five years, a third of all doctor visits required both formal and "under the table" on-the-spot payments. The informal system extracted a greater price from those least able to pay. The poor spent 252 percent of their monthly wages for hospital care compared to the middle class, who paid 52 percent for the same service.

LITHUANIA: An experiment in freedom is bearing good fruit. Government permission for doctors to open private practices apart from the government is spreading. As the number of those practices increased, the number of "under the table" arrangements correspondingly decreased.

CZECH: Similar to Lithuania, a new private sector is growing, and the line between government doctors and private doctors is sharpening. The private doctors make more money than their government counterparts—no surprise there—and the quality of care is superior.

GOVERNMENT SPAWNS CHEATING: Desperate people will go to any lengths to get the things they want. The normal growth of bureaucratic institutions always leaves holes the desperate will exploit.

Socialized medicine and its many fatal flaws inadvertently generate an underground market of exchange, influence peddling, and outright theft. The free-market private insurance companies, on the other hand, are better motivated to protect profits, and are more efficient at catching abuse and dishonesty.

5. DEATH PANELS

There is a misunderstanding about "panels" in the political dialogue of health care. Many Americans understand the *panel* to be a committee controlling medical decisions between doctor and patient—making life-and-death choices by restricting access to certain life-saving medical treatments.

In Europe, the traditional panel system is different. In the 1800s, workers formed voluntary associations to meet the needs of emergency illness or disaster. Control was local and managed by the participants. These were the original "panels"—German *krankenkassen*, the French *caisses de maladie*, the Dutch *ziekenfondsen*, Danish sick clubs, Swedish orders, the Friendly Societies, and more.[419] They formed the backbone of voluntary care for the sick and needy.

In England, for example, the Friendly Societies were 100 percent voluntary and grew to 14 million members by 1909. They pooled the risk of medical care without government "help."

INTRUSION: Eventually, European governments got involved and made panel membership compulsory, laying the foundations for most national health care throughout the continent. Exceptions include the U.K., where the panel system was completely abandoned in 1946 and replaced by the National Health Service.

---

419 Palyi, Ibid., p. 34.

"The assumption that spending more of the taxpayer's money will make things better has survived all kinds of evidence that it has made things worse. The black family—which survived slavery, discrimination, poverty, wars and depressions—began to come apart as the federal government moved in with its well-financed programs to 'help.'"—Thomas Sowell

PATIENTS COME IN ALL FORMS—rich and poor, healthy and chronically ill, nearby or far away. The panel system evolved to the point where managers could mix and match the various patients so no single doctor had all the rich and healthy who paid their bills, and no one doctor was stuck with all the poor and sick who didn't pay. This created opportunity for graft, where a doctor sought to negotiate (or bribe) his way into being assigned a "good panel."

RUINED BY GOVERNMENT: Today, government intervention in most country's panel systems has destroyed them. Regulations have created exactly what people feared—"death panels," committees rationing resources to save money, to weigh one expensive treatment against another. In essence, to decide between life and death. If an option to purchase life-saving care was made available, the fear and criticism would not be as warranted.

❖ **FAT PEOPLE LOSE OUT**: In 2011, three Suffolk (U.K.) primary care trusts started rejecting patients because of their weight. They produced a list of ten procedures (such as knee and hip replacement) they would no longer perform if a patient's body mass index (BMI) was over 30. Average BMI is 18.5-24.9. Officials admitted it was a cost-cutting decision.[420]

IN 2007, NEW ZEALAND denied immigration permission to Richi Trezise of the U.K. because he was too fat. With more than half of New Zealand's adults and a third of the children overweight or obese, the country's health-care system cannot afford to add overweight immigrants. After Trezise lost some pounds, he was allowed to resettle, but his wife remained overweight and had to stay in Wales until she worked her weight down. High blood pressure and diabetes is over-taxing New Zealand's socialist health-care system.[421]

IN 2008, JAPAN imposed a maximum waistline standard (age 40 and older) of 33.5 inches for men and 35.4 inches for women. This was part of a national campaign to reduce health-care costs. Those who grow too fat must, by law, undergo counseling. Companies that fail to reduce the number of overweight

---

420   BBC News, *Obese patients denied operations*, November 23, 2005.
421   U.K. Daily Mail, as quoted in FoxNews, *New Zealand Denies Immigration to U.K. Wife Because She's Too Fat*, November 17, 2007.

people on their payrolls are penalized with higher payments into the national health-care program.[422]

✦ **BABIES LOSE OUT**: Abortion is permitted in most countries, and proves—with ultimate finality—the power of government over life and death. In 2011, Russia reined in its policy of free abortion *at any term* in the pregnancy to rescue its shrinking population. The new rules made abortion permissible only during the first 12 weeks (longer for the poor). The law was intended to stem the steep decline in population, attributed to more than an estimated 6 million abortions per year. Since 1992, Russia's population has declined by 5.7 million to 143 million.[423]

✦ **MS PATIENTS LOSE OUT**: In Sweden, a man with multiple sclerosis was denied a new drug that cost 33% more than the older drug because it was too expensive. When the patient offered to pay for the drug himself, he was denied—regulators said it would lead to unequal access to medicine, a bad precedent for the whole country.[424]

THE TERM: "Death Panels" is a moniker spawned by the idea that committees will rise up to ration health care based on cost, leaving some without—to die. In reality, *all* health care is rationed one way or another, both private and public—there is no such thing as an unending supply of medical care. Rationing, however, comes in two forms:

✦ **PUBLIC MINIMUMS**: The government is motivated to ration health care for a *minimum* level of care for a maximum number of people—typically paid for by the most inefficient means possible—*taxes*. Are taxes any different from co-pays and premiums universally extracted from everyone? No. As long as payments, by whatever name the regime gives them, continue to flow, public caregivers have no fear of ever going out of business, and therefore have little incentive to maximize their efforts.

✦ **PRIVATE MAXIMUMS**: The private sector is motivated to ration health care so there is a *maximum* level of the best care

---

422 David Nakamura, *Fat in Japan? You're breaking the law,* GlobalPost, June 16, 2010.
423 Washington Post (AP), *Russia's Parliament Adopts Law Restricting Abortions to 12 Weeks,* October 21, 2011.
424 Sven R. Larson, *Lessons from Sweden's Universal Health System: Tales from the Health-care Crypt,* vol. 13 number 1, Spring 2008, pp. 21-22.

"Gun control? It's the best thing you can do for crooks..." Interview with former Mafia member Sammy Gravano, in Howard Blum, "The Reluctant Don," Vanity Fair, 1999.

money can buy. It is paid for by as many participants as the insurance companies can entice. It is persistently motivated by competition with other companies to be efficient, affordable, and innovative—or it goes out of business.

Health care is a luxury. It always has been. Whether paying the local shaman to offer chants in exchange for a dead chicken, or mortgaging the house for chemotherapy, the same principle applies: health care is a need, not a personal right.

Excellent health care is available because of the hard work and unleashed creativity of doctors, chemists, nurses, inventors, business developers, and other professionals all uniting their efforts to make a living in exchange for their services. While rationing is a harsh reality for health care, stepping aside and allowing free-market incentives to induce both the giver and receiver to participate creates more advantage, progress, participation and cooperation than the stagnation of compulsory care.

6. ADMINISTRATIVE FAILURE

Top-down control of health care is pure Marxism: "Each patient gets care according to his needs from each doctor according to his ability."[425] Here are some samples of administrative failures that the vibrant, unhindered free-market approach is better at eliminating.

◊ **CANADA:** A comparison of Canadian national health care vs. U.S. regulated health care reveals government meddling created varied wait times for doctor appointments.

ROUTINE: To see a doctor in 2005, about 36 percent of Canadians waited 6 days or more, versus 23 percent in the U.S.

E.R. VISITS: When Canadian patients raced to the emergency room for urgent help, 24 percent had to wait more than 4 hours or more to be seen, versus 12 percent in the U.S.

SPECIALISTS: If Canadians required a specialist, 57 percent had to wait 4 weeks, versus 23 percent in the U.S.

ELECTIVE: If Canadians wanted elective surgery, 33 percent had to wait 4 months, versus 8 percent in the U.S.

---

425   Quoted from Lin Zinser and Paul Hsieh, *Moral Health Care vs. "Universal Health Care,"* The Objective Standard, vol. 2, no. 4, 2007..

RISING COSTS: On the 20th anniversary of Canada's national health-care services, hospital costs had skyrocketed 424 percent—cost of doctor care rose 71 percent. They had too many specialists and not enough general practitioners. Doctors were hard to find in rural areas and non-existent in inner cities. They also were paying more for "free" government health care than they would have paid for a free-market system.[426]

"ADVERSE EVENTS": The term means mistakes, errors, poor management, or out-right *mis*management of health care leading to unnecessary illness, injury, or death. Government impositions destroy local efficiencies. Some samples:

❖ **UNITED STATES:** A Harvard study showed that 3.7 percent of hospital admissions in New York had adverse events. Most of the problems were minor, but 7 percent created permanent damage, and in 14 percent of the cases, the patients died.[427] A study in Colorado and Utah showed similar results.[428]

A Health and Human Services study in 2011 found that hospital employees reluctantly reported only one out of every seven medical errors they made at hospitals receiving Medicare funds. HHS estimates 130,000 Medicare patients experience some type of adverse event per month, such as over-medication (pain killers, usually), hospital-acquired infections, and severe bedsores. Some of the more serious adverse events led to death.[429]

❖ **UNITED KINGDOM:** A 2001 study of two London hospitals found almost 12 percent of the patients experienced adverse events—at least half of these were judged preventable. A third of the mistakes led to greater disability or death. The researchers estimated the added costs for such problems would exceed £1 billion ($1.6 billion) a year.[430]

❖ **AUSTRALIA:** Almost 17 percent of hospital admissions in New South Wales and South Australia experienced adverse events—half

---

426   *National Health Insurance—It Doesn't Work & It's Not Free*, American Cause, Inc., Vol. IV, No. 9, October 1978.
427   Brennan, Leape, Laird, et al, *Incidence of Adverse Events and Negligence in Hospitalized Patients—Results of the Harvard Medical Practice Study I*, February 7, 1991.
428   Gawande, Thomas, Zinner, Brennan, et al, *The incidence and nature of surgical adverse events in Colorado and Utah in 1992*, Department of Surgery, Brigham and Women's Hospital, Boston, MA, 1999.
429   U.S. Department of Health & Human Services, Report OEI-06-09-00091, *Hospital Incident Reporting Systems Do Not Capture Most Patient Harm*, January 5, 2012.
430   Charles Vincent, Graham Neale, Maria Woloshynowych, Adverse events in British hospitals: preliminary retrospective record review.

of them were considered preventable. About 14 percent were permanently disabled and 5 percent died. Keeping people in the hospital because of these problems accounted for 8 percent of Australia's total hospital bed days, adding $4.7 billion a year in unnecessary costs.[431]

❖ **SWEDEN**: In 2006, a couple rushed to the emergency room with their 3-year-old son who was suffering from diarrhea and had been vomiting for two days. A doctor sent them to a pediatric clinic for intravenous fluids, but the nurses there had no time for him— too many patients, too little time, they said. The parents' repeated pleas were met with the same excuses. Six hours later, the boy died of heart failure. This event is one of too many that result from budget cuts meant to somehow meet national needs for full medical coverage in socialist Sweden.[432]

In 2007, Sweden's third-largest city, Malmo, had only two public clinics available to serve its 280,000 residents. The clinic visit was required before a patient would be allowed to see a specialist. Only one clinic is open after business hours. It becomes so crowded, security guards are stationed in the waiting room to keep the crowds from becoming unruly after waiting several hours to see the doctor—and to prevent new patients from entering. The government limits how many can wait.[433]

❖ **CHINA**: In 2009, China abandoned a medical system they called 'capitalistic' and 'profit driven,' and started implementing a top-down, government-run regulated system. According to several interviews by Jeffrey Kaye for PBS,[434] the transition has been anything but smooth—

> In an interview with Dr. Chen Zhu, Chinese Minister of Health, the country now boasts about 94 percent of the population with insurance coverage—that's about 1.2 billion people. One of the architects of China's health reforms, Gordon Liu, said the overcrowding at the health-care facilities is so severe, even those with money in their pockets and insurance cannot get into

431 Wilson, Runicman, Gibbert, et al, *The Quality in Australian Health Care Study*, The Medical Journal of Australia, November 6, 1995.
432 Sven R. Larson, Journal of American Physicians and Surgeons, vol. 13, no. 1, Spring 2008, pp. 21-22.
433 Ibid. p. 21.
434 See PBS NewsHour, *China Struggles With Health Care Reform Amid Growing Demand*, April 14, 2011.

a hospital quickly for a diagnosis. People start lining up early in the morning to get appointments for the following day.

Doctors see 50 or more patients a day.

Emergency rooms become so crowded, the staff is forced to set up beds in the hallways.

In 2008, before the transition to socialized medicine, Meng Xianan, a freelance writer in Beijing, said going to the hospital would take up to half a day.[435]

Until recently, hospitals made 60% of their income from prescribing and dispensing medications. China is the world leader in per capita use of I.V. fluids to dispense drugs, and patients everywhere are seen hooked up to the bottle. To combat the abuse, the government limited the price on such drugs, and hospitals may not make more than 50 percent of their incomes from the sale of pharmaceuticals.

WHAT IS THE WORTH OF ONE LIFE?

The principle underlying good medical care, good government, and good economic growth is the same—local control.

When the people most affected by any issue are empowered to deal with it on the lowest possible level, the most efficient solutions emerge.

A doctor and a patient are the most qualified people to make important medical decisions. A government employee in some office a million miles away giving the stamp of approval or rejection based on a balance sheet of check boxes is not.

Despite the bloated, inefficient, and profligate unraveling of the world's national health-care systems, the freedom and free-market alternatives remain anathema. The people in charge in any place at any level continue their ceaseless mantra—the government owes you everything.

U.N. CALLS FOR SOCIALIZED MEDICINE

In 2010, the World Health Organization published its *World Health Report*. The Director-General of the WHO, Dr. Margaret Chan, wrote a message pleading with the world to adopt socialistic measures for medical care. She declared socialized medicine the best,

---

435   Maureen Fan, *Health Care Tops List of Concerns in China*, Washington Post, Jan. 10, 2008.

"A higher standard of living also brings about a higher standard of culture and civilization."—Ludwig von Mises

and a pursuit—she was proud to declare—that was well underway. She wrote:

> "Concerning the path to universal coverage, the report identifies continued reliance on direct payments, including user fees, as by far the greatest obstacle to progress. Abundant evidence shows that raising funds through required prepayment is the most efficient and equitable base for increasing population coverage. In effect, such mechanisms mean that the rich subsidize the poor, the healthy subsidize the sick."[436]

❖   In the first sentence, she calls the free-market system "the greatest obstacle." In the second sentence she states that "required prepayment" (that is, *forced*) is the quickest way to get everyone insured. In the third sentence she channels Marx, declaring that taking from the "haves" and giving to the "have nots" is perfect for health care: "...the rich subsidize the poor," in her words.

❖   On page 13: "...Contributions need to be compulsory..."

❖   On page 14: "Ultimately, universal coverage requires a commitment to covering 100% of the population...."

❖   On page 19: "To allow the poorest countries to scale up more rapidly, external partners will need to increase contributions ..." In other words, the U.S. taxpayer, she implies, has a moral obligation to pay more for everyone else.

LEARNING TO RECOGNIZE SOCIALISM

The power of national health care to ruin individual rights is already at work in the welfare-state nations. The economist Melchior Palyi points out this corruption is ancient. He called it "the systematic dispensing, through political channels and without regard to productivity, of domestic wealth."[437] Dispensing wealth, he said, could one day control the world:

TYRANTS LOVE WELFARE: "All modern dictators have at least one thing in common. They all believe in Social Security, especially in coercing people into governmentalized medicine."

WELFARE IS ANCIENT: "The essential idea of the Welfare State is as old as known history. Its concept and mechanism ... were at

---

436   World Health Organization, *World Health Report, Executive Summary*, 2010.
437   All quotes: M. Palyi, *Compulsory Medical Care and the Welfare State*, 1949.

Socialist Sweden learns hard lesson: "Carl Bildt, Sweden's new 42-year-old conservative prime minister [1992], aims to steer Sweden back into the family of free market nations. 'Collectivism and socialism have been thrown ...'" (cont'd)

the very core of the Greco-Latin city states, of the medieval city, and of the post-Renaissance absolute monarchy."

FIGHTING OVER WHO DISPENSES BENEFITS: "In the city republics ... their constantly recurring violent quarrels about constitutional issues [caused] bitter class-warfares to seize the power that was dispensing all benefits. Most of them went on the rocks of their internal struggles for economic privileges."

CAN'T BE STOPPED: "Once the principle is accepted that the general taxpayer has to participate in the cost, the basic barrier to expanding the system—from a limited medical insurance to an all-embracing medical security—is scrapped."

Expanding welfare coverage requires enormous taxes and tight control of the national treasury. How would the agents of socialism get control of the money? They found a way, a clever way, almost by accident. It started with John Law.

Part XIII

SOCIALIZING THE MONEY

"There is something behind the throne greater than the king himself."

—Sir William Pitt—

CHAPTER 71:
JOHN LAW'S TRILLION DOLLAR IDEA

About 70 years before Alexander Hamilton pushed for a strong central bank, a clever scheme was unfolding in The Netherlands. At the hands of John Law, a Scottish economist, the scheme grew into a creature that would eventually infiltrate every bank around the world, collapse the U.S. economy, and saddle all national economies with feeble attempts at managing growth. All of the necessary pieces didn't come together overnight—in fact, it required a couple of centuries to catch on. Today, John Law's get-rich-quick scheme is called fractional reserve banking.

CULPRIT: John Law (1671-1729)[438]
IMPACT: Implemented fractional banking in France
STORY: In 1694, John Law was sitting in prison. He was just convicted for murder. It was a shooting duel over the affections of a young lady, and the competing beau died in the contest. Law was arrested and sentenced to death, but the dead man's brother appealed the sentence—murder was reduced to manslaughter, and Law was spared. And then one day, Law managed to escape his English prison and fled across the channel to Amsterdam. That's where it all started.

One thing Law had going for himself was a brilliant mathematical mind. He discovered great success as a professional gambler. He could win card games by calculating the odds in his head, and made a pretty good living at it.

But a much bigger game presented itself that whetted Law's appetite—it was the risk of a lifetime, but worth millions.

The Bank of Amsterdam, he saw, was essentially a warehouse for gold. Merchants deposited their gold for safe keeping and were given a receipt to reclaim the gold at their pleasure. The bankers made their money by charging a storage fee.

---

438   The Encyclopedia Britannica, *John Law,* Thirteenth Edition, vol. 16, pp. 297-299, 1926.

"The individual has always had to struggle to keep from being overwhelmed by the tribe. If you try it, you will be lonely often, and sometimes frightened. But no price is too high to pay for the privilege of owning yourself."—Friedrich Nietzsche

ROCKS, PAPER, SCISSORS

And then Law caught wind of a strange pattern in human behavior. With very predictable regularity, the merchants rarely went to "the warehouse" to claim their gold. Using the paper in the pocket was more convenient than taking a carriage ride downtown, withdrawing a purse sagging with heavy coins or bullion, and carrying it about around the neck or bulging in a pocket. Trading receipts was so much easier, so simple.

THE TEN PERCENT

By this time, the clerks at the Bank of Amsterdam were already working this curious tendency to their advantage. In fact, they had been keeping track. At any given time, only 10% of the merchants actually took their gold. The other 90% seemed content with trading around their paper, secure in the knowledge that their gold was always there inside the bank vault.

The bankers then got the idea they could print up more receipts than they had gold. They could go about town, swapping a receipt for groceries, a horse, maybe a new boat. Or why not make loans? Now there's an idea—if the people believed they were actually borrowing real gold, but got receipts instead—and then had them pay back the loan with real gold, what a fantastic way to make some fast cash.

A MILLION FOR A BILLION?

John Law saw an amazing phenomenon unfolding. Since only a small percentage, a small fraction of people, worried enough to retrieve their gold, could not an entire economy be built on this human tendency? Could a country prosper with only a million in gold but a billion in paper?[439]

John Law tried for 20 long and frustrating years to sell his scheme of fractional banking to other European governments, but nobody took the bait. He assured them that if at least 10 or 20% of the gold was kept in the vault, 80 or 90% of it could be loaned out.

FIRST UP: KING LOUIE'S COURT

Law's luck finally changed in 1715.[440] France was grinding down into financial failure. King Louis XV was desperate. He summoned

---

439 A billion from a million is an exaggeration to make a point. "Deposit multiplication" is a complex subject, and lending on a 1:1000 basis would be deemed too risky for banks today.
440 See John T. Flynn, *Men of Wealth*, 1941.

John Law to his chambers for details on how to make fractional banking work in France. The scheme sounded risky, but workable, so Louis put John Law in charge of the whole thing and sent him on his way to repair France's troubles.

John Law's scheme started out great. All the country's gold and silver was steered and enticed into his banks. Paper money was suddenly in fashion for all business transactions.

As bails of money were printed, John Law became wealthy and France prospered—everyone exchanging receipts thought to be equal to actual deposits.

RAINY DAY FUNDS ON RAINY DAYS

And then circumstances threw a wrench into the works. A growing number of people who picked up their gold didn't turn around and deposit it again. Some took it with them and moved out of the country. Others shipped it away to invest in foreign activities or to pay off debts. And others stuffed it at home under the mattress. It was becoming more difficult to keep enough actual gold in the vaults to keep the wheels of fractional banking turning.

IGNORE THAT MAN BEHIND THE CURTAIN

How did John Law respond? To stop the flow of gold of the country, he arranged to outlaw private ownership of gold. The receipts were still good, he assured everyone—you just can't trade them for gold or silver right now. That did not sit well with some people and they demanded their gold. Word spread and suddenly there was a run on the banks—those first in line emptied all the vaults. Everyone else was left holding millions in worthless receipts. Like a rock thrown off the yet-to-be-built Eiffel Tower, France's economy collapsed overnight.

John Law had to flee the country in 1720, chased away by hordes with a hangman's rope. He survived and managed to get along for a few more years, only to die in poverty in 1729.

NATIONAL BANKS TO THE RESCUE

John Law's experience demonstrated some important points that were later adopted by European bankers.

⋄   First, he demonstrated the power of illusion. So long as people were convinced that the system working their money was too complex to be understood, the average layman felt secure. All they cared about was receiving money when they wanted it. How many banks carry "trust" in their name?

❖ Second, John Law showed the power of a central, all-powerful bank. If bank customers worried there wasn't enough cash in the vault, a central bank could calm a potential run by shoveling in more—it could dispatch a coach hauling gold or freshly printed bills to the back door and have the clerks carry the boxes into the vault. With plenty of coin or cash to disburse on demand, the appearance of security and strength remained, and people calmed down.

"THEY WROTE IT DOWN—IT MUST BE TRUE!"

Creating the appearance of stability was done by tracking everyone's transactions in ledger books and pass books and receipts showing balances left in an account—people could "see" their balances were securely noted in ink, officially scrawled on official bank documents, official proof that they had that much money stashed somewhere ... officially.

DECEPTION BECOMES POLICY

Today, the ruse is no longer hidden. In fact, allowing banks to lend the same money over and over again is an established policy for banks worldwide. They must keep a certain reserve of cash on hand "for the 10 percent," or more—whatever reserve their circumstances require.

The socialists loved this idea. Some 200 years ago, Nathan Rothschild said,

> "The great body of people mentally incapable of comprehending the tremendous advantages that the capital derives from the system, will bear its burdens without even suspecting that the system is inimical to their interests."[441]

Karl Marx made this scheme of top-down financial control an important goal for implementing socialism. His fifth of 10 communist planks espoused "Centralization of credit in the hands of the State, by means of a national bank with State capital as an exclusive monopoly."[442] That goal has been met.

---

441 This quote has been attributed to the Rothschilds—see *National Economy and The Banking System of the United States*, Document No. 23, 76th Congress, 1st Session, 1939.
442 Ibid., *The Communist Manifesto*.

CHAPTER 72:

THE RULING POWER OF CENTRAL BANKS

The principles of socialism are well exercised in international banking. Their entangling alliances give the appearance of extreme complexity—financial labyrinths no person could ever unravel. The truth is, cutting away the centuries of barnacles and shrouds, the vulnerabilities of modern banking are seen resting on the very same pillar that has wreaked havoc since the dawn of humanity—*monopoly*.

POWER BEHIND THE THRONE

Holding monopolies is how rulers retain power. The question is, do rulers control every monopoly? What could possibly be operating behind the scenes, then, to prompt such admissions as these—

❖ **KING NOT OMNIPOTENT?**: "There is something behind the throne greater than the king himself."—Sir William Pitt, House of Lords, writing in 1770.[443]

❖ **BANKERS AND ARMIES**: "I sincerely believe, with you, that banking institutions are more dangerous than standing armies..."—Thomas Jefferson[444] in a letter to John Taylor, May 28, 1816.

❖ **SMOKE AND MIRRORS**: "The world is governed by very different personages from what is imagined by those who are not behind the scenes."—Benjamin Disraeli, writing in 1844.[445]

❖ **RULERS IN AMERICA**: "The real truth of the matter is ... that a financial element in the large centers has owned the government since the days of Andrew Jackson."—Franklin D. Roosevelt, 1933[446]

❖ **INVISIBLE GOVERNMENT**: "Behind the ostensible government sits enthroned an invisible government owing no allegiance and acknowledging no responsibility to the people. To destroy this invisible government, to befoul this unholy alliance between corrupt

---

443   Quoted by Lord Mahon, *History of England*, vol. v., p. 258.
444   Thomas Jefferson Randolph, editor, *Memoirs, Correspondence, and Private Papers of Thomas Jefferson*, vol. 4, 1829, pp. 285-288.
445   Benjamin Disraeli, *Coningsby*, Book 4, Chapter 15, 1844.
446   Elliott Roosevelt, *F.D.R.: His Personal Letters, 1928-1945, 1950*, p. 373.

"The right of a nation to kill a tyrant, in cases of necessity, can no more be doubted, than to hang a robber, or kill a flea. But killing one tyrant only makes way for worse, unless the people ..." (cont'd)

business and corrupt politics is the first task of statesmanship."
—Theodore Roosevelt, 1912.[447]

THE REAL RULER IS A CENTRAL BANK

The references to *powers behind the throne* point to privately-run central banks that concentrate financial power in just a few private hands. This is far from "power by the people" the Founders wanted, who rejected such scheming completely.

Before the American War for Independence, England's King George tried to force the colonies to set up their currency by borrowing from the Central Bank of England. The Americans refused. Benjamin Franklin listed this demand as one of five major reasons for the Revolution.[448] He said the king's "prohibition of making paper money among themselves [the colonies]" helped turn the colonists against Parliament and king alike.[449]

WHY WERE THEY SO OPPOSED?

Central banks have only one purpose: to create debt. Debt means power—power to earn an income from interest, and power to guide national policy, politics, and finance. Put a nation under the thumb of a banker and everything else must follow. Voluntarily surrendering that much power to the bankers is the central bank's first major hurdle. Afterwards, it's all downhill from there:

❖ **CREATE CURRENCY**: The bank's job is to print money, control how much is in circulation, and control interest rates.

❖ **CREATE DEBT**: A central bank doesn't just give money to the government. A nation must borrow it—and pay interest.

❖ **CREATE MORE DEBT**: The interest owed must come from somewhere. The government doesn't go out and print it up itself—that printing job is the central bank's. So, that *somewhere* ends up becoming more borrowed money from the same central bank—with more interest due on the new loan. As a result, the country is forever borrowing, forever in debt, forever at the whims and behest of bankers.

---

447 Theodore Roosevelt, *The Progressive Covenant With the People*, a speech given in 1912.
448 Franklin's five reasons include restraining trade, prohibiting paper money, the Stamp Act, removing trials by juries, and refusing to hear the colonists' petitions.
449 William Jennings Bryan, editor, *The World's Famous Orations, America: 1. (1761-1837)*, [Benjamin Franklin] *His Examination Before the House of Commons, 1766*, New York: Funk and Wagnalls, 1906.

(cont'd) "... have sense, spirit and honesty enough to establish and support a constitution guarded at all points against the tyranny of the one, the few, and the many."—John Adams

❖ **CREATE BOOM AND BUST CYCLES**: When the central bank allows a lot of money to circulate, loans are cheap. Everyone runs out to buy that car or house or start a business because interest rates are low. But when the central bank pulls money out of the system, money is scarce—interest rates go high, and many people stop borrowing until rates drop again.

❖ **CREATE FALSE AUTHORITY**: It's critical that the central bank appear to be a branch of the government. This is necessary to retain confidence in the system. When confidence collapses, there are runs on the banks, people hoard money, black market bartering systems emerge, and the bankers lose their power, influence, and profits. Instead of blaming the banks for inflation, deflation, recessions, etc., people must be led to believe that the banks are rescuing them from regular and painful business cycles that operate beyond anyone's control.

Appearing official is why private central banks around the world adopt such names as The Central Bank of England, The U.S. Federal Reserve System, The Central Bank of Argentina, Reserve Bank of Australia, National Bank of Poland, Central Bank of Cuba, National Bank of Rwanda, etc.

For almost every country in the world there exists at least one such bank with National, Central, or Reserve in its name serving as its central bank. Only two countries remain independent—Andorra and Monaco have no central bank.

HOW MUCH DO WE OWE CENTRAL BANKS?

According to estimates accumulated by the Joint External Debt Hub,[450] the CIA Factbook, the U.S. Census Bureau, the International Monetary Fund,[451] the World Development Indicators,[452] and others, the total on-the-books external indebtedness of all nations combined, and payable to their financial masters, those central banks, is a staggering $74.1 trillion in 2011 dollars—$16 trillion of that owed by the U.S. alone.

---

450   World Bank Group, The Joint External Debt Hub, www.jedh.org.
451   International Monetary Fund, www.imf.org.
452   World Bank Group, World Databank, http://databank.worldbank.org.

Potemkin Villages ("fake villages") are alive and well in the U.S. New York, Cleveland and Chicago tried to brighten up slum areas by having cheery windows and doors painted on wood panels boarding up the windows and doors to make them look occupied and hide the blight.

CHAPTER 73:
PROGRESSIVES FINALLY GET THEIR CENTRAL BANK

They called it "The Federal Reserve"—it was, however, neither federal nor reserved.

Putting a central bank in America had been a goal since Alexander Hamilton first encouraged it. After decades of start-stop and succeed-fail, the opportunity to wrest control of America's money supply and interest rates came in 1907 on the heels of recent frustrations with the banking system and the economy in general.

AT THE TURN OF THE CENTURY: Powerful financial forces were at work in the U.S. by 1900, fiercely competing against each other for power and control. People watching the maneuvering developed a deep sense of suspicion about these Wall Street titans—it was a tripwire of panic tautly stretched.

PANIC OF 1907

In October 1907, an attempt to corner the market on copper failed. Blamed for the run was Union Copper. The market punished it by selling off stock. Prices plummeted from $60 to $10. As brokers dashed about making repairs, the rest of the stock market reacted badly. The New York Stock Exchange fell almost 50 percent.

J.P. Morgan stepped in at this point and announced he feared his Knickerbocker bank was so damaged in the massive money transfers that this bank would close.

Panicked patrons rushed the bank and cleaned out the vaults. Like tumbling dominoes, a crisis of confidence spread nationwide. There were runs on banks, businesses went bankrupt, and reports came in of rioting in the streets.

Thousands of banks bristling at the hordes of customers demanding their deposits back suddenly needed fast cash. Notifications by their head offices ordered the widely disbursed branches to pull in as much money as they could—foreclose on loans, limit withdrawals, limit payouts, etc. Sen. Robert Owen later gave a congressional committee an idea what these orders looked like. A demand from the National Banker's Association that became known as "Panic Circular of 1893" instructed him, "You will at once retire one-third of your circulation and call in one half of your loans..."[453]

And that's what they did, demanding loans be repaid—many of which, ultimately, were not. People lost homes, businesses, and those with cash hoarded it as their last ounce of security.

J.P. Morgan rescued the system by injecting $200 million of his own money into one of the last major banks still open. He issued certificates to mingle with the millions of IOUs that people were exchanging for lack of greenbacks.

Eventually, the certificates restored confidence, and people began spending cash again. As for the banks, the small ones died, the bigger ones absorbed those customers, and life went on—some wallets fatter, other wallets reamed out to the seams.

A writer for *Life Magazine* summarized the whole sordid affair in 1949. Frederick Lewis Allen described how J.P. Morgan caused the panic to further his own financial controls.

> "Oakleigh Thorne, the president of [The Trust Company of America] testified later before a congressional committee that his bank had been subjected to only moderate withdrawals ... that he had not applied for help and that it was the (Morgan) 'sore point' statement alone that had caused the run on his bank. From this evidence, plus other fragments of other supposedly pertinent evidence, certain chroniclers have come to the ingenious conclusion that the Morgan interests took advantage of the unsettled conditions during the autumn of 1907 to precipitate the panic, guiding it slow as it progressed so that it would kill off rival banks and consolidate the pre-eminence of the banks within the Morgan orbit."[454]

CONGRESS GOT THE MESSAGE: Senator Nelson W. Aldrich (R-RI) was dispatched to investigate exactly why the panic happened. His committee reviewed banking policies in America and decided the country needed central banking to prevent these kinds of damaging panics.

So, off he went to Europe with his committee, spending $300,000 for two years so they could study the national banking schemes in operation in all the major countries.

---

453   Gary Allen, quoted in *None Dare Call It Conspiracy*.
454   Frederik Lewis Allen, Life Magazine, April 25, 1949.

Upon his return, Aldrich convened a secret meeting in November of 1910. He invited several powerful investment bankers and financial leaders. The gathering was super-secret—all travel was done at night, names and faces were hidden from others—*secrecy*. The meeting place was off the coast of Georgia at Jekyll Island.

THE PLAN: The Jekyll Island group produced a plan to create a "National Reserve Bank." It took two years of debate and refinement to get Congress to consider the idea. As enthusiasm for the central bank grew, word spread that *this is a great idea!*

HARD P.R. PUSH: The public relations campaign that followed was intense and enormous. Pressure by politicians to win support erupted on the House and Senate floors hundreds of times. For example, a promise that the new system would miraculously stop inflation was proclaimed from the Senate and Congress more than 50 times. How many of their promises failed?

◇ "Interest rates will always be low."—Rep. Oscar W. Underwood (D-Ala),[455] Dec. 22, 1913

◇ "It will be easy to obtain loans for as much money as the borrower thinks is reasonable, and at all times."—Rep. Samuel J. Tribble (D-GA),[456] September 16, 1913

◇ "Farmers will get easy loans at any time, especially during harvest season or planting time."—Rep. Michael E. Burke (D-Wis.),[457] Sept. 17, 1913

◇ "Financial panics will be impossible."—Sen. Claude A. Swanson (D-VA),[458] Dec. 8, 1913

◇ "America will have permanent prosperity."—Rep. William A. Cullop (D-Ind.),[459] Sept. 17, 1913

◇ "Federal Reserve notes will be more secure than any currency in the history of the world."—Sen. Robert L. Owen (D-Okla.),[460] Dec. 15, 1913

◇ "A Federal Reserve note is not real money."—Rep. Louis

---

455   Congressional Record, 63rd Congress, 2nd session, vol. 51, pt. 2, p. 1459.
456   Ibid., 1st session, vol. 50, pt. 7, p. A309.
457   Ibid., p. A293.
458   Ibid., 2nd session, vol. 51, pt. 1, p. 430.
459   Ibid., 1st session, vol. 50, pt. 7, p. A332.
460   Ibid., 2nd session, vol. 51, pt. 1, pp. 901-902.

Socialism in Venezuela: In 2010, Hugo Chavez ordered all television stations to broadcast a government message. When six privately-owned cable channels refused, one of which was openly anti-Chavez, he ordered all six taken off the air.

Fitzhenry (D-Ill.),[461] Sept. 17, 1913

❖ "All Federal Reserve notes can ultimately be redeemed in gold."—Rep. Finly Gray (D-Ind.),[462] Sept. 17, 1913

❖ "The Federal Reserve will redeem notes with its own gold, not with gold owned by the government."—Sen. John Shafroth (D-Colo.),[463] Nov. 25, 1913

❖ "America will never have to worry about a strain on her gold reserves."—Sen. John Shafroth (D-Colo.),[464] Nov. 25, 1913

❖ "Federal Reserve notes will be as valuable as gold itself."—Rep. Michael E. Burke (D-Wis),[465] Sept. 17, 1913

❖ "However, some Federal Reserve notes may be backed merely with other Federal Reserve Notes."—Sen. James A. Reed (D-Mo.),[466] Dec. 4, 1913

❖ "The Federal Reserve automatically prevents inflation, but only if a gold reserve is maintained."—Rep. Adolph J. Sabath (D-Ill.),[467] Dec. 22, 1913

❖ "The Federal Reserve Board will see to it that Americans have stable prices."—Rep. Finly Gray (D-Ind.),[468] Sept. 12, 1913

❖ "The Federal Reserve system will destroy the powerful 'Money Trust' on Wall Street so that it will no longer control American Finances."—Rep. Claude Weaver (D-Okla.),[469] Sept. 17, 1913

❖ "Government control over all banking transactions will be strengthened."—Rep. Michael E. Burke (D-Wis.),[470] Sept. 17, 1913

❖ "The Federal Reserve Board will represent the American people."—Rep. Lawrence B. Stringer (D-Ill.),[471] Sept. 18, 1913

❖ "Federal Reserve Board members are just as trustworthy as the justices on the Supreme Court."—Rep. Michael E. Burke (D-Wis.),[472]

461 Ibid. 1st session, vol. 50, pt. 7, p. A331.
462 Ibid., p. 301.
463 Ibid., pt. 6, p. 6028.
464 Ibid.
465 Ibid., pt. 7, p. A294.
466 Ibid., 2 session, vol. 51, pt. 1, p. 174.
467 Ibid., pt. 17, p. A32.
468 Ibid., 1st session, vol. 50, pt. 7, p. A297.
469 Ibid., p. A310
470 Ibid., p. A291.
471 Ibid., p. A314.
472 Ibid., pp. A295-296.

Socialism Payback: In 2012, Bank of America Corp. announced it would donate $50 billion over the next 10 years to fight global warming. In 2008-09, U.S. taxpayers gave the bank a bailout of $45 billion that was eventually paid back with interest. It pays to have friends in high places

Sept. 17, 1913

◆ "The Federal Reserve Board will be completely beyond political control and manipulation."—Rep. William A. Cullop (D-Ind.),[473] Sept. 17, 1913

◆ "The powers of the Federal Reserve Board will be safely limited by the act."—Sen. Thomas Sterling (R-S.D.)[474]

◆ "However, another proponent of the act admits that the power of the Federal Reserve Board is arbitrary, drastic, and extraordinary."—Sen. Knute Nelson (R-Minn.),[475] Dec. 9, 1913

◆ "The absolute control of the system by the Federal Reserve Board is not a danger, but a safeguard."—Sen. John F. Shafroth (D-Colo.),[476] Dec. 18, 1913

◆ "The work of the Federal Reserve Board will be given full publicity."—Sen. Henry F. Hollis (D-N.H.),[477] Dec. 12, 1913

◆ "The Federal Reserve Board will prevent depressions."—Sen. Claude A. Swanson,(D-Va.),[478] Dec. 8, 1913

◆ "The Fed will increase overseas trade so greatly that a Democratic victory in the next election is guaranteed."—Rep. Oscar W. Underwood (D-Ala.),[479] Dec. 22, 1913

◆ "If all the bank vaults are emptied, the Fed will still have power to pay depositors by printing more 'notes.'"—Sen. John F. Shafroth (D-Colo.),[480] Nov. 25, 1913

◆ "The Fed has the right to take privately owned deposits in order to bail out any bank in financial trouble."—Sen. John F. Shafroth (D-Colo.),[481] Dec. 12, 1913

WHO HAS THE POWER?

The Founding Fathers made every aspect of a central bank unconstitutional. That's why it required a combination of crisis, an unwary public, and a progressive-minded Congress and president to

---

473 Ibid., p. A332.
474 Ibid., 2nd session, vol. 51, pt. 1, p. 773.
475 Ibid., p. 521.
476 Ibid., pt. 2, p. 1121.
477 Ibid., pt. 1, p. 782.
478 Ibid., p. 432.
479 Ibid., p. 1460.
480 Ibid., 1st session, vol. 50, pt. 6, p. 6026.
481 Ibid., 2nd session, vol. 51, pt. 1, p. 789.

Since 1960, the U.S. has raised the limit on its national "credit card" 78 times. In 2012, that limit exceeded $15 trillion, plus some change.

push it through—and that's what they did. On December 23, 1913, the Federal Reserve Act became law.

Aside from all of the laudatory assurances by Congress, there lurked beneath the establishment of the Federal Reserve something more sinister than any promise and assurance—

❖ **JAMES A. GARFIELD**, one of the writers of the original Federal Reserve Act, said,

"Whoever controls the volume of money in any country is absolute master of all industry and commerce."[482]

❖ **MAYER AMSCHEL ROTHSCHILD** made the same observation a century earlier:

"Permit me to issue and control the money of a nation and I care not who makes its laws."[483]

❖ **CHARLES A. LINDBERGH, SR.** deeply despaired the unstoppable signing of the Federal Reserve Act—

"When the President signs this bill, the invisible government of the monetary power will be legalized .... the worst legislative crime of the ages is perpetrated by this banking and currency bill."[484]

PROMISES: After more than 100 years, the Federal Reserve has proven itself a ravenous monster that is eating the labors of the people with wanton disregard. It is ruining businesses and nonmember banks, heaping billions of unearned fortunes into private, elitist hands, and is manipulating at will the greatest economic power on earth. With its soft and flimsy flaxen cord of false authority loosely looped around America's neck, it is leading her down into the gaping jowls of cold misery and financial hell.

---

482 Attributed to James A. Garfield in *The American Plutocracy*, by Milford Wriarson Howard, Chapter 16, p. 156.
483 Attributed to Mayer Amschel Rothschild (1744-1812) in *Money Creators* (1935) by Gertrude M. Coogan.
484 Attributed to Charles A. Lindbergh, Sr., December 23, 1913.

"The Democrats are the party that says government will make you smarter, taller, richer, and remove the crabgrass on your lawn. The Republicans are the party that says government doesn't work and then they get elected and prove it."—P.J. O'Rourke

CHAPTER 74:

BROKEN PROMISES OF THE FEDERAL RESERVE

Like a silent partner in a massive Ponzi scheme, the Federal Reserve has been mute about its collapse of the U.S. economy.

T he Federal Reserve is the financial arm of the socialist government of the United States. It has emerged as the modern rendition of Alexander Hamilton's original concept of a strong central bank, and it brought all the tyranny, regulation and economic misery that was long ago predicted.

UNDER THE INFLUENCE: The influence of progressivism was thick in Washington in the early 1900s. Had they stopped to put the Federal Reserve Act to the constitutional test, it would have failed. Article 1.8.5 clearly states that Congress is mandated to "coin money [and to] regulate the value thereof." Congress was not to delegate this to another party. When they did, and that party was not even a government agency but a private business, they violated the Constitution. Nevertheless, with unconstitutional powers exclusively in hand, the Federal Reserve went about to break all 12 of its promises.

1 **PROMISE: NO MORE DEPRESSIONS**—In 1921, a severe depression was caused by the Federal Reserve. They did it ✦ again in 1929, causing the worst depression in American history, lasting 1929-1939. Since World War II, the Federal Reserve's policies created eleven avoidable recessions.

2 **PROMISE: INTEREST RATES WILL BE KEPT LOW**—A week before Christmas in 1980, the interest rate charged by ✦ banks to their most credit-worthy customers—the prime rate— rose to 21.5 percent, its highest in America's history. That record-breaking "usury fee" capped a rocky but steady climb that began right after WWII.[485]

3 **PROMISE: NO INFLATION**—Since World War II, the Federal Reserve's inflationary policies have gutted the dollar, ✦ causing it to lose 92% of its value. For example, a very nice

---

485 Federal Reserve Board, 2011.

"The democracy will cease to exist when you take away from those who are willing to work and give to those who would not."—Thomas Jefferson

suit that cost $50 right after the war would cost $625 today.[486]

4. PROMISE: SUBMIT TO DIRECT SUPERVISION—
Originally, the proposal was to put government leaders on
the Board "which shall consist of seven members, including the Secretary of the Treasury and ... five members appointed
by the President" so there was some degree of oversight.[487] Almost
immediately after the Federal Reserve Act was passed, more than
200 amendments were added, its structure changed, and instead of
transparency, it meets to control the economy in absolute secrecy.

5. PROMISE: STABILIZE THE MONEY SUPPLY—The
Federal Reserve's mismanagement contributed to the Great
Depression. In 1928, it tightened the money supply and
forced interest rates up. The resulting recession triggered the stock
market crash in 1929. It raised interest rates again in 1931, lowered
them, and then raised them again in 1932, collapsing the U.S. economy. This foolishness continues today, costing Americans billions
if not trillions with each attempt to force the free market to follow
their short-range solutions to long-range problems.

6. PROMISE: KEEP CLEAR OF WALL STREET—The
original Federal Reserve Act stipulated, "No director ... shall
be an officer, director, or employee of any bank."[488] However, subsequent actions proved that Wall Street investment bankers benefitted the most, and the Board of Governors and the secret
Federal Open Market Committee have been dominated by Wall
Street bankers. In its first 15 years, Paul Warburg and Benjamin
Strong, both Wall Street bankers, ruled the Federal Reserve to their
advantage. Any form of Wall Street neutrality was long ago abandoned except for perhaps in the strictest token sense.

7. PROMISE: NO CHARGE TO GOVERNMENT—In 1941,
Rep. Wright Patman (D-TX), the chairman of the House
Banking and Currency Committee, asked the chairman of the
Federal Reserve Board, Marriner Eccles: "Wasn't it intended when
the Federal Reserve Act was passed that the Federal Reserve Bank
would render this service without charge—since under the Act the

---

486   Calculated at 8% of prices in 1945, or 12.5 times more costly today.
487   Federal Reserve Act, section 10, 1913.
488   Federal Reserve Act, section 4, 1913.

government would give them the use of government credit free?" Eccles seemed insulted: "I wouldn't think so!"[489]

8. PROMISE: HELP FARMERS SURVIVE—The government destroyed the U.S. farmers' independence. The first error ◆ was promising wheat farmers $2 a bushel during World War I. This fixed price drove farmers to borrow and buy more land to enlarge their wheat farms. After the war, demand plummeted and so did their income. On May 18, 1920, the Federal Reserve raised interest rates on agriculture loans to 7 percent. Many couldn't pay—and so began the Agricultural Depression of 1920-21. Thousands lost their farms, homes—everything. This process was repeated, with higher taxes, in the early 1930s. An estimated 25 percent of bankrupt farms were sold for failure to pay taxes.[490] Taxes were so high that by 1933, farmers were essentially working 2 days a week for the government.[491]

9. PROMISE: HELP SMALL BUSINESS SURVIVE—The Federal Reserve's constant yanking on the national economy ◆ destroyed thousands of small businesses. In 1925, unemployment was about 3 percent. When the Great Depression hit thousands of businesses closed, unemployment was around 25 percent—that's 13 million by 1933. New York City police estimated that 7,000 people over age 17 were shining shoes for a living. Congress was forced to enact lending agencies to rescue as many small businesses as possible. Ben Isaacs, a Chicago clothier, sold his car for $15 to buy food. "I would bend my head low [in the relief line] so nobody would recognize me."[492]

10. PROMISE: PROTECT BANKS FROM COLLAPSE— The unpredictable policy changes of the Federal Reserve ◆ kept most banks operating on the razor's edge. Since its enactment, and by exercising powers of regulation to control inflation and money, at least 3,970 U.S. banks have failed since 1934, directly because of the Federal Reserve. Some put the number at

---

489   House Committee on Banking and Currency, June 24, 1941.
490   James Bovard, *Hoover's Second Wrecking of American Agriculture*, Freedom Daily, 2005..
491   B.H. Hibbard, *Taxes A Cause of Agricultural Distress*, Journal of Farm Economics, Vol. XV, No. 1, January 1933, pp. 1-10.
492   Suds Terkel, *Hard Times: An Oral History of the Great Depression*, Pantheon Books, 1970.

"When we get piled upon one another in large cities, as in Europe, We shall become as corrupt as Europe."—Thomas Jefferson

more than 15,000.[493]

11. ♦ PROMISE: PROTECT U.S. ECONOMY FROM FOREIGN ENTANGLEMENTS—The Federal Reserve makes no secret that it links U.S. fortunes to international developments. From its website: "The Federal Reserve formulates policies that shape, and are shaped by, international developments. It also participates directly in international affairs."[494] A 2011 audit showed the Federal Reserve provided hundreds of billions, or more, in financial assistance to foreign corporations ranging from South Korea to Scotland.[495] Analysts accuse the Federal Reserve of escalating U.S. interest rates to make up for bad investments in international investments. Spending other people's money is always easy.

12. ♦ PROMISE: KEEP BANKING DECENTRALIZED—For banking purposes, America is divided into twelve banking regions across the U.S. Despite this regional leadership, the entire structure gravitates toward the decision-making power in New York. The Board policies and money-market decisions all originate in New York with the Open Market Committee. People had suspected favoritism toward the New York investors all along.

Finally, after years of preventing an examination of its books, a little light was shed on the complex system in 2011.

WHAT THE AUDIT REVEALED

Up until 2011, the Federal Reserve had never been independently audited and scrutinized. It was well protected from snooping eyes. Even though its books were opened for examination for the first time in 2011, not all the books were examined. Nevertheless, the examiners found plenty of problems that simply can't be excused or ignored.

INSIDER HELP

The auditors found that during the financial crisis of 2010-11, emergency funds dispatched by the Federal Reserve went to more than a dozen banks and companies that had ties to regional Federal Reserve boards. Why them and why not others? This violated the promises the Federal Reserve would stand independent from high

---

493   FDIC, *Federal Deposit Insurance Corporation Failures and Assistance Transactions,* 1934-2011.

494   Federal Reserve, www.federalreserve.gov/pf/pdf/pf_4.pdf, p. 51.

495   GAO Report to Congressional Addressees, *Federal Reserve System, Opportunities Exist to Strengthen Policies and Processes for Managing Emergency Assistance,* July 2011.

Christmas Tree Tax—In 2011, the Obama administration imposed a 15-cent charge on all fresh Christmas trees. After a huge public outcry, the charge was withdrawn the next day.

finance bankers and not show favoritism.

THE BUDDY NETWORK

The Government Accountability Office found 18 current or former board members of the Federal Reserve connected to businesses that received emergency lending. On that list are General Electric, JP Morgan, Chase, and Lehman Brothers.

RIDDLED WITH CONFLICT

Jeffrey Immelt, CEO of GE (General Electric), was serving on the board of the Federal Reserve when a $16 billion emergency loan was given to GE.[496] Sen. Bernie Sanders (D-VT) said of this and other self-serving violations, the Federal Reserve is "riddled with conflicts of interest."[497]

"UNDER THE TABLE" LOANS

It was also confirmed that between 2007 and 2008, about $1.2 trillion was lent to 300 banking and financial institutions that had close ties to New York "headquarters." These loans were separate from the TARP bailout money approved by Congress during that same time frame (2008).[498]

IS THERE RULER'S LAW IN FINANCE?

The Federal Reserve is America's central bank. The formula for controlling economies by central banks has been known, developed, and deployed for centuries. As a monarch may control a nation's political fate, so does the central bank control a nation's economic fate. When these two forces combine, the death of freedom, individual rights, and ultimately, prosperity, is assured. Political control means saddling the people with whatever rules and laws the dictator demands. Financial control means those dictatorial forces in power may set interest rates for borrowing to buy a house or start a business, or sell overseas. Such regimentation is among the reasons why America's early colonists broke from England.

---

496 Huma Khan, ABCNews, *Federal Reserve Board Rife with Conflict of Interest*, GAO *Report*, October 19, 2011.
497 GAO Report to Congressional Addressees, *Federal Reserve System, Opportunities Exist to Strengthen Policies and Processes for Managing Emergency Assistance*, July 2011.
498 Ibid.

"Single acts of tyranny may be ascribed to the accidental opinion of a day; but a series of oppressions, begun at a distinguished period, and pursued unalterably through every change of ministers, too plainly prove a deliberate, systematical plan of reducing us to slavery."—Thomas Jefferson

CHAPTER 75

THE GREAT CONCESSION

Ten steps toward gutting the Constitution

B efore the Great Depression, there was the Great Concession. This was the era of dismantling the Constitution, an era that some call *progressive*. It started sometime in the mid-1800s, then picked up a lot of steam by 1900, rushed into the 1920s with expansion of the government that culminated with the "New Deal Constitution" in the 1930s. It was a time when America naively conceded, surrendered, and traded her hard-won birthright of freedom for a mess of tyrannical pottage. It was the prelude to a meltdown.

Along the way, there were some interesting proofs of the free system that came along. Had people been paying attention, these signals of what worked and what didn't might have saved the Constitution.

LEARNING TO STOP THE RUN

One of the main reasons people wanted a central bank was to reduce the number of recessions and depressions, and stop runs on the bank.

As mentioned earlier, a run on the bank can be devastating. In the Panic of 1907, some of the banks saw the coming run and used a savvy technique that saved them from losing all their cash. That technique was a simple sign in the window that declared, "Sorry, no payments today."

THE POWER OF AN I.O.U.

Restricting payments helped the banks keep precious cash piled up in the vault. If a depositor demanded $1,000, the banks in 1907 said sorry, here's $100, or here's $10, or here's *nothing* until we re-open. The goal was to keep people trusting in the banks. Customers might have turned around frustrated, but they firmly believed that somewhere in that bank building was their stack of money. They didn't know where or how or why, but they had a piece of paper proving it, so they remained wary but hopeful.

For those banks that had their vaults emptied, it was catastrophic. Not only did they lose their ability to give out loans and earn interest income to pay their bills and stay in business, but they lost the confidence of the people who lost their money. Rumors of such nasty losses spread quickly, and nobody wanted to do business there ever again—and another bank had to close its doors.

The banks that survived the Panic of 1907 kept money in their vaults and closed for a few days until the panic cooled off. After a day or two, customers were back, confidently depositing and withdrawing as usual.

The depression in 1907 was very hard—businesses failed and people suffered—but it was short-lived. Recovery started in 1908.

PANIC OF 1921

A similar event took place after the end of World War I. With peace in Europe, employment was hard to come by. Millions of veterans headed for home had to find a job. Millions more employed in war materials manufacturing were laid off, and had to find new work. And sales of wheat and goods to overseas consumers went through a roller coaster of demand that eventually just died. With high unemployment, reduced sales to overseas markets, a surplus of goods, and too few dollars to buy them, another panic set in—and money began leaving bank vaults across America.

FEDERAL RESERVE TO THE RESCUE?

The Federal Reserve could have helped. It could have lent more cash to the banks. Most banks only had, on average, $12 cash for every $100 of deposits. The Fed could have lowered interest rates to make it easier to take out loans to start new businesses or farms or to buy some land—to buy and re-sell—to *do* something to create jobs. But it didn't.

Instead, the Federal Reserve did just the opposite. In just a few short months, the interest rate was pushed up from 4.75% to 7%, making it harder to get loans. The interest hike had the effect of removing $15 billion from the economy—that's $170 billion in today's dollars.[499] And the effect was ruinous.

BY THE NUMBERS

From January 1920 until July 1921, wholesale prices dropped almost 37%. Automobile manufacturing dropped off 60%. Industrial

---

499 Bureau of Labor Statistics, CPI Inflation Calculator, www.bls.gov/data/inflation_calculator.htm.

production was down 30%. The stock market dropped 47%. More than 5,400 banks failed, thousands of businesses closed, and almost half a million farmers lost their land—13 million acres valued at $20 billion had to be abandoned. Unemployment climbed to almost 12%.

WHO "WON"?

When the dust settled, the giant banks went tiptoeing through the wreckage, buying the assets of the broken banks for 5-7 cents on the dollar. Land was snatched up for a fraction of its value, and bankrupt businesses were absorbed by corporations tightly connected to the same giant banks.[500] The massive transfer of wealth from private to central bankers' hands was too enormous to calculate.

After 18 grueling months, the Federal Reserve began reducing rates, half a point at a time, starting in July 1921. By November, the rates were back to 4.5%, and just like that, the depression ended. Was there collusion by the Fed and the large banks to reduce competition and increase their financial hold on America? That suspicion has been hotly debated.

THE GREAT CONCESSION

After the great Roaring Twenties about a decade later, another cycle of collapse started. It was different. This one was aggravated by government intrusion, making it last longer than it otherwise might have. There were 10 critical events during moments of crisis that softened up the people for the gutting of the Constitution during this crisis—

1. CONSEQUENCES OF WWI

STORY: The U.S. loaned billions of dollars to our European allies, and wanted it paid back. At the end of the war, a few countries did start paying. As foreign payments came in, the American economy calmed down and after the 1921 panic, the roaring twenties began.

From 1929 to 1932, Europe changed its mind. Many countries decided they wouldn't pay back their loans to America. One of the major complaints was a nearly exact replica of a complaint the colonies leveled at England during the Revolution: If the king wouldn't let our merchants freely trade to make profits, how could the colonies pay their debts? The Europeans made the same

---

500   Freemen Report, *Story Behind the 1929 Crash*, Vol. III. No. 22, pp. 2-6.

claim. What was preventing them from making profit to pay back America? It was reason number two—

2. SMOOT-HAWLEY TARIFF ACT

STORY: In an effort to strengthen sales of U.S. goods inside America, a new tariff was imposed on 3,218 imported items. For almost 900 of these the tax was severely increased. When word of this new tax reached foreign shores, America's trading partners were incensed. They retaliated with boycotts and by charging high tariffs on American-made imports. The tariff war between nations reduced world trade by 33% and contributed to the ongoing recession.[501] When Smoot-Hawley was passed, unemployment in the U.S. was 7.8—by 1933, it was 25.1 percent. Already dragging the economy was another attempt at an income tax—

3. 16TH AMENDMENT, FEBRUARY 12, 1913—INCOME TAX

STORY: Originally designed to "soak the rich," the 16th Amendment ended up soaking everyone. It bypassed the tax-revenue system in Article 1.2.3, and allowed the federal government to confiscate as much as 94% of a person's income. In 1943, President Roosevelt created "withholding," so taxes were taken at the payroll window before they were even due. Today, income tax has become the principle source of government income, and is an enormous drag on the economy. Where were the checks and balances keeping an eye on federal usurpation of rights? They had been blinded by the 17th Amendment—

4. 17TH AMENDMENT, APRIL 8, 1913—SENATORS:

STORY: As discussed in Chapter 34, the state legislature held the chain of representative government by appointing a senator to Washington. The senators were supposed to concentrate on protecting states' rights and maintain the established order. They were supposed to balance the budget, keep taxes low, and temper the radicalism of the congressmen who came every two years. The 17th amendment severed the leash held by legislatures and freed senators to hide from the voters for five years, emerging in the sixth to trumpet their achievements and then promise, "Vote for me, and think how much money I can bring to the state." The peoples' watchdogs were *put down* by the 17th Amendment.

---

501 Jakob B. Madsen, *Trade Barriers and the Collapse of World Trade during the Great Depression*, Southern Economic Journal 67 (4), pp. 848-868, 2001.

Socialism in America: In 2012, *Chief Executive's* 8th annual survey of the best states in which to do business, Texas ranked #1, California ranked #50. Texas enjoyed the highest net migration while California lost 1.5 million. Most of the top 20 were right-to-work states.

5. FEDERAL RESERVE ACT, DECEMBER 23, 1913

STORY: And then came the Fed riding atop a Trojan Horse, promising economic peace and calm and prosperity, but hiding regimentation and manipulation of freedom on the inside. "Power by the people" was dealt a fatal blow when control of money and its value was transferred to a private central banking cartel through passage of the Federal Reserve Act in 1913. The Federal Reserve's record for calming the economy has been suspiciously volatile.

6. FEDERAL RESERVE AND THE MONEY SUPPLY

STORY: From 1921-1927, the Federal Reserve inflated the money supply by 62%, sparking a rapid rise in stock prices and encouraging investors to buy stocks with borrowed money (margin loans). In 1928, the Federal Reserve began a year-long program to pull money out of circulation. This pushed interest rates up and triggered the stock market crash in 1929. To make matters worse, the Federal Reserve increased interest rates again in 1931. Overall, around one-third of the money supply was removed from America's economy, and helped entrench the misery of the Great Depression.

In 1936-37, the Federal Reserve required banks to double the reserves of cash they kept in the vault. This reduced even more the cash in circulation, and triggered a short recession during the Depression.

7. LEGITIMIZING THE UNIONS

STORY: Perhaps the most damaging and longest-lasting corruption in the market's ability to cleanse itself of extremes came next. The power of unions to extract higher wages and force employees to join the union received the force of law in the 1930s.

The Davis-Bacon Act (1931) forced minimum wages on government projects. It also favored white workers in white-only unions. At the time, blacks were not as educated and skilled and were therefore excluded from white-dominated unions.

The Norris-LaGuardia Act (1932) allowed unions to form and stopped new hires from pledging to never join a union as a condition of employment.

The Wagner Act (1935) legalized the formation of unions, collective bargaining, and strikes. Later, it was amended to set minimum wages and eliminate child labor. Increased government costs had to be supported with increased taxes.

"The inherent vice of capitalism is the unequal sharing of blessings; the inherent virtue of socialism is the equal sharing of miseries."—Winston Churchill

Forcing unions on America made the Great Depression last longer because higher wages were extracted with strikes and union actions. This hurt business and slowed the recovery of the economy.

8. INCREASED TAXES

STORY: Painful tax increases severely damaged the ability of some companies to hire new people. In 1932, unemployment stood at a staggering 23.6%. The Revenue Act (1932) pushed the top tax bracket from 25 percent to 63 percent. Corporate taxes rose from 12 percent to 13.75 percent.

Four years later, taxes went up again in 1936. The top tax rate climbed to 79 percent, and business profits were taxed at 42 percent. By this time, unemployment fluctuated between 16.9% in 1936 and 19% by 1938. The incentives to work, invest, create savings, and be more productive were all chilled, contributing to the length of the Great Depression. Not until World War II did unemployment drop back to single digits (4.7% in 1942).

9. PRESIDENT: Herbert Hoover (served 1929-1933)
LEGACY: Grandfather of the New Deal
STORY: Hoover created a train wreck of the country with his attempted "scientific regulation" of business, industry, farming, and the economy. He doubled federal spending, forced wages to stay artificially high, created a world-wide trade war and collapse with his Smoot-Hawley tariff, and increased taxes that depressed productivity. He even tried to subsidize farmers, but when that flopped he paid them not to produce so prices would stay high. He imposed the Reconstruction Finance Corporation, and enacted or paved the way for every New Deal program that was yet to be deployed.

The so-called "Hoover New Deal" gave birth to a massive failure of government control, manipulation and intervention—the epitome of power run amok. The monument to his utopian fantasies was a ruined economy and the Great Depression.

10. PRESIDENT: Franklin D. Roosevelt (served 1933-1945)
LEGACY: Father of the New Deal
STORY: Roosevelt is best remembered for his intense regulation of America with the largest expansion of government power since the country was established. His fundamental change was called the New Deal.

"Devaluing currency" is another way of saying how a country makes its products cheaper for foreign nations to buy its cars, so more start selling ... brings in fast cash.

Roosevelt's programs prolonged the Great Depression with intrusions into the free market that slowed recovery. His multitude of bureaucratic hurdles created additional drags on the economy that prior panics and depressions had overcome naturally when government was kept out of the process.

His Acts and implementation of progressive ideals in the form of the New Deal put off recovery for at least a whole decade. Not until the massive public works spending during World War II did the economy ever recover.

CONSPIRACY OR SOMETHING ELSE?

Many millions of words—often contradictory—have been published to explain why the U.S. economy crashed in 1929. For this examination, the point isn't to discuss if the Federal Reserve *did* or *didn't* break the U.S. economy or prolong the Depression. The point here is to highlight the fact that top-down intervention in national economies worldwide created a dismal mess. The panics of 1907 and 1921 were examples before the Great Depression which illustrated that if left alone, the economy corrects itself. Yes, there are losses and pain, but nothing compared to when the government tries to fix everything.

Finance and economics textbooks expand the Great Depression's details in so many volumes, but the important message is that central bank meddling always destroys. The twisted wreckage of the world's economy after the Crash of 1929 left little escape except through more of the same—*more* government controls and *more* government regulations. It was as if the Constitution of guaranteed rights and limited government had been replaced by a book of fantasy laws that were so stringent, even King George might have taken pause. It was the New Deal Constitution.

CHAPTER 76:

THE "NEW DEAL CONSTITUTION"

J ames Madison knew how government leaders would destroy the Constitution using a crisis as the excuse. He warned, "You will understand the game behind the curtain too well not to perceive the old trick of turning every contingency into a resource for accumulating force in the government."[502] And accumulating force is exactly what most presidents did—especially FDR.

AMERICA ELECTS A NIGHTMARE

On March 4, 1933, Franklin D. Roosevelt took office with a promise to reverse America's economic meltdown. His promised fix wasn't the kind of fix America needed. Roosevelt's New Deal prevented the free market from sloughing off excesses and repairing itself as it had a dozen times previously. Instead, Roosevelt's approach stifled growth, stifled recovery, prolonged the Depression, and intertwined into American culture a long list of socialistic controls beyond the reach of constitutional repair.

It took a friendly Congress and a friendly Supreme Court (eventually) backing him up, but Roosevelt was able to exploit the emergencies of the Great Depression to fundamentally transform the United States into a democratic socialist republic.

The great energy of America's production and willpower has long masked the continued drag of government intrusion on freedoms. Today, after more than 80 years of the New Deal, the strain on the American economy has finally and fatally broken the budget. Today, balancing the budget means borrowing multiples of trillions of dollars to cover the shortfalls.

A sampling of the stepping stones through the crisis of the Great Depression and the New Deal deployment includes—

❖ **BANK HOLIDAY**: After his first day in office, Roosevelt forced all banks to take a holiday to stop those vault-emptying runs that were beginning. This act was unconstitutional (many banks were privately owned).

---

502   Ralph Louis Ketcham, *James Madison: A Biography*, 1990, p. 351.

"If you tell a lie big enough and keep repeating it, people will eventually come to believe it." Joseph Goebbels, Nazi Propaganda Minister (1933-45)

◆ **INVENTS FDIC**: Roosevelt promised everyone that their deposits were safe, and were backed up by the government. This was comforting and calming, but placed an unconstitutional obligation on taxpayers to insure complete strangers.

◆ **NO GOLD**: Roosevelt declared that Americans could no longer own gold. Later, FDR made it a criminal act to own gold—unconstitutional confiscation of private property without due process.

◆ **PAID TO SIT**: Roosevelt paid farmers for not growing crops. This kept prices higher at the market, forcing consumers to pay more while profiting the farmers so they wouldn't lose their farms. There is no federal right to re-distribute wealth to help one sector of the economy, or to violate the freedom to fail.

◆ **FEDERAL FAVORITISM**: Roosevelt made sure that only banks affiliated with the Federal Reserve were protected by the government. This was unconstitutional favoritism against private, non-Federal Reserve banks.

◆ **REGULATORY POWER**: Roosevelt usurped law-making power by giving his agencies power to pass laws under the misnomer of "regulations." This was the unconstitutional transfer of legislative power to the executive branch.

◆ **USURPED STATES' RIGHTS**: Forced brokerage firms, even those operating within state boundaries, to obey federal rules on stock trades—here he intruded, unconstitutionally, on states' rights.

◆ **GOVERNMENT LENDING**: Started lending tax dollars to farmers and struggling homeowners at low interest rates, but wouldn't make similar concessions to other industries in harm's way—unconstitutional use of public funds to intrude into the free market.

◆ **BAILOUTS**: Pushed for a law that protected farmers who were late on mortgage payments from having their property repossessed for three years. This was the unconstitutional violation of private contracts, and control of private property (preventing private investors' money loaned to farmers from being collected).

◆ **FEDERAL RAILROADS**: Declared the railroads to be public property and assigned the first rail czar to save money by destroying duplicated facilities—this was an unconstitutional nationalization of private property.

♦ **FEDERAL COAL**: Roosevelt tried to control wages, prices, production, union participation, and rules for all coal mines across America. The Supreme Court knocked him down on this one, calling the action unconstitutional.

♦ **FEDERAL ELECTRICITY**: In 1933, Roosevelt used the Tennessee Valley Authority Act (TVA) to take over the means of production and distribution of electricity in that area. Massive projects were started to build dams, reservoirs, power lines, etc., to create fertilizer and sell surplus power. In the end, 98% of the country paid for the electrical power of the other 2%. Recent studies reveal TVA retarded economic development of Tennessee compared to its neighboring states.[503]

♦ **FEDERAL HOME LOANS**: Gave government power to lend tax dollars to people in danger of losing their homes, or to help others buy a home. This violated Article 1.8 of the Constitution, giving Congress the power to pick winners and losers by spending public tax dollars on some home mortgage loans, excluding others.

♦ **CONTROL COMMUNICATIONS**: The 1934 Communications Act regulated the airwaves, controlling at first interstate radio and later television. It was expanded in 1982 to include the airwaves inside specific states in violation of the interstate commerce clause.

♦ **UNION DICTATORSHIP**: Roosevelt pushed through legislation that gave unions unprecedented control to coerce business owners to capitulate to their demands—rule by the workers, just as Karl Marx had envisioned it.

LEARNING TO RECOGNIZE SOCIALISM

The New Deal saga was the legislative destruction of the American system. The seeds planted by Roosevelt have been sprouting over the decades as tyranny and dictatorship of the individual and the community—a slow smothering of the human spirit to invent and invest. And yet, despite this wholesale negation of several rights and freedoms, the strong work ethic of the American entrepreneur fought through the dredges and chains to grow enterprises that changed the world.

---

503 William U. Chandler, *The Myth of TVA: Conservation and Development in the Tennessee Valley, 1933-1980,* 1984, pp. 50-53.

Subsequent generations of Americans born since the New Deal have expanded those federal powers to lethal proportions. Unrestrained powers at the highest levels now jeopardize the economy and culture of the United States. Unrecoverable debt, reckless spending, decaying virtue, and a widespread suspicion of fellow Americans are the poisonous fruits of the New Deal tsunami. Modern socialists in the form of Barack Obama, Bill and Hillary Clinton, George Soros, and all the infamous names and faces lending their support to this demise are the leaders of destruction, and the perpetrators of the greatest crime in history—the death of freedom.

The welfare state, socialism, and cradle-to-grave government care are self-fulfilling catastrophes. Whether it be for a small cluster of medieval villages, a confederation of jungle communes, or a giant megatropolis of hundreds of millions, certain basic principles still apply: a community of people must consistently support the production of a surplus or they will collapse. Producing a surplus is an act of free will that the government cannot force, the laws cannot force, and the free market cannot force.

Perpetual prosperity lies in the voluntary industry of the individual worker coupled with the rigid protection of property rights. Hard work that bears good fruit that is untouchable by the government's taxing or redistribution power is how nations become strong—and stay that way.

Only when individuals break free from their addictions to government handouts will the countries that shelter them escape the unaffordable and ever-rising flood of entitlement demands.

Only when individuals rise up and throw off the tyrannical forms to which they have become accustomed can they ever hope to enjoy prosperity in their lifetimes.

As long as there are welfare benefits to be found, the retired, the unemployed, and the lazy will forever make their demands on other taxpayers and producers to support them.

As long as there is power and cronyism (favoritism) to be found, tyrants will forever abuse the people with Ruler's Law to retain their own support.

Freeing the economies of all nations to create jobs, and then stepping aside so that new opportunities can develop on their own, goes hand in glove with hard work and personal industry. The one cannot happen without the other.

The addiction to the welfare state by both ruler and slave is powerful and hard to break, but it *can* be broken—just ask Star Parker (see Chapter 85, the story of Star Parker, a remarkable woman who successfully escaped a life on welfare relief, and worked hard to help others do the same.)

The result of government-supported welfare is that the people allow corrosive influences to infiltrate the schools, the media, the business world, the unions, the churches, and the culture. Self-sufficiency and independence have become less important—citizens lay the task on their leaders to provide everything for everyone. Too many people have stopped thinking about freedom.

Big Brother in the U.K.: In 2012, a government electronic listening agency was approved allowing listening in on phone calls, email and text messages in real time. Warrants are needed beforehand.

Part XIV

SOCIALISM TODAY IN AMERICA

"It is impossible to introduce into society a greater change and a greater evil than this: the conversion of the law into an instrument of plunder."

—Frederic Bastiat—

CHAPTER 77:

THINKING LIKE A SOCIALIST

Reducing the definition of socialism to "government force to change society" helps measure how far leaders are moving their national fortunes and populations away from protected rights. Each day, the headlines shout new messages about all the consequences and problems from government force being used to address problems that are more easily solved with freedom and liberty. Socialists never see it that way—that is not how they think. "There ought to be a law" is their motto, and they go about making sure that happens in every way possible.

BEGIN WITH AMERICA

U.S. presidents who impose socialistic ideas are defended by their supporters who place *blame* (i.e., capitalism doesn't work), *guilt* (i.e., look at all the suffering), and *well, that's his job* (i.e., he must do what is necessary regardless of Congress or the Constitution), as reasons for a leader's failings. They believe *only* government has the answers.

Defenders of socialistic leaders try to distance their president from others of ill-repute. For example, they point to Eugene Debs or Norman Thomas (both famous socialists), or the Socialist Party, or Karl Marx, or Soviet Stalinism, and say that *this* president was totally opposed to *that* man or *that* political party. They'll also defensively declare how "even Republicans" did *this* or *that*, as if party affiliation made a difference—and then ask blankly *How then could you possibly call him a socialist?*

ANSWER: Words are cheap, words are easy, words win applause and headlines. But actions say everything.

The socialism that most Americans fear isn't necessarily some party or platform. Americans fear an ever-expanding federal government that consumes more and more labor and taxes. Such expansion has swelled under the name of almost every political party and declaration since the Civil War.

In America, socialism is a uniquely crafted product. It must be slipped into the mainstream in a fashion that does not arouse suspicion or objection. Here are some examples of how that happened.

Free Speech in Thailand: In 2012, a website editor was convicted for allowing users of her website to make comments that caused "damage to the reputation of the king, queen and heir-apparent," essentially making webmasters enforcers and censors for the government.

CHAPTER 78:

U.S. PRESIDENTS AND SOCIALISM

—Lincoln, Cleveland, Teddy Roosevelt—

In both peace and war, the ruling executives of the United States are bound by oath to uphold, defend and protect the U.S. Constitution. Did they?

PRESIDENT: Abraham Lincoln (served 1861-1865)
EVENT: Unconstitutional actions during the Civil War?
STORY: As Commander in Chief during the Civil War, Lincoln declared war and established war policies (Congress's job), suspended habeas corpus (Congress's job), imposed martial law on Kentucky (Violates Article 4, Sections 2 and 4), tried civilians in military tribunals where they were convicted and punished by the military (Judiciary's job), and exercised strong prerogatives thought by many to exceed his authority.

After the Union armies started gaining the upper hand in 1862-63, the constitutionality of Lincoln's actions was finally brought to the Supreme Court in the Prize Cases.

The Court sided with Lincoln. It acknowledged that the president does not have power to start a war, but an insurrection within the country's midst that "sprung forth suddenly" bound him to "meet it in the shape in which it presented itself." The Court said Lincoln "was bound to accept the challenge without waiting for any special legislative authority ... He must determine what degree of force the crisis demands."[504]

Dissenters in the case said the president didn't have the power to change the nation from "a state of peace to a state of war ... this power belongs exclusively to the Congress ..."

Lincoln lamented that Congress and existing laws were sorely inadequate to deal with rampant preparations by the South to break away, including spying, stealing of war materials, and splitting legislatures to favor the rebellion. Lincoln felt compelled to take drastic action to save the Union.[505]

---

504 Justice Robert Grier, 67 U.S. 635 (1862).
505 Kelly & Harbison, *The American Constitution*, p. 438.

"If our community does not beget men who have the power to make sound social principles generally acceptable, civilization is lost, whatever the system of government may be."—Ludwig von Mises

"I have never understood that the presidency conferred upon me an unrestricted right to act," Lincoln wrote in 1864. "I did understand, however, that my oath to preserve the Constitution to the best of my ability imposed upon me the duty of preserving, by every indispensable means, that government—that nation, of which the Constitution was the organic law."[506]

The Constitution is largely a peace-time document with little detail on war powers. By war's end, however, many questions and lapses about Federal power—for better or worse—were resolved.

PRESIDENT: Grover Cleveland (served 1893-1897)
LEGACY: Pro-Constitution, pro-free market
STORY: President Cleveland demonstrated how a man of integrity will refuse pressure by Congress to approve unconstitutional projects simply to gain votes. His administration was an example of how a president can function as a check and balance to counter an over-zealous Congress.

◆ **NO "GIFTS"**: When Cleveland vetoed a Senate pension plan for Elizabeth S. DeKraft, he complained that the Senate had buried him with 400 such "special interest bills," and said he would continue to disapprove "gifts of public money" to people with no legal constitutional claim.

◆ **NO HANDOUTS**: He vetoed House Bill #10203 that provided seeds to drought-stricken Texas. "I can find no warrant for such an appropriation in the Constitution, and I do not believe that the power and duty of the General Government ought to be extended to the relief of individual suffering which is in no manner properly related to the public service or benefit."[507]

◆ **STOP THE SPLURGE**: Cleveland rejected needless spending, over-taxation, accumulation of surplus money in the Treasury, bequeathing federal grants to states as means to buy control, and other finance schemes that plundered the people's national treasury.

◆ **CONTROL THE POWER**: Cleveland withdrew the treaty granting the U.S. takeover of the Hawaiian monarchy. He said the U.S. used methods that were morally wrong, and there shouldn't be

---

506   Abraham Lincoln letter to A. G. Hodges, April 4, 1864.
507   Messages and Papers of the Presidents, vol. IX, p. 301.

Socialism in New York: In 2012, NY Mayor Michael Bloomberg decided to combat obesity by banning sodas and sugary drinks that exceeded 16 oz. at public venues. Free refills, where allowed, were granted immunity.

"one law for a strong nation and another for a weak one...."[508]

Cleveland's story stands as an example of how a president should avoid the tempting traps to expand the government. Unfortunately, after Cleveland had to leave the White House with his correct perspective on freedom, things were never the same in Washington. It was the beginning of a slow decline into abusive political power, corruption, and struggle.

PRESIDENT: Teddy Roosevelt (served 1901-1909)
LEGACY: A progressive who dismantled restraints
STORY: A great wave of reform was sweeping the nation when Roosevelt took office. His energetic personality fit the times nicely. He emulated Hamilton's vision of a strong monarch in the executive position—a head of state beholden to no one including, in the strictest sense, the Constitution.

◆ **AMERICA'S STEWARD**: Roosevelt appointed himself "steward" over America's welfare, and used executive orders to take independent action outside his constitutional boundaries. He believed he could do anything that wasn't specifically forbidden by the Constitution.

"I declined to adopt the view that what was imperatively necessary for the nation could not be done by the President unless he could find some specific authorization for it. My belief was that it was not only his right but his duty to do *anything* that the needs of the nation demanded unless such action was forbidden by the Constitution or by the laws ..."[509]

◆ **WHAT CONSTITUTION?** When Roosevelt was challenged by Congress about usurping Congress's authority to seize private property (in this case, the coal mines), Roosevelt shrugged them off with, "The Constitution was made for the people and not the people for the Constitution!"[510]

◆ **GRADUATED TAXES**: Roosevelt supported Karl Marx's idea of graduated taxes, especially on large fortunes, inherited fortunes, and corporations.

---

508   *Annals of America*, vol. II, p. 481.
509   Theodore Roosevelt, *The Autobiography of Theodore Roosevelt*, 1913, emphasis added.
510   Attributed to Roosevelt but may have been taken from Albert J. Beveridge's speech to the Senate on January 9, 1900. See Congressional Record, Senate, 56th Congress, 1st session, January 9, 1900, pp. 704-712.

In 2012, two reporters for *The Sun* bluffed their way into North Korea. At a massive 65-foot bronze statue of departed leaders, the men were prevented from taking photos too close lest any body part be cut out of the frame, "a very grave offence," their tour guides warned.

❖ **FEDERAL CONTROLS**: Roosevelt enlarged the power of the federal government to interfere in the marketplace. He pushed the Department of Commerce and Labor to oversee large corporations, and his Bureau of Corporations had police power to go after businesses that Roosevelt deemed too big and too powerful. He ordered his attorney general to file 44 lawsuits against such corporations.

❖ **LAND GRABS**: Roosevelt fenced off more than 170 million acres as national parks and monuments, leaving them immune to private development or control by the states that held the lands in their boundaries. He thrust the federal government into the role of activist to take over water management and reclamation.

❖ **PROGRESSIVE PARTY**: After Roosevelt left the White House, he founded the Progressive Party—his so-called Bull Moose Party—and called for a government that intervened in people's lives and businesses on multiple levels to regulate and control them. Breaking restraints on the federal government was necessary to achieve this.

RULER'S LAW: Roosevelt called for a faster, easier way to amend the Constitution, he smothered states' rights, he forced minimum wages and child labor laws, he restricted work hours for women, he imposed the eight-hour work day, he called for Social Security insurance for everyone, and he granted legal protections of unions. All of these fell into the category of Ruler's Law, and gave foundation to the New Deal that would come 20 years later.

"Dutch Disease"—After the discovery of oil in North Sea, the value of Dutch currency rose making exports too expensive, causing its industry to decline and a de-industrialization of its economy.

CHAPTER 79:

U.S. PRESIDENTS AND SOCIALISM
CONTINUED

—Taft, Wilson, Hoover, FDR, Truman—
In both peace and war, the ruling executives of the United States
are bound by oath to uphold, defend and protect
the U.S. Constitution. Did they?

By the first decade of the 1900s, freedom in the United States was being threatened—not by an outside force, but by the American people themselves. It seemed people were willing to abandon some of their rights in exchange for a more secure, but regimented, way of living. It was the beginning of the loss of freedom that would bear costly fruit in the decades that followed.

PRESIDENT: William Howard Taft (served 1909-1913)
LEGACY: A progressive beholden to the Constitution
STORY: Taft was a mixed Progressive. On the one hand, he worked to expand the power of the federal government and judges to create law rather than to apply law. On the other hand he put more emphasis toward constitutional restraints on the presidency.

"The true view of the Executive functions is," he wrote in 1916, "as I conceive it, that the President can exercise no power which cannot be fairly and reasonably traced to some specific grant of power or justly implied and included within such express grant as proper and necessary to its exercise. Such specific grant must be either in the federal Constitution or in an act of Congress..."[511]

❖ **INCOME TAX, 1913**—In 1909, Taft proposed a change to the Constitution to raise more revenue. He pushed for removing the apportionment requirement (sharing identically) so that a personal income tax could be legally taken from every working American. This amendment later became law on February 3, 1913.

The new income tax had seven brackets. The lowest bracket was 1% on incomes up to $20,000 (equal to $435,292 in 2011

---

511 *Our Chief Magistrate and His Powers*, NY: Columbia University Press, 1916.

In 2012, Canada upped the retirement age to 67 in an effort to balance the budget and afford its socialist programs of old age security and guaranteed income supplement benefits, effective 2013.

dollars). The highest bracket was 7% on incomes above $500,000 (equal to $11.3 million in 2011 dollars).[512]

P RESIDENT: Woodrow Wilson (served 1913-1921)
LEGACY: Human nature and Constitution must evolve
STORY: Wilson thought the original Constitution was designed for a simpler time and looked to abolish the restrictions that prohibited him from meeting the challenges of the modern day.

He wanted Congress to delegate some of its law-making responsibilities to "the experts" in the executive branch. He was an elitist and believed people were too ignorant to understand the complexities of politics—they needed government to do for them all those things that were necessary and good.

Wilson's mastermind was Colonel E. Mandell House, an advocate of Marxist socialism, and the man Wilson called "my second personality. He is my independent self. His thoughts and mine are one. If I were in his place I would do just as he suggested."[513]

Through the formation of federal agencies, Wilson exerted vast amounts of power without direct accountability. From that framework, Wilson proceeded to subvert the Constitution with a long list of progressive reforms that forever changed America.

❖ **FEDERAL RESERVE ACT, 1913**—In violation of the Constitution, this Act delegated away Congress's authority to "coin Money, regulate the Value thereof"[514] to so-called experts on the Federal Reserve—men who didn't have to worry about being reelected. The president could appoint the board and chairman, but the Senate had to confirm them.

❖ **PROGRESSIVE INCOME TAX**—The actual progressive income tax law (different tax rates for different incomes) was passed during President Taft's administration, but fleshing out the law and putting it into operation fell to Wilson.

❖ **FEDERAL TRADE COMMISSION ACT, 1914**—In violation of the Constitution, this Act delegated a lot of legislative power

---

512   *U.S. Federal Individual Income Tax Rates History, 1913-2011,* Nominal and Inflation Brackets.
513   Charles Seymour, *The Intimate Papers of Colonel House, Vol. 1,* pp. 114-115.
514   U.S. Constitution, Article 1 Section 8.

Freedom of Spit in Russia: In 2012, Dmitry Karuyev, 20, was thrown in jail for spitting on a portrait of President Vladimir Putin. He was found guilty of "breaching public order and showing clear disrespect for society." Karuyev's defense? "I sneezed."

to the executive branch agencies—in particular, power to break up corporations it deemed an interference to free trade.

❖ **CLAYTON ANTITRUST ACT, 1914**—Gave government politically corruptible power to prevent certain types of business activity it deemed detrimental to free trade.

❖ **FEDERAL FARM LOAN ACT, 1916**—Created a nationwide network of tax-backed lending agencies for farmers.

❖ **CHILD LABOR LAW, 1916**—Wilson's heavily-promoted Keating-Owen Child Labor Act was passed by Congress but the Court declared it an unconstitutional intrusion into states' rights.

❖ **THE 8-HOUR WORK DAY, 1916**—The Adamson Act of 1916 forced an 8-hour work day for activities that were related to interstate commerce. The Supreme Court deemed it constitutional, but its dissenters said it violated the property and contract rights of employers and employees willing to work more hours, if desired.

❖ **POWER LET LOOSE**: Wilson believed Congress could do whatever it pleased. "Government does now whatever experience permits or the times demand," he said.[515]

❖ **PRESIDENTIAL POWER**: "The President is at liberty," Wilson wrote, "both in law and conscience, to be as big a man as he can. His capacity will set the limit ..."[516]

❖ **SUPPORTED SOCIALISM**: "...No line can be drawn between private and public affairs which the State may not cross at will," Wilson wrote. "That omnipotence of legislation is the first postulate of all just political theory."[517]

❖ **UNALIENABLE RIGHTS OLD-FASHIONED**: "The competent leader of men cares little for the internal niceties of other people's characters: he cares much—everything—for the external use to which they may be put. ...Men are as clay in the hands of the consummate leader."[518]

❖ **CHANGE BY FORCE**: Wilson asked, "...Must not government lay aside all timid scruple and boldly make itself an agency

---

515　Woodrow Wilson, *The State*, D.C. Heath & Co., 1889, p. 651, para. 1255.
516　Woodrow Wilson, *Constitutional Government in the United States*, The Columbia University Press, p. 70, 1908.
517　Woodrow Wilson, *Socialism and Democracy*, 1887.
518　Woodrow Wilson, *Leaders of Men*, 1890.

Potemkin Villages ("fake villages") are alive and well in North Korea. In the 1950s, the communist government built Gijeong-dong, an expensive and *uninhabited* village to encourage South Korean defectors, and to occasionally house soldiers manning military posts on the border.

for social reform as well as for political control? 'Yes,' say the democrats, 'perhaps it must.'"[519]

❖ **WAR-TIME CIVIL RIGHTS**: In 1918, Wilson pushed a set of amendments to the Espionage Act of 1917 that added personal opinion and speech to the list of crimes punishable by law. It made it a crime to "utter, print, write or publish any disloyal, profane, scurrilous, or abusive language" that referenced the military, the U.S. flag, or the U.S. government in an unpatriotic way. Even the mailman wasn't required to deliver materials that were anti-American. Although the Court later declared the Act constitutional, Congress repealed Wilson's amendments in 1921.

PRESIDENT: Herbert Hoover (served 1929-1933)
LEGACY: Grandfather of the New Deal
STORY: Hoover was a Progressive at heart, a benevolent socialist, and believed that top-down control of the economy could avert recessions and bring about prosperity. In 1921, he was appointed secretary of commerce where he began his intervention ideas, and later led America into economic ruin.

❖ **CREATED PERSONAL KINGDOM**: As secretary of commerce, Hoover hired 3,000 government bureaucrats, expanded his department's budget by 50%, and organized 30 new divisions to manage industry, production, and distribution.

❖ **ADOPTED SOVIET MODEL**: Just like the Russian central planners of the same time period, Hoover believed administrative manipulation of the economy—central planning—was more effective than any of the long-respected natural laws of economics.[520]

❖ **INTERVENED IN COMPETITION**: With his massive influence as secretary, Hoover worked to eliminate what he called "lawlessness" and "destructive competition" that created too much economic waste. His best answer to free competition was more regulation.[521]

❖ **PUSHED FOR SHORTER WORK WEEK**: Hoover intruded on the rights of employers to make contracts with employees.

---

519 Woodrow Wilson, *Socialism and Democracy*, unpublished essay, 1887.
520 William J. Barber, *From New Era to New Deal: Herbert Hoover, The Economists, and American Economic Policy*, 1921-1933, New York: Cambridge University Press, 1985, p. 15.
521 Herbert Hoover, address to Congress, December 2, 1930.

When he was secretary of commerce the working hours for 75% of industry was 54 hours per week. "When I left the White House," Hoover wrote, "only 4.6 percent were working 60 hours or more."[522]

❖ **PROMOTED STIMULUS SPENDING:** After the Stock Market Crash in 1929, Hoover worked for more spending by federal, state and local governments for public roads, shovel-ready jobs, bridges, and his namesake, the Hoover Dam. With tax revenues collapsing, the government's redistribution of the wealth to pay for such projects folded up.

❖ **GAVE UNIONS FEDERAL BACKING**: Hoover helped draft the Railway Labor Act in 1926 to guarantee railway unions the right to form unions. This tied the business owners' hands if they tried to resist the "legal" unionization of their employees, or resisted subsequent union demands. He signed the Norris-LaGuardia Act that quick-started union organizing. This doubled the number of strikes in Hoover's last year. He bragged that during the 1920s, union wages grew 40% compared to non-union wages at 6%,[523] illustrating how the use of force can circumvent the natural rise in wages that results when workers create more value.

❖ **DIDN'T UNDERSTAND WAGES**: Hoover was convinced higher wages meant more spending and therefore more prosperity. He twisted industry's arm to keep wages high, rather than leave the free market to set wages. Writing to Congress in December 1929, Hoover said, "I have instituted ... systematic ... cooperation with business ... that wages and therefore earning power shall not be reduced...."

❖ **TAX HIKE IN A DEPRESSION?** In 1932, Hoover raised the top income tax rate from 25% to 63%, and the lowest rate from 1% to 4%. All his meddling slowed productivity. Tax revenues dropped from $834 million in 1931 to $427 million in 1932. By 1933 it was $353 million.

❖ **SUPREME REGULATOR**: Hoover pushed the Agricultural Marketing Act and the Federal Farm Board to control prices. The plan backfired. For example, prices for U.S. wheat ended up double the price of Canada's wheat, and nobody wanted it. To keep farmers in business, Hoover bought their wheat for $300 million,

---

522 Herbert Hoover, *The Memoirs of Herbert Hoover, Volume 2: The Cabinet and the Presidency 1920-1933*, p. 104.
523 Bureau of the Census, 1976.

"Socialism means justice, means the wealth of the society shared among the individuals of that society."—Moammar Qadhafi, Libyan dictator killed in 2011, who had $200 billion stashed away.

and ended up throwing it away or dumping it on foreign markets—at the peak of the Depression when many Americans were going hungry.

✦ **HOOVER'S NEW DEAL**: Hoover's flawed programs pushed a recession into the Great Depression. When Roosevelt took over, his New Deal programs were really a continuation and expansion of Hoover's original proposals.

PRESIDENT: Franklin D. Roosevelt (served 1933-1945)
LEGACY: Father of the New Deal, New Nationalism
STORY: Before Roosevelt took office, signs were present that the Depression had bottomed out and the economy was on the rise. This wasn't unusual—the economy had recovered from dozens of prior problems without any big government intervention. Despite all the stark suffering with millions of people out of work and billions of dollars lost in savings and investments, there still remained a large 75% of the private economy that continued to crank away, offering the same kinds of recovery potential as it had in panics past.

Roosevelt's New Deal programs scared many business people. Their comfort level for investing in new activities rose and fell with their confidence in the system.

STRANGER DANGER: The more Roosevelt intervened with his plethora of programs, the more nervous he made the investors. His policies created an unpredictable investment world with property rights evaporating and various schemes of price fixing, wage fixing, production limitations, and reduction of farm acreage all justifying a great deal of doubt and worry.

"Business leaders sincerely believed that the government was in evil hands," said Herman Krooss in 1970. It led people to believe the government was "preparing the way for socialism, communism, or some other variety of anti-Americanism."[524]

In 1939, Joseph Schumpeter took note of this phenomenon of fear. "They *are* not only, but they *feel* threatened," he said.[525]

IF IT AIN'T BROKE DON'T FIX IT: With the economy slowly recovering when Roosevelt took office, the sudden onslaught of his

---

524　Hermaqn E. Krooss, *Executive Opinion: What Business Leaders Said and Thought on Economic Issues, 1920s-1960s,* 1970.
525　Joseph A. Schumpeter, *Business Cycles: A Theoretical, Historical, and Statistical Analysis of the Capitalist Process,* 1939.

New Deal legislation panicked investors, and millions of Americans became bewildered and confused. Dozens of new laws and regulations would bury the "old way" forever, and foolishly prolonged the Great Depression by years. By the end of the long Depression, America was less free, and socialism was here to stay.

ECONOMIC BILL OF RIGHTS: In 1944, Roosevelt declared the Constitution and the Bill of Rights "inadequate to assure us equality in the pursuit of happiness."[526] The solution he proposed was a new Bill of Rights that included economic guarantees.

Every American, he said, has a *right* to a job, a "living wage," freedom from unfair competition, a home, medical care, an education, unemployment protection, and retirement security through generous tax-supported Social Security. His list of ideas was a nice taste of double-talk—all promises but no attention to the dissolution of individual rights that implementing such ideas would require.

Before he was finished, Roosevelt used government force to change America in a very fundamental and permanent way.

PRESIDENT: Harry S. Truman (served 1945-1953)
LEGACY: Father of Fair Deal, grandfather of health care
STORY: Truman's major steps toward socialism included his so-called Fair Deal. One of its major promises was a national health-care program. It was an enormous proposal. Truman wanted to build hospitals and clinics all over the U.S., guarantee wages for doctors and nurses so it didn't matter where they worked, and create a branch of government that would oversee who got the money and if standards were being met.

The most controversial part of the plan was national health insurance—available to everyone, and run by the government. The proposal came to Congress as an expansion of the Social Security Act, and was called the W-M-D bill. It failed to win passage.[527]

Truman tried to remove recently imposed controls on unions set by the Taft-Hartley Act of 1947. The Act restricted unions' ability to strike and controlled how their funds could be used in elections. It also allowed states to bypass unions with their own right-to-work

---

526   Franklin D. Roosevelt, *State of the Union Message to Congress,* January 11, 1944.
527   See *President Truman's Proposed Health Program, November 19, 1945,* Harry S. Truman library, www.trumanlibrary.org

laws. The Act gave employees the right to get a job without being forced to join a union. Truman tried to veto the Act but failed.

Truman's other activities to expand the government were carried forward as if the enumerated powers of Article 1.8 didn't really exist. By the close of his administration, his actions helped underscore the assumed power of the federal government to use its enormous financial resources to shape the growth of America in whatever direction it pleased.

* * * * *

GOING FORWARDS?

The word "forward" has long carried special meaning for socialists. For decades it has often been used as a name for socialist and communist publications. For example:

Vpered (Russian for "Forward," Lenin's publication started in 1905)

Avante! (Portuguese for "Forward," the Portuguese Communist Party publication)[528]

Avanti! (Italian for "Forward," the Italian Socialist Party publication)[529]

Voorwaarts! (Dutch for "Forward," a Netherlands Communist Youth Movement publication)[530]

Vorwarts (German for "Forward," the Social Democratic Party of Germany publication)[531]

Vorwarts! (Printed from Paris in 1844, a publication for the Communist League)[532]

Forward, the 2012 re-election campaign slogan for incumbent U.S. President Barack Obama.[533]

---

528   See http://avante.pt.
529   Ivone Kirkpatrick, *Mussolini: A Study In Power,* Hawthorne Books, 1964.
530   See www.voorwaarts.net.
531   Geschichte schreiben, Zukunft gestalten. 125 Jahre vorwärts (as part of: vorwärts, Oktober 2001, Berlin).
532   Karl Marx (1992). Early writings. Penguin. pp. 402.
533   Victor Morton, *New Obama Slogan has long ties to Marxism, socialism,* The Washington Times, April 30, 2012.

CHAPTER 80:

U.S. PRESIDENTS
AND SOCIALISM
CONTINUED

—*Kennedy, Johnson, Nixon, Carter, Reagan*—

*In both peace and war, the ruling executives of the United States
are bound by oath to uphold, defend and protect
the U.S. Constitution. Did they?*

As America moved into the baby-boomer era, the government was no longer a manager of the post-war growth spurt of a rapidly growing nation. It had become the financial savior and instigator of all things "progressive." The presidents who came along during this period not only wanted to expand their executive power into building an empire, but they discovered they could do it with relative ease. The checks and balances that should have stopped presidential expansion of power had long been sterilized.

PRESIDENT: John F. Kennedy (served 1961-1963)
LEGACY: New Frontier and unfinished business
STORY: Kennedy's expansion of government continued to socialize the nation, but with some surprisingly conservative actions that subsequent democrats failed to embrace (see next page).

❖ **INCREASED** minimum wage to $1.25, "which is still much too low," Kennedy said, and expanded its coverage to 3.5 million more workers "which is still too little."[534]

❖ **INCREASED** Social Security benefits to those who could retire by age 62.

❖ **EXTENDED** unemployment benefits to 3 million workers.

❖ **GRANTED ADDITIONAL MILLIONS** for public assistance to hundreds of thousands of children of unemployed fathers.

❖ **INCREASED** Social Security payments and federal funds to help farmers and home builders.

---

534   John F. Kennedy, *The Work Done and the Work Still To Do*, a speech before the AFL-CIO Convention, November 15, 1964.

(cont'd) " ...the leaders of the Social Democrats; and that the Communists might not have been able to seize power if they had not first shared it with the Social Democrats."—Ivor Thomas, 1951.

❖ **FOOD STAMPS**: In 1961, Kennedy's first executive order was to initiate a food stamp pilot program to help distribute food to the needy. The idea had been passed around for a long time, but Kennedy was the first to finally implemented it. In just one generation, it snowballed into a $75 billion program that now supports more than 46,000,000 Americans—that's 1 out of every 7.[535]

❖ **KENNEDY'S "BULLY PULPIT" POWER** was demonstrated when the major steel companies, caught in a wage dispute with unions, agreed to give workers a 2.5% raise. Kennedy was happy. But then the companies turned around and raised prices on steel by 3.5% to pay for it. Kennedy was furious and unleashed a nationwide blitz in Congress and the press, even turning loose the FBI to interview steel company executives. The Wall Street Journal castigated Kennedy, saying he acted "by naked power, by threats, by agents of the state security police."[536] His bully pulpit tactic worked and the steel companies caved in and their reduced prices.

Despite those actions, Kennedy took very positive steps to reduce federal power over the country.

❖ **TAX CUT**: He proposed an $11 billion tax reduction bill to stimulate the economy. "Lower rates of taxation will stimulate economic activity and so raise the levels of personal and corporate income as to yield within a few years an increased—not a reduced—flow of revenues to the federal government."[537]

❖ **TOOK POWER FROM FEDERAL RESERVE**: He signed Executive Order 11110 that gave the Treasury authority to issue silver certificates and to coin silver dollars. This removed from the Federal Reserve some of its control over American currency and returned at least that much control back to Congress.[538]

❖ **LOWER TAX RATES**: Kennedy proposed lowering income tax rates from an inexcusably high of 91% down to 65%, and corporate taxes from 52% to 47%. "The final and best means of strengthening demand among consumers and business," Kennedy said, "is to

535   See *SNAP Annual Statistics* provided at www.fns.usda.gov.
536   Michael O'Brien, *John F. Kennedy: A Biography*, 2005.
537   John F. Kennedy, *Annual Budget Message to the Congress*, January 17, 1963.
538   John F. Kennedy: "Executive Order 11110 - Amendment of Executive Order No. 10289 as Amended, Relating to the Performance of Certain Functions Affecting the Department of the Treasury," June 4, 1963.

What's in a name? Marxist-Leninist communist countries refer to themselves as socialist republics in their constitutions. They claim a one-party system, allegiance to Marxism-Leninism, and that all power resides in the working class—in all actuality, it doesn't, but that's beside the point.

reduce the burden on private income and the deterrents to private initiative which are imposed by our present tax system; and this administration pledged itself last summer to an across-the-board, top-to-bottom cut in personal and corporate income taxes to be enacted and become effective in 1963."[539]

❖ **DECREASE SPENDING**: Kennedy proposed reducing spending and removing hurdles to grow the economy. "In short, to increase demand and lift the economy," Kennedy said, "the federal government's most useful role is not to rush into a program of excessive increases in public expenditures, but to expand the incentives and opportunities for private expenditures."[540]

PRESIDENT: Lyndon Johnson (served 1963-1969)
LEGACY: Perpetuated New Deal with "Great Society"
STORY: Johnson's expansion of government and injection of socialism did more to prove the negative consequences of socialism in America than anyone since FDR.

❖ **VIETNAM WAR**: In 1964, Johnson rammed through Congress the Gulf of Tonkin Resolution that gave him broad powers to "take all necessary steps, including the use of armed force"[541] to stop aggression in Vietnam. It gave Johnson authorization to use conventional military force to wage war that had not been constitutionally authorized. He micro-managed the war, even selecting bombing targets, to play a political chess game of wits that eventually took 58,000 American lives.

❖ **CIVIL RIGHTS ACT OF 1964**: Despite its good intentions of racial equality, the fatal flaw in Johnson's Act was that it replaced "equal rights" with "equal outcome." Forcing equal outcome produced an ugly process called quotas—the percentage of blacks at the workplace and in schools had to be in the same proportion to meet the quota as to what existed in the surrounding population, regardless of skills or achievement.

Johnson's Act led to forced busing, forced housing, reverse discrimination, and the violation of constitutional protections to negotiate contracts and control property.

---

539   John A. King, John R. Vile, *Presidents from Eisenhower through Johnson, 1953-1969* p. 95.
540   *Congressional Quarterly*, Volume 1, 1945-1964 (1965) p. 434.
541   *Public Law 88-408*, by the 88th U.S. Congress.

Supreme or Supremacy Pizza? In 2012, Papa John's Pizza, the world-wide pizza chain with 4,000 outlets in all 50 states and 33 countries, announced it would have to pass along price increases of at least 14 cents per pizza, due to increased costs from Obama's health care law.

The issue has never become free from doubt and debate. With case after case, the Supreme Court forced a situation that would have fared much better had it evolved naturally *without* government force. Improved racial harmony has grown in spite of the Civil Rights Act, not because of it.[542]

❖　**WAR ON POVERTY, 1964**: Johnson's efforts to take from the "haves" and give to the "have nots" with his *Economic Opportunity Act of 1964*, among others, exploded into a monster that today eats almost half of America's total annual production.

IN 1964, welfare spending was around $40 billion. Today it exceeds a trillion dollars—a 13-fold increase even after adjusting for inflation.[543] The "war" failed to contain costs.

IN 1964, children born to unwed mothers was at 10%. By 2010, it was 41%.[544] The "war" failed to heal this and other root perpetuations of poverty in America.

WELFARE FOR 2012: President Obama's 2012 budget for welfare exceeded $1.5 trillion (Social Security—$754.5 billion; Medicare—$484.3 billion; Medicaid—$274.5 billion)—about 41% of the total budget.[545] Johnson's socialistic "war" failed to stem the snowballing effect of welfare growth.

SINCE THE 1960s, the U.S. has spent more than $16 trillion on welfare, and President Obama proposed another $10.3 trillion for the decade of 2009-2018. Poverty under socialism is here to stay.

Johnson's war on poverty was a colossal failure. The whole fabric of society was polluted beyond repair, and millions of lives were ruined because of the entitlement mentality. His program made things worse, for lack of—

DECREASED SPENDING: Johnson's programs did not roll back welfare spending or offer fixes and solutions.

WORK REQUIREMENT: His programs did not ask for *so many hours of work* in exchange for *so much assistance*.

542　Alfred H. Kelly and Winfred A. Harbison, *The American Constitution, Its Origins and Development*, 1970, pp. 914-973.
543　Congressional Office of Management and Budget.
544　U.S. Department of Health and Human Services, *National Vital Statistics Report*, December 2010.
545　U.S. Office of Management and Budget, *Budget of the U.S. Government, Fiscal Year 2012: Historical Tables*, pp. 73-74, (figures adjusted for inflation).

LOAN OPTION: He did not offer aid in the form of loans. Instead, the checks were generously doled out—no strings attached.

CORRECT INCENTIVES: He offered more welfare for each baby born out of wedlock, but did not similarly try to encourage marriage as a means of stemming unintended pregnancies and to support the family with an income.

IMMIGRATION CONTROL: Johnson didn't restrict immigration to those with higher education who could bring marketable value to the country instead of instant dependency.

❖ **MEDICARE AND MEDICAID, 1965**: From 1776 until 1965, most Americans did not need to depend on the federal government for health care. The exceptions were those in the military or employed by the government. Johnson changed that in 1965.

Medicare became a nationwide health-care program paid for by income taxes. It was set up to help the elderly receive health care, to kick in at retirement with Social Security benefits.

Medicaid was a welfare program set up to help the poor and disabled. Because it matched a state's health-care expenses it inadvertently created an incentive for states to spend more on the poor. Medicaid pays doctors much less than other insurances, so few physicians can afford to accept Medicaid patients.

These two programs are the natural outcome of a culture so inoculated against the aspirations of freedom that its people became dependent on the government for survival. Wherever such dependency becomes the accepted norm, the dependent feel trapped and will always vote for the candidates who will assure the continuation of their welfare support.

This kind of system is automatically doomed to failure. The needs of the consumers will always outgrow the capacity of the producers—it is a basic law of economics that is usually ignored.

PRESIDENT: Richard M. Nixon (served 1969-1974)
LEGACY: Inflated regulatory controls
STORY: Nixon expanded the reach of federal agencies more deeply into business and commerce than any president since World War II. When he resigned in 1975, the *Federal Register*—the record of new regulations for businesses—had doubled in size, becom-

ing that much more of an anchor slowing America's expansion and prosperity.

❖ **EPA**: Nixon's 1970 Environmental Protection Agency Act started small but next to the IRS, became the worst example of Soviet-style central planning in existence today. In the name of environmental protection, the EPA enforces direct violation of constitutionally protected states' rights and personal freedoms to acquire, develop, and dispose of property.

Billions in private projects and jobs have been voided by the EPA, and that same form of control has been expanding globally. Versions of the EPA are uniting advocates through the U.N. to put U.S. freedoms under the jurisdiction of a single ruling international body.

❖ **CLEAN AIR ACT (1970), CLEAN WATER ACT (1972)** imposed federal control over state-level air and water quality issues. States were obligated to request federal approval for their plans to meet federal guidelines. States had to show compliance and enforcement of those programs. Since then, the Supreme Court has upheld the EPA's authority to regulate greenhouse gas emissions, and thereby intrude into additional states' rights issues.

❖ **OSHA**: In 1970, Nixon formed the Occupational Safety and Health Administration with power to impose safety regulations on almost every commerce activity in America. While safety in the workplace and food safety is everyone's goal, this level of regulatory power at the federal level has grown into a tyrannical law-making body that extracts untold billions from business and industry for compliance. No-knock inspection power, forcing companies to pay for home improvements so at-home employees have a "safe" work environment, fining companies for breaking rules they don't even know exist, and adding to a tower of regulations that today form a pile of laws that stands *17 feet high* are realities of the king-like controls this agency has over Americans. States are better suited to handle those issues.

❖ **NATIONALIZED RAILROADS**: In 1970, Nixon put the cost for rescuing the failing passenger railroads on the backs of taxpayers. His new National Railroad Passenger Corporation was a safety net that was supposed to rescue the railroads from financial collapse.

Socialism kills—Mao's *Great Leap Forward* in China during 1958-1961, used brutal coercion, terror and systematic violence on the population to kill at least 27,000,000 —some estimates put the slaughter as high as 45,000,000.

Private rail owners doubted it would work, but were happy to reap profits where profits could be made and let the taxpayers cover the losses.

❖ **WAGE AND PRICE CONTROLS**: Nixon's unprecedented peacetime wage and price freeze was supported by many as a reasonable way to stop raging inflation. Nixon imposed a freeze in 1971 and again in 1973. Neither attempt solved anything. The strategy was a monumental failure, and only made things worse.

❖ **NO MORE GOLD**: In 1971, Nixon announced the dollar could no longer be converted to gold. U.S. currency would henceforth be fiat money, or money backed by nothing. Today, the gold-less U.S. dollar is deified as an omnipotent paper of faith.

❖ **NATIONAL HEALTH CARE**: Nixon attempted to introduce various forms of national health care. He proposed that these programs be paid for with tax dollars invested in various forms, or through government partnerships with state or private insurance. His vision for national health care didn't go anywhere.

PRESIDENT: Jimmy Carter (served 1977-1981)
LEGACY: A thrifty socialist who just wanted peace
STORY: Carter's turn at the Oval Office came during a tumultuous period of high inflation, a recession, and an energy crisis. In the midst of these, Carter took significant steps toward reining in government spending and issuing new regulations.

❖ **DEREGULATION**: Carter moved positively to reduce the government's hand in the open market. He deregulated the airline industry (Airline Deregulation Act, 1978), trucking (Motor Carrier Act, 1980), rail (Staggers Rail Act, 1980), finance industries (Depository Institutions Deregulation and Monetary Control Act, 1980), and took stabs at deregulating oil, gas, and communications—among others.[546]

❖ **PORK BARREL REDUCTION**: Several of Carter's efforts to reduce spending were rebuffed by his own party which controlled both houses at the time. He tried to scrap several water projects but was overturned. He issued a "hit list" of 19 projects that he deemed wasteful "pork-barrel" expenses, and vowed to veto any legislation supporting them. Congress hated him for it and turned against him.

---

546   A popular myth that Carter deregulated the beer industry grew out of a misinterpretation of H.R. 1337, a bill signed by Carter in 1978 to amend the IRS code regarding excise taxes. H.R. 1337 did several things, including lifting excise taxes on home-brewed beer and wine if certain conditions were met. The bill didn't deregulate the commercial aspects.

People are too dumb to know what's good for them: "If Socialism can only be realized when the intellectual development of all the people permits it, then we shall not see Socialism for at least five hundred years."—Vladimir Lenin

◆ **NATIONAL PARKS**: In 1978, Carter grew impatient with the failure of Congress to pass his Alaska National Interest Lands Conservation Act (1980) that would cut off 103 million acres from economic development. Carter used the Antiquities Act to justify an executive order that locked up the land as a national monument— in gross violation of Alaska's state right and the rights of others seeking mineral, gas and oil extraction rights.

◆ **HEW**: Carter's new Department of Health, Education and Welfare (1978) was a multi-billion-dollar regulatory agency with the nondescript purpose of protecting the health, well-being and safety of Americans. In 30 years its annual budget has grown to $75 billion, and today employs 67,000 workers.

◆ **DEPARTMENT OF EDUCATION**: Carter's education program was separated from HEW to become its own cabinet-level position in 1979. Its purpose was to enforce federal laws in local schools, and otherwise dispense money to schools and students— all of this in direct violation of Article 1.8, the 10th Amendment, and others. Today, the Department of Education has a budget exceeding $71 billion. President George W. Bush's No Child Left Behind Act was the first to piggyback into local state-controlled curricula and standards by way of Carter's federal agency.

◆ **FOREIGN AFFAIRS**: Carter helped negotiate a peace treaty between Egypt and Israel in 1978 (The Camp David Accords), and normalized relations with China, but then he gave away an expensive and strategic American waterway critical for U.S. military and cargo ships—the Panama Canal. The 48-mile trench cost taxpayers $375 million to build. For national security reasons, not to mention regular maintenance and upkeep, the canal should have remained U.S. property.

◆ **ENERGY CRISIS**: A reduction in oil imports from the Middle East created long lines at gas stations and exorbitant prices. Carter gave his famous "malaise speech" to draw attention to over-consumption by Americans, and said the impact of OPEC's production cutbacks was made worse by Americans' sloppy use of energy resources. Side note to baby boomers: Carter did not instigate the 55 mph regulation to save gas—that was an Act signed by Nixon on January 2, 1974.[547]

---

547 See New York Times, *Nixon Approves Limit of 55 MPH*, January 3, 1974.

Adolf Hitler (1939): "If the international Jewish financiers in and outside Europe should succeed in plunging the nations once more into a world war, then the result will not be the Bolshevizing of the earth, and thus the victory of Jewry, but the annihilation of the Jewish race in Europe!"

PRESIDENT: Ronald Reagan (served 1981-1989)
LEGACY: Conservative Constitutionalist who won Cold War
STORY: Reagan was the first in a long time to attempt to turn
the country back to its fundamental roots. His so-called "Reagan-
omics" called for lowering taxes to stimulate the economy. He survived an assassination attempt, and brought a new level of respect-
ful dignity to the executive office, mixed with self-effacing humor
that endeared him to leaders around the world.

Reagan was tough, smart, better read than most people realized,
and exhibited leadership principles that caught most critics off
guard. He is remembered for igniting prosperity that carried into
future administrations, salvaging and energizing American morale,
and reducing their dependence on the government. He crushed the
Soviet empire with a spending program that dug a deep deficit but
ended decades more of exorbitant spending.

❖ **AS GOVERNOR**: Reagan launched his two terms as California's governor (1967-1975) by intending to shrink welfare rolls—"to
send the welfare bums back to work."[548] He froze government hiring
and balanced the budget by raising taxes. He clamped down hard
on campus riots, particularly at Berkeley where he sent 2,200 state
National Guard troops for two weeks to stop student rioting.

A mistake he regretted was signing the legislature's pro-abortion
act. He said later he should have vetoed it. Reagan maintained
a strong pro-life position from that time forward. He was also
pro-capital punishment, anti-welfare, and in favor of shrinking the
government and lowering taxes.

❖ **AIR TRAFFIC CONTROLLERS' STRIKE**: As president in
1981, the air traffic controllers—all federal employees—went on
strike. Reagan told them if they didn't return to work in 48 hours he
would fire them. They refused, and on August 5, 1981, Reagan fired
all 11,345 union members. David Schultz wrote in the Encyclopedia
of Public Administration and Public Policy (2004) that Reagan's
actions "not only demonstrated a clear resolve by the president to
take control of the bureaucracy, but it also sent a clear message to
the private sector that unions no longer needed to be feared."

❖ **REDUCED TAXES, SPURRED PROSPERITY**: Firing up the
economy was one of Reagan's priorities. He lowered the top tax

---

548   Jeffery Kahn, NewsCenter, UCBerkeley News, June 8, 2004.

bracket from 70% to 50% so the rich could create more jobs, and the lowest bracket from 14% to 11%. Inflation decreased and 16 million new jobs were created.

◆ **TRICKLE-DOWN**: Reagan's labors to reduce the size of government included freezing the minimum wage at $3.35 an hour, and cutting federal dollars to local governments for welfare programs by 60%. The impact was more money invested and rising employment.

◆ **CUT GOVERNMENT PROGRAMS**: Reagan was a strong supporter of the military. He initiated ground and space-based defense systems to defeat the Soviet's nuclear missile buildup. At the same time, he cut the budgets of the EPA, federal education programs, food stamps, and Medicaid. Reagan had promised to dismantle the unconstitutional Department of Education, but with a Democrat-controlled Congress and Secretary of Education Ted Bell, the department was doubled in size. Today, it is another massive government bureaucracy that redistributes people's money to violating states' rights, telling them how to teach their children, or else lose the government handout.

To finance federal programs while stimulating the economy, the national debt grew from $997 billion to $2.85 trillion, a burden Reagan described as the greatest disappointment of his presidency.

◆ **ENDING THE COLD WAR**: Reagan and U.S. allies brought several pressures to bear against the USSR to end the cold war. Reagan's so-called "Star Wars" anti-missile defense system helped, and was viewed by the Soviets as a "very successful blackmail. ...The Soviet economy could not endure such competition."[549] The war in Afghanistan was made more expensive with U.S. shoulder-launched missiles delivered to freedom fighters who could drop multi-million dollar Soviet helicopters out of the sky with the squeeze of a trigger.[550] Reagan's consistent messages opposing the Soviet's tyranny, and his famous, "Mr. Gorbachev, tear down this wall!" call to end the division between East and West Germany, led the way for the eventual demise of the USSR.

Ronald Reagan changed world history for the better.

---

549   Richard Lebow and Janice Stein, *Reagan and the Russians*, The Atlantic, February 1994.
550   See James M. Scott, *Deciding to Intervene: The Reagan Doctrine and American Foreign Policy*, Duke University Press, 1966, p. 63.

In a single day (May 14, 2012), Greeks withdrew $900 million from banks out of fear the country would abandon the euro for a return to the devalued drachma. Trusting its economic strength in the euro had prevented Greece from stimulating its economy.

CHAPTER 81:

U.S. PRESIDENTS AND SOCIALISM

CONTINUED

—*Bush, Clinton, G.W. Bush*—

In both peace and war, the ruling executives of the United States are bound by oath to uphold, defend and protect the U.S. Constitution. Do they?

After Reagan rescued the economy and national spirit by winning the Cold War, subsequent presidents and congresses acted as if growing the size and intrusion of government was their most important job. No longer was it the goal of politicians to shrink entitlement programs to the point of elimination, no longer was it allowing unregulated innovation and growth, no longer was it the private sector doing all the expansion—instead, it was all about taxes. How many new programs could government invent to justify more taxes, more spending, more borrowing? The Founding Fathers' most abstract nightmares had at last become formalized and institutionalized. It was the new American way.

PRESIDENT: George H. W. Bush (served 1989-1993)
LEGACY: Implemented additional civil rights socialism
STORY: Bush had big shoes to fill. Reagan had just broken the back of the Soviet Union so freedom could rush in, his deficit-spending programs had to be curtailed, and there were tyrants loose in the world. Besides growing taxes, spending, government, and negotiating NAFTA, Bush pushed America away from freedom with another New Deal program—

AMERICANS WITH DISABILITIES ACT OF 1990 (ADA)

The ADA falls into the category of civil rights socialism. The Act, another attempted "one size fits all" program, forces anyone dealing with the public to comply with rules set by the federal government, or be exposed to a costly law suit. The courts protected this position and allowed untold thousands of legal proceedings against companies failing to meet the rules.

VIOLATED INTERSTATE COMMERCE: Telling a state how to conduct its business, create its infrastructure, or protect its citizens was not a federal prerogative prior to the Progressive period. Such power in the ADA is a continuation of the same New Deal/Great Society expansion of federal power.

VIOLATES TENTH AMENDMENT: The Founders left nearly everything to the states because they knew how top-level government grows to abuse the people. The states do a better job of discovering reasonable solutions to problems than do far-removed regulatory agencies. Contrary to its legislative intent, the ADA and its close cousin, the Equal Employment Opportunity Commission, actually reduced employment of the disabled by 10% in the first five years after the ADA's enactment.[551]

REVERSE DISCRIMINATION: The ADA discriminates against the able bodied, forcing them to expend resources to accommodate other people. These additional expenses made hiring the disabled too expensive, and many employers avoided those added costs by turning to other solutions.

EXAMPLE OF FABIAN SOCIALISM: The Fabians promote socialism in this stealth-like fashion—not specifically the ADA, but as an over-all goal to replace individual freedoms with friendly-sounding Acts. Who could possibly be against a bill that prevents discrimination against people with disabilities? That is how Fabian socialism does its work. With Bush's signature on the ADA, more liberty was lost—but "for a good cause," his supporters said.

PRESIDENT: Bill Clinton (served 1993-2001)
LEGACY: A folksy socialist plagued with womanizing
STORY: Clinton and Al Gore's opening agenda was called "Putting People First." It was, in reality, a campaign to put government first. Toward the end of his second term he made his intentions more clear.

"Our government is a progressive instrument of the common good," he said in his 1999 State of the Union address, "... determined to give our people the tools they need to make the most of their lives."

The only tools his administration gave the American people were more taxes, more regulations, and more controls.

---

551 Thomas DeLeire, *The Unintended Consequences of the Americans with Disability Act,* Regulation magazine, Volume 23, No. 1, 2000, pp.21-24.

A glimpse of the American flag sways voters, including Democrats, to vote Republican or have attitudes and beliefs more Republican, according to a 2-year study by Chicago, Cornell, and Hebrew universities.

◆ **ERODING 2ND AMENDMENT**: Clinton was a master at double talk, saying what people wanted to hear, and he tended to pay more attention to marketing than substance. In declaring his support for Second Amendment gun rights, he slipped in justification to violate that very same right:

> "We can't be so fixated on our desire to preserve the rights of ordinary Americans to legitimately own handguns and rifles—it's something I strongly support—we can't be so fixated on that that we are unable to think about the reality of life that millions of Americans face on streets that are unsafe..."[552]

◆ **REDISTRIBUTION OF WEALTH**: Clinton enjoyed budget surpluses in his second term, and proposed giving an equal piece of the surplus to each American to start a personal savings account. Even those who didn't pay taxes would receive a check.

◆ **VIOLATING STATES' RIGHTS:** Clinton's Goals 2000: Educate America Act of 1993 laid out an ambitious wish list of education goals that rewarded participation with special grants.[553] Clinton wanted to remove from the states the power to set their own standards of performance.

◆ **DIRECT INCOME TAXES**: In 1993, Clinton raised the highest income tax rate to 36%, added a 10% surcharge on the highest incomes, made the Medicare payroll tax apply to all income, added 4.3 cents per gallon on fuel taxes, increased taxes on certain Social Security benefits, raised the corporate income tax rate to 35%, and phased out certain deductions and exemptions.

◆ **NATIONAL HEALTH CARE**: Clinton submitted his 1,342-page national health-care program to Congress in 1993, calling for universal coverage, regulation of the private market, and requiring, among other things, that employers provide insurance. It was rejected by Congress.

◆ **NATIONAL WELFARE:** Children in families that didn't qualify for tax-funded Medicaid could qualify for tax-funded CHIP (also known as SCHIP), another expansion of government not authorized by the Constitution. CHIP served as a precursor to the national health-care reform passed in 2010.

---

552 Bill Clinton, remarks in New Brunswick, New Jersey, March 1, 1993.
553 103rd Congress, H.R. 1804, *Goals 2000: Educate America Act.*

As of 2012, the "red tide" of communism claims only five nations, down form 25 before 1960: The People's Republic of China, the Republic of Cuba, the Democratic People's Republic of Korea, Lao People's Democratic Republic, and the Socialist Republic of Vietnam.

❖ **GOVERNMENT WELFARE JOBS:** Americorps was Clinton's attempt to put low-skilled labor to work as paid volunteers. It has since grown into a $700 million program that supports 88,000 people. A long string of theft, deceit, and abuses, plus a growing list of questionable activities (organizing Pink Proms for gay youth, and lobbying for democrat candidates, etc.) illustrate the futility of government "make work" entitlement programs.[554]

❖ **IGNORING CONSTITUTION:** An example of Clinton's imperial presidency was when he deployed American troops as peacekeepers with guns to militarily occupy Haiti and Bosnia—without prior approval of Congress.

❖ **REFUSED TO ENFORCE LAW:** In the 1988 Beck decision, the Supreme Court declared it unconstitutional to force workers to pay union dues that are used to support political candidates. George H. W. Bush issued an order that these Beck rights be posted for workers to see. Bill Clinton rescinded the order in 1993. George W. Bush reinstated his father's order in 2001, and Barack Obama rescinded it yet again in 2009.

❖ **ABOVE THE LAW:** Accusations of moral corruption, back-room politicking, and deal-making followed Bill and Hillary Clinton for decades—

"WHITEWATER"—While Bill was governor of Arkansas, the Clintons were accused of political improprieties in a failed Arkansas real estate venture.

"TRAVELGATE"—The Clintons were charged with misuse of the FBI to bring fraudulent charges against White House employees whom the Clintons wanted fired.

"FILEGATE"—The Clintons were accused of collecting and storing confidential background FBI files on former White House employees.

PAULA JONES sued Clinton for sexual harassment. Clinton claimed he was protected from private lawsuits by presidential immunity until his term expired. The Supreme Court disagreed. By a vote of 9-0, the Court said Clinton could not postpone the

---

554   For example, see Gregory Korte, *AmeriCorps fraud seldom followed up*, USA TODAY, February 8, 2011, Jim Bovard, *Bush's AmeriCorps Fraud*, Freedom Daily, September 2007.

"In practice, socialism didn't work. But socialism could never have worked because it is based on false premises about human psychology and society, and gross ignorance of human economy."—David Horowitz

trial while serving as president. Clinton ultimately settled out of court for $850,000. Other sexual harassment cases came to light (Juanita Broaddrick, Gennifer Flowers, Kathleen Willey, Elizabeth Ward Gracen, and Sally Perdue, among others.)

LEWINSKY—Depositions from the Paula Jones case exposed Clinton's sexual relationship with 22-year-old White House intern Monica Lewinsky from 1995-1997. He was impeached by the House of Representatives for perjury and obstruction of justice.

Does character matter? Does a president's private life impact his public life? The Founders thought so and with constitutional restraints they chained down the government so human flaws, jealousies, vices, and passions would not play out on the national scene. But the Constitution can only go so far—personal virtue and work ethic must fill in the rest.

Since the erosion of those values, people like the Clintons have been free to work the system to attack opponents, subvert fairness, and promote their private agendas through force and intimidation. Where they were found innocent of such manipulations, public confidence in their integrity was seriously eroded, and doubt and debate have followed the Clintons ever since.

PRESIDENT: George W. Bush (served 2001-2009)
LEGACY: Grew government and undermined rights
STORY: When Bush ordered the invasion of Iraq in response to the terrorist attacks of September 11, 2001, circumstances seemed to justify tolerating some temporary war-time powers. However, the intrusion into private lives that followed was unprecedented.

While some elevated Bush as highly conservative for invading Iraq and cutting U.S. taxes, Bush ran on a different frequency. "We have a responsibility," he said, "that when somebody hurts, government has got to move"—a concisely enunciated declaration of socialism's moral article of faith that big government should serve as everyone's savior.[555]

George W. Bush hurt America with policies of protectionism, increased federal spending, enormous budgets, massive bailouts, and nationalized portions of the economy.

---

555   George W. Bush, Labor Day remarks, 2003, to the Ohio Operating Engineers.

"It is incumbent on every generation to pay its own debts as it goes. A principle which, if acted on, would save one half the wars of the world."—Thomas Jefferson

These actions, among others, exposed the Bush Administration as just another in a long line of leadership behaving as if the chore of expanding government's power was correct and needful.

❖ **VIOLATING STATES' RIGHTS:** The No Child Left Behind Act forced schools receiving government money (notice how Bush ignored any "interstate commerce" criteria) to meet certain testing requirements and follow certain teaching standards. Failing schools would lose money. The scramble for federal dollars resulted in cheating to meet standards, "teaching to the test," and working the system to retain federal funds.

The Act removed local control and imposed a one-size-fits-all approach. For all of its positive intentions, it earns a failing grade from the Founding Fathers' better idea of leaving it to the states.

❖ **REDISTRIBUTING WEALTH:** The Threatened Asset Relief Program (TARP) authorized an initial $700 billion to buy shares and protect taxpayers from bad investments, loans, and foreclosures. With millions of investors and billions of decisions, the Act prevented free-market forces from making those adjustments. It expanded government power into private banking. With billions of TARP dollars suddenly flowing, huge amounts of fraud that resulted from such programs buried the FBI in thousands of cases.[556]

❖ **NATIONAL PRESCRIPTIONS:** Modernizing Medicare was Bush's expansion of government to cover prescription drugs. The program made good sense to a socialist—why hand out hospital care, but not the drugs? The program also reimbursed corporations for their drug expenses. The Wall Street Journal reported some gigantic private reimbursements—General Motors, $4 billion; Verizon, $1.3 billion; BellSouth, $572 million; U.S. Steel, $450 million; American Airlines, $415 million, John Deere, $400 million, among others.[557] Those reimbursements translated into company profits. A million saved is a million earned, thanks to taxpayer "generosity."

❖ **PORK-BARREL SPENDING:** According to Citizens Against Government Waste, Bush didn't veto any spending bills, and signed into law more pork-barrel projects than ever before in U.S.

556   See, for example, *FBI targets fraud in TARP, stimulus fund*, Reuters, June 2, 2009.
557   Ellen E. Schultz, Theo Francis, *How Cuts in Retiree Benefits Fatten Companies' Bottom Lines*, The Wall Street Journal, March 16, 2004; Bruce Bartlett, *Impostor*, 2006, p. 78.

"If the government is big enough to give you everything you want, it is big enough to take away everything you have."—Gerald Ford

history—from 2001, he signed 6,333 new projects for $18.5 billion, with a steady increase to 13,999 projects in 2005 for $27.3 billion.[558] Some observers believed if he had vetoed just one such bill early in his administration, Congress would have reined back its orgy of profligate spending.

❖ **GROWING THE RULING CLASS**: Bush expanded the federal budget by $700 billion and added more than $2.8 trillion to the public debt to finance federal promises and retain loyalty among voters. He shares $2.6 trillion of new debt with President Obama that was accrued in 2009.

❖ **VIOLATING PRIVACY**: The Patriot Act was enacted to track down terrorists hiding in America. The Act freed law enforcement agencies to examine private communications, voice mail, library records, books, papers, documents, telephone records, email, financial, and medical records. It allowed indefinite detention of suspected aliens, the examination of some Canadians' records, and more. Some of these investigations required a search warrant or court order.

The 9/11 attacks illustrated how national security has become an extremely complex process for America's open society. Nevertheless, a solution better safeguarding constitutional rights should replace the Patriot Act.

❖ **CONTROLLING PRIVATE MARKET**: Sarbanes-Oxley (SOX) was formed in 2002 to regulate how companies select and police their directors to prevent scandals such as the Enron and Tyco International fiascoes. SOX created a new quasi-public regulatory agency that keeps an eye out for trouble or collusion between companies. Since its passage, many new startup companies have refused to submit to SOX, refused to be listed on the New York Stock Exchange, and moved overseas to the London Exchange to avoid those regulatory powers—taking billions of dollars with them.

---

558 *Citizens Against Government Waste, Critical Waste Issues,* www.cagw.org.

Socialism in Venezuela: In 2010, Hugo Chavez nationalized the Exito supermarket chain, accusing it and 200 other stores of breaking the law on price controls. Chavez suggested the store chain become part of a "Corporation of Socialist Markets" offering everything from restaurants to car dealerships.

CHAPTER 82:
U.S. PRESIDENTS AND SOCIALISM
CONCLUSION

—Obama—

*In both peace and war, the ruling executives of the United States
are bound by oath to uphold, defend and protect
the U.S. Constitution. Did he?*

The tragedy of President Barack Obama is that he made another of those blatant reaches for power so many presidents have in the past by offering everything to everyone. Basic economic restraint was rejected for the bailout, raising the debt ceiling, the borrowing, the numerous dictatorial rulings outside the controls of Congress to support political activism instead of political stability. By the end of four years, the president had cut an ugly swath through the heart of United States with increased racism, class warfare, and unrecoverable indebtedness exceeding $5 trillion—all of this a virulent poison of entitlement he blithely minted as "hope and change."

PRESIDENT: Barack Obama (served 2009-)
LEGACY: A brutality of elitism, a shameful low point
STORY: The Obama administration campaigned on "hope and change" without ever specifying what change they had in mind except to "fundamentally change America." As the months unfolded into years, a supportive Congress (until 2011) and Senate made it abundantly clear—Obama's goal was to close the doors on numerous constitutional freedoms. Instead of moving to solve the nation's complex problems, Obama created class warfare. He divided the nation along economic lines using envy to stir demand for forceful redistribution of the wealth. Instead of uniting people of all political persuasions behind common goals—a sign of wisdom and seasoned leadership—he pitted one against the other, using bully tactics of the worst kind.

Obama's administration will be remembered as a sorry low point in U.S. history, when the fruits and lessons of socialism had

Does socialism lead to communism? It did in Italy and France: "In Italy and France, communists have not been able to seize power, but the history of these two countries since the ..." (cont'd)

not yet been fully realized in America. In the aftermath of his vapid understanding of prosperity and freedom, millions were left suffering.

Acting out Alexander Hamilton's grandest visions of a president with all power, Obama plunged the nation into unrecoverable debt and regulation, all in the name of benevolent welfare socialism. A random sampling from his imperialistic presidency, in no particular order, includes—

* **BYPASSED CONSTITUTION:** The president is allowed to appoint federal officers when Congress is in recess (see Article 2.2.2). Obama broke this law on January 4, 2012, when he made four recess appointments when the Senate was *not* in recess. In his words, "But when Congress refuses to act, and as a result, hurts our economy and puts our people at risk, then I have an obligation as President to do what I can without them."[559] The Constitution forbids this.

* **THE MIND OF MARX**: In 2001, when Obama was a senator in the Illinois state legislature, he complained that the Warren Court failed to redistribute the wealth—to have all things in common. Obama blamed the civil rights movement for failing to create power groups that could force redistribution—that is, taking from the "haves" in violation of property rights—in defiance of elected representation that was established to ensure an orderly America.

> "One of the ... tragedies of the civil rights movement," Obama said on radio, "was ... because the civil rights movement became so court focused I think there was a tendency to lose track of the **political and community organizing and activities on the ground that are able to put together the actual coalition of powers through which you bring about redistributive change**. In some ways we still suffer from that." [560]

* **TAKING FROM THE "HAVES"**: Senator Obama voted for TARP on October 1, 2008, giving his approval to the federal government to buy shares in banks, among other activities, to prevent their collapse. Five months later Obama denied it. "I did think it might be useful to point out," he said in an interview with

---

559   Barack Obama, speech at Shaker Heights High School, Shaker Heights, Ohio, recorded by C-SPAN, January 4, 2012, emphasis added.
560   WBEZ interview of Senator Barack Obama, 2001, emphasis added.

(cont'd) " ... first world war shows no less convincingly that socialism cannot be an effective barrier to communism; they show rather that socialism opens the way to communism."—Ivor Thomas, 1951

the New York Times, "that it wasn't under me that we started buying a bunch of shares of banks."[561]

❖ **NATIONAL HEALTH CARE:** Obama's 2010 health-care plan forced Americans to buy into government health insurance, leaving free-market providers to fade away. The nationalizing of the health insurance industry came with trillions in new costs. The resulting chain reaction is destined to regulate the entire American health-care industry into another government-run utility, destroying along the way American medicine's highly revered initiative, efficiency, and inventiveness.

TEAM SPOKESMAN—Taking from the "haves" and giving to the "have nots" is a primary pillar of socialism. Sen. Max Baucus (D-Montana), explained how Obama's health care achieved exactly that—a redistribution of wealth using health care. Baucus said the bill was to be "an income shift ... a leveling to help lower-income middle income Americans. Too often ... the mal-distribution of income in America is gone up way too much, the wealthy are getting way, way too wealthy, and the middle income class is left behind. Wages have not kept up with increased income of the highest-income Americans. This legislation will have the effect of addressing that mal-distribution of income in America."[562]

FRIENDS OF THE REGIME—Unfair preference is allowed for some businesses to opt out of ObamaCare. Thousands of waivers have been issued, the bulk going to labor unions. In 2011, about 20% went to businesses in Nancy Pelosi's district (she was the House leader pushing ObamaCare). Harry Reid's home state (Nevada) received a blanket waiver (he led the Senate push to pass ObamaCare).

DEATH PANELS—The Independent Payment Advisory Board is a group of 15 people the president appointed to shrink Medicare. Their decisions are law, reversible only by a 3/5ths majority vote in the Senate. They are beholden to no one and have power to reduce Medicare checks.

561   The New York Times, *Obama's Interview Aboard Air Force One,* Transcript, published March 7, 2009.
562   Max Baucus, speech on Senate floor, March 25, 2010, recorded by C-SPAN.

Socialism in Zimbabwe: During President Robert Mugabe's 88th birthday fest at Sakubva Stadium, construction worker Richmore Jazi was in a nearby bar and jokingly asked a local resident if Mugabe had the strength to blow up his own balloons. ... (cont'd)

NOT INTERSTATE—Obama claimed authority to regulate national health insurance based on Article 1.8 of the Constitution that allows congressional control over interstate commerce. The flaw here is that insurance isn't interstate—it is offered and serviced inside state boundaries. In 2012, the Supreme Court supported that pro-Constitution position, saying the personal mandate in ObamaCare was not constitutional, although it allowed it on the basis of Congress's power to tax.

UNCHANGEABLE?—Language in the health-care bill banned future Congresses from changing or amending the bill. This violates Article 1.1 that states only Congress is authorized to make law, including the right to alter, amend, and change the health-care bill. To deny this power is to violate Article 5 which outlines the amendment process—the only means whereby Congress could be stripped of its duty.

❖ **VIOLATED RIGHTS OF RELIGION:** In 2012, Obama expanded his health-care program to force church-affiliated hospitals, social services groups, and colleges to pay for their employees to have access to birth control and the morning-after abortion pill that kills a fertilized egg. Under normal circumstances, these institutions could and would refuse for religious and moral reasons. The First Amendment says "Congress shall make *no* law respecting an establishment of religion, or prohibiting the free exercise thereof." Obama violated the Constitution with this government mandate that prohibited the free exercise of religious freedom to establish hospitals founded on Christian principles.

❖ **VIOLATED PROPERTY RIGHTS:** In 2010, Obama required money lenders to slash or eliminate the monthly mortgage payments of people who were struggling financially or unemployed. Banks would have to reduce payments to 31% of a borrower's income. The reductions were to last 3-6 months.[563] Similar to the New Deal bankruptcy acts that prevented foreclosures, this action violated the contracts that lenders had with borrowers.

❖ **USURPED LAW-MAKING POWER:** Obama's so-called czars are appointees who report to no one but the president. They

---

563   Renae Merle and Dina ElBoghdady, *Obama Readies Steps To Fight Foreclosures, Particularly For Unemployed*, The Washington Post, March 26, 2010.

(cont'd) ...The resident told the police about the derogatory comment and Jazi was arrested on allegations of undermining Mugabe's authority. Jazi was just one of dozens arrested for violating the so-called "insult laws."—Nehanda Radio, February 29, 2012

are un-elected decision makers who direct agencies that make laws to regulate America. The Constitution holds the legislative branch responsible for making laws.

❖ **GIVING TO THE "HAVE NOTS"**: Making the populous dependent on the government took a big step forward with Obama's $787-billion stimulus bill, passed in 2009. After a year, it failed to stimulate anything except government job growth, and didn't slow the rising rate of unemployment. His answer was to pay out more taxpayer money (borrowed) to extend unemployment welfare payments to 99 weeks.

❖ **IMPERIAL PRESIDENT**: In 2009, Obama appointed himself chairman of the U.N. Security Council. This rotating assignment normally goes to the U.S. Ambassador to the U.N. Article 1.9 of the Constitution forbids the president from accepting any gift, foreign office, or title from a foreign country or a foreign potentate unless it is specifically authorized by Congress. The Founders wanted to prevent deal-making, corruption and foreign influences from affecting America's internal affairs. Obama ignored the Constitution.

❖ **CASH FOR CLUNKERS**: Obama's illegal grants of cash rebates to car buyers cost taxpayers $6 billion. The $4,500 rebates went to encourage people to junk their clunkers and buy more fuel-efficient vehicles. Follow-up analysis showed the program did nothing to stimulate the economy and put many people into additional debt by encouraging them to purchase cars that they otherwise would not have bought during those bad economic times of 2009. Granting funds selectively to purchase vehicles violates Articles 1.2 and 1.8.

❖ **TAKEOVER OF STUDENT LOANS:** For years, U.S. students could choose from 2,000 private lenders to obtain college loans. In 2010, Obama nationalized the process with a government takeover. The Health Care and Education Reconciliation Act authorized the Department of Education to lend to students directly, bypassing private banks and lenders. The Department borrows money at 2.8% and lends it to students at 6.8%. The 4% "profit" will go toward Obama's national health-care program. Resulting job losses for Americans in the private lending industry was estimated at 31,000.[564]

---

564 Obama Signs Overhaul of Student Loan Program, The New York Times, March 30, 2010; Sen. Lamar Alexander (Tenn.) who was a former U.S. Secretary of Education.

Comparing hammers and sickles: "Marxists like to compare a theoretically perfect version of socialism with practical, imperfect capitalism which allows them to claim that socialism is superior to capitalism."—Mark J. Perry

❖ **ENLARGED RULING CLASS**: To keep the government in power, Obama enlarged its numbers, influence, and intrusion. In his first 18 months in office, he added 140,000 workers to the federal payroll.[565] Obama's 2012 budget added 15,000 more federal jobs, including 4,182 new IRS employees—more than 1,000 of those to enforce ObamaCare.[566]

❖ **IGNORED NATIONAL BORDERS**: Article 4.4 states the U.S. shall protect the states from invasion. In 2010, Arizona grew weary of Obama's failure to prevent a flow of illegal immigrants from crossing into the state, so it passed SB 1070, giving local authorities the power to enforce federal responsibilities. Obama's derelict government not only refused to take action as required by law to protect national borders, it turned around and sued Arizona. The state is burdened with the crushing influx of an estimated 400,000 illegal aliens consuming state services. The Supreme Court later found Arizona could police its own borders, but couldn't perform the federal government's enforcement duties..

❖ **INCREASED DEPENDENCY**: Under Obama's watch, food-stamp recipients grew from 26 million to 46 million in 2011—that's one in seven Americans.[567] The percentage of Americans receiving federal benefits grew to 47%, its highest level in U.S. history. Unemployment was 7.8% when Obama took office. Six months later it rose above 9%, where it fluctuated for 25 of the following 27 months. The real unemployment rate including those working part time and wanting full time jobs, and those who had given up looking, skyrocketed to 16.2% under Obama's watch.

Obama's Healthy, Hunger-Free Kids Act of 2010 provided free lunches for 100% of students in schools where at least 40% were on welfare, regardless if the other 60% qualified or not. If there were illegal children enrolled at the school, that percentage could be added to the number of welfare kids in order to achieve the qualifying 40%.[568]

---

565 Ed O'Keefe, Eric Yoder, *Boerner's Comments Revive Debate On How To Tally Federal Workers*, The Washington Post, February 17, 2011.
566 Lachlan Markay, *IRS Requests Army of Bureaucrats to Facilitate ObamaCare Implementation*, The Washington Examiner, February 17, 2011.
567 See SNAP Annual Statistics provided at www.fns.usda.gov.
568 See Public Law 111-296-Dec. 13, 2010, at www.gpo.gov.

In North Korea, no one is paid a wage. Workers receive an apartment to live in with free electricity, although it frequently cuts out. There's an 11 pm curfew. The lavishly-decorated subway system is too expensive for most commuters. The elite Party members ride in special cars from Germany.

❖ **DODD-FRANK BILL**: Signed by Obama on July 22, 2010, this Act destroyed another aspect of Congress's authority of "power of the purse." Dodd-Frank created a financial partnership between big banks and the government. The government promised them they wouldn't ever fail, and the big banks promised to obey the government's every word. The Act also created an agency (the Consumer Financial Protection Bureau) that could reach into such transactions as real estate loans and appraisals, leases, credit, check cashing, check guarantees, gathering private reports on consumers, debt collecting, and more. The agency is funded by the Federal Reserve, and is not controlled directly or indirectly by Congress or the president. Dodd-Frank takes more freedom and economic power from the free market and consolidates it under Ruler's Law.[569]

❖ **VIOLATED CONSTITUTION ON IMMIGRATION**: On June 15, 2012, Obama announced the U.S. would no longer deport young illegal immigrants. This new law impacted an estimated 800,000 illegal immigrants. Article 1.8.4 puts the burden of immigration on the shoulders of Congress: "The Congress shall have power ... to establish an uniform Rule of Naturalization. ..." While the president does have power to "grant Reprieves and Pardons for Offenses against the United States" (Article 2.2.1), this authority must apply only to certain named individuals and not a class of people. Actions impacting a class of people is, by definition, a *law*, and only Congress can make laws. Obama justified his actions because Congress would not comply with his demands for an amnesty program, the so-called DREAM Act. "I've said this time and again to Congress," he said. "Send me the DREAM Act, put it on my desk, and I'll sign it."[570] For lack of congressional obedience, Obama ignored and violated the Constitution to get his way. It also served to attract an untold number of Hispanic voters to his reelection campaign.

❖ **FAST AND FURIOUS**: In 1995, U.S. Attorney Eric Holder told a crowd at the Women's National Democratic Club that he wanted to "really brainwash people into thinking about guns in a vastly different way."[571] His idea of a "different way" was made possible

---

569   See Peter J. Wallison, *The Dodd-Frank Act: Creative Destruction, Destroyed*, American Enterprise Institute, July-August 2010.

570   FoxNews and AP, *Obama suspends deportation for thousands of illegals, tells GOP to pass DREAM Act*, June 15, 2012.

571   C-SPAN, January 30, 1995, brought to light in 2012 by researchers at Breitbart.com.

"Gentlemen, you will permit me to put on my spectacles, for, I have grown not only gray, but almost blind in the service of my country."—George Washington, 1783

when Holder was appointed U.S. Attorney General. Overseeing a program dubbed "Fast and Furious," some 2,000 guns were delivered to Mexican drug cartels, by way of "straw purchasers." The stated goal was to expose illegal gun trafficking routes and suppliers. When the secret operation came to light, charges were made that Holder did this to incite gun violence, put the spotlight on the ease of drug traffickers to obtain weapons, and then generate hostility toward American citizens' 2nd Amendment right to own a gun.

The ulterior motive became clear when Holder's anti-gun supporters spoke up in his defense. For example: "And the problem is, anybody can walk in and buy anything," Senator Dianne Feinstein (D-CA) said. "...So, the question really becomes, what do we do about this?"[572]

Fast and Furious was responsible for putting guns into the hands of people who killed a U.S. Border Patrol agent, most likely a U.S. Immigration and Customs Enforcement agent, and hundreds of Mexican citizens. Holder denied knowledge and then documents emerged showing he did know, and had lied to Congress. When Congress asked for 1,300 pages of documents that might shed some light on the smoking gun, Obama invoked executive privilege, preventing the transfer, thus raising more questions that the president himself might be implicated.[573]

IS HE A SOCIALIST?

When a chorus of angry voices called President Barack Obama a socialist, they weren't necessarily pointing to his scurrilous affiliations, his secretive history, or his influential mentors who declared themselves adherents to communism. They may not even have pointed directly at the dictionary definition of socialism, or party affiliation.

They were responding with fear to suspicions about his ulterior motives. They had been frightened by his declared goal to "fundamentally change America." They saw him empowered to do as he pleased by exploiting an emerging American aristocracy empowered by greed, bent on micromanaging private lives beyond the control of the people. They saw him erode the free market with

---

572   Fred Lucas, *Feinstein Uses Fast and Furious to Make Case for National Gun Registration*, CNSNews.com, November 1, 2011.

573   David Jackson, *Obama claims executive privilege, Holder held in contempt*, USA TODAY, June 20, 2012.

Socialists proclaim entitlement. Americans proclaim ennoblement.

uncontrollable government force beyond the bounds of the original Constitution. They saw him smother every aspect of American life beneath growing mountains of new regulations, controls, and unrecoverable debt to purchase with indulgences the temporary salvation for each of his supporters. They watched him turn America into Europe, and worse.

Barack Obama, with support from Nancy Pelosi in the House, Harry Reid in the Senate, and some 69 million American voters, established a new order of elitist authority in the United States that will—like all other attempts at socialism—assuredly, predictably, and eventually collapse in failure.

Those who are producing all the wealth and prosperity in America will not carry on their backs so many millions of stagnated welfare consumers for much longer. Higher taxes, more regulations, continued flaunting of constitutional restraints, frequent excusing of corrupted public officials, disparaging common values—all of these added together are bringing about the accelerated slide into national bankruptcy of America's economy and America's honored virtues. The nation's producers are not able to long stand against such a tide reared up against them, especially when it mocks and ridicules their work from behind the iron fist of government force.

Socialism is a rainbow of gray that frowns across America in shades of guilt and envy, promising no pot of gold, but to the rulers. Obama's raid on the treasury was like no other before him. He doled out his rewards and favors like an addictive drug to followers whose American dreams had been dashed upon the rocks of a corrupted economy, failed work ethic, and loss of hope—all at a time when the culture of America stood in greatest need of correction and a course turned back to its fundamental principles. Obama failed to see that necessary corrective action, and did just the opposite.

EATING THE ELEPHANT A TEASPOON AT A TIME

The preceding sampling of U.S. presidents and their advancement of socialism is by no means complete, nor is it intended to give equal time to the positives of each man. It serves to illustrate how quickly a nation founded on principles of property rights and individual freedoms can lose them when the virtues of self reliance are abandoned.

Socialism kills: In 1984, the Marxist-Leninist regime of Ethiopia was so busy consolidating its power and fighting a civil war that food meant to stave off starvation went to troops. Drought, crop disease, and government diversion led to the starvation deaths of 1 million.

Is it fair, then, to call a president who enabled the loss of so many freedoms, who used government force to change society, who expanded power and eroded liberty, a true-blue dyed-in-the-wool, through and through *socialist*?

GREAT NATIONS FALL FIRST FROM WITHIN

For most of America's first 200 years, there was no external force in the world that could take her down. Peace and prosperity were confidently guaranteed.

In retrospect, it is also clear the many troubles that plague the United States today never would have materialized had the country stayed true to its founding principles, but the country didn't stay true.

The changes that voided the warranty on liberty didn't come all at once. The leftward list toward Ruler's Law came by small degrees, even fractions of degrees over its first 225 years. It came in the form of unrestrained expansions of presidential power, unrestrained taxation and spending by Congress, unrestrained legislation by the Supreme Court and re-interpretation of the Constitution. It came by the loss of national virtue, that common corruption that tends to follow prosperity, and the subsequent rewriting of the Constitution— not by amendment as much as by neglect.

"AS A MAN THINKETH ..."

Therefore, even if a president's unconstitutional imposition on the American people is not a declared act of socialism, it is proof he is certainly *thinking* like a socialist—ever seeking government force to change society, to create the United States in his own image. Said Obama in August 2012, "Do we go forward towards a new vision of an America in which prosperity is shared?"[574] *Sharing prosperity*—the ages-old promise of all socialist-minded dreamers, and the verbal poison that destroys, *always destroys*, without fail. And yet many entitlement-minded Americans loved hearing it.

As the ancient poet of Proverbs[575] and the more modern philosopher of truths James Allen[576] both astutely observed, "They themselves are makers of themselves ... for as a man thinketh in his heart, so is he."

---

574   Barack Obama, said during a fund-raiser speech in Chicago, Ill, August 12, 2012.
575   Proverbs 23:7 (KJV).
576   James Allen, *As A Man Thinketh*, 1903.

"To achieve world government, it is necessary to remove from the minds of men their individualism, loyalty to family tradition, national patriotism, and religious dogmas."—Alger Hiss, G. Brock Chisholm

Part XV

SOCIALISM AROUND THE WORLD

"... Vagabonds and beggars have of long time increased, and daily do increase ... being whole and mighty in body, and able to labour ... there to put himself to labour, like as a true man oweth to do."

—King Henry VIII—

CHAPTER 83:
THE RISE AND FALL OF SOCIALIST EUROPE

There is an eerie similarity between today's decaying European Union and the failed Soviet Union. Both attempted to amalgamate a variety of sovereign nations, each with its own unique culture, history, economy, resources, and national work ethic, into a single economic and political power.

❖ Both empires adopted a common currency—the ruble for the Soviets, and the euro for the Europeans.

❖ Both adopted central ruling bodies to act in behalf of the individual nations—the Politburo/Central Committee/Party Congresses, and the European Parliament/Council/Commission.

❖ And both started to crack up after about six decades.

STORY: After centuries of wars and conflict, six of Europe's nations decided to form a compact of cooperation. The goal was to prevent Germany and France from slugging it out in another of their costly conflagrations. Their hope was to keep the peace by intertwining mutual goals, and reviving their war-ravaged heavy industries of coal and steel production.

It started in 1950 when the nations of Belgium, France, West Germany, Italy, Luxembourg, and the Netherlands sent delegates to a round table and formed the European Coal and Steel Community. In 1957, they expanded their cooperation by treaty to become the European Economic Community. Some 36 years later, in 1993, they evolved into the European Union (EU).

ECONOMIC POWERHOUSE: The EU grew into one of the largest and most powerful economies in the world. By 2007, it had 492 million people in 27 nations, with a cumulative GDP of $14.8 trillion, ranking it first in the world (2010 estimate).[577]

KEEPING PEACE: Managing the EU has been convoluted by political party voting blocs, infighting, power grabs, widely divergent views on social issues, and political standoff's.

---

577   The CIA World Factbook, *European Union*, 2011.

Canada stopped producing the penny in 2012 to save $11 million in annual production costs.

The EU is ruled by a parliamentary system at the highest levels, fraught with political infighting that makes some nations threaten to leave. Germany is the heavyweight on the block, holding sway on many EU decisions because of its productivity, money, and influence.

THE EURO BURROW

In 1999, a common currency was created called the euro. As of 2012, only 17 of 27 EU nations adopted it, and for a while the euro was on track to become the premier currency on the planet. And then came the 2009 debt crisis in Greece, among others.

With all EU nations taxed to support all other EU nations, and all EU nations borrowing from each other to give each other loans, it is no wonder that a toppling of any single member of that circle of dominoes could bring them *all* down. Saving Greece from collapse was an act of survival for the entire EU. But that wasn't the root of the EU's real problem. They had to save the euro. As Germany's Merkel declared, the single currency euro was "the glue that holds Europe together."

Rescuing the euro required massive bailouts by other banks. George Papandreou, prime minister of Greece, turned for help to higher taxes: "We need a mechanism which can be funded through different forms and different ways," he said, calling on nations to kick in "a financial tax or carbon dioxide taxes" to meet their needs.[578] People watching on the sidelines wondered why taxes had to be raised. Why not stop spending? Lenders demanded austerity programs before shoveling over billions in rescue money, but the heart of the people was so accustomed to the generations of generous entitlements that cutting back was too abrupt, too archaic, too mean.

STANDING IN THE BUCKET

Most people know that standing in a bucket and pulling up on the handle doesn't lift anything, not even a little. That is the problem the EU was facing with its mutual and individual country economies. The debt crisis that began around 2008 put the EU in the awkward position of borrowing from itself to lend to itself— pulling on the handle and expecting to rise.

---

578   Montreal Gazette, *Euro under siege as now Portugal hits panic button*, Nov. 15, 2010.

Socialist Europe: In 2012, the EU's carbon tax became effective on the airlines of all member nations. India and China refused to comply, calling it an attempt to control free trade. When the EU refused to back down, China cancelled orders for the Airbus, killing thousands of jobs.

THE EUROPEAN SNAKE EATING ITS TAIL

The European dispensers and recipients of social welfare and social justice have long boasted of an elevated life style—shorter work weeks, generous holidays, universal health care, early retirements, full pensions, and cradle-to-grave care of the highest order. Much of this luxury has been paid for by ever-increasing taxes and the money the EU saves by not carrying the full load of self-defense—the cost of military protection has been left largely to the alliances with NATO and the American nuclear umbrella.

So, life in most of Europe was relatively rosy for many years until it all came to a screeching halt at the foot of reality.

THE WORLD-WIDE DEBT CRISIS

When the international debt crisis of 2008-09 forced the EU to examine its profligate ways, the long-ignored wreckage was massive—deeply entrenched unemployment, shrinking tax revenues, bloated budgets, growing numbers of retirees, inflating pensions, and heavy welfare demands.

People weren't dying fast enough. Longer life expectancy, lower birth rates, low economic growth, lack of productivity, too much reliance on services, lack of manufacturing, and all the problems and complexities that followed, exacerbated the rapid drain on the treasuries.

THE MANY FACES OF A MELTDOWN

❖ **PENSIONS**: When the Union initially formed in the 1950s, each retiree in member nations was supported by taxes from seven workers, a ratio of 7:1. By 2050, that ratio will evaporate to 1.3 workers for every 1 retiree.

❖ **POLITICALLY CORRECT MEDICINE**: In 1999, multiple sclerosis patients in Belgium seeking money to pay for a new drug were ignored, even after widespread public protests. Meanwhile, AIDS patients making similar demands for their highly expensive medical treatment were given immediate attention. In Europe, the "politically correct sick" are more equal than others.

❖ **EVER-RISING COSTS**: Nationalized health care is the norm among EU nations. The confederation hasn't controlled escalating costs. In Germany, for example, a person was taxed 13.1% in 2000 for health care. By 2010, it was 15.4%, and by 2040, it will reach a conservatively estimated 23.1%.

Get MORE with socialism: more debt, more taxes, more misery.

❖ **FROZEN CURRENCY**: When Greece, Italy, Spain, and other EU members fell into hard economic times, they couldn't bring in extra cash because they were tied to the euro. A way to bring in more cash is to make things cheaper for foreigners to buy. If a $1,000 new car suddenly was suddenly only $500, more cars would be exported, and more cash would flow into the country. The mechanism to achieve that is devaluing the currency—make more of Greece's drachma (Greece's currency) available for the same number of dollars. But, being committed to the inflexible euro, Greece was stuck with no way to increase its income from exports.

❖ **BANKRUPT**: By 2011, the EU's money ran out, all the treasuries were being raided, no more easy credit was available, and the alliance was in general economic collapse. As a side note, the rules said that no EU nation could settle the debt of another with loans, but everyone knew it happened all the time anyway.

❖ **CONSOLIDATING POWER**: The U.S. Constitution seeks maximum distribution of power over the greatest number of people. The EU concentrated the power into one body of 27 un-elected commissioners thought to be experts in economic affairs. They weren't. In 2012, Germany's Angela Merkel called for the creation of a European political union with member nations ceding more national powers to a central EU government, a strengthened bicameral European parliament, and creation of a European supreme court—a new world order.[579]

❖ **NOT READY**: The utopian dream of a united Europe, a forerunner to how one-world government might be established, crumbled in 2005. An effort to bind EU member states collapsed when France and the Netherlands rejected it. The EU's muddled and imprecise constitution had 448 articles (the U.S. constitution has 7), and tried to cover every contingency and make everyone happy. Two years after the failure, the Treaty of Lisbon in 2007 achieved many of the same desired goals.

❖ **OUTLAW KEYNES**: A positive outcome of the EU debt crisis was the choice to abandon Keynesian economics. From 2012 onward, there was to be no more "borrowing to spend" to kick start economies. Austerity was the new demand—cut expenses, control

---

579 The Guardian, *Angela Merkel Casts Doubt on Saving Greece From Financial Meltdown*, January 25, 2012.

Thomas Jefferson once wrote "To compel a man to furnish contributions of money for the propagation of opinions which he disbelieves is sinful and tyrannical."

taxes, issue limited bailouts, pay them back, set debt ceilings, control budgets, and punish future fiscal sinners.[580] It highlights the ages-old and common-sense approach of pay for what you get, and avoid debt like the plague—the *black plague*, something Europe is already familiar with.

❖ **BAILOUTS**: In 2011, a one-trillion euro loan was secured to bail out failing banks in Ireland, Spain, Portugal, Italy, and Greece. The cost for that loan was placed on the taxpayers in those same countries, plus the rest of the EU. The result was puzzling. The people who were guaranteeing that the loans would be paid back were those same people receiving the loans from which they would pay back the guaranteed loans. There was no new money coming in—the classical Ponzi scheme at work—the hungry snake getting satisfaction from eating its own tail, and accepting the pain as part of the new deal.

SAME THING ALL OVER AGAIN

In 2010, an economics student in Athens was quoted in the New York Times expressing his resentment that he had to pay higher taxes for his government's extravagance. "They sit there for years," Aris Iordanidis, 25, said, "drinking coffee and chatting on the telephone and then retire at 50 with nice fat pensions. As for us, the way things are going we'll have to work until we're 70."[581]

Iordanidis' comment echoed the same complaints from Plymouth, Jamestown, Harmony, and a thousand other failed socialist experiments: "Why do I have to work and pay for someone else's luxury? Why don't they work and pay for their own?"

Such is the nature of socialism in Europe and around the globe. People come to expect certain services from their governments—services that must be paid for somehow. And when taxes and borrowing don't do the job, economic reality forces governments to take a few steps back and reduce health coverage, pension plans, insurances, support for assorted projects, etc. And how do the people respond? With riots in the streets. It takes very little time for the entitlement mentality to grow oblivious to basic economic realities.

---

580   The Guardian, ibid..
581   Steven Erlanger, *Europeans Fear Crisis Threatens Liberal Benefits*, The New York Times, May 22, 2010.

Socialism creates shortages. In the Soviet Union during the 1970s, it was an accepted norm that Soviet women daily spent two hours in line, seven days a week.

CHAPTER 84:

GRANDMA WAS RIGHT

*Hampered markets slow the world economies like broken-down busses
on the freeway of prosperity—proudly limping with their
bewildered cargo to the nearest exit ramp. If they were
smart, they would let their passengers off to board
the freedom express—it stays on the freeway.*

In 1977, the French scholar and politician Alain Peyrefitte (1925-1999), identified a characteristic of hampered markets that always leads them to eventual collapse. He called it "the French Illness."

"The state wants to assure the happiness of its citizens in spite of themselves," Peyrefitte said. "Everything is decided at the top, far from those areas where the decisions will be imposed. Economies based on such authoritarian practices have always found it difficult to move forward. Our administration ... prefers to set prices, fix quotas, create new establishments rather than to make sure that the laws of competition are faithfully followed."[582] Peyrefitte saw in his day the eternal constant that when it comes to national economies, top-down manipulation never works. Decision makers removed from the realities of the day-to-day market activities are in no position to factor in everything necessary to make things work. He said, in short, distance makes the smart go wander.

KEYNES LAYS THE TRAP

John Maynard Keynes (1883-1946) gave "the French illness" some economic authority when he convinced most of the industrialized nations that spending money is what makes the world go 'round. When one person spends, Keynes pointed out, another person earns. *That* person spends, and another person earns. This is supposed to produce prosperity for everyone. But when one person decides to stop spending and save the money, this theoretically prevents others from earning, and the whole cycle slows to a halt ... he said.

Keynes theorized that in hard economic times, going into debt was the best way to keep this cycle going. By spending for things using credit cards (even if the credit limits are in the trillions of dollars), Keynes' idea was that more money would continue circulating, creating more opportunity for earning, spending, earning, spending, and so forth.

---

582   International Herald Tribune, *Happiness Decreed From on High—'The French Illness'*, Paris, May 1977.

"Socialism feeds a man for a day, freedom feeds him forever."—Author

But that's not what happened. Those who indulged in that philosophy spent too much and everyone went bankrupt.

GRANDMA WAS RIGHT

The free market handles life with greater efficiency. Grandma's traditional and time-proven principles of austerity, living within one's means, pay-as-you-go, and working to pay off frugally-enacted loans creates healthier markets and nations. This lesson is obvious to any household or business owner, but for some reason, that clarity of prosperity becomes lost to politicians worldwide.

Managing the conflicting ideas of Keynes and the free market gave birth to decades of top-down control, central banks, and fully embracing the seven pillars of socialism—all of these working to control the markets for maximum production. Billions of people have been seduced to endure, embrace, and encourage those failed ideas.

RULER'S LAW IS EASIER

There is not a purely socialist state in the world today. Every nation has a degree of free-market activity taking place, some clearly more free than others. Even in places like China, Vietnam, North Korea, Cuba, Africa, and some eastern European countries, where freedom has been ground to dust, there remain some open market or black market activities that keep the government-controlled economies propped up and limping along.

EVER PROMISING, NEVER DELIVERING

The world's descent into socialism is a loss of efficiency. Heavier tax burdens are placed on the populations. Dissatisfaction increases, crime rates rise, clashes with the government increase, and in some instances, full-scale rebellion breaks out and rulers are toppled. While the Middle East underwent regime changes after the first decade of 2000, most nations have continued to absorb the tyranny, giving validity to Jefferson's observation that "Mankind are more disposed to suffer, while Evils are sufferable, than to right themselves by abolishing the Forms to which they are accustomed."[583]

What are some of these *forms* people would rather suffer through than abolish? How have the people fared under the "Forms to which they are accustomed"?

---

583   Thomas Jefferson, *The Declaration of Independence*, July 4, 1776.

Soviet resurrections? In 2004, eleven of the twenty sitting presidents of nations formerly in the Soviet Union were also former Communist party insiders (called nomenklatura).

CHAPTER 85:

A SNAP SHOT OF WORLD SOCIALISM

—*Australia, Argentina, Canada, China, Cuba*—

*In bad economic times, nothing is more easily rationalized
than a welfare check from the government.*

STAR PARKER is a black American woman who fought her way out of crippling addictions to drugs and welfare. For much of her adult life she cheated the system to receive food stamps, a couple of welfare checks each month, free public housing, rent, and medical treatment. And then one day, she woke up hating the life she was living. She loathed what the free handouts were doing to her, and decided that welfare was as much an addiction as were her drugs. She said her life, her happiness, and her sense of satisfaction was "spiraling into a little dark hole."

As a result, Parker got herself clean. She fought to rid herself from drugs, got a job, and started paying her own way. And then one day, finally, life started to have meaning, she said. She decided others were in a similar circumstances, and she wanted to help. That's when she founded CURE (Coalition of Urban Renewal) to pull black families out of the entitlement trap she was in, a trap she blames on President Lyndon B. Johnson's massive entitlement program:

> "After the war on poverty in the '60s," Parker said in 2011, "we began to see the unraveling of the entire black community because the family collapsed. During the '60s, the black family was pretty healthy. Seventy-eight percent of husbands were in their homes with their wives raising their children. But after this lure to government that said 'you don't have to work, you don't have to save, you don't have to get married,' over time marriage stopped occurring to where now 7 out of 10 black children are born outside of marriage—and what happens when you don't have that intact family is your values change. So your culture changes. So your community changes."[584]

---

584   Star Parker, *Welfare Dependency Destroys Black Families*, August 9, 2011, urbancure.org.

Marx on transition from capitalism to socialism: "You will have to go through fifteen, twenty or fifty years of civil wars and international conflicts, not only to change existing conditions, but also to change yourselves and to make yourselves capable of wielding political power."—Karl Marx

PARKER SAID WELFARE CAN BE BLAMED FOR:

❖ More than 600,000 blacks in American jails or prisons

❖ 60% of black children growing up in fatherless homes

❖ More than 300,000 black babies aborted annually

❖ 50% of all new AIDS cases sprouting in the black community

❖ Almost 50% of black men in America neither working nor attending school.

In addition to the terrible toll on families that welfare exacts, the ugly truth that compulsory care doesn't work hits hardest in the national wallet. Reining in the enormous costs is an exercise in painful reconciliation that is hard on every economy. In most countries, the political party stuck with the dirty work to bring entitlement spending under control nearly always gets booed out of office, or killed. The entitlement mentality is a viciously vengeful vassal that can rise up against its masters, even those attempting to fix problems, and exact its displeasure at a moment's notice.

NOSE DIVE

The modern welfare state is in a death spiral. It has created an expectation among the populous it can't easily escape. The result has been varying degrees of enormous national debt, complicated by aging populations, low birth rates, huge budget deficits, and national demands for more government intervention to solve the mess. That's what socialists do.

The only viable answer for these economic plagues and the associated pillars of socialism is to emulate the example of people like Star Parker. She knows how to restart the dead engines of personal incentive and escape to freedom.

"INCENTIVE TO WORK"

Shrinking the welfare rolls in any nation begins with pushing the unemployed back to work. The term "incentive to work" was often used during the world debt crisis as code for "It's time for the government to cut your monthly check—in half ... so get off the couch and get a job."

Such calls to labor created a great hue and cry across the many nations as appeals were made to show mercy and compassion for the sick, young, elderly, disabled, and under-qualified—but those

Russia's enormous bureaucracy: During the administration of Boris Yeltsin, 1991-1999, more than 18 million people were employed by the State, from a population of 147 million.

were not the people targeted by the various austerity plans. It was the able but non-working people who needed to be encouraged, re-trained, and enticed off the dole into real jobs. The world can simply no longer afford the costly welfare state.

Reining in run-away entitlement spending has a familiar ring to it, almost as if the ghost of Henry VIII and his Poor Laws of 1530 had returned to go after "...vagabonds and beggars [who] have of long time increased, and daily do increase ... being whole and mighty in body, and able to labour ... there to put himself to labour, like as a true man oweth to do."[585]

Some samples of socialism's ruinous impact on nations,[586] and the pains of "compulsory care withdrawal" include—

COUNTRY: Argentina (41 million people)
BELOW POVERTY LINE: 12 million (30%)
WELFARE COSTS: Not available
NATIONAL DEBT: $136 billion (#36 in world)
STORY: As of 2012, Argentina remains steeped in corruption and heavy-handed political intrusions that have plagued the country for years. The election of Nestor Kirchner to the presidency in 2003, and later his wife in 2007, continued the problems that have since grown worse. The country's appearance of a booming economy was created in part by government intervention in the free market, nationalizing various industries, and data manipulation. Popular support continues despite the continued corruption at the highest levels and violations of personal rights that further entrench the ruling powers.[587]

Samples of tyrannical control include Mrs. Kirchner's takeover of the country's statistics bureau and replacing its director to stop the reporting of bad economic news. She also had the top staff fired. The manipulation of data became evident when some time later the government reported 7% inflation. Outsiders laughed it off, saying it had to be more like 22% and on its way to 30% in 2012.[588]

---

585   Ibid., Pictorial History of England.
586   For more information on the world-wide impact of socialization of nations as discussed in this section, see CIA World Factbook, 2012.
587   Alexei Barrionuevo, *Kirchner Achieves an Easy Victory in Argentina Presidential Election*, The New York Times, October 23. 2011.
588   Matt Moffett, *Economists Quake as Argentina Votes*, Wall Street Journal, October 22, 2011.

"I offer my opponents a bargain: if they will stop telling lies about us, I will stop telling the truth about them."—Adlai Stevenson, campaign speech, 1952.

To balance the budget in 2008, Mrs. Kirchner seized private savings, similar to America's 401(k) programs, to the tune of $30 billion, nationalizing the private savings industry at the same time. The move sent the Buenos Aires stock-exchange index plummeting by 24% in two days. Despite this and other interventions by Mrs. Kirchner, the country's economic growth nevertheless continued to slow and inflation continued to climb.

To keep food, oil, and gas from being exported, she imposed a 35% tax on food and a 100% tax on oil sold above $45 a barrel. She limited how much farmland could be held by foreigners, heavily taxed beef exports to keep it in county, and put a cap on all utility prices—this latter intervention drove the U.K. and French energy companies out of the country. In 2012, Mrs. Kirchner seized YPF Gas, part of Spain's energy giant Reposol Butano SA, making it an Argentina-owned public utility. In 1999, Spain invested $15 billion to buy YPF to help the then-struggling Argentina privatize its economy and get back on its financial feet. The 2012 takeover sent Spain's YPF stock prices plummeting more than 70%.[589]

When the Central Bank president wouldn't give Mrs. Kirchner the $6.6 billion held in the bank's reserves so she could pay off foreign debt to keep confidence with lenders, she fired the president to make things easier. The president resisted, saying only Congress could fire him. It went to court and the judge ruled in favor of the bank president. A few days later the judge found the police standing on her doorstep with questions. She was watched and followed for weeks. Eventually, Mrs. Kirchner got her way—and a new bank president.

To silence the press, she shut down the main Internet provider and nationalized the newsprint providers, forcing newspapers critical of her to pay higher fees for the paper.

Do Argentinians love socialism? They're evidently too afraid to think otherwise—Mrs. Kirchner was re-elected in 2011.

The Kirchner's ruined Argentina's budding marketplace, causing it to fall from the 19th freest economy in 1998, just prior to them taking power, to 135th in 2010.[590]

---

589   Liliana Samuel, *Argentina Seizes Gas Firm Owned by Repsol*, AFT news, April 19, 2012.
590   Wall Street Journal, *Heritage Foundation Index of Economic Freedom*, 2012.

"Men always strive for an improvement in their conditions and always will. This is man's inescapable destiny."— Ludwig von Mises

COUNTRY: Australia (21.8 million people)
BELOW POVERTY LINE: Not available
WELFARE COSTS: 18% of GDP (#22 in world)
NATIONAL DEBT: $1.4 trillion (#13 in world)
STORY: In 2011, Prime Minister Gillard prepared to slash spending on social welfare, which is her country's largest single-ticket item. She estimated that at least 2 million would be encouraged back to work from the ranks of: 800,000 part-time workers who wanted longer hours; 800,000 who were unemployed and discouraged, but took no welfare; and 620,000 unemployed who were officially on welfare at a cost of $11 billion every year.[591] Gillard was castigated by the press and politicians. Had there been enough pitchforks, her capital gates would have been stormed. The Australians love socialism.

COUNTRY: Canada (34 million people)
BELOW POVERTY LINE: 3.2 million (9.4%)
WELFARE COSTS: 17.8% of GDP (#24 in world)
NATIONAL DEBT: $1.2 trillion
STORY: An interesting decline in Ontario's welfare recipients took place in 1995 when welfare payments were reduced by 22%. In eight months about 80,000 welfare recipients fell off the rolls, saving the province $499 million a year.[592] Critics argued that the 80,000 were forced to take jobs that were not appealing. Well, wasn't employment the point, to return able-bodied workers to the workforce? It appears that at least some Canadians love socialism.

COUNTRY: China (1.3 billion people)
BELOW POVERTY LINE 36 million (at least)
WELFARE COSTS: Not available
NATIONAL DEBT: $635.5 billion
STORY: It is difficult to measure the demeanor of 1.3 billion people fully dominated by the totalitarian state of China. Statistics are always skewed by the prosperity of Hong Kong, the most vibrant part of China's overall economy. Excluding that oasis of capitalism, the rest of the country suffers under the sluggish regimentation of communist rule.

---

591   The Sydney Morning Herald, *PM's Dodgy Maths on Welfare Dreams*, March 23, 2011.
592   The Ottawa Times, December 1995, *Welfare cuts force thousands back to work*,
       reprinted by Freedom Party of Ontario, Freedom Flyer 29, March 1996.

"A better world is possible—a world where people come before profits. That's socialism. That's our vision. We are the Communist Party USA."—Communist Party USA website:

But in January 2012, the little fishing village of Wukan, only 12,000 strong, held free elections to replace the dictatorship of crooked communists and police. What ended up being a recall election was ignited when local Communist Party members seized the villagers' farmland, sold it for enormous profits, and invited into their quiet piece of the world all the trappings of China's growing wealth—luxury homes, shopping centers, golf courses, and more. When an earlier protest was lodged against these confiscations, the protester's leader, Xue Jinbo, was arrested and died while in police custody. In a fit of rage, the villagers attacked the police and drove them out and wouldn't let them return.

For the people in Wukan, withdrawing from the abuses of socialism and communism was worth risking the wrath of the central Communist Party. It remains to be seen how far this rebellion will spread before the ruling powers crack down.[593]

HISTORICAL PERSPECTIVE: In 1994, R.J. Rummel estimated the body count from socialism's tyranny in China to be 72,260,000, probably a low-ball figure, tallied from 1949-1980. Chairman Mao Tse-Tung's "Great Leap Forward," his push to make China a military superpower in just five years, cost at least 27,000,000 deaths from famine and another 5,680,000 deaths by execution.[594] Mao's massive push created a tremendous strain, diversion of resources, and severe conditions of living and overworking. Giant communes for grain production were organized, with tens of thousands of families grouped at the farmlands, with all things communal.[595]

C**OUNTRY**: Cuba (11 million people)
BELOW POVERTY LINE: not available
WELFARE COSTS: not available
NATIONAL DEBT: $21 billion (77th in world)
STORY: The Communist state of Cuba was dependent on the Soviet bloc for decades. When the Soviet Union fell, Cuba was left hanging without the financial support to keep its socialist economy running. Despite the U.S. blockade, sprinklings of help arrived such as oil from Venezuela.

---

593   Brian Spegele, *Chinese Village Vote Tests Waters on Reform*, WSJ, February 2, 2012.
594   Jung Chang and Jon Halliday, *Mao: The Unknown Story*, Alfred A. Knoph, 2005,
       p. 438.
595   Rummel, R.J., *Death By Government*, New Brunswick, NJ, Transaction Publishers, 1994.

A prayer on the White House: "I pray Heaven to bestow the best of blessings on this house and all that shall hereafter inhabit it. May none but honest and wise men ever rule under this roof."—John Adams

Having all things in common means rationed food. Today, the basics such as milk, bread, rice, eggs, and beans can be bought if there are any in the stores—otherwise, it's a long wait in line to get small portions. Families are allotted 1 liter of milk per child per day. These scarcities drive a large black market for the basics.

Teachers suffer on a salary of $15 a month and cannot obtain pencils, paper, crayons, or books, not to mention computers.

Medical supplies are scarce, and modern medical technology such as MRI and CAT scanning equipment are almost unheard of. The water is turned off from midnight to 6 a.m. to save on energy, chemicals, and the machinery to pump it.

Technology helps increase freedom. For example, while impoverished Haiti had cell phones (40.03%) and Internet access (10-11%), Castro's utopia had only 8.9% with a cell phone and 1.7% on the Internet.[596] The people of Haiti enjoy much more freedom than Cubans.

Crime is rampant—corruption, prostitution, drugs, white collar crime. Tourists are often victims of robberies or pickpockets.

The Castro regime used torture, arbitrary imprisonment, false trials, and executions to keep the population under control. Civil activists protesting the communist leadership are routinely arrested and imprisoned. Next to China, Cuba has the second highest number of journalists in prison.[597]

In 2010, The Raul Castro government announced that Cubans could build their own houses. The following year, Cuba announced it was thinking about free enterprise—the legalizing of buying and selling property—as a way to restart the economy. What a novel idea.

Cuba's enslaved and threatened population has little option but to support socialism. To do otherwise means prison—or death.

HISTORICAL PERSPECTIVE: In 1997, R.J. Rummel estimated the body count from socialism's tyranny in Cuba over the years 1949-1987 to be about 70,000 dead.[598]

---

596   The World Bank, cited in Mike Gonzalez, *Bringing the Light of Freedom to Cuba*, March 21, 2012.

597   Committee to Protect Journalists, *2008 Prison Census: Online And In Jail*, December 4, 2008.

598   R.J. Rummel, *Statistics of Democide: Genocide and Mass Murder Since 1900*.

CHAPTER 86:
A SNAP SHOT OF WORLD SOCIALISM
CONTINUED

—France, Germany, Greece, Iran, Ireland, Italy—
In bad economic times, nothing is more easily rationalized
than a welfare check from the government.

COUNTRY: France (65 million people)
BELOW POVERTY LINE: 5.3 million (8.2%)
WELFARE COSTS: 28.5% of GDP (#3 in world)
NATIONAL DEBT: $5.6 trillion
STORY: The second largest economy in Europe was stagnating by 2011, teetering on the brink of a major recession. In response, France turned to raising the retirement age from 60 to 62, eligibility for pensions from 65 to 67, raising corporate taxes, and raising taxes on consumable goods (except groceries). But welfare and pension expenses had already crushed the nation's ability to prosper. French workers boasted that they spent more of their lives in retirement than did their counterparts in other countries. However, by 2011, those costly pension plans could no longer be sustained.

Rigid austerity plans were imposed on most EU nations looking for bailouts. Despite the dire necessity, the public was outraged at the announced cutbacks. Trade unions reacted violently to protect their hard-won social rights. Strikes of 1 to 2 million people took place several times across the country that included school students, truck drivers, teachers, train drivers, postal workers, trash collectors, and more—all in response to the government's attempt to cut back spending and borrowing and spending and borrowing and spending and ....

In the streets of Paris and elsewhere during 2011, protesting citizens made it abundantly clear: the French love socialism.[599]

---

599   BBC, *French Strikes Over Pension Reform*, November 10, 2010.

Capitalism didn't fail, it was strangled to death by regulations.

COUNTRY: Germany (81 million)
BELOW POVERTY LINE: 12.6 million (15.5%)
WELFARE COSTS: 27.4% of GDP (#4 in world)
NATIONAL DEBT: $5.6 trillion
STORY: Before World War II, the Weimar government tried to control the growth of towns and cities all across Germany. They believed the city life was overcrowded, too disorderly, and sorely unchangeable. The better answer, they said, was to build smaller, more easily controlled and organized communities in fertile areas where both farm and factory could thrive.

Just before the war, the new National Socialist government took the country just the opposite direction. They wanted to create beautifully ordered cities with large, but controlled, populations.

The back-and-forth of these growth models so disrupted the people that they rejected central planning altogether. When Ludwig Erhard came to power right after the war, he was fully expected to install a highly regimented socialistic government to control Germany's war-ravaged economy. Instead, with the stroke of a pen, he abolished socialism and installed instead a free market.

Today there remains great bitterness and resentment toward central planners who take away local decisions and desires. Although socialist parties occasionally rise to take power, the Germans jealously guard their freedoms, and have worked hard to prosper despite the impositions of government.

The Germans probably hate socialism, but they've embraced many of the same costly government security nets that are crushing other economies in Europe and around the world.

HISTORICAL PERSPECTIVE: Before Germany's liberation from one of the most murderous socialists in history, Adolf Hitler, his regime began a state-sponsored systematic killing of at least 3,200,000 Jews in concentration camps, and at least 2,800,000 more—men, women and children—were exterminated and cremated with the help of Nazi collaborators in other nations. The Hitler regime called it "the final solution to the Jewish question." The war Hitler helped foment ultimately killed between 62-78 million, or 2.5% of the world's population, the deadliest war ever.[600]

---

600   Donald L. Niewyk, *The Columbia Guide to the Holocaust*, Columbia University, 2000.

The more the Federal government has swelled into places the Constitution originally forbade it, the worse off our nation has become economically, morally and culturally.

COUNTRY: Greece (10.8 million)
  BELOW POVERTY LINE: 2.2 million (20%)
  WELFARE COSTS: 24.3% of GDP (#10 in world)
NATIONAL DEBT: $583 billion
STORY: The ruinous outcome of over-promising a mountain of
perks and pensions and national care took center stage in 2011-12.
Faced with half-a-trillion dollar debt, the Greek parliament tried to
cut back its expenses so the nation wouldn't default on its loans and
thereby cause a chain reaction of defaults throughout Europe (many
were invested in Greece).

The outgoing socialist government of Papandreou failed on his
promise to privatize many nationalized parts of the economy—a
promise made to stimulate economic growth. The new government
promised they would fix things. In return for more borrowed money
to stay afloat, the government promised to cut public spending by
$20 billion, and raise taxes by the same amount over a five-year
period.

The resulting burden placed on society was grating. Property
taxes had to go up, consumption taxes at restaurants and bars
rose from 13% to 23%, new taxes on luxury items were imposed,
some tax exemptions were eliminated, taxes on fuel, cigarettes,
and alcohol went up more than 30%, public wages were cut by
20%, about 30,000 public workers were to get only 60% of pay,
all temporary public-sector workers were to be laid off, health-
care spending and Social Security were all reduced, pensions were
to be cut by 20%, the retirement age was raised to 65, and the
government planned to sell off nationally-owned utilities to private
investors.

The reaction of the people? With unemployment over 18%, there
were bloody riots and protests that lasted for weeks. The Greeks
made it clear they love socialism.

COUNTRY: Iran (78 million people)
  BELOW POVERTY LINE: 14.6 million (18.7%)
  WELFARE COSTS: not available
NATIONAL DEBT: $18 billion
STORY: Iran's ruling Islamic regime has been forcing its people
to obey religious tenets since the 1979 revolution. In the name
of religious purity, the strait and rigid rules of oppression have

crushed political dissidents, journalists, students, bloggers, advocates for women's rights and human rights, and people of minority faiths. Those speaking out against the regime are followed and harassed, arrested and imprisoned, and sometimes stoned or hanged.

Ever since Ahmadinejad became president in 2005 and his questionable reelection in 2009, his regime has worried more about the indirect "soft war" that threatens to change the culture than any outside military attack. While imposing its purified Islam on the populous, it must crush all attempts to inject change. Silencing so many voices is a burdensome chore.

The rulers dictate everything—what people may wear, the books they may read, what television and movies they may watch, how they groom themselves, cut their hair, the food they eat, the company they keep. Journalists are jailed, movie makers are jailed, university instructors are jailed, anyone caught defaming the Supreme Leader or the declared tenets of Islam are jailed—or worse.

With nuclear weapons on the horizon, Iran became the new strategic threat to Israel and other western allies in the region.

Every pillar of socialism is present in Iran. The people are abused to such an extent that another revolution will be hard for the government to prevent unless they loosen the hard-line rules of complete obedience to the regime.

HISTORICAL PERSPECTIVE: In 1988, Iran's Ayatollah Khomeini issued a fatwa that led to the killing of 30,000 in Iran during a two-month purge. Some were children as young as 13, hanged from cranes, six at a time. It is unknown how many more have died for the purification of the culture. Socialism in religion is alive and lethal in Iran.[601]

COUNTRY: Ireland (4.7 million)
BELOW POVERTY LINE: 260,000 (5.5%)
WELFARE COSTS: 13.8% of GDP (#27 in world)
NATIONAL DEBT: $2.4 trillion
STORY: Like most of Europe in 2011, Ireland was buried under state welfare that supported the third highest EU unemployment rate of 14.6 percent—or 440,000. Half of those were long-term jobless who received benefits of £188 ($297) a week.

---

601   Grand Ayatollah Hossein-Ali Montazeri, *The Memoirs of Grand Ayatollah Hossein Ali Montazeri*, published privately, 2001.

Socialism kills—In 1994, Jean Kambanda, Prime Minister of Rwanda, distributed weapons to commit the mass murder of at least 800,000 people, almost 20% of the population, in just 100 days—all in the name of ethnic competition to gain control and keep political power.

Cuts to wages for low-paid workers and restricting overtime pay on Sundays was floated as a solution, much to a cacophony of complaints. Working on Sunday always earned more per hour than weekdays, so all over Europe, people loved that extra opportunity to line the wallet. In Ireland, that Sunday pay was one of the very highest, a full 34 percent more than in England.

The Organization for Economic Cooperation and Development (OECD) chided the country for not reducing benefits as a means to encourage the job hunt. Said Education Minister Ruairi Quinn, "It doesn't make sense for people to be better off by not working than by working."[602] The Irish love socialism.

COUNTRY: Italy (61 million)
    BELOW POVERTY LINE: Not available
    WELFARE COSTS: 24.4% of GDP (#9 in world)
NATIONAL DEBT: $2.7 trillion
STORY: Similar to Greece, the financial crisis that hit Italy extracted enormous costs and forced a turnover in the government. The two-decade reign of Berlusconi came to an end when he couldn't salvage the country with cuts and increased taxes. The public debt at Berlusconi's departure was almost $2.4 trillion, or 120% of GDP. Cuts across the board, plus increased taxes and shrinking the government, was their latest plan. And what did the Italians think of their bloated government's efforts to rein in the extravagances? Riots and protests in the streets—a demonstration that Italians love socialism.

HISTORICAL PERSPECTIVE: Benito Mussolini, Italian leader and founder of fascist socialism who carried Italy into World War II, helped Hitler exterminate Jews and worked to kill political prisoners both before and during WWII. At least 225,000 deaths are attributed to his dictatorship, deaths of Italians and people in Ethiopia, Libya, Yugoslavia, and Greece, among others.[603]

---

602   Thomas Molloy, The Independent, May 26, 2011.
603   Rummel, R.J., *Death by Government—Genocide and Mass Murder*, 1994; also Mark Mazower, *Dark Continent: Europe's Twentieth Century* (1998).

The innovation unleashed by liberty means longer life. Life expectancy in 35,000 B.C. was estimated at about 18 years. By A.D. 1200, it was only 30 years. By 1850, it was 43 years. Today, the average life expectancy around the world is roughly 78 years.

CHAPTER 87:

A SNAP SHOT OF
WORLD SOCIALISM
CONTINUED

—North Korea, Peru, Portugal, Russia, Spain—
*In bad economic times, nothing is more easily rationalized
than a welfare check from the government.*

COUNTRY: North Korea (24.5 million)
BELOW POVERTY LINE: Not available
WELFARE COSTS: Not available
NATIONAL DEBT: $12.5 billion (2001 estimate)
STORY: By all standards of measurement, North Korea is the most
oppressed nation on earth. Its government is a dictatorship that
controls every part of a person's life, including how much weeping
was sufficient when the late Kim Jong Il died in 2011 (replaced by his
son, Kim Jong Un). Television cameras swept past farcical staged
mourners in orderly lines all weeping in unison.

The government operates 450,000 "Revolutionary Research
Centers" where citizens are indoctrinated on a weekly basis to
believe the new leader. Kim Jong Un has all power, supernatural
power, with other mystical traits worthy of the people's worship.

The citizens are divided into 51 social castes[604] based on their
loyalty to the Dear Leader. The general caste is three levels deep—
trustworthy loyalists are called "core," followed by the "wavering,"
and then the "hostile." The hostile group are all those the regime
doesn't trust or like. They are denied employment and food.

People are required to spy on each other. If someone is arrested
for disobeying the Dear Leader's dictates, he or she goes to one
of 210 detention centers, 210 labor camps, 27 holding facilities, 23
prisons, 6 political prison camps, or 5 indoctrination camps. There
they join an estimated 200,000-250,000 prisoners held indefinitely
for torture or execution.[605] The casualty rate at the roughest concentration camps is estimated at 25% per year.[606]

---

604 The Economist, *Deprive and Rule, Why does North Korea's dictatorship remain so
entrenched despite causing such hunger and misery?*, September 17, 2011.
605 The Chosunilbo, *200,000 Political Prisoners Held in N. Korean Camps*, 1/21/2010.
606 The Korea Times, *NK Defector Testifies to Horrors at Concentration Camp*, 3/16/2011.

**The free market works: In 2011, Walmart had 9,600 retail stores in 28 countries, and served
200 million customers per week.**

Malnutrition is an ongoing problem. In the 1990s, some 3.5 million starved to death. The average 7-year-old is about 2 inches shorter than a South Korean child the same age.[607]

All media outlets, from print to electronic to church sermons, are controlled by the regime, and all messages must praise Dear Leader. Listening to foreign broadcasts or traveling outside the proscribed boundaries can result in a trip to the concentration camp.[608]

North Korea is desperately dependent on trade with China to keep the economy going. In 2010, the trade between the two nations was estimated to be at $3.5 billion, up from $2.5 billion in 2009.

In the capital city, nervous escorts guard visiting foreigners so they see only what is meant to be seen. The air is unpolluted, but that is for lack of industry and automobiles in the barren city. Photos of Dear Leader are everywhere. Sparsely placed dim lights illuminate the ghost-town feel of what once was a large metropolis. Under communism, North Korea is dying. But at least they have their 1.3 million-man army to protect their ruins.

HISTORICAL PERSPECTIVE: In 1994, R.J. Rummel estimated the body count from socialism's tyranny in North Korea to be about 3,163,000 since 1948.[609] The U.S. Committee for Human Rights in North Korea estimated in 2006 that socialist policies caused the starvation deaths of about 2,500,000 between 1995-1998.[610]

COUNTRY: Peru (29.3 million)
BELOW POVERTY LINE: 10.2 million (34.8%)
WELFARE COSTS: not available
NATIONAL DEBT: $38 billion
STORY: After decades of extreme totalitarian governments and ruthless insurgencies, such as the Shining Path, positive changes came to Peru. The economy was freed to promote business and the government was finally decentralized. This triggered a wave of sustained economic growth.

---

607   Economics & Human Biology, *The biological standard of living in the two Koreas*, Vol. 2, Issue 3, December 2004, pp 511-521.
608   Oppression in North Korea, http://jeresearchtopics.blogspot.com/2011/01/oppression-in-north-korea.html.
609   Rummel, R.J. *Death by Government*, New Brunswick, NJ: Transaction Publishers, 1994.
610   U.S. Committee for Human Rights in North Korea, *Failure to Protect, A Call for the U.N. Security Council to Act in North Korea*, DLA Piper U.S. LLP, 2006.

The free market really works: In 2010, New Yorkers living in Zip Code 10104 paid an average $1,045,692 in taxes. How many jobs would that have created were it not flowing into the coffers of the U.S. Treasury?

From 2003-2011, the country averaged a 7% growth rate, one of the fastest in the world. At the same time, Peru cut its poverty rate in half. The economy was also booming, thanks to the country's rich mineral wealth in gold, silver, tin, iron, zinc, and copper. People in the interior where such resources were found finally gained some wealth and a voice in national affairs.

Taxes on those mines rose to 30% in recent years, but the money went to regional governments instead of Lima. That was a good sign—proof the country was finally pulling down barriers and decentralizing the socialist government.

China is Peru's biggest customer for raw resources. The trade became so rich, Peru embarked on a massive road construction project to link its Pacific coast with Brazil. The road made transporting exports to the east coast easier and cheaper. The Peruvians predicted the road would not only bypass the Panama Canal, but replace it as the shortcut of choice.

Peru gave credit for its economic turnaround to a political choice: Instead of following its neighbors—Venezuela, Ecuador, and Bolivia—into socialism, a dark place it admits was its worst modern-day nightmare, the country instead chose freedom. "We've learned from our mistakes," says Francisco Sagasti, an analyst in Lima. "No one is pushing for nationalization here. Everyone here knows that you have to have sensible economic policies from top to bottom."[611] Peruvians hate socialism.

COUNTRY: Portugal (10.8 million)
BELOW POVERTY LINE: 1.95 million (18%)
WELFARE COSTS: 21.2% of GDP (#15 in world)
NATIONAL DEBT: $548 billion
STORY: Resisting austerity measures to save the economy was handled much more peacefully among Portugal's 10.6 million people in 2011. Instead of rioting in the streets, they were content with a 24-hour general strike—and then got back to business.

But the ruling socialist party didn't fare so well. It was kicked out of office in 2011 and replaced by the Social Democrats. The new leaders were faced with the daunting task of cutting wages in an already depressed economy, forcing the laborers to work

---

611 Matthew Clark, *Latin America's surprise rising economic star: Peru*, The Christian Science Monitor, January 5, 2010.

longer hours, and slashing retirement benefits. Unemployment in 2011 climbed to over 12% with signs the trend would continue for the near term.

Fernanda Lopes, 60, who ran a fruit and vegetable stand in Porto, told CNN, "We are from a generation that has been through a lot before. We've been through a dictatorship when the country was very poor. The younger people haven't been through so much, they are not used to this type of impoverishment."[612]

COUNTRY: Russia (138 million people)
     BELOW POVERTY LINE: 18 million (13.1%)
     WELFARE COSTS: not available
NATIONAL DEBT: $519 billion
STORY: The motherland continued to suffer from the remnants of its abandoned socialistic heritage long into the new millennium. With reforms more than two decades in the making, the basics of property rights and protections continued to elude the nation.

People expecting protection of individual rights found the judicial system sadly unpredictable, corrupt, and unable to handle sophisticated cases. Foreigners arriving to create business contracts couldn't get them enforced. Borrowing to buy a home was a massive exercise in bureaucracy, and any kind of intellectual property was thinly protected from piracy.

After all those years of climbing out of the shadow of Communist dictatorship, Prime Minister Vladimir Putin started turning back the clock in 1999. He retained the undercover forces of secret police to run things. He was accused of enriching his inner circle with profits from oil revenues. Most of the industry was privatized in the 1990s, but some were re-nationalized later.

Russia has enormous energy resources. In 2011, it became the world's leading oil producer, passing Saudi Arabia, and is the world's second largest producer of natural gas and has the world's second largest coal reserves. The country pushes manufacturing, and is the world's third-largest exporter of steel and primary aluminum. To insulate itself from the boom and bust cycles of world demand, Russia is focusing on high technology. For a decade, the economy

---

612   Laura Smith-Spark, Portugal: *When there's no light at the end of the tunnel*, CNN, December 20, 2011.

Socialism erodes virtue: First, Congress piles on taxes so heavy, many struggle to pay them and most of it doesn't strengthen society, but saps it of strength by supporting entitlement welfare. Second, the struggle to pay creates dishonesty among otherwise ... (cont'd)

averaged 7% growth until the 2008-09 world economic crisis. [613]

Russia has reduced its unemployment and rate of inflation, but its shrinking labor force, high levels of corruption, and aging infrastructure are remnants of its old ways that need urgent attention.

HISTORICAL PERSPECTIVE: In 1994, R.J. Rummel estimated the body count from socialism's tyranny for all of the Soviet Union, not just Russia, to be about 58,627,000 from 1922-1991. An earlier confederation called the Russian Soviet Federated Socialist Republic killed 3,284,000 from 1918-1922. This does not count at least 6,210,000 killed in the civil war of 1918-1920.[614] Robert Conquest, a Stalin biographer, estimated that Stalin's administration killed 18 million with famines, executions, imprisonment, show trials, purges, and forced collectivization. Victor Kravchenko, author of *I Choose Freedom* (1946), said 19.8 million "enemies of the people" were arrested. Of these, 7,000,000 were shot in prison and untold thousands of others died in camp. Stalin killed most of the Soviet military officer corps and almost all of his inner circle. He was preparing an anti-Semitic purge, but died before it got underway.[615]

COUNTRY: Spain (46.7 million)
BELOW POVERTY LINE: 9.2 million (19.8%)
WELFARE COSTS: 19.6 of GDP (#20 in world)
NATIONAL DEBT: $2.57 trillion
STORY: Unemployment was Spain's biggest problem in 2011, where it stood at 21%—the highest in Europe. Unemployment among the youth was at 46%. When bailout money was offered to restart the economy, along with many austerity requirements to cut back on spending, the people got mad. The rich were angry for the higher taxes, the population was mad because overall spending was cut by 8%, employees were mad because salaries were frozen, and other measures were met with widespread mobs and riots. The Spaniards also love socialism.

---

613   CIA, The World Factbook, *Russia*, 2012.

614   Rummel, R.J. *Death by Government*, New Brunswick, NJ: Transaction Publishers, 1994.

615   Victor A. Kravchenko, *I Chose Freedom*, Angell Press, 2007.

(cont'd) ...honest people to avoid payment in any way possible. And third, the IRS then resorts to rewarding whistle blowers who expose tax cheats with a percentage of the "take." People are incentivized to spy on one another, and national virtue slides toward fascism.

CHAPTER 88:
A SNAP SHOT OF
WORLD SOCIALISM
CONCLUSION

—Sweden, U.K., U.S., Venezuela, Vietnam, Zimbabwe—
In bad economic times, nothing is more easily rationalized than a welfare check from the government.

C **OUNTRY**: Sweden (9.1 million)
BELOW POVERTY LINE: Not available
WELFARE COSTS: 28.9% of GDP (#2 in world)
NATIONAL DEBT: $1.02 trillion
STORY: This nation of nine million enjoys a degree of prosperity but at a huge personal cost. The county owes an enormous debt of $1.02 trillion (15th highest in the world),[616] and its people carry a load of taxes that consumes up to 60% of the average income. Add to this the sales tax of 25% built into the price of consumer goods (VAT—Value Added Tax), plus 1/5th of the working-age people on welfare, a third of everyone working for the government, and a population growth rate almost flat (.163%), and Sweden is headed for trouble.[617]

Sweden is often celebrated as an example of how social-ism can create prosperity. Closer to the truth is the fact that a small, homogeneous society of hard-working, law-abiding and well-educated people can overcome the drags of socialistic controls.

Sweden was an impoverished nation before the 1870s, losing many of its citizens who began migrating to the United States. The country persevered by adopting principles of the free market—protecting property rights, establishing a clean set of laws, and focusing hard on expanding education of the work force. The result was a nation growing richer into the early 1900s. During that time period, world-respected companies were created, such as Volvo, IKEA, Electrolux, Ericsson, and Alfa Laval, among others.[618] Up

616 CIA, The World Factbook, *Sweden,* 2012.
617 Ibid.
618 Nima Sanandaji, *Sweden: A Role Model for Capitalist Reform?,* Captus 2011.

It took 60 years, from 1789 to 1848, for the U.S. Government to spend its first $1 billion. Toward the end of Barack Obama's administration, the government was spending $1 billion every 2 hours 22 minutes.

until 1936, Sweden had the world's highest economic growth rate among the industrialized nations. And then came the socialists.

Between about 1936 to 2008, the effects of the welfare state—larger government, more promises, higher taxes—began to slow Sweden's growth. By 2008, it had dropped to 18th among 28 industrialized nations.

The cultural differences that helped Sweden do so well were reflected in their successes in other countries. The 4.5 million Swedes in America[619] in 2008 earned on average $10,000 more than the average American.[620] The poverty rate among American Swedes was about 6.7% in 2010, and in Sweden, also about 6.7%.[621]

Starting in the 1990s, Sweden began scaling back its socialist government from the oppressive heavy-handedness of the 1960s. The results were outstanding. School vouchers created competition among educators to improve quality. Health care and pensions became partially private, giving flexibility to people's choices for when they could retire. The public transportation systems were returned to the private sector, including the rail lines. The center-right government that came to power in 2006 was reelected in 2010 with goals to continue privatization and reduce taxes.

A majority of Swedes still love socialism, but with each move toward economic liberty, the country grows stronger.

COUNTRY: United Kingdom (62.7 million)
BELOW POVERTY LINE: 8.8 million (14%)
WELFARE COSTS: 21.8 % of GDP (#14 in world)
NATIONAL DEBT: $9.8 trillion
STORY: In 2010, Britain worked to reduce its yearly welfare costs of £190 billion ($300 billion). With 1.4 million receiving jobseekers' allowance, the new plan required that each welfare recipient perform at least 30 hours a week in mandatory work activity for a month. If they didn't put in the hours, they would risk having their welfare checks stopped for at least 3 months.

By 2011, conditions worsened and Britain planned to cut 490,000

---

619 U.S. Census Bureau, *Selected Social Characteristics in the U.S.: 2008, ACS 2008 1-Year Estimates.*
620 Nima Sanandaji, Robert Gidehag, *Is Sweden A False Utopia?*, www.newgeography.com, May 2, 2010.
621 Ibid., Sanandaji.

government jobs, cut about 20% from government departments, and raise the retirement age to 66 by 2020.

Slashing the disability living allowances and other welfare payments was expected to push 400,000 back to work. Another 200,000 whose housing benefits would be capped were expected to leave their pricey subsidized homes for the suburbs. Housing benefits cost taxpayers more than £21 billion ($33 billion) in 2010.

Said one Labour MP, "It is tantamount to cleansing the poor out of rich areas—a brutal and shocking piece of social engineering."[622] Spoken like a true socialist.

Public uproar to the proposed cuts was huge—demonstrations numbering 250,000 people or more broke out in London and elsewhere, proving that the English love socialism.

COUNTRY: United States (313.2 million)
BELOW POVERTY LINE: 47.3 million (15.1%)
WELFARE COSTS: 14.8% of GDP (#26 in world)
NATIONAL DEBT: $16 trillion
STORY: America's welfare system is enormous. It involves six top-level departments that run more than 70 programs. Many recipients of welfare receive funds from several departments at the same time.

Welfare in the U.S. has become an enormous drain. Plan after plan offering huge cash payments to the jobless was forced on the American people in 2008-2011—to the tune of hundreds of billions of borrowed dollars. This reckless abandonment of sound economic principle gave scholars ample opportunity to study the impact of historically unprecedented incentives for people to remain on the dole. Their findings showed:

❖ **INCENTIVE TO FIND A JOB:** The average unemployed American spends 41 minutes a day looking for work, compared with 12 minutes for Europeans. Why? Because unemployment insurance runs out quicker in the U.S. than overseas.[623] Therefore, an American's hunt for a job remained more intense.

❖ **PROCRASTINATION WOES:** Efforts to find a job peaked just about when that last unemployment check arrived at week 26.

---

622   Gerri Peev, MailOnline, *Welfare Payments Cuts 'will force 200,000 benefits claimants out of London and into suburbs'*, October 25, 2010.
623   Alan B. Krueger, et al, *Job Search and Unemployment Insurance: New Evidence from Time Use Data*, CEPS Working Paper No. 175, August 2008.

Samuel Webster, 1777: "Encroachments on the people's liberties are not generally made all at once, but so gradually as hardly to be perceived by the less watchful; ... [cont'd]

At week 27, after the benefits stopped rolling in, job-search efforts dropped off dramatically. Scholars supposed that people became discouraged, and if no job was found after increased searching in weeks 22-26, what's the point of trying in week 27 and beyond?[624] When benefits were extended to 79 and then 99 weeks, people procrastinated in the same fashion, putting off until the end their best efforts to find a job.

❖ **BENEFITS DESTROY GOOD INCENTIVES:** Why did unemployment suddenly rise in 2009 from 7.2 percent to 10.2 percent in just ten months? Because in February of that year, another of those "stimulus bills" of $40 billion in benefits was handed over at no cost to the states. Suddenly, the unemployed could afford to stay unemployed that much longer—hundreds of thousands of them re-enrolled for benefits. Before that rescue package was passed by Congress, the average length people remained unemployed was 10 weeks. After the extension, the average length of unemployment grew to 18.7 weeks.[625]

❖ **BENEFITS CREATE BAD INCENTIVE:** Unemployment benefits give incentives to stay unemployed. At least 2 percent of the U.S. unemployment figures are blamed on bailouts or extensions of unemployment benefits. Study after study, expert after expert, all said the same: When people are paid not to work, that's exactly what they'll do.[626]

COUNTRY: Venezuela (27.6 million)
BELOW POVERTY LINE: 10.5 million (38%)
WELFARE COSTS: Not available
NATIONAL DEBT: $90 billion
STORY: When Hugo Chavez became president in 1999, he promoted his "21st Century Socialism" as the great solution to alleviate all social ills. At the same time, he attacked America, capitalism, and democracy. The fruits of his brilliant solution rose no higher than all other failed socialist schemes.

Reckless government interference in the economy, rampant corruption, price controls on nearly all goods and services, a corrupted legal system, a lack of respect for property ownership

---

624 Ibid.
625 Alan Reynolds, *The 'Stimulus' for Unemployment*, Cato Institute, November 17, 2009.
626 Brookings Institution, cited in *Incentives Not to Work*, Wall Street Journal, 4/13/2010.

(cont'd) "...and all plaistered over, it may be, with such plausible pretenses, that before they are aware of the snare, they are taken and cannot disentangle themselves."

and contracts, and the constant threat of government confiscation of wealth and property has almost killed prosperity.

Chavez trampled on human rights, outlawed free speech, abolished property rights, took over successful private businesses and nationalized them, exhausted the national treasure to build up the military, and made his neighboring countries angry.

The country had the highest inflation rate in all of Latin America at 29% (in 2011). The government-run infrastructure produced chronic power outages, shortages of food, housing shortages, escalating crime, and anemic economic growth outside of its oil-supported activities.

Venezuela's oil industry produces almost 95% of its total export income, and provides 60% of total federal revenue. Even so, Chavez's brilliant program forces the government to borrow money every year (he runs a deficit 5% of GDP), while creating a welfare class with 10 million of his 27.6 million below the poverty line.

On August 23, 2011, Chavez nationalized the gold industry. Foreign companies had to keep 50% of all the gold they mined inside the country. The only large foreign gold miner was Russia's Agapov family, who produced 100,000 ounces in 2010. Chavez also withdrew $11 billion in gold reserves from U.S. and European banks so he could keep the metal closer to home.

COUNTRY: Vietnam (90.5 million)
BELOW POVERTY LINE: 9.6 million (10.6%)
WELFARE COSTS: not available
NATIONAL DEBT: $37 billion
STORY: Inflation is a continual problem for this repressed country, averaging more than 18 percent between 2006-08. By summer 2011, it jumped to 22% and was rising. The constant irritant to the Vietnam market was the government and its typical tyrannical manipulations—price fixing, regulation, subsidies, and ownership of business, enterprises, banks, and utilities. Corruption at all levels continued to be a big problem for this country of 90.5 million. The regime reaped benefits from the state-owned enterprises at the expense of the very workers it claimed to be rescuing from the ravages of the free market.

Vietnam depends on tourism and exports to bring needed growth, and has enjoyed an economic boom in recent years. This was the result of miniscule efforts to reform the economy and start benefitting from the fruits of capitalism, without admitting as much. In its proclaimed socialist society, the top producers are taxed at 35% and corporations at 25%. Everyone must pay a value-added tax on goods, and property tax. And, like everyone else, the government overspends every year and now has a national debt that is more than half its total output.

Without protection of private property rights, contracts, intellectual property rights, and a judicial system bogged down with corruption and manipulation, outsiders are wary of investing.

Withdrawal from compulsory care will be a long time coming for Vietnam, but signs of letting that wretched enemy called capitalism benefit all sectors in the country prove the people may be open to something better than tyrannical socialism.

HISTORICAL PERSPECTIVE: In 1994, R.J. Rummel estimated the body count from socialism's tyranny in Vietnam to be about 1,670,000 since 1975.[627]

COUNTRY: Zimbabwe (12.6 million)
BELOW POVERTY LINE: 8.2 million (68%)
WELFARE COSTS: Not available
NATIONAL DEBT: $6 billion
STORY: This resource-rich country was once the breadbasket of the region before the regime of Robert G. Mugabe took power in 1979. His tyrannical rule has ruined the nation.

In 2000, Mugabe embarked on redistribution of the land. This drove out white farmers and ruined the economy. Massive shortages followed.

In 2005, Mugabe's political machine corrupted the constitution so his regime could amend it at will. That same year he embarked on "Operation Restore Order," and in the name of urban renewal he destroyed 700,000 homes and businesses of his political opponents and those who voted for them.

In 2007, Mugabe imposed price controls that panicked the nation, and store shelves were emptied in hours—and stayed that way for months. Inflation shot up to 1,700% and unemployment (and

---

627 Rummel, R.J. *Death by Government*, New Brunswick, NJ: Transaction Publishers, 1994.

Socialism in America: Spending on U.S. "dependence programs" grew to 70.5% of the federal budget under President Barack Obama (as of 2010).

underemployment) stood at 95%.[628]

A rising political opposition leader, Morgan Tsvangirai, was subjected to multiple arrests and beatings by Mugabe's men. In 2007, for example, he was arrested and hauled to prison. When his wife saw him, he was sorely injured, with gashes and a swollen eye. A freelance cameraman, Edward Chikombo, smuggled in a camera and broadcast images of the injuries. Chikombo was later kidnapped and his body was found the following weekend. Beatings and killings have been typical of the Mugabe regime.

In the 2008 elections, neither man received 50% of the vote so a run-off election was going to be held. Instead, Tsvangirai was made prime minister and Mugabe was made president, the positions now held as of 2012.

HIV/AIDS is a massive problem, with an estimated 1.2 million of the population infected. Zimbabwe has the 5th highest death rate from AIDS in the world. Life expectancy is one of the lowest in the world, averaging 51 years for both men and women.

Zimbabwe is a source of men, women, and children trafficked for forced labor, drug smuggling, and sexual exploitation. Some of these are forced into South Africa for additional sexual exploitation.

SOCIALISM NEEDS A HOST: THREE EXAMPLES

Like all other freeloaders, socialism requires help to stay alive. It doesn't innovate, invent, or produce. Every system ends up with the consumers out-consuming the ability of the producers to provide. Regular infusions of cash or help is a normal activity for highly socialized nations.

All socialistic schemes rise on the backs of prosperity. Once free enterprise builds a strong economy, the socialists show up demanding equality for the lazy, the less fortunate, and the impoverished masses.

British Prime Minister Margaret Thatcher said it best: "Socialist governments traditionally do make a financial mess. They always run out of other people's money."[629] Or, to paraphrase, socialism works until it runs out of other people's money.

---

628   The Economist, *Zimbabwe: The Face of Oppression*, May 15, 2007.
629   Margaret Thatcher, in a TV interview for *Thames TV This Week*, February 5, 1976.

Looks can be deceiving—Super model Elle MacPherson on why she supported Barack Obama for President (quoted in 2012): "I'm socialist ... what do you expect?"

COUNTRY: Cuba
DESPERATE ACT: Huge State Farms Fail—2009
STORY: In this small island where the Communist government sets wages and prices, where farmers are forced to produce without capitalistic profit incentives, the country is starving. Having lost its Soviet host to sustain them in recent years, the Cuban government has been forced to turn to free-enterprise economics. The St. Petersburg Times reported,

"Despite being an agricultural nation with plentiful sun, soil and rain, Cuba produces barely 30 percent of the food it needs, due to an acute lack of resources and the inefficiency of its state farm sector. About 250,000 small family farms and 1,100 cooperatives till only about one-quarter of the land, yet still manage to outperform the state farms, producing almost 60 percent of crops and livestock, according to official figures."[630]

COUNTRY: The Soviet Union
DESPERATE ACT: Private Plotters create emergency produce
STORY: Before the USSR finally collapsed in 1991, common scenes in cities all across the land were the farmer's markets. They were necessary to keep the populations fed. The government looked askance at these capitalistic activities because of their tremendous good. The markets offered a huge quantity and wide variety of agriculture goods—sold at a profit.

An example was a 78-year-old-woman in Kiev who rented a table at the Hay Market to sell her home-grown apples, pears, and berries. She charged a high price, and got it. Nearby, a 70-year-old man sold homegrown onions and garlic. Next door, another sold watermelons grown on private land by a group of cooperating farmers. What did these farmers do for their day job? The very same type of work on the less-efficient state farm. Others at the market sold cabbage, tomatoes, onions, apples, eggs, churned butter, beef, pork, poultry, cottage cheese, ducks, and geese—all of it privately raised, prepared, and brought to market.

"Every city in the Soviet Union has a similar market where farmers can sell their produce," said a writer for in the Kansas City Star and Times in 1978, "... not at state-regulated prices but for whatever the market will bring. These tiny enclaves of free

---

630   St. Petersburg Times, August 17, 2009.

Socialism in America: In 2010, more than $2.1 trillion, or 66% of the federal budget, was spent on government handouts (Medicare, Medicaid, Social Security, unemployment, food stamps, earned income).

enterprise, while they may be frowned on officially, are welcomed and even encouraged by the Soviet government, in practice because they add so much to the national food supply."[631]

Agriculture experts in both the U.S. and Soviet Union calculated that thousands of small gardens, accounting for a miniscule 3-4 percent of the cultivated land, produced a whopping 27 percent of all food grown in the Soviet Union, including 62 percent of all potatoes, 37 percent of all eggs, 31 percent of all meat and poultry, 30 percent of all milk, and 1 percent of all grain (sweet corn).

COUNTRY: North Korea
DESPERATE ACT: Making ends meet by counterfeiting
STORY: North Korea was once a powerhouse of productivity. Today, its people are starving to death. While their neighbor to the south thrives with a relatively free economy, socialism has flattened North Korea's ability to produce. Today it relies on desperate measures. It sells its coal and minerals to China, and sells the right for Chinese fishermen to work Korean waters. It sends workers to other foreign lands as cheap labor to return whatever funds are possible.

Before he died, Dictator Kim Jong II required at least $1 billion a year to meet his needs, and dispensed worthless currency to the people to live on.

To compensate for the country's inability to prosper, Kim and company might have supported or tolerated counterfeiting and money laundering to the tune of millions every year. Defectors claim in uncorroborated statements that the government of North Korea is indeed directly involved, despite public denials to the contrary. No one knows if or how the current regime has carried on that work.

Three primary facilities poured out at least $25 million in phony $100 bills every year for the past 25 years. The bills circulate primarily through Korea and China, sometimes making their way to Europe and the U.S. Locally, people buy $100 bills for $40 and try to pawn them off as real U.S. tender. If print quality is especially accurate, counterfeiters can get up to $70 each.

There exists some doubt that the socialist country has the technology to reproduce $100 bills. The government claims no involvement, and gave evidence by publicly executing two convicted counterfeiters in 2006.

---

631 Reprinted in *The Palm Beach Post*, Nov. 5, 1978.

Compared to national needs ($1 billion annually), and the total quantity of U.S. currency in circulation at any given time ($800 billion worldwide), $25 million a year in bogus bills doesn't seem to make much of a dent. But the U.S. dollars are not the only lucrative trade coming out of North Korea. Some estimates put the value of counterfeited currency at more than $100 million a year.[632] The fact that the practice continues poses the question: In what other ways is North Korea benefitting by counterfeiting currencies other than the U.S. dollar?[633]

North Korea can't feed itself. With the fall of the Soviet Union, the country has been dependent on China for food and energy. According to a study by Heather Smith and Yiping Huang, China has been supplying North Korea with millions of tons of grains, coal, and oil. Between 1996 and 2000, for example, China sent more than 1.2 million tons of grain, 2.3 million tons of crude, and 2.5 million tons of coal.[634]

LEARNING TO RECOGNIZE SOCIALISM

All the world's nations are plagued with powers and forces that feed the rulers and starve the people. This self-perpetuating abuse of human nature continues despite the widespread belief held almost universally in all the world today: *The government can solve all my problems.*

How many more billions of people must be born onto the earth to establish the universal truth that government can't "solve all my problems"? That each and every attempt ends in failure? That governments of any kind can sink or rise no further than the people's lowest vices and their highest ideals? That a corrupt people stands in need of more masters, but *only* a virtuous people can govern themselves?

---

632 Economist Intelligence Unit, *Country Profile 2003, South Korea, North Korea*, p. 85.

633 Dick K. Nanto, *North Korean Counterfeiting of U.S. Currency*, Congressional Research Service, June 12, 2009.

634 Heather Smith and Yiping Huang, *Achieving Food Security in North Korea*, presented at the Ladau Network/Centro di Cultura Scientifica A. Volta conference, June 2000.

In 2012, a study exposed bias in claims that same-sex parenting produces comparable results as biological parents. Seven flaws were discovered including trying to compare wealthy, well-educated lesbian couples with problem-prone single-parent heterosexual families, as if they were the "same."

Part XVI

THE 46 GOALS OF SOCIALISM

The goal of socialism
is communism:

"What is usually called
socialism was termed
by Marx the 'first,'
or lower, phase of
communist society."

—Vladimir Lenin—

CHAPTER 89:

THE 46 GOALS OF SOCIALISM

The opportunities change, but the goals remain the same.

The biggest mistake in recent decades by the world's free people is their indulgence in a prolonged mental demise into apathy, stagnation, and neglect. In many circles the former yearning for freedom is smothered under a desperate frenzy for government bailouts, the dole, the loan, the tax break—anything, as if governments were saviors of last resort with limitless resources.

Within a single lifespan the world has changed from hope to hype, concern to contempt, cautious to callous, from helping neighbors to fearing them. This can't last. Many scholars believe it is time for a revolutionary change in our state of mind. What went wrong with the world's state of mind?

First and foremost, we have been thinking the way the socialists want us to think—that is, *we are thinking like socialists.*

We want to change the world, but not ourselves. We want everything and anything, except the consequences. We want the government to force all things right. We impatiently want it all. Our motto has become "There ought to be a law ..."—and today, there usually is. Our slogan is, "Choose the right—*or else.*"

Western culture has been adopting socialist thinking for a very long time—but not in a vacuum. Guiding it along have been a number of objectives, targets, and goals. They come in the form of friendly solutions that play on our natural human weaknesses. They promise something for nothing—an easier life, all the benefits without the cost, a fix for all things, fairness, and social justice—just give socialism a try. These objectives and goals have a great world-wide following today.

Most people don't realize that these goals are designed to soften them up, to prepare them for the final collapse of freedom and the birth of global Ruler's Law, international socialism, a *new world order.* For lack of understanding, many loyal defenders of freedom are supporting these goals. The goals in the following list are derived from the vast collection of writings, both ancient and

Decade of Greed? During the 1980s, anti-welfare people were criticized for being heartless. But was cutting government welfare really that heartless? After Reagan cut the marginal tax rate in 1981, charitable giving grew 55% higher than in the prior 25 years. ... (cont'd)

modern, from reformers and dreamers throughout history. Some could be quoted directly, others are surmised by actions being undertaken today. Some modern socialists bravely deny they would ever want to upset the culture, such as calling for the elimination of the family or religion, but as shown in the prior pages, given enough time, all socialism must and does eventually lead to those extremes.

THE 46 GOALS OF SOCIALISM[635]

NOTE: Referenced in the footnotes are a few examples of plans, proposals, or arguments that carry forward the on-going or eventual enactment of the 46 goals of socialism.

1. PROMOTE SOCIAL DEMOCRACY: Eliminate laws and the popular stigma against socialism. Promote socialism as the best alternative to capitalism. "Once the vast majority makes the decision in favor of socialism," says *World Socialism*, "then it will elect socialist representatives or delegates to ... administer the elimination of capitalism and the creation of socialism."[636]

2. PROMOTE THE U.N.: Renew popular support of the U.N. as the only hope for the world. Rewrite its charter so it can establish a single global democracy[637] with its own independent military force.[638]

3. A WORLD WITH NO NATIONAL BOUNDARIES: Eliminate all borders and national sovereignty. "Socialism will be a world without countries," says *World Socialism*. "Borders are just artificial barriers that belong to a past and present that is best left behind."[639]

4. INSTALL ENVIRONMENTAL RULERS: Support U.S. acceptance of a "global green economy" and the U.N.'s World Summit on Sustainable Development. Compel the U.S. to accept the cap-and-trade market for carbon.[640]

---

635   These goals were compiled by the author from the vast accumulation of writings on socialism, and from national and U.N. efforts now underway to further these causes.
636   WorldSocialism.org, Socialist Party of Canada, *Frequently Asked Questions,* 2012.
637   See Jean-Philippe Therien, *The United Nations and Global Democracy, From Discourse to Deeds, Cooperation and Conflict,* December 2009, vol. 44 no. 4, pp. 355-377.
638   United Nations, *U.N. body urges support for treaty regulating private military, security companies,* U.N. News Centre, April 30, 2010.
639   WorldSocialism.org, Socialist Party of Canada, *Frequently Asked Questions,* 2012
640   See *Outcomes on Human Settlements,* www.un.org.

(cont'd) ... Overall giving grew 56 percent. Giving exceeded the expected and predicted amount every year, averaging $16 billion a year. The lesson is when people have more money in their pockets, they give more to the needy.

5. ONE-WORLD CURRENCY: Create a new "global currency" to replace the dollar, euro, yen, and all other national currencies. The "global currency" would be managed by a "Global Reserve Bank."[641]

6. CONTROL OF INTERNET: Form a specialized agency of the U.N. to absorb or replace ICANN (Internet Corporation for Assigned Names and Numbers), and regulate all Internet traffic, prices, and taxes—and censor content according to the ever-changing mandates from U.N. charter nations. Also, mandate construction of wide-area networks covering the entire inhabited world.[642]

7. ESTABLISH ECONOMIC RULERS: Use the European Union model to create a super-legislature under the auspices of the U.N.'s economic development and social councils. Infuse the super-legislature with power to bypass economic decisions of its member nations, and subordinate to it all laws and constitutions.

8. UNIVERSAL EQUALITY: Use the U.N.'s Declaration on Social Justice to force all nations to guarantee employment, protection, participation, and uniform labor practices regardless of gender, age, race, ethnicity, religion, culture, or disability.

9. KING OF AMERICA (U.S.): Codify the general use of Executive Orders to enact presidential decrees "so I can fulfill my promises to the electorate" without checks and balances interference from Congress or the Supreme Court.

10. RENDER CONGRESS IRRELEVANT (U.S.): Increase the number and powers of regulatory agencies of the executive branch as the primary law-making bodies of the federal government. Bypass Congressional authorization—instead of seeking permission and approval, obligate Congress to override any new laws and rules enacted by the many agencies with majority votes.[643]

---

641   See Decian McCullagh, *United Nations Proposes New "Global Currency,"* CBSNews.com, September 9, 2009.

642   Numerous proposals to this end have been offered. In September, Russia, China, among others, petitioned the U.N. General Assembly for "an international code of conduct for information security." See Trent Nouveau, *Pentagon Opposes U.N. Regulation of the Internet*, TGdaily.com, October 21, 2011.

643   See W. Mark Crain, et al, *The Impact of Regulatory Costs on Small Firms*, SBA, September 2005; Administrative Procedure Act, Title 5, United States Code, Chapter 5,

11. SUBORDINATE LOCAL GOVERNMENT: Use technical decisions by the courts to bypass the laws and court decisions made by local and state governments. Make all decisions dependent on approval by leaders further up the chain of control.[644]

12. DESTROY REPRESENTATION (WORLD): Resist any attempt to allow free elections that dethrone the ruling parties.

13. SUSTAIN 17TH AMENDMENT (U.S.): Inflame suspicion about repealing the 17th amendment, warning that making senators beholden to the state legislatures will unleash back-door deal making and collusion. Keep this link of representation cleanly severed because it otherwise brings too much control by the people over the federal government.[645]

14. DEFLATE CONSTITUTIONAL CONVENTION (U.S.): Spread fear that a constitutional convention would open the Constitution to a complete re-write and destruction. Hide the mechanics of protection the Founders gave to this act of last resort.[646]

15. REGULATE TRANSPORTATION: Nationalize the transportation industries. Create cooperatives with car and truck makers to force fuel efficiency and to meet pollution limits. Expand mass transit into all major cities.[647]

16. REGULATE ALL ENERGY: Nationalize energy production and prices using as an excuse the terror of pollution and the fairness of equal access to every nation's natural resources.[648]

Sections 511-599.

644 See World Socialist Movement goals at www.worldsocialism.org.

645 Typical of numerous scare tactics is this from Gerry Connolly running for Congress in Virginia, "Repealing the 17th Amendment would strip your right to vote for your U.S. Senators and allow political insiders in Richmond to decide who represents us in the Senate." See http://gerryconnolly.com/blog/129. He avoids mention that the state legislature is more accessible than Washington DC, and therefore more responsive to constituent demands. The Founders knew this and created that direct link to the federal levels through the legislature.

646 Multiple references are available on the Internet. Nearly all promise the immediate destruction of the Constitution should such a convention be held. Close to none explain the parameters necessary to prevent a runaway convention. Progressive socialists win by paralysis, and America's great escape clause remains unused—it's as good as repealed.

647 Ibid., Marx, Engels, *Communist Manifesto.*

648 See *United Nations Development Programme, United Nations Environment Programme, United Nations Division of Environmental Law and Conventions,* among dozens of others.

(cont'd) ... Of that enormous regulatory burden, U.S. businesses paid $221 billion toward obedience to environmental regulations.

17. ELIMINATE PRIVATE PROPERTY: Adopt the U.N.'s land policy (1976), "Land ... cannot be treated as an ordinary asset, controlled by individuals ... Private land ownership is also a principle instrument of accumulation and concentration of wealth and therefore contributes to social injustice ... The provision of decent dwellings and healthy conditions for the people can only be achieved if land is used in the interests of society as a whole."[649]

18. DESTROY FAMILY CULTURE: Encourage the collapse of ties between husband and wife, children and parents, people and church by promoting pornography as a right granted by freedom of speech.[650]

19. REDEFINE NORMAL AND HEALTHY: Present homosexuality, degeneracy, and promiscuity as "normal, natural, healthy." In 2011, the U.S. backed a successful U.N. resolution endorsing the rights of gay, lesbian and transgender people.[651]

20. DESTROY SANCTITY OF MARRIAGE: In the name of equality, remove all authority from church marriages. Only those unions decreed by a clerk of the court according to established laws and requirements, with properly signed papers, may constitute a marriage.[652]

21. DISCREDIT THE FAMILY: Dilute natural family structure by compelling by law the acceptance of any union of consenting adults without regard to gender, gender preference, or numbers involved.[653]

22. DESTROY GENDER DISTINCTIONS: Compel all institutions to recognize, accommodate, and facilitate any individual regardless of gender or sexual identification. Blur the biological differences between men and women and eliminate any requirements based on that distinction.[654]

---

649   *Report of Habitat: United Nations Conference on Human Settlements*, Conference Report, Vancouver, May 31-June 11, 1976.

650   See Ginsberg vs. New York, Miller vs. California, New York vs. Ferber.

651   Associated Press, *U.N. Gay Rights Protection Resolution Passes, Hailed as 'Historic Moment,'* June 17, 2011.

652   Marriage licenses serve positive purposes (underage, close relations, disease issues, etc.). Elimination of the church is to remove the authority of the marriage sacrament—a serious and sacred commitment for life—and replacing it with a ticket to be intimate without disdain from the public. One day it will become a tool of "out of sight, out of mind."

653   For example, see *Respect for Marriage Act*, H.R. 1116, S. 598 (2011); polygamy, see The U.N. Refugee Agency, Refworld, *Polygamy.*

654   The U.N. Human Rights Council, *Human rights, sexual orientation and gender identity,*

As a president thinketh in his heart, so is he.

23. UNIVERSAL ACCESS TO ABORTION: Transfer protection of reproductive rights to the U.N. In 2011, the U.N. said, "States must take measures to ensure that legal and safe abortion services are available, accessible, and of good quality. ...Criminal laws and other legal restrictions that reduce or deny access to family planning goods and services, or certain modern contraceptive methods, such as emergency contraception, constitute a violation of the right to health."[655] In 2012, Barack Obama obeyed the order by forcing U.S. insurance companies to provide free contraceptives and "day after" abortion drugs.

24. LIMIT FAMILY SIZE: Remove all tax advantages from parents for their dependent children. Promote "responsible" family planning to reduce world population.[656]

25. EMASCULATE RELIGION: Infiltrate the pulpits to create a "social religion" that promotes social and political agendas. Inject the mainstream with messages of moral guilt for all aspects of progress. Promote a neutral belief system founded on financial and material goals.[657]

26. DESTROY CHURCH ECONOMIES: Eliminate tax-exempt status for church properties and associated employees. Eliminate tax deductions for charitable donations.[658]

27. TRANSITION TOWARD WORLD WITHOUT CASH: Expand the network of electronic banking into every nation, allowing a digital economy with centralized electronic records to be kept of all transactions; make accessible to appropriate authorities as needed.[659]

June 14, 2011.

655   Arnand Grover, *Right of Everyone to the Enjoyment of the Highest Attainable Standard of Physical and Mental Health*, U.N., A/66/254, August 3, 2011; Sarah Boseley, *U.N. States Told They Must Legalize Abortion*, The Guardian, October 24, 2011.

656   For example, U.N. *Agenda 21*, www.un.org/esa/dsd/agenda21, 1992 and 2002; U.N. Population Division Policy, March 2009; World Population Report, Facing a Changing World: Women Population and Climate," 2009.

657   For example, Jeremiah Wright, expounder of inflammatory rhetoric, ABC News, *Obama's Pastor: God Damn America, U.S. to Blame for 9/11*, March 13, 2008.

658   For example, Diana B. Henriques, *Religion-based Tax Breaks: Housing to Paychecks to Books*, The New York Times, October 11, 2006; Proposed by Bipartisan Policy Center, *Restoring America's Future*, November 17, 2010.

659   In 2012, Sweden completed major steps toward a cashless economy, leading the world

28. INTERNATIONAL HEALTH CARE: Nationalize health care in every nation and place it under an international board of control. The U.N. World Health Organization said, "In the 21st century, health is a shared responsibility, involving equitable access to essential care and collective defense against transnational threats."[660] *Shared* and *equitable access* means government control.

29. OBEY THE WORLD COURT: Expand the international role of a world court system with power to bypass state and national laws and constitutions. Today, it exists in part as the U.N.'s International Court of Justice (also called the World Court), headquartered at The Hague, Netherlands.[661]

30. CREATE ONE-WORLD SUPER-LEGISLATURE over the environment. Gain control of economic development by gaining control of the environment.[662]

31. WORSHIP MOTHER EARTH: Lift environmental issues to a level that is equivalent or higher than human rights. Put forward the claim that preservation of the environment for the good of all living things must take priority over human needs.[663]

32. NATIONALIZE ALL NATURAL RESOURCES: Assume ownership and regulatory power over all national resources regardless of who owns the property on which the resource is found. Use this assumed control to promote *ecologically correct* choices—low- or non-flush toilets, battery-powered cars, low-energy light bulbs, recyclable containers and packaging, mandatory recycling, low-energy appliances, rationed energy access, and more—all of this mandated by government, not driven by free-market incentives and invention.[664]

33. UNILATERALLY DESTROY NUCLEAR WEAPONS: Develop the illusion that dismantling all nuclear weapons would

---

toward electronic payments for everything from bus rides to church donations. See Associated Press, *Sweden moving toward cashless economy*," March 18, 2012.

660   United Nations World Health Organization, *About Who*, 2012.

661   See the United Nations Charter; Articles 92-96; Article 93 makes all 193 U.N. members ipso facto (automatic) parties to the statute of the World Court.

662   The U.N. Environment Programme is already in place to "provide leadership ..."

663   See the United Nations World Trade Organization; *Earth Day; International Mother Earth Day*.

664   See U.N. Environment Programme, and World Conservation Monitoring Centre for blame on the "industrial age" for pollution, over harvesting, and climate change.

be a demonstration of moral strength. In February 2012, President Obama announced he was contemplating destroying up to 80% of America's deployed nuclear weapons.[665]

34. NEUTRALIZE ISRAEL: Resolve the Israeli-Palestinian issue by U.N. fiat and force Israel to surrender all disputed lands, including half or more of Jerusalem, to the Palestinians.[666]

35. NATIONALIZE ALL INDUSTRY: In the name of ecological sanity, grant regulatory authority to the U.N. over all heavy industry such as steel, mining, automobiles, machinery, railroads, airlines, etc.

36. SYNC ANIMAL RIGHTS WITH HUMAN RIGHTS: Legalize human rights in animals. Tax meat out of the marketplace. Prohibit all medical testing of animals, and human use of animal products for any purpose.

According to a writer for PETA, who was responding to a U.S. judge denying the animal rights organization its petition that the 13th amendment be applied to captive whales:

"Women, children, and racial and ethnic minorities were once denied fundamental constitutional rights that are now self-evident, and that day will certainly come for the orcas and all the other animals enslaved for human amusement."[667]

37. INFILTRATE AND REGULATE EDUCATION: Get control of the schools. Promote socialism's goals and ideologies. In 1992, the U.N. adopted Agenda 21 as a blueprint of action to reduce human impact on the environment. Thoroughly indoctrinating the world's children in how to sustain the environment is one of the U.N.'s mandates for every member nation.[668]

38. CONTROL INFORMATION: Infiltrate the media. Promote the successes of the new order and disparage the inhibiting drag of the old order. Ridicule the old order, celebrate the new, hide the

---

665   Associated Press, *U.S. Weighing Options for Future Cuts in Nuclear Weapons, Including 80% Reduction,* February 14, 2012.
666   Israel Today, *U.N. to Israel: Surrender,* March 30, 2011.
667   Jennifer OConnor, *The Case Forever Known as Tilikum vs. SeaWorld,* The PETA files, the official blog, February 9, 2012.
668   Rosalyn NcKeown, et al, *Education for Sustainable Development Toolkit,* July 2002.

In 1961, Fidel Castro forced his country into solitary confinement when he declared, "Within the Revolution: Everything. Outside of it: Nothing." After 50 years, that is precisely what he got: everything turned to nothing.

excesses of the ruling class.

39. INFILTRATE AND REGULATE LABOR: Unionize all labor at all levels, and rule them by an international body of regulators. Install overseers to ensure that government mandates are obeyed.

In 1999, the U.N.'s International Labor Organization declared its purpose to provide "a strong social dimension to globalization [of labor] in achieving improved and fair outcomes for all ... to accelerate progress in the implementation of the Decent Work Agenda at the country level."[669]

40. UPHOLD ALL LABOR AS OPTIONAL: Make labor voluntary by providing financial safety nets for unemployment, illness, and retirement.

41. DISCREDIT THE U.S. CONSTITUTION: Re-educate the people regarding the American Constitution to cast it as inadequate and old-fashioned, a hindrance to cooperation between countries worldwide.

42. DISCREDIT FREEDOM HEROES: Discredit America's Founding Fathers and other heroes of freedom—cast them as elitists whose selfish desires left them no concern for "the little people."

43. DISCREDIT THE GREAT ENLIGHTENMENT AND AMERICAN CULTURE: Remove knowledge about the advances coming out of the Great Enlightenment and subsequent American Revolution, and white-wash U.S. history as relatively insignificant flotsam on the tides of history, an awkward child of the great enlightenment, 1500-1800. Emphasize the rich histories of other countries such as China, India, and Australia.

44. PROMOTE GOVERNMENT REGULATION: Support any movement that seeks government control over education, welfare, mental health clinics, social agencies, the arts, etc.

45. INSTALL SOCIALISM EVERYWHERE: For any emerging nation, move quickly to install socialism. Promote it as the most efficient model to achieve political and economic stability.

---

669   U.N., *ILO Declaration on Social Justice for a Fair Globalization*, June 10, 2008.

Socialists see light at the end of the tunnel as an excuse to buy more tunnel.

46. CREATE CRISIS: Trigger widespread disorder to justify massive changes in the governments of the world. Use periodic chaos as the means to expand top-down control and restrict personal rights.

LEARNING TO RECOGNIZE SOCIALISM

To most people it appears an almost impossible task to unravel, unwind, untwist, and dismantle the machinations of brute power.

The workings of socialism in all its assorted flavors and dispensations operate upon the same foundation: they take government control away from the people and use it to force change.

Controlling government force to respond to the people's will is what the U.S. Constitution offered the world. It was a magnificent proposition, based on faith in the people to be their own managers, to rule themselves according to natural law, to protect among one another the rights of property and choice.

So long as virtue exists among the people, so long as the cultural codes of honesty and decency live in the hearts of the people, so long as Christian patience and forgiveness and forbearance are nurtured among the races and cultures and alliances of all people, this proposition of self-mastery on a national level is viable, workable, and proven possible. When corruption enters the people's private lives, such corruption spreads to government— and suddenly, trust withers away, desperation, panic, and the ugly rawness of survival-greed take over, and everyone begins looking to get something for nothing—by force, if necessary. It's an ancient pattern that will forever repeat and re-invent itself until some day, one day, personal and national virtue returns once again. It will be a new beginning.

In 1933, Stalin's collective farming policy lead to the seizure of privately owned and farmed goods in and around Ukraine. This resulted in the starvation of 7 million people, an estimated 3 million of which were children. Today it is known as the Black Famine.

Part XVII

THE PROPER ROLE OF GOVERNMENT

"Government may not possess more rights than those held by the individual. The individual may delegate certain rights—defense, justice, and raising revenue—but the government may not simply assume them. When it does, that is tyranny."

—Author—

CHAPTER 90:

THE PROPER ROLE OF GOVERNMENT

The proper role of government is to protect unalienable rights and clear the way for people to prosper without violating those rights.

As illustrated in the previous chapters, governments throughout history have routinely followed the same patterns of usurpation to gain power over the masses. History shows a broad spectrum of assorted beginning places, but their ultimate ending places have been, more or less, all the same. Each has enthroned itself according to the seven pillars of socialism—and at the terrible expense of failing to protect the natural rights of its citizens.

When the U.S. Constitution was discussed and debated, its very design and purpose was to abolish that ages-old abuse of natural rights.

It created watchmen that were built right into its very fabric—a clearly-defined set of checks and balances—to jealously guard the actions of all handlers of government power. That structure of self-correcting tensions and counterbalancing forces was universal in its application across all national, cultural, and racial boundaries. All that it required to function was a minimal level of personal and national virtue.

As Franklin said, "As nations become more corrupt and vicious, they have more need of masters." When it comes to freedom, virtue is everything.

Sadly, because of corruption, neglect, and a constant chipping away at its foundations, the Constitution has lost much of its moral authority to guide America's affairs—not just by the letter of the law, but the spirit, as well.

For America, and for the world at large, to regain control over run-away governments, there needs to be a clear, common starting place. The following is a good one to consider:

In 1968, Ezra Taft Benson, former Secretary of Agriculture under President Dwight Eisenhower, gave a speech outlining the proper

---

"Society cannot exist, unless a controlling power upon the will and appetite is placed somewhere; and the less of it there is within, the more there must be without."—Edmond Burke

role of government. Each point of his message was a sermon by itself, and the very antithesis of all that socialism strives to do:

1. **FOUNDED ON GOD**: "I believe that no people can maintain freedom unless their political institutions are founded upon faith in God and belief in the existence of moral law."

2. **RIGHTS**: "I believe that God has endowed men with certain unalienable rights as set forth in the Declaration of Independence and that no legislature and no majority, however great, may morally limit or destroy these; that the sole function of government is to protect life, liberty, and property and anything more than this is usurpation and oppression."

3. **LAW IS SUPREME**: "I believe that the Constitution of the United States was prepared and adopted by men acting under inspiration from Almighty God; that it is a solemn compact between the peoples of the States of this nation which all officers of government are under duty to obey; that the eternal moral laws expressed therein must be adhered to or individual liberty will perish."

4. **RESPONSIBILITIES**: "I believe it a violation of the Constitution for government to deprive the individual of either life, liberty, or property except for these purposes:

"(a) Punish crime and provide for the administration of justice;

"(b) Protect the right and control of private property;

"(c) Wage defensive war and provide for the nation's defense;

"(d) Compel each one who enjoys the protection of government to bear his fair share of the burden of performing the above functions."

5. **CAN'T DELEGATE FALSE RIGHTS**: "I hold that the Constitution denies government the power to take from the individual either his life, liberty, or property except in accordance with moral law; that the same moral law which governs the actions of men when acting alone is also applicable when they act in concert with others; that no citizen or group of citizens has any right to direct their agent, the government to perform any act which would be evil or offensive to the conscience if that citizen were performing the act himself outside the framework of government."

"When the righteous are in authority, the people rejoice: but when the wicked beareth rule, the people mourn." Proverbs 29:2

6. **RELIGION, ARMS, PROPERTY**: "I am hereby resolved that under no circumstances shall the freedoms guaranteed by the Bill of Rights be infringed. In particular I am opposed to any attempt on the part of the federal Government to deny the people their right to bear arms, to worship and pray when and where they choose, or to own and control private property."

7. **LEGALLY ANTI-COMMUNIST**: "I consider ourselves at war with international Communism which is committed to the destruction of our government, our right of property, and our freedom; that it is treason as defined by the Constitution to give aid and comfort to this implacable enemy."

8. **LEGALLY ANTI-SOCIALISM**: "I am unalterably opposed to Socialism, either in whole or in part, and regard it as an unconstitutional usurpation of power and a denial of the right of private property for government to own or operate the means of producing and distributing goods and services in competition with private enterprise, or to regiment owners in the legitimate use of private property."

9. **FAIR TAXES**: "I maintain that every person who enjoys the protection of his life, liberty, and property should bear his fair share of the cost of government in providing that protection; that the elementary principles of justice set forth in the Constitution demand that all taxes imposed be uniform and that each person's property or income be taxed at the same rate."

10. **COINAGE**: "I believe in honest money, the gold and silver coinage of the Constitution, and a circulation medium convertible into such money without loss. I regard it as a flagrant violation of the explicit provisions of the Constitution for the federal government to make it a criminal offense to use gold or silver coin as legal tender or to use irredeemable paper money."

11. **SOVEREIGN STATES**: "I believe that each State is sovereign in performing those functions reserved to it by the Constitution and it is destructive of our federal system and the right of self-government guaranteed under the Constitution for the federal government

to regulate or control the States in performing their functions or to engage in performing such functions itself."

12. **POLITICAL WELFARE**: "I consider it a violation of the Constitution for the federal government to levy taxes for the support of state or local government; that no State or local government can accept funds from the federal and remain independent in performing its functions, nor can the citizens exercise their rights of self-government under such conditions."

13. **ANTI-FOREIGN AID**: "I deem it a violation of the right of private property guaranteed under the Constitution for the federal government to forcibly deprive the citizens of this nation of their property through taxation or otherwise, and make a gift thereof to foreign governments or their citizens."

14. **NO FOREIGN CONTROL**: "I believe that no treaty or agreement with other countries should deprive our citizens of rights guaranteed them by the Constitution."

15. **STRONG DEFENSE**: "I consider it a direct violation of the obligation imposed upon it by the Constitution for the federal government to dismantle or weaken our military establishment below that point required for the protection of the States against invasion, or to surrender or commit our men, arms, or money to the control of foreign or world organizations of governments."

"These things I believe to be the proper role of government."

THE PROPER ROLE OF GOVERNMENT CAN'T EVOLVE

For the same reason that human nature doesn't change, neither should the authority granted to governments ever change.

Government may not possess more rights than those held by the individual. The individual may delegate certain rights—defense, justice, and raising revenue—but the government may not simply assume them. When it does, that is tyranny.

With these ideals in mind, what are the next steps forward?

(cont'd) "... socialism in the United States through a series of New Deals. ...If socialism (i.e. the ownership of the state of all significant means of production) is to preserve democracy, it must be brought about step by step. ..."—Arthur Schlesinger, Jr.

Part XVIII
THE NEW BEGINNING

"Happily for America, happily we trust for the whole human race, they pursued a new and more noble course. They accomplished a revolution which has no parallel in the annals of human society."

—James Madison—

CHAPTER 91:
THE NEW BEGINNING

There is a strong basis for abolishing socialism from the earth—not just temporarily, but completely and for all time. It has something to do with birds, frogs, snakes, and raccoons.

LETTING OTHERS DO THE WORK

One specie of the cuckoo bird has an interesting laziness to her nature. Perhaps it's not laziness, maybe it's her clever exploitation of circumstances—it is difficult to read nature at this level.

When the cuckoo hen needs to lay her egg, sometimes she flies about to locate the nests of other birds. She will wait patiently until the nest is unguarded, and then swoop in, lay her egg, and leave it for tending by other birds. This frees her from nest duty. She is free to fly. The unsuspecting nest owner returns to see the egg, or if it's among her own, maybe not notice, and plops down to warm and protect them, keeping the eggs safe until hatching.

This trick doesn't always work. Some birds recognize the strange addition and remove the egg completely. Nevertheless, it's a great way to get what the cuckoo hen wants without the responsibilities and consequences—or so it would seem.

"CAREFUL, THAT WILL LAND YOU IN HOT WATER!"

There's the old story of the frog standing on his hind legs in the pot of water that was just placed over a hot stove. At first, the water is cool, a temperature typical for any pond or gentle stream he is familiar with—just like home. So, the frog is content to stay for a minute. He senses no urgency to leap away.

As the water becomes warmer, a relaxing embrace of summertime comfort entices the frog to bask in the delicious lure, and his eyes go half closed—he thinks a short nap would be nice, and does not leap away.

As the water gradually becomes hot, the frog suddenly realizes he is in danger. His instinct is to leap away but his legs and muscles have become too weak—he tries, but fails to find the strength. The heat quickly overcomes him and he dies in the boiling broth.

YOU KNEW I WAS A SNAKE WHEN YOU PICKED ME UP

In an adaptation of Aesop's fable, a hiker is working his way off a mountain and comes upon a snake. The snake addresses the hiker and pleads for a ride down to the valley below. The hiker hesitates, but eventually agrees to do this favor for the snake.

Upon arriving at the bottom, the hiker sets the snake down and is promptly bitten. As the hiker falls to the ground, shocked and saddened at the sudden betrayal, the snake replies, "Why are you surprised? You knew I was a snake when you picked me up."

HOW CURIOSITY KILLED THE RACCOON

The classic children's book *Where the Red Fern Grows*, tells the heartwarming story of a boy and his two Redbone Coonhound hunting dogs. Early in the book, author Wilson Rawls unfolds an exchange where Grandpa explains to his young grandson Billy how to catch a raccoon with a simple trap.

The trick, Grandpa said, is to bore a deep hole in a log and pound four nails around the outside at an angle so their points pierce the inside of the hole. The idea is to leave just enough space for a raccoon's paw to fit through. Put a shiny piece of tin at the bottom and the raccoon's curiosity will get the best of him—

"It'll catch him all right," Grandpa said, "and it won't fail. You see, a coon is a curious little animal. Anything that is bright and shiny attracts him. He will reach in and pick it up. When his paw closes on the bright object it balls up, and when he starts to pull it from the hole, the sharp ends of the nails will gouge into his paw and he's caught."

Billy thinks it over a bit and decides Grandpa is telling a big joke. Growing angry, he gets up to leave but Grandpa calls him back and tells about a time when as a boy he had his own pet raccoon, and how he learned his pet would do exactly that—ball up his fist when he got hold of something he wanted, and refuse to let go. He told how the whole family had to hold down the raccoon to release his grip on a pat of butter he grabbed by reaching into the the small hole in the lid of a butter churn. His balled-up fist was too big to pull back through, and he was caught.

Billy becomes convinced and goes to the nearby woods to give the idea a try. The next morning, he finds a raccoon stuck with its paw in the trap. It hisses and growls as Billy approaches, but won't let go. Billy calls his family to come see, and they're all surprised that grandpa's idea really worked. Billy's father kills the raccoon and goes about releasing it from the trap.

> After Papa had pulled the nails, he lifted the coon's paw from the hole. There, clamped firmly in it, was the bright piece of tin.

> In a low voice Papa said, "Well, I'll be darned. All he had to do was open it up and he was free, but he wouldn't do it. Your grandfather was right.[670]

LETTING GO OF SOCIALISM

Comfort, ease, and security are difficult to let go for the sake of long term prosperity. Most people in countries ruined by socialism are in that trap. They don't want to let go of their pensions, monthly checks, food stamps, insurance, housing, transportation, or anything coming to them gratis from the government. Like the cuckoo hen, people on welfare grow content to leave the burden of their financial and medical care in the nest of another's labors.

But like the frog's trap, socialism's promise of an easy life feels good until enough time has passed and financial reality sneaks up hot and boiling, and quickly turns deadly.

Like the snake's ulterior motives, the appeal to embrace the hopes for an easier life may seem right at first. But when a socialistic takeover has reached its goal, there is deadly betrayal for which hundreds of millions have been sacrificed already.

And like the raccoon, that shiny bit of tin—the hope for free money from everyone else, a bit of nothing that seemed so important and desirable at first, soon turns out to be a trap holding fast those who can't let go, from which the only escape is death.

THE BIRTHING GROUNDS OF FREEDOM

In the 1770s, the rugged settlers of a rough-hewn agrarian society, grossly underrated as mere *American colonists*, launched a unique and unprecedented revolution against the world's greatest military power.

From these humble beginnings, pockmarked with risk and resistance, grew an uprising of the noblest kind.

Their ensuing shout for freedom was no coincidental gasp of the beleaguered. It was a brilliant declaration of principle. It was

---

670   All excerpts by Woodrow Wilson Rawls, *Where the Red Fern Grows*, 1961.

founded not on guns and cannon fire, nor bayonets and open fields of slaughter. This revolution was rooted in the simple but eloquent words of Jesus, "... know the truth and the truth shall make you free."[671]

What is this truth that exposes and reveals so much with such liberating strength as to serve the cause to "make you free"?[672] Has truth the fortitude to abolish socialism?

The truth is, the "laws of Nature and of Nature's God" are at the foundation of all good government. It is a condition of liberty that natural law be honored and sustained, and the people have a natural affinity and love for "Nature's God," God's laws of justice, and their fellow man.

The truth is, self-mastery is necessary for freedom. It is a condition of liberty that "Only a virtuous people are capable of freedom," because "as nations become corrupt and vicious, they have more need of masters."[673]

The truth is, religion is the most efficient structure to elicit individual self-restraint and selflessness for an orderly and peaceful society. It is a condition of liberty that religion be freely allowed to work its refining influence on the people—without force or compulsion—as the means to prepare leaders and followers with the highest caliber of integrity, honesty, compassion, virtue, and ethics.

The truth is, all people possess unalienable rights that no other has the moral authority to abrogate. It is a condition of liberty that rights be jealously guarded and preserved as the well-spring from which solutions to all problems will emerge.

The truth is, all men are created equal, but that's all. After birth, the only equality is in the eyes of God, in the eyes of the law, and in the endowment of unalienable rights. It is a condition of liberty that life's struggles remain unimpeded by government intervention except to rectify violations of moral law.

The truth is, equal things are impossible. The expectation of equal outcomes and material items is the work of envy. Envy doesn't build or create—it is mortality's second worst enemy next to death. A condition of liberty is the firm rooting of free choice in all

---

671   John 8:32 KJV.
672   For an expanded discussion how truth creates freedom, see Ezra Taft Benson, *The Proper Role of Government*, 1975.
673   Smyth, *Writings of Benjamin Franklin*, 9:569.

human action within the boundaries of moral law—even the freedom to fail.

The truth is, those who shirk their responsibilities will forever look to government to take from those who "have" and give it over by force to those who "have not." It is a condition of liberty that each person acquires a strong work ethic, stand on his or her own feet, prepare for emergencies, and work for their lives.

The truth is, compassion for others and a spirit of service and charity is a condition of liberty. Experience and reason prove that delegating to the government the natural human trait to alleviate suffering will inevitably destroy a nation's economy. A condition of liberty is leaving the care of the needy in private hands.

The truth is, the government may possess no more rights than those possessed by the individual. A condition of liberty is a strongly worded written constitution binding the government from mischief, and a process of checks and balances to ensure that the government does not stray from those boundaries.

The truth is, international alliances that take private property from the people and lend or gift it to other governments is an unjust theft of private labor. It is a condition of liberty that a nation's sovereign laws never become subordinate to foreign powers.

The truth is, every person who is blessed with the protection of his or her life, liberty, and property is obligated to carry their portion of the cost for such protection. It is a condition of liberty that taxes taken from the people for these purposes are uniform and are taken from the people at the same rate.

The truth is, private control over public money will profit those private managers and their friends at the taxpayers' expense, and lead to mismanagement and disaster. It is a condition of liberty that the people themselves manage their national money supply.

The truth is, duties delegated to the central government must be few and defined, while duties for local government are many and undefined. It is a condition of liberty that prosperity grows from the lowest levels of society upwards—from individual labors, not from government regulation, management, and meddling.

All regimes now standing cannot survive an examination of their behaviors with the light of such truths spotlighting their abuses.

The truth is, being free to choose is the only answer that endures—being free to let go of those shiny pieces of government-minted tin and escaping into the vast potential of self-made opportunity is the power of freedom, and it must be protected.

Creating our own opportunities is the reason we exist.

The obscure Quaker Isaac Potts, an otherwise unknown and insignificant figure in history, told of a poignant moment he personally witnessed during the ravages of the early days of America's War for Independence. It was a scene at Valley Forge—amply recreated in paintings, drawings and popular media—of George Washington, the general of the American army, a bowed man whose shoulders carried the burdens of freedom through that grist mill of defeat and deprivation, dropping to his knees in final desperation to lay his petition for relief before God.

Quaker Potts is the sole source of the details of this event, telling it to family and associates, a tale of lasting endurance drawn from the frozen mud of stark discouragement and death among the dwindling hovels of troops who then sustained the cause of freedom that wintry day.

Seldom mentioned about this lowest point of that slogging struggle is that after his fervent and private communion with his Father in Heaven, General Washington gathered about himself what remained of his faith, his courage, and his inner resolve—and the man stood up.

He stood up against the arrogance of an all-powerful ruler who had dispatched death to smother the embers of freedom.

He stood up against the arbitrary chains of abject obedience forged around the throats of people wanting nothing more but their liberty and their lives.

He stood up against the tyrant who held the executioner's axe that forced Washington and his troops into this forge of the worst kind.

He stood up against an impotent Congress, rendered chaotic and inept to unify the colonies or materially support the war because of their Articles of Confederation.

He stood up against the consuming collapse of a broken heart for the losses of men about him, suffering through starvation, disease, and the cold, leaving nameless bloody tracks in the snow as monuments to their passages through the great struggle for freedom.

He stood up against the fear for his own existence, his neglected labors at Mount Vernon, his Martha, his family, his personal fortune, the things a man labors for to sustain and secure him through such crushing times as these.

He stood up against all that would destroy and enslave and end the great cause that brought them to this place in the snow, this Valley Forge, where the only sentinel preventing an escape was his own personal resolve. And all around him, the powers of the cold, the elements, the collapsing decay of mortality and conflict, squeezed away the last drops of ability and hope, and callously poured them into the frozen earth—leaving just threadbare fingers of faith clutched in humble prayer. For this, George Washington stood up this one last time—for his life, for his liberty, and for his sacred honor.

And when he stood up, others in their rags and illness saw it. Taking courage, they stood up with him.

Every person *must* stand up who desires freedom—stand up against the forces that are drowning human capacity. It begins, simply enough, at home—No more borrowing, no more debt, no more personal vices and temptation, no more slavery to bad habits, no more lethargy toward political participation, no more fear of a neighbor or a neighbor's needs, no more tolerance of tyrannical force—but a renewed devotion to a humble reliance on God, and the gifts and talents He bestows on each of us. And to the extent that individuals are willing to live worthy of true freedom and liberty, so rises a nation, patterned after the divine, and created in *their* image, a reflection of a people's willingness and choice to live the virtues necessary for freedom.

The impact of this personal pursuit of private virtue spreads easily—from individual to family, to friends, to communities and regions—then across countries, across the sea, and around the world. The promise of freedom, the freedom to choose in this world of oppression and force, assuredly opens the very powers of the universe into this mortal sphere, bringing all of the joys, liberties, and satisfactions possible in this life. The promise, if we want it, is freedom for all mankind, and freedom in our day. The beginning place is in our homes, in our private lives, and in the depth of our very souls. The virtues of freedom must first be found in us.

The cycle of
socialism.

The Ouroboros—from the Greek meaning
"tail" (ouro) and "eating" (boros)

THE OUROBOROS

" . . . Socialism
progresses like a snake
eating its tail . . . .
Let them pray, therefore,
that their tail be
very, very long."

—Author—

APPENDIX

- The Day the Socialists Took My Honey and Nectar
- "ObamaCare"
- A President's Private Army?
- Why is Socialism So Appealing?
- Sample Fruits of Socialism
- It Takes A Family
- A Khrushchev Quote
- Acknowledgements
- About the Author
- Selected Bibliography
- Quotes on Section Headers
- "Factoids"
- Index

THE DAY THE SOCIALISTS TOOK MY HONEY AND NECTAR

The finest example of socialism's beautiful promise is not in Russia, China, Venezuela, Sweden, or Cuba. If you really want to see the utopia that socialists long for, of no war, no want, no discord, and no conspiracy to overthrow, then stop over at Paul's place.

Late July in the western United States is the best time to see this goal of perfect socialism in action. To witness it yourself, let Paul give you a tour of his manufacturing facility. It only takes a few minutes.

You'll recognize it instantly—thousands of socialists perfectly organized, never complaining, and faithfully on the job. Paul says they've been living for decades in exactly what the socialists envision.

NO INTERVENTION REQUIRED

Paul reports that no outsider intervenes or disciplines the workers—they take care of everything themselves, from food and housing to employment and work assignments, police and community defense, public utilities, equality for all females, sewage disposal, and cradle-to-grave care and compensation.

The only disruption in their well-ordered society is when Paul comes to take away their honey—honeybees don't like that.[674]

DO BE A DO-BEE—DON'T BE A DON'T-BEE

They call it an apiary. Paul's is a stack of three wooden boxes painted white. The top box has a lid the bees glue down with a mysterious bee-epoxy. It's their futile attempt to keep him from stealing the fruits of their labors.

Inside each box are ten wooden frames hanging side by side holding a plastic sheet whereon the bees feverishly build their wax honeycomb. The frames are spaced just right so the workers can comfortably move about with ease and tend to chores.

Paul says he doesn't see any deviation from the way the bees do things. They always make their wax cells the same way, six-sided,

---

674   Based on Author's personal experience raising honeybees.

identical size. Some cells receive the honey—the honey comb. The others receive the queen's eggs—the brood comb.

UNIVERSAL EMPLOYMENT

Honeybees are social insects that work together to stay alive. Each bee has a job. Several thousand are out during the daylight hours to visit flowers and blossoms, harvesting as much nectar as they can carry. The other bees are back at the hive cleaning out the cells or sealing them up with wax. Some bees are busy at the bottom of the boxes carrying out the garbage—dead bees, bee parts, sticks, grass, other insects, the usual beehive rubbish.

SELF-POLICING

The hive's front door is watched by the guard bees. In the heat of summer the guards stand at the entrance and with hundreds of others lined up in the hive, they ventilate by beating their wings. They also watch for illegals trying to get inside—flies, spiders, foreign bees, crawly things. The guards will sting them to death.

Outside, the bees control certain air space that leads to the hive. The bees decide the boundaries: Paul estimates theirs to be about 15 feet in all directions, and as high as his head. During peak production, the bees entering this space are loaded down and tired. They want to go directly to the entrance without interference. The guard bees ensure that the flight path is clear.

IT TAKES A COLONY TO RAISE HONEY

This huge cooperative supports the entire colony. As Marx envisioned socialism, each bee labors according to her ability and eats according to her needs. True to the promise of socialism, when each is doing her job, there is just enough honey for their needs.

RULER AND CASTE SYSTEM

Paul says his bees have a natural caste system: the fertile queen, the infertile female workers, and the couch-potato male drones.

The queen is the supreme ruler. She stings other bees to get her way, but usually she's too busy. She is guarded, groomed, and watched. When she leaves the hive, sometimes half the bees go with her. If she's accidently killed or stops laying eggs, the worker bees feed royal jelly to a new female bee still in larvae stage and grow themselves a new queen. The queen can live through half a dozen winters, unlike the worker bees. In the middle of the summer many workers can be seen with damaged or frayed wings. They literally work themselves to death in just a few weeks.

The worker bees are all infertile females. They typically number 20,000-30,000, or more. These girl bees do all the heavy lifting: they guard the hive, make thousands of trips for nectar, turn it into honey, seal the cells, take out the trash, do the dishes—just about everything necessary to survive.

And the male drones? There are usually 100-200, not many, and they just eat honey and stay out of the way, drifting from hive to hive—unless there's a new queen that needs to be fertilized. Fertilizing the queen are the drones' only purpose for living. It happens in mid-flight, then he falls to the ground and dies.

All bees know where they fit in the universal order of things, and stick to their jobs until they die.

INFORMATION AND THINGS IN COMMON

Paul uses the old smoke trick to take the bees' honey. Somehow bees know about smoke. He has a small tin can with smoldering sticks or leaves. A bellows on the side lets him puff the smoke into the apiary. The smell and pollution mask the bees' silent alarm system and trigger an "abandon the hive" panic.

The honey is their common storehouse for survival. They eat as much as they can, storing it in their honey stomach for regurgitation later. This gorging makes them very distracted and somewhat passive. The result is that they don't fly—they just crawl around. The old smoke trick fools them into a panic—and that's when Paul pops the lid, grabs their honeycomb and runs.

REGULATION AND FORCE

Overpopulation is handled by the bees themselves. When the hive becomes overcrowded, they grow a new queen, launch her on a maiden voyage, and half the bees move out with her. That's bad for a beekeeper because honey production drops off until the population builds up again.

Several new queens are "grown" at the same time. The first to hatch from her cell will sting the unhatched queens to death, perhaps even hunt down the old queen and kill her. It's survival of the fittest among queen bees.

Then the new ruler queen goes buzzing away to celebrate out on the town. Her pheromones will attract drones from other hives for mating. Why drones from other hives? So the problems of inbreeding don't ruin the family reputation.

NO INDIVIDUAL RIGHTS—When winter comes, the drones are kicked out and the girl bees bunch up in a giant ball around the queen to protect her from the cold. Inside the ball, the temperature stays at least 85 degrees F. Bees stay warm by eating honey and vibrating—burning calories to generate heat. The unfortunate bees on the outside of the ball perish from the dangerous freezing temperatures and drop to the bottom of the hive. But the queen is safe.

Everyone depends on the queen doing her job, and the queen depends on everyone doing their jobs. At the expense of a few bees willing to sacrifice their lives, the colony continues to survive—the perfect socialist society.

INSECT MENTALITY WITH A HIGHER IQ? In theory, socialists dream that all of humanity can be organized to function like honeybees. The socialist philosophers believe that humans can be trained to be more concerned about their society, their apiary, than they are with their own selfish pursuits—and to become content with tending to the immediate needs that are assigned to them.

CAN IT WORK FOR HUMANS? The critical question is whether or not these processes observed in nature can translate over into the human world as government force to change society.

Bees perform the same unchanging chores all the time. They have one goal. It is well defined and is the same from one bee to the next, generation after generation. Humans are, of course, entirely different in every regard. They have goals unique to each—one wants a big family, to live in the city, and drive a Suburban. Another wants to live alone in a cabin, hunt and fish, not wear deodorant and raise honeybees. Bees in the hive are interchangeable—humans in the world are not.

Unlike bees, humans are hard wired with tremendous powers of reason, judgment, analysis, memory, survival, compassion, and an unquenchable desire to prosper. These tools of survival are unique to humans, and allow them to become independent of others. That's not good for the "human apiary"—socialism depends on predictable cooperation. What they want is a world patterned after the insects, the bees, the ants, or some other example in nature that perpetuates the specie. For human beings, the only world that will stand the test of time is one built on freedom within the boundaries of constitutional liberty. It's not any more complicated than that.

"OBAMACARE"

President Obama's Patient Protection and Affordable Care Act
forced America to open a vein and dive into shark-infested waters.

Signed into law March 23, 2010, the so-called ObamaCare
national health care was the United States' first serious foray
into national health care. It was intended to extend health
insurance to millions of uninsured, and correct some inequalities
in current insurance coverage. The final bill of 2,100+ pages was
not read by most of Congress prior to passage. It does not take a
Supreme Court decision to see that it is unconstitutional.

The built-in flaws inherent in ObamaCare include:[675]

❖ **TRILLIONS IN NEW DEBT**: Supporters project the cost to
reach $940 billion by 2019. More realistic estimates put the figure at
$2.5 trillion, at least.[676] As illustrated earlier, Congress' record for
predicting future costs is abysmally poor.

❖ **AVOIDS REAL PROBLEM**: The root cause of rising health
care costs are not dealt with by ObamaCare. Instead, the bill forces
coverage to increase by millions of people, premiums to increase by
as much as 13 percent,[677] and overall health care costs to increase by
a minimum $222 billion by 2019.[678]

❖ **NEW TAXES**: At least two dozen new taxes are imposed on
Americans with the passage of ObamaCare. These range from
penalty taxes for non-participants, to employer penalties for not
offering health coverage. Investors will suffer a new tax of 3.8
percent. It is estimated new taxes will reduce household income by
more than $17 billion a year, probably more.[679]

---

675   See Kathryn Nix, *Top 10 Disaster of ObamaCare*, The Heritage Foundation, No. 2848, March 30, 2010.

676   James C. Capretta, *ObamaCare Will Break the Bank, Not Reduce the Deficit*, The Foundry, March 18, 2010.

677   Congressional Budget Office, An Analysis of Health Insurance Permiums Under the Patient Protection and Affordable Care Act, November 30, 2009.

678   Richard S. Foster, Chief Actuary, Centres for Medicare and Medicaid Services, *Estimated Financial Effects of the 'Patient Protection and Affordable Care Act,' as Passed by the Senate on December 24, 2009*, January 8, 2010.

679   Karen Campbell, Guinevere Nell, *The President's Health Proposal: Taxing Investments Undermines Economic Recovery*," Heritage Foundation WebMemo No. 2817, February 25, 2010; Americans for Tax Reform, *Comprehensive List of Tax Hikes in ObamaCare*, January 14, 2011.

◆ **MANDATED COVERAGE**: The healthcare bill forces minimum coverage requirements on all private insurance programs, and sets up the government's plan to compete directly with private insurance.[680]

◆ **EXPANDED MEDICAID**: By 2019, some 32 million would be added to the national insurance program, and at least half would be covered by Medicaid. Anyone with an income of less than 133 percent of the federal poverty level will be covered.[681]

◆ **STATES BEAR THE LOAD**: States would pay up to half of the expenses for Medicaid with the federal government matching the costs. The new bill relaxes how many people qualify for Medicaid, and fails to cover increased administrative costs. Projected *new* costs for just the states alone, from 2013-2019, will probably exceed $60 billion, or about $1.2 billion per state.[682] In 2012, the Court struck down the requirement that states expand Medicaid as part of ObamaCare, saying states may choose whether to accept grants for these purposes, or not.[683]

◆ **UNCONSTITUTIONAL**: The arguments for and against national health care center on these constitutional principles:

WELFARE CLAUSE: Article 1.8 does not include health care as a valid use of taxpayers' money. In 2012, the Supreme Court upheld this position, rejecting the personal mandate on this basis. However, the Court allowed the personal mandate on the basis of Congress's power to "lay and collect taxes" (also Article 1.8) whether we participate in health care or not.

INTERSTATE COMMERCE: Article 1.8 allows regulation of commerce between states. Insurance is a state-by-state negotiation not traded with other states. Calling ObamaCare a tax successfully steps around this problem because taxation falls within Congress's powers, the Court said in 2012.

NINTH & TENTH AMENDMENTS: Powers not given to the federal government, such as national insurances of any type, belong to the states (such as already practiced by Tennessee, Massachusetts, and Hawaii)

---

680   Ibid., Kathryn Nix.
681   Congressional Budget Office, *H.R. 4872, Reconciliation Act of 2010.*
682   Edmund Haislmaier, *Expanding Medicaid: The Real Costs to the States*, Heritage Foundation WebMemo No. 2757, January 14, 2010.
683   See supra, slip op., at 58.

COMPULSION: There is *no* constitutional authority in the slightest degree to force citizens to purchase a commodity such as health care. The Court continued the New Deal slide towards uncontrolled federal control over states and individual rights, and the people have become relatively powerless to do a thing about it. Europe's slide into financial ruin now lays in America's future, and it was completely avoidable. The only option is a new action by Congress to revoke ObamaCare in total, and revisit the issues on the state level.

A PRESIDENT'S PRIVATE ARMY?

Part of a dictator's climb to power is a private enforcement army that stands outside the law but obeys an emperor's every whim. Such an army helps consolidate power, especially in the throes of a national crisis.

On July 2, 2008 in Colorado Springs, Barack Obama sent cold shivers of alarm down 100 million spines when he called for a private civilian guard. Said he, "We cannot continue to rely on our military in order to achieve the national security objectives we've set. We've got to have a civilian national security force that's just as powerful, just as strong, just as well-funded."

NO, HE DIDN'T—A first knee-jerk reaction to what a civilian national security force meant was discounted by some observers as a poorly phrased idea actually meant to turn America into a giant community of millions of tax-funded "volunteer" groups. That theory had support from both Obama's plan to fund his civilian guard, and the general thrust of his policy to dismantle American culture, tradition, and ethics.

YES, HE DID—But the other interpretation surmises that Obama wanted to create a giant police force. If Obama wasn't talking about a police force, then why did he use perfect descriptors such as: a "national security force"; "just as powerful"; and "just as well-funded"?

"Force" against others means doing it against someone's will—a strange declaration in a country where the power is supposed to be in, by, and from the people.

"Strong," in that context must mean there's a use of weapons.

And "funding," he implied, must be comparable to the defense budget ($600 billion).

Any discussion that includes the words "community organizing" is a real yawner, so let's not waste space on that. But the primary theory about installing a private police force or army is not without precedent. Here's how others did it.

HISTORY: In ancient Rome, a commander over an army deployed to the field was called a praetor. His tent or house was called a praetorium. For reasons of personal protection from assassination by some other leader or to intimidate challengers, a powerful military leader would hand-pick some soldiers to guard his house and person, trusted men he could count on both when he slept and in the midst of a crisis, men to "watch his back." This band of protectors became known as his praetorian guard.

The Praetorian Guard was unconditionally loyal and fiercely attached to powerful people to help them stay in power.

When Augustus became the first emperor of Rome in 27 B.C., he decided such a guard could help him politically as well as militarily. He set up nine large units in Rome to provide around-the-hourglass protection. He sent others to patrol neighboring towns and the borderlands for signs of rebellion or conspiracy.

HONORS AND ACCOLADES—It was a huge honor to a soldier and his family to be picked out of the regular ranks to serve in the guard. The selection process was sometimes elaborate and well paraded. It didn't matter if the man was a foot soldier or cavalry because both were needed.

Rome's Praetorian Guards were grouped in 60, 80, and sometimes 100 men forming a century. Six of those made up a cohort (500-600 men). Ten of those made up a Legion (5,000-6,000 men).

The Praetorian Guard evolved from a military roll to having a strong political function. Sometimes they assassinated weak leaders to install someone stronger. With all the problems going on in Rome, this military junta served to keep things relative stable despite the ruthless manner whereby they carried out an emperor's wishes. Constantine I disbanded the guard around A.D. 312.

NAPOLEON'S PRAETORIAN GUARDS—The idea of a private security force has kept tyrants in power for a long time. Napoleon's small but elite guard was organized in 1799, first as his personal bodyguard, and second to protect the executive offices of the French Republic. Napoleon was cautious about sending them out into battle. He treated them well, giving them more pay and better equipment and accommodations than the regular army. They also had their own artillery and cavalry. Beginning with only 1,000 men, Napoleon expanded it to more than 100,000 in 1812. In 1815 at the Battle of Waterloo, Napoleon sent in his Imperial Guard at the last moment to attempt a victory, but was forced to retreat. The British destroyed both the guard and the regular French army. Napoleon was defeated, and his vaunted personal guard, his Praetorian Guard, was decimated.

WHY IS SOCIALISM SO APPEALING?

The experts explain their dream for happy living.

Q. **WILL I NEED MONEY?**
A. No. "In socialism," the World Socialist Party says, "people would obtain the food, clothes and other articles they needed for their personal consumption by going into a distribution center and taking what they needed without having to hand over either money or consumption vouchers."[684]

Q. May I still buy things?
A. Not any more. The Socialist Party of Great Britain explains: "In a socialist society there will be no market, no buying and selling, and no money. Exchange can have no function where everything belongs to everyone. All people will have free access to the goods

---

684   The World Socialist Party—www.wspus.org.

and services available."[685]

Q. With no money, do we all barter?

A. No, all things are everyone's. "In a socialist society, there will be no money and no barter," says WorldSocialism.org. "Goods will be voluntarily produced, and services voluntarily supplied to meet people's needs. People will freely take the things they need." [686]

Q. How do I buy a house?

A. You don't. "Houses and flats would be rent-free," says The World Socialist Party, "with heating, lighting and water supplied free of charge. Transport, communications, health care, education, restaurants and laundries would be organized as free public services. There would be no admission charge to theatres, cinemas, museums, parks, libraries and other places of entertainment and recreation. The best term to describe this key social relationship of socialist society is free access, as it emphasizes the fact that in socialism it would be the individual who would decide what his or her individual needs were."[687]

Q. That means equal shares for everyone?

A. No, but according to your needs. The Socialist Party of Canada explains, "People are different and have different needs. Some needs will be more expensive (in terms of resources and labour needed to satisfy them) than others."[688]

Q. What if people want too much?

A. Then it won't work. WorldSocialism.org explains that "In a socialist society 'too much' can only mean 'more than is sustainably produced.' If people decide that they (individually and as a society) need to over-consume then socialism cannot possibly work."[689]

Q. Am I forced to participate?

A. It's voluntary. The World Socialist Party says, "Work in socialist society could only be voluntary since there would be no group or organization in a position to force people to work against their will."[690]

---

685 The Socialist Party of Great Britain—see www.worldsocialism.org/spgb.
686 World Socialism—www.worldsocialism.org.
687 The World Socialist Party—see www.wspus.org.
688 World Socialism—www.worldsocialism.org.
689 Ibid.
690 Ibid.

Q. Yes, but really, am I forced or not?

A. Well, on second thought... Super-socialist George Bernard Shaw takes exception to the World Socialist Party: "You would be forcibly fed, clothed, lodged, taught, and employed whether you liked it or not," Shaw wrote in 1928. "If it were discovered that you had not character and industry enough to be worth all this trouble, you might possibly be executed in a kindly manner; but whilst you were permitted to live you would have to live well."[691]

Q. Does socialism free me from religion?

A. Yes, a glorious freedom. "Religion is the sigh of the oppressed creature," Karl Marx said, "the sentiment of a heartless world, as it is the spirit of spiritless conditions. It is the opium of the people."[692]

Q. Will the government still persecute me?

A. No, there will be no government. "The state, then, is ... simply a product of society at a certain stage of evolution," Friedrich Engels said. "It is the confession that this society has become hopelessly divided against itself, has entangled itself in irreconcilable contradictions which it is powerless to banish."[693]

Q. What does Einstein think about socialism?

A. He likes it. The smartest man in the world would do better sticking to physics. "A planned economy, which adjusts production to the needs of the community," Albert Einstein explained, "would distribute the work to be done among all those able to work and would guarantee a livelihood to every man, woman, and child."[694]

Q. Does socialism free me from the Bible?

A. Yes, it will free you at last. "With him (the communist) the end justifies the means," said William Z. Foster, an avowed communist. "Whether his tactics be 'legal' or 'moral' or not, does not concern him, so long as they are effective. He knows that the laws as well as the current code of morals are made by his mortal enemies . . . Consequently, he ignores them insofar as he is able, and it suits his purposes. He proposed to develop, regardless of capitalist conceptions of 'legality,' 'fairness,' 'right,' etc., a greater power than his capitalist enemies have . . ." Vladimir Lenin summarized it best:

---

691   George Bernard Shaw, "The Intelligent Woman's Guide to Socialism and Capitalism," 1928, p. 470.
692   Karl Marx, *Critique of Hegel's Philosophy of Right.*
693   Friedrich Engels, *The origin of the family, private property and the State*, p. 206.
694   Albert Einstein, *Why Socialism?*, Monthly Review, May 1949.

"We say that our morality is wholly subordinated to the interest of the class-struggle of the proletariat." Engels declared: "We therefore reject every attempt to impose on us any moral dogma whatever . . ."[695]

Q. Is it wrong to want things under socialism?
A. Only if it somehow hurts others. The World Socialist Movement says, "Socialism will be a society in which satisfying an individual's self interest is the result of satisfying everyone's needs. It is enlightened self-interest."[696]

Q. What if I don't want my neighbor's cows?
A. They're yours anyway. Paul Hubert Casselman says in the Labor Dictionary that "[Socialism is] an economic theory which holds that ownership of property should be in the group and not in the individuals who make up the group. Collectivism may be partial or complete."[697]

Q. May I stake a claim and be on my own?
A. No, we're in this together. "[Socialism] therefore aims at the reorganization of Society," says Anne Fremantle, "by the emancipation of Land and Industrial Capital from individual ownership, and the vesting in them in the community for the general benefit ... for the transfer to the community ... of all such industries as can be conducted socially."[698]

Q. Can I still save a little to get ahead?
A. No, it's no longer about you. Norman Thomas said, "[Socialism is] control of economic processes for human use rather than for individual profit."[699]

Q. Can I stop worrying about my future?
A. Yes, socialism covers everything. "Under capitalism and the previous systems," the Socialist Party of Canada explains, "people have good reason to worry about tomorrow—they can lose their jobs, or be injured, or grow old, and need a cushion of wealth to fall back on. In a socialist society, everyone is entitled to have their

---

695 William Z. Foster, *Syndicalism*, pg. 3.
696 World Socialist Movement, 2006.
697 Paul Hubert Casselman, Labor Dictionary, New York: Philosophical Library, 1949, p. 63.
698 Anne Fremantle *This Little Band of Prophets: The British Fabians*, p. 263 (Note: The Fabians coat-of-arms is a wolf in sheep's clothing).
699 Norman Thomas, *America's Way Out: A Program for Democracy*, p. 54.

needs met. They won't be kicked out onto the street, or forced to give up the pleasures of life. There will be no poverty. The 'cushion' will be cooperatively provided by all."[700]

Q. Could I be arrested for stealing?

A. There's no such thing as 'stealing.' Engels wrote that the Ten Commandments, in particular "Thou Shalt Not Steal" and "Thou Shalt Not Covet," were examples of the exploiters forcing respect for private property onto the masses. "Thou shalt not steal," Engels said. "Does this law thereby become an eternal moral law? By no means."[701]

Q. Don't the rich owe me some help?

A. They do, and socialism shares that around. "The vast majority of workers are not paid according to the full value of what they produce," The Marxist Encyclopedia declares. "If all workers in a workplace were paid this full value, then the boss would have nothing to survive on, since labour is the source of all value!"[702]

Q. Are unions part of socialism?

A. Yes, a union is democracy in the workplace—one worker, one vote, regardless of who owns the business. The Marxist Encyclopedia answers: "The vast majority of workers in the world are over-worked: required to put in more hours than is socially necessary in order to create profits. ... Unions can force the boss to hire more workers, instead of constantly increasing the burdens on existing employees. The union can also ensure that in emergency cases where someone must work over time, they are fairly compensated for (contrary to popular understanding—overtime compensation is compulsory only for unskilled workers in a handful of countries)."[703]

Q. Will there need to be national borders?

A. Not any more. "According to its basic principles," socialist Eric Fromm said, "the aim of socialism is the abolition of national sovereignty, the abolition of any kind of armed forces, and the establishment of a commonwealth of nations."[704] "[Socialism] insists on a comradeship of the workers which transcends racial or nation-

---

700   See www.worldsocialism.org.
701   Friedrich Engels, *Herr Eugen During's Revolution in Science*, 1894.
702   Encyclopedia of Marxism, *Wage & Benefits*.
703   Encyclopedia of Marxism, *Unions*.
704   Erich From, *Let Man Prevail*, 1960, p. 26.

alist lines," said Norman Thomas. "It is therefore international in outlook."[705]

Q. What if I don't want to work?

A. Obviously you have to do something! "People will have to work, but it will be voluntary," says WorldSocialism.org. "If people didn't work society would obviously fall apart. To establish socialism the vast majority must consciously decide that they want socialism and that they are prepared to work in socialist society."[706]

Q. What if I change my mind about living in socialism?

A. Depends on whose socialism is used. The Socialist Party of Canada tries to have it both ways: "Those who disagree will be treated like anyone else. If a person or group decided to start promoting a return to capitalism, or some other class-divided social form, they would be free to do so. If however, a person or group was damaging society (beating people up, or blowing up buildings, etc.) then society will take appropriate action against them."[707]

Q. Must there be violence to switch to socialism?

A. It depends on how willing people are through the transition. Lenin called for a war for power among the masses to impose the dictatorship of the proletariat—"an organization for the systematic use of violence by ... one part of the population against another ... [and then] there will vanish all need for force, for the subjection of one man to another."[708]

Q. How does socialism get started?

A. Three simple steps. Engels explains: "By limiting private property in such a way that it gradually prepares the way for its transformation into social property, e.g., by progressive taxation, limitation of the right of inheritance in favor of the state, etc., etc. By employing workers in national workshops and factories and on national estates. By educating all children at the expense of the state."[709]

---

705 Norman Thomas, *America's Way Out: A Program for Democracy*, p. 55.
706 See www.worldsocialism.org.
707 Ibid.
708 Joseph Stalin, *Problems of Leninism*, pp. 26-27.
709 Friedrich Engels, *Draft of a Communist Confession of Faith*.

SAMPLE FRUITS OF RULER'S LAW

To what end does socialism extend its utopian
goals of universal happiness?

W hen people consent to Ruler's Law and a king in whatever form he is presented, they assume they will retain certain controls and guidelines over the ruler. History and current events show the opposite is true. Here are some samples of socialistic absurdities at work—behaviors far out of line with the expectations of the masses who are obligated to submit to the arrogance of misguided authority. These are the inflated decisions of people in charge who go looking to build private kingdoms of power—

SOCIALIST ABSURDITY: No hoarding of food
PRINCIPLE VIOLATED: Freedom to acquire property
STORY: In May 1918, Francis Smith Nash and his wife were charged with violating Section 6 of the U.S. government's Food Control act for storing a large supply of flour, sugar, and other foodstuffs in their home.

The 1917 Food and Fuel Act allowed Americans to store only a 30-day supply, an amount that Food Administrator Herbert Hoover deemed a "reasonable one." The purpose, Hoover said, was to keep the troops overseas supplied. The Nash's food stash, legally purchased over time, was valued at $1,923.36 ($31,700 in 2012 dollars). For this crime, the judge set their bail at $3,000 ($50,000 in 2012 dollars) each.

To escape punishment Nash tried to distribute the food to charity. The Food Administration said they would prosecute all food hoarders to the fullest extent of the law regardless of a hoarder's social standing or efforts to dispose of the evidence.[710]

SOCIALIST ABSURDITY: Forced recycling of trash
PRINCIPLE VIOLATED: Freedom to dispose of property
STORY: In 2010, Cleveland residents were warned that their curb side trash would soon be monitored to make sure they were recy-

---

710   The New York Times, May 30, 1918.

cling. If they didn't comply, they would be fined $100.[711]

Trash carts for recyclables were distributed with identification chips and bar codes. City workers started monitoring the activity of all such carts. If a cart was not wheeled to the curb for a few weeks in a row, this gave the Trash Czars automatic permission to dig through the companion trash cart's contents. Whenever more than 10% recyclable waste was discovered, the owners were fined $100.

Chip-embedded carts are in use in others parts of the U.S., England, and are catching on elsewhere.

SOCIALIST ABSURDITY: Banning lemonade stands
PRINCIPLE VIOLATED: Freedom to try, buy, sell, and fail
STORY: Julie Murphy was only 7 years old when Multnomah County (Oregon) shut down her lemonade stand for failing to obtain a $120 temporary restaurant license.

A health inspector patrolling the monthly art fair in northeast Portland confronted the girl for failing to produce a proper license and threatened her with a $500 fine.

Nearby booth people told Julie to stand her ground, but two inspectors came back a short time later and forced her to shut down. A growing crowd protested, and Julie started crying while her mother gathered up Julie's hand-made sign, her bottled water, and Kool-Aid and wheeled it away for home. Eric Pippert from the Oregon public health division vapidly responded with a bland, "Our role is to protect the public."[712]

The summer of 2011 saw half a dozen such cases across the U.S.

SOCIALIST ABSURDITY: New Black Panthers threaten voters
PRINCIPLE VIOLATED: Equal rights and responsibilities
STORY: On Election Day 2008, three New Black Panther party members intimidated voters with threats and coercion. They were dressed in military clothing, brandished batons, and stood menacingly outside a Philadelphia polling place. They threatened and verbally harassed black Republicans and whites who came to cast their votes. Their message was clear: vote for Obama or else.

Evidence of the Panthers' violation of the Voting Rights Act

---

711 Cleveland.com, August 20, 2010, "High-tech carts will tell on Cleveland residents who don't recycle ... and they face $100 fine."

712 Oregonlive.com, August 4, 2010, "Portland lemonade stand runs into health inspectors, needs $120 license to operate."

made it an open-and-shut case for President George Bush's Department of Justice.[713] But when President Barack Obama came to power, he appointed Eric Holder as attorney general. Holder dropped the charges after the thugs agreed to a plea deal not to do it again in that same city. The length of the probation? Only a couple of years, just in time to do it all over again for the 2012 elections.

The three walked free.

SOCIALIST ABSURDITY: National health care—Sweden
PRINCIPLE VIOLATED: Freedom to choose
STORY: In 2010, a bleeding man named "Jonas" who was waiting in a Swedish emergency room took matters into his own hands by sewing up a deep cut in his leg.

"It [waiting] took such a long time," Jonas told the Sundsvall Tidning Daily.

He said he first went to the regular health clinic, part of the socialized health-care program for which Sweden is so famous—it was closed. He called for help and was told the clinic wasn't supposed to be closed. That's when Jonas went to the emergency room of a hospital much farther away, but waited there more than an hour as his wound bled down his leg.

Deciding he had to take some kind of action, he sought out a sterile needle and thread and stitched the wound himself. Hospital staff caught him doing the procedure and reported him to the authorities. The charge was suspicion of arbitrary conduct for having used hospital equipment without authorization.[714] Socialism failed Jonas and punished him for disobeying control.

SOCIALIST ABSURDITY: National health care—Canada
PRINCIPLE VIOLATED: Freedom to choose
STORY: In July 2010, Christine Handrahan was nine weeks pregnant when she started bleeding. Fearing for her unborn baby's safety, her husband rushed her to Queen Elizabeth Hospital's new emergency room.

She sat waiting unattended in a packed waiting room for three hours, with blood seeping out of her jeans and tears of panic rolling down her cheeks. Finally fed up with the wait, the husband pushed

---

713 Department of Justice press release, January 7, 2009, "Justice Department Seeks Injunction Against New Black Panther Party."
714 "Jonas, 32 sewed up his own leg after ER wait," *The Local* (Sweden), August 4, 2010.

her wheelchair back to the parking lot where he helped her into their truck to make a 45-minute drive to Prince County Hospital, where Christine was given the sorry news that she had miscarried.

"Somebody should have cared enough to say, 'Oh my goodness, you're going through a miscarriage, do you need some quiet time?'" Christine said. "What bothered me the most was the fact that I had to sit in public going through a miscarriage."[715] Over-taxed national health care in Canada failed Christine.

SOCIALIST ABSURDITY: National health care—Britain
PRINCIPLE VIOLATED: Freedom to choose
STORY: Britain's famed National Health Service (NHS) has been around since 1948, the oldest and most socialized health-care system in the world. Though it has had more than 60 years to sort out the bugs and become lean and efficient, just the opposite has unfolded. It is a bloated, redundant, government-run institution that employs 1.5 million, is immune from change, and is losing money left and right. With few free-market forces to impose corrections, some real problems have erupted.

◆ **RUSHED—2007**: A doctor at St. Ann's Hospital, examining an 18-month-old baby, failed to notice that the child's back was broken. The baby died two days later. An investigation was squashed by the hospital's chief administrator. An independent report earlier warned that St. Ann's Hospital was "clinically risky."[716]

◆ **ELDER CARE—2011:** Some 100,000 terminally ill Englanders do not get proper care and run up costs by dying in the hospital instead of at home. New socialist measures are being deployed to grant each patient a pot of money based on circumstances to handle end-of-life expenses. Not mentioned is what happens when the pot of money runs dry.[717]

◆ **TOO SAD TO BE SAD—2011**: Rachael Dobson, 22, suffering from post-natal depression, was denied access to the U.K.'s NHS support group for post-natal depression sufferers because, they told her, she was too sad.[718] Her health visitor referred her to a community practice nurse from the mental health team. That nurse told Rachael to "work through it on your own."

715   The Guardian, "Christine Handrahan describes hours of tension in ER," 7/29/10.
716   Stephen Adams, "Doctors ask: Did Great Ormaond Street boss cover up hospital's role in Baby P Affair?", The Telegraph, October 16, 2011.
717   Andy Bloxham, "100,000 terminally ill ...'," The Telegraph, July 1, 2011.
718   Mail Online, *"You can't join NHS post-natal depression support group"*, June 30, 2011.

◆ **SELLING NAME LISTS—2011**: Legal firms offering to represent patients in law suits to win damages have been receiving private patient names and phone numbers after the patients leave the hospital. The hospitals denied that names were being sold for profit.[719]

◆ **HIDING INCOMPETENCE—2011**: European Union laws prevent Britain from verifying qualifications of foreign doctors. Many European countries refuse to reveal malpractice information, putting patients in England at risk from under-qualified doctors. A recent case involved a German-qualified cosmetic surgeon who accidently gave his 70-year-old patient a tenfold overdose of painkillers in 2008, killing the man. The doctor was found guilty. He moved back to Germany to continue practicing medicine.[720]

◆ **INCENTIVES TO WORK—2011**: Doctors receiving more money for performing certain treatments tended to ignore other activities that did not lead to extra money, a survey discovered. Quality of care that was not incentivized went down, while rewarded care went up.[721]

◆ **"THE SYSTEM" TRUMPS SANITY—2010**: A five-year-old girl suffering from 3rd degree burns that required skin grafts was turned away from Coventry's University Hospital. Her parents were forced to drive her 25 miles to a burn specialist.[722]

◆ **MEAT MARKET MEDICINE—2010**: A man was left infertile when surgeons removed the wrong testicle. After the mistake was discovered, the doctors had to remove the other, the cancerous one. A hospital spokesman responded with, "The safety of our patients is our number one priority." A consultant suggested the hospital give clearer instructions on how to mark and verify sites.[723]

◆ **STAR-STRUCK SLOPPY—2010**: A British movie star died of cervical cancer because NHS doctors failed to notice a tangerine-sized tumor.[724]

And the list goes on.

---

719   Stephen Adams, "Hospitals leaking patient data to 'no win no fee' firms, claims MEP," The Telegraph, June 28, 2011.

720   Nick Collins, "Rules on Foreign doctors 'put patient safety at risk,'" The Telegraph, 6/29/11.

721   Jenny Hope, "GP bonuses 'lead to poor patient care,'" MailOnline, June 29, 2011.

722   The Telegraph, "Burned girl 'turned away' from hospital," March 21, 2010.

723   The Telegraph, "Man left infertile after wrong testicle removed," March 29, 2010.

724   Sara McCorquodale, "Jade's death unnecessary," MailOnline March 20, 2010.

SOCIALIST ABSURDITY: Prohibition (1919-1933)
PRINCIPLE VIOLATED: Freedom to choose; property
STORY: Prohibition in the U.S. was the constitutional outlawing of the manufacture, sale, and transport of alcohol to curb the abuse of drinking—"for our own good." A majority of Americans believed that using force to prevent drinking was a good idea, a principled idea, a *constitutional* idea.

The result? People demanded their freedom to choose, and some began a private revolution. Thousands of "speak-easies" or their equivalents sprang up overnight. Underground railroads and black market exchanges began moving illegal goods across the country. Violence, shooting, raids, mobs, fighting, killing, and destruction exploded in the major cities. The idea of forcing people into abstinence was the deployment of socialist ideas of compulsion against human nature in violation of unalienable rights. The whole thing flopped and was repealed.[725]

SOCIALIST ABSURDITY: Complete Submission to Master Race
PRINCIPLE VIOLATED: All natural rights and freedoms
STORY: Primo Levi was a survivor of Auschwitz, and described in his memoirs the utter brutality of an existence in the concentration camp where life and civilization had been stripped from everyone. He said each inmate was ultimately alone in his heart and mind, although surrounded by hundreds of others. The men could either fight to survive, mentally and emotionally, or give up—"drowning," as he called it, the easy way out.

Living was a daily battle, an unending hourly struggle. Those who surrendered their human will and relied on what was given to them became the "drowned." They soon died from starvation, disease, back-breaking labor, or from the death of hope.

"Precisely because the lager was a great machine to reduce us to beasts we must not become beasts," Levi wrote. "We must want to survive ... to bear witness." Their hearts, their minds, and their very human nature remained the one place the Nazis couldn't reach. The freedom to choose was the freedom to survive.[726]

725　18th amendment ratified January 16, 1919; repealed by 21st amendment ratified December 5, 1933.
726　"Survival in Auschwitz," Primo Levi.

IT TAKES A FAMILY

Socialists must destroy parts of human nature to achieve the
cooperation they deem necessary for the perfect socialist society.

The act of dehumanizing individuals by forcing them into an anonymous beehive existence may facilitate Ruler's Law, but it destroys human capacity and society.

The four major attributes of human nature cannot survive in a vacuum. There is an irreplaceable component of human relations necessary from the earliest age onward. Without a strong family unit, the human species does not develop to its fullest capacity and potential. The question is: Can a village replace mother and father?

A fascinating study published in 1967 by German researcher Irenaus Eibl-Eibesfeldt shows how infants deprived of the bonding love of a mother and father can wither and die[727]—

FIRST TRUST: "It is especially in the second half of the first year of life [6-12 months] that a child establishes personal ties with its mother or a person substituting for her (a nurse, a matron). This contact is the precondition for the development of 'primary trust,' the basis for the attitude toward oneself and the world. The child learns to trust his partner, and this positive basic orientation is the foundation of a healthy personality."

CREATING DISTRUST: "If these contacts are broken, 'primary distrust' develops. A prolonged stay in the hospital during the child's second year may, for example, lead to such results. Though the child will try even there to establish close contact with a mother substitute, no nurse will be able to devote herself intensively enough to an infant for a close personal tie to be established. Nurses constantly change, and so the contacts that arise are constantly broken."

BREAKING A CHILD'S HEART: "The child, deceived in his expectations of contact, falls into a state of apathy after a brief outburst of protest. During the first month of his stay in the hospital, he whines and clings to anyone available. During the second month, he usually cries and loses weight. During the third month, such children

---

727   Irenaus Eibl-Eibesfeldt, *Grundriss der vergleichenden Verhaltensforschung, Ethologie, Muhich*, 1967, p. 234, as quoted by Shafarevich, p. 271.

only weep quietly and finally become thoroughly apathetic. If after three to four months' separation they are taken home, they return to normal. But if they stay in the hospital longer, the trauma becomes irreversible ...."

DEATH BY ABANDONMENT: "... In one orphanage where R. Spitz studied 91 children who had been separated from their mothers in the third month of their lives, thirty-four died before they reached the age of two. The level of development of the survivors was only 45 percent of normal and the children were almost like idiots. Many of them could neither walk nor stand nor speak at age four."

CONSEQUENCES

Depriving a child from bonding with a parent can ruin a life. The assorted problems that are created by breaking up the family show up as the child develops. Rebecca O'Neill completed a study in 2002 about the removal of the father from that structure. Her results include:[728]

EARLY TROUBLES: Children without a father struggle more in school, have more health problems, are at greater risk of being victims of physical, emotional, or sexual abuse, and are more prone to run away from home.

TEENAGERS: Teens without fathers are more prone to abandon structured settings. They are more likely to become teenage parents, have problems with their own sexuality, are more inclined to take up smoking, alcohol, drugs, act out at school, be expelled, and are more likely to drop out of school by age 16.

YOUNG ADULTS: This age group is more likely to wander through the preparatory college years, failing to obtain qualifications for advancements in school or employment. They are more likely to be on welfare or without a job. They tend to have lower incomes, will spend time on the street as homeless beggars, and are more likely to be caught in criminal activity and spend time in jail. They are also more likely to have emotional problems and health problems. They're more likely to rotate through multiple relationships and cohabitations, and have children outside of marriage or a committed partnership.

---

728 Rebecca O'Neill, *Experiments in Living: The Fatherless Family*, The Institute for the Study of Civil Society, 2002.

UNRAVELING OF ORDERLY SOCIETY

The impact on society of children without fathers includes an increase in crime and violence, divorces, unwanted pregnancies, and a renewed cycle of dependence on welfare.

These social problems raise the question, could these failings be attributable to the mother injecting anti-social behavior into her children? No, it is the balancing influence of a devoted father—despite his many imperfections—who is supremely suitable compared to no father at all. Devoted dads help gather the scattered pieces of a child's life and make it whole.

The socialists promote nurture as the means whereby individuals can be torn from the family structure so the family can be destroyed. However, all instances of violating these natural needs and desires have backfired. Children naturally need and desire all that the family provides. Children naturally respond positively to the guidance of parents. They'll rebel and push and resist, but only loving parents are best suited to guide those natural impulses and help children grow into responsible adults. Interrupting that process with social experimentation produces a life of misery and distrust that is difficult to correct. Many valiant children manage to escape the dredges of difficult living in a broken home, and many single parents who succeed at such herculean tasks are the saviors of the planet. But nothing replaces a loving mother and father.

INDIVIDUAL RIGHTS ARE HARD WIRED

The extraordinarily complex and interwoven components of the human soul are unconquerable by the socialists.

Human nature is why people will never permanently adapt to the beehive mentality. They know and understand at their deepest levels of conviction that each and every person enjoys a common set of rights that no other has permission to deny. The family has proven its worth for eons. Only a committed mother and father are best suited to convey the lessons of history and experience to the next generation. It is all about learning to get along and learning to respect individual rights. It is all about rights.

A KHRUSHCHEV QUOTE

Detractors[729] have brought into question the reliability of a quote by Nikita Khrushchev, provided below. The man who heard the statement from Khrushchev's own mouth, former Secretary of Agriculture, Ezra Taft Benson, shared the encounter at a meeting in 1978. Here is a transcript of his comments:

"It may surprise many of you when I tell you that I spent half a day with Mr. Khrushchev when he was here. ...They told me point blank to my face, that my grandchildren will live under Communism. When Mr. Khrushchev said that to me, I responded, 'Mr. Chairman, if I have my way, your grandchildren and every grandchild will live under freedom.' He said, 'Oh, you Americans. You are so gullible. You won't accept Communism outright, but we'll keep feeding you small doses of Socialism until one day you will wake up and find you already have Communism. We won't have to fight you. We'll weaken your economy and infiltrate your economy until you fall like overripe fruit into our hands.' I didn't realize it then, but he was only repeating the prophecy—that last part in particular—which his predecessors, Lenin and Stalin, had said before him."[730]

Khrushchev was reported to have made that statement, or words similar prior to the Benson meeting in 1959, for example: "We cannot expect the Americans to jump from capitalism to communism, but we can assist their elected leaders in giving Americans small doses of socialism, until they suddenly awake to find they have communism."[731]

Khrushchev's messages proved prophetic as America found herself deeply ensnared in socialism by 2012, with only the dithering of a fickle electorate standing between freedom and collapse.

---

729   Paul F. Boller, John H. George, *They Never Said It: A Book of Fake Quotes, Misquotes, and Misleading Attributions*, Oxford University Press, 1990, pp. 59-60.
730   Ezra Taft Benson, first given publicly October 25, 1966, at BYU, and repeated in informal remarks on December 30, 1978, Sandy, Utah—a transcript is on file with the author.
731   Ezra Taft Benson, *The Red Carpet: Socialism*, 1962, p. 65.

ACKNOWLEDGEMENTS

Dedicated to the heirs of *liberty*, that supernally perfect gift made available by the simple and divine happenstance of living in the United States of America. And, to my loving and supportive wife, Kathy, who persevered with kind patience to smooth the way so these many years of research could be concluded—a contribution of untold importance. And, to my ten children, their spouses and offspring, and all other freedom-loving patriots. May they become a staff of knowledge and understanding and direction upon which the nation may lean, that together the people of the United States may bear the Constitution away from the forces of destruction described in these pages. May they live to see the day when liberty is restored and confidence in constitutional government rebuilt, so that freedom may once again reign supreme, and prosperity flourish.

It seems appropriate to acknowledge powerful guides, influences and sources of enlightenment. First, the tremendous scholarship and labors of my father, W. Cleon Skousen, who paved the way for this treatment on socialism, a project he prepared for but didn't get a chance to write.

And, my mother, Jewel P. Skousen, who, at the age of 94, still retained her amazing talent for editing and thoughtful suggestion. She is one of those rare, precious souls who knows how to spin gold from an exhausted writer's literary straw.

And, Igor Shafarevich, Ludwig von Mises, Milton Friedman, F.A. Hayek, James Madison, Thomas Jefferson, Ezra Taft Benson, a few hundred authors and scholars, and all the American Founding Fathers whose insights, writings, and willingness to face the monsters of this mortal sphere with wisdom, courage, and patience, brought insight and understanding to these troublesome times in which the world finds itself.

Dozens of family members and several great friends were willing to review the text for suggestions and corrections, including the studious attentions of editor Tristi Pinkston, and the encouraging suggestions of Benjamin C. Skousen, Michelle K. Kennedy, Joseph M. Skousen, Jacob P. Skousen, Tim and Wendy McConnehey, Joshua B. Skousen, Mary Ramirez, Sharon Krey, and students from my classes at the university—to them my profound gratitude and appreciation. Also lending valuable suggestions were Patricia S. Taylor, Julie S. Mason, MaryAnn S. Hill, and the constant encouragement from Elisabeth Skousen who lent excellent and timely historical context. And for the brilliant cover and illustration ideas powerfully originated and designed by Arnold Friberg, conceptualized for socialism by J. Rich Skousen, and recreated by Benjamin C. Skousen.

There are others, but like the subject matter at hand, there must be an ending to the writing, and here it is.

ABOUT THE AUTHOR

Paul B. Skousen was an analyst and intelligence officer for the Central Intelligence Agency (1982-1987). For two of those years, he worked in the White House Situation Room for President Ronald Reagan. He is a journalist by training, a writer, published author, and teacher. He has a B.A. in journalism and communications from Brigham Young University, and an M.A. in National Security Studies from Georgetown University (1982). He teaches journalism and communications at Utah Valley University.

SELECTED BIBLIOGRAPHY

Adams, John, "The Works of John Adams," *Boston: Little, Brown and Co., 1856.*

Adler, Mortimer J. & Charles Van Doren, "Annals of America," *Encyclopaedia Britannica, 2007.*

Alchon, Suzanne Austin, "A Pest in the Land: New World Epidemics in a Global Perspective," *University of New Mexico Press. 2003.*

Allen, Gary, "None Dare Call It Conspiracy," *Buccaneer Books, 1976.*

Allen, James, "As A Man Thinketh," *Devorss & Company, 1948.*

Aristophanes, The Ecclesiazusae, *Kessinger Publishing, 1994,*

Aristotle, "The Athenian Constitution," *translated by Sir Frederic G. Kenyon, Penguin Classics, 1984.*

Aspinall, Arthur, "English Historical Documents, 1783-1832," *Oxford University Press, 1959.*

Aveling, Edward, "Charles Darwin and Karl Marx: A Comparison," *The Twentieth Century Press, 1897.*

Bales, J.D. Bales, "What is Socialism?," *unpublished text in possession of the author.*

Barber, William J., "From New Era to New Deal: Herbert Hoover, The Economists, and American Economic Policy, 1921-1933," *New York: Cambridge University Press, 1985.*

Barry, John Stetson, "The History of Massachusetts, The Colonial Period," *Phillips, Sampson and Company, 1855.*

Bartlett, Bruce, "How Excessive Government Killed Ancient Rome," *The Cato Journal, Vol. 14 Number 2, Fall 1994.*

Baskerville, Geoffrey, "English Monks and the Suppression of the Monasteries," *New Haven, Connecticut, Yale University Press, 1937.*

Bastiat, Frederic, "The Law" [1850], *Ludwig von Mises Institute, Auburn, Alabama, 2007.*

Bastiat, Frederic, "Justice and Fraternity" [1848], *in Journal des Économistes, June 15, 1848.*

Baudin, Louis, Daily Life of the Incas, *Courier Dover Publications, NY, 2003.*

Baudin, Louis, "A Socialist Empire: The Incas of Peru," *D. Van Nostrand Company, 1961.*

Benedictow, Ole J., "The Black Death, 1346-1353, The Complete History," *The Boydell Press, Woodbridge, 2004.*

Benson, Ezra Taft, "The Proper Role of Government," *Hawkes Publishing, 1975.*

Bentham, Jeremy, "The Works of Jeremy" Bentham, *Simpkin, Marshall, & Co., London, 1839.*

Bergh, Albert Ellery, "The Writings of Thomas Jefferson," *The Thomas Jefferson Memorial Association, 1907.*

Bernardi, Aurelio, "The Economic Problems of the Roman Empire at the Time of Its Decline," *edited by Carlo M. Cipolla, in The Economic Decline of Empires, Methuen, London, 1970.*

Bezold, Friedrich von, "Geschichte der deutschen Reformation [History of the German Reformation]," *AMS Press, 1971.*

Bible, King James Version.

Bogucki, Peter, "The Origins of Human Society," *Blackwell Publishers, 1999.*

Bovard, James, "Hoover's Second Wrecking of American Agriculture," *Freedom Daily, 2005.*

Boyd, Julian P., editor, "The Papers of Thomas Jefferson," *20 volumes, Princeton University Press, 1950-.*

Bradford, William, "Of Plymouth Plantation," *New York: Charles Scribner's Sons, 1908.*

Bucholz, R. O., "Early Modern England, 1485-1714," *Wiley-Blackwell, 2003.*

Buckler, John, "A History of World Societies," *Houghton Mifflin Company, 1996.*

Buddhadasa Bhikkhu, "No Religion," *Buddha-Dhamma Meditation Center, Hinsdale, IL, 1993.*

Buddhadasa Bhikkhu, "Dhammic Socialism—Political Thought of Buddhadasa Bhikkhu," *The Chulalongkorn Journal of Buddhist Studies, Vol. 2 No. 1, 2003.*

Burton, E., Guilds, in "The Catholic Encyclopedia," *New York: Robert Appleton Company, 1910.*

Bryan, William Jennings, editor, "The World's Famous Orations, America: 1 (1761-1837), [Benjamin Franklin] His Examination Before the House of Commons, 1766," *New York: Funk & Wagnalls, 1906.*

Carson, Clarence B., "The Utopian Vision," *The Freeman, pp. 20-34, February 1965.*

Casselman, Paul Hubert, "Labor Dictionary," *New York: Philosophical Library, 1949.*

Chambers, Whittaker, "Witness Whittaker Chambers," *New York: Random House, 1952.*

Chandler Tertium, "Four Thousand Years of Urban Growth: An Historical Census," *St. David's University Press, 1987.*

Chandler, William U., "The Myth of TVA: Conservation and Development in the Tennessee Valley, 1933-1980," *Cambridge, Mass.: Ballinger, 1984.*

Chang, Jung, "Mao: The Unknown Story," *Alfred A. Knoph, 2005.*

Charvat, Petr, "Mesopotamia Before History," *Routledge, 2002.*

Cherry, Conrad, "God's New Israel," *Prentice-Hall, Englewood Cliffs, N.J., 1971.*

Clark, John, "The Anarchist Moment," *Montreal: Black Rose, 1984.*

Cobban, Alfred, "Dictatorship, Its History and Theory," *New York: Charles Scribner's Sons, 1939.*

Cole, Margaret, "The Story of Fabian Socialism," *Toronto, Heinemann, 1961.*

Constitution, U.S., U.S. National Archives, *Washington, DC.*

Coogan, Gertrude M., "Money Creators," *Noontide Press, 1986.*

Corwin, Edwin S., editor, "The Constitution of the United States, Annotated," *Library of Congress, 1953.*

Cottrell, Robert C., "Baldwin, 'From the Harvard Classbook,' June 1935, vol. 763, ACLU Papers; Roger Nash Baldwin and the American Civil Liberties Union," *New York: Columbia University Press, 2000.*

Craik, George Lillie, et al., "The Pictorial History of England," *Charles Knight and Co., 1839.*

Crain, W. Mark, "The Impact of Regulatory Costs on Small Firms,"

Small Business Administration Office of Advocacy, September 2005.

Croly, Herbert, "The Promise of American Life," New York, The Macmillan Company, 1909.

Davis, William T., "Bradford's History of Plymouth Plantation," New York: Charles Scriber's Sons, 1908.

Declaration of Independence, U.S. National Archives, Washington, DC.

Deschamps, Dom, "La Verite ou le Veritable Systeme," Moscow, 1973.

Dewey, John, "Democracy and Education," Free Press, 1997.

Dexter, Henry Martyn, "Mourt's Relation Or Journal of the Plantation at Plymouth," John Kimball Wiggin, 1865.

Dickman, Howard, "Industrial Democracy In America, Ideological Origins of National Labor Relations Policy," Open Court, 1987.

Disraeli, Benjamin, "Coningsby," Kessinger Publishing, 2010.

Douglas, David Charles, "English Historical Documents, 1783-1832," Oxford University Press, 1959.

Dross, Fritz, "Hygiea Internationalis: The Price of Unification—The Emergence of Health & Welfare Policy in Pre-Bismarckian Prussia," Linkoping University Electronic Press, 2007.

Durant, Will, "The Story of Civilization, The Age of Faith," New York: Simon and Schuster, 1950.

Durant, Will, "The Story of Civilization: Our Oriental History," New York: Simon and Schuster, 1935.

Durant Will, "The Story of Civilization, The Reformation," New York: Simon and Schuster, 1957.

Ebenstein, Alan O., "Great Political Thinkers: From Plato to the Present, Wadsworth Publishing, 6th edition, 1999.

Eckersley, Robyn, "Environmentalism and Political Theory," Albany, NY: SUNY Press, 1992.

Einstein, Albert, "Why Socialism? Monthly Review—An Independent Socialist Magazine," May 1949

Emery, Noemie, "Alexander Hamilton, An Intimate Portrait," Putnam, 1982.

Encyclopedia Britannica, 1913 Scholars Edition, second edition 1926.

Engels, Friedrich, "Communist Manifesto," Penguin Classics, 2002.

Engels, Friedrich, "Draft of a Communist Confession of Faith," Marx/Engels Collected Works, by Progress Publishers (Moscow), Lawrence and Wishart (London), and International Publishers (New York), copyright 2005.

Engels, Friedrich, "Herr Eugen During's Revolution in Science," New York International Publishers, 1894.

Engels, Friedrich, "The origin of the family, private property and the state," Marx/Engels Selected Works, Hamburg, 1969.

Engels, Friedrich, "Socialism: Utopian and Scientific," International Publishers, New York, 1935.

Engels, Friedrich, "Sochineniia," Marx/Engels Collected Works, by Progress Publishers (Moscow), Lawrence and Wishart (London), and International Publishers (New York), copyright 2005.

Engels, Frederick, "Works," Moscow: Progress Publishers, London: Lawrence and Wishart, and New York: International Publishers, 2005.

Flynn, John T., "Men of Wealth: The Story of Twelve Significant Fortunes from the Renaissance to the Present Day," *Simon and Schuster, New York, 1941.*

Foster, John Belemy, "Marx's Ecology in Historical Perspective," *International Socialism Journal, Winter 2002.*

Foster, William Z., "Syndicalism," *Chicago, W. Z. Foster, 1913.*

Freeman Report, "Story Behind the 1929 Crash," *Vol. III. No. 22, 1973.*

Fremantle, Anne, "This Little Band of Prophets: The British Fabians," *New York: The New American Library, 1959.*

Friedman, Milton and Rose, "Free To Choose, A Personal Statement," *Harcourt Brace Jovanovich, Inc., 1980.*

From, Erich, "Let Man Prevail," *New York: The Call Association, 1960.*

Gavi, Philippe, "The Right to Rebel," *1974, public domain.*

Geddes, Joseph A., "The Mormons, Missouri Phase: An Unfinished Experiment," *Deseret News Press, 1924.*

Gerrard Winstanley, "The True Levelers Standard Advanced," *Benediction Books, 2010.*

Great Britain Parliament, "The Parliamentary Debates, Vol. 41 (Nov. 23, 1819 to Feb. 28, 1820)," *T.C. Hansard, 1820.*

Gress, Stefan, "Private Health Insurance in Germany: Consequences of a Dual System," *Longwoods Publishing Corporation, 2006.*

Guyot, Yves, "Socialistic Fallacies," *London: Cope and Fenwick, 1910.*

Halliday, Jon, "Mao: The Unknown Story," *Alfred A. Knoph, 2005.*

Hamilton, Alexander, "The Federalist Papers," *Signet, 2000.*

Hamor, Ralph, "A True Discourse of the Present State of Virginia," *Richmond Virginia State Library, 1957.*

Hardin, Garrett, "The Tragedy of the Commons," *Science, vol. 162, December 13, 1968.*

Harrison, Winfred A., "The American Constitution—Its Origins and Development," *WW Norton & Company, 1948, Fourth Edition 1970.*

Hayek, Friedrich A., "The Road to Serfdom," *Chicago: University of Chicago Press 1944.*

Hegel, G. W. F., "Philosophy of History," *Prometheus Books, 1990.*

Hegel, G. W. F., "Philosophy of Law," *Pringer, 1995.*

Henry VIII, "Calendars of State Papers: Letters and Papers, Foreign and Domestic, Henry VIII," *Longman, Green, Longman, & Roberts, 1875.*

Herbermann, Charles George, Catholic Encyclopedia, *Robert Appleton Company, 1912.*

Hew, Chee, "Healthcare in China," *IBM Institute for Business Value, 2006*

Hibbard, B.H., "Taxes A Cause of Agricultural Distress," *Journal of Farm Economics, Vol. XV, No. 1, January 1933.*

Hill, Bennett D., "A History of World Societies," *Houghton Mifflin Company, 1996.*

Hippolytus, "Refutation of All Heresies," *Kessinger Publishing, 2004.*

Holborn, Hajo, "A History of Modern Germany—1840-1945," *Princeton University Press, 1969.*

Holyoake, George Jacob, "The History of Co-operation in England," *Clapham Press, 2010.*

Hoover, Herbert, "The Memoirs of Herbert Hoover," *Macmillan, 1952*

Horowitz, Carl F., "Union Corruption: Why it Happens, How to Combat It," *National Institute for Labor Relations Research, 1999.*

Howard, Milford Wriarson, "The American Plutocracy," *Nabu Press, 2010.*

Howe, John R., "The Changing Political Thought of John Adams," *Princeton University Press, 1966.*

Hsieh, Paul, "Moral Health Care vs. Universal Health Care," *The Objective Standard, vol. 2, no. 4, 2007.*

Irenaeus, "Against Heresies," *Kessinger Publishing, 2004.*

Jay, John, "The Federalist Papers," *Signet, 2000.*

Jefferson, Thomas, "The Anas," *Kessinger Publications, LLC, 2007.*

Jefferson, Thomas, "Memoir, Correspondence, and Miscellanies From the Papers of Thomas Jefferson," *H. Colburn and R. Bentley Publishers, 1829.*

Jessee, Dean C., "The Personal Writings of Joseph Smith," *Deseret Book, 2002.*

Johnson, E. A. J., "American Economic Thought in the Seventeenth Century," *New York: Russell & Russell, Inc., 1961.*

Jones, A. H. M., "Taxation in Antiquity," *published in The Roman Economy: Studies in Ancient Economic and Administrative History, Oxford: Basil Blackwell, 1974.*

Josephus, "Jewish Antiquities," *Cambridge MA: Harvard University Press, Loeb Classics, 1998.*

Josephus, "The Wars of the Jews, Antiquities of the Jews," *Penguin Classics, 1984.*

Keil, C. F. & P. Delitzsch, "Commentary on the Old Testament," *vol. 1, Grand Rapids: Eerdmans, 1975.*

Keller, Ludwig, "Johann von Staupitz un die Anfange der Reformation [Johann von Staupitz and the Beginnings of the Reformation]," *Nabu Press, 2010.*

Kelly, Alfred H., "The American Constitution—Its Origins and Development," *WW Norton & Company, 1948, Fourth Edition 1970.*

Kennedy, David M., "Over Here: The First World War and American Society," *Oxford University Press, 2004.*

Kenyon, John, "Medieval Fortifications," *Continuum International Publishing Group, 1990.*

Ketchem, Ralph Louis, "James Madison: A Biography," *The University Press of Virginia, 1990.*

Key, Newton, "Early Modern England, 1485-1714," *Wiley-Blackwell, 2003.*

Khan-ad-Din, Felinah Memo Hazara, "Common Misconceptions about Medieval England," *Caidan Penthathlon, March 2003.*

King, John A., "Presidents from Eisenhower through Johnson, 1953-1969," *Greenwood, 2005.*

Knight, Charles, "Penny Cyclopaedia of the Society for the Diffusion of Useful Knowledge," *London: Knight & Co, 1858.*

Koch, Adrienne, "The American Enlightenment," *Cornell University, 1961.*

Kovel, Joel, "The Enemy of Nature," *Zed Books, 2002.*

Kravchenko, Victor A. "I Chose Freedom" [1946], Transaction Publishers, 1988

Krooss, Herman E., "Executive Opinion: What Business Leaders Said and Thought on Economic Issues, 1920s-1960s," Garden City, NY: Doubleday, 1970.

Larson, Andrew Karl, "I Was Called to Dixie," Deseret News Press, 1961.

Larson, Sven R., "Lessons from Sweden's Universal Health System: Tales from the Health-care Crypt, Journal of American Physicians and Surgeons," vol. 13 number 1, Spring 2008.

Levi, Primo, "Survival in Auschwitz," Summit Books, New York, 1986.

Levy, Robert A., "The Dirty Dozen: How Twelve Supreme Court Cases Radically Expanded Government and Eroded Freedom," Sentinel, Penguin Group publishing, 2008.

Lippmann, Walter, "A Preface to Morals," New York: The Macmillan Co., 1929.

Livingston, David P., citing Emil Friedrich Kautzsch, Heilige Schrift des Alten Testaments, J.C.B. Mohr, 1894 (3rd edition, 1908-10).

Locke, John, "An Essay Concerning Human Understanding," see The Great Books, The University of Chicago, 1952 .

Macek, Josef, "Tabor in the Hussite Revolutionary Movement," vol. 2, Prague, 1952.

Madison, James, "The Federalist Papers," Signet, 2000.

Madison, James, "The Writings of James Madison," Library Reprints, 2000.

Madsen, Jakob B., "Trade Barriers and the Collapse of World Trade During the Great Depression, Southern Economic Journal 67 (4), pp. 848-868, 2001.

Malthus, Robert, "An Essay on the Principle of Population," London: J. Johnson, St. Paul's Church-Yard, 1798.

Marcuse, Herbert, "Eros and Civilization. A Philosophical Inquiry into Freud," Routledge & Kegan Paul Ltd., England, 1956.

Marique, P., "Guilds," in The Catholic Encyclopedia, New York: Robert Appleton Company, 1910.

Marx, Karl, "Communist Manifesto," Penguin Classics, 2002.

Marx, Karl, "Critique of the Gotha Program," published after Marx's death, 1875.

Marx, Karl, "Critique of Hegel's Philosophy of Right," Cambridge University Press, 1970.

Marx, Karl, "Works," Moscow: Progress Publishers, London: Lawrence and Wishart, and New York: International Publishers, 2005.

Maspero, Henri, "Ancient China," Folkestone, Dawson, 1927.

Mazower, Mark, "Dark Continent: Europe's Twentieth Century," Vintage, 2000.

McBriar, A. M., "Fabian Socialism and English Politics, 1884-1918," Cambridge: University Press, 1962.

McDonald, Forest, "Alexander Hamilton," New York: W. C. Norton & Company, 1979.

McHenry, James, "The Life and Correspondence of James McHenry: Secretary of War Under Washington and Adams," Cornell University Library, 2009.

McKay, John P., "A History of World Societies," Houghton Mifflin Company, 1996.

Merriam, Charles Edward, "A History of American Political Theories," The MacMillan Company, 1915.

Mill, John Stuart, "Principles of Political Economy with some of their Applications to Social Philosophy," London: Longmans, Green and Co., 1909.

Mises, Ludwig von, "Socialism, An Economic And Sociological Analysis," 2nd Edition, Indianapolis: Liberty Fund, 1981.

Montazeri, Grand Ayatollah Hossein-Ali, "The Memoirs of Grand Ayatollah Hossein Ali Montazeri," published privately, 2001.

Morison, Samuel Eliot, "Of Plymouth Plantation, 1620-1647," Knopf, 1952

Muhammad ibn Ismail al-Bukhari, "Sahih Al-Bukhari," IBT, 2002.

Muravchik, "Joshua, Heaven on Earth: The Rise and Fall of Socialism," San Francisco: Encounter, 2002.

Nettles, Curtis P., "The Roots of American Civilization," New York: F.S. Crofts Company, 1938.

Nietzsche, Friedrich, "The Gay Science," Cambridge University Press, 2001.

Niewyk, Donald L., "The Columbia Guide to the Holocaust," Columbia University, 2000.

Nissen, Hans J., "The Early History of the Ancient Near East, 9000-2000 BC," University of Chicago Press, 1990.

O'Brien, Michael, "John F. Kennedy: A Biography," Thomas Dunne Books, 2005

Ogg, Frederic Austin, "Social progress in Contemporary Europe," The MacMillan Company, 1912.

Oliver, Frederick Scott, "Alexander Hamilton: An Essay on American Union," G.P. Putnam's Sons, 1918.

Page, Walter Hines, "The World's Work," Doubleday, 1914.

Page, Arthur Wilson, "The World's Work," Doubleday, 1914.

Pak, Sunyoung., "The biological standard of living in the two Koreas," Economics & Human Biology, Volume 2, Issue 3, December 2004.

Paley, Baildon William, "Great Britain, Court of Chancery, Select Cases in Chancery, A.D. 1364 to 1471," London, B. Quaritch, 1896.

Palyi, Melchoir, "Compulsory Medical Care and the Welfare State," National Institute of Professional Services, Inc., Chicago, 1949.

Pavin, Abraham, "The Kibbutz Movement, facts and figures," Central Bureau of Statistics, State of Israel, 2006.

Peters, Rudolph, "Jihad in Medieval and Modern Islam," Brill, 1977.

Pietrusza, David, "1920: The Year of Six Presidents," Carroll & Graf, New York, 2007.

Pinker, Steven, "The Blank Slate: The Modern Denial of Human Nature," New York: Viking, 2002.

Piper, DLA (Firm), "Failure to Protect, A Call for the U.N. Security Council to Act in North Korea," DLA Piper, 2006.

Plato, "Apology," Classics of Western Philosophy, 6th ed., edited by Steven M. Cahn, Hackett Publishing Company, Inc., 2002.

Plato, "The Dialogues of Plato," translated by Benjamin Jowett, Modern Library, 2001.

Plato, "The Republic," Benjamin Jowett, Charles Schribner's Sons, NY, 1908.

Plutarch, "The Life of Solon," translated from the Greek by Aubrey Stewart,

M.A., London: George Bell & Sons, 1894.

Pohlmann, Robert von, "The Sunny Islands," *Geschichte des antiken Kommunismus und Sozialismus*, 2 vols., 1893-1901.

Popper, Karl Raimund, "The Open Society and Its Enemies: The Spell of Plato," *Princeton University Press*, 1971.

Powell, Jefferson, "Our Chief Magistrate and His Powers," *New York: Columbia University Press*, 1916.

Prescott, William H., "History of the conquest of Peru, with a preliminary view of the civilization of the Incas," *Philadelphia: J. B. Lippincott & Co.*, 1883.

Rambaut, William, translator of "Ante-Nicene Fathers," *vol. 1 edited by Alexander Roberts, James Donaldson, and A. Cleveland Coxe, Buffalo, NY: Christian Literature Publishing Co.*, 1885.

Rand, Ayn, "The Ayn Rand Lexicon," *edited by Harry Binswanger, Meridian*, 1986.

Rand, Ayn, "The Monument Builders," *in For the New Intellectual, Signet, New York*, 1963.

Rawls, Woodrow Wilson, "Where the Red Fern Grows," *New York: Random House Inc./Laurel-Leaf*, 1961.

Renard, George Francois, "Guilds of the Middle Ages," *General Books LLC*, 2010.

Rives, John C., "Abridgment of the Debates of Congress, from 1789 to 1856," *vol. V,, New York: D. Appleton & Company*, 1857.

Roberts, Alexander, translator of "Ante-Nicene Fathers," *vol. 1 edited by Alexander Roberts, James Donaldson, and A. Cleveland*

Coxe, Buffalo, NY: Christian Literature Publishing Co., 1885.

Robinson, James Harvey, "An Introduction to the History of Western Europe," *Ginn and Company 1902*, 1946.

Roosevelt, Elliott, "F.D.R.: His Personal Letters, 1928-1945," *Duell, Sloan and Pearce*, 1950.

Roosevelt, Theodore, "The Autobiography of Theodore Roosevelt," *NY: Schribner's*, 1913.

Roosevelt, Theodore, "Progressive Principles, Selections from Addresses," *London: Effingham Wilson, 1913*

Rostovtzeff, Mikhail, "The Social and Economic History of the Roman Empire," *Biblo & Tannen Publishers*, 1926.

Roth, Cecil, editor, "Encyclopedia Judaica," *Coronet Books Inc*, 1994.

Roux, Georges, "Ancient Iraq" *(3rd ed.), Penguin*, 1992.

Rummel, R.J., "Death By Government," *New Brunswick, JJ, Transaction Publishers*, 1994.

Rummel, R.J., "Statistics of Democide: Genocide and Mass Murder Since 1900," *Charlottesville, Virginia, Transaction Publishers*, 1997.

Sarte, Jean-Paul, "The Right to Rebel," *1974, public domain*.

Savine, Alexander, "English Monasteries on the Eve of the Dissolution," *Oxford, The Clarendon Press, 1909*.

Scheidel, Walter, "Real wages in early economies: Evidence for living standards from 1800 BCE to 1300 CE," *Princeton/Stanford Working Papers in Classics*, 2009.

Schumpeter, Joseph A., "Business Cycles: A Theoretical, Historical, and Statistical Analysis of the Capitalist Process," *Martino Publishing, 2005.*

Seymour, Charles, "The Intimate Papers of Colonel House," *Kessinger Publishing, 2005.*

Shafarevich, Igor, "The Socialist Phenomenon," *foreword by Aleksandr I. Solzhenitsyn, in Russian in 1975 by YMCA Press; in English by Harper & Row, 1980.*

Shang, Yang, "The Book of Lord Shang," *translated by J. J.-L. Duyvendak, The Lawbook Exchange, Ltd., 2003.*

Shaw, George Bernard, "The Intelligent Woman's Guide to Socialism and Capitalism," *1928.*

Shotwell, James T., "An Introduction to the History of Western Europe," *Ginn and Company 1902, 1946.*

Skousen, Mark, "The Making of Modern Economics," *M.E. Sharpe, New York, 2001.*

Skousen, W. Cleon, The Five Thousand Year Leap, *Utah: SCCS, 1981, 2009.*

Skousen, W. Cleon, "The Majesty of God's Law, It's Coming To America," *Utah: Ensign Publishing, 1996, 2010.*

Skousen, W. Cleon, "The Making of America," *National Center for Constitutional Studies, Utah: Ensign Publishing, 2010.*

Skousen, W. Cleon, "The Naked Communist," *Utah: Ensign Publishing, 1958, 1960, 2007.*

Slack, Paul, "The English Poor Law, 1531-1782," *London: Macmillan, 1990.*

Smith, John, "Captain John Smith: Writings with Other Narratives of Roanoke, Jamestown, and the First English Settlement of America," *Library of America, 2007.*

Smyth, Albert Henry, "The Writings of Benjamin Franklin," *The Macmillan Company, 1906.*

Spalding, Franklin Spencer, quoted *in* Radicalism in the Mountain West "1890-1920," *The Christian Socialist, November 1914.*

Stalin, Joseph, "Problems of Leninism," *Foreign Languages Publishing House, 1947.*

Taft, William H., "Our Chief Magistrate and His Powers," *NY: Columbia University Press, 1916.*

Terkel, Suds, "Hard Times: An Oral History of the Great Depression," *Pantheon Books, 1970.*

Thapar, Romila, "Ancient Indian Social History: Some Interpretations," *Hyderabad: Orient Longman Ltd., 1984.*

Thaplyal, Kiran Kumar, "Guilds in Ancient India," *New Age International, 1966.*

Thomas, Ivor, The Socialist Tragedy, *New York: MacMillan Co., 1951.*

Thomas, Norman, "America's Way Out: A Program for Democracy," *New York: The MacMillan Co., 1931.*

Thomas, Norman, "A Socialist's Faith," *New York: W. W. Norton and Co. Inc. 1951.*

Thomsen, Rudi, "Ambition and Confucianism: A biography of Wang Mang," *Aarhus University Press, 1988.*

Tiumenev, Aleksandr Ilich, "The Economy of Ancient Sumer," *Moscow-Leningrad, 1956.*

Tocqueville, Alex de, "Democracy in America," *Rochelle, New York; Arlington House, 1840.*

Transparency International, "Global Corruption Report 2006," *Pluto Press, December 2005.*

Tucker, Benjamin, "State Socialism and Anarchism: How Far They Agree, and Wherein They Differ," *North American Review, 1886.*

Tyler, Lyon Gardiner, "Narratives of Early Virginia," *New York: Barnes and Noble, Inc. 1907.*

United States Presidents, "Messages and Papers of the Presidents," *Government Printing Office, 1897.*

U.S. Constitution, National Archives, Washington, DC.

Utley, Jon Basil, "Obama and the Alternative Energy Fiasco," *Reason.com, May 13, 2009.*

Victor, P., "The Right to Rebel," *1974, public domain.*

Vile, John R., "Presidents from Eisenhower through Johnson, 1953-1969," *Greenwood, 2005.*

Wallechinsky, David & Irving Wallace, "Peoples Almanac," *New York: William Morrow and Company, 1978, 2:400.*

Ward, Lester F., quoted in "American Thought: Civil War to World War I," *New York: Holt, Rinehart & Winston, Inc., 1957.*

Warren, Josiah, "The Motives for Communism—How It Worked and What It Led To," *Woodhull and Claflin's Weekly, IV, 15, Feb. 24, 1872.*

Webster, Noah, "An American Dictionary of the English Language," *1828, republished in facsimile edition by Foundation for American Christian Education, 1967.*

Wells, H. G., "The New World Order," *Filiquarian Publishing, LLC, 2007.*

Wells, William V., "The Life and Public Services of Samuel Adams," *Boston: Little, Brown, and Company, 1888.*

Whalen, Michael L., "A Land-Grant University," *Cornell University, May 2001.*

Wherry, Rev. E. M., "A Comprehensive Commentary on the Quran and Preliminary Discourse," *Taylor & Francis, Inc., 2001.*

Wilhem, Eugen, "Die Homosexualitat des Prinzen Heinrich von Preussen, des Bruders Friedrichs des Grossen," *Zeitschrift fur Sexualwissenschaft 15, 1929;*

Wilson, Edwin H., "The Genesis of a Humanist Manifesto," *Humanist Press, 1995.*

Wilson, Woodrow, "Socialism and Democracy," *edited by Ronald J. Pestritto, Lexington Books, 2005.*

Woolsey, Theodore, "Political Science," *C. Schribner's Sons, 1900.*

World Health Organization, "World Health Report," *Executive Summary, 2010.*

Zinser, Lin, "Moral Health Care vs. Universal Health Care," *The Objective Standard, vol. 2, no. 4, 2007.*

QUOTES ON MAJOR SECTION HEADINGS

xiv. **Part I: What is Socialism?** *"Socialism is government force to change society."—Author*

xv. **Ouroboros** *"Socialism progresses like a snake eating its tail."—Author*

27. **Part II: Socialism in Ancient History** *"Socialism is a time-released poison pill with a 100% success rate."—Author*

49. **Part III: Socialism in Classical History** *"From Rome to ruins, the classical forms marched bravely toward the chasm, determined and assured that all was well."—Author*

73. **Part IV: Socialism in the Middle Ages** *"They advocated having all things in common—including wives. Early Church fathers stated, 'They lead lives of unrestrained indulgence' ..."—Author*

121. **Part V: Socialism in the Americas** *"The sober and godly men ... evince the vanity of that conceit of Plato's ... as if they were wiser then God."—Gov. William Bradford, cited in Samuel Eliot Morison, Of Plymouth Plantation, 1620-1647, p. 120*

143. **Part VI: Socialism in Religion** *"All major world religions have experienced periods when members or its leaders practiced Ruler's Law in one form or another."—Author*

175. **Part VII: The Miracle That Stopped Socialism** *"The Utopian schemes of leveling ... are arbitrary, despotic, and in our government, unconstitutional."— Samuel Adams, 1768 letter to Massachusetts's agent in London.*

223. **Part VIII: Revolution of the Socialists, Section 1** *"When the people find that they can vote themselves money, that will herald the end of the republic."— Often attributed to Benjamin Franklin, though not validated.*

249. **Part IX: Revolution of the Socialists, Section 2** *"When virtue suffers neglect and death, the historian knows an end to the whole is not far behind."—Author*

279. **Part X: Revolution of the Socialists, Section 3** *""God is dead. God remains dead. And we have killed him. How shall we comfort ourselves, the murderers of all murderers?"—Friedrich Nietzsche, The Gay Science, section 125*

325. **Part XI: The Last Temptation: Compulsory Care** *"The surest path to dictatorship is braced with the promises of universal care."—Author*

347. **Part XII: The Last Temptation: Health Care** *"All modern dictators believe in coercing people into governmentalized medicine."—Melchior Palyi, Compulsory Medical Care and The Welfare State, National Institute of Professional Services, Inc., Chicago, 1949.*

371. **Part XIII: Socializing the Money** *"There is something behind the throne greater than the king himself."—Sir William Pitt, 1770, quoted by Lord Mahon, History of England, vol. v., p. 258.*

403. **Part XIV: Socialism Today in America** *"It is impossible to introduce into society a great change and a greater evil than this: the conversion of the law into an instrument of plunder." —Frederic Bastiat, The Law, Ludwig von Mises Institute, Auburn, Alabama, 2007, p. 7 (paragraph 31)*

445. **Part XV: Socialism Around the World** *"... Vagabonds and beggars have of long time increased, and daily do increase ... being whole and mighty in body, and able to labour ... there to put himself to labour, like as a true man oweth to do." —King Henry VIII, George Lillie Craik, et al., The Pictorial History of England, Charles Knight and Co., 1839.*

481. **Part XVI: The 46 Goals of Socialism** *The goal of socialism is communism:* "What is usually called socialism was termed by Marx the 'first,' or lower, phase of communist society."—Vladimir Lenin, The State and Revolution, Chapter 5: The First Phase of Communist Society.*

493. **Part XVII: The Proper Role of Government** *"Government may not possess more rights than those held by the individual. The individual may delegate certain rights—defense, justice, and raising revenue—but the government may not simply assume them. When it does, that is tyranny."*

499. **Part XVIII: The New Beginning** *"Happily for America, happily we trust for the whole human race, they pursued a new and more noble course. They accomplished a revolution which has no parallel in the annals of human society."—James Madison, The Federalist No. 14, November 30, 1787*

508. **The Ouroboros** *"... Socialism progresses like a snake eating its tail . . . . Let them pray, therefore, that their tail be very, very long."—Author*

"FACTOIDS"

At the bottom of each page are short news items or quotes about socialism or freedom. Each has been cited and sourced by page number. To reduce page count, these have been moved to the official web page. See www.thenakedsocialist.com.

Index

Note: To locate any particular *factoid* (the short facts or quotes found at the bottom of every page) find them listed last under their corresponding keyword entry.

A

Abolishing the Pillars of Socialism, 181
Abortion, 126, 198, 354
 States' Rights issue, 198, 287
 Roe vs. Wade (1973), 295
 Russia restricts abortion to boost population, 363
 Reagan regrets supporting abortion, 425
 Obama imposes morning after pill, 437
 Abortion is goal of socialism, 487
 Factoid: Democrats in U.S. favor sex-selective abortion, 87
 Factoid: What age for abortion? Murder? 332
ACLU, 310
 Roger Nash Baldwin, a founder, 165
 Clarence Darrow, leading member, 310
ADA (Americans With Disabilities Act), 427
Adamites
 Christian heretics, 90
Adams, John
 ∗Comment on Plato, 59
 "Liberty ... general knowledge", 141
 America founded on religion, 155
 "America ... in Providence", 179
 "...Treason against the hopes", 180, 193
 "Liberty once lost", 217
 "Democracy never lasts long", 219
 Challenges Hamilton's monarchy views, 232
 America founded on "principles of Christianity", 273
 "Property is ... sacred", 196, 214
 Against socialism, 214–217
 Factoid: Government of laws not men, 97
 Factoid: Dare to read, think, speak, write, 243
 Factoid: Constitution for moral and religious, 258

Factoid: Morality and religion necessary for freedom, 330
Factoid: Virtue necessary for freedom, 341
Factoid: Stop arbitrary power to preserve liberty, 358
Factoid: Fear is foundation of government, 365
Factoid: Constitution guards against tyranny, 377
Factoid: Prayer over the White House, 458
Adamson Act (1916), 411
Adams, Samuel
 "Religion of America ...", 155
 Socialism is "in our government, unconstitutional.", 194, 214–216
Africa, 128, 323, 452, 476
 Julius Nyerere, "ujamaa" or familyhood, 102
Agencies, government, 9, 307, 387, 398, 428, 484
 Power to make law, 296, 410
 Nixon expands power, 421
 Patriot Act, impact of, 433
 Czars, appointed by Obama, 437
Agnew, Spiro T.
 Resigned as Vice President, 289
Agricultural Depression of 1920-21, 387
Agricultural Marketing Act, 413
Alcoholic Liquor
 Prohibition (18th Amendment), 286-287, 305, 529
 Food and Drug Administration, 319
 Taxes, in Greece, 462
 Increased abuse in fatherless homes, 531
Aldrich, Nelson W., 380
Al-Farabi, Abu Nasr
 The Virtuous City (book), 274
Allen, James
 "As a man thinketh ...", 443
Amalric of Bena
 Pioneer of Middle Ages heresies, 84
Amendment 1, 201
 And Unions, 256
 Obama violates by forcing religions 437
Amendment 1-10, 178, 196-198, 204-208
 Bill of Rights, 206

Amendment 2, 441
    Guns rights curtailed by S. Court, 296
    Clinton erodes gun rights, 429
Amendment 4
    Privacy, 282
Amendment 5, 196, 280, 295-296, 318
Amendment 9
    Rights don't deny or disparage others,
      200
Amendment 10, 200, 318, 424, 515
    All Other Powers Go to States, 198
    Garcia vs. San Antonio Metro. Transit
      Authority (1985), 295
    ADA violates the tenth Amendment,
      428
Amendment 13, 280, 489
Amendment 14
    "Bad Amendment", 280-282
Amendment 16
    Article 1.2.3, 186
    Marxist idea, 269, 277, 283
    Tax violates equal protection, 281
    "Bad Amendment", 282
    Goal of progressives, 304
    A cause of Great Depression, 393
    Graduated income taxes, 407
Amendment 17, 283-286
    Ruins representative government, 182,
      183
    "Bad amendment", 283
    Replaces Republic with Democracy, 303
    The "Great Concession", 393
    Footnote: Typical defense of 17th, 485
    Goal of socialism, 485
Amendment 18
    "Bad amendment", 286
    Eliminating free choice, 305
Amendment 19
    John Dewey and suffrage, 271
    Replaces Republic with Democracy, 303
Amendment 21, 287
Amendment 23
    "Bad amendment," 288-289
Amendment 25, 288-290
    Allows un-elected president, 289
Amendments, "Bad" *See also* individual
    Amendments
    14th, overrides states rights, 280
    16th, income tax, 282
    17th, popular vote for senators, 283
    18th, prohibition, 286
    23rd, turning DC into city-state, 287

    25th, allows un-elected president, 288
Amendments, Suggested
    Abolish the power to borrow, 221
    Restrict General Welfare Clause to
      enumerated powers, 221
    Veto Supreme Court with 3/5ths states'
      vote, 190, 297
American Revolution, 110, 167, 177, 189,
    230, 377, 490, 505
    Factoid: Washington changes the world,
      334
Americorps, 430
Ameringer, Oscar
    Factoid: Politics is gentle art of ..., 379
Amtrak
    Factoid: Releases gay-friendly ad
      campaign, 462
Anabaptists
    Christian heretics, 91-92
Ananias
    And "Christian" socialism, 160-161
Anarchy
    Examples of (no law), 8
    Sliding scale of political power, 176-177
    No property rights leads to, 196, 214,
      273
Anchor Babies, 281
Andrews, T. Coleman
    Against 16th Amendment, 283
Anglo-Saxons, 13
    People's Law practiced by, 178
    Enacted representative government, 193
    Numbered among successful republics,
      220
Animal Rights
    Goal of socialism, 489
Anti-begging Law (1495), 333
Antoinette, Marie
    Wife of Louis XVI, 108
    Extravagant living, 109
    Death of, 116
Apathy
    Among the Incas, 127
    Factor in socialism's advances, 71, 482
    Abandoned infants falling into a state
      of, 531
Apostolic Brethren
    Christian heretics, 86
Argentina
    Part of Inca empire, 123
    Snapshot of socialism in, 455
Aristophanes, ancient playwright, 62

Aristotle, 50, 56
  Factoid: "Equality only among slaves", 19
Article 1, 23
  Duties of Congress, 184
  Violation of, 185, 186, 305, 321, 348,
    385, 399, 416, 424, 436, 438
  Limits on Congress, 184–187
  Enumerated powers, 186, 198
  Limits on States, 188
  Equal taxation, 196
  Property rights protected, 196
  Foreign commerce, 197
  Interstate commerce, 198
  Journal, congress to keep, 202
  "Congress has not unlimited powers,"
    Jefferson, 215
  "...detail of power," Madison, 215
  Unions violate commerce clause, 255
  Anti-slavery provision, 280
  Taxation, Article 1.2.9, 282
  Health care not government duty, see
    Article 1.8, 348
  Federal Reserve violates, 385
  Factoid: Jefferson accuses Congress of
    violating commerce clause, 24
  Factoid: Obama illegal immigration
    policy, 207
Article 2
  Duties of the President/Executive,
    183-184
  State of the Union address required, 202
  Violations of, 435, 440
Article 3, 202
  Duties of Supreme Court, 190
  Republican form guaranteed, 193
  Restrictions on Supreme Court, 291
Article 4
  14th Amendment repeats, 280
  Citizens guaranteed rights, 280
  Violation of, 405, 439
Article 5
  Violations of, 437
Articles of Confederation, 505
  On the sliding scale of government
    power, 8
  Failure of, 176-177
  Too little Federal power, 188
  Authority without power is ..., 199
  Three kinds of republics, 220
  Factoid: Main reason for failure of, 364
Assemble, freedom to, 201
  Bill of Rights, 206

  Congress may not interfere, 206
  Democracy, too much assembling, 219
  Unions may peacefully assemble, 254
Assyria, Ancient Socialism, 42
Auschwitz
  Primo Levi describes, 529
Australia, 323, 378, 490
  Health care in, 366
  Snapshot of socialism in, 457
Austria
  Anabaptists in Austria, 91
  War with Prussia, 114
  Health care in, 352
Aveling, Edward
  Son-in-law of Karl Marx, 268
Azerbaijan
  Health care, 360

B

Bacon, Francis
  New Atlantis (book), 276
Bailouts, 4-6, 22, 64, 233, 256, 323, 389,
    398, 431, 434, 447, 460, 473, 482
  For European banks, 450
  Spain, 469
Baldwin, Roger Nash
  Defines socialism, 165
  Founder of ACLU, 165
Ball-Point Pen Story, 212
  Factoid: Fisher Space Pen, 211
Bank Holiday
  Roosevelt declares, 1933, 397
Bank of America
  Factoid: Donates billions to "global
    warming" fight, 382
Bank Reserves, 394, 456
  John Law's Trillion Dollar Idea, 372
Banks, Central, 379-384. *See
    also* **Federal Reserve**
  Hamilton promotes in America,
    233-234
  Combined with welfare, health care,
    323
  John Law, 372–378
  Power behind the throne, 376
  Motivated to create debt, 377
  How much does world owe them? 378
  United States establishes its first
    central bank, 379-380
  Congressional promises about central
    banks, 380-384

Broken promises by the Federal Reserve, 385
Panic of 1921, 391
Panic of 1907, 390
Run on the bank, 390
Argentina, government takes over, 456
Barry, John S., 137
Bastiat, Frederic, 403
Defines socialism, 166
Against state welfare, 329-332
"Law ... instrument of plunder", 403
Bastille, Storming the, 112
Baucus, Max
Redistribution of wealth, quote, 436
Baudin, Louis
Socialism destroyed the Inca, 18
Bavaria, State Welfare, 339
Bebel, August
Factoid: Human sex no different than animal sex, 110
Bees
Socialists in the wild, 510
Belgium
Cathars driven from, 84
Prussians liberate, 1792, 115
Rance conquers, 1794, 117
Founding member of European Union, 446
Treating the politically correct sick, 448
Factoid: Leopold slaughters in Congo, 185
Benson, Ezra Taft
Proper role of government, 494
Bill of Rights must be protected, 496
Nikita Khrushchev, "...small doses of socialism...", 533
Bible, 31, 146, 195, 202, 261, 269, 272, 294, 334
King, qualifications for described in Bible, 10
Does socialism free me from Bible? 25
Story about socialism in Bible Nimrod, 36
Jonah and Nineveh, 43
Divine Right of Kings, 54
Dead Sea Scrolls, 65
Essenes, 65
John Wycliffe and Reformation, 89
Anabaptists reject non-Bible sacraments, 91
Forced religion, Shadrach, et al, 144
Did Early Christians Practice Communism? 159-162
No Biblical morals in socialism, 520
Socialists reject B., 520
Ten Commandments condemned by Engels, 522
Factoid: Hosea 4:6, thou rejected knowledge, 4
Factoid: Bible translated into 2,287 languages, 59
Factoid: Proverbs, No vision means people perish, 215
Biden, Joseph
Threatening government force, 20
Factoid: Take from haves, give to have nots, 266
Big Mac
Factoid: Minutes of work to earn a, 14
Bill of Rights, 178, 196, 198, 496
And Natural Law, 204
List of protected rights, 206
Washington assures passage of, 206
Supreme Court forced Bill of Rights on states, 294
Roosevelt's "Economic Bill of Rights", 415
Bismarck, Otto Van
Modern welfare in Prussia, 339–342
Attacks social democrats, 340
First modern state welfare, 340
Factoid: Questions settled by iron and blood, 190
Black Death (1348-1350)
Kills millions in Europe, 330–331
Factoid: Rats and fleas no longer blamed, 333
Black Panthers, New
Intimidating voters, 525
Blacks in America
Davis-Bacon Act favors whites in unions, 394
Civil Rights Act, 1964, 419
Welfare destroys black families, 454
Factoid: Black family began to collapse after welfare, 361
Blair, Tony
"I am a socialist ...", 46
Fabian socialist, 169
Bonaparte, Napoleon
French revolution leads to emperor, 117
Comes to power in France, 241
Europe, after Napoleon toppled, 243

Napoleonic Code, 241-243
Praetorian guard, 518
Books Promoting Socialism
Al-Madina al-Fadila, AD 900 (The
   Virtuous City), 274
Peach Blossom Spring, (AD 376), 274
The Republic (380 BC), 274
Utopia (AD 1516), 275
City of the Sun (1602), 275
How the Other Half Lives (AD 1890),
   276
New Atlantis (AD 1624), 276
The Law of Freedom (AD 1652), 276
Communist Manifesto (1848), 277
The Communist Manifesto (1848), 277
The Jungle (AD 1906), 277
Boundaries
Jesuit priests give Paraguay natives strict
   boundaries, 129
Europe, after Napoleon toppled, 243
Interstate commerce problems, 317, 318,
   319, 398, 408, 437
North Korea, controlling broadcasts
   over boundaries, 466
Abolishing all national B., 483
Goal of socialism, 483
Bradford, William
Governor of Plymouth Colony, 135
"Indolent would labor only when
   compelled", 137
"Retard much employment", 137
"They deemed it a kind of slavery", 137
"Vanity of ... Plato", 139
Brazil
Factoid: Pays government employees
   56% more than private, 165
Factoid: Media is subsidized, 255
Factoid: Brazilian taxes averages 55%,
   307
Bread and Circuses
America, 64
Rome, 64, 71
Russia, 64
Spain, 64
Brethren of the Free Spirit
Christian heretics, 84
Brezhnev, Leonid
Factoid: List of luxury cars owned, 328
Britannica, Encyclopaedia
Definition of socialism, 163
Buchanan, James, 344
Buddhadasa
"Look at the birds", 148

Socialism is a natural state, 148
Buddhism
Socialism in, 148
Bulgaria
Factoid: Vampire myth and information
   control, 128
Health care in, 360
Burgess, John, 303
No God, only earthly perfection, 303
State must totally control individuals,
   303
Burke, Edmond
Factoid: "Intemperate minds cannot be
   free", 126
Factoid: If power is not within, it will be
   without, 494
Burke, Michael E.
Promoted Federal Reserve, 381
Bush, George H. W.
Acts of socialism, 427
Bush, George W.
Acts of socialism, 431
Medicare expansion, 432
No Child Left Behind Act, 432
Pork barrel spending, 432
TARP, 432
Sarbanes-Oxley (SOX), 433
The Patriot Act, 433
Businesses, small, 387
Right to start a, 14
France allows, for a fee, 102
Right to privacy in, 207
Guilds create strength in, 250
Unions more important than property
   owners, 254
Taxes, if they destroy business, 318
Taxes force layoffs, 326
Butter Makers Force Tax, 318

C

Cambodia
Factoid: Death count, 2.6 million, 109
Campanella, Tommaso
City of the Sun (book), 275
Canada
Health care in, 356, 364
Snapshot of socialism in, 457
Socialist Party of, 519, 521, 523
Socialist absurdity, 526
Factoid: Raised retirement age, 3
Factoid: Health care, 1 in 13 will fall
   victim to malpractice, 101

Factoid: Stopped producing the penny in 2012, 446

Capital, Das Kapital
Book by Marx, 269

Capitalism, 45, 102, 162, 165, 167-170, 244, 266-269, 277, 283, 340-342, 343, 404, 457, 473, 475, 483, 521-523, 529, 533
Factoid: Castro, "Where is success of capitalism?" 58
Factoid: Marx, "Dethrone God ... destroy capitalism, 67
Factoid: Lenin, "Violence needed to topple capitalism" 310
Factoid: Churchill, "The inherent vice of capitalism is ..." 394
Factoid: Lenin, "Socialism grows out of capitalism ..." 415
Factoid: Capitalism didn't fail, was strangled, 460

Carlovingians, 99

Carolinians, 99

Carpocratians, Christian Socialists, 75

Carter, Jimmy
Acts of socialism, 423
Airline Deregulation Act (1978), 423
Alaska National Interest Lands Conservation Act (1980), 424
Attempts to shrink government, 423
Depository Institutions Deregulation and Monetary Control Act (1980), 423
Motor Carrier Act (1980), 423
Pork barrel spending reduction, 423
Staggers Rail Act (1980), 423
The Camp David Accords (1978), 424

Casselman, Paul Hubert
Defines socialism, 163
No private property, 521

Castes, 29, 31-32, 35, 44, 56, 59, 80, 86, 96, 154, 188, 210
Second pillar of socialism, 5-6
India, 60-61
France, 104-105
Incas, 124-125
Abolishing Pillar #2, the Caste, 192-193
North Korea, 465
Beehive, 511

Castro, Fidel, 4, 459
Factoid: "Where is success of capitalism?" 58
Factoid: In Castro's Cuba, it's a crime to..., *176*

Factoid: Forced Cuba into solitary confinement, 489

Cathars, Christian Socialists, 82, 145

Catholic Church
Model for socialists? 74
Cathars oppose C., 84
Brethren of the Free Spirit, 85
Apostolic Brethren oppose C., 87
Dolcino opposes C., 87
Taborites oppose C., 88
Reformation, 88, 146
Adamites oppose C., 90
Hussite wars, 90
Anabaptists oppose C., 91
French Revolution, 104
Socialism in Christianity, 145
Socialism in Religion, 145-149
Napoleon abolished cloisters, 242
Pro-union encyclical, 263-264
Roots of modern welfare, 330
French Popes challenge Rome, 1319-1418, 330-334
Battle over true pope, 332
Guttenberg's printing press, 333

Central Bank of England, 378

Central Banks, 233-234, 323, 327, 375, 385, 389, 452, 456
The ruling power of, 376
How much do we owe?, 378
Progressives finally get theirs, 379
Congress assures America, quotes, 381
Role in the Great Depression, 390–396

Chavez, Hugo
Factoid: Bans guns to stop murders, 107
Factoid: Controls all television, 380
Factoid: Nationalizes grocery stores, 432

Checks and Balances
France and parlement, 106
Description of, 183
U.S. and Congress, 183
Hamilton, "...a double security", 200
Failed to stop passage of 16th Amendment, 393
Socialist goal, nullify with Executive Orders, 484

Child Labor Act (1916), 321
Wilson's version unconstitutional, 411

China
Ancient China, 1750 BC, 38
Dynasties of socialism, 38
Shang Yang, how to make the people weak, 40
Wang Mang, failed socialist, 66

One-child policy, 267
National health care, 355
Health care in, 355, 366
Over-prescribing I.V. fluids, 367
Camp David Accords, 424
President Carter, 424
Snapshot of socialism in, 457
Socialism in modern C., 457
North Korea dependent on, 466
Peru trade, 467
History of China used to discredit U.S.,
    490
Factoid: Forcing farmers to meet
    environmental code, 80
Factoid: pre-marital relations punished,
    129
Factoid: Children indoctrinated at
    young age, 150
Factoid: Scrubs Internet of references to
    blind dissident, 162
Factoid: Abandons socialism to survive,
    195
Factoid: 7-month pregnancy terminated,
    2012, 260
Factoid: Death count 1949-2010, 269
Factoid: Blocking Internet to control
    information, 296
Factoid: Switched to fingerprint ID, 299
Factoid: May join communist party at
    age 18, 308
Factoid: Blocks Korean soaps that
    "distorts" history, 318
Factoid: Communist part necessary for
    socialism, 322
Factoid: Fake villages built in Tibet, 342
Factoid: 8 cars per 1,000 people, 343
Factoid: Ideological education necessary,
    344
Factoid: 70% of illegal copies made in
    China, 353
Factoid: Party members required in
    Walmart stores, 355
Factoid: Must have faith in Party, 400
Factoid: Socialism death toll in Great
    Leap Forward, 422
Chisholm, G. Brock
Destroy the individual, 17
Factoid: "Remove family, individualism,"
    443
Choice
Force versus choice, 3, 71, 157, 199
Denied under socialism, 22

Unalienable right to choose, 15, 24
Religion, choice versus force, 144
'All in common' violates choice, 194
Ball-point pen, example of C., 212
Prohibition, violated freedom of C., 286,
    305, 529
Neo-progressives seek to eliminate free
    Choice, 305
Choice limited in national health care,
    361
Socialism: What if I change my mind?,
    523
Christian, Christian Church
Did Early Christians Practice
    Communism? 159-161
Christian socialism defined, 165
Christianity, America founded on
    (Adams), 273
Factoid: What's mine is yours ..., 201
Christian Socialists, 145
Nicolaites, 75
Churchill, Winston
Factoid: "All things are simple ...
    freedom, justice, honor...", 246
Factoid: Socialism is equal sharing of
    misery, 394
Cicero
Natural Law explained, 204
Rights, right reason quote, 208-209
Factoid: Importance of learning history,
    323
Civil Rights Act (1964), 419
Civil War, 405
Flat tax during, 304
Roots of American welfare, 343
Lincoln and socialism, 405
Factoid: Death count, 427
Clayton Antitrust Act, 411
Clean Air Act (1970), 422
Clean Water Act (1972), 422
Cleveland, Grover
No gifts, no handouts, 406
Resisted socialism, 406
Climate
Advantages of harsh C., 131
Clinton, Bill
"Limit freedom if needed," 21
Threatening government force quotes,
    21
Acts of socialism, 428
As president, 428

National Health Care proposal, 429
Taxes, raises, 429
Goals 2000: Educate America Act
   (1993), 429
Americorps, 430
Filegate, 430
Paula Jones, 430
Refused to post union dues message,
   430
Travelgate, 430
Whitewater, 430
Monica Lewinsky, 431
Clinton, Hillary
"Rich not paying enough," 19
Quotes promoting envy, 19
Quote, we'll take things from you, 21
Threatening government force, 21
Factoid: "I am a progressive," 265
Colonists, Early American, 502
Jamestown, 131
Plymouth, 135
Combination Act of 1799, 240
Commerce
Role of Congress to regulate, 186
States may not tax states, 189
Interstate commerce, 197
With foreign nations, 197
Madison, federal role, 199
Declaration of Independence, 205
National Labor Relations Board, 255
Robert Fulton steamboat, 293
State railroads, 305
Lottery Act, 317
Child Labor Act, 321
Communications Act, 399
Teddy Roosevelt, 408
Wilson and 8-hour workday, 411
Herbert Hoover, Sec. of Commerce, 412
Nixon, OSHA, 422
H. W. Bush, and ADA, 427
G. W. Bush, No Child Left Behind, 432
National Health Care, 437
Factoid: Jefferson says Congress
   violated, 24
Common, All Things
Aristophanes, 62
Catholic monasteries, 74
Carpocrates, 75
Nicolaites, 75
Manicheism, 76
Cathars, 82
Brethren of the Free Spirit, 84
Taborites, 90

Diggers, 92
Ranters, 94
Jesuit Priests in Paraguay, 129
Jamestown, 131
Plymouth, 135
Did Jesus teach that? 156
Did the Early Christians Practice
   Communism?, 159
Abolishing Pillar #3, 194
Sidney Rigdon, 261
Obama disappointed Supreme Court
   failed to, 435
Communism
Condemned at Plymouth, 139
Defined with socialism, 167–169
Robert Owen, 246
Karl Marx, 269
Communist Manifesto, 277
Americans feared Roosevelt was
   preparing for, 414
China, 457
Cuba, 458
North Korea, 465
U.S. is legally anti-communist, 496
Factoid: Naming of book "The Naked
   Communist", xiv
Factoid: "Meet needs of majority", 13
Factoid: Theory of communism means
   no private property, 71
Factoid: Socialism is path to C., 82
Factoid: C. Party formed in 1919, 280
Factoid: Decline of communist nations
   by 2012, 429
Factoid: "People come before profits",
   457
Communist Manifesto, 3, 269, 277, 283,
   304, 329, 375, 485
Factoid: Lennon's song, Imagine, is
   Communist Manifesto, 103
Communist, The Naked, 159-161, 168
Factoid: Naming of the book, 1
Compagnonnages, Secret Societies, 101
Compassion, 17, 19, 22, 147, 210, 349, 454
An unalienable right, 16, 24
Christian tenet, 78-79, 145
Taught by Jesus, 157
Being forced is not compassion, 158
Destroyed by state welfare, 330–337
Concession, The Great, 390-396
Confederation, Articles of, 8, 199
Weakness of Articles, 176-177
Were too weak, 188
Three kinds of republics, 220

Congress, 1, 5, 23, 114, 176-78, 197-203, 234, 246, 285, 291-293, 315-320, 357, 380-384, 358, 389, 397-399, 405-420, 429-443, 473, 514-516
Job description, 182
Chains on Congress, 184-189
Restrictions on in Bill of Rights, 206-209
Obama bypasses congress with immigration, 207
Founders quotes on restrictions of Congress, 214–217
Control, a goal of socialism, 484
Supreme Court allows Congress to break chains, 255, 281, 291-300, 304-308
Factoid: Jefferson accuses congress of violating Constitution, 24
Factoid: 2nd Continental Congress met at Guild hall, 224
Conservative, 288, 308, 417, 425, 431
Factoid: Worried most about liberal's grandson, 281
Constitution, 11-12, 21-25, 50, 71, 108, 111, 131, 134, 173, 178-179, 183, 187-217, 240
Balance between tyranny and anarchy, 8
Property rights, 196
Protects rights, 205
Is it old fashioned?, 218
Jefferson, "Not a blank paper," 299
Original Intent, 299
Scalia, "Enduring Constitution," 315
Dismantle Constitution by amendment or interpretation, 316
Destroy Constitution, goal of socialism, 490
Factoid: Judicial activism unconstitutional, 225
Factoid: Not a lot of compromises, 240
Factoid: Doesn't create law, 247
Factoid: How to remember 7 articles, 251
Factoid: Made for moral and religious people, 258
Factoid: FDR seeks to ignore it, 366
Constitutional Convention, 1787, 177, 193, 225, 284
The Hamilton Plan, 228
Constitutional Convention of States
Socialist goal: Prevent at all costs, 485
Continental Dollar
After the war, 177
Hamilton proposes buy back, 234

Contracts, 81, 135, 189, 205, 233, 255, 314, 321, 398, 411-412, 419, 437, 468, 474-75
Protection of destroyed, 296
Coolidge, Calvin
Constitution not old fashioned, 218
Stop Federal encroachment, 320
Corn
Factoid: U.S. produces 44% of world's supply, 250
Corruption
Defined by Jefferson, 232
Craft Guilds, 98
Crisis, Chaos, 306
Means to install socialism, 491
Croly, Herbert
Promoted progressive movement, 313
Cromwell, Thomas, 335
Crusades, 146
Cuba
Health care in, 359
Snapshot of socialism in, 458
Socialism needs a host, 477
Factoid: Illegal to meet, report, travel, etc., 176
Factoid: Most prisoners jailed for black market, 345
Factoid: Castro forces country into isolation, 489
Cuckoo Bird
Socialism in nature, 500
Cullop, William A., 381, 383
Currency
Washington on depreciation, 203
Euro, problems with, 449
Goal of socialism, 484
Goal of socialism, all electronic, 488
Proper role of government, 496
Factoid: Lenin, debauch currency to ruin capitalism, 264
Czars, 7
Railroad czar, 398
Barack Obama appointed czars, 437
Trash can czars, 525
Factoid: Joseph Goebbels, Hitler's propaganda czar, on truth, 5
Factoid: Food czars fine high school for selling soda, candy, 154
Czechoslovakia
Factoid: Socialism leads to communism, 416

Czech Republic
Jan Hus, 89
Health care in, 360

D

Dale, Sir Thomas
Rescues Jamestown, 132
Daniels, Robert V.
Defines socialism, 164
Darrow, Clarence, 310
Darwin, Charles
Theory of evolution, 267
Friends with Karl Marx, 268
Factoid: Marx compliments Darwin's
research, 304
Davis-Bacon Act
Minimum wages for government
workers, 394
Dead Sea Scrolls, 65
Dean, Howard
Promoting envy, quote, 20
Death Count from Socialism, 71
Cambodia, 109
China, 269, 458
Great Leap Forward, 422
Cuba, 459
Germany, 461
Iran, 463
Italy, 464
North Korea, 466
Russia, 469
Vietnam, 475
Death Panels, 361
Debs, Eugene V.
Biography, 309
Factoid: He who controls my bread ...,
390
Declaration of Independence
Mankind disposed to suffer, 201
Natural Law, 205
Protects equality, 205
Is it old fashioned? 218
Not old fashioned, 218
Describes proper role of government,
495
Factoid: Adopted in Carpenter's hall, 224
Factoid: Makes reference to God four
times, 241
**Declaration of the Rights of Man and
of the Citizen (France),** 108, 113

Defense
An unalienable right, 16, 24
Proper role of government, 497
Delegate (assign) Rights, 208, 211, 221,
385, 410, 495, 497
Definition of Socialism, 163-173
DeMille, Cecil B.
Factoid: Names Naked Communist,
xiv-1
Democracy, 51, 57, 71, 117, 152, 163, 192,
275, 300, 473
Adams, "Democracy never lasts long,"
219
Defined, 219
Democracy vs. republic, 219-220
Failed in Greece, 450 BC, 219
Replace Republic with democracy, 303
Social democracy goal of socialism, 483
Unions are "democracy in the
workplace," 522
Factoid: Democracy is like 2 wolves and
a lamb..., 252
Factoid: Democracy will cease when you
take from the workers, 385
Denmark
Factoid: Taxes higher than U.S., 64
Depression
Caused by Federal Reserve, 385
Depression of 1907, 391
Unions and the Great Depression, 395
Prolonged by Roosevelt's programs, 396
Herbert Hoover raises taxes during
Depression, 413
Franklin D. Roosevelt, 414
Deschamps, Dom
Destroy the individual, 18
Dewey, John
Biography, 271
Abandon God, 271
Humanist Manifesto, 271
Nature vs. Nurture, 271
Supported evolution, 271
Freedom, natural rights not natural, 301
Diggers, Christian socialists, 92
Dingell, John
Threatening government force, 21
Diodorus, Ancient Historian, 63
Disraeli, Benjamin
"World is ruled by others," 376
Dodd-Frank Bill, 440
Dolcino
Christian heresy, 86

Draco, Ancient Socialist, 50
Durant, Will
  Factoid: Age and money cures socialism,
    68

E

Eccles, Marriner, 386
Economic Control
  Goal of socialism, 485
  Factoid: Reagan, "Gov't must control
    people to control economy," 78
Ecosocialism
  Socialistic control of an economy, 170
Education, 224, 244, 269, 299
  Michelle Obama, "got to give up
    something" for education, 20
  In Plato's Republic, 97
  Polybius on education, 71
  Inca refuse education to outcasts, 126
  Bastiat and education, 166
  Northwest Ordinance, 202
  John Dewey on education, 272
  Religious education challenged in court,
    294
  Law schools abandon Constitution,
    312-315
  Land Grants to support education, 344
  Department of Education, 424
  Jimmy Carter and, 424
  Ronald Reagan and, 426
  Bill Clinton and, 429
  Barack Obama and, 438
  Student loans nationalized, 438
  Regulate all, goal of socialism, 489
  Factoid: Lenin, "Give me four years", 38
  Factoid: Florida lowered passing grade
    so more could pass, 95
  Factoid: Chinese children indoctrinated
    at early age, 150
  Factoid: Fichte, "Education should aim
    at destroying free will...", 218
  Factoid: China seeks unity with
    ideological education, 344
Edward VI, 332
  Imposed penalties on beggars, 336
Egypt, Ancient, 10, 33, 193, 424
  Moses leaves with tribes of Israel, 11
  Pharaoh, the Demi-God Socialist, 33-35
Eibl-Eibesfeldt, Irenaus
  Study on infants, 530
Einstein, Albert
  Supports socialism, quote, 520

Eliot, W. Charles
  Harvard president, 312
Emergency Rooms
  Abuse of, 352, 364, 366-367, 526
Endura, suicide ritual, 84
Energy, 108, 170, 304, 362, 423-424, 456,
    468, 474, 479, 488
  Regulate, goal of socialism, 485
  Factoid: U.S. dependency on Middle
    East? 362
  Factoid: U.S. is 3rd top oil producer, 467
Engels, Friedrich, 329, 520-523
  Rebellions turn to sexual liberties, 95
  Inspired by Robert Owen, 245
  Communist Manifesto, 269, 277
  No state under socialism, 520
  No Biblical morals, 521
  How to implement socialism, 523
  Factoid: "Abolish private property," 71
England outlaws monasteries,
    1536-1540, 335
Enumerated Powers
  Article 1, Section 8, 198
Environment, *see also* Green Movement
  Environmental socialism, 170
  Goal of socialism, 483, 488
  Factoid: China takes over private
    gardens to control E., 80
  Factoid: EPA in U.S. bypassing Congress
    with new regulations, 122
  Factoid: San Francisco outlaws plastic
    bags, 2007, 124
  Factoid: China refuses EU's carbon tax,
    447
Envy, 19-21, 118, 158, 264, 304, 324, 434,
    442
  Factoid: Envy wounds itself, 50
  Factoid: Socialism is envy, 51
EPA, Environmental Protection Agency,
    422
Equality
  An unalienable right, 16, 24
  Goal of socialism, 484
  Factoid: Aristotle, "Equality exists only
    among slaves.", 19
  Factoid: Lieber, "leads to communism.",
    19
  Factoid: Created equal ends at birth., 23
  Factoid: Hamilton, "Inequality always
    here," 43
Espionage Act (1917), 412
Essenes, Ancient Jewish Sect, 65

Estates General, 111
Ethiopia
  Factoid: 1 million starved to death in 1984, 442
Euro, 426, 446-447, 450
European Parliament, 446
European Union (EU)
  Formation of, 1950, 446
  Consolidating power, 449
  Constitution, failed attempt at, 449
  Treaty of Lisbon, 449
  Factoid: China refuses EU's carbon tax, 446
Everson vs. Board of Education, 294
Evolution, 56
  Scientific socialism, 168
  Industrial Revolution really an evolution, 237
  Charles Darwin theory on, 267–268
  John Dewey and evolution, 271
  Karl Marx and evolution, 269-270
  Supreme Court, evolving power of, 292
  John Scopes, Monkey Trial, 311
  Engels says state is product of evolution, 520
Executive Branch, 182-183, 290, 398, 410-411, 484
Executive Order
  Roosevelt bans gold, 304
  Teddy Roosevelt bypasses Congress, 407
  Kennedy and food stamps, 418
  Kennedy and silver coins, 418
  Jimmy Carter and Antiquities Act, 424
  Goal of socialism, 484
Executive Privilege
  Invoked by Obama over botched *Fast and Furious*, 441

F

Fabian Socialism, 234, 345, 428, 521
  Explained, 168-169
Facebook
  Factoid: Facilitates a crime every 40 minutes, 180
Failure, 65, 128, 138-39, 176, 186, 197, 244, 364, 420, 479
  An unalienable right, 17, 24
Fair Deal
  Program of Harry Truman, 415
Family, 28, 35, 52-55, 61, 74, 102, 150-152, 192, 219

Destroy family and marriage, goal of socialism, 17, 78, 83, 86, 95, 127, 169, 269, 277, 421, 486, 530
  Black families destroyed by welfare, 453
  Homosexuality, 486
  Limit size as "responsible" planning, 487
  Impact of no father, 531
  Factoid: Same-sex parents have more problems, 40
  Factoid: Family is main obstacle to good mental health, 79
  Factoid: India day-care center takes children 24x7, 125
  Factoid: Give me a baby, I'll make him anything you want, 147
Farmers, 30, 70, 81, 93, 235, 304, 381, 411
  Independence destroyed, 387, 413
  Paid not to grow crops, 392, 398
  Factoid: 75% of people grow food to survive, 10
Fascism
  Fascism explained, 169
Fast and Furious, 441
Father
  Impact of no father on family, 531
FDIC (Federal Deposit Insurance Corporation), 398
Federal Farm Board, 413
Federal Farm Loan Act, 411
Federal Lottery Act (1895), 317
Federal Register, 421
  Factoid: Grew to 81,405 pages in 2010, 7
  Factoid: Obama adds thousands of new rules, 217
Federal Reserve, 234, 378-381, 440
  Congressmen, senators push for passage, 381–382
  Broken promises of, 385-389
  Federal Reserve Board, 386
  Not to charge government interest, 386
  Audit, the first in 2011, 388
  Riddled with conflict, 389
  Panic of 1921, 391
  Great Depression, 394, 396
  Favors member banks over others, 398
Federal Reserve Act, 384, 385
  Pushed by Woodrow Wilson, 410
Federal Trade Commission Act, 410
Feinstein, Dianne
  Anti-gun stance from operation Fast and Furious, 441

Fief, 81

Finland, 354-355
  Factoid: No job growth under socialism,
    61
  Factoid: Taxes higher than U.S., 64

Fitzhenry, Louis, 382

Flag, America, 307, 412
  Factoid: Sight of influences voters, 420

Food, 4, 14, 25, 28-29, 34, 60, 64-68,
    93, 102, 123, 148, 266, 287, 319,
    330-332, 387, 518, 529
  Anti-hoarding laws, 304, 524

Food and Drug Act, 319

Food and Fuel Control Act, 304

Food Stamps, 37, 158, 502
  Under Kennedy, 418
  Under Reagan, 426
  Under Obama, 439

Force, 15-25, 71
  Measuring political force, 8
  Self defense, 16
  Force and Envy, 19
  Socialism is force, examples, 21
  Can force be used for good things?, 157
  Abolishing Pillar #5, 199
  George Bernard Shaw on force, 520
  Surviving concentration camps, 529

Ford, Gerald R.
  Un-elected president, 289
  Factoid: Big government can take
    everything, 433

Foreign Aid
  Proper role of government, 497

Forests
  Government control over, 320

Foster, William Z.
  All morals self-defined, not Biblical, 520

Founding Fathers, 22-23, 46, 134, 155
  Sliding scale of political power, 8, 176
  Identified rights, 13-17
  How they stopped socialism, 176-211
  Against socialism, quotes, 59, 214
  America's first progressive, 227-236
  Discredit, goal of socialism, 490

France
  Declaration of the Rights of Man and of
    the Citizen, 113
  Member of EU, 446
  Snapshot of socialism in, 460
  Factoid: Marie Antoinette needed 80
    staff for baby, 6
  Factoid: Joseph Guillotin sought more

  humane execution, 116
  Factoid: Socialists take over government,
    2012, 268

Franklin, Benjamin, 46, 193, 494
  The universal religion, 155
  Against socialism, 216
  "A republic if you can keep it," 225
  Against state welfare, 327-328
  Central Banks a reason for war, 377
  "More need of masters," 494

Freedman's Bureau, 344

Free Economy
  Factoid: Milton Friedman, freedom
    gives what people want, 187
  Factoid: Freedom increases life
    expectancy, 464
  Factoid: New Yorkers in Zip Code 10104
    paid 1+ million in taxes, 466

Fremantle, Anne
  Private property taken away, 521

French Revolution, 80, 105, 110, 117
  How the French revolutionized
    socialism, 103-118

Freud, Sigmund
  Factoid: "Religion is an illusion", 149

Friedman, Milton
  Factoid: "Free economy gives people ...",
    187
  Factoid: One-man system is bad, 359

Frog in boiling pot, 500

Fromm, Eric
  No national borders, 522

Frothingham, Richard
  Self-government under attack, 193

Fulton, Robert
  Steamboat violates states' rights, 293

G

**Garcia vs. San Antonio Metro. Transit
    Authority,** 295

Garfield, Harry, 304

Garfield, James A., 384
  Speaks on Federal Reserve, 384

Gaulle, Charles de
  Factoid: Politics too serious for
    politicians, 331

General Welfare Clause. *See
    also* **Welfare,** 196-198, 215, 221,
    255, 305, 321, 348, 358, 385, 399,
    416, 424, 436, 440
  Webster defines welfare, 184

Hamilton's comments, 185
Jefferson's comments, 185
Madison's comments, 185
Article 1.8, 186
"If Congress can apply money indefinitely ...", 188
Supreme Court declares it a blank check, 294
Georgia (former USSR)
Health care in, 360
Germany, 84, 91-92, 99-102, 172, 231, 242, 334, 339, 340-342, 446
Health care in, 355
Snapshot of socialism in, 461
Factoid: WWII, human brains delivered to Nazi doctors, 138
Factoid: Hitler kills mentally ill, 262
Gibbons vs. Ogden, 293
Gimbels, Ball-Point Pen Story, 212
Goals of Socialism, the 46, 482
God, 10-11, 75, 144, 194-196, 330
Nimrod, 36-37
Jonah, 43
Divine Right of Kings, 54
Essenes, 65
Evil God, Good God, 82-84
"Render unto God ..." 156-158
Author of natural law, 204-209
Dewey says science trumps God, 271
Banned from schools, 294
God is dead, 302-303
All law founded upon God, 495
Factoid: Ionesco, "God is dead, Marx is dead, and I'm ...", 141
Factoid: Declaration references God, 241
Goebbels, Joseph
Factoid: How to make people believe a lie, 397
Gold, 10, 12, 53, 58, 66, 124, 131, 188, 270, 382, 474, 496
Currency should be based on G., 202-203
John Law sees gold warehoused, 372-375
Ownership outlawed by Roosevelt, 304-05, 398
Nixon stops conversion of dollar to, 423
Golden Mean, 8
Government
Expansion of government, 296
Limited government, 302
Control local government, a goal of socialism, 485
Proper role of, 494

Responsibilities of, 495
Must not evolve outside people's control, 497
Factoid: Plato quote, why decent men accept power, 127
Factoid: Warren, "Government help for me is good, for others is socialism," 148
Factoid: Jefferson, too much government is bad government, 338
Factoid: Adams, "Fear is foundation of government," 365
Factoid: To achieve world government, 443
Factoid: Failure follows expanding government, 461
Gray, Finly, 382
Great Concession
Surrendering to progressives, 390
Great Depression
16th Amendment adds to, 393
Smoot-Hawley Tariff Act, 393
Unions, 394
Federal Reserve adds to, 386, 394
Increased taxes make worse, 395
Revenue Act (1932) adds to, 395
Greece
Member of EU, 447
Snapshot of socialism in, 462
Factoid: Run on banks as economy teetered, 426
Green Movement
A type of socialism, 170
Nixon forms EPA, the Environment Protection Agency, 422
Goal of socialism, control all environments, 483, 488–489
Guilds, 96–101
Decline of, 250
Forerunners of unions, 251
Guillotine, 115-117
Factoid: Napoleon's doctor could amputate leg in 13 sec., 117
Gun Rights
Curtailed by S. Court, 296
Fast and Furious, 441
Factoid: Gun ownership reduces crime, 45
Factoid: Hugo Chavez bans guns to reduce murder rate, 107
Factoid: Jefferson, "Retain arms to defend against tyranny," 339

Factoid: Mafia members likes gun control, 363

Gutenberg's Printing Press, 91, 333

H

Habeas Corpus
In U.S. Constitution, 187-188
Abraham Lincoln suspended, 405

Habeas Corpus, French Declaration, 113

Hamilton, Alexander, 227-236
Promoted Central Government, 1
"Constitution changes the world," 179-180
Quotes on welfare, 185
Encroaching national and state government, 200
Problems from listing rights, 206
"Constitution is a list of restraints," 211
America's first progressive, 227
Considered Constitution too weak, 228
Desires to be Prime Minister, 231
Says it makes government practical, 232
Sets up private controlled central bank, 233
Adultery and death, 235
Factoid: "Inequality will always exist", 43

Harmor, Ralph
Jamestown survivor, 133

Harrison Narcotics Tax Act (1914), 321

Hayek, F.A.
Socialists don't "have a leg to stand on", 55
Factoid: Freedom means the unknown, 263
Factoid: Liberty means being responsible, 391

Health Care, 20, 169, 256, 339-340
Not a natural right, 14
How to test legitimacy as a right, 23-25
Supreme Court opens door to ObamaCare, 294
Part of 3-pronged takeover, 323
Death by national health care, 348-349
Flaws in universal health care, 350
Unsustainable on national level, 351
ObamaCare, 357
Worldwide abuse, fraud, 358
U.N. calls for, 368
National health care in EU, 448
Politically Correct medicine in Belgium, 448

International, goal of socialism, 488
Factoid: Obama makes deal with drug makers for support of, 77
Factoid: Prostate cancer survival lower in Europe than U.S., 90
Factoid: Security guards in Swedish health clinics, 351
Factoid: Free care guaranteed in constitution, 375

Healthy, Hunger-Free Kids Act of 2010, 439

Hegel, Georg Eihelm
Factoid: We learn from history we don't, 91

Hegel, Georg Wilhelm Friedrich, 302

Henry VIII
Outlaws the monasteries, 332
Poor Laws, 455

Heresy, Heresies, 74

HEW (Health, Education and Welfare), 424

Hinduism, 60-61, 153-155

Hiss, Alger
Factoid: Put aside traditional ways, 273
Factoid: To achieve world government, 443

History, 71
Factoid: Ayn Rand, "Every major horror", 39
Factoid: We learn from history that we don't, 91

Hitler, Adolf, 220, 464
Deaths, responsible for, 461
Factoid: "I use emotion ...", 34
Factoid: "Hitlers" in phone book after WWII, 35
Factoid: Killed 6,000,000 Jews, 118
Factoid: "We are socialists ...", 192
Factoid: "Providence allowed our victory", 271
Factoid: No freedom of speech, 289
Factoid: World war will lead to killing Jews, 424

Holder, Eric, 440

Hollis< Henry F., 383

Homosexuality
Prussia's Prince Henry, 230
Goal of socialism, 486
Factoid: Same-sex parents have more problems, 40

Factoid: Arkansas U. ordered to allow sex-change student to use women's rest room, 96

Factoid: Amtrak releases gay-friendly ad campaign, 462

Factoid: Same-sex parenting proven inferior, 479

Honeybees
Socialists in the wild, 510

Hoover, Herbert
Anti-hoarding laws, 304, 524
Contributed to Great Depression, 395
Grandfather of New Deal, 395
Acts of socialism, 412

Horowitz, David
Factoid: Socialism based on lies, won't work, 425

House, Colonel E. Mandell
Marxist-minded advisor to Woodrow Wilson, 410

House of Representatives
Description of, 182

Humanist Manifesto, 272, 302

Human Nature
John Stuart Mill quote, 32
Crushing initiative
Inca, 127
Paraguay Indians, 130
Humans similar to cuckoo bird, 500
Humans similar to frogs in hot water, 500
Humans similar to hiker and snake, 501
Humans similar to raccoons, 501
Importance of family, 530
Factoid: Bebel says sexual activity neither moral nor immoral, 111

Hungary
Factoid: Socialism led to Communism, 327

Huntington, Ellsworth
Climate study, 131

Hus, Jan, 89, 146
Factoid: meaning of "Your goose is cooked", 89

Hussite Wars, 89

I

Immigration
Obama violates Constitution with 2012 waiver, 440
Responsibility for in the Constitution, 440

Factoid: Illegal immigrants to U.S. collected $4.2 billion, 135

Impeachment
Supreme Court Justices, 291
Bill Clinton, 431

Incas
Model socialists, 123-128
The Inca Affect, 140

Incentives, 132, 194, 230, 277, 298, 326, 349, 364, 421, 528
Importance of, 15
Robert Owen and incentives, 245, 266
Flawed incentives in health care, 355-356
Incentives and WWII, 395
Kennedy on, 419
Star Parker on, 454
Incentive to stay unemployed, 472-473

Income Tax, 393

India
Factoid: Refused to comply with EU carbon tax demands, 74
Factoid: Day-care center takes children 24x7, 125
Factoid: Young girl sacrificed for harvest, 2011, 274

Indians, of North America, 122

Individual, 46, 53, 61, 68, 97-99, 124, 163, 176, 179, 183, 192, 195, 200, 237, 260, 270, 302-303, 313, 415, 428
Independent Individual, a right, 15-19, 24
And religious beliefs, 144-156
Protect individual rights, 206-211
Government's role to create individual rights, 302-303
Taxing individual income, 304, Frederic Bastiat on individuals, 329
Factoid: Socialists blame Individual for suffering, 256

Industrial Revolution, 237

Industry
Nationalize all worldwide, 489

Infants
Impact of no love, 530

Inflation
Caused by Federal Reserve, 385

Information
Abolishing Pillar #6, 201
Constitution protects freedom of, 201
Control all, goal of socialism, 490

Inquisitions, 146

Insurance, 367, 415, 429
  Takeover by U.S. government, 20
  Obama care, forces America to buy, 296,
    436-437, 487, 514-515
  Insurance starts in Prussia, 340-342, In
    Sweden, 354
  in Germany, 355
  in U.S., SCHIP, 357
  Unemployment insurance, 472
  Accident, in Prussia, 341
  Health, in Prussia, 341
  Old age and disability, in Prussia, 342
Internet
  Factoid: U.N. wants to tax U.S. web sites,
    33
  Goal of socialism, 485
Ionesco, Eugene
  Factoid: "God is dead, Marx is dead, and
    I'm ...", 141
Iran, 97
  Snapshot of socialism in, 462-463
  Factoid: Taxis not allowed to pick up
    immodest women, 144
  Factoid: Khomeini executes 30,000, 232
  Factoid: "Vulgar" dressed women
    arrested, 233
Ireland
  Snapshot of socialism in, 463
Isaacs, Ben, 387
Islam, 84, 148-151, 156, 274, 462-463
  Qur'an, 149
  Factoid: Freeway sign says non-muslims
    not allowed in Mecca, 85
  Factoid: Women forbidden to drive or
    ride bikes, 86
  Factoid: Honor killings continue in
    Islam, 199
  Factoid: Book says, wife beatings okay,
    203
  Factoid: Honor killings in Pakistan, 206
  Factoid: Khomeini executes 30,000, 232
  Factoid: Arab socialism differs from
    Soviet socialism, 244
Israel, 424
  Ancient Israel wanted a king, 10
  Moses leads ancient Israel, 11-12
  People's Law in Israel, 12-13, 178-179,
    193, 220
  Essenes, 65
  Socialism in modern Israel, 151-153
  Religious leaders not religious
    government, 156
  Assault on by U.N., 489

Italy
  Factoid: Mussolini's death toll, 374
  Member of EU, 446
  Snapshot of socialism in, 464

J

Jamestown, socialism in, 131-134, 194,
    210, 450
Japan
  Health care in, 359
  Limited waistline, 362-363
Jarvis, William Charles
  Jefferson letter to, on S. Court, 298
Jefferson, Thomas
  Student of Anglo-Saxon government, 13
  Dismissed Plato, 59
  In France in 1780s, 106
  "Religion unites us," 155
  Constitution is world's best hope, 179
  "Divide the power," 181-182
  Guard power jealously quote, 183
  Quotes on "general welfare", 185
  "Constitution not a blank paper,"
    189-190
  Wards work best quote, 192
  "Mankind more disposed to suffer," 201,
    452
  Base currency on gold quote, 203
  Against socialism, 214-217
  Challenges Hamilton's views, 229-232
  Warns Washington about Hamilton,
    233-235
  How to control Supreme Court, 293-300
  Bankers more dangerous (quote), 376
  Factoid: Quote, "...soon want for bread.",
    16
  Factoid: Accuses Congress of violating
    commerce clause, 24
  Factoid: "Mankind not born with
    saddles", 42
  Factoid: "True foundation is protection
    of rights, property," 198
  Factoid:"Liberties are a gift of God," 200
  Factoid: Liberty is a precious blessing,
    219
  Factoid: Weapons protect against
    tyranny, 227
  Factoid: No castes in land of free, 234
  Factoid: Coined "monocrat", 272
  Factoid: Hamilton's financial plan bad,
    282
  Factoid: Too much government is bad
    government, 338

Factoid: Bear arms against tyrannical government, 339

Factoid: Kill democracy by taking from workers, 385

Factoid: Large cities lead to corruption, 387

Factoid: Acts of tyranny lead to slavery, 389

Factoid: Pay debts, keep peace, 431

Factoid: Don't compel men to support opposing opinions, 449

Jekyll Island, 381

Jesuit Priests
In Paraguay, 129

Jesus
Drove out money changers, 78
Socialism in Christianity, 145
Was Jesus a socialist? 156
Keep religion and government separate, 156
"Know the truth" quote, 503

Jews, 424
Factoid: Hitler killed 6,000,000, 118

Joachim of Fiore, 84

Johnson, Andrew
Gave pardon to southerners, 281

Johnson, E. A. J.
Communism and Plymouth, 139

Johnson, Lyndon
Acts of socialism, 419
Civil Rights Act (1964), 419
Vietnam war, 419
War on Poverty, 420
Medicaid, 421
Medicare, 421

John Stuart Mill, 270, 273

Jonah, Avoids Nineveh, 43

Judaism, 151, 424

Judicial Activism, 293, 311, 314
Factoid: Washington—Don't let court change Constitution, 225

Judicial Review
Authority to review Congressional Acts, 292
Jefferson comments on, 297

Judiciary, International
Create one-world court, 488

Judiciary, U.S.
Description of, 183
Chains on the Judiciary, 189
Jefferson wants chains on S. Court, 189

Jumonville Glen, Battle of
Factoid: World's most important battle, 334

K

Kazakhstan
Health care in, 360

Kelo vs. New London, 295, 296

Kennedy, John F.
Acts of socialism, 417
Bully pulpit power, 418
Cut taxes in recession, quote, 418
Food stamps, 418
Factoid: "Those who make revolution impossible ...", 237

Keynes, John Maynard, 449, 451

Khomeini, Ayatollah
Deaths responsible for, 463

Khrushchev, Nikita
Quote: "...small doses of socialism ...", 533
Factoid: "Coexistence ... develops ... socialism", 32
Factoid: Build a bridge over no river, 267

Kibbutz, 152

King
Always a bad idea, 10
Described in the Bible, 10
Hamilton supports king in U.S., 230

King Louis XIV, 105

King Louis XV, 374

Kirchner, Nestor and Cristina
Socialize Argentina, 455

Knowledge, 13, 238
Socialism cultivates ignorance, 41, 54, 71
"Knowledge necessary for freedom," Adams, 141; also, 202;
Humanist Manifesto: Abandon traditional knowledge, 272
Factoid: Madison, "Knowledge governs ignorance," 31
Factoid: Florida lowers passing grade so more could pass, 95
Factoid: Cherish knowledge, John Adams, 243

Korea, 466
Factoid: Soaps "distorting" history blacked by China, 318

Krooss, Herman
Americans feared Roosevelt's New Deal, 414

L

Labor, *see also* **Unions**
Regulate all, goal of socialism, 490
Laissez Faire, 109, 360
Factoid: Von Mises, "Man's failings are
government's failings," 81
Langdell, Christopher Columbus
Introduced "casebook method", 313
Law, 280-281, 292-298
See also **People's Law, Ruler's Law**
Law is supreme, 495
Law, John
Trillion dollar idea, 372
Law Schools, 312-315
Abandon Constitution, 306, 312
Charles W. Eliot, Harvard president,
312
Christopher Columbus Langdell, 313
Herbert Croly, 313
Roscoe Pound, 314
Legal Formalism, 314
Legal Realism, 314
Legislative Branch, U.S., 182
Legislature, World
Goal of socialism, 488
Lemonade Stands Banned, 525
Lending
Government lends to some, not others,
398
Lenin, Vladimir
French Revolution, observation about,
115
Morals decided by people, 520
Factoid: Death count under Lenin, 17
Factoid: "Give me four years", 38
Factoid: "Destroy family, you destroy
country", 196
Factoid: Freedom of press is backwards,
230
Factoid: Press is collective propagandist,
236
Factoid: Debauch currency to destroy
capitalism, 264
Factoid: Violence accompanies collapse
of capitalism, 310, 523
Factoid: Socialism grows out of
capitalism, 415
Factoid: People too dumb to value
socialism, 423
Factoid: Imperialism comes before
revolution, 459

Lennon, John
His song, "Imagine," is Communist
Manifesto, 3-4
Factoid: "Imagine" is anti-western
culture, but accepted because its
sugar coated, 102
Levi, Primo
Surviving concentration camps, 529
Levy, Robert A.
Court cases harmful to America, 296
Lewis, C. S.
Factoid: Good men make good society, 2
Libya
Factoid: Qadhafi's bodyguards all
women, 284
Lincoln, Abraham
Freedman's Bureau, 344
Acts of socialism, 405
Lindbergh, Charles A., Sr.
Warning about Federal Reserve, 384
Lithuania
Health care in, 360
Locke, John
Attributes of God, 19
Describes property rights, 195
Lott, John R. Jr.
Factoid: Gun ownership reduces crime,
45
Louis XVI, 103, 105, 108, 112, 115, 374
Factoid: 80 staff required to tend to
princess baby, 6
Ludd, Ned
Broke machines with hammer, 239
Luddites, 240
Luther, Martin, 334
Factoid: Government may compel
children to attend school, 189
Luxembourg
Member of EU, 446
Lying
Plato allows lying to keep order, 58

M

MacPherson, Elie
Factoid: Why she voted for Obama, 476
Madison, James, 178
Quotes on welfare, 184-188
Push power to lowest levels possible, 192
Republican form of government is best,
192
Property rights and liberty, 196

"Powers few and defined," 199
Gradual encroachment quote, 200
Against socialism, 215–216
Supreme Court settles Madison' fight
 with Hamilton over welfare clause,
 294
Warns that government uses crisis to take
 more power, 397
"Happily for America,", 499
Factoid: "Knowledge governs ignorance",
 31
Mafia
 Factoid: Mafia turncoat once supported
  gun control, 293
Magna Carta
 Factoid: Was never officially signed, 157
Malthus, Robert
 Uncontrolled population growth, 266
Mandela, Nelson
 Factoid: Some socialism necessary to
  catch up, 170
Mang, Wang, 66
Manicheism, Christian Socialists, 76
Manifest Destiny, 179
Mann Act (1910), 319
Mao Zedong
 Factoid: "Socialism will replace
  capitalism," 84
 Factoid: Army must become one with
  people, 99
 Factoid: "Where do correct ideas come
  from?", 146
 Factoid: Rockefeller praised Mao's killings
  as successful experiment, 158-159
 Factoid: Before killing millions, declared
  to "Serve people heart and soul", 166
 Factoid: Rulers needed at all levels of
  society, 178
 Factoid: Communist Party is core of
  socialistic cause, 322
 Factoid: Control of information needed
  to reach goals, 344
Marbury vs. Madison, 293
 Jefferson objects to, 298
Marcuse, Herbert
 Destroy the individual, 17
Margarine Tax, 318
Marshall, John
 Role in Supreme Court evolution, 292
Martial Law
 Imposed by Lincoln, 405

Martin vs. Hunter's Lessee, 293
Marxist Encyclopedia
 Labor is 100% of value, 522
Marx, Karl, 269-270
 Marx's Manifesto put to music, 3
 "I will stride through the wreckage," 5
 Destroy the individual, 17
 Influenced by Joachim, 85
 "From each according to his ..." 131-132,
  364, 511
 Marxist socialism, 168
 Influenced by Robert Owen, 245
 Evolution, support of Darwin, 268
 Capital, 269
 Plato, shared ideas with, 269
 Thoughts and teachings, 269
 Communist Manifesto, 269, 277, 329, 407
 Flawed theories, thinking, 270
 Herr Werner Sombart calls Marx
  contradictory, 270
 Marx's ideas of graduated income tax,
  283, 304, 407
 Marx's tax idea included in 16th
  Amendment, 283
 Religion is opium of the people, 520
 Factoid: Peace is accepting socialism, 54
 Factoid: "Dethrone God ...", 62
 Factoid: Theory of communism means no
  private property, 71
 Factoid: "Workers of the world unite", 145
 Factoid: "I am not a Marxist", 151
 Factoid: Harvard only place where
  Marxists still survive, 183
 Factoid: Marx's failed prophecies don't
  stop his followers, 295
 Factoid: Kimball "Marx's predictions were
  wrong," 298
 Factoid: Quote, praises Darwin, 304
 Factoid: Decades of war needed for
  socialism, 453
Massachusetts, 137
 State supreme court legalizes labor, 253
 Hopedale, Mass., utopian society, 260
 Health Care fraud, 358
 Factoid: School banned tag, 285
 Factoid: Bake sales banned, too fattening,
  301
 Factoid: Environmental Police close ice
  cream stand, 313
 Factoid: Day-care children required to
  brush teeth, 398
Mayflower Compact, 135

Mazdakians, Christian Socialists, 77
McCorvey, Norma
  As Jane Roe in Roe vs. Wade, 295
Meat Inspection Act, 277, 319
Medicare, 365, 421
  Free for nothing attitude, 353
  Congress's inability to predict costs, 357
  ObamaCare and Medicare, 357, 420-421, 436
  Fraud and false claims, 359
  And Bill Clinton, 429
  And George Bush, 432
  Factoid: Entitlements cost $102 trillion, 202
  Factoid: Medicare is $25 trillion liability, 270, 326
Medicine
  UN calls for socialized medicine, 368
Merriam, Charles, 301
  Force western culture on others, 306
Mexico
  Factoid: Minutes to earn a Big Mac in, 14
  Factoid: Consumers pay 16% sales tax, 94
  Factoid: If you discover oil, you must surrender land, 108
  Factoid: Only communist or socialist political parties, 155
  Factoid: Socialized medicine delays surgery, 226
  Factoid: Knee joint patient had to buy own surgical hardware, 300
Mill, John Stuart
  Competition a part of human nature, 32
Ming, Tao Yuan
  Peach Blossom Spring (poem), 274
Minimum Wages, 394, 408, 426
  Fabians proposed, 169
  and Pope Leo XIII, 263
  and progressives, 306-308
  and Kennedy, 417
  and Reagan, 426
Mises, Ludwig von
  Defines socialism, 164
  Factoid: "Innovators defy school," 28
  Factoid: "Only individual thinks", 36
  Factoid: No freedom in art if ..., 67
  Factoid: "If one rejects laissez faire", 81
  Factoid: "Men will always strive to improve", 184
  Factoid: "Change involves risks", 194
  Factoid: "Only the individual thinks", 242

Factoid: All achievements because of liberty, 357
Factoid: High standards equals high culture, 367
Factoid: Importance of "selling" freedom, 405
Factoid: Men always strive for improvement, 456
Monasteries, 74, 89-90
  Dissolution of the Monasteries, 335-338
Money, 81, *see also* Banks, Central
  Ananias and Sapphira cheat Peter, 160-161
  Reasons to raise money (taxes), 186-216
  Madison: Restricted use of money, 188
  States may not coin own, 188
  Washington cautions about taxes, 197
  Manipulation by government, 202-203
  Congressman's term of 2 years to prevent abuse of money, 230
  Using money to corrupt, 232, 353
  Regulation of money, 234-35, 353
  Socializing the money, 371-401
  Power behind the throne is money, 376
  Banks motivated to create debt, 376
  Great depression extended, 394
  Factoid: Took 60 years to spend first billion, 470
Montesquieu, 108
  Separation of Powers, 181
Moran, Jim
  Threatening government force, 20
More, Thomas
  Utopian socialism, 167
  Utopia (book), 275
Morgan, J.P.
  Knickerbocker bank, 379
Morrill Land Grant Act, 344
Moses, 75, 85, 149
  and People's Law, 11-14, 156, 178
  Organizing families of 10s, 50s, 100s..., 193
Movies, Socialism in, 128
Mugabe, Robert, 475
  Factoid: Arrested man who made casual joke, 436
Mussolini, Benito
  Deaths responsible for, 464
  Factoid: Death count by Mussolini regime, 374
  Fascism explained, 170

N

Napoleon Bonaparte, *see* Bonaparte, Napoleon
Napoleonic Code, 241
National Borders
No borders under socialism, 522
National Debt
Of various nations, 453-476
Hamilton supports monetizing, 228, 233-235
and Reagan, 426
and Obama 434-443
Factoid: Interest costs per month, 191
Factoid: Jefferson opposes national debt, 282
National Health Care
Canada, Emergency Room disaster, 526
Sweden, Emergency Room disaster, 526
Britain, mistakes and sloppiness, 527
National Health Service (NHS), 353, 356, 362, 527-528
National Labor Relations Board, 255
National Reserve Bank, 381
Natural Law, 195, 317, 491
Anglo-Saxons, 178
Cicero, 204-209
Natural Resources
Goal of socialism, 488
Nature vs. Nurture, 244
Nazi
Factoid: WWII, human brains delivered to Nazi doctors, 138
Factoid: Goebbels teaches how to tell a lie, 397
Nelson, Knute, 383
Neo-Progressives, 301
Netherlands
Member of EU, 446
New Deal, 323, 348, 395
H.G. Wells, New Deal is the socializing of America, 165
and Hoover, 395, 412-414
and Roosevelt, 395-401, 414-415
and Johnson, 419-421
and G.H.W. Bush, 427-428
and Obama, 437
"New Deal" Constitution, 390, 397
Factoid: Schlesinger, New Deal was socializing of U.S., 496-497
New Harmony, Indiana, 266

Robert Owen's failed experiment, 246
New Jersey
Factoid: Pets ordered to be in seat belts, 179
Factoid: Man charged for displaying flags, 182
New World Order
Factoid: Right major crisis will lead to, 254
New York
Factoid: Mayor bans sodas, sugary drinks, 406
New Zealand
Health care in, 362
NHS, see National Health Services
Nicolaites, First Christian Socialists, 75
Nietzsche, Friedrich, 303
God is dead, 303
Factoid: Price to own yourself is steep, 372
Nimrod, Ancient Ruler, 36
Nineveh, 43
Nixon, Richard M.
Acts of socialism, 421
National health care proposal, 423
Wage and price controls, 423
Gerald Ford, un-elected president, 289
Norris-LaGuardia Act, 394
North Dakota
Factoid: Eliminates property tax, 373
North Korea
Prisons and re-education camps, 465
Snapshot of socialism in, 465
Socialism needs a host, 478
Factoid: Reporters discover ghost cities, 92
Factoid: Arrests are high so police can get more bribes, 119
Factoid: Women yells at cop demanding bribe, 136
Factoid: 67 North Korea negotiators were murdered by Dear Leader, 140
Factoid: 3 million starved to death after U.S.SR dissolved, 161
Factoid: Drivers licenses more expensive for foreign motorcycles, 167
Factoid: Soldiers ordered to shoot people escaping, 172
Factoid: Television broadcasts Dear Leader 24 x 7, 283
Factoid: Socialism caused 3 million famine deaths, 302

Factoid: Dependent on China for food and energy, 320
Factoid: Chronic malnutrition, 348
Factoid: Reporters sneak in, see 65-foot statue, 407
Factoid: No wages, sporadic services, elitists get the best, 439
Northwest Ordinance, 202
Norway
  Factoid: Sales tax added to food, 12
  Factoid: Bus ride tax, 46
  Factoid: Tax on non-food items, 52
Nuclear Weapons
  Goal of socialism, 489
Nurture
  Nature vs. nurture, 245
Nyerere, Julius
  Socialism is natural, 102

O

Obama, Barack
  Quotes promoting envy, 19
  Threatening government force, 21
  Acts of socialism, 434
  Organize power to force change, 435
  Recess appointments, violating, 435
  TARP, 435
  Death panels, 436
  Ignored Legislative Branch, 437
  National Health Care, 1, 436
  Violating freedom of religion, 437
  Violating property rights, 437
  Cash for Clunkers, 438
  Stimulus bill, 2009, 438
  Student loans, nationalizing, 438
  U.N., appointing self to, 438
  Healthy, Hunger-Free Kids Act of 2010, 439
  Federal employment roles, expanding, 439
  Illegal immigrants, 439
  Dodd-Frank Bill, 440
  Fast and Furious gun walking operation, 441
  Is he a socialist?, 441
  Wanted a Praetorian Guard?, 516
  Factoid: Strikes deal with drug makers for health care support, 77
  Factoid: In three years, Obama increased national debt $4.7 trillion, 88
  Factoid: Vandalized on-line presidential biographies, 153

Factoid: Declares young illegals won't be deported, 207
Factoid: Adds thousands of new rules, 217
Factoid: Obama tries to bribe Pastor Wright to keep quiet, 314
Factoid: Christmas tree tax, 388
Factoid: Spent $1 billion every 2.3 hours, 470
Factoid: Welfare spending grew 70.5%, 475
Factoid: Dependency shot up 23% in 2 years, 474
Factoid: Giddy voter relieved no more mortgage, 488
ObamaCare, 357-358, 436-439, 514-516
  Supreme Court sidesteps Constitution and allows, 296
Obama, Michelle
  Promoting class envy, 20
Oleomargarine Act (1886), 318
O'Neill, Rebecca
  Impact of no father, 531
OPEC
  And oil crisis during Carter, 424
Opium, 322
Oranges
  Factoid: Millions dumped to keep prices high, 113
Original Intent, 299
O'Rourke, P.J.
  Factoid: The democrats are ... the republicans are ..., 384
Orwell, George
  Factoid: Wrote 'Animal Farm' to expose socialism, 311
OSHA, 22, 422
Ouroboros, xiv, 508
Owen, Robert, 260-261, 266, 381
  Biography, 244-246
  Belief in incentives, 245, 266
  and Marx, 245
  and Engels, 245
  New Harmony, failed experiment, 246
  and Frederick Maurice, 260

P

Packer, Boyd K.
  Factoid: "Old men talk of the past because ...", 303

Pakistan
  Factoid: Honor killings in 2011, 206
Palyi, Dr. Melchior
  Political power from health care, 348
Panama Canal
  Carter signs away, 424
Panic of 1907, 379, 390
Panic of 1921, 391
Papa John's Pizza
  Factoid: Costs go up due to Obama
    health care, 419
Papandreou, George, 447
Parker, Star, 401
  Escaped welfare trap, 453-454
Parlement, French Parliament, 106,
  110-111
Parliament, English, 99, 106
  Rulers bypass parliament, 5
  One of three powers in government, 108
  Three kinds of Republics, 220
  and Hamilton, 232
  and the monasteries, 334-347
  European Union, 446-447
Patman, Wright, 386
Patriot Act, 433
Pelosi, Nancy
  Acts of socialism, 436
Penn, William
  Factoid: Men will be governed by God or
    tyrants, 63
People's Law, 11-19, 178-180
  Eleven traits of People's Law, 12
Pericles,
  Democracy was a disaster, 219
Peru
  Conquered by Pizarro, 123
  Snapshot of socialism in, 466
Peter, Apostle
  And early Church, 160
  Did Early Christians Practice
    Communism? 159-162
Petition, freedom to, 201
Peyrefitte, Alain
  French illness, 451
Pharaoh, Egyptian Ruler, 33
Pilgrims, 135-141
Pillars, Abolishing the Seven, 181-211
  See **Seven Pillars of Socialism**
Pitt, Sir William
  Banks greater than king (quote), 376
Pizarro, 123

Plato, 53
  Biographical sketch, 56-59
  Rejected by Founders, 59
  Rejected at Plymouth, 139
  The Republic (book), 274
  Factoid: "Tyrant comes first as protector",
    44
  Factoid: Why decent people accept
    power, 127
Plymouth, Socialism in, 135
Poland
  Factoid: Socialism led to communism,
    286
Polio
  Factoid: Taliban threatens to withhold
    vaccinations, 20
Politburo, 446
Polybius
  Describes socialism's deadly cycle, 71
  How Power is Spread Out, 181
Ponzi Scheme, 385, 450
Poor Laws, 1500s-1800s, 336-338, 455
Pope 79, 84-85, 87-89, 105, 146, 334
  Who is real Pope? 89, 330
  Pope Leo XIII, pro-union encyclical,
    1891, 263-264
  French popes challenge Rome, 330-334
Pope John Paul II
  Factoid: Quote, Socialism increases
    inefficiency, 171
Population Growth
  Malthus' theories on, 266
  Goal of socialism, 487
Pork Barrel
  Carter tries to reduce spending on, 423
Portugal
  Snapshot of socialism in, 467
Postal Roads, 186
Potemkin Village
  Factoid: WWII, Germany builds fake
    villages, 231
  Factoid: "Fake villages" alive in Tibet, 342
  Factoid: Fake villages in the U.S., 378
  Factoid: North Korea built village to
    encourage immigrants, 411
Potts, Quaker Isaac
  Sees Washington pray, 505
Pound, Roscoe
  Started "legal realism", 314
Poverty
  Factoid: Poverty has no cause, prosperity
    does, 205

Factoid: Poor in U.S. have TVs, AC, computers..., 208
Factoid: Poverty not bad until there was prosperity, 360
Power
Founding Fathers' sliding scale of political power, 8, 176
Separation of power, Polybius, 71, 181
Divide the power, Jefferson quote, 181-182
Guard power jealously, Jefferson quote, 183
Push power to lowest level, Madison quote, 192
Enumerated powers in U.S., 176-211, 198
Power not delegated belongs to people, 208
Can lead to socialism, Jefferson quote, 217
Evolving power of the Supreme Court 292
Government uses crisis to take power, 397
Power behind the throne is money, 376
Health Care changes who has power, 348
Regulation leads to unfair power, 296, 410
Obama uses power to force change, 435
EU consolidates power, 449
Factoid: Plato, who decent men accept power, 127
Praetorian Guards
Protect dictators, 516
President
Chains on the President, 183-184
25th Amendment allows un-elected president, 289
U.S. presidents and socialism, 405-443
Lincoln, 405-406
Cleveland, 406-407
Teddy Roosevelt, 407-408
Taft, 409-410
Wilson, 410-412
Hoover, 412-414
Franklin D. Roosevelt, 414-415; *see also* **New Deal**
Truman, 415-416
Kennedy, 417-419
Johnson, 419-421
Nixon, 421-423

Carter, 423-424
Reagan, 425-426
George H. W. Bush, 427-428
Clinton, 428-431
George W. Bush, 431-433
Obama, 434-443
Price Controls
French regulations, 116
and Theodore Roosevelt, 305
and Nixon, 423
Priests
Jesuit Priests in Paraguay, 129-130
Printing Press, 91, 333
Privacy, 207, 282, 348, 431, 433, 440
Wilson says no line between private and public, 411
Violated by 16th Amendment, 282
Clinton: does private life impact public life? 431
Progressives, 301
History of progressivism, 225
Hamilton is first progressive, 227
Progressive Party Platform of 1912, 306
Prohibition
18th Amendment ratified, 286
Goal of socialism, 305
As an example of force, 529
Factoid: Saloons grew in NY, 37
Factoid: Mark Twain, "Prohibition drives drunkenness behind...", 55
Propaganda
Factoid: Joseph Goebbels quote, 5
Property, Freedom To
3rd Unalienable Right, 15
Saves Jamestown, 134
Saves Plymouth, 139
In Bill of Rights, 207
Kelo vs. New London (2005), 295, 296
Forced to surrender property, 297
Food and Fuel Control Act of 1917, 304
Hoover and Garfield violate, 304
Eliminate, goal of socialism, 486
Prosperity
Prosperity and compassion, 16
Prosperity eludes Jamestown, 131-134
Prosperity eludes Plymouth, 135-141
Ayn Rand, socialism delivers opposite of prosperity, 172
Webster defines, 184
Unions ruin prosperity, 256, 297
Europeans lured to American prosperity, 341-342

Obama promises sharing the prosperity, 443
Factoid: Poverty has no cause, Prosperity does, 205
Factoid: Poverty wasn't bad until there was prosperity, 360
Protestants
Abused by Catholics, 105
Prussia, 339
War with Austria, 114
Prussians liberate Belgium, 1792, 115
Modern welfare born in Prussia, 339–342
Prussia's lewd Prince Henry considered for king of America, 230

Q

Qadhafi, Moammar
Factoid: Female bodyguards, 284
Factoid: Preached sharing, hoarded billions, 413

R

Raccoon
Where the Red Fern Grows, 501
Race
Violation of equal protection, 297
Railroads
Shreveport Rate Case (1914), 305
Raleigh, Sir Walter, 131
Establishes colony at Roanoke, 131
Rand, Ayn
Definitions of socialism, 171
Factoid: "Every major horror", 39
Ranters, Christian socialists, 94
Rawls, Wilson
Where the Red Fern Grows, 501
Reagan, Ronald
Abortion, 425
Air traffic controllers' strike, 425
Governor, 425
Attempts to shrink government, 426
Education, Department of, 426
National debt grows, 426
Role in ending Cold War, 426
"Tear down this wall," 426
Factoid: Government must control people to control economy, 78
Factoid: Politics similar to world's oldest profession, 421
Factoid: Cut taxes, charity increased, 482
Reed, James A., 382

Regulation, 186, 294, 345
and EU, 4
and Nimrod, 37
and China, 39
and India, 60
and the heretics, 76
and France, 103
and Inca, 125-27
Abolishing Pillar #4—Regulation," 197-198
Jefferson: Be free to self-regulate, 214
Hamilton's central bank regulated money supply, 234
Expanding power of, 296
and WWI, 304
Regulating food, 319
Regulating money, 165
Bypasses legislative branch, 398
Federal Reserve Act, 412
EPA regulations, 422
and Carter, 423
Sarbanes-Oxley, 433
ObamaCare and regulating the nation, 436-437
Goal of socialism, 491
Factoid: Cost of U.S. regulation agencies, 337
Factoid: Costs of regulations and impact, 484
Reid, Harry
Acts of socialism, 436, 442
Reisman, George
Factoid: "Socialists are slaves but no one's property," 98
Religion
Socialism in Religion, 144
Franklin's "universal religion", 155
Freedom of Religion in France, 114
United States, 201
Abolishing Pillar #6, 201
America founded on Christianity, John Adams quote, 273
Everson vs. Board of Education (1947), 294
Protected in Bill of Rights, 206
Religious revivalists, 260
Adin Ballou, 260
Frederick Denison Maurice, 260
Pope Leo XIII, 263
Sidney Rigdon, 261
Eliminate tax advantages, 487
Goal of socialism, 487

Proper role of government, 495
Factoid: Freeway sign bans non-muslim drivers from entering Mecca, 85
Factoid: Adams, "Morality and religion needed for freedom," 330
Factoid: Alger Hiss, to achieve world government ..., 443
Representation
and Moses, 11-13, 113-114, 179, 193
and Bastiat, 166
U.S. Congress, 182-183
Abolishing Pillar #2—The Caste, 192
Madison quote, republican form works best, 192
Bill of Rights, 207
Democracy vs. republic, 219-221
Senator no longer represents state, 283-286
Representatives for District of Columbia, 287-288
Justice Antonin Scalia on, 315
Goal of socialism, 483
Destroy representation, a goal of socialism, 485
Republic
Replace republic with Democracy, 303
Republican form of Government
Constitution guarantees it, 193
Three kinds of republics, 220
Republic, The
By Plato, 274
Resources, Natural
Goal of socialism, 488
Revenue Act, 395
Rights
Vested rights, defined, 13
Independent individual, 14
Natural rights, 14
Three parts of, 14
Unalienable rights, defined, 14
The Eight Rights, 14
  Independent individuals, 14
  Association, 15, 24
  Choice, 15, 24
  Property, 15, 24
  Compassion, 16, 24
  Defense, 16, 24
  Equality, 16, 24
  Failure, 17, 24
  Use the 8 rights to test truthfulness of a bill or act, 23-25

Abolishing Pillar #7, 204
Hamilton questions listing rights, 206
Protected in Bill of Rights, 208
Delegation of individual rights to the government, 495
Endowed by God, 495
Rights, Using As A Test of Truthfulness, 23-25
Riis, Jacob
How the Other Half Lives (book), 276
Roaring Twenties, 392
Robespierre, 116
Rockefeller, David
Factoid: Praised Mao's death toll as "successful", 158
Factoid: Right major crisis leads to new world order, 254
Rockefeller, Nelson A.
Un-elected vice president, 289
Roe vs. Wade (1973), 295
Romania
Health care in, 360
Factoid: Giant palace costs $4.5 billion, 228-229
Rome, Ancient, 64
How socialism killed Rome, 67, 71
Fall of Rome and Feudalism, 80
Roosevelt, Franklin D.
Quotes promoting envy, 20
Outlaws gold ownership, 304
Bankers own government (quote), 376
Father of New Deal, 395, 397
Acts of socialism, 414
Economic Bill of Rights, 415
Factoid: Tries to ignore Constitution, 366
Roosevelt, Theodore, 316
Bankers are invisible government, 377
Acts of socialism, 407
"America's Steward", 407
National parks and monuments, 408
Progressive Party (Bull Moose), 408
Rothschild, Mayer Amschel
On controlling money, 384
Rousseau, Jean Jacques, 108
Ruler, Ruler's Law
First pillar of socialism, 5-6
Ten traits of Ruler's Law, 8-10
During middle ages, 80
Abolishing the Ruler, 181
Examples of, 71, 524

Rummel, R.J.
China death count, 458
Cuba death count, 459
Italy death count, 464
North Korea death count, 466
Russia death count, 469
Vietnam death count, 475
Rushdie, Salman
Factoid: Without freedom to offend ...,
238
Russia
Snapshot of socialism in, 468
Factoid: 75% grow food to survive, 10
Factoid: Abortion restricted, 354
Factoid: Government privatized 20,000
enterprises, 356 *Factoid:* Free health
care part of constitution, 375
Factoid: Man in jail for spitting on
portrait of Putin, 410
Factoid: 18 million government workers,
454
Rwanda
Factoid: Mass murder of 800,000 to
retain power, 463

S

Sabath, Adolph J., 382
Salt Tax, 104, 110
Samuelson, Paul
Factoid: Quote, USSR proof socialism
works (just before it fell), 93
Sapphira
and socialism, 161
Sarbanes-Oxley (SOX), 433
Sartre, Jean-Paul
Destroy the individual, 18
Scale
Founders' measure of political force, 8
Scalia, Antonin, 315
Schakowsky, Jan
Threatening government force, 21
Schlesinger, Arthur Jr.
Factoid: No stopping the advance of
socialism, 497
Scopes, John, 311
Sedition Act of 1918, 307
Seditious Assembling Act of 1795, 240
Senate
Description of, 182
Hamilton's idea for lifetime appointment,
229

17th Amendment destroys
representation, 283, 393
Progressives push for direct vote of, 303
The great concession, 393
Goals of socialism, 485
Separation of Powers
Separation of power, Polybius quote, 181
Divide the power, Jefferson quote,
181-182
Seven Pillars of Socialism
Diagram, xi
Seven Pillars Listed and explained, 5
Abolishing the Pillars, 181–209
Seventeenth Amendment, 182, 485
Sexual Activity Unrestrained
Nicolaites, 75
Carpocratians, 76
Manicheism, 76
Mazdakians, 78
Cathars, 83
Apostolic Brethren, 86
Taborites, 90
Adamites, 90
Anabaptists, 91
Ranters, 94
Engels observes rebellions usually turn
to sexual liberties, 95
Factoid: Bebel says sexual activity is
neither moral nor immoral, 111
Shafroth, John, 382
Shaw, Chief Justice Lemuel
Rules in Bootmakers Strike, 1839, 254
Shaw, George Bernard
Socialism is forced, 520
Shreveport Rate Case
Private control over rails lost, 305
Sinclair, Upton
The Jungle (book), 277
Factoid: Americans will take socialism
but not the label, 75
Skousen, Paul B.
About the author, 535
Skousen, W. Cleon
Did the Early Christians Practice
Communism? 159
The 286 rights in Constitution, 205
Factoid: Cecil B. DeMille names Naked
Communist, xiv
Slavery
Anti-slavery, "3/5ths", 280
Small Business, 387
Smoot-Hawley Tariff Act, 393-395

Snake
Fable of hiker picking up snake, 501
"Socialism progresses like ....", 508
Social Democracy
Goal of socialism, 483
Socialism
What is socialism? 3
Socialism in ancient history, 27
Socialism in classical history, 50
Socialism in the middle ages, 74
Christianity and socialism
Nicolaites, AD 100, 75
Carpocratians, AD 200, 75
Manicheism, AD 300, 76
Mazdakians, AD 400, 77
Cathars, AD 1100, 82
Brethren of the Free Spirit, AD 1200,
84
Taborites, AD 1300, 74, 88, 91
Apostolic Brethren, 86
Anabaptists, AD 1525, 91
Diggers, AD 1640, 92
Ranters, AD 1649, 94
Socialism in the early Americas, 121
Christian Socialists, 145
Socialism in Religion, 144
Definitions from multiple sources, 163
Socialism du jour, 167
Types of socialism
Democratic socialism, 167
Utopian socialism, 167
Fabian socialism, 168
Market socialism, 168
Marxism, 168
Scientific socialism, 168
Christian socialism, 169
Fascism, 169
Environmental socialism, 170
Ayn Rand quotes on socialism, 171
Miracle that stopped socialism, 176
Founding Fathers speak against, 214
Socializing the U.S., 224
Socializing the money, 372
Thinking like a socialist, 71, 404
Socialism and U.S. presidents, 405-443
Socialism today in the World, 446
46 Goals of socialism, 482
Socialism needs a host, 476
U.S. is legally anti-socialist, 496
Bees—socialism in the wild, 510
Violence necessary to adopt, 71, 523
Factoid: Prager, "Socialism values
equality...", 11

Factoid: Lenin, "Goal of socialism is ...",
17
Factoid: Mailer, "Purpose is to raise
suffering," 29
Factoid: Khrushchev, "Peaceful
coexistence," 32
Factoid: Plato, "Tyrant comes first as
protector", 44
Factoid: Socialism is squalor of envy, 51
Factoid: Sandlin, "wealth and misery
redistributed," 53
Factoid: Marx, "Peace is accepting
socialism", 54
Factoid: Lord Acton, "Socialism means
slavery", 56
Factoid: Socialism is born inside a man,
57
Factoid: Castro quote on failure of
capitalism, 58
Factoid: Low taxes equals more jobs., 61
Factoid: Promises of S. delectable to
fast-food mentality, 70
Factoid: Americans will take S. but not
the label, 75
Factoid: Quote, Mao, socialism will
replace capitalism, 84
Factoid: Prostate cancer survival lower
than U.S., 90
Factoid: Two reporters discover ghost
cities in North Korea, 92
Factoid: Samuelson boasts USSR
socialism works, just before it fell,
93
Factoid: Socialists are slaves, but no one's
property, 98
Factoid: Socialism is amoral, they decide
what is right and wrong, 100
Factoid: In Mexico, hiding oil discovery
is crime, 108
Factoid: Millions of U.S. oranges
dumped to keep prices high, 112
Factoid: Unions balked at Obama
pollution rules in 2011, 114
Factoid: California traffic camera caught
cheating to get more tickets, 115
Factoid: Arrests in North Korea high
because guards get more bribes,
119
Factoid: In U.S., Obama had 4,257 new
regulations planned, 123
Factoid: San Francisco bans plastic bags
in 2007, 124
Factoid: India day care takes children
24x7, 125

Factoid: Government help for me is good, for others is socialism, 148

Factoid: Religion teaches opposite of equality, 152

Factoid: Some socialism necessary for South Africa to catch up, 170

Factoid: Pope John Paul II, socialism makes things worse, 171

Factoid: "Pink tide" of socialism in South America, 173

Factoid: New Jersey orders pets be put in seat belts, 179

Factoid: Thinking like a socialist, woman tweets Obama, 186

Factoid: When survival threatened, socialism is abandoned, 195

Factoid: Socialism only works in heaven and hell, 197

Factoid: Honor killings in Islam continue, 199

Factoid: Revolutions put on same robes as deposed, 204

Factoid: Only four socialist nations in 2012, 212

Factoid: Quote, "Socialism leads to Communism...", 213

Factoid: "A liberal is a person whose interests ...", 221

Factoid: Arab socialism is different from Soviet socialism, 244

Factoid: Slave more virtuous than master, 245

Factoid: India girl sacrificed for harvest, 274

Factoid: Political terms, "socialism" disliked, 276

Factoid: Welfare abuser steals $1.2 million, 277

Factoid: Socialism led to Communism in Poland, 286

Factoid: Synonyms for socialism, 294

Factoid: Famine deaths in North Korea, 302

Factoid: U.S. entitlements cost $102 trillion, 202

Factoid: Socialism kills, Soviet Union death toll, 305

Factoid: Ruler of Turkmenistan makes golden statue of self, 309

Factoid: Lenin quote, violence accompanies rise of socialism, 310

Factoid: Violence accompanies rise of socialism, 310

Factoid: Orwell wrote 'Animal Farm' to expose socialism, 311

Factoid: Massachusetts police close ice cream stand, 313

Factoid: "Socialism is the religion people get when ...", 316

Factoid: U.S. liabilities in detail, 326

Factoid: Socialism leads to communism in Hungary, 327

Factoid: Hypocrisy of leaders, Brezhnev's luxury cars, 328

Factoid: Oxymoron, "peace through governance", 336

Factoid: Cost of regulatory agencies, 337

Factoid: Stalin, Socialism is to consolidate power, 340

Factoid: Freedom is strength, S. is weakness, 350

Factoid: Security guards in Sweden's health clinics, 351

Factoid: Socialism abandoned in Sweden, 1992, 368

Factoid: Bailed out bank donates to global warming fight, 382

Factoid: Churchill, socialism is sharing of misery, 394

Factoid: Socialism grows out of capitalism, 415

Factoid: I can understand communism, but not socialism, 428

Factoid: Socialism leads to communism in Italy and France, 434

Factoid: Marxists compare best of socialism to worst of capitalism, 438

Factoid: Socialism creates shortages, standing in line, 450

Factoid: When socialists see light, they buy more tunnel, 490

Factoid: Schlesinger says no stopping socialism in the U.S., 497

Socialism In History

Sumer, 4000 BC, 29

Egypt, 2600 BC, 33

Nimrod, 2200 BC, 36

China, 1750 BC, 38

Assyria, 750 BC, 42

Sparta, 650 BC, 52

Draco, 621 BC, 50

Aristophanes, 400 BC, 62

India, 400 BC, 60

Plato, 400 BC, 56

Rome, 140 BC, 64, 71

Essenes, 100 BC, 65

Diodorius, 100 BC, 63
China, Wang Mang, AD 9, 66
Christianity, AD 30, 74
Feudalism, middle ages, 80
Socialism, Learning To Recognize, 70-71
Destroying status of individual, 17
In Ancient Times, 45
Early Christian heresies, 79
Christian Heresies, 94
French Revolution, 118
Portrayed in modern media, 128
Various definitions, 166
Impact of various groups, 171
Stopped by a miracle, 209
Federal government abandoned
Constitution, 221
In religion, 264
Socialism, Snapshot of World
Argentina, 455
Australia, 457
Canada, 457
China, 457
Cuba, 458
France, 460
Germany, 461
Greece, 462
Iran, 462
Ireland, 463
Italy, 464
North Korea, 465
Peru, 466
Portugal, 467
Russia, 468
Spain, 469
Sweden, 470
United Kingdom, 471
United States, 472
Venezuela, 473
Vietnam, 474
Zimbabwe, 475
Socialist Party of America, 309
Socialist Party of Canada, 519, 521, 523
Socialist Party of Great Britain, 518
Social Security
And anchor babies, 281
Modern dictators believe in, 369
Teddy Roosevelt calls for, 408
Under Kennedy, 417
FDR pushes for, 415
Under Johnson, 421
Factoid: Entitlements cost $102 trillion,
202

Society
Importance of family, 532
Soviet Union, 446
Health care in, 354, 359
Socialism needs a host, 477
Black market saves the empire, 529
Factoid: Death count under Stalin, 15
Factoid: Samuelson brags USSR
economy works, just before it fell,
93
Factoid: Death count from 1922-1991,
305
Factoid: Standing in line was normal,
450
Factoid: Former Party leaders rule
"freed" nations, 452
Sowell, Thomas
Factoid: Socialism's failure is so blatant
that ..., 65
Factoid: Welfare destroyed black family,
361
Spain
Snapshot of socialism in, 469
Spalding, Franklin Spencer
Defines socialism, 165
Sparta
Warrior Socialists, 52
Factoid: 25,000 citizens with 500,000
slaves, 106
Speech, Freedom of, 201
France, 114
Eroding freedom of speech, 296

Stalin, Joseph
Soviet death county under Stalin, 15
(Factoid), 469
Factoid: Socialism is to consolidate
power, 340
Factoid: Undermine three areas to
topple U.S., 471
Factoid: Collective farming caused
"Black Famine", 491
State Legislatures
Description and role, 183
State of the Union
Requirement to report on, 202
States, 182, 186-187, 196-200
Chains on the States, 188-189
States may not tax states, 189
Veto Supreme Court with 3/5ths states'
vote, 190, 297
Abortion is states' rights issue, 198, 287

10th Amendment, all other powers go to states, 198

Right-to-work states, 257-259

14th amendment overrides states rights, 280

Supreme Court forced Bill of Rights on states, 294

States' rights usurped by Roosevelt, 398

Sovereign, 496

Factoid: Best states are right to work, 393

Sterling, Thomas, 383

Stevenson, Adlai

Factoid: Stop telling lies, I'll stop telling truth, 455

Storehouse

Sumer, 29-31

Egypt, 34

China, 44

Inca, 123-124

Jamestown, 131

Plymouth, 135

Honeybees, 512

Stringer, Lawrence B., 382

Strong, Benjamin, 386

Sumer

Socialism in the culture, 29

Super Legislature

Supreme Court overrides Congress, 292

Supremacy, Judicial

Supremacy of Supreme Court, 292

Supreme Court

Chains on the Supreme Court, 190

Anti-Constitution cases, 291

Restrictions on, Article 3 of Constitution, 291

Evolution of power, 292

Gibbons vs. Ogden (1824), 293

Martin vs. Hunter's Lessee (1816), 293

Marbury vs. Madison (1803), 293

Everson vs. Board of Education (1947), 294

United States vs. Butler (1936), 294

Garcia vs. San Antonio Metro. Transit Authority (1985), 295

Roe vs. Wade (1973), 295

Kelo vs. New London (2005), 295, 296

Jefferson amendment to override Supreme Court, 297-298

Destroy democracy, Jefferson quote, 300

Judicial Activism, 311

Factoid: Washington quote, judicial activism unconstitutional, 225

Factoid: Cited international law in murder case, 312

Factoid: What age for abortion? Murder?, 332

Sutherland, George

Right of or to property?, 195

Swanson, Claude A., 381, 383

Sweden

Health care in, 354, 366

Expensive drugs denied, 363

Snapshot of socialism in, 470

Factoid: 12 weeks to see doctor, 60

Factoid: No job growth under socialism, 61

Factoid: Taxes higher than U.S., 64

Factoid: Average wait for medical care after doctor, 12 weeks, 66

Factoid: Security guards in health clinics, 351

Factoid: Prime minister abandons socialism, 368

T

Taborites

Christian heresy, 88

Taft-Hartley Act, 415

Taft, William Howard

Acts of socialism, 409

Income tax amendment, pushed for, 409

Taliban

Factoid: Threatens to withhold polio medications, 20

Taney, Roger B.

Role in Supreme Court evolution, 292

Tariffs, 109

Progressives promote tariffs, 306

Smoot-Hawley Act, 393-395

TARP, 389, 432

Taxes

Equal taxation, 196

Tax violates equal protection, 281

16th Amendment, income tax, 282

Income tax during Civil War, 304

Contribute to Great Depression, 395

Graduated income taxes, 407

Progressive Income Tax, 410

Proper role of government, 496

Factoid: Taxes lower in U.S. than many socialist nations, 64

Factoid: North Dakota eliminates property taxes, 373

Factoid: New Yorkers pad $1 million in taxes, 466

Factoid: Cutting taxes increased charitable giving, 482

Ten Commandments
Engels condemns as capitalistic, 522

Thailand
Factoid: Criticizing monarch punishable by prison, 404

Thanksgiving, 135

Thatcher, Margaret
Socialists always run out of other people's money, 476
Factoid: Socialism is like curing leukemia with leeches, 69

Thomas, Norman
No national borders under socialism, 523
No private property allowed, 521

Thorne, Oakleigh, 380

Toast, Early America
Factoid: "Equal rights for all ...", 315

Tocqueville, Alexis de
Defines socialism, 163

Tolstoy, Leo
Factoid: Change the world, not one's self? 386

Torture, 146

Tragedy of the Commons, 351

Transportation
Regulate, goal of socialism, 485

Trash
Government monitoring of, 524
Trash Czar, 524
Factoid: Istanbul scavengers find treasure in, 21
Factoid: Miami forces recycling, or pay, 22

Treaty
Proper role of government, 497

Tribble, Samuel J., 381

True Levellers (The Diggers), 93

Truman, Harry S.
Acts of socialism, 415
Fair Deal, 415

Truth
Jefferson, "We hold these truths to be self-evident," 205

Is truth outdated? Which truths? Calvin Coolidge comments, 218

Know the truth, 503

Factoid: Washington, truth will ultimately prevail, 239

Try, buy, sell, and fail, 250

Tucker, Benjamin
Defines socialism, 164

Turkmenistan
Factoid: Niyazov erects golden statue, declares "President for Life", 309

Tyrant
All tyrants are on left side of Founders' scale of political power, 8-11
Factoid: "Collective tyrant no different than single...", 18

U

Unalienable Rights, 23, 79
Rejected by progressives, 7, 9, 301
and vested rights, 13-19
Islam denies unalienable rights, 150
sustained by Anglo-Saxons, 178-180

Unconstitutional
Jefferson on Supreme Court decisions, 299

Underwood, Oscar W., 381, 383

Unions, 250
and the King, 1700-1800s, 240
guilds were forerunners to unions, 251
Colonial period, 252
Strikes made legal, 252
Bootmakers strike leads to legalization of forming unions, 254
Clayton Antitrust Act, 254
Norris-La Guardia Act, 1932, 254, 394
National Labor Relations Act, 255
Violence, damage is legal, 255
Misuse union dues, 256
Unions bankrupt companies, 256
Unions ruin prosperity, 256, 297
Decline of the unions, 257
Right-to-work states, 259
Wagner Act (1935), 394
Davis-Bacon Act (1931), 394
Integral part of socialism, 522
Factoid: Unions rebelled at Obama pollution rules in 2011, 114
Factoid: Forced Twinkies into bankruptcy, 290
Factoid: Public sector unions growing, 291

Factoid: Private sector unions shrinking, 292

Factoid: Right to work states do better, 393

United Kingdom
Health care in, 353, 355, 356, 362, 365
Snapshot of socialism in, 471
Factoid: Privacy violation: Gov't. listens to calls, e-mail in real time, 401

United Nations
Calls for socialized medicine worldwide, 368
Obama appoints self to Security Council, 438
Promote U.N. as body of international control, *see* **Goals of Socialism**, 483-491
Factoid: U.N. seeks to tax U.S. web sites, 33

United States, 156, 179, 185, 191, 193, 198-200, 215-217, 220, 231
Constitution of the U.S., 205-209
Conspiracy to socialize U.S., 224
Un-elected president of, 289-290
and tariffs, 306
Health care in, 353, 357, 358, 365
New Deal Constitution, 397-401
Presidents and socialism, 405-443
Snapshot of socialism in, 472
Destroy culture, goal of socialism, 490
Factoid: U.S. produces 50% of soybeans, 9
Factoid: Produces 44% of world's corn, 47
Factoid: Taxes lower in U.S. than many socialist nations, 64
Factoid: Under Obama, national debt grew $4.7 trillion in 3 years, 88
Factoid: Pentagon does study on study on studies, 104
Factoid: Orange prices kept high by dumping millions to rot, 112
Factoid: California traffic camera caught cheating to increase income, 115
Factoid: EPA issuing regulations, bypassing Congress, 122
Factoid: Obama plans 4,257 new regulations in 2011, 123
Factoid: Government employs 2.6 million people, 130
Factoid: State government employs 19 million, 131
Factoid: Illegal immigrants collected $4.2 billion, 135

Factoid: Food czars fined high school for candy machine, 154
Factoid: Salaries for government workers $40K higher than private, 156
Factoid: Lethal injection drugs rejected by FDA as untested, 168
Factoid: American flag sways voters to conservative, 235
Factoid: Entitlement spending biggest part of budget, 270
Factoid: 49% of households have welfare, 288
Factoid: Total liability, $61.6 trillion, 317
Factoid: U.S. total liability in detail, 326
Factoid: Cost of regulatory agencies, 337
Factoid: $2 trillion move across U.S. every day, 349
Factoid: U.S. raises debt limit 78 times, 381
Factoid: Right to work states do better, 393

United States vs. Butler (1936), 294
USSR *see* **Soviet Union**

V

Valley Forge, 177, 505
Vampire
Factoid: Superstitions left skeletons with stakes in heart, 128
Venezuela
Snapshot of socialism in, 473
Factoid: Murder rate climbed during Chavez leadership, 107
Factoid: Unregulated dairy products in greater abundance, 132
Factoid: Chavez bans "violent photographs", 306
Factoid: Chavez controls television, 380
Factoid: Chavez nationalizes grocery stores, 432
Vietnam
Vietnam War, 419
Snapshot of socialism in, 474
Factoid: Death count, 30
Virginia
Benefits of climate, 131
Virtue 491, 494
A part of People's Law, 12, 224
Abandoned in ancient China, 40
Lack of cultural virtue leads to misery, 151, 400, 431, 442
Clarence Darrow, 311

Factoid: Adams says virtue necessary for freedom, 341
Factoid: Socialism erodes virtue, 468
Factoid: More virtue means less government, 494
Virtuous City, the
Book by al-Farabi, 900 AD, 274
Voltaire (1694-1778), 107
Vote
Voters intimated by Black Panthers, 525

W

Wagner Act (1935), 394
Walmart
Factoid: Operated 4,400 stores in U.S., 160
Factoid: Good example that capitalism works, 216
Factoid: Sales almost $430 billion in 2011, 319
Factoid: China requires Party members in stores, 355
Factoid: Serves 200 million customers a week, 465
Factoid: Employes 2.1 million, 487
Wang, Ancient Chinese Leader, 38
Warburg, Paul, 386
Ward, Lester F.
Destroy the individual, 18
Warren, Josiah
Victim of Robert Owen's socialism, 246
Washington, George
Articles of Confederation failed him, 176
At Valley Forge, 177, 505
Fire cakes, 177
Opposes price controls, 197
Depreciation of currency quote, 203
Problems from listing rights, 206
Warned about Hamilton, 235
Prays at Valley Forge, 505
Factoid: Washington Monument tallest in DC, 214
Factoid: Judicial activism unconstitutional, 225
Factoid: "Truth will ultimately prevail...", 239
Factoid: World's most important battle, 335
Factoid: "Gentlemen, permit me to put on my spectacles ...", 440

Waters, Maxine
Threatening government force, 20
Watson, John B.
Factoid: "Give me a baby and I'll make him anything," 147
Weaver, Claude, 382
Webster, Samuel
Factoid: Imperceptible growth of socialism, 472
Weeks Act, 320
Welfare
Noah Webster's definition, 184
Franklin comments against, 327
Modern state welfare begins in Prussia, 341-342
American welfare, roots of, 343
War on Poverty, 420
Food stamps
and Nimrod, 37
and Kennedy, 418
and Reagan, 426
and Obama, 439
and Star Parker, 453
letting go of, 502
Damage to American blacks, 453
Proper role of government, 497
Factoid: Jefferson accuses Congress of violating commerce clause, 24
Factoid: Seattle couple abuses welfare, 277
Factoid: 49% of U.S. receives welfare, 288
Factoid: As of 2011, 100 million Americans on welfare, 321
Factoid: Welfare blamed for breakup of black family, 361
Factoid: Pizza prices rise from Obama Health Care, 419
Factoid: Under Obama, dependency shot up 23%, 474
Factoid: Welfare spending in U.S. great 70% under Obama, 475
Factoid: 66% of U.S. budget spent on welfare, 477
Factoid: Cutting taxes increased charitable giving, 482
Wells, H. G., 169
Defines socialism, 165
West Germany
Member of EU, 446
Wheat
In Egyptian diet, 35
Bread and circuses, 64

"Wheatless Mondays," 304
Fixing prices, 391, 413
USSR buys from U.S. 529
Factoid: U.S. produces 18%, 253
Factoid: 228,000 bushels per hour in
    U.S., 396
Where the Red Fern Grows, 501
White Slave Traffic Act (1910), 319
Wilson, Woodrow
Acts of socialism, 410
Socialism is necessary, quote, 411
Winstanley, Gerrard
Leader of "The Diggers", 93
The Law of Freedom (book), 276
Women
Excluded from Indian castes, 61
Forced to marry by Inca, 125
Human sacrifices, 126
Wives in Common
    Nicolaites, 75
    Carpocratians, 76
    Manicheism, 76
    Mazdakians, 78
    Cathars, 83
    Apostolic Brethren, 86
    Brethren of the Free Spirit, 86
    Adamites, 90
    Anabaptists, 91
    Ranters, 94
Factoid: Forbidden to drive or ride bikes
    in Iran, 86
Factoid: U.S. democrats favor
    sex-selective abortion, 87
Factoid: Bebel says woman may leave
    sex partner anytime, 110
Factoid: North Korean woman yells at
    cop demanding bribe, 136
Factoid: Taxis not allowed to pickup
    immodest women in Iran, 144
Factoid: Honor killings in Islam, 199
Factoid: Islam book says wife beatings
    okay, 203
Factoid: Honor killings in Pakistan, 206
Factoid: "Vulgar" dressed women
    arrested, 233
Woolsey, Theodore, 302
WorldSocialism.org, 519, 523
World Socialist Movement, 521
World Socialist Party, 518, 519
World War I
And prohibition, 287
Consequences of, 392

Contributed to Great Depression, 392
Wright, Jeremiah
Factoid: Bribed to stop talking, 314
Wycliffe, John, 88

Z

Zedong, Mao, *see* **Mao Zedong**
Zhu, Dr. Chen, 367
Zimbabwe
Snapshot of socialism in, 475
Factoid: Mugabe regime arrests
    disrespectful citizens, 436
Ziggurat of Ur, 30
Zizka, Ian, 90
Zoroastrians, 76-78